Contemporary Readings
in Social Psychology

D1536249

The Nelson-Hall Series in Psychology

Stephen Worchel, Consulting Editor
Texas A & M University

Contemporary Readings in Social Psychology

David A. Schroeder
University of Arkansas

David E. Johnson
John Brown University

Thomas D. Jensen
University of Arkansas

EDITORS

Nelson-Hall Publishers
nh Chicago

LIBRARY OF CONGRESS CATALOGING IN PUBLICATION DATA

Main entry under title:

Contemporary readings in social psychology.

  Includes bibliographies.
  1. Social psychology—Addresses, essays, lectures.
I. Schroeder, David A.   II. Johnson, David E.
III. Jensen, Thomas D.
HM251.C689 1985   302   84-19027
ISBN 0-8304-1093-7

Manufactured in the United States of America

10 9 8 7 6 5 4 3 2 1

The paper is this book is pH neutral (acid-free).

To our families:
Susie, Lisa, and Kevin;
Simone and Deron;
Karen

Contents

Preface

NUMEROUS SURVEY TEXTS ARE available that provide excellent overviews of the field of social psychology. By necessity, these volumes must omit many details of the research upon which their presentations are based, with the result that students are often deprived of the opportunity to trace a researcher's idea from hypothesis to experiment to conclusion and application. The present text is offered in an attempt to rectify this state of affairs by providing the student in social psychology with an exposure to the issues being investigated and the methods being utilized in the field today.

The articles that we have chosen to include in this book of readings were selected on the basis of four criteria. First, each article was evaluated for its readability (e.g., Are the issues being addressed and the hypotheses being tested readily discernible? Are the methodology and statistical analyses understandable for the social psychology neophyte?) Second, the centrality of each article was considered; an attempt was made to select articles that represented the major topics and issues that define the field of social psychology today. Third, a judicious mix of applied and basic research reports was sought. Current trends in the field suggest that both perspectives are now receiving considerable attention, often from researchers who are active in both domains. We have attempted to capture the spirit of this integration. Finally, it was deemed necessary that the selections reflect the current status of work in social psychology. Ninety-four percent of the articles included were published since 1980.

To facilitate the use of this text, short introductory comments precede the articles presented within each chapter. These comments are not intended to replace the material presented in basic social psychology texts but rather to provide a context for the student to understand how the selected articles relate to the particular area of research being considered. Our goal is to relieve the instructor from having to "set the stage" for the articles that might be assigned from this set of readings.

We believe that collections of readings can make a positive contribution to students' training and that the characteristics that we have incorporated into this text will make it a useful supplement. It will promote students' understanding and appreciation of social psychology as a science and as an action-oriented discipline.

Putting this book together has been a social exercise to no lesser an extent than the various social phenomena that are described in this text. Our collaboration has not been without differences of opinion, but the net result of our work together has been rewarding and satisfying. With each of us approaching this project from somewhat different perspectives due to differences in our professional experiences (e.g., large university, small college, marketing department), the outcome may be considered a tribute to our understanding of social dynamics brought about by our training in social psychology. We tried to be altruistic and helpful, we avoided violence and aggression, we were able to resolve intragroup conflicts amiably, and, most importantly, we have remained good friends.

Although it would seem that the division of labor among three individuals would leave few tasks for others, we were not efficient enough. We needed help from our friends. Two of these individuals are particularly deserving of recognition. Lynn Mosesso and Cindy Hansen made a major contribution to this project during its initial stages by helping to identify possible articles for inclusion and then winnowing the list down to a manageable number. We are deeply indebted to them. Several of our undergraduate students reviewed our "next to final" selections to ensure that the articles we felt should be included were appropriate for our target market; in particular, we want to thank Amy Marr, Lisa Koty, and Karen Cunningham for their valuable assistance.

We would also like to express our appreciation to the editors and staff of Nelson-Hall for giving us the opportunity to undertake this project. Steve Worchel served as the initial contact and was an invaluable critic of our original prospectus. Ron Warnecke encouraged our progress and provided his expertise. Dorothy Anderson and the editorial and production staffs brought the project to completion. We thank them all.

Finally, we would each like to thank our families who supported and tolerated us while we worked on this project—Susie, Lisa, and Kevin; Simone and Deron; and Karen. We hope that their retrospective view of this episode will be one of only minor inconvenience.

1 Social Psychology: Perspectives and Methods

SOCIAL PSYCHOLOGY IS THE study of behavior within a social context. Social psychologists are interested in the impact that the presence, attitudes, and actions of persons have on the attitudes and actions of other individuals. We are also interested in understanding the processes by which we interpret the actions of those whom we observe and form unified perceptions of others. Topics such as these have constituted the field of social psychology since its inception with the research of Triplett in the late 1890s and the work of McDougall in the early 1900s.

Although much has remained the same in social psychology for the past ninety years, there have also been many changes as researchers have expanded the scope of their investigations to explore such topics as social perception, altruism, aggression, and group processes. These changes are the consequences of many forces: methodological advances, the exigencies of wars and social unrest, sensitivities to important social issues, and the continued contributions of exceptional women and men in the field. In addition, social psychology has undergone change because of the field's willingness to engage in constructive self-criticism. In the first article in this chapter, William McGuire offers a critique of the dominant research methods utilized in social psychology. He presents prescriptions for reorienting the field to make it more responsive to the needs of those who rely on our discipline and more able to address and answer important questions about social behavior. Although not all of McGuire's suggestions have been adopted by social researchers in the ten years since the original publication of his article, it would be difficult not to attribute many of the the the changes that have taken place during this period to his insightful comments.

The most recent trend in social psychology, however, has raised a more fundamental issue with respect to the research methodology utilized by psychologists who study social phenomena. This involves generalizing the results of social psychological research to "real-world" problems. Some researchers have suggested that the problem of generalizing research findings can be avoided at the time the research is designed. Bobby Calder, Lynn Phillips, and Alice Tybout suggest that there are two types of generalizability—one that involves specific practical application of the findings obtained and another that involves a more general application of the underlying processes that are identified. These authors further suggest that the researcher must decide which type of generalizability is of primary import prior to the selection of a research design and the development of the procedures to be employed. The second article in this chapter describes their solutions to the problem of designing research for application.

Finally, we realize that many students enrolled in introductory social psychology classes that might be using this text have not previously completed courses in research methods and have not been exposed to original research articles such as those that comprise the remainder of this volume. In an attempt to help these students derive the maximum benefit from this book, we have prepared a brief article that discusses the typical composition of research reports. This article is not intended to provide a thorough introduction to research methodology, but it should give the reader a good sense of what kind of material is presented in each section of a research report and what information should be derived from each section as one reads the articles in this volume. We have tried to make our explanation relatively nontechnical and to avoid jargon whenever possible . We hope you will find it beneficial.

The Yin and Yang of Progress
in Social Psychology: Seven Koan

William J. McGuire

We describe the current dissatisfactions with the paradigm that has recently guided experimental social psychology—testing of theory-derived hypotheses by means of laboratory manipulational experiments. The emerging variant of doing field experiments does not meet the criticisms. It is argued that an adequate new paradigm will be a more radical departure involving, on the creative side, deriving hypotheses from a systems theory of social and cognitive structures that takes into account multiple and bidirectional causality among social variables. On the critical side, its hypotheses testing will be done in multivariate correlational designs with naturally fluctuating variables. Some steps toward this new paradigm are described in the form of seven koan.

THE PARADIGM RECENTLY GUIDING EXPERIMENTAL SOCIAL PSYCHOLOGY

When the XIXth Congress met 3 years ago in London, and certainly a half-dozen years back at the Moscow Congress, social psychology appeared to be in a golden age. It was a prestigious and productive area in which droves of bright young people, a sufficiency of middle-aged colonels, and a few

"The Yin and Yang of Progress in Social Psychology: Seven Koan" by W.J. McGuire, 1973, *Journal of Personality and Social Psychology, 26,* pp. 446-456. Copyright 1973 by the American Psychological Assn. Reprinted by permission of the publisher and author. This paper is based on an address given at the Nineteenth Congress of the International Union of Scientific Psychology at Tokyo in August 1972.

grand old men were pursuing their research with a confidence and energy that is found in those who know where they are going. Any moments of doubt we experienced involved anxiety as to whether we were doing our thing well, rather than uncertainty as to whether it needed to be done at all.

The image of these golden boys (and a few, but all too few, golden girls) of social psychology, glowing with confidence and chutzpah only 6 years back at the Moscow Congress, blissfully unaware of the strident attacks which were soon to strike confusion into the field, brings to mind a beautiful haiku of Buson that goes

Tsurigane-ni
Tomarite nemuru
Kochō kana

which I hasten to translate as follows

> *On a temple bell*
> *Settled, asleep,*
> *A butterfly.*

We social psychology researchers know all too well that the peaceful temple bell on which we were then displaying ourselves has now rudely rung. During the past half-dozen years, the vibrations which could be vaguely sensed at the time of the Moscow meeting have gathered force. Now the temple bell has tolled and tolled again, rudely disturbing the stream of experimental social psychological research and shaking the confidence of many of us who work in the area.

The first half of this paper is devoted to describing the three successive waves of this current history. First, I shall describe the experimental social psychology paradigm that has recently guided our prolific research. Second, I shall discuss why this recent paradigm is being attacked and what, superficially at least, appears to be emerging in its place. Third, I shall say why I feel the seemingly emerging new paradigm is as inadequate as the one we would replace. Then, in the second half of this paper I shall offer, in the form of seven koan, my prescriptions for a new paradigm more radically different from the recent one, but more in tune with the times and the march of history than is the variant that is supposedly emerging.

The Old Paradigm

What was the experimental social psychology paradigm which until recently had been unquestioningly accepted by the great majority of us but which now is being so vigorously attacked? Like any adequate paradigm it had two aspects, a creative and

a critical component (McGuire, 1969, pp. 22-25). By the creative aspect, I mean the part of our scientific thinking that involves hypothesis generation, and by the critical aspect, I mean the hypothesis-testing part of our work.

The creative aspect of the recent paradigm inclined us to derive our hypotheses from current theoretical formulations. Typically, these theoretical formulations were borrowed from other areas of psychology (such as the study of psychopathology or of learning and memory), though without the level of refinement and quantification which those theories had reached in their fields of origin.

The critical, hypothesis-testing aspect of the recent paradigm called for manipulational experiments carried out in the laboratory. The experimental social psychologist attempted to simulate in the laboratory the gist of the situation to which he hoped to generalize, and he measured the dependent variable after deliberately manipulating the independent variable while trying to hold constant all other factors likely to affect the social behavior under study. In brief, the recent paradigm called for selecting our hypotheses for their relevance to broad theoretical formulations and testing them by laboratory manipulational experiments. McGuire (1965) presented an emphatic assertion of this recent paradigm in its heyday.

Assaults on the Old Paradigm

During the past several years both the creative and the critical aspects of this experimental social psychology paradigm have come under increasing attack. The creative aspect of formulating hypotheses for their relevance to theory has been denounced as a mandarin activity out of phase with the needs of our time. It has been argued that hypotheses should be formulated for their relevance to social problems rather than for their relevance to theoretical issues. Such urgings come from people inside and outside social psychology, reflecting both the increasing social concern of researchers themselves and the demands of an articulate public for greater payoff from expensive scientific research. While many of us still insist with Lewin that "There is nothing so practical as a good theory," the extent to which the pendulum has swung from the theoretically relevant toward the socially relevent pole is shown in the recent upsurge of publications on socially important topics of ad hoc interest, such as bystander intervention, the use of local space, the mass media and violence, the determinants of love, responses to victimization, nonverbal communication, etc.

At least as strong and successful an assault has been launched on the critical aspect of the recent paradigm, namely, the notion that hypotheses should be tested by manipulational laboratory experiments. It has been urged that laboratory experiments are full of artifacts (such as experimenter bias, demand character, evaluation apprehension, etc.) which make their results very hard to interpret. Ethical questions also have been raised against the laboratory social experiments on the grounds that they expose the participants to an unacceptable amount of deception, coercion, and stress.

In place of the laboratory manipulational experiment, there has been a definite trend toward experiments conducted in field settings and toward correlational analysis of data from naturalistic situations. A variety of recent methodological advances (which we shall list under Koan 5) has made alternative hypothesis-testing procedures more attractive.

The attacks on the old paradigm of theory-derived hypotheses tested in laboratory manipulational experiments have certainly shaken confidence in that approach. At the same time, there is some suggestion of an emerging new paradigm which has as its creative aspect the derivation of new hypotheses for their ad hoc interest and social relevance. And in its critical aspect, this new paradigm involves testing these hypotheses by field experiments and, where necessary, by the correlational analysis of naturalistic data. McGuire (1967, 1969) described in more detail the worries about the recent paradigm and the nature of the purportedly emerging one. Higbee and Wells (1972) and Fried, Gumpper, and Allen (1973) suggested that reports by McGuire, by Sears and Abeles (1969), etc., of the demise of the recent paradigm may be exaggerated, but perhaps they have underestimated the time that must intervene before a change of vogue by the leaders shows up in mass analysis of the methods used in published research.

MORE BASIC QUESTIONS REGARDING BOTH THE RECENT AND EMERGING PARADIGMS

My own position on the relative merits of the recent paradigm and this supposedly emerging new paradigm is a complex and developing one which I have detailed in print (McGuire, 1965, 1967, 1969) so the reader will be spared here a recital of my Byzantine opinions on this issue. Instead, I am raising the more fundamental issue of whether or not both the recent and the seemingly emerging paradigms which I have just described fail to come to grips with the deeper questions which lie behind our present unease. It seems to me that any truly new paradigm that ultimately arises from the present unrest is going to be more radically different from the recent one than is the supposedly emerging paradigm I have just depicted. It will represent a more fundamental departure on both the creative and the critical sides.

Inadequacies on the Creative Side

The switch from theory relevance to social relevance as the criterion in the creative, hypothesis-generating aspect of our work seems to me to constitute only a superficial cosmetic change that masks rather than corrects the basic problem. Socially relevant hypotheses, no less than theoretically relevant hypotheses, tend to be based on a simple linear process model, a sequential chain of cause and effect which is inadequate to simulate the true complexities of the individual's cognitive system or of the social system which we are typically trying to describe. Such simple a-affects-b hypotheses fail to catch the complexities of parallel processing, bidirectional causality, and reverberating feedback that characterize both cognitive and social organizations. The simple sequential model had its uses, but these have been largely exploited in past progress, and we must now deal with the complexities of systems in order to continue the progress on a new level.

The real inadequacy of the theory-derived hypotheses of the recent paradigm is not, as those now advocating socially relevant hypotheses insist, that it focused on the wrong variables (those that were theory rather than problem relevant). Rather, the basic shortcoming of the theory-relevant and the socially relevant hypotheses alike is that they fail to come to grips with the complexities with which the variables are organized in the individual and social systems.

Inadequacies of the Critical Aspect of the Recent Paradigm

The critical, hypothesis-testing aspect of the purportedly emerging paradigm also has the defect of being but a minor variant of the recent experimental social psychology paradigm rather than the fundamental departure which is called for. Let me first describe some of the deep epistemological uneasiness some of us have been expressing about the manipulational laboratory experiment that was the hypothesis-testing procedure of the recent paradigm. The crux of this objection is that we social psychologists have tended to use the manipulational laboratory experiment not to test our hypotheses but to demonstrate their obvious truth. We tend to start off with an hypothesis that is so clearly true (given the implicit and explicit assumptions) and which we have no intention of rejecting however the experiment comes out. Such a stance is quite appropriate, since the hypothesis by its meaningfulness and plausibility to reasonable people is tautologically true in the assumed context. As Blake said, "Everything possible to be believ'd is an image of truth."

The area of interpersonal attraction will serve to illustrate my point. The researcher might start off with a *really* obvious proposition from bubba-psychology, such as "The more someone perceives another person as having attitudes similar to his own, the more he tends to like that other person." Or a somewhat more flashy researcher, a little hungrier for novelty, might hypothesize the opposite. That is, he could look for certain circumstances in which the generally true, obvious hypothesis would obviously be reversed. He might hypothesize exceptional circumstances where attitudinal similarity would be anxiety arousing and a source of hostility; for example, if one loves one's wife, then one might actually dislike some other man to the extent that one perceives that other as also loving one's wife. Or another exceptional reversal might be that some people may think so poorly of themselves that they think less well of another person to the extent that the other person is like themselves. If the negative relationship is not found, we are likely to conclude that the person did not have a sufficiently low self-image, not that the hypothesis is wrong. Both the original obvious hypothesis and the obvious reversed hypothesis are reasonable and valid in the sense that if all our premises obtained, then our conclusion would pretty much have to follow.

Experiments on such hypotheses naturally turn out to be more like demonstrations than tests. If the experiment does not come out "right," then the researcher does not say that the hypothesis is wrong but rather that something was wrong with the experiment, and he corrects and revises it, perhaps by using more appropriate subjects, by strengthening the independent variable manipulation, by blocking off extraneous response possibilities, or by setting up a more appropriate context, etc. Sometimes he may have such continuous bad luck that he finally gives up the demonstration because the phenomenon proves to be so elusive as to be beyond his ability to demonstrate. The more persistent of us typically manage at last to get control of the experimental situation so that we can reliably demonstrate the hypothesized relationship. But note that what the experiment tests is not whether the hypothesis is true but rather

whether the experimenter is a sufficiently ingenious stage manager to produce in the laboratory conditions which demonstrate that an obviously true hypothesis is correct. In our graduate programs in social psychology, we try to train people who are good enough stage managers so that they can create in the laboratory simulations of realities in which the obvious correctness of our hypotheses can be demonstrated.

It is this kind of epistemological worry about manipulational laboratory experiments that a half-dozen years back caused a number of observers (e.g., McGuire, 1967) to urge social psychology to search for interrelations among naturally varying factors in the world outside the laboratory. Out of these urgings has come the critical aspect of the apparently emerging paradigm which I have described above, calling for research in the field rather than in the laboratory.

Inadequacies of the Critical Aspects of the Purportedly Emerging New Field-Experiment Paradigm

Recently, I have come to recognize that this flight from the laboratory manipulational experiment to the field study, which I myself helped to instigate, is a tactical evasion which fails to meet the basic problem. We would grant that in the field we put the question to nature in a world we never made, where the context factors cannot be so confounded by our stage management proclivities as they were in the laboratory. But in this natural world research, the basic problem remains that we are not really testing our hypotheses. Rather, just as in the laboratory experiment we were testing our stage-managing abilities, in the field study we are testing our ability as "finders," if I may use a term from real estate and merchandising. When our field test of the hypothesis does not come out correctly, we are probably going to assume not that the hypothesis is wrong but that we unwisely chose an inappropriate natural setting in which to test it, and so we shall try again to test it in some other setting in which the conditions are more relevant to the hypothesis. Increasing our own and our graduate students' critical skill will involve making us not better hypothesis testers or better stage managers but rather better finders of situations in which our hypotheses can be demonstrated as tautologically true. Though I shall not pursue the point here, other objections to the laboratory experiment, including ethical and methodological considerations, that have been used (McGuire, 1969) to argue for more field research could similarly be turned against experiments conducted in the natural environment.

What I am arguing here is that changing from a theory-relevant to a socially relevant criterion for variable selection does not constitute a real answer to the basic problem with the creative aspect of our recent social psychology paradigm. And again, the switch from laboratory to field manipulation does not meet the basic objection to the critical aspect of the old paradigm. Neither the recent paradigm nor the supposedly emerging one really supplies the answer to our present needs. The discontent is a quite healthy one, and we should indeed be dissatisfied with the recent paradigm of testing theory-derived hypotheses by means of laboratory manipulational experiments. But our healthy discontent should carry us to a more fundamentally new outlook than is provided by this supposedly emerging variant paradigm of testing socially relevant hypotheses by experiments in natural settings.

SOURCES OF THE NEW SOCIAL PSYCHOLOGY

The Ultimate Shape of the New Paradigm

What I have written in the previous section suggests my general vision of what the more radically different new paradigm for social psychology will look like. On the creative side, it will involve theoretical models of the cognitive and social systems in their true multivariate complexity, involving a great deal of parallel processing, bidirectional relationships, and feedback circuits. Since such complex theoretical formulations will be far more in accord with actual individual and social reality than our present a-affects-b linear models, it follows that theory-derived hypotheses will be similar to hypotheses selected for their relevance to social issues. Correspondingly, the critical aspect of this new paradigm involves hypothesis testing by multivariate time series designs that recognize the obsolescence of our current simplistic a-affects-b sequential designs with their distinctions between dependent and independent variables.

But I feel somewhat uncomfortable here in trying to describe in detail what the next, radically different paradigm will look like. It will be hammered out by theoretically and empirically skilled researchers in a hundred eyeball-to-eyeball confrontations of thought with data, all the while obscured by a thousand mediocre and irrelevant studies which will constitute the background noise in which the true signal will be detected only gradually. Trying to predict precisely what new paradigm will emerge is almost as foolish as trying to control it.

But there is a subsidiary task with which I feel more comfortable and to which I shall devote the rest of this paper. I have come to· feel that some specific tactical changes should be made in our creative and critical work in social psychology so as to enhance the momentum and the ultimate sweep of this wave of the future, whatever form it may take. I shall here recommend a few of these needed innovations and correctives, presenting them as koans and commentaries thereon, to mask my own uncertainties.

Koan 1: The Sound of One Hand Clapping . . . and the Wrong Hand

One drastic change that is called for in our teaching of research methodology is that we should emphasize the creative, hypothesis-formation stage relative to the critical, hypothesis-testing stage of research. It is my guess that at least 90% of the time irl our current courses on methodology is devoted to presenting ways of testing hypotheses and that little time is spent on the prior and more important process of how one creates these hypotheses in the first place. Both the creation and testing of hypotheses are important parts of the scientific method, but the creative phase is the more important of the two. If our hypotheses are trivial, it is hardly worth amassing a great methodological arsenal to test them; to paraphrase Maslow, what is not worth doing, is not worth doing well. Surely, we all recognize that the creation of hypotheses is an essential part of the scientific process. The neglect of the creative phase in our methodology courses probably comes neither from a failure to recognize its importance

nor a belief that it is trivially simple. Rather, the neglect is probably due to the suspicion that so complex a creative process as hypothesis formation is something that cannot be taught.

I admit that creative hypothesis formation cannot be reduced to teachable rules, and that there are individual differences among us in ultimate capacity for creative hypothesis generation. Still, it seems to me that we have to give increased time in our own thinking and teaching about methodology to the hypothesis-generating phase of research, even at the expense of reducing the time spent discussing hypothesis testing. In my own methodology courses, I make a point of stressing the importance of the hypothesis-generating phase of our work by describing and illustrating at least a dozen or so different approaches to hypothesis formation which have been used in psychological research, some of which I can briefly describe here, including case study, paradoxical incident, analogy, hypothetico-deductive method, functional analysis, rules of thumb, conflicting results, accounting for exceptions, and straightening out complex relationships.

For example, there is the intensive case study, such as Piaget's of his children's cognitive development or Freud's mulling over and over of the Dora or the Wolf Man case or his own dreams or memory difficulties. Often the case is hardly an exceptional one—for example, Dora strikes me as a rather mild and uninteresting case of hysteria—so that it almost seems as if any case studied intensively might serve as a Rorschach card to provoke interesting hypotheses. Perhaps an even surer method of arriving at an interesting hypothesis is to try to account for a paradoxical incident. For example, in a study of rumors circulating in Bihar, India, after a devastating earthquake, Prasad found that the rumors tended to predict further catastrophes. It seemed paradoxical that the victims of the disaster did not seek some gratification in fantasy, when reality was so harsh, by generating rumors that would be gratifying rather than further disturbing. I believe that attempting to explain this paradox played a more than trivial role in Festinger's formulation of dissonance theory and Schachter's developmnt of a cognitive theory of emotion.

A third creative method for generating hypothesis is the use of analogy, as in my own work on deriving hypotheses about techniques for inducing resistance to persuasion, where I formulated hypotheses by analogy with the biological process of inoculating the person in advance with a weakened form of the threatening material, an idea suggested in earlier work by Janis and Lumsdaine. A fourth creative procedure is the hypothetico-deductive method, where one puts together a number of commonsensical principles and derives from their conjunction some interesting predictions, as in the Hull and Hovland mathematico-deductive theory of rote learning, or of the work by Simon and his colleagues on logical reasoning. The possibility of computer simulation has made this hypothesis-generating procedure increasingly possible and popular.

A fifth way of deriving hypotheses might be called the functional or adaptive approach, as when Hull generated the principles on which we would have to operate if we were to be able to learn from experience to repeat successful actions, and yet eventually be able to learn an alternative shorter path to a goal even though we have already mastered a longer path which does successfully lead us to that goal. A sixth approach involves analyzing the practitioner's rule of thumb. Here when one observes that practitioners or craftsmen generally follow some procedural rule of thumb, we assume that it probably works, and one tries to think of theoretical implications of its effectiveness. One does not have to be a Maoist to admit that the basic researcher can learn something by talking to a practitioner. For example, one's programmed simulation of chess playing is improved by accepting the good player's heuristic of keeping control of the center of the board. Or one's attitude change theorization can be helped by noting the politician's and advertiser's rule that when dealing with public opinion, it is better to ignore your opposition than to refute it. These examples also serve to remind us that the practitioner's rule of thumb is as suggestive by its failures as by its successes.

A seventh technique for provoking new hypotheses is trying to account for conflicting results. For example, in learning and attitude change situations, there are opposite laws of primacy and of recency, each of which sometimes seems valid; or in information integration, sometimes an additive or sometimes an averaging model seems more appropriate. The work by Anderson trying to reconcile these seeming conflicts shows how provocative a technique this can be in generating new theories. An eighth creative method is accounting for exceptions to general findings, as when Hovland tried to account for delayed action effect in opinion change. That is, while usually the persuasive effect of communications dissipates with time, Hovland found that occasionally the impact actually intensifies over time, which provoked him to formulate a variety of interesting hypotheses about delayed action effects. A ninth creative technique for hypothesis formation involves reducing observed complex relationships to simpler component relationships. For example, the somewhat untidy line that illustrates the functional relationship between visual acuity and light intensity can be reduced to a prettier set of rectilinear functions by hypothesizing separate rod and cone processes, a logarithmic transformation, a Blondel-Rey-type threshold phenomenon to account for deviations at very low intensities, etc.

But our purpose here is not to design a methodology course, so it would be inappropriate to prolong this list. Let me say once again, to summarize our first koan, that we have listened too long to the sound of one hand clapping, and the less interesting hand at that, in confining our methodology discussion almost exclusively to hypothesis testing. It is now time to clap more loudly using the other hand as well by stressing the importance of hypothesis generation as part of psychological methodology.

Koan 2: In This Nettle Chaos, We Discern This Pattern, Truth

I stress here the basic point that our cognitive systems and social systems are complex and that the currently conventional simple linear process models have outlived their heuristic usefulness as descriptions of these complex systems. In our actual cognitive and social systems, effects are the outcome of multiple causes which are often in complex interactions; moreover, it is the rule rather than the exception that the effects act back on the causal variables. Hence, students of cognitive and social processes must be encouraged to think big, or rather to think complexly, with conceptual models that involve parallel process-

ing, nets of causally inter-related factors, feedback loops, bidirectional causation, etc.

If we and our students are to begin thinking in terms of these more complex models, then explicit encouragement is necessary since the published literature on social and cognitive processes is dominated by the simple linear models, and our students must be warned against imprinting on them. But our encouragement, while necessary, will not be sufficient to provoke our students into the more complex theorizing. We shall all shy away from the mental strain of keeping in mind so many variables, so completely inter-related. Moreover, such complex theories allow so many degrees of freedom as to threaten the dictum that in order to be scientifically interesting, a theory must be testable, that is, disprovable. These complex theories, with their free-floating parameters, seem to be adjustable to any outcome.

Hence, we have to give our students skill and confidence and be role models to encourage them to use complex formulations. To this end we have to give greater play to techniques like computer simulation, parameter estimation, multivariate time series designs, path analysis, etc. (as discussed further in Koan 5 below), in our graduate training programs.

Koan 3: Observe. But Observe People Not Data

In our father's house there are many rooms. In the total structure of the intelligentsia, there is a place for the philosopher of mind and the social philosopher, as well as for the scientific psychologist. But the scientific psychologist can offer something beside and beyond these armchair thinkers in that we not only generate delusional systems, but we go further and test our delusional systems against objective data as well as for their subjective plausibility. Between the philosopher of mind and the scientific psychologist, there is the difference of putting the question to nature. Even when our theory seems plausible and so ingenious that it deserves to be true, we are conditioned to follow the Cromwellian dictum (better than did the Lord Protector himself) to consider in the bowels of Christ that we may be wrong.

But I feel that in our determination to maintain this difference we have gone too far. In our holy determination to confront reality and put our theory to the test of nature, we have plunged through reality, like Alice through the mirror, into a never-never land in which we contemplate not life but data. All too often the scientific psychologist is observing not mind or behavior but summed data and computer printout. He is thus a self-incarcerated prisoner in a platonic cave, where he has placed himself with his back to the outside world, watching its shadows on the walls. There may be a time to watch shadows but not to the exclusion of the real thing.

Perhaps Piaget should be held up as a role model here, as an inspiring example of how a creative mind can be guided in theorizing by direct confrontation with empirical reality. Piaget's close observation of how the developing human mind grapples with carefully devised problems was much more conducive to his interesting theorizing than would have been either the armchair philosopher's test of subjective plausibility or the scientific entrepreneur's massive project in which assistants bring him computer printout, inches thick.

The young student typically enters graduate study wanting to do just what we are proposing, that is, to engage in a direct confrontation with reality. All too often, it is our graduate programs which distract him with shadows. Either by falling into the hands of the humanists, he is diverted into subjectivism and twice-removed scholarly studies of what other subjectivists have said; or, if he falls under the influence of scientific psychologists, he becomes preoccupied with twice-removed sanitized data in the form of computer printout. I am urging that we restructure our graduate programs somewhat to keep the novice's eye on the real rather than distracting and obscuring his view behind a wall of data.

Koan 4: To See the Future in the Present, Find the Present in the Past

One idea whose time has come in social psychology is the accumulation of social data archives. Leaders of both the social science and the political establishments have recognized that we need a quality-of-life index (based perhaps on trace data, social records, self-reports obtained through survey research, etc.). Such social archives will also include data on factors which might affect subjective happiness, and analyses will be done to tease out the complex interrelations among these important variables. The need for such archives is adequately recognized; the interest and advocacy may even have outrun the talent, energy, and funds needed to assemble them.

In this growing interest in social data archives, one essential feature has been neglected, namely, the importance of obtaining time series data on the variables. While it will be useful to have contemporaneous data on a wide variety of social, economic, and psychological variables, the full exploitation of these data becomes possible only when we have recorded them at several successive points in time. Likewise, while a nationwide survey of subjective feelings and attitudes is quite useful for its demographic breakdowns at one point in time, the value of such a social survey becomes magnified many times when we have it repeated at successive points in history. It is only when we have the time series provided by a reconstructed or preplanned longitudinal study that we can apply the powerful methodology of time series analyses which allow us to reduce the complexity of the data and identify causality.

Hence, my fourth koan emphasizes the usefulness of collecting and using social data archives but adds that we should collect data on these variables not only at a single contemporaneous point in time, but also that we should set up a time series by reconstructing measures of the variables from the recent and distant past and prospectively by repeated surveys into the future.

Koan 5: The New Methodology Where Correlation Can Indicate Causation

If we agree that the simple linear sequence model has outlived its usefulness for guiding our theorizing about cognitive and social systems, then we must also grant that the laboratory manipulational experiment should not be the standard method for testing psychological hypotheses. But most graduate programs and most of the published studies (Higbee & Wells, 1972) focus disproportionately on descriptive and inferential statistics appropriate mainly to the linear models from the recent paradigm. The methods taught and used are characterized by obsolescent procedures, such as rigorous distinction between dependent and independent variables, two-variable or few-variable designs, an assumption of continuous variables, the setting of equal numbers and equal intervals, etc.

It seems to me that we should revise the methodology curriculum of our graduate programs and our research practice so as to make us better able to cope with the dirty data of the real world, where the intervals cannot be preset equally, where the subjects cannot be assigned randomly and in the same number, and where continuous measures and normal distributions typically cannot be obtained. In previous writings in recent years, I have called attention to advances in these directions which I mention here (McGuire, 1967, 1969), and Campbell (1969) has been in the forefront in devising, assembling, and using such procedures.

Our graduate programs should call the student's attention to new sources of social data, such as archives conveniently storing information from public opinion surveys, and to non-reactive measures of the unobtrusive trace type discussed by Webb and his colleagues.

Our students should also be acquainted with the newer analytic methods that make more possible the reduction of the complex natural field to a manageable number of underlying variables whose interrelations can be determined. To this end, we and our students must have the opportunity to master new techniques for scaling qualitative data, new methods of multivariate analysis, such as those devised by Shepard and others, and the use of time series causal analyses like the cross-lag panel design. More training is also needed in computer simulation and techniques of parameter estimation.

Mastery of these techniques will not be easy. Because we older researchers have already mastered difficult techniques which have served us well, we naturally look upon this retooling task with something less than enthusiasm. We have worked hard and endured much; how much more can be asked of us? But however we answer that question regarding our obligation to master these techniques ourselves, we owe it to our students to make the newer techniques available to those who wish it, rather than requiring all students to preoccupy themselves with the old techniques which have served us so well in reaching the point from which our students must now proceed.

Koan 6: *The Riches of Poverty*

The industrial countries, where the great bulk of psychological research is conducted, have in the past couple of years suffered economic growing pains which, if they have not quite reduced the amount of funds available for scientific research, at least have reduced the rate at which these funds have been growing. In the United States, at least, the last couple of years have been ones of worry about leveling scientific budgets. It is my feeling that the worry exceeds the actuality. In the United States' situation, psychology has in fact suffered very little as compared with our sister sciences. As an irrepressible optimist I am of the opinion that not only will this privileged position of psychology continue but also that the budgetary retrenchment in the other fields of science is only a temporary one and that, in the long run, the social investment in scientific research will resume a healthy, if not exuberant, rate of growth. I recognize that this optimism on my part will do little to cheer scientists whose own research programs have been hard hit by the financial cuts. To my prediction that in the long run social investment in science will

grow again after this temporary recession, they might point out (like Keynes) that in the long run we shall all be dead.

I persist in my Dr. Pangloss optimism that things are going to turn out well and even engage in gallows humor by saying that what psychological research has needed is a good depression. I do feel that during the recent period of affluence when we in the United States could obtain government funds for psychological research simply by asking, we did develop some fat, some bad habits, and some distorted priorities which should now be corrected. While we could have made these corrections without enforced poverty, at least we can make a virtue of necessity by using this time of budgetary retrenchment to cut out some of the waste and distraction so that we shall emerge from this period of retrenchment stronger than we entered it.

The days of easy research money sometimes induced frenzies of expensive and exhausting activity. We hired many people to help us, often having to dip into less creative populations, and to keep them employed the easiest thing to do was to have them continue doing pretty much what we had alreay done, resulting in a stereotyping of research and a repetitious output. It tended to result in the collection of more data of the same type and subjecting it to the same kinds of analyses as in the past. It also motivated us to churn out one little study after another, to the neglect of the more solitary and reflective intellectual activity of integrating all the isolated findings into more meaningful big pictures.

Affluence has also produced the complex research project which has removed us from reality into the realm of data as I discussed in Koan 3. The affluent senior researcher often carried out his work through graduate assistants and research associates, who, in turn, often have the actual observations done by parapsychological technicians or hourly help, and the data they collect go to card-punchers who feed them into computers, whose output goes back to the research associate, who might call the more meaningful outcome to the attention of the senior researcher who is too busy meeting the payrolls to control the form of the printout or look diligently through it when it arrives. A cutback in research funds might in some cases divert these assistants into more productive and satisfying work while freeing the creative senior researcher from wasting his efforts on meeting the payroll rather than observing the phenomena.

I am urging here, then, that if the budgetary cutbacks continue instead of running ever faster on the Big-Science treadmill, we make the best of the bad bargain by changing our research organization, our mode of working, and our priorities. I would suggest that rather than fighting for a bigger slice of the diminishing financial pie, we redirect our efforts somewhat. We should rediscover the gratification of personally observing the phenomena ourselves and experiencing the relief of not having to administer our research empire. Also, I think we should spend a greater portion of our time trying to interpret and integrate the empirical relationships that have been turned up by the recent deluge of studies, rather than simply adding new, undigested relationships to the existing pile.

Koan 7: The Opposite of a Great Truth Is Also True

What I have been prescribing above is not a simple, coherent list. A number of my urgings would pull the field in opposite directions. For example, Koan 1 urges that

our methodology courses place more emphasis on the creative hypothesis-forming aspect of research even at the cost of less attention to the critical, hypothesis-testing aspect, but then in Koan 5 I urged that we, or at least our students, master a whole new pattern of hypothesis-testing procedures. Again, Koan 3 urges that we observe concrete phenomena rather than abstract data, but Koan 4 favors assembling social data archives that would reduce concrete historical events to abstract numbers. My prescriptions admittedly ride off in opposite directions, but let us remember that "consistency is the hobgoblin of little minds."

That my attempt to discuss ways in which our current psychological research enterprise could be improved has led me in opposite directions does not terribly disconcert me. I remember that Bohr has written, "There are trivial truths and great truths. The opposite of a trivial truth is plainly false. The opposite of a great truth is also true." The same paradox has appealed to thinkers of East and West alike since Sikh sacred writings advise that if any two passages in that scripture contradict one another, then both are true. The urging at the same time of seemingly opposed courses is not necessarily false. It should be recognized that I have been giving mini-directives which are only a few parts of the total system which our psychological research and research training should involve. Indeed, I have specified only a few components of such a total research program. Any adequate synthesis of a total program must be expected to contain theses and antitheses.

I have asserted that social psychology is currently passing through a period of more than usual uneasiness, an uneasiness which is felt even more by researchers inside the field than by outside observers. I have tried to analyze and describe the sources of this uneasiness as it is felt at various levels of depth. I have also described a few of the undercurrents which I believe will, or at any rate should, be part of the wave of the future which will eventuate in a new paradigm which will lead us to further successes, after it replaces the recent paradigm which has served us well but shows signs of obsolescence.

A time of troubles like the present one is a worrisome period in which to work, but it is also an exciting period. It is a time of contention when everything is questioned, when it sometimes seems that "the best lack all conviction, while the worst are full of passionate intensity." It may seem that this is the day of the assassin, but remember that "it is he devours death, mocks mutability, has heart to make an end, keeps nature new." These are the times when the "rough beast, its hour come round at last, slouches toward Bethlehem to be born." Ours is a dangerous period, when the stakes have been raised, when nothing seems certain but everything seems possible.

I began this talk by describing the proud and placid social psychology of a half-dozen years back, just before the bell tolled, as suggesting Buson's beautiful sleeping butterfly. I close by drawing upon his disciple, the angry young man Shiki, for a related but dynamically different image of the new social psychology which is struggling to be born. Shiki wrote a variant on Buson's haiku as follows:

> *Tsurigane-ni*
> *Tomarite hikaru*
> *Hotaru kana.*

Or,

> *On a temple bell*
> *Waiting, glittering,*
> *A firefly.*

REFERENCES

Campbell, D. T. Reforms as experiments. *American Psychologist,* 1969, 24, 409-429.

Fried, S. B., Gumpper, D.C., & Allen, J.C. Ten years of social psychology: Is there a growing commitment to field research? *American Psychologist,* 1973, 28, 155-156.

Higbee, K. L., & Wells, M. G. Some research trends in social psychology during the 1960s. *American Psychologist,* 1972, 27, 963-966.

McGuire, W. J. Learning theory and social psychology. In O. Klineberg & R. Christie (Eds.), *Perspectives in social psychology.* New York: Holt, Rinehart & Winston, 1965.

McGuire, W. J. Some impending reorientations in social psychology. *Journal of Experimental Social Psychology,* 1967, 3, 124-139.

McGuire, W. J. Theory-oriented research in natural settings: The best of both worlds for social psychology. In M. Sherif & C. Sherif (Eds.), *Interdisciplinary relationships in the social sciences.* Chicago: Aldine, 1969.

Sears, D. O., & Abeles, R. P. Attitudes and opinions. *Annual Review of Psychology,* 1969, 20, 253-288.

Designing Research for Application

Bobby J. Calder, Lynn W. Phillips, and Alice M. Tybout

Two distinct types of generalizability are identified in consumer research. One entails the application of specific effects, whereas the other entails the application of general scientific theory. Effects application and theory application rest on different philosophical assumptions, and have different methodological implications. A failure to respect these differences has led to much confusion, regarding issues such as the appropriateness of student subjects and laboratory settings.

There is always the expectation in conducting research that the findings ultimately will be useful in addressing situations beyond the one studied. Yet, there exists a concern that much of consumer research, and behavioral research in general, is not generalizable. It frequently is argued that research procedures, particularly the use of student subjects and laboratory settings, necessarily limit the application of findings. Underlying this contention is a failure to recognize that generalizability is not a single issue. Two distinct types of application may be identified in consumer research. The purpose of this paper is to examine the two types of application, and to specify their implications for research design.

The first type of generalizability, which we term *effects application,* maps observed data directly into events beyond the research setting. That is, the specific effects obtained are expected to mirror findings that would be observed if data were collected for other populations and settings in

the real world.[1] The second type, which we term *theory application,* uses only scientific theory to explain events beyond the research setting. Effects observed in the research are employed to assess the status of theory. But, it is the theoretical explanation that is expected to be generalizable and not the particular effects obtained.

The paper begins by elaborating the distinction between the goals of effects application and theory application. Then, the ramifications of this distinction are discussed by addressing the following questions:

- What specific research procedures are appropriate when each type of application is intended?
- What are the resulting implications of these differences in research procedures for methodological controversies in the literature regarding the use of student subjects and laboratory settings?
- What philosophical assumptions underlie each type of application, and what then should be done to improve our ability to make each type?

In examining these issues, it is shown that the two types of application lead to different priorities when designing studies.

The authors thank Joel Cohen, Claes Fornell, Louis W. Stern, and Brian Sternthal for comments on earlier drafts of this paper.

"Designing Research for Application" by B.J. Calder, L.W. Phillips & A.M. Tybout, 1981, *Journal of Consumer Research, 8,* pp. 197-207. Reprinted by permission of The Journal of Consumer Research, Inc.

It is argued that the failure to distinguish between the research designs optimum for each type has led to inappropriate conclusions regarding the impact of student subjects and laboratory settings on generalizability. Finally, it is observed that, despite the need for both effects application and theory application in consumer research, each rests on assumptions and can be improved by consideration of the validity of these assumptions.

DISTINGUISHING RESEARCH GOALS

Effects application and theory application have common elements as well as distinguishing features. Research seeking either type of generalizability necessarily involves some framework or reasoning that might be loosely referred to as "theory." And in both instances, research entails observations of some "effects" related to the theoretical framework. The distinction lies in whether the researcher's primary goal is to apply the specific effects observed or to apply a more general theoretical understanding. In this section, we examine the goals and procedures for achieving each type of generalization.

Effects application is based on a desire for knowledge about the events and relationships in a particular real-world situation. The primary goal of this type of research (hereafter referred to as "effects research") is to obtain findings that can be applied directly to the situation of interest. A theoretical framework may be used to identify and measure effects.[2] But it is the effects themselves that are generalized rather than being linked by inference to theoretical constructs and the hypothesized

theoretical network then used to deduce patterns of outcomes.

Application of effects calls for correspondence procedures. It is necessary to assess effects in a research setting that corresponds to a real-world situation. Complete correspondence is difficult to achieve, however. The mere fact of data collection usually distinguishes the research setting from its real-world counterpart. And, because interest rarely is limited to present situations, temporal differences often exist as well. These differences, and others, between the research setting and the real world are inevitable. Effects application, nonetheless, is characterized by the premise that there is *sufficient* correspondence to expect the effects observed to be repeated in the real world.

In contrast, theory application is based on a desire for scientific knowledge about events and relationships that occur in a variety of real-world situations. The primary goal of such research (hereafter referred to as "theory research") is to identify scientific theories that provide a general understanding of the real world. Theory applications call for falsification test procedures. These procedures are used to test a theory by creating a context and measuring effects within that context that have the potential to disprove or refute the theory. The research context and effects are not of interest in their own right. Their significance lies in the information that they provide about the theory's adequacy. Theories that repeatedly survive rigorous falsification attempts are accepted as scientific explanation (subject to further more stringent testing), and are candidates for application.[3] Scientific theories typically are universal and, therefore, can explain any real-world situation within their domain.

The actual application of theory entails

using the scientific explanation to design a program or intervention predicted to have some effect in the real world. In a marketing context, the intervention may take the form of a product, price, communication strategy, etc. It is crucial to note that, whatever the strategy, the process of translating from theory to intervention is necessarily a creative one. Theories neither specify how their abstract constructs can be embodied in real-world interventions nor identify the level(s) that uncontrolled theoretical variables will assume in a particular application. Moreover, theories are always incom-

EXHIBIT 1
Summary of Two Approaches to Applicability

	Effects application	Theory application
Research goal	To obtain findings that can be generalized directly to a real-world situation of interest.	To obtain scientific theory that can be generalized through the design of theory-based interventions that are viable in the real world.
Research procedure	Generalizing effects requires procedures to ensure that the research setting accurately reflects the real world. These are termed *correspondence procedures.*	Generalizing theory requires two stages of *falsification procedures.* First, *theory falsification procedures* are used to ensure that the abstract theoretical explanation is rendered fully testable. Theories that survive rigorous attempts at falsification are accepted and accorded scientific status.
		Accepted theory is used as a framework for designing an intervention. Then, *intervention falsification procedures* are used to test the intervention under conditions that could cause it to fail in the real world. Only interventions surviving these tests are implemented.

plete—they deal with a subset of variables that exist in the real world. Consequently, the design process must rely on some assumptions about the operation of both theoretical and nontheoretical variables.

Because intervention design is creative, basing an intervention on theory that has survived rigorous falsification attempts is not sufficient to ensure that the intervention will yield the theoretically predicted outcome. Separate falsification procedures are required to test a theory and a theory-based intervention. Perhaps an example can best illustrate this. Theories of aerodynamics explain the processes underlying flight. It is not possible, however, to design an airplane solely from aerodynamic theory. Any number of stress studies and the like are necessary to calibrate the theory to conditions in a particular real-world situation. These studies, which we term efforts at intervention falsification, systematically subject the intervention to conditions that might cause it to fail in a particular situation. If the intervention does not perform as predicted by

the theory, then its weaknesses are exposed. As in theory testing, failures are more informative than successes. But, the failure of an intervention need not imply inadequacies in the theory. Indeed, failure of the theoretical explanation can be implied only when theory falsification procedures are employed.[4] Theory falsification procedures are, thus, the foundation of any effort to apply theory.

If it succeeds, confidence that the intervention is viable increases. As a result, the intervention may be used in the real world. In contrast to effects application, however, *no attempt is made to generalize any particular outcomes observed in testing the theory or the intervention.* It is only the theoretical relationship that the intervention is presumed to represent that is applied beyond the research setting.

The goals of research leading to effects application and to theory application are summarized in Exhibit 1. As we have indicated, different research procedures are necessary to achieve each of these goals.

TABLE 1

Summary Table of Analysis of Variance for Belief Change

Source	SS	df	MS	F
Disc (A)	160.07	2	80.03	36.67
Own (B)	450.82	2	225.41	103.26
Source (C)	452.62	2	226.31	103.67
A × B	236.24	4	59.06	27.06
A × C	141.24	4	35.31	16.18
B × C	97.42	4	24.36	11.16
A × B × C	170.24	8	21.28	9.75
Error	530.45	243	2.18	
Total	2,239.12	269		

Note: All *F* values are significant at $p < .01$.

TABLE 2

Mean Belief Change Scores as a Function of Discrepancy, Source Confidence, and Own Confidence

| Source confidence | Own confidence | | | | | | | | | |
| | High discrepancy | | | Moderate discrepancy | | | Low discrepancy | | | |
	High	Moderate	Low	High	Moderate	Low	High	Moderate	Low	M
High	1.8	5.6	13.0	2.3	5.3	5.4	2.2	2.5	2.8	4.54
Moderate	1.7	1.6	6.1	.5	2.1	4.1	1.7	1.9	2.4	2.45
Low	.7	1.1	2.8	.9	1.5	1.8	.8	1.0	2.3	1.43
M	1.4	2.77	7.3	1.23	2.97	3.77	1.57	1.8	2.5	

We now examine these research procedures in greater detail.

COMPARISON OF CORRESPONDENCE AND FALSIFICATION PROCEDURES

Effects application relies on research methods not only different from, but also largely incompatible with, the methods leading to theory application. The former requires correspondence procedures to ensure that all features of the real world are represented in the research setting. The latter requires falsification procedures to ensure, first, that the abstract scientific explanation is rendered fully testable, and, second, that the concrete theory-based intervention is viable under conditions present in the real world.

In this section, research procedures leading to effects application and those leading to theory application are compared with respect to selecting respondents, operationalizing variables, choosing research settings, and selecting research designs. This entails contrasting correspondence, theory falsification, and intervention falsification procedures. Primary consideration is given to the comparison of correspondence and *theory* falsification procedures because they are maximally different, and their differences are particularly relevant to methodological controversies in the literature. Theory falsification procedures also are emphasized because they lie at the heart of any theory application. Discussion of the distinguishing features of intervention falsification procedures is deferred until the end of the section. (See Exhibit 2 for a comparison of all three procedures.)

Selecting Respondents

When effects application is the goal, correspondence procedures require that research participants match individuals in the

EXHIBIT 2

Comparison of Research Procedures Optimal for Correspondence, Theory Falsification, and Intervention Falsification

Methodological issues	Correspondence procedures	Falsification procedures	
		Theory	Intervention
Selection of respondents	Use a sample statistically representative of the real-world population.	Use a sample homogeneous on nontheoretical variables.	Use a sample that encompasses individual differences that might influence performance of the intervention.
Operationali- zation of key variables	Operationalize variables in the research to parallel those in the real world.	Ensure that empirical opera- tionalization of theoretical constructs cannot be construed in terms of other constructs.	Operationalize variables to reflect the manner in which an intervention is to be implemented in the real world.
Selection of a research setting	Choose a research setting statistically representative of the environmental variation present in the real world.	Choose a setting that allows operationalization of theoretical constructs and is free of extraneous sources of variation.	Choose a setting encompassing en- vironmental heterogeneity that might influence the performance of the intervention.
Selection of a research design	Use a design that preserves the correspondence between the research environment, and provides the type of information required for decision making (e.g., descriptive, correlational, causal).	Use a design that affords the strongest possible inferences about the relationships between theoretical constructs.	Use a design that affords the strongest possible test of the intervention subject to constraints imposed by the need to represent real-world variation.

real world setting of interest. Ideally, this is accomplished by carefully defining the relevant population for the effects of interest, and then employing in the investigation a strictly representative sample of individuals from this target population.[5] This procedure is necessary if any generalization from the sample to the population is to be statistically valid. But, because strict statistical sampling often is not feasible, other procedures may be invoked to enhance the representativeness of individuals in the research. For example, it may be possible to replicate the study with different subgroups of the target population. Alternatively, one might purposively sample individuals who vary on important dimensions that characterize members of the target population. Some degree of representativeness could even be achieved by sampling only the most prevalent type of individual in the target population (Cook and Campbell 1975).

The underlying theoretical framework may be useful in determining important dimensions for any nonrepresentative sample. When alternatives to statistical sampling are employed, however, the application of the results must rest on belief that the sample(s) accurately reflects the population and not on any statistical principle. Thus, confidence in generalizing is severely weakened when statistical sampling is not used.

The criteria are quite different when theory application is the goal. The theory falsification procedures, which underlie this type of generalization, require only that research participants be selected to provide a rigorous test of the theory at issue. Because most scientific theories are universal in scope, any respondent group can provide a test of the theory's predictions (Kruglanski 1973; Webster and Kervin 1971).[6] The ideal theory falsification procedure, however, is to employ maximally homogeneous re-spondents.[7] This entails sampling from groups of individuals that are similar on dimensions likely to influence the variables of theoretical interest. (For example, for some theories, students or housewives with similar profiles on relevant dimensions may qualify as homogeneous respondents.)

Homogeneous respondents are desired for two reasons. First, they permit more exact theoretical predictions than may be possible with a heterogeneous group. For instance, by employing a homogeneous student sample it might be possible to predict that purchases of a particular product known to be used by students would decrease with advertising exposure. In contrast, if a more heterogeneous sample were selected it might be possible only to predict a decline in some broad category of products. The greater variability in behavior associated with a heterogeneous group makes precise predictions more difficult. This makes failure of the theory harder to detect. Thus, heterogeneous respondents may weaken the theory test.

Homogeneous respondents also are preferred because they decrease the chance of making a false conclusion about whether there is covariation between the variables under study. When respondents are heterogeneous with respect to characteristics that affect their responses, the error variance is increased and the sensitivity of statistical tests in identifying the significant relationships declines. Thus, heterogeneous respondents constitute a threat to statistical conclusion validity (Cook and Campbell 1975). They increase the chance of making a Type II error and concluding that a theory was disconfirmed when, in fact, the theoretical relationship existed but was obscured by variability in the data attributable to nontheoretical constructs. By selecting maximally homogeneous samples, or by conducting full or partial replications of the research for each level or "block" of a respondent characteristic believed to inflate error variance, these random sources of error can be controlled, and the likelihood of making a Type II error decreased (Cook and Campbell 1975; Winer 1971). As a result, the researcher can be more confident that any negative results reflect failure of the theoretical explanation.

It should be noted that nothing in the theory falsification procedure rules out statistical sampling from a relevant population. But a representative sample is not required because *statistical* generalization of the findings is *not* the goal. It is the theory that is applied beyond the research setting. The research sample need only allow a test of the theory. And, any sample within the theory's domain (e.g., any relevant sample), not just a representative one, can provide such a test.

In summary, effects application requires correspondence between the research sample and the population of interest. This is best achieved through statistical sampling. Only such sampling justifies statistical generalization of the research findings. In contrast, theory application requires a research sample that permits falsification of the theory. Although any sample in the theory's domain can potentially falsify the theory, homogeneous samples are preferred because they typically provide a stronger test of the theory. Only the theory is applied and its applicability is determined by its scientific status, not by statistical sampling principles.

Operationalizing Independent and Dependent Variables

Whether the goal is effects application or theory application, valid operationalizations of the independent and dependent variables are necessary. The two types of application differ, however, in the nature of the variables they strive to capture and, thus, in their criteria and procedures for achieving this objective. When the goal is theory application, theory falsification procedures require that the operationalization of constructs (i.e., the independent and dependent variables) render the theory testable. This involves making certain that there is a high degree of correspondence between the empirical operationalizations and the abstract concepts they intend to represent, and that the empirical indicators used to represent the theory's constructs cannot be construed in terms of other constructs. This is necessary to ensure that any failure to disconfirm the theory is not due to the use of empirical operationalizations not measuring the theoretical constructs and, thus, not testing the relationship of interest. This mislabeling of operationalizations in the theory-relevant terms is referred to as a threat to the construct validity of research results (Cook and Campbell 1975).[8]

Attaining construct validity in theory research requires rigorous definition of the theoretical constructs so that empirical measures can be tailored to them. Further, because single exemplars of any construct always contain measurement components that are irrelevant to the theoretical construct of interest, validity is enhanced by employing multiple operationalizations of each construct (Campbell and Fiske 1959; Cook and Campbell 1975). Multiple exemplars of each construct should demonstrably share common variance attributable to the target construct, and should differ from each other in unique ways (Campbell and Fiske 1959). Such "multiple operationalism" allows one to test whether a theoretical relationship holds even though measurement error is present in each operationalization (Bagozzi 1979).

When the goal is effects application, the

operationalization of variables is determined by the need for correspondence. Indices of the independent and dependent variables in the research setting are chosen to parallel events in the real world. They are not tailored to abstract theoretical constructs that these variables may be presumed to represent.

Similarity between the operationalizations of variables and their real-world counterparts is maximized by using naturally occurring events in the target setting as independent variables, and naturally occurring behaviors in the target setting as dependent variables (Tunnell 1977; Webb, Campbell, Schwartz, and Sechrest 1966). Events and behaviors are considered to be "natural" if they occur in the real world. This does not necessarily imply that such events will be uncontrolled by the researcher. Price, advertising strategy, etc., are determined by decision-makers; thus, their systematic variation for research purposes would not compromise naturalness, provided that their variations reflected any real-world constraints (e.g., any practical constraints preventing disentangling related components of a marketing program in the real world). On occasion, however, the researcher may be concerned with effects on variables for which no naturally occurring measures are available, e.g., attitudes. Then, measures must be designed to assess these variables, while still preserving the correspondence between the research setting and the real world. Generally, this is achieved by making these measures as unobtrusive as possible. Regardless of the variables being examined, measurement error is a concern. Therefore, multiple measures of variables also are desirable in research leading to effects application.

The objectives when operationalizing variables for theory research are largely incompatible with the objectives when operationalizing variables for effects research. As just noted, the correspondence needed for effects application is achieved best by employing naturally occurring events and behaviors as variables, whenever possible. However, naturally occurring events and behaviors generally are inappropriate variables in research testing theory. They do not permit the researcher much latitude in tailoring operationalizations to theoretical constructs. Moreover, naturally occurring events often serve as indicators of a complex package of several theoretically-distinct constructs. Rarely can they be taken as indicators of a single unidimensional construct. Theory falsification procedures aim to untangle these packages into several distinct variables that can be labeled in theoretical terms. Correspondence procedures aim to preserve these packages as single variables to reflect events in the real world more accurately. Thus, these two types of construct validity typically cannot be pursued simultaneously.

Choosing a Research Setting

The goals of effects application and theory application also imply different criteria in choosing a research setting. The correspondence procedures associated with effects application lead to maximizing the similarity between the research setting and the real-world situation of interest (Ellsworth 1977; Tunnel 1977). This real-world situation usually is heterogeneous on a number of background factors. For example, it may include variation in the time of day, the season, the complexity of the products involved, or the characteristics of salespersons who deliver influence attempts. To enhance transfer of the research findings to the real world, the research setting must reflect the heterogeneity of the background factors. Ideally, a random sampling of background factors present in the real world would be employed (Brunswik 1956). From a statistical perspective, only this method of treating the heterogeneity in such factors allows generalizing the results from the research to the real world.

Often it is infeasible, if not impossible, to represent systematically all the variation in the real-world setting within a single study. In such circumstances, the researcher may try to identify the background factors most likely to impact the effects of interest. The underlying theoretical framework may be used for this purpose. Then, these factors may be represented in several ways. The study may be replicated in settings representing different levels of these background factors. Alternatively, variation on significant factors may be built into a single study without randomly sampling such factors. Or, some degree of representativeness might be achieved by including only the most frequent or typical setting factor(s) found in the real world (Cook and Campbell 1975). When these approaches are employed, however, generalization of the effects must rest on judgment that all important background factors have been properly represented, and not on a statistical principle.

Regardless of which procedure for treating setting heterogeneity is followed, representativeness is best achieved through field research. Field research refers to "any setting which respondents do not perceive to have been set up for the primary purpose of conducting research" (Cook and Campbell 1975, p. 224). The idea is to conduct the research in the real world with as little intrusion as possible. When effects research must be conducted in nonfield (i.e., laboratory) contexts, efforts should be made to incorporate the critical background factors from the real-world setting into the laboratory setting (Sawyer, Worthing, and Sendak 1979).

The theory falsification procedures associated with theory application lead to selection of an entirely different research setting. To test a theory, its constructs must be tied to a particular set of observables in a specific circumstance. It is not important, however, that these events be representative of some set of events that occur in another setting. Rather, the particular events at issue in the research setting are only important as operationalizations of the theory. What is required is that a theory's operationalization in the test setting allow it to be falsified. Typically, this involves choosing a research setting relatively free of extraneous sources of variation, e.g., free of variation on variables not of theoretical interest, and free of variation in treatment implementation. Extraneous variation can produce spurious effects on the dependent variable, and, at a minimum, inflates error variance (Cook and Campbell 1975). To the extent that theoretically irrelevant factors are at work, significant relationships between the phenomena under study may be obscured and the risk of Type II error may be increased. Insulated test settings minimize such irrelevancies.

Most often, the best procedure for reducing the number of random irrelevancies is to employ a controlled laboratory setting. In contrast to field settings, laboratory settings facilitate the use of standardized procedures and treatment implementation, and allow the researcher to control rigorously the stimuli impinging upon respondents. Moreover, laboratory settings possess other inherent advantages, relative to field settings, in conducting the strongest possible test of a theory. Homogeneous respondents are obtained more easily in the laboratory, because the investigator typically has greater control over who participates in a study. Similarly, the laboratory provides greater latitude for tailoring empirical operationalizations to the constructs they are meant to represent, because operationalizations in the laboratory are only limited by the ingenuity of the investigator, and not by naturally occurring variation and real-world constraints. And, the laboratory possesses greater potential for achieving multiple operationalizations of independent and dependent variables, because the expense associated with exposing individuals to a number of independent variables and administering a number of dependent variable responses typically is lower for the laboratory than for the field. Thus, laboratory settings generally are better geared to achieving high degrees of statistical conclusion validity and theoretical construct validity.

The advantages of the laboratory in terms of increasing statistical power and enhancing construct validity are not without limit. Tests of certain theoretical hypotheses may lead to the field if they involve variables not easily examined in laboratory settings. Thus, the advantages of insulated settings may sometimes have to be given up in order to achieve adequate empirical realizations of a theory's constructs. Nevertheless, such limits to the utility of employing laboratory settings in theory tests do not contradict our thesis. They simply reaffirm the general rule that settings yielding the strongest test of the theory should be employed when the goal is theory application. In many cases, this will be the laboratory.

Selecting a Research Design

The choice of a research setting either determines or is determined by the research design to be used. For example, laboratory research is usually associated with "true" experimental designs wherein respondents are randomly assigned to treatments (Camp-

bell and Stanley 1966; Cook and Campbell 1975). When the goal is theory application, and theory testing is being conducted, true experimental designs are preferred because they allow the strongest test. Unlike other designs, such as the survey method or the case study, true experiments permit the investigator to minimize the possibility that third variables cause any observed relation between the independent and dependent variables. This is necessary to ensure that any failure to disconfirm the theory linking the variables is not due to the spurious impact of irrelevant third variables. Moreover, true experiments allow the investigator to establish that the independent variable precedes the dependent variable in time, thus ruling out the possibility that the dependent variable initiates changes in the independent variable, rather than vice versa. The capacity for establishing temporal antecedence and for ruling out third variable rival explanations enables true experiments to eliminate most plausible threats to internal validity, i.e., threats to the conclusion that a demonstrated statistical relationship between the independent and dependent variables implies causality (Cook and Campbell 1975). This is a critical aspect of theory falsification procedures because most theories are stated in a causal framework. True experiments, by ranking higher than other research designs on internal validity, allow the strongest test of causality.[9]

The general preference for true experimental procedures does not mean that all research testing theory will employ such designs. On occasion, the independent variable(s) of interest is not subject to manipulation by the researcher, and conditions prevent random assignment of respondents to different treatments. When this occurs, correlational or quasi-experimental designs must be employed. In certain cases, these designs permit causal inferences (Bagozzi 1979; Cook and Campbell 1975), and even when they do not, they are often of sufficient probing value to be worth employing. However, research designs of less efficiency than true experiments should be used only when true experiments are not feasible (Campbell and Stanley 1966). This is in keeping with the criterion that the research design chosen be the one that offers the strongest test of the theory.

When the goal is effects application, the need for correspondence necessitates different research design priorities. The design depends on the nature of the event structure of interest and the particular information needed regarding that structure. If it is important to establish the causal sequence of the events in the real world, then true experiments are preferred whenever possible. Yet, true experiments may not be feasible to examine certain variables. And, true experiments may seriously compromise the naturalness of the research setting. In these circumstances, or when causal statements regarding the event structure are not required as a basis for decision making, research seeking effects application should opt for correlational or quasi-experimental designs. Such designs are far less intrusive and, hence, enhance correspondence between the research setting and the real-world situation.

Summary

Effects application and theory application differ sharply in the research procedures upon which they depend. When effects application is the goal, correspondence procedures are required to ensure that the findings are generalizable to some real-world situation of interest. These procedures allow *nothing* to be done that might cause an important mismatch between the research and the real-world situation. Ideally, this goal is achieved by employing a representative sample of respondents, using natural events and behaviors as variables in a field context, and selecting a research design that preserves the natural setting (see Exhibit 2). To the extent that similarity between the research and the real-world is achieved, the empirical outcomes observed may be applied in the real world.

When theory application is the goal, falsification procedures are required to assess the scientific status of the theory. These procedures allow *anything* to be done that will ensure a rigorous test of the theory. Such a test is provided when internal, construct, and statistical-conclusion validity are maximized. As summarized in Exhibit 2, this entails selecting homogeneous respondent samples, tailoring multiple empirical operationalizations to the abstract theoretical concepts that they are meant to represent, and conducting true experiments in laboratory or other settings that are relatively free of extraneous sources of variation. If research provides a strong test of the theory, and if the theory escapes refutation, then the theory is accepted as a scientific explanation of real-world events.

Theory application is done through the design of a theory-based intervention. But, before such an intervention is implemented in the real world, intervention falsification procedures are required to test its performance. Like theory falsification procedures, intervention falsification procedures seek the most rigorous test possible. But, in contrast to a theory test, a rigorous intervention test is not provided by minimizing variation on nontheoretical factors. Instead, such a test is obtained by exposing the intervention to real-world variability that might cause it

to fail. Thus, internal, construct, and statistical-conclusion validity are pursued
within limits created by the need to reflect
important dimensions of the real world. As
summarized in Exhibit 2, this entails selecting research respondents and choosing
a research setting that are heterogeneous on
variables likely to affect intervention outcomes, operationalizing variables to reflect
the manner in which the intervention would
be implemented in the real world, and employing the most rigorous research design
possible given the need to capture aspects
of real-world variability. Only interventions
that yield outcomes predicted by the theory
in such a test situation are applied in the
real world.

Although superficially similar, intervention falsification procedures and correspondence procedures are distinct. Correspondence procedures demand that the
research provide an *accurate representation* of the real-world situation of interest.
This is necessary because the goal is to apply the particular effects observed in the
research to the real world. Intervention falsification procedures only require that the
research subject the intervention to *levels
of variability* that it might encounter in the
real world. The research need not mirror
the real world because it is the theoretical
relationship represented by the intervention, and not the particular effects observed
in the research, that is applied.

THE METHODOLOGICAL
LITERATURE

Much confusion in the methodological
literature has resulted from a lack of realization that different procedures are optimal
for achieving the two types of generalizability. This confusion is particularly evident
in criticism of laboratory studies with stu-

dent respondents. It is instructive to review
this criticism with the research procedures
underlying effects application and theory
application in mind.

Objections to laboratory studies have traditionally centered on the "artificiality" of
the findings obtained (Aronson and Carlsmith 1968; Opp 1970; Webster and Kervin
1971). But in recent years these objections
have manifested themselves in two specific
lines of criticism (Kruglanski 1975). One
has been the concern that because much
research employs student, volunteer, and
other convenience samples, it cannot be
generalized to broader population groups.
In consumer research, this concern has
prompted a number of investigations attempting to determine whether students' responses to marketing stimuli are representative of the responses made by individuals
comprising some larger target population,
such as housewives, businessmen, etc. (Albert 1967; Cunningham, Anderson, and
Murphy 1974; Enis, Cox, and Stafford
1972; Khera and Benson 1970; Park and
Lessig 1977; Sheth 1970; Shuptrine 1975).
Moreover, it has led to the appeal for use
of more relevant and more representative
subject samples in laboratory research (Ferber 1977; McNemar 1946; Rosenthal and
Rosnow 1969b; Schultz 1969; Shuptrine
1975). Relevance refers to the need for samples or target populations appropriate to the
topic under investigation (Ferber 1977).
Representativeness refers to how accurately
the sample reflects characteristics of the target population.

A second major line of criticism has been
the argument that, because the laboratory
is characterized by unique features not
found in the real world, laboratory studies
necessarily yield nongeneralizable results.
The unique features most commonly referred to include the unrealistic character of

the interaction between the experimenter and the subject (Orne 1962; Reicken 1962; Silverman 1968; Sawyer 1975; Venkatesan 1967), and the unrealistic contextual features that make up the laboratory background (Banks 1965; Cox and Enis 1969; Green 1966; Uhl 1966). For example, it is often contended that studies of persuasion in laboratory settings differ from real-world persuasion situations in terms of such contextual factors as audience involvement, attention, noise, exposure time, motivation, and opportunity to make cognitive responses (Gardner 1970; Greenberg 1967; Ray 1977) and, thus, are limited in their relevance to the real world. This argument has been the impetus for suggestions that true experiments be conducted in field settings whenever possible (Banks 1965; Caffyn 1964; Cartwright and Zander 1968, p. 36; McGuire 1969; Ross and Smith 1968; Tunnell 1977; Uhl 1966), and that when laboratory settings are employed, research procedures be altered to take into account the real-world dimensions of the phenomenon under investigation (Fromkin and Streufert 1975; Ray 1977).

When effects application is the goal, the above concerns are well-founded. Correspondence between the subjects and the setting used in the research and those in the real world is a necessary condition for effects application. To the extent that the use of student or other convenience samples and laboratory settings undermines this correspondence, applicability of the effects observed is limited. Thus, procedures that enhance the match between the research environment and the real world, such as the use of relevant representative samples and field settings, are appropriate when effects application is desired.

Yet, when the goal is theory application, the call for research subjects and settings representative of the real world is inappropriate. The foundation of theory application is rigorous theory testing. It is a mistake to assume that the people and events in a theory test must reflect people and events in some real-world situation. Rather, the test circumstance simply must provide the strongest test of the theory possible. Features of the test are only constrained by the requirement that they not undermine the degree to which any demonstrated construct relationship can be generalized to other settings not ruled out by the theory. Any sample is relevant if it permits operationalization within the domain of the theory. Homogeneous convenience samples may thus be employed in theory research. In fact, homogeneous samples are preferred because their use enables more precise predictions and enhances statistical-conclusion validity, thereby increasing the rigor of the theory test.

Similarly, laboratory settings generally are desirable in theory testing research. The controlled environment of the laboratory typically allows the researcher to employ true experimental designs, to tailor variables to abstract theoretical constructs, and to minimize extraneous sources of variation. These features lead to high internal, construct, and statistical-conclusion validity, thereby providing a strong theory test.

The only damaging criticisms of the laboratory setting are those that specify why its unrealistic features might operate as plausible threats to internal, construct, or statistical-conclusion validity. For example, if the artificiality of the laboratory facilitates participants in guessing the experimental hypothesis, then internal validity may be threatened and the theory test weakened. If valid arguments can be made to this effect, generalizability of the observed construct relationship is impaired. Otherwise, the use of insulated environments, standardized procedures, and other "unrealistic" features may constitute perfectly acceptable theory-testing procedures.

Recommendations for alternatives to the controlled laboratory setting, such as the suggestions that true experiments be conducted in field settings or that real-world features be introduced into the laboratory, are detrimental to achieving a rigorous theory test. Conducting true experiments in field settings is likely to reduce internal validity because there are numerous obstacles to forming and maintaining randomly constituted groups in the field (Cook and Campbell 1975). Construct validity also may be lower because tailoring operationalizations to abstract constructs may be difficult in the field. In addition, statistical-conclusion validity is likely to suffer because the field affords less opportunity for using standardized procedures and controlling stimuli.

Likewise, attempts to incorporate real-world features into the laboratory may undermine construct and statistical-conclusion validity. These features can represent plausible sources of distortion regarding the theoretical labeling of the independent variables, as well as uncontrolled sources of error variance in dependent variable responses (Aronson and Carlsmith 1968; Cook and Campbell 1975; Webster and Kervin 1971). Thus, because these strategies could potentially decrease the internal, construct, and statistical-conclusion validity of research results, they should be avoided in theory-testing research whenever possible. Their implementation could compromise the severity of the theory test.

The conclusion is not that variation in people and events found in the real world is irrelevant to theory application, however.

On the contrary, it simply assumes a different role than in effects application. In theory application, accepted theory is used to design an intervention. This intervention, then, must be shown to perform successfully in the face of variability that it is likely to encounter in the real world. To test the performance of an intervention, it may be implemented in an uncontrolled environment such as a field setting, or it may be exposed to extreme levels of important variables in a controlled (laboratory) environment. But, as we observed earlier, the test environment need not be *representative* of any particular real-world situation (as is the case when effects application is sought); it only must expose the intervention to stress that could cause it to fail. Repeated failure of interventions based on a particular theory may suggest the need for a better explanation. However, testing procedures for any new theory remain controlled. The applicability of an explanation is never improved by weakening its test.

PHILOSOPHIES UNDERLYING THE TWO TYPES OF APPLICABILITY

Clarification of the procedural implications of the two types of applicability does much to resolve the confusion in the methodological literature. The distinction between effects application and theory application is more than a procedural one, however. Also at stake are two basic philosophies of how to go about application. Discussion rarely gets beyond the vague perception of research pursuing effects application as "intuitively practical" and research pursuing theory application as "academically respectable." Not surprisingly, many studies end up trying to embrace both, with little appreciation that they represent different philosophies. Accordingly, it is appropriate to end the present discussion with an explicit statement of the philosophical rationale underlying each approach to application.

Traditionally, the application of effects has rested philosophically on the principle of induction. The notion that observed effects will be repeated in the real world, given the use of correspondence procedures, is an inductive argument. The observation that something has happened is said to imply that it (or something similar) will happen again.

It must be pointed out, however, that, although intuitively plausible, induction turns out, on close examination, to be an extremely hollow form of argument. Induction actually has no basis in logic. With any logical argument, true premises should yield true conclusions. Yet even though the sun has come up every day so far, whether or not it comes up tomorrow is not a matter of logical necessity. True premises may yield a false conclusion. Induction is not a logical argument.

The intuitive appeal of an inductive argument is such that many researchers are willing to subscribe to it as a matter of experience, if not logic. After all, the sun appears to come up every day. Even the appeal from experience, however, is suspect. It amounts to using induction to justify itself. Because induction has seemed to work before, it will work in the future. The circularity of such reasoning is devastating in the case of effects application. The researcher has only a few observations on which to base conclusions. Conclusions about the real world must really be based on an uncritical faith in induction rather than any experience with observations.

It might seem that the problem of induc-

tion could be escaped by resorting to probabilistic conclusions. Given observed effects, the occurrence of a real-world event is not proven, but it is made more highly probable. Under any standard concept of probability, however, this turns out to be not very helpful. In principle, the researcher could observe an effect an infinite number of times. The number of observations actually available is obviously finite. Thus, the probability of any effect must be zero if the number of possible observations of the effect is infinite. Probabilities are not meaningful in the context of infinite possibility.

Our conclusion must be that effects application rests on very soft grounds. While this approach appears to be the epitome of rigorous application, it is mostly a matter of blind faith. Induction itself cannot support going from observed effects to conclusions about the real world.

Effects application might better be viewed as reasoning by analogy. There is no logical principle involved. Rather, outcomes observed in the research are related to outcomes of the real world. If the research conditions seem to be analogous to events in the real world, then the analogy is completed by concluding that observed effects will hold in the real world. Reasoning by analogy depends, not on logic, but on the researcher's insight. Although correspondence procedures may provide some basis for analogy, this process is ultimately qualitative in nature.[10] This argument cannot be pursued here; however, it is our opinion that effects application could be improved by the increased use of qualitative methods (Calder 1977).

In contrast to effects application, theory application rests on the logical principle that it is possible for observed effects to contradict a theory, thereby falsifying it. Theories are tested in situations where they can possibly fail. Only those that survive these tests, then, are accepted and are candidates for application.

The logical principle of falsification requires that theory testing be bound to formal methodological procedures. These procedures are designed to expose the theory to refutation, and should follow directly from the theoretical explanation itself. It is only where theory fully dictates observation that observation can contradict theory. Thus, qualitative methods are not essential in testing theory.

The falsification procedures employed to test theory are not sufficient to ensure successful theory application, however. Accepted theories can provide only a framework for designing interventions. These interventions also must be tested before they are applied in the real world. Again the logic of falsification is invoked. Research procedures are designed to expose the intervention to refutation. These procedures should follow directly from the underlying theory *and* the real-world circumstances that the intervention will face. If the intervention performs as predicted by the theory, it may be implemented. If, however, the intervention does not lead to expected outcomes, it must be modified. Careful assessment of theoretical and nontheoretical variables as part of the testing process may provide insight for this redesign.

Application of theory often stops short of efforts to falsify interventions. It is mistakenly assumed that accepted theories will yield usable interventions without further work. But, whereas such theories do provide efficient frameworks for design, testing the intervention designed is still necessary. Theory application in consumer research would be greatly improved by recognition of the need for, and role of, intervention falsification procedures.[11]

CONCLUSION

Consumer researchers pursue two distinct types of generalizability. One involves the application of specific effects observed in a research setting. The other involves the application of a general scientific theory. Although both types of generalization are tenable, it is important to determine which will be the primary goal prior to designing a study. Effects application and theory application are based on different philosophical assumptions and, therefore, require different research procedures.

Effects application rests on the presumption of correspondence between the research and some real-world situation of interest. If these two situations are analogous, then the outcomes observed in one can be expected to occur in the other. When effects application is the goal, the research subjects, setting, and variables examined must be representative of their real-world counterparts. Any procedures likely to impair the match between the research and the real world, such as convenience samples and laboratory settings, should be avoided. Because objective correspondence is impossible to achieve fully, and can never ensure equivalent *experience,* qualitative insight may assist the researcher in judging whether or not the research experience matches that of the real world.

Theory application rests on the acceptance of the scientific explanation itself. This acceptance is determined by the logical principle of falsification. Theories that survive rigorous efforts at disproof are accepted. The only requirement for research testing theory is that it provide the strongest test possible. Because homogeneous samples and laboratory settings often lead to a stronger test of the theory than heterogeneous samples and field settings, they may be preferred in this type of research. But, theory tests alone are not sufficient for theory application. Accepted theories must be calibrated to the real world through the design and testing of interventions.

In sum, the research procedures optimal for effects application and theory application are incompatible. This does not mean that there cannot be synergy between research pursuing each type of applicability. It does mean that research procedures can only be evaluated with reference to the type of generalizability being pursued. To do otherwise only leads to needless criticism and poor communication within the discipline.

NOTES

1. The term "real world" is employed in reference to all situations not constructed for, or altered by, the conduct of research. It is not meant to imply that research settings do not have their own reality.

2. The theoretical framework underlying effects research can be either scientific (i.e., a general theory that has survived rigorous testing) or intuitive (i.e., a theory generated to address a particular situation, which may be consistent with informal observations, but which has not undergone any rigorous testing). This is in contrast to theory research, which is restricted to the examination of general scientific theories. Although we subscribe to the view that scientific theory has advantages over intuitive theory even in effects research, this is obviously a debatable issue. Moreover, because this issue is only tangentially related to ones surrounding the conduct and application of effects research, we leave its discussion to some other forum.

3. It should be noted that the view of theory testing outlined here is a falsificationist one (Popper 1959; 1963). Theories are not proven. They are accepted pending further research. Although many issues surround the falsificationist

perspective (Kuhn 1970; Lakatos 1970), they are largely peripheral to the concerns of this paper. The important point is that theory tests must attempt to expose theories to refutation by observed data, and must be conservative in accepting theories that escape refutation.

4. This is not to say that intervention-falsification procedures might not sometimes suggest theory-falsification procedures. Nor does it mean that in some cases the two procedures might not be identical.

5. Although for ease in exposition we use the term "individuals" to refer to respondents, the issues discussed apply equally when the units of analysis are groups.

6. Although any respondent group can be used to test a universal theory, characteristics of the particular group chosen affect, or are affected by, the operationalizations of theory variables. Operationalizations that are relevant for the subject population (Ferber 1977) should be employed to avoid the possibility that Type II errors will weaken the theory test.

7. An exception to this preference for homogeneity occurs when an individual difference variable that cannot be manipulated by the researcher (e.g., extroversion) is of theoretical interest. Here, testing the theory requires that variability be achieved by sampling individuals who differ on the dimension of interest. This exception is consistent with providing the strongest possible test of the theory.

8. For a more comprehensive discussion of construct validity, see Bagozzi (1979, Chap. 5).

9. The major threats to internal validity that remain in laboratory experiments are participants uncovering the hypothesis and responding to it rather than to the independent variables alone, or participants responding to demand characteristics, i.e., to inadvertent cues given by the experimenter regarding the appropriate behavior. Procedures such as carefully constructed cover stories, between subjects' designs, and "blind" experimenters can be used to reduce the plausibility of these threats; see Rosenthal and Rosnow (1969a) for a discussion of these procedures.

10. See Wright and Kriewall (1980) for an empirical demonstration of the need for effects research to capture individuals' "state-of-mind" in the real-world setting of interest.

11. O'Shaughnessy and Ryan's (1979) discussion of the distinction between science and technology in some ways parallels and complements our discussion of the difference between theory testing and intervention design and testing.

REFERENCES

Albert, Bernard 1967. "Non-Businessmen as Surrogates for Businessmen in Behavioral Experiments," *Journal of Business*, 40, 203-207.

Aronson, Elliot, and Carlsmith, J. Merrill 1968. "Experimentation in Social Psychology," in *Handbook of Social Psychology, Vol. 2*, eds. Gardner Lindzey and Elliot Aronson, Reading, MA: Addison-Wesley Publishing Co.

Bagozzi, Richard 1979. *Causal Models in Marketing*, New York: John Wiley & Sons.

Banks, Seymout 1965. *Experimentation in Marketing*, New York: McGraw-Hill Book Co.

Brunswik, Egon 1956. *Perception and the Representative Design of Psychological Experiments*, 2nd edn., Berkeley: University of California Press.

Caffyn, J. M. 1964. "Psychological Laboratory Techniques in Copy Research," *Journal of Advertising Research*, 4, 45-50.

Calder, Bobby J. 1977. "Focus Groups and the Nature of Qualitative Marketing Research," *Journal of Marketing Research*, 14, 353-64.

Campbell, Donald, and Fiske, Donald 1959. "Convergent and Discriminant Validation by the Multitrait-Multimethod Matrix," *Psychological Bulletin*, 56, 81-105.

———, and Stanley, John 1966. *Experimental and Quasi-experimental Designs for Research*, Chicago: Rand McNally & Co.

Cartwright, Dorwin, and Zander, Alvin 1968. *Group Dynamics*, New York: Harper and Row.

Cook, Thomas, and Campbell, Donald 1975. "The Design and Conduct of Experiments and Quasi-experiments in Field Settings," in *Handbook of Industrial and Organizational Research*, ed. Martin Dunnette, Chicago: Rand McNally & Co.

Cox, Keith, and Enis, Ben 1969. *Experimentation for Marketing Decisions*, Scranton, PA: International Textbook Co.

Cunningham, William, Anderson, W. Thomas Jr., and Murphy, John 1974. "Are Students Real People?" *Journal of Business*, 48, 399-409.

Ellsworth, Phoebe 1977. "From Abstract Ideas to Concrete Instances: Some Guidelines for Choosing Natural Research Settings," *American Psychologist*, 32, 604-15.

Enis, Ben, Cox, Keith, and Stafford, James 1972. "Students as Subjects in Consumer Behavior Experiments, *Journal of Marketing Research*, 9, 72-4.

Ferber, Robert 1977. "Research by Convenience," *Journal of Consumer Research*, 4, 57-8.

Fromkin, Howard, and Streufert, Siegfried 1975. "Laboratory Experimentation," in *Handbook of Industrial and Organizational Psychology*, ed. Marvin Dunnette, Chicago: Rand McNally & Co., pp. 415-63.

Gardner, David 1970. "The Distraction Hypothesis in Marketing," *Journal of Advertising Research*, 10, 25-30.

Green, Paul 1966. "The Role of Experimental Research in Marketing: Its Potentials and Limitations," in *Science, Technology, and Marketing*, ed. Raymond Haas, Chicago: American Marketing Association, pp. 483-94.

Greenberg, Allan 1967. "Is Communications Research Really Worthwhile?" *Journal of Marketing*, 31, 48-50.

Khera, Inder, and Benson, James 1970. "Are Students Really Poor Substitutes for Businessmen in Behavioral Research?" *Journal of Marketing Research*, 7, 529-32.

Kruglanski, Arie 1973. "Much Ado About the 'Volunteer Artifacts,' "*Journal of Personality and Social Psychology*, 28, 348-54.

———1975. "The Two Meanings of External Invalidity," *Human Relations*, 28, 653-9.

Kuhn, Thomas 1970. *The Structure of Scientific Revolutions*, Chicago: University of Chicago Press.

Lakatos, Imre 1970."Falsification and the Methodology of Science Research Programs," in *Criticism and the Growth of Knowledge*, eds. Imre Lakatos and Alan Musgrave, London: Cambridge University Press.

McGuire, William 1969. "Theory-oriented Research in Natural Settings: The Best of Both Worlds for Social Psychology," in *Interdisciplinary Relationships in the Social Sciences*, eds. M. Sherif and C. Sherif, Chicago: Aldine Publishing.

McNemar, Quinn 1946. "Opinion-Attitude Methodology," *Psychological Bulletin*, 43, 289-374.

Opp, Karl-Dieter 1970. "The Experimental Method in the Social Sciences: Some Problems and Proposals for its More Effective Use," *Quality and Quantity*, 34, 39-54.

Orne, Martin 1962. "On the Social Psychology of the Psychological Experiment with Particular Reference to Demand Characteristics and Other Implications," *American Psychologist*, 17, 776-83.

O'Shaughnessy, John, and Ryan, Mile 1979. "Marketing, Science and Technology," in *Conceptual and Theoretical Developments in Marketing*, eds. O. C. Ferrell, Stephen Brown, and Charles Lamb, Chicago: American Marketing Association.

Park, W. Whan, and Lessig, V. Parker 1977. "Students and Housewives: Differences in Susceptibility to Reference Group Influence," *Journal of Consumer Research*, 4, 102-10.

Popper, Karl R. 1959. *The Logic of Scientific Discovery*, New York: Harper Torchbooks.

———1963. *Conjectures and Refutations*, New York: Harper Torchbooks.

Ray, Michael 1977. "When Does Consume' Information Processing Actually Have Anything to Do with Consumer Information Processing?" in *Advances in Consumer Research*, Vol. 4., ed. William Perreault, Jr., Atlanta: Association for Consumer Reserach.

Riecken, Henry 1962. "A Program for Research on Experiments in Social Psychology," in *Decisions, Values and Groups, Vol. 2*, ed. Norman Washburn, New York: Pergamon Press, pp. 25-41.

Rosenthal, Robert, and Rosnow, Ralph 1969a. *Artifact in Behavioral Research*, New York: Academic Press.

———, and Rosnow, Ralph 1969b. "The Volunteer Subject," in *Artifact in Behavioral Research*, eds. Robert Rosenthal and Ralph Rosnow, New York: Academic Press, pp. 61-112.

Ross, J., and Smith, P. 1968. "Orthodox Experimental Designs," in *Methodology in Social Research*, ed. Hubert Blalock and Ann Blalock, San Francisco: McGraw-Hill Book Co.

Sawyer, Alan 1975. "Demand Artifacts in Laboratory Experiments in Consumer Research," *Journal of Consumer Research*, 1, 20-30.

———, Worthing, Parker, and Sendak, Paul 1979. "The Role of Laboratory Experiments to Test Marketing Strategies," *Journal of Marketing*, 43, 60-7.

Schultz, Duane 1969. "The Human Subject in Psychological Research," *Psychological Bulletin*, 72, 214-28.

Sheth, Jagdish 1970. "Are There Differences in Dissonance Reduction Behavior Between Students and Housewives?" *Journal of Marketing Research*, 7, 243-5.

Shuptrine, F. Kelly 1975. "On the Validity of Using Students as Subjects in Consumer Behavior Investigations," *Journal of Business*, 48, 383-90.

Silverman, Irwin 1968. "Role-Related Behavior of Subjects in Laboratory Studies of Attitude Change," *Journal of Personality and Social Psychology*, 8, 343-8.

Tunnell, Gilbert 1977. "Three Dimensions of Naturalness: An Expanded Definition of Field Research," *Psychological Bulletin*, 84, 426-77.

Uhl, Kenneth 1966. "Field Experimentation: Some Problems, Pitfalls, and Perspectives," in *Science, Technology, and Marketing*, ed. Raymond Haas, Chicago: American Marketing Association, pp. 561-72.

Venkatesen, M. 1967. "Laboratory Experiments in Marketing: The Experimenter Effect, *Journal of Marketing Research*, 4, 142-7.

Webb, Eugene, Campbell, Donald, Schwartz, Richard, and Sechrest, Lee 1966. *Unobtrusive Measures: Nonreactive Research in the Social Sciences*, Chicago: Rand McNally & Co.

Webster, Murray, and Kervin, John 1971. "Artificiality in Experimental Sociology," *Canadian Review of Sociology and Anthropology*, 8, 263-72.

Winer, B. J. 1971. *Statistical Principles in Experimental Design*, New York: McGraw Hill Book Co.

Wright, Peter, and Kriewall, Mary Ann 1980. "State-of-Mind Effects on the Accuracy with which Utility Functions Predict Marketplace Choice," *Journal of Marketing Research*, 17, 277-94.

Reading Research Reports: A Brief Introduction

David A. Schroeder, David E. Johnson, and Thomas D. Jensen

To many students, the prospect of reading a research report in a professional journal elicits so much fear that no information is, in fact, transmitted. Such apprehension on the part of the reader is not necessary, and we hope that this article will help students understand more clearly what such reports are all about and will teach them how to use these resources more effectively. Let us assure you that there is nothing mystical or magical about research reports, although they may be somewhat more technical and precise in style, more intimidating in vocabulary, and more likely to refer to specific sources of information than are everyday mass media sources. However, once you get beyond these intimidating features, you will find that the vast majority of research reports do a good job of guiding you through a project and of informing you of important points of which you should be aware.

A scientific research report has but one purpose: to communicate to others the results of one's scientific investigations. To ensure that readers will be able to appreciate fully the import and implications of the research, the author of the report will make every effort to describe the project so comprehensively that even a naive reader will be able to follow the logic as he or she traces the author's thinking through the project.

A standardized format has been developed by editors and authors to facilitate effective communication. The format is subject to some modification, according to the specific needs and goals of a particular author for a particular article, but, in general, most articles possess a number of features in common. We will briefly discuss the six

major sections of research articles and the purpose of each. We hope that this selection will help you take full advantage of the subsequent articles and to appreciate their content as informed "consumers" of social psychological research.

HEADING

The heading of an article consists of the title, the name of the author or authors, and their institutional affiliations. Typically the title provides a brief description of the primary independent and dependent variables that have been investigated in the study. This information should help you begin to categorize the study into some implicit organizational framework that will help you keep track of the social psychological material. For example, if the title includes the word *persuasion*, you should immediately recognize that the article will be related to the attitude-change literature, and you should prepare yourself to identify the similarities and differences between the present study and the previous literature.

The names of the authors may also be important to you for at least two reasons. First, it is quite common for social psychologists to use the names of authors as a shorthand notation in referring among themselves to critical articles. Rather than asking, "Have your read 'Videotape and the attribution process: Reversing actors' and observers' points of view'?", it is much easier to say, "Have you read the Storms (1973) article?" In addition, this strategy gives the author(s) credit for the material contained in the article. Second, you will find that most researchers actively pursue programs of research that are specific to a particular area of interest. For example, you will eventually be able to recognize that an article written by Albert Bandura is likely to be about social learning processes, while an article by Leonard Berkowitz is probably going to discuss aggression and violence. Once you begin to identify the major researchers in each area, you will find that you will be able to go beyond the information presented within an article and understand not only how a piece of research fits into a well-defined body of literature but also how it may be related to other less obvious topics.

ABSTRACT

The Abstract is a short (often less than 150 words) preview of the contents of the article. The Abstract should be totally self-contained and intelligible without any reference to the article proper. It should briefly convey a statement of the problem explored, the methods used, the major results of the study, and the conclusions reached. The Abstract helps to set the stage and to prepare you for the article itself. Just as the title helps you place the article in a particular area of investigation, the Abstract helps pinpoint the exact question or questions to be addressed in the study.

INTRODUCTION

The Introduction provides the foundation for the study itself and therefore for the remainder of the article. Thus it serves several critical functions for the reader. First, it provides a context for the article and the study by discussing past literature that is relevant to and has implications for the present research. Second, it permits a thorough discussion of the rationale for the research that was conducted and a full description of the independent and dependent variables that were employed. Third, it allows the hypotheses that were tested to be stated explicitly, and the arguments on which these predictions were based to be elucidated. Each of these functions will be considered in detail.

The literature review that is typically the initial portion of the Introduction is not intended to provide a comprehensive restatement of all the published articles that are tangentially relevant to the present research. Normally, a selective review is presented—one that carefully sets up the rationale of the study and identifies deficiencies in our understanding of the phenomena being investigated. In taking this approach, the author is attempting to provide insights into the thought processes that preceded the actual conducting of the study. Usually the literature review will begin by discussing rather broad conceptual issues (e.g., major theories, recognized areas of investigation) and will then gradually narrow its focus to more specific concerns (e.g., specific findings from previous research, methods that have been employed). It may be helpful to think of the introduction as a funnel, gradually drawing one's attention to a central point that represents the critical feature of the article.

Following the review of the past literature, the author typically presents the rationale for his or her own research. A research study may have one of several goals as its primary aim: (1) it may be designed to answer a question specifically raised by the previous literature but left unanswered. (2) It may attempt to correct methodological flaws that have plagued previous research and threaten the validity of the conclusions reached. (3) It may seek to reconcile conflicting findings that have been reported in the literature, typically by identifying and/ or eliminating confounding variables by exerting greater experimental control. (4) It may be designed to assess the validity of a scientific theory by testing one or more hypotheses that have been deduced or derived from that theory. (5) It may begin a novel line of research that has not been previously pursued or discussed in the literature. Research pursuing any of these five goals may yield significant contributions to a particular field of inquiry.

After providing the rationale for the study, the author properly continues to narrow the focus of the article from broad conceptual issues to the particular variables that are to be employed in the study. Ideally, in experimental studies, the author clearly identifies the independent and dependent variables to be used; in correlational studies, the predictor and criterion variables are specified. For those readers who do not have an extensive background in research methodology, a brief explanation of experimental and correlational studies may be in order.

Experimental studies. An experimental study is designed to identify cause-effect relationships between independent variables that the experimenter systematically manipulates and the dependent variable that is used to measure the behavior of interest. In such a study, the researcher controls the situation to eliminate or neutralize the effects of all extraneous factors that may affect the behavior of interest in order to assess more precisely the impact of the independent variables alone. In most instances, only the tightly controlled experimental method permits valid inferences of cause-effect relationships to be made.

Correlational studies. In some circumstances the researcher cannot exert the degree of control over the situation that is necessary for a true experimental study. Rather than giving up the project, the researcher may explore alternative methods that may still permit an assessment of his or her hypotheses and predictions. One such alternative is the correlational approach. In a correlational study, the researcher specifies a set of measures that should be related conceptually to the display of a target behavior. The measure that is used to assess the target behavior is called the criterion variable; the measure from which the researcher expects to be able to make predictions about the criterion variable is called the predictor variable. Correlational studies permit the researcher to assess the degree of relationship between the predictor variable(s) and the criterion variable(s), but inferences of cause and effect cannot be validly made because the effects of extraneous variables have not been adequately controlled. Correlational studies are most frequently used in naturalistic or applied situations in which researchers must either tolerate the lack of control and do the best they can under the circumstances or give up any hope of testing their hypotheses.

After the discussion of these critical components of the study, the author explicitly states the exact predictions that the study is designed to test. The previous material should have set the stage sufficiently well for you as a reader to anticipate what these hypotheses will be, but it is incumbent on the author to present them nonetheless. The wording of the hypotheses may vary, some authors preferring to state the predictions in conceptual terms (e.g., "The arousal of cognitive dissonance due to counterattitudinal advocacy is expected to lead to greater attitude change than the presentation of an attitude-consistent argument.") and others preferring to state their predictions in terms of the actual operationalizations that they employed (e.g., "Subjects who received a $1 incentive to say that an objectively boring task was fun are expected to subsequently evaluate the task as being more enjoyable than subjects who were offered a $20 incentive to say that the task was interesting.")

In reading a research report, it is imperative that you pay attention to the relationship between the initial literature review, the rationale for the study and the statement of the hypotheses. In a well-conceived and well-designed investigation, each section will flow logically from the preceding one; the internal consistency of the author's arguments will make for smooth transitions as the presentation advances. If there appear to be discontinuities or inconsistencies throughout the author's presentation, it would be wise to take a more critical view of the study—particularly if the predictions do not seem to follow logically from the earlier material. In such cases, the author may be trying to present as a prediction a description of the findings that were unexpectedly uncovered when the study was being conducted. Although there is nothing wrong with reporting unexpected findings in a journal article, the author should be honest enough to identify them as what they really are. As a reader, you should have much more confidence in the reliability of predictions that obtain than you do in data that can be described by postdictions only.

METHOD

To this point, the author has dealt with the study in relatively abstract terms, and has given little attention to the actual procedures used in conducting it. In the Method section, the author at last describes the operationalizations and procedures that were employed in the investigation. There are at least two reasons for the detailed presentation of this information. First, such a presentation allows interested readers to reconstruct the methodology used, so that a replication of the study can be undertaken. By conducting a replication using different subject populations and slightly different operationalizations of the same conceptual variables, more information can be gained about the validity of the conclusions that the original investigator reached. Second, even if a replication is not conducted, the careful description of the method used will permit you to evaluate the adequacy of the procedures employed.

The Method section typically comprises two or more subsections, each of which has a specific function to fulfill. Almost without exception, the Method section begins with a subject subsection, consisting of a complete description of the subjects who participated in the study. The number of subjects should be indicated, and there should be a summary of important demographic information (e.g., numbers of male and female subjects, age) so that you can know to what populations the findings can be reasonably generalized. Sampling techniques that were used to recruit subjects and incentives used to induce volunteering should also be clearly specified. To the extent that subject characteristics are of primary importance to the goals of the research, greater detail is presented in this subsection, and more attention should be directed to it.

A procedures subsection is also almost always included in the Method section. This subsection presents a detailed account of the subjects' experiences in the experiment. Although other formats may also be effective, the most common presentation style is to describe the subjects' activities in chronological order. A thorough description of all questionnaires administered or tasks completed is given, as well as any other features that might be reasonably expected to affect the behavior of the subjects in the study.

After the procedures have been discussed, a full description of the independent variables in an experimental study, or predictor variables in a correlational study, is typically provided. Verbatim descriptions of each of the different levels of each independent variable is presented, and similar detail is used to describe each predictor variable. This information may be included either in the procedures subsection or, if the description of these variables is quite lengthy, in a separate subsection.

After thoroughly describing these variables, the author usually describes the dependent variables in an experimental study, and the criterion variables in a correlational study. The description of the dependent and/or criterion variables also requires a verbatim specification of the exact operationalizations that were employed. When appropriate and available, information about the reliability and validity of these measures is also presented. In addition, if the investigator has included any questions that were intended to allow the effectiveness of the independent variable manipulation to be assessed, these manipulation checks are described at this point. All of this information may be incorporated in the procedures subsection or in a separate subsection.

After you have read the Method section, there should be no question about what has been done to the subjects who participated in the study. You should try to evaluate how representative the methods that were used were of the conceptual variables discussed in the Introduction. Manipulation checks may help to allay one's concerns, but poorly conceived manipulation checks are of little or no value. Therefore, it is important for you as a reader to remember that you are ultimately responsible for the critical evaluation of any research report.

RESULTS

Once the full methodology of the study has been described for the reader, the author proceeds to report the results of the statistical analyses that were conducted on the data. The Results section is probably the most intimidating section for students to read, and often the most difficult section for researchers to write. You are typically confronted with terminology and analytical techniques with which you are at best unfamiliar, or at worst totally ignorant. There is no reason for you to feel badly about this state of affairs; as a neophyte in the world of research, you cannot expect mastery of all phases of research from the start. Even experienced researchers are often exposed to statistical techniques with which they are unfamiliar, requiring them either to learn the techniques or to rely on others to assess the appropriateness of the procedure. For the student researcher, a little experience and a conscientious effort to learn the basics will lead to mastery of the statistical skills necessary.

The author's task is similarly difficult. He or she is attempting to present the findings of the study in a straightforward and easily understood manner, but the presentation of statistical findings does not always lend itself readily to this task. The author must decide whether to present the results strictly within the text of the article or to use tables, graphs, and figures to help to convey the information effectively. Although the implications of the data may be clear to the researcher, trying to present the data clearly and concisely so that the reader will also be able to discern the implications is not necessarily assured. In addition, the author is obligated to present all the significant results obtained in the statistical analyses, not just the results that support the hypotheses being tested. Although this may clutter the presentation and detract from the simplicity of the interpretation, it must be remembered that the researcher's primary goal is to seek the truth, not to espouse a particular point of view that may not be supported by the data.

DISCUSSION

The Discussion section is the part of the manuscript in which the author offers an evaluation and interpretation of the findings of the study, particularly as they relate to the hypotheses that were proposed in the Introduction. Typically the author will begin this section with a brief review of the major findings of the study and a clear statement of whether the data were consistent or inconsistent with the hypotheses. The discussion will then address any discrepancies between the predictions and the data, trying to resolve these inconsistencies and offering plausible reasons for their occurrence. In general, the first portion of the Discussion is devoted to an evaluation of the hypotheses that were originally set forward in the Introduction, given the data that were obtained in the research.

The Discussion may be seen as the inverse of the introduction, parallelling the issues raised in that section in the opposite order of presentation. Therefore, after discussing the relationship of the data with the hypotheses, the author often attempts to integrate the new findings into the body of research that provided the background for the study. Just as this literature initially provided the context within which you can understand the rationale for the study, it subsequently provides the context within which the data can be understood and interpreted. The author's responsibility at this point is to help you recognize the potential import of the research, without relying on hype or gimmicks to make the point.

The Discussion continues to expand in terms of the breadth of ideas discussed until it reaches the broad, conceptual issues that are addressed by the superordinate theoretical work that originally stimulated the past research literature. If a particular piece of research is to make a significant contribution to the field, its findings must either clarify some past discrepancy in the literature, identify boundary conditions for the applicability of the critical theoretical work, reconcile differences of opinion among the researchers in the field, or otherwise contribute to a more complete understanding of the mechanisms and mediators of important social phenomena.

Once the author has reached the goals that are common to most journal articles, attention may be turned to less rigorous ideas. Depending on a particular journal's editorial policy and the availability of additional space, the author may finish the article with a brief section about possible applications of the present work, implications for future work in the area, and with some restraint, speculations about what lies ahead for the line of research. Scientists tend to have relatively little tolerance for conclusions without foundation and off-the-cuff comments made without full consideration. Therefore authors must be careful not to overstep the bounds of propriety in making speculations about the future. But such exercises can be useful and can serve a heuristic function for other researchers if the notions stated are well conceived.

Finally, particularly if the article has been

relatively long or complex, the author may decide to end it with a short Conclusion. The Conclusion usually simply restates the major arguments that have been made throughout the article, reminding the reader one last time of the value of the work.

As we suggested earlier, not all articles will follow the format exactly. Some latitude is allowed to accommodate the particular needs of the author and the quirks of the research being described. Given that the goal is effective communication of information, it would not be reasonable for the format to dictate what could and could not be included in a manuscript. We hope that this introduction will help to demystify research articles and provide you with some insights into what an author is trying to accomplish at various points in the report. Let us end with a word of encouragement: Your enjoyment of social psychology will be enhanced by your fuller appreciation of the sources of the information to which you are being exposed, and, to the extent that you are able to read and understand these original sources for yourself, your appreciation of this work will be maximized.

REFERENCE

Storms, M. D. Videotape and the attribution process: Reversing actors' and observers' points of view. *Journal of Personality and Social Psychology,* 1973, **27,** 165-175.

2   Attitudes and Behavior

HISTORICALLY, SINCE L. L. THURSTONE'S early demonstrations that attitudes could be reliably measured, the field of social psychology has investigated the nature of attitudes and attitude change more thoroughly than any other area of research. As early as 1935, Gordon Allport suggested that the concept of an attitude was the keystone of social psychology, and social psychologists' interest in attitudes did not wane for the next quarter of a century. Throughout the 1940s and the 1950s, the work of Carl Hovland and others associated with the Yale Communication Program and of Leon Festinger and his colleagues at Minnesota and Stanford continued to expand our understanding of the factors affecting attitude formation and attitude change.

During the late 1960s and the 1970s, however, a shift in the field found attitude research beginning to take second place to more cognitive-oriented approaches to social processes, particularly with the work stimulated by the attribution theories of Jones and Davis (1965) and Kelley (e.g., 1967, 1973); the selections in chapter 4 will introduce this area of research. It appears that the decline of interest in attitudes may have been only a temporary fluctuation, for attitude research has experienced something of a rebirth in the past several years, with investigators reexamining the classic theories and models as well as proposing new theories to explain attitude-related phenomena.

The studies in this chapter were selected to reflect this reexamination and to exemplify the new theoretical work that is being pursued. The first study, by Eugene Borgida and Bruce Campbell, investigates the role of belief relevance in attitude-behavior relationships. These researchers argue that global attitude measures often fail to predict subsequent behaviors because these attitudes do not suggest the behavioral implications of a particular attitudinal position. Cognitive manipulations that encourage subjects to consider such implications have been shown to be effective in increasing the attitude-behavior relationship in various contexts, and Borgida and Campbell seek to assess the effectiveness of such cognitive manipulations compared to having the behavioral implications suggested by the subject's own previous actions.

The second article, by Joel Cooper and Diane Mackie, takes a somewhat different tack in terms of the relationship between attitudes and behaviors. While Borgida and Campbell suggest that attitudes may guide subsequent behaviors, Cooper and Mackie demonstrate that, under certain circumstances, one's behaviors may affect the attitudes that one holds. Taking a traditional cognitive dissonance approach, these researchers argue that attitude-discrepant behaviors may lead to attitude change, but only to the extent that the attitude in question is important to an individual in some way, such as defining one's membership in a valued group.

In the final article in this chapter, James Jaccard proposes a new theory of persuasive communications and subsequent attitude change. Tracing the research on persuasive communications back to Carl Hovland and the Yale group, Jaccard suggests that differential processing takes place for simple assertions that lack supporting arguments, and for complex persuasive communications that do include supporting evidence. After providing a comprehensive description of his theory, Jaccard reports the results of a study that is consistent with his proposal.

Belief Relevance and Attitude—Behavior Consistency: The Moderating Role of Personal Experience

Eugene Borgida and Bruce Campbell

This experiment examines whether belief relevance enhances the degree of attitude-behavior consistency when the behavioral implications of a global attitude contradict the behavioral implications of prior personal experience in a pertinent action domain. It was generally expected that belief relevance would only promote attitude-behavior consistency for those individuals with little prior personal experience. As predicted, enhancing cognitive accessibility increased substantially the consistency between global environmental attitudes and petition-signing behavior, but only for those subjects who had minimal prior personal experience with the consequences of an on-campus parking shortage. For those individuals with relatively extensive personal experience, cognitive accessibility did not increase attitude-behavior consistency. The theoretical importance of considering the nature and extent of respondents' prior personal experiences in attitude behavior research is discussed.

The extent to which attitudes are predictive of social behavior has long been controversial in social psychology (cf. Ajzen & Fishbein, 1977; Cialdini, Petty, & Cacioppo, 1981; Schuman & Johnson, 1976; Wicker, 1969, Zanna, Higgins, & Herman, in press). Early pessimism about the predictive validity of attitudes, however, has recently given way to the suggestion that strong attitude-behavior relations can indeed be obtained under certain conditions.

Fazio and Zanna (1981) have framed this shift by asking: Under what conditions do what kinds of attitudes of what kinds of individuals predict what kinds of behavior? Substantial evidence for the predictive validity of attitudes has been found under conditions of methodological correspondence between attitudinal and behavioral measures (Ajzen & Fishbein, 1977), when the cognitive accessibility of attitudes has been primed (Snyder & Swann, 1976), and when various mediating context factors such as immediate situational pressures and normative constraints have been taken into consideration (Ajzen & Fishbein, 1980). Research on the kinds of attitudes (Fazio & Zanna, 1981; Norman, 1975; Schwartz, 1978), the kinds of individuals (McArthur, Kiesler, & Cook, 1969; Schwartz, 1977; Zanna, Olson, & Fazio, 1980), and the kinds of behaviors (Fishbein & Ajzen,

This research was supported by a grant from the Graduate School of the University of Minnesota to Eugene Borgida. The authors acknowledge the assistance of LaRaye Osborne, Nancy Brekke, and Diane Hanson and the comments of Robert Abelson, Susan Fiske, Linda Heath, and Richard Nisbett.

"Belief Relevance and Attitude-behavior Consistency: The Moderating Role of Personal Experience" by E. Borgida & B. Campbell, 1982, *Journal of Personality and Social Psychology, 42,* pp. 239-247. Copyright 1982 by the American Psychological Assn. Reprinted by permission of the publisher and authors.

1975) has also provided support for the strength of attitude-behavior relations.

The present research examines more closely one of the conditions that previous research has identified as an important determinant of attitude-behavior consistency. Specifically, it has been argued that global attitudes (i.e., attitude toward the object) often may not predict specific behaviors because the behavioral implications of these global attitudes simply may not be salient or cognitively accessible to people in the behavioral choice situation. Investigators who have essentially made this argument (Pryor et al., 1977; Snyder & Swann, 1976; Tesser, 1978) have successfully manipulated the cognitive accessibility of such global attitudes and have shown that, either by making the behavioral implications of global attitudes more salient or by encouraging people to think about the behavioral implications of their attitudes, the degree of attitude-behavior consistency can be improved dramatically.

One might conclude from these findings that cognitive manipulations that make the behavioral implications of global attitudes salient and accessible generally ought to be effective in promoting consistency between global attitudes (toward an object) and specific behaviors. But suppose that the implications of one's personal experience in a given behavioral domain conflict with or even directly contradict the implications of a more global attitude that one also holds for the specific behavioral choice in question. Would a belief-relevance manipulation that underscores the behavioral implications of one's global attitude still be effective in promoting attitude-behavior consistency under these conditions?

Consider, for example, the chronic plight of a university student who regularly commutes to campus in his or her car for classes. Greeted by hopelessly long lines or

"Lot Full" signs at various on-campus parking facilities and with few minutes to spare before class gets underway, our harried commuter must seek out and probably settle for some marginally legal or clearly unauthorized parking space in the campus vicinity. What is at risk, of course, is the likelihood of yet another parking ticket or perhaps even the possibility of a costly car towing. But classes must be attended and the daily inconvenience and hassle associated with the on-campus parking shortage at least tolerated until parking facilities are expanded by an administration undoubtedly hard pressed for funds. Based on our commuter's daily experiences with the parking shortage, one might well expect him or her to strongly favor expansion of on-campus parking facilities and perhaps to be quite willing to take some sort of action designed to encourage the administration to build new parking facilities.

Suppose, however, that our frustrated and hassled student commuter were to realize (through some sort of thought or belief-relevance manipulation) that his or her proenvironmental beliefs and attitudes conflict with the experience-based desire for increased on-campus parking, since increased air pollution would surely accompany expanded parking facilities at the University. Would our commuter's realization that his or her favorable attitude toward the environment is relevant to his or her stance on the parking issue actually increase the likelihood that he or she would act in line with the behavioral implications of the global proenvironmental atttitude? Or, would our commuter's personal experience with the parking shortage lead him or her to act in ways that are inconsistent with a proenvironmental attitude despite an awareness of the relevance of those proenvironmental beliefs?

Previous research on the cognitive accessibility of attitudes would suggest that consistency between global environmental attitudes and overt behaviors concerning the parking issue should be enhanced under these conditions. By contrast, however, there is also substantial evidence that suggests that previous direct behavioral experience with an attitude object should be quite predictive of subsequent behaviors (Fazio & Zanna, 1978a; 1978b; Fazio, Zanna & Cooper, 1978; Regan & Fazio, 1977; Songer-Nocks, 1976). The extent to which people are personally involved in a given attitude issue should also moderate the degree of attitude-behavior consistency (Cialdini, Petty, & Cacioppo, 1981) and, in turn, the effectiveness of any cognitive manipulation that underscores the behavioral implications of global attitudes.

The present experiment addresses for the first time the question of whether belief relevance and cognitive accessibility will in fact be effective when the behavioral implications of a global attitude contradict or conflict with the implications of prior personal experience in a given behavioral domain. It was generally expected that belief relevance and cognitive accessibility would only promote attitude-behavior consistency for individuals with relatively little prior personal experience in the pertinent behavioral domain.

METHOD

Subjects

Sixty-eight male and female University of Minnesota undergraduates enrolled in general psychology were recruited as participants for a two-part student opinion survey. Subjects received extra course credit for their participation. Thirty-two subjects

were randomly assigned to the belief-relevant condition and 36 subjects were assigned to the belief-nonrelevant condition.

Procedure

Part 1: Administering the Student Opinion Survey. Subjects arrived at the Laboratory for Research in Social Relations in groups ranging in size from three to seven. Upon arrival, they were met by a female experimenter who explained the basic purpose of the survey as an in-depth attempt to examine how "students feel about several state and national issues, as well as to determine how students feel about some very specific issues pertaining to the operation of the University and the quality of student life." The experimenter, who was blind to experimental condition, went on to explain that since the survey was rather long and would take more than 1 hour to complete, the questionnaire had been divided into two parts, which was why subjects had been asked to sign up for two sessions on consecutive days. In addition, since the first section of the survey would not require the full experimental hour, subjects were also being asked to participate in an unrelated person-perception experiment being conducted by a colleague.

After this introduction, the first section of the Student Opinion Survey (SOS) was distributed and completed, on the average, within 25 minutes.

Stimulus materials: Part 1 of the Student Opinion Survey. The first section of the SOS consisted of 67 items. Forty of these were attitude items evaluated along 5-point Likert scales that assessed subjects' attitudes toward environmental issues, the Equal Rights Amendment, abortion rights, the Boundary Waters Canoe Area dispute in northern Minnesota, and administrative priorities at the University. The remainder of the first section of the survey consisted of 27 demographic items that were included to enhance the face validity of the survey rather than for use on data analysis.

Part 1: The person-perception task. Upon completion of the first section of the SOS subjects were reminded to return to the same room on the following day to complete the second section of the survey. They were then escorted to a different experimental room where the person-perception task was being conducted. There subjects were greeted by a male experimenter. After subjects completed a research consent form associated with this new task, the experimenter explained that as part of a larger study in person perception, subjects would be asked to listen to three brief tape-recorded conversations and to note their impressions of one of the two people from each tape. Specifically, they were to rate their impressions of the person who spoke second (the target) in each of the three dialogues. The experimenter then proceeded to play three tape-recorded conversations, pausing 3-4 minutes after each dialogue to allow subjects to complete their ratings. In each case, the personality ratings were based on the second or target conversant. After the third dialogue was rated, all subjects filled out structured and free-recall measures for each of the three dialogues. Finally, the experimenter distributed an explanation of the design and purpose of the person-perception task to all participants. This debriefing feedback had been carefully constructed to seem as plausible and convincing as possible to allay any suspicions about a connection between the SOS and the person-perception task.

Stimulus materials: The person-perception task. For the person-perception task, 10 male colleagues were enlisted to enact five conversations. These conversations concerned downtown restaurants, motorcycle safety, summer jobs, racquetball, and parking at the university, and were initially written in script form. The dialogues were rehearsed and modified until the conversations sounded spontaneous and unrehearsed to a pilot group of subjects. Each conversation lasted approximately 4 minutes.

Belief-relevant dialogues. Subjects in the belief-relevant condition always heard the parking at the university dialogue as the second conversation in the series of three. For half of the subjects in the belief-relevant condition, the downtown restaurants dialogue was heard first and the motorcycle safety dialogue was last in the sequence. For the other half of the belief-relevant subjects, the order of the downtown restaurants and motorcycle safety dialogues was reversed.

The parking at the university dialogue conveyed the critical belief-relevance manipulation. The motorcycle safety dialogue was about the hazards of helmetless motorcycling and bore a structural similarity to the parking at the university dialogue in that one participant in the former dialogue encouraged his partner to think more carefully about the implications of supporting a repeal of the law requiring motorcyclists to wear helmets. The downtown restaurants dialogue was merely a filler conversation about the virtues of various downtown restaurants.[1]

In the parking at the university dialogue, the conversation began with some small talk about the movie *Close Encounters of the Third Kind.* After a few comments about that movie's technical gimmickry, the conversation shifted to a discussion of the overcrowded parking situation at the University. The target's conversation partner mentioned that he was worried about the time on his parking meter, since he did not want to get another parking ticket. He went on to complain about the hassle and inconvenience of finding on-campus parking and criticized the university administration for not taking steps to remedy it. At this point in the conversation, the target conversant pointed out that in his opinion the decision to build more parking facilities might have some ramifications that his partner had not considered. Moreover, if his partner gave more thought to the situation, then he might not be so eager for the construction of additional parking facilities.

The target went on to point out that the construction of more on-campus parking would encourage more people to drive to the university rather than to use mass transit and that such a change could be accompanied by increased pollution and energy consumption. The target also pointed out that this influx of cars in search of parking would perhaps intensify the safety problems on campus. Finally, he pointed out that new parking facilities would be extremely expensive and that the money could be better used in ways more directly related to educational objectives. The conversation concluded with the target's partner stating that he had "never really thought about those things before."

Belief-nonrelevant dialogues. Subjects in the belief-nonrelevant condition always heard the same three filler dialogues in the same order. The first conversation in the sequence was the downtown restaurants dialogue, followed by the summer jobs dialogue and the racquetball dialogue. The lat-

ter two conversations involved a discussion between two students of summer job plans and experiences and a conversation about the merits of racquetball and other recreational sports, respectively. None of the three dialogues in the belief-nonrelevant condition mentioned environmental issues or the parking situation at the university.[2]

Dependent measures: The person-perception task. To enhance the credibility of the person-perception task, subjects rated each target conversant on 10 bipolar trait-adjectives, judged "How effectively does this person express his ideas?" and "How favorable is your overall impression of this person?" and completed an open-ended item that asked them to describe their impression of the target. Upon completion of these ratings, subjects' recall of the target's conversation in each of the three dialogues was assessed. Finally, subjects were asked to summarize each conversation in their own words as they would in order to "give a friend a good idea of what this conversation was about." These measures are not pertinent to the hypotheses examined in the actual experiment and therefore will not be discussed further.

Part 2: Administering the Student Opinion Survey. When subjects returned on the second day to complete the SOS, they were met by the same female experimenter who had distributed the survey in the first session. She reminded them to use the same subject code number that they had used on the previous day and then distributed Part 2 of the survey. Subjects were also informed that they should remain seated after completing the survey because departmental policy required that the experimenter fully explain the purpose of the research. Upon completion of the survey, the experimenter began to discuss the research when, as if it were an afterthought, she mentioned that:

> This student group on campus got wind of the fact that we were including questions concerning parking on our questionnaire, and asked that I give each of you a copy of their petition for consideration. Why don't I gather up my surveys before I hand out these sheets so that I can keep my materials separate from theirs. . . . And why don't you just put these petitions in a pile on the table when you've looked them over.

The petitions, which had been lying face down on a small table near the door throughout the session, were then distributed to subjects. The experimenter appeared to be totally disinterested in whether anyone signed these petitions. Whenever a subject asked a question about the content of the petition, for example, she always responded by saying, "I haven't even taken a look at it," at which time she glanced over the petition and said, "I really don't know." Whenever a subject asked a question about who would use the petitions, the experimenter always responded, "I haven't even taken a look at it. I really have nothing to do with it. I really don't know."

After a few minutes, subjects were told to leave their materials on the table and were taken to another lab room for a complete debriefing about the experiment. During this final debriefing, not one subject spontaneously suggested that there was a link between administration of the SOS and the interpolated person-perception task, nor did anyone voice suspicion about the student petition.

Stimulus materials: Part 2 of the Student Opinion Survey. Part 2 of the SOS consisted of 32 items that inquired about the nature and extent of subjects' experience with various university programs and services and their satisfaction with each service. These items dealt with financial aid, the student employment service, the student health service, transportation to and from the university, and the university library system. On the average, subjects were able to complete this part of the survey in 20 minutes.

Direct Experience Measure

There were 11 items in one section of the SOS/Part 2 that dealt with parking at the university. Seven of these items solicited information such as whether the subject owned a car, and if so, how frequently they drove to campus; whether they had received parking tickets or had ever been towed for illegal parking; how far away from campus they typically had to park; and how much time they spent searching for a parking space when they did drive to campus. This latter measure was the primary direct experience measure. Respondents were asked: "When you drive to the U, how long on the average do you usually have to spend looking for a place to park and/or waiting in line at a parking lot? (Less than 2 minutes, 2-5 minutes, 5-10 minutes, more than 10 minutes)."

Dependent Measures

The primary dependent measure in the present experiment was whether the subject signed one or both of two petitions recommending an increase in parking facilities at the university. The two petitions differed in terms of the strength of public commitment that they required (Brannon et al., 1973). The first petition was carefully typed and had an official appearance. It followed the last page of the survey booklet and was attached to Part 2 of the SOS by a paper clip. At the top of the page, subjects read that the administration was "currently giving careful consideration to the issue of whether or not plans to construct extensive new parking facilities should be implemented" and that "a memorandum reporting the overall percentage of students (not individual names) who endorse the following request" would be forwarded to the university committee that was currently considering the parking issue. Beneath this explanation was a statement requesting that "plans for the construction of additional new parking facilities . . . be adopted and implemented as soon as possible," and a space for the subject's signature.

In contrast, the second petition, which was presented to subjects at the end of the second session, was designed to convey the impression of a rather low-budget, hastily produced student petition campaign. It was dittoed rather than mimeographed like the first petition (and the entire SOS). It clearly had been typed on an old manual typewriter and the heading at the top of the page was handwritten: "TIRED OF LOSING THE BATTLE FOR PARKING SPACES? WANT TO SEE SOMETHING DONE ABOUT IT??" Beneath this heading was a paragraph that explained that the student group that was soliciting signatures for this petition was not a political organization and had no affiliation with student government or any other organized group. It stated that they were simply a small group of students who were tired of the inconvenience caused by the shortage of on-campus parking and intended to publish their petition, along with the names of every other student who was willing to sign it, as a full-page ad in the campus newspaper.

Following this explanation were the reproduced signatures of seven fictitious students along with their college affiliation within the university. At the bottom of the page was their petition urging the university to make a firm commitment to provide additional parking facilities, along with a space for the subject's signature.

In addition to its distinctly different appearance and sponsorship, signing the second petition clearly involved public, and hence, stronger commitment to one's beliefs about the parking situation at the university than the commitment entailed by an endorsement of the first petition.

RESULTS

Table 1 presents the correlations between Environmental Concern and petition-signing for participants who were high and low in direct experience by experimental condition. The environmental concern measure is a sum-score index composed of eight environmental attitude items from the first section of the SOS (scale $M = 30.43$, $sd = 3.79$, Cronbach's alpha $= .59$, $n = 68$).[3] The petition-signing measure was constructed by assigning participants who signed the first but not the second petition a score of 1, and assigning participants who signed both petitions a score of 2.[4] Categorization of participants as high or low on direct experience was based on their responses to the item "When you drive to the U, how long on the average do you usually have to spend looking for a place to park and/or waiting in line at a parking lot?" Participants who answered with "less than 2 minutes" or "2-5 minutes" were categorized as low in direct experience; participants who answered either "5-10 minutes" or "more than 10 minutes" were categorized as high in direct experience.[5]

It may be seen in Table 1 that, as predicted, in the belief-nonrelevant condition there is no reliable relationship between the strength of the participants' global environmental attitudes and their petition-signing behavior at *either* level of direct experience (for low experience, $r = -.03$, *ns;* for high experience, $r = .29$, *ns*). Within the belief-relevant condition, by contrast, whether environmental attitudes are closely related to petition-signing behavior clearly depends on the level of direct experience. Specifically, for participants high in direct experience, there is no reliable relationship between environmental attitudes and willingness to sign petitions recommending increased on-campus parking ($r = -.07$, *ns*). For participants low in direct experience, however, there is a highly significant inverse correlation between the strength of proenvironmental attitudes and petition-signing behavior ($r = -.62$, $p = .004$).

The pattern of correlations presented in Table 1 strongly suggests that, as predicted, global environmental attitudes are related to petition-signing behavior only for those participants who are low in direct experience and who had been previously exposed to the belief-relevance manipulation. Computation of these correlations, however, does not provide the most rigorous test of our theoretical predictions. Accordingly, we tested the correspondence between our theoretical predictions and the data presented in Table 1 by a single planned comparison within a 2 (belief relevance) $\times$ 2 (direct experience) analysis of variance.

In this analysis of variance, the product-moment correlation between the environmental concern measure and the petition-signing measure (calculated separately for each of the four cells within the 2 $\times$ 2 factorial design) constitutes the dependent measure. Each correlation is first transformed to a z score. The within-cells variance of the samples that these z scores rep-

TABLE 1

Correlations Between Environmental Concern (Attitude) and Petition-Signing (Behavior) by Level of Direct Experience and Experimental Condition.

	Experimental condition	
Direct experience	Belief nonrelevant	Belief relevant
Low		
r	$-.03$ (*ns, n* = 24)	$-.62$ ($p = .004, n = 17$)
M attitude	30.08, $\sigma^2 = 4.16$	30.35, $\sigma^2 = 4.18$
M behavior	1.42, $\sigma^2 = .65$	.71, $\sigma^2 = .85$
High		
r	.29 (*ns, n* = 12)	$-.07$ (*ns, n* = 15)
M attitude	30.50, $\sigma^2 = 3.18$	31.00, $\sigma^2 = 3.46$
M behavior	1.83, $\sigma^2 = .39$	.81, $\sigma^2 = .83$

Note: All reported *r*s are Pearson product-moment correlations.

resent (given unequal n) is calculated from the formula $\sigma^2 = 1/\bar{n} - 3$, where $\bar{n}$ represents the harmonic mean of the number of paired observations contributing to each correlation coefficient (Fisher, 1946). This known within-cells variance is then used in constructing an F ratio to test the significance of the planned comparison that tests the theoretical predictions.

In this research, a substantial correlation between environmental concern and petition-signing in the belief-relevant, low direct-experience cell, but a trivial correlation in each of the remaining cells was predicted. Therefore, a weight of $+3$ was assigned to the z score representing the correlation from the belief-relevant, low direct-experience cell and weights of -1 were assigned to the z scores representing each of the other three correlations. Calculation of the appropriate F test reveals that this planned comparison is significant, $F(1, \infty) = 6.102$, $p = .02$. Furthermore, an F test calculated on the residual was clearly not significant, $F(2, \infty) = .550$, ns. Thus, the contrast representing the theoretically predicted pattern of correlations accounts for a highly significant amount of systematic variation in the actually obtained pattern of correlations and there was no significant amount of systematic variation remaining beyond that accounted for by the theoretically predicted pattern.

Direct Experience Versus Relevant Beliefs

The pattern of correlations presented in Table 1 is further explicated by Table 2 which presents the frequency of petition-signing as a function of direct experience and environmental concern. As predicted, subjects who were high on direct experience but low on environmental concern tended

to sign either or both of the petitions, regardless of experimental condition, Fisher's exact $p = .12$. Likewise, the belief-relevance manipulation did not significantly affect the frequency of petition-signing for participants who were high on direct experience and high on environmental concern, Fisher's exact $p = .10$. Nor did belief relevance make a significant difference for those subjects who were low on environmental concern and low in direct experience, Fisher's exact $p = .17$. By contrast, belief relevance has a significant and substantial effect for those subjects who were high on environmental concern but low on direct experience. Whereas only 2 of 12 subjects refused to sign in the belief-nonrelevant condition, 7 of 8 refused to sign in the belief-relevant condition ($p = .003$).

DISCUSSION

This investigation examined attitude-behavior consistency in a context where the behavioral implications of subjects' global attitudes directly contradicted the behavioral implications of their prior personal experience in the pertinent behavioral domain. Specifically, the results showed that belief relevance or cognitive accessibility was effective in substantially increasing the consistency between global environmental attitudes and petition-signing behavior but *only* for those subjects who had relatively little personal experience with the consequences of the on-campus parking shortage. For subjects with relatively extensive personal experience, the belief-relevance manipulation, as expected, did not increase attitude-behavior consistency.

The results of this research, therefore, provide strong support for the proposition that the degree to which global attitudes and their behavioral implications are cognitively accessible may be a key determinant of attitude-behavior consistency. In fact, the results of the present study provide perhaps the most compelling evidence for this proposition to date. In contrast to previous studies that have also examined belief relevance (e.g., Pryor et al., 1977; Snyder & Swann, 1976), subjects in our research were never explicitly instructed by the experimenter to think through the implications of their attitudes for the impending behavioral choice. Neither, for that matter, did the experimental procedure include a specific period of time just prior to the behavioral choice situation in which subjects were free from other task demands and left to contemplate their own attitudes. Instead, subjects in the present study merely listened (in the context of what they believed was an entirely separate experiment) to a previously recorded conversation in which one discussant pointed out to his partner the relevance of a proenvironmental attitude for the on-campus parking issue. In further contrast to other studies of belief relevance, the present study also entailed a 24-hour delay between subjects' exposure to this rather unobtrusive manipulation and the experimental session in which the behavioral measures were obtained. Nevertheless, as predicted, an impressive increase in attitude-behavior consistency attributable to the belief relevance manipulation was clearly demonstrated for those subjects who were low in personal experience.

More importantly, however, the results of the present research strongly suggest that the effects of increasing the cognitive accessibility of global attitudes and their behavioral implications depend in a crucial way on the type and extent of individuals' prior personal experience in the particular behavioral domain under consideration. Whereas the belief-relevance manipulation

TABLE 2

Frequency of Petition-Signing as a Function of Direct Experience and Environmental Concern

	Experimental condition	
Behavior	Belief nonrelevant	Belief relevant
High direct experience/ Low environmental concern		
Refused to sign	0	3
Signed 1 or 2 petitions	7	5
High direct experience/ High environmental concern		
Refused to sign	0	3
Signed 1 or 2 petitions	5	4
Low direct experience/ High environmental concern		
Refused to sign	2	7
Signed 1 or 2 petitions	10	1
Low direct experience/ Low environmental concern		
Refused to sign	0	2
Signed 1 or 2 petitions	12	7

Note: The median score of the sample was 30.00. Scores less than or equal to 30 were classified as low; scores of 31 and above were classified as high. For subjects high on direct experience but low on environmental concern, Fisher's exact $p = .12$. For subjects high on direct experience and high on environmental concern, Fisher's exact $p = .16$. For subjects low on direct experience but high on environmental concern, Fisher's exact $p = .003$. For subjects low on direct experience and low on environmental concern, Fisher's exact $p = .17$.

was impressively effective in increasing attitude-behavior consistency for those subjects who were relatively low in personal experience with the on-campus parking shortage, it was remarkably ineffective for subjects who were high in personal experience. Apparently, then, making individuals well aware of the behavioral implications of their global attitudes will not necessarily increase the consistency between global attitudes and actual behavior if their prior personal experience in the pertinent behavioral domain predisposes them to engage in actions that are inconsistent with their attitudes. Interestingly, such a conclusion seems entirely in line with the implications of recent work by Bentler and Speckart (1979) who demonstrated, using structural equation models, that measures of previous behavior contribute significantly to the prediction of a variety of socially important actions independently of the influence of prior behavior on attitudes, intentions, or subjective norms.

But why were the effects of the belief-relevance manipulation in this research so strikingly dependent on the extent of prior personal experience with the parking shortage? The answer to this question may lie in the extent to which subjects viewed important personal outcomes as potentially being affected by their choice of whether to sign the petitions advocating increased on-campus parking. It seems reasonable to assume that subjects who had little personal experience with the hassles and inconvenience associated with the on-campus parking shortage probably anticipated that a decision to build additional parking facilities would not benefit them in personally important ways. To the extent that they perceived the implications of their global environmental attitudes for their position on the parking issue, these individuals should

have experienced relatively little conflict between their personal interests vis-à-vis the parking situation and the implications of their global proenvironmental attitudes. Thus, when faced with the choice to sign or not to sign the petitions, individuals who were low in prior personal experience were likely to follow the dictates of their global environmental attitudes to the extent that they were made aware of the behavioral implications of their environmental beliefs.

By contrast, those individuals who were high in prior personal experience probably anticipated that the success or failure of efforts to persuade the university administration to build additional parking facilities would have relatively important implications for their own personal outcomes in the future. For these individuals, acting in the service of their strong personal interests necessarily conflicted with acting in accordance with the implications of their proenvironmental beliefs. Thus, for individuals high in prior personal experience, making the behavioral implications of their environmental beliefs more cognitively accessible probably made them more aware of the conflict between their personal interests and their environmental beliefs. However, this awareness did not guarantee that they would resolve their behavioral dilemma in favor of their environmental beliefs.

One clear implication of this analysis is that those individuals who stand to benefit the most from engaging in behaviors that are *congruent* with their attitudes should be most likely to demonstrate substantial attitude-behavior consistency. This was precisely what Sivacek and Crano (Note 1) recently found in a study of vested interest as a moderator of attitude-behavior consistency. Respondents who perceived that they would be most directly and personally affected by the consequences of an impending legislative referendum were most likely to act in accordance with their **attitudes**.

Although the foregoing analysis is speculative, the results of the present investigation make one point very clearly. When examining the effects of increased cognitive accessibility of global attitudes on attitude-behavior consistency, social psychologists should take into consideration the nature and extent of respondent's prior personal experience in the behavioral domain under consideration.

NOTES

1. Since the belief-relevant condition always included the parking at the university and motorcycle safety dialogues and the belief-nonrelevant condition did not include either of these dialogues, it is not possible to estimate to what extent the effects, if any, of the belief-relevance manipulation are due to the parking at the university dialogue as opposed to the motorcycle dialogue. However, this poses no unique interpretive problem. Even if the presence or absence of the parking dialogue had been the only difference between the two experimental conditions, it still would have been impossible (and uninteresting from our perspective) to determine what particular aspect or element of the parking dialogue was responsible for producing any observed effects of the belief-relevance manipulation.

2. There was no reason whatsoever to suspect that any of the filler dialogues in the belief-nonrelevant condition could possibly alter the accessibility of either global environmental attitudes or the specific behavioral implications of those attitudes with respect to the parking issue. Thus it seemed highly implausible that the order in which subjects were exposed to these innocuous conversations could possibly affect their petition-signing behavior. Accordingly, the order of dialogue presentation was not counterbalanced in the belief-nonrelevant condition.

3. These eight items dealt with the extent to which subjects felt pollution was affecting them

personally, their beliefs about governmental regulations designed to curb pollution, their beliefs about antipollution organizations, and their sense of personal responsibility for taking steps to slow down pollution.

4. This scale construction was of course based on the assumption that there was an increase in the strength of public commitment from the first to the second petition. Consistent with this assumption, not one subject signed the second petition without also having signed the first petition. In contrast, 21 subjects signed the first but not the second petition, and 30 subjects signed both.

5. The correlation between environmental concern and the direct experience measure was not statistically reliable, $r = .12$, ns, $n = 68$.

REFERENCE NOTE

1. Sivacek, J., & Crano, W.D. *Vested interest and attitude-behavior consistency.* Unpublished manuscript, Michigan State University, 1979.

REFERENCES

Ajzen, I., & Fishbein, M. Attitude-behavior relations: A theoretical analysis and review of empirical research. *Psychological Bulletin,* 1977, *84,* 888-918.

Ajzen, I., & Fishbein, M. *Understanding attitudes and predicting social behavior.* Englewood Cliffs, N.J.: Prentice-Hall, 1980.

Bentler, P. M., & Speckart, G. Models of attitude-behavior relations. *Psychological Review,* 1979, *86,* 452-464.

Brannon, R., Cyphers, G., Hesse, S., Hesselbart, S., Keane, R., Schuman, H., Viccaro, T., & Wright, D. Attitude and action: A field experiment joined to a general population survey. *American Sociological Review,* 1973, *38,* 625-636.

Cialdini, R. B., Petty, R. E., & Cacioppo, J.T. Attitude and attitude change. *Annual Review of Psychology,* 1981, *32,* 357-404.

Fazio, R. H., & Zanna, M. P. Attitudinal qualities relating to the strength of the attitude-behavior relationship. *Journal of Experimental Social Psychology,* 1978, *14,* 398-408. (a)

Fazio, R. H., & Zanna, M. P. On the predictive validity of attitudes: The roles of direct experience and confidence. *Journal of Personality*, 1978, *46*, 228-243. (b)

Fazio, R. H., & Zanna, M. P. Direct experience and attitude-behavior consistency. In L. Berkowitz (Ed.), *Advances in experimental social psychology* (Vol. 14). New York: Academic Press, 1981.

Fazio, R. H., Zanna, M. P., & Cooper, J. Direct experience and attitude-behavior consistency: An information processing analysis. *Personality and Social Psychology Bulletin*, 1978, *4*, 48-51.

Fishbein, M., & Ajzen, I. *Belief, attitude, intention and behavior*. Reading, Mass.: Addison-Wesley, 1975.

Fisher, R. A. *Statistical methods for research workers* (10th ed.). London: Oliver and Boyd, 1946.

McArthur, L. A., Kiesler, C. A., & Cook, B. P. Acting on an attitude as a function of self-percept and inequity. *Journal of Personality and Social Psychology*, 1969, *12*, 295-302.

Norman, R. Affective-cognitive consistency, attitudes, conformity, and behavior. *Journal of Personality and Social Psychology*, 1975, *32*, 83-91.

Pryor, J. B., Gibbons, F. X., Wicklund, R. A., Fazio, R., & Hood, R. Self-focused attention and self-report validity. *Journal of Personality*, 1977, *45*, 513-527.

Regan, D. T., & Fazio, R. On the consistency between attitudes and behavior: Look to the method of attitude formation. *Journal of Experimental Social Psychology*, 1977, *13*, 28-45.

Schuman, H., & Johnson, M. P. Attitudes and behavior. *Annual Review of Sociology*, 1976, *2*, 161-207.

Schwartz, S. Normative influences on altruism. In L. Berkowitz (Ed.), *Advances in experimental social psychology* (Vol. 10). New York: Academic Press, 1977.

Schwartz, S. Temporal instability as a moderator of the attitude-behavior relationship. *Journal of Personality and Social Psychology*, 1978, *36*, 715-724.

Snyder, M., & Swann, W. B., Jr. When actions reflect attitudes: The politics of impression management. *Journal of Personality and Social Psychology*, 1976, *34*, 1034-1042.

Songer-Nocks, E. Situational factors affecting the weighting of predictor components in the Fishbein model. *Journal of Experimental Social Psychology*, 1976, *12*, 56-69.

Tesser, A. Self-generated attitude change. In L. Berkowitz (Ed.), *Advances in experimental social psychology* (Vol. 11). New York: Academic Press, 1978.

Wicker, A. W. Attitudes versus actions: The relationship of verbal and overt behavioral responses to attitude objects. *Journal of Social Issues*, 1969, *25*, 44-78.

Zanna, M. P., Higgins, E. T., & Herman, C. P. (Eds.), *Consistency in social behavior: The Ontario symposium* (Vol. 2). Hillsdale, N.J.: Erlbaum, in press.

Zanna, M. P., Olson, J. M., & Fazio, R. H. Attitude-behavior consistency: An individual difference perspective. *Journal of Personality and Social Psychology*, 1980, *38*, 432-440.

Cognitive Dissonance in an Intergroup Context

Joel Cooper and Diane Mackie

Student members of a campus group supporting Ronald Reagan in the 1980 presidential election participated in a study of the effects of group membership on dissonance reduction. In a 2 × 2 factorial design, half of the subjects were asked to write arguments contrary to their attitudes, whereas the other half were required to write such arguments. Half of the subjects were asked to advocate a position that was counter to the attitude that defined their membership in the group. The other half produced arguments that were counter to attitudes relevant to, but not definitional of, group membership. It was predicted that attitude change would be used as a way to reduce dissonance only by those subjects who freely wrote arguments counter to nondefinitional attitudes. Attitude change was not possible, however, for subjects who freely produced arguments counter to a definitional attitude; these subjects were expected to misattribute their arousal to the existence of a competing out-group and to reduce their dissonance by derogating that group. The results supported these predictions. The importance of group membership in affecting attitude change is discussed.

Consider the situation of typical participants in an experiment on the effects of cognitive dissonance. Dissonance is aroused by having subjects advocate publicly a position that is contrary to their private attitudes. When participants feel free to refuse to perform the task but nonetheless agree to do so, significant attitude shifts toward the advocated position are found. Such changes are thought to be due to subjects' desires to restore consistency among their cognitions and thereby reduce the unpleasant tension state of dissonance.

In reaching this understanding of dissonance-mediated attitude change, it has been heuristically useful to consider only those events that impinge upon the participant during the experimental session. Even when social factors have been incorporated into dissonance research, the social contexts constructed for the subject have usually been temporary and artificial. Subjects interact with colleagues or confederates who have no place in the ongoing network of relationships outside the laboratory (e.g., Cooper, Zanna, & Goethals, 1974; Festin-

This research was supported by Research Grant #BNS76-19384 from the National Science Foundation and was carried out while the second author was the recipient of a Winifred Cullis Grant from the International Federation of University Women. The authors would like to thank Linda Worcel for her convincing role as the second experimenter.

ger & Carlsmith, 1959); they participate as members of artificial committees and groups formed in the laboratory and made to seem real for the brief period of interaction (Aronson & Mills, 1959). The world created in the laboratory is designed specifically to have an impact on the attitudes of participants. But for the subject, this is not the only world of importance. Subjects bring with them into the laboratory a world of interlocking social relationships and group memberships that may interact with the events produced in the laboratory to affect the motivations, perceptions, and ultimately the attitudes of the participants. In the present context, we wish to reunite these two worlds. We wish to consider in a systematic fashion the way in which the ongoing social groups to which subjects belong influence their perception and management of the events that occur in the research setting.

Membership groups have a powerful influence on the individual's attitudes and behavior. The social groups with which individuals identify affect their self-esteem, with members of valued groups having more positive self-regard (Doise & Sinclair, 1973). Individuals show a strong loyalty to their groups, consistently preferring members of their group to members of others, evaluating their own group more positively, adhering more closely to the normative standards of their own group, and favoring their group over others in the allocation of rewards and resources (see Brewer, 1979, and Tajfel, 1982, for reviews). Such behavior seems to be the result of a social identification mechanism that appears to be activated when categorization of the social world into identity-relevant groups is salient. Individuals attempt to maintain high self-esteem by positively evaluating, liking, and conforming to the social groups with which they identify and by distinguishing themselves from and discriminating against groups to which they do belong (Tajfel, 1978; Tajfel & Turner, 1979).

Of fundamental importance to such categorization and evaluation are dimensions on which membership in a group can be defined and distinguished from membership in other groups. Attributes represented on these dimensions may be called *definitional*, as possession of them is a necessary condition of group membership. They can be contrasted with *associated* attributes which may be possessed by most or even all members of the group, without defining group membership. Such attributes may be associated with the group, but failure to possess them does not automatically preclude membership in it.

Supporting a candidate's election to office, for example, is an attitude definitional of membership in a group dedicated to his or her election. In principle, not wanting the candidate elected precludes membership in the group. However, it is possible to belong to a group campaigning for a candidate and yet not favor one of the candidate's platforms. Support for the issue would be an attribute associated with, rather than definitional of, group membership. The relative importance of definitional and associated attributes is not relevant to the distinction. Possession of an associated attribute may be just as important to individual members of the group as possession of definitional ones. Group membership, however, depends on the presence or absence of the latter.

How might membership in an ongoing social group interact with a subject's perception and handling of the events occurring in the typical dissonance study? Suppose, for example, that in 1980, members of a student group campaigning for Ronald Reagan's election as president of the United States are asked to provide strong and forceful reasons to support Jimmy Carter's reelection. They agree to do so and find that the task is performed in the presence of other members of their Youth for Reagan group. This situation produces clearly discrepant cognitions: the perception of free choice to engage in the task and the salience of being a member of a group supporting Reagan but nevertheless supplying arguments in support of Carter's reelection.

Focusing on the events occurring in the research session alone allows a clear prediction from dissonance theory to be made. The inconsistent cognitions will produce arousal and, consequently, attitudes will change toward the advocated position. This will occur in the service of reducing the arousal by rendering the cognitions consonant with one another.

When the impact of these events on the subject's social affiliations is also considered, however, the situation looks quite different. Group membership is very salient, and subjects must deal with the implications of their behavior for this membership. In such circumstances, increased liking for the in-group, increased disliking for the out-group, and increased conformity to group norms could be expected. Subjects are more likely to move away from the nonnormative advocated position and adhere even more rigidly to their original, normative position.

How might our Reagan supporters deal with this conflict? On the one hand, there are the compelling demands of group membership and the need to maintain social relationships and adhere to the norms regulating them. Group membership cannot be maintained if there is a change in the definitional attitude, so subjects are strongly motivated to resist abandoning their pro-Reagan position. On the other hand, subjects feel a need to reduce the uncomfortable arousal associated with their inconsistent behavior. How can the dissonance resulting from inconsistent cognitions be dealt with and positive social identity be maintained? It seems to us that our subjects might achieve both these ends by misattributing any arousal to their dislike for a salient, and in the circumstances somewhat threatening, out-group.

A number of experiments have consistently supported the proposition that the uncomfortable arousal state of dissonance can be misapplied to other factors in the environment, particularly if circumstances make other stimuli salient or if it is difficult to reduce dissonance by altering attitudes (see Zanna & Cooper, 1976, for a review). For example, Gonzales and Cooper (cited in Zanna & Cooper, 1976) found that members of various campus clubs who were induced to write statements attacking those clubs came to believe that it was the lights in the experimental room that made them uncomfortable. When it was difficult to change their attitudes toward their own organization, these subjects found another stimulus to explain their discomfort. Similarly, Fazio, Zanna and Cooper (1977) demonstrated that political conservatives who advocated liberal positions and liberals who advocated conservative positions also preferred to believe that their discomfort was due to some disturbing aspect of the room in which they were questioned. Negative feeling states that had been aroused by the subjects' attitude-discrepant statements were not attributed to those statements but rather were misattributed to conditions in the experimental room.

We believed that members of Youth for Reagan who advocated the election of Jimmy Carter would be proscribed from changing their attitude about the person who should be elected president. Following the lead of previous research, we predicted that members of the Youth for Reagan group would seize upon the intergroup context to deal with their uncomfortable arousal. If the existence of an opposing group (Carter supporters) was made salient, we believed it would serve as a convenient focus for the misattribution of arousal. This led us to make three main predictions.

1. We expected to replicate the findings of previous induced-compliance experiments when subjects made statements counter to an attitude that was associated with, but not definitional of, group membership. When subjects were induced to support extending government-funded health programs, we predicted attitude change toward the advocated position when participation in the experiment was perceived as having been freely chosen.

2. When, under otherwise identical conditions, subjects were induced to make statements counter to an issue that defined their group membership, however, we predicted that attitude change would be blocked. Subjects in the high-choice condition were expected to experience the dissonance associated with making attitude-discrepant statements but would be precluded from dissipating that tension by rejecting the defining norm of an important membership group.

3. When dissonance was experienced but attitude change blocked, we expected misattribution of arousal. Targeting a salient and relevant out-group for dissonance misattribution would not only reduce tension but would reaffirm group membership and maintain positive social identity. We predicted that subjects who freely choose

to make statements counter to a defining norm of their group would misattribute their discomfort to relations with an out-group rather than change their attitudes. We expected this misattribution to be evidenced by increased derogation of and disliking for the relevant out-group in the high-choice/definitional-issue condition.

METHOD

Subjects

Forty-two male and female members of a Princeton University group supporting Ronald Reagan in the 1980 presidential election agreed to participate in a study of political attitudes and social perception. Participants received $3.50 for attending two experimental sessions. Subjects were run in groups of three to six in both sessions and were randomly assigned to experimental conditions.

Overview

In the first session, all subjects completed a three-page questionnaire that served as a premeasure of political attitudes and perceptions of the in-group and of other groups. Subjects were told that supporters of all three presidential candidates would be participating in the study. At the end of the first session, subjects were scheduled to return approximately 8 days later to complete a similar follow-up questionnaire. The experimental variables were manipulated in a "second experiment" immediately preceding this follow-up session. Subjects agreed to produce arguments counter to an item that was either definitional of or associated with group membership under conditions of high or low choice for a different experimenter. The follow-up questionnaire

included the postmeasure of attitudes and group liking. In all phases, the intergroup context was stressed by having other members of the in-group present, by referring to out-groups, and by asking subjects to deal with issues related to their group membership.

Procedure

Initial attitude measurement. The first questionnaire asked subjects to indicate how long they had belonged to the group and what activities, such as canvassing and organizational support work, they did on the group's behalf. Subjects were also asked to indicate how important membership in the group was to them on an 11-point scale, where 1 indicated low importance and 11 indicated high importance.

Subjects' support for or opposition to 12 political issues was also assessed. Subjects responded on 31-point scales to items ranging from the election of Ronald Reagan and the Kemp-Roth proposal to desegregation and busing. Each of these 12 items was followed by a 5-point scale (with 1 marked "not at all important" and 5 marked "very important") on which subjects indicated how important the preceding issue was to them.

Four other items on the initial questionnaire were of importance. Subjects were asked to indicate, on 11-point scales, how positively or negatively they felt toward members of their own Youth for Reagan group, "typical Reagan supporters," members of an equivalent group (Students for Carter), and "typical Carter supporters." High scores on these scales indicated liking for the target group.

Choice of definitional and associated attitude items. Because all subjects belonged to the Youth for Reagan group, the item deemed to be definitional of group membership was the one dealing with support for or opposition to Reagan's election as President. To oppose Reagan's election and yet be a member of Youth for Reagan was impossible. On the initial questionnaire, subjects' mean score on this item was 26.03, with a standard deviation of 3.37, where 31 indicated maximum support for Reagan's election. The mean importance rating assigned to the item was 3.13., indicating that the subjects indeed felt that it was important that Reagan be elected.

Responses to the other items on the questionnaire were examined to identify those with a similar distribution of attitude and importance responses. The item asking subjects about their attitude toward the "establishment of government-funded national health programs" proved to have a mean of 26.95 (where 31 indicated maximum opposition to the issue) and a standard deviation of 4.15, indicating a pattern of responses very similar in extremity and spread to that of the definitional item. Moreover, the mean importance rating given the item was 3.37 out of a possible 5, again very similar to the Reagan item. As a high score on the Reagan item indicated support for Reagan's election whereas a high score on the health item indicated opposition to government-funded health programs, high scores on both items indicated a conservative pattern of responding consistent with group norms. In fact, neither attitude responses nor importance ratings for the two issues differed: For the attitude items, $t(78) = 1.04$, $p < .29$; for the importance ratings, $t(78) = 1.17$, $p < .24$. The health care item was selected as the associated attitude item, an issue clearly associated with group membership and of equal importance to group members but not

definitional of such membership. One could argue for extension of governmental health programs and still support Reagan's election.

Manipulation of dissonance. When subjects arrived for the second session, they were met by a new experimenter who explained that the original experimenter had been held up and would be about 10 minutes late. The new experimenter then mentioned that she was also involved in some work related to the election that subjects could do while waiting. The degree of dissonance subjects experienced was manipulated by varying the degree of decision freedom subjects were given to participate, once the nature of the task was known. In both the high- and the low-choice conditions, the experimenter explained that she was studying the effect of information on decisions about political issues using taped debates as stimuli. All subjects were told the following:

> to make sure all possible points are raised in the debates we've found the best way is to ask people to present strong and forceful arguments for one side of an issue only. It makes no difference which side of the issue you actually support. The important thing is to concentrate on making forceful points for one side. The debates I'm preparing are on the military draft issue, the Presidential election, extension of government health programs and modifying the electoral college.

While scanning a list of topics, the experimenter announced which issues she still needed arguments for and whether arguments for or against the issue were needed. In the high-choice condition, she then said, "What I'd like from you are arguments supporting the _____ issue. Would you be willing to help me out? It shouldn't take more than 10 minutes." In the low-choice condition she said, "I need you to give me arguments supporting the _____ issue. It shouldn't take more than 10 minutes.

Manipulation of the nature of the attitude. Within each session, the second experimenter randomly assigned subjects to the definitional and associated attitude conditions. Half the subjects were asked to produce arguments supporting Carter's reelection (behavior inconsistent with an attitude definitional of group membership) and half to produce arguments supporting extension of government-funded health programs (behavior inconsistent with an attitude associated with but not definitional of group membership). In both conditions, paper was provided on which the instructions reappeared and on which subjects were asked to write their name, the issue they were supporting, and eight strong and forceful arguments for this position.[1]

Dependent measures. Approximately 10 minutes later, the original experimenter arrived. The second experimenter gathered the argument sheets, thanked the subjects, and then left. The original experimenter passed out the second questionnaire on which, in addition to answering several new attitude issues, subjects were again asked to indicate their attitude toward the election of Reagan and the establishment of government-funded health programs; their liking for members of their own Reagan support group, members of a rival Carter support group, and "typical" Reagan and "typical" Carter supporters; and how important membership in their group was to them. For half the subjects, the items dealing with perception of the in-group and the similar group (typical Reagan supporters) preceded the items dealing with perceptions of Carter supporters, whereas this order was reversed for the rest of the subjects.

Check on manipulations and debriefing. When subjects completed the questionnaire, they were asked to fill out a short questionnaire required by the Psychology Department of all experimental subjects as a check on ethical standards. This comprised seven items asking subjects to indicate on 11-point scales their feelings about various aspects of the experiment. The important item here read, "How much choice did you feel you had to participate in the study?" In distributing the questionnaire, the experimenter noted that subjects would be familiar with the questionnaire because they had filled it out for the other experimenter. When told that this was not the case, the experimenter instructed subjects to fill it out "thinking about that exercise and that experimenter"—they could then do one for the present experimenter. When subjects had completed the evaluation of the first experiment, which allowed the success of the choice manipulation to be checked, they were thoroughly debriefed.

RESULTS

Check on the Manipulations

Several relevant items on the initial questionnaire allowed us to check that our subjects did in fact identify with their Youth for Reagan group. Subjects indicated that they had belonged to the group on the average for 4½ months; as the group had been formed especially for the election, this meant that many had been members from its inception. Members spent approximately 2½ hours a week canvassing, soliciting new members, or doing some other form of support work for the group. Many held positions of responsibility in the group, positions that ranged from chairman/coordinator of the group to dorm captain. When the initial attitude measure was taken, subjects reported that membership in the group was of considerable importance to them ($M = 6.3$ on an 11-point scale, where 11 indicated high importance). By the time the experimental session was run, membership had increased in importance ($M = 7.22$). We were thus able to verify that group membership was indeed both relevant and salient to our subjects.

We were also able to evaluate the effectiveness of the dissonance manipulation by checking subjects' responses to the perceived-choice item on the "ethical standards" questionnaire. Subjects in the choice condition apparently felt that their participation had been completely voluntary ($M = 7.55$, where 11 indicated high choice and 1 indicated no choice). In contrast, subjects in the no-choice condition felt significantly less freedom of choice ($M = 3.0$), $F(1, 39) = 22.29, p < .0001$. The manipulation of perceived choice appeared to have been successful.

There were no differences among subjects assigned to different conditions on any of these indicators.

Attitude Change

The associated item. Our first hypothesis concerned the way in which subjects making counterattitudinal statements on an issue associated with group membership would reduce the resulting dissonance. Because a position on the issue of government health care did not define group membership, it was predicted that subjects who produced pro-health-care arguments under conditions of high choice would reduce their dissonance by changing their attitudes to make them consistent with their behavior. The data presented in Table 1 are the adjusted means for subjects' attitudes toward government-funded health care following the argument-producing situation.

TABLE 1

Mean Postexperimental Attitude Toward Government-Funded Health Care (Associated Item), Adjusted by Initial Attitude

	Argument	
Choice	Pro Carter	Pro health care
High	25.66$_{a,b}$	24.37$_a$
Low	27.72$_b$	27.72$_b$

Note: High scores indicate support for government funding. Means with no common subscripts differ at $p < .05$.

Initial attitudes on the issue serve as the covariate.

The first column of Table 1 presents the data for subjects who did not produce arguments on the health care issue but had been asked instead to support Carter's reelection. The second column presents the data for subjects who had produced pro-health-care arguments. The prediction was that subjects in the free-choice/health-care condition would differ from their low-choice counterparts on their final rating of the health care item. The analysis of covariance indicates that this prediction was confirmed. The mean attitude in the high-choice/health-care condition differed from that of the low-choice/health-care condition, $t(18) = 2.90, p < .004$. Moreover, the high-choice/health-care condition differed significantly from the combined mean of the other three conditions, $t(34) = -2.22, p < .03$. The overall pattern of data also revealed a strong main effect for choice, $F(1, 39) = 11.21, p < .002$.

These results are consistent with often-replicated induced-compliance findings.

Subjects who produced counterattitudinal arguments in high-choice conditions demonstrated attitude change in the direction advocated by their arguments.

The definitional item. Our second hypothesis concerned subjects induced to argue against a position that defined their membership in an important group. Although we expected these subjects to experience dissonance if they had freely chosen to produce the counterattitudinal arguments, we predicted that membership in the group would preclude attitude change as a means of reducing this tension. Table 2 presents the adjusted means (adjusted by subjects' initial attitudes) for subjects' postmanipulation attitudes toward Ronald Reagan's election. The first column of Table 2 presents the attitude data from subjects who produced pro-Carter arguments. The second column presents the attitudes of subjects who had been asked to support the health care issue but not the presidential issue.

The analysis of covariance indicates that

FIGURE 1

Mean postexperimental attitudes for items on which counterattitudinal statements were made.

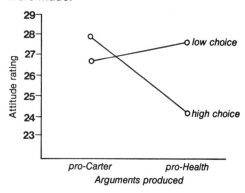

there were no main effects or interactions. Clearly, the subjects in the high-choice/ Carter condition did not change their attitude in the direction of their advocacy. If anything, these students strengthened their pro-Reagan stand relative to the subjects in the low-choice/Carter condition (but this difference did not reach significance).

Combined analysis. Further support for the confirmation of Hypotheses 1 and 2 can be seen in Figure 1, which presents the results of the attitude assessment on the item relevant to the subjects' counterattitudinal statements.[2] For subjects who produced pro-Carter arguments, adjusted mean posttest responses to the question, "How strongly do you feel Reagan should be elected president?" are represented in Figure 1. For subjects in the pro-health-care conditions, the depicted data are adjusted mean responses to the question, "How strongly do you feel that government-funded health programs should be established?"

An analysis of covariance reveals a sig-

TABLE 2

Mean Postexperimental Attitude Toward the Election of Ronald Reagan (Definitional Item), Adjusted by Initial Attitude

	Argument	
Choice	Pro Carter	Pro health care
High	28.02	26.68
Low	26.91	26.58

Note: High scores indicate support for Reagan. Means did not differ significantly.

nificant main effect for the topic of the essay. $F(1, 39) = 7.46, p < .01$, and a significant interaction between topic and choice, $F(1, 39) = 5.34, p < .05$. The main effect indicates that our Youth for Reagan subjects changed their attitudes far more when federally subsidized health care was the relevant question than when the reelection of Jimmy Carter was the relevant issue. The interaction reveals that the attitude change following counterattitudinal behavior was a function of the combination of the type of item (associated rather than definitional) and high choice. Also, as predicted, it was the high-choice/pro-health-care condition that contributed most prominently to the interaction. The mean for this cell differs significantly from a combination of the means in the other three conditions, $t(39) = 3.54, p < .001$.

Attractiveness of Groups

Our third prediction was linked to the apparent blocking of attitude change on membership-definitional issues. The results of the attitude measure indicate that subjects who produced counterattitudinal arguments under high-choice conditions reduced dissonance by changing their attitude if that attitude was associated with, rather than definitional of, group membership. In the latter case, subjects held tightly to their initial attitudes, despite their discrepant behavior. If dissonance was aroused in subjects who produced arguments advocating Jimmy Carter's reelection, how was that dissonance reduced?

We predicted that the intergroup context would provide the avenue for dissonance reduction. Specifically, we expected that those subjects who produced pro-Carter arguments under conditions of high choice would deal with their dissonance by attributing their negative arousal to an out-group.

TABLE 3

Mean Liking for Democrats ("Liking for Students for Carter" and "Liking for Typical Carter Supporters" Items Combined), Adjusted by Initial Liking

	Argument	
Choice	Pro Carter	Pro health care
High	6.23$_a$	8.20$_b$
Low	8.50$_b$	9.30$_b$

Note: High scores indicate dislike. Means with different subscripts differ at $p < .05$.

In this instance, subjects were asked to express their opinions of Democrats and of a specific pro-Carter group on the university campus. Table 3 presents the results of the two items combined.

Subjects who produced counterattitudinal arguments on the health care issue do not differ in their attitudes toward Democrats as a function of the degree of choice they had in writing the essay. However, subjects who came up with pro-Carter arguments did express more negative feelings about Democrats if those arguments had been produced under high-choice as compared with low-choice conditions, $t(18) = 2.40, p < .02$. The analysis of covariance also indicates a strong main effect for choice and a strong main effect for topic. It is clear that these main effects are due primarily to the high degree of disliking in the high-choice/pro-Carter condition. Subjects in that condition differed markedly from a combination of the other three cells, $t(37) = 2.58, p < .01$, whereas no other conditions differed from one another.[3]

Subjects were also asked about their feelings toward their own (Youth for Reagan) group after producing the counterattitudinal arguments. The results did not demonstrate systematic differences in in-group liking as a function of experimental conditions.[4]

The number of arguments produced by each student was assessed. No differences among experimental conditions were found. In addition, no significant correlations were found between the number of arguments produced and attitude change in any condition.

DISCUSSION

The data from the experiment offered support for our three major hypotheses. We predicted that attitude change would occur following counterattitudinal advocacy if that advocacy was made under conditions of high choice and if the position advocated was not definitional of group membership. The data confirmed again the importance of the choice variable in arousing dissonance and also confirmed the importance of the group context. Attitudes that were associated with group membership were changed as a function of freely agreeing to produce attitude-discrepant arguments. However, attitudes that were definitional of group membership were not changed by counterattitudinal advocacy whether it occurred freely or not. Members of a Youth for Reagan group did not become more inclined to support Jimmy Carter even if they had publicly supported his reelection with arguments written under high-choice conditions.

What, then, happened to the dissonance that Youth for Reagan members experienced after producing their pro-Carter arguments? We predicted that group members who supported a discrepant position on a definitional attitude would misattribute

their resulting unpleasant tension state to some other aversive element. In the context of the present study, the likely targets of misattribution were the members of rival Carter support groups, the most salient out-group. Indeed, the data showed that Youth for Reagan members denigrated the members of Students for Carter and typical Carter supporters if and only if they had made pro-Carter arguments under high-choice conditions. Subjects who had produced pro-Carter arguments under low-choice conditions and subjects who argued for government-funded health care under high- or low-choice conditions did not denigrate the out-group.

These results highlight the importance of considering the intergroup context in understanding the effects of cognitive dissonance. There is evidence that taking a counterattitudinal position under high-choice conditions evoked the unpleasant state of dissonance in all conditions. But it would have been an error to predict attitude change as a function of dissonance without taking the intergroup situation into account. Members of the Youth for Reagan group simply could not change their attitudes when the attitude in question was definitional of their membership in their group. Thus, they needed another means of dealing with this discomfort. The salient out-groups in this situation proved a convenient vehicle for dissonance reduction. Out-groups were perceived negatively and were therefore appropriate stimuli to which to attribute one's aversive arousal.

The results also have implications for the study of social groups. Group membership has been found to be an antecedent of strong in-group preference and out-group discrimination. People come to like their own group and to dislike an out-group, even when the groups are arbitrarily created.

Controversy exists as to whether differential treatment of the in-group and the out-group following social categorization is due to an increase in attractiveness of the in-group (Brewer, 1979), a decrease in attractiveness of the out-group, or both (see Tajfel, 1982). The results of this study suggest that under these conditions at least, the in-group is distinguished from the out-group by decreasing the attractiveness of the out-group. In the condition in which dissonance could not be reduced by attitude change, intergroup differences were created more by a denigration of the opposing group than by the increased attractiveness of one's own group. As pointed out above, there is some evidence that dissonance is experienced as having a negative quality, and our research shows that negative feelings created by one source can cause group members to transfer or misattribute those feelings to another possible source. It may be that intergroup discrimination is expressed through denigration of the out-group in our experiment because it is the most appropriate way of dealing both with dissonance reduction and with maintenance of group membership.

Finally, we would like to take note of the irony that results from the consideration of group membership and dissonance arousal. Those subjects who freely agreed to support Jimmy Carter's election might have been expected to become more pro-Carter or, by generalization, more favorable to Carter supporters if the intergroup context had not been considered. But because of the subjects' ongoing membership in a group that was important to them, producing arguments favorable to Carter resulted in an opposite phenomenon. Pro-Carter advocators in this condition became more hostile, rather than more favorable, toward Students for Carter and other Carter supporters.

The implication of our results is not that the intergroup context limits dissonance arousal. Rather, it is that a consideration of ongoing social memberships is crucial in understanding the consequences of such arousal. Divorcing dissonance from the social context in which it occurs allows predictions of attitude change to be made. But considered within the social context of group membership and identity, the very same dissonance that is aroused by induced compliance may have effects that are very different from, and even contradictory to, the consequences of dissonance in a setting devoid of social context.

Notes

1. Although all subjects agreed to produce arguments, one subject in fact produced arguments opposing the issue and another produced no arguments at all. As these subjects presumably experienced no dissonance, they were replaced.

2. Because examination of pretest responses on both items revealed that the means and standard deviations were similar, it was considered appropriate to present the two items in the same analysis.

3. As can be seen in Table 1, there was also an increase in support for government health care in the high-choice/pro-Carter condition. Change on this item in a direction consistent with the pro-Democrat position advocated may also have been used by subjects in this condition to reduce dissonance when attitude change on the membership-definitional issue was precluded.

4. The order in which group-liking items were presented interacted with in-group liking in a rather complex manner. Members of the Youth for Reagan group reported more liking for their own group if they had already responded to the items concerned with the attractiveness of the various Democrat out-groups. There were no order effects on subjects' feelings about the out-group, and liking for the in-group did not increase if subjects stated their feelings about in-groups before answering the out-group items.

This finding is inconsistent with previous suggestions that out-group denigration is a function of in-group favoritism (Brewer, 1979).

REFERENCES

Aronson, E., & Mills, J. The effect of severity of initiation on liking for a group. *Journal of Abnormal and Social Psychology*, 1959, *59*, 177-181.

Brewer, M. In-group bias in the minimal intergroup situation: A cognitive-motivational analysis. *Psychological Bulletin*, 1979, *86*, 307-324.

Cooper, J., Zanna, M., & Goethals, G. Mistreatment of an esteemed other as a consequence affecting dissonance reduction. *Journal of Experimental Social Psychology*, 1974, *10*, 224-233.

Doise, W., & Sinclair, A. The categorization process in intergroup relations. *European Journal of Social Psychology*, 1973, *3*, 145-157.

Fazio, R., Zanna, M., & Cooper, J. Dissonance and self-perception: An integrative view of each theory's proper domain of application. *Journal of Experimental Social Psychology*, 1977, *13*, 464-479.

Festinger, L., & Carlsmith, J. Cognitive consequences of forced compliance. *Journal of Abnormal and Social Psychology*, 1959, *58*, 203-210.

Tajfel, H. (Ed.). *Differentiation between social groups: Studies in the social psychology of intergroup relations*. London: Academic Press, 1978.

Tajfel, H. Social psychology of intergroup relations. *Annual Review of Psychology*, 1982, *33*, 1-40.

Tajfel, H., & Turner, J. An integrative theory of intergroup conflict. In W. Austin & S. Worchel (Eds.), *The social psychology of intergroup relations*. Monterey, Calif.: Brooks/Cole, 1979.

Zanna, M., & Cooper, J. Dissonance and the attribution process. In J. Harvey, W. Ickes, & R. Kidd (Eds.), *New directions in attribution research* (Vol. 1). Hillsdale, N.J.: Erlbaum, 1976.

Toward Theories of Persuasion and Belief Change

James Jaccard

Research trends on the effects of persuasive messages on attitude change were reviewed. It was concluded that new orientations to this area are required, and two general directions for theories of persuasion were proposed: (a) a theory of the acceptance of assertions and (b) a theory of the acceptance of complex messages. An empirical investigation on the former supported the viability of the proposed approach.

Research on attitude change has typically focused on two change strategies representing major research traditions in the attitude area. The Yale Communication Program, under the direction of Carl Hovland, focused research efforts on the effects of persuasive communications on attitudes. Research in the Hovland tradition has involved the manipulation of source variables (e.g., expertise, trustworthiness, sex, race of the source), message variables (e.g., discrepancy, order effects, fear appeals), and/

"Toward Theories of Persuasion and Belief Change" by J. Jaccard, 1981, *Journal of Personality and Social Psychology, 40*, pp. 260-269. Copyright 1981 by the American Psychological Assn. Reprinted by permission of the publisher and author.

or audience variables (e.g., intelligence, self-esteem, cognitive complexity) with corresponding analysis of the relationship of these manipulations to attitude change. Summaries of this research may be found in McGuire (1969), Triandis (1971), Fishbein and Ajzen (1972, 1975), and Himmelfarb and Eagly (1973).

The second tradition, characterized by the work of Festinger (1957) and other dissonance theorists, has examined the effects of behavioral performance on attitude change. The classic research paradigm is that of "forced compliance" (e.g., Festinger & Carlsmith, 1959), in which an individual is induced to perform a counterattitudinal behavior. Research in this tradition has typically attempted to specify those conditions in which the performance of a counterattitudinal behavior will produce attitude change versus those conditions in which attitude will remain relatively unaffected.

The present analysis focuses on research in the Hovland tradition, namely the attempt to understand the effects of a communication on attitudes. During the 1950s and 1960s, research activity in this important area was considerable. However, numerous scholars (e.g., Fishbein & Ajzen, 1975; Himmelfarb & Eagly, 1973) have noted that theoretical and empirical interest in this area has waned. A major reason for this has been the accumulation of largely inconsistent data regarding the influence of source, message, and audience variables on attitude change. As Himmelfarb and Eagly (1973) note:

After several decades of research, there are few simple and direct empirical generalizations that can be made concerning how to change attitudes. In fact, one of the most salient features of recent research is the great number of studies demonstrating that the empirical generalizations of earlier research are

not general, but contingent on conditions not originally apparent. (p. 594)

It will be argued in the present article that the communication situation as studied by Hovland and others has a level of complexity such that few empirical generalizations will be realized in this area of inquiry. New frameworks and approaches to the area are necessary, and specific suggestions for the direction that these approaches should take will be provided. Finally, a theory of persuasion will be tentatively developed as a first step toward applying these orientations to the persuasion literature.

THE DEPENDENT VARIABLE IN PERSUASION RESEARCH

A major source of inconsistent data in persuasion research concerns the nature of the dependent variable used in empirical studies of "attitude." Persuasion research in the Hovland tradition has generally used diverse concepts as dependent variables. Fishbein and Ajzen (1972) noted over 500 different operationalizations of attitude over a 2-year review period. These authors have convincingly argued for the necessity to distinguish between four variables—beliefs, affect, behavioral intentions, and behavior. According to Fishbein and Ajzen, the determinants of each of these types of variables may be different, and hence, they may respond to experimental manipulations differentially. To fully understand persuasive attempts, we must therefore understand what these determinants are, since they may moderate the influence of the manipulation on attitude.

The development of sophisticated social psychological theories of the determinants of these variables as well as their interrelationships has been lacking. To be sure, several theorists (e.g., Fishbein & Ajzen, 1975; Triandis, 1977) have developed preliminary frameworks, but considerable empirical and theoretical issues remain. Much of the inconsistent data in the persuasion literature can be understood by applying the taxonomy of Fishbein and Ajzen. However, even when the type of dependent variable is held constant, inconsistent data still result.

The present article is concerned with developing a persuasive theory concerning belief change (as opposed to affect change, intention change, or behavior change). There are several reasons for doing so. First, most persuasive messages in the experimental literature are composed of a set of belief statements (i.e., information) and hence are designed to change beliefs. When an investigator uses affect, behavioral intention, or behavior as the dependent measure, he or she is implicitly assuming that changes in these target beliefs will lead to changes in the dependent measure (an assumption that may be incorrect). Essentially, the researcher has implicitly used a theory of the relationships between beliefs and the variable in question. The focus of the present approach on beliefs simplifies the analyses so as to eliminate the need to take these implicit assumptions into account. Nevertheless, the relationship among beliefs, affect, behavioral intentions, and behavior is a critical one for understanding the ultimate impact of manipulations on dependent measures that are more removed from the persuasive communication (for interesting approaches to this problem, see Fishbein & Ajzen, 1975; Jaccard, Knox, & Brinberg, 1979; Wyer, 1974). Second, a large number of theorists in social psychology are increasingly relying on beliefs (or constructs very similar to them) as major variables in the development of theoretical networks concerning social behavior and social judgment. This trend justifies restricting the initial analysis to this key variable in these theories.

THE INDEPENDENT VARIABLE IN PERSUASION RESEARCH

Research in persuasion has typically manipulated a source variable, message variable, or audience variable and examined its effects on belief change. Even a cursory reading of *Psychological Abstracts* reveals the rather large number of variables that have been investigated. Among the different source variables that have been investigated are the expertise of the source, the trustworthiness of the source, the sex of the source, the race of the source, the attractiveness of the source, the social status of the source, the friendliness of the source, the religion of the source, the similarity of the source, the power of the source, the intentions of the source, the occupation of the source, and the posture of the source.

The list of audience variables is equally diverse. Among these variables are those such as the ego involvement of the audience, the sex of the audience, the intelligence of the audience, the authoritarianism of the audience, the social class of the audience, the race of the audience, the dogmatism of the audience, the internality-externality orientation of the audience, the status of the audience, the age of the audience, the religiosity of the audience, the liberalness of the audience, and the religion of the audience.

Finally, message variables have also been numerous. Message topics have included birth control, brushing one's teeth, cigarette smoking, sleep, psychology, punishment practices in schools, increasing tuition, police, racial differences in intelligence, attendance at school, football, elections, psychology experiments, and so on. The structural characteristics of these messages has also varied considerably including simple, one-statement messages, complex messages, messages designed to arouse fear, logical versus illogical messages, emotional versus unemotional messages, specific versus general messages, and so on.

In principle, there are hundreds of dimensions and characteristics of the source, message and audience that could be relevant in a change situation. To the extent that the relevant characteristics within a given class of variables (e.g., source characteristics) interact with each other to influence belief change, empirical studies that ignore *any* dimension may produce potentially inconsistent results. Similarly, if interactions occur between classes of variables (e.g., Source Variables × Message Variables), then failing to consider a relevant dimension may result in inconsistent data. The impact of a manipulation of any one variable will depend not only on the values of the other variables that are manipulated by the experimenter but those that are held constant as well. In studies of source credibility, for example, message content is usually held constant within a study but not between studies. If one study holds message discrepancy constant at a low level and another study holds message discrepancy constant at a high level, the two studies may yield drastically different results. This applies to *all* potentially relevant dimensions of source, message, and audience characteristics.

The above considerations suggest that simple relationships among the independent variables traditionally studied by Hovland and others and belief change will not be easily found. This has generally been borne out by the empirical data (Himmelfarb & Eagly, 1973). Any given persuasion study is always conducted with reference to the population of potential source, message, and audience characteristics relevant to belief change. The study essentially represents a "sampling" from these populations in which some of the dimensions are manipulated, some are held constant, and some are ignored. If the appropriate dimensions happen to be selected in the right combination, then belief change will manifest itself, and the theoretical prediction, whatever it might be, can be "verified." However, if one of the appropriate dimensions has been (unknowingly) excluded, "inconsistent" data may result. A pessimistic viewpoint might even go so far as to suggest that in those areas in which consistent data do exist, it is simply a matter of time until new conditions are (implicitly and randomly) "sampled" that yield inconsistent data. The act of communication is obviously complex, and research that assumes simple relationships may be problematic. This applies not only to research in persuasion via the Hovland tradition but *any* area that studies communication. Communication, by definition, involves a source, a message, and a recipient. Be it in a persuasive context, an interpersonal one, or otherwise, the above problems exist.

TOWARD GENERAL THEORIES OF PERSUASION

It seems unlikely that continued research investigating source, message, and audience variables in the Hovland tradition will yield a cumulative body of knowledge in the persuasion area. The *prediction* of belief change seems a difficult enterprise, since it is impossible to identify and measure all of the potentially relevant source, message, and audience variables in a given study. It is suggested here that an alternative (more precisely, a complementary) approach is required. This involves the specification and development of a small set of psychological variables that will, in essence, summarize or reflect all of the relevant source, message, and audience dimensions. Rather than having to measure or comprehend the hundreds of variables that might operate via the Hovland analysis, the measurement of these summary variables should allow for relatively precise predictions of belief change. In short, it seems necessary to develop a theory of the more immediate psychological determinants of belief change that will allow us to predict when change will occur and when it will not, and to help us understand the effectiveness or ineffectiveness of certain experimental manipulations. The present article considers some initial theoretical and empirical work in this direction.

Persuasive Messages

It would seem useful to develop persuasive theories in the context of two types of messages an individual may receive. At the simplest level, a source may make an assertion with no supporting arguments or evidence. The message simply consists of an assertion, such as "smoking cigarettes does not cause cancer." At a more complex level, a source may not only make an assertion but may present arguments or evidence in support of that assertion. An individual might be told that A is true because of B, C, and D, that B is true because of E and F, and that C is true because of G. In the former situation, concern is with the types of variables that influence the acceptance of a simple assertion. In the latter situation, concern is with how the individual perceives the logical structure of the message and then integrates this into his or her own logical structure with respect to the target belief. At some point, a complex message does contain statements that are simple assertions (in the above example, Statements D, E, F, and G would represent assertions for which no supporting evidence is given). Thus a theory of the acceptance of assertions would ultimately serve as the foundation for building a more elaborate theory of complex messages. Most research in the persuasion area has used complex messages, a research strategy that may be premature without a theoretical base in the acceptance of assertions and integration processes of own versus message logical structures. In fact, relatively little persuasion research, with the possible exception of investigations on counterarguing, has considered logical structures of the individual relative to the structure of message information and its implications for belief change.

A Theory of Persuasion at the Level of Assertions

Any communication involves a source, a message, and a receiver. A theory that attempts to delineate key summary variables of persuasion must therefore address each of these facets of communication. A critical message variable at the level of assertions would seem to be the position of the source on the target belief. If the target belief is "smoking causes cancer," a source might assert an extreme position ("smoking definitely causes cancer" or "smoking definitely does not cause cancer") or more moderate positions (e.g., "smoking may cause cancer," "smoking probably causes cancer," etc.). Thus one variable of interest is the perceived position of the source (PS) on the target belief. This variable should be influenced primarily by the language a source uses in making an assertion and, to a lesser extent, certain individual difference variables. In terms of linguistics, the polarizing effects of adverbs such as "definitely," "probably," "may," and so on, can greatly influence perceptions of the source's position. Using psychophysical scaling procedures such as the method of successive intervals (see Cliff, 1959), the precise effects of these adverbs can be isolated. Similarly, different types of verbs ("causes," "leads to," "influences") may have differential polarizing effects in interaction with specific adverbs. Again, methods developed in psychophysical scaling can yield relatively precise answers to these issues.

Sherif and Hovland (1961) have suggested that the processes of *assimilation* and *contrast* may affect perceptions of source positions. Assimilation focuses on the tendency for individuals to perceive a source's position as being closer to their own position than it actually is, whereas contrast focuses on the tendency for individuals to perceive a source's position as being farther from their own position than it actually is. Research in this tradition is directly applicable to understanding variations in perceptions of source positions.

In the present theory, the influence of the perceived position of the source on belief change is assumed to operate in the context of its *discrepancy* from the position of the individual (PI). Thus, discrepancy (D) is defined as PS − PI and represents a key construct in the theory. Qualitative distinctions between types of discrepancy will be introduced later, but they are not considered here for the sake of presentation.

In terms of the receiver, an individual may hold a particular belief for many reasons. He or she may believe that several lines of evidence (or reasoning) all suggest that a particular belief is true. The individual may have considerable support among his or her peers, who also think the belief is true. Similarly, the person may be highly ego involved in the issue and have considerable personal investment in it. For all of these reasons, and others, individuals will be more or less confident in the position they have taken. A second variable in the present theory, which is said to reflect receiver characteristics, is the *confidence* an individual has in his or her belief. Some individuals are highly confident in the positions they take, whereas other individuals may be less confident. This confidence will, in turn, have some influence on whether an individual is likely to accept or reject an assertion.

Several researchers have suggested that the confidence individuals have in their own belief will be systematically related to the extremity or polarity of the belief (e.g., Wyer, 1974). Individuals who strongly agree with the statement "smoking causes cancer" or who strongly disagree with this statement will be relatively confident in their beliefs. Others with less extreme positions will be less confident. Although this relationship has been observed by some researchers, others have failed to find any systematic relationship between these variables (cf. Johnson, 1955; Lee, 1972; Wyer, 1974).

Just as an individual may have confidence in his or her own position, he or she may have a generalized confidence in the source of the communication. Given a source who is perceived as being knowledgeable, trustworthy, an expert who is well respected by important others, and so forth, the individual may have considerable confidence in the source in terms of what he or she might say with respect to the target belief. This confidence in the source, which mediates the relevant source characteristics, represents another major variable in the present theory.

To summarize, three variables have been suggested thus far as the immediate psychological determinants of belief change: (a) the discrepancy (D) of the source's position from the individuals' own opinion, (b) the confidence an individual has in his or her own position (CO), and (c) the confidence an individual has in the source (CS). Once an assertion is made, an individual can (a) change his or her initial position, (b) change the confidence he or she has in that position, or (c) change the confidence he or she has in the source. The exact function relating D, CO, and CS to each of these reactions is an empirical question, but is undoubtedly complex.

To date, one laboratory experiment has been conducted to isolate the function relating the three variables to belief change. The results of this experiment are sufficiently promising to warrant further investigation of the approach. The initial experiment was conducted using a laboratory situation whereby relatively precise control over variables could be achieved. This required orthogonally manipulating discrepancy, confidence in one's own belief, and confidence in the source, all with respect to the same target belief. Such a factorial design permits identification of the function relating these variables to belief change as well as goodness of fit. Consideration of the present approach relative to other theories of persuasion will be treated in the Discussion section.

METHOD

Subjects

Subjects were 270 female students enrolled in introductory psychology classes. Participation in the experiment satisfied a course requirement.

Design and Procedure

A three-way ($3 \times 3 \times 3$) factorial design was used with all between-subjects factors. The first factor represents the manipulation of confidence in the source (high, moderate, or low), the second factor represents the manipulation of confidence in one's own belief (high, moderate, or low), and the third factor represents the manipulation of discrepancy (high, moderate, or low).

The experiment was conducted on a microcomputer for the purpose of stimulus control and feedback. Each subject was seated at the computer and told that the study concerned aviation safety and job performance of an air traffic controller. They were further told that the specific research question was whether a controller could make better judgments working alone or in cooperation with a co-worker, and how each team member uses the information supplied by her partner. The task was then described as a visual perception problem involving numerosity judgments of arrays of dots. They were told that a random array of dots would be flashed on the screen and that they were to estimate the number of dots that appeared. The "team" structure was then outlined for each subject. These instructions were designed to assure the subject that her judgments would be anonymous. Subjects were told that they were a member of two different, two-person teams, an A team (with members a_1 and a_2) and a B team (with members b_1 and b_2). The first member in each team (a_1 and b_1) was told that she would view and judge each stimulus without any help. The second person in each team (a_2 and b_2) was told that she would see both the stimulus and her partner's judgment of that stimulus before making her own judgment. Each subject was also told that she was team member b_1

and a_2 and that her anonymous partner, a_1, had completed the series of judgments a few days earlier, whereas her other anonymous partner, b_2, would do so several days later. It was explained that she would view the stimulus, make her judgment as b_1, receive a_1's judgment, and then make her judgment as a_2.

Each subject was then shown an example array and performed 10 practice trials. A practice trial involved the presentation of an array of dots and then an estimate by the subject as to how many dots appeared in the array. These estimates were made on a scale with eight interval sizes, 11–15, 16–20, 21–25, 26–30, 31–35, 36–40, 41–45, and 46–50. Thus, subjects did not estimate the exact number of dots, but rather, the interval that contained the number of dots displayed. After the 10 trials, subjects were given false feedback on how well they performed. Subjects were told they either obtained 8 correct trials, 5 correct trials, or 2 correct trials. This was designed to manipulate the confidence in their own belief (high, moderate, or low). The duration of presentation and nature of the array (e.g., number of dots, placement on screen) were extensively pretested to make this feedback plausible. For example, in the "2 correct trials" feedback condition, the presentation rate was sufficiently fast and the array complex enough to (a) ensure that subjects would be unable to determine their own accuracy level and (b) demonstrate that the task was a difficult one. In the "8 correct trials" feedback condition, the "self-feedback" was less ambiguous (but still sufficiently so that the false feedback was plausible), and the task was relatively easy.

Subjects were then provided information as to how their partner performed on these same 10 practice trials. Specifically, they were told that their partner obtained 8 cor-

rect trials, 5 correct trials, or 2 correct trials. This constituted the manipulation of confidence in the source. A measure of confidence in the source was then obtained on a 10-point scale ranging from not at all confident (1) to extremely confident (10). This scale was completed in response to the question, "How confident are you that your partner's judgments will be accurate?" This measure served as a manipulation check.

Each subject was then presented the first array and asked to estimate the exact number of dots that was displayed. The duration of presentation and nature of the array was similar to that of the practice trials. A measure of their confidence in this judgment was then obtained on the 10-point scale as described above. This measure served as a manipulation check for the own-confidence factor. Subjects were then shown the judgment of their partner. This judgment was either 5, 10, or 15 dots discrepant from their own estimate and represented the discrepancy manipulation (low, moderate, or high). They were then asked to provide their second judgment of the number of dots as well as their confidence in their partner's estimate (postmeasure of source confidence). Only one postpractice trial was used for purposes of analysis of the experiment. Ten subjects participated in each cell of the design.

RESULTS

Manipulation Checks

To ensure that manipulations of own and source confidence were effective, a 3 × 3 × 3 analysis of variance was performed on each of the preassertion measures of confidence.[1] The analysis of own confidence ratings yielded a significant main effect, $F(2, 243) = 775.20$, $p < .01$, for the own confidence factor. None of the other effects in the analysis were significant. Similarly, the analysis of the source confidence ratings yielded a significant main effect, $F(2, 243) = 868.86$, $p < .01$, for the source confidence factor. None of the other effects in the analysis were significant. Newman-Keuls tests indicated that both manipulations achieved the desired differences between the experimental groups. To ensure that the pretest beliefs did not differ as a function of the manipulations (due to sampling error in random assignment), a 3 × 3 × 3 analysis of variance was performed on the pretest belief scores. None of the effects in the analysis were statistically significant.

Belief Change

A 3 × 3 × 3 analysis of variance was conducted on change scores (postassertion judgment minus preassertion judgment) for the beliefs.[2] Table 1 presents the summary table for this analysis and Table 2 the means. All main effects and interaction effects were statistically significant. An interesting trend reveals itself in the means in Table 2. Whenever the person's confidence in her own belief exceeded the confidence in the source, relatively little belief change occurred. In the high, moderate, and low discrepancy conditions, when the subject was more confident in herself than in the source, the mean belief change was only 1.17, .97, and 1.17, respectively. When the confidence in herself was roughly equal to that of the source, the corresponding means were 2.07, 2.07, and 2.13. Thus, slightly more belief change occurred, but it was still similar across discrepancy levels. When the individual had more confidence in the source than herself, considerable belief change occurred, and this was directly related to the discrepancy of the assertion. In the high, moderate, and low discrepancy conditions, the mean change scores for individuals who had more confidence in the source than themselves was 8.23, 4.93, and 2.57, respectively.

TABLE 1

Summary Table of Analysis of Variance for Belief Change

Source	SS	df	MS	F
Disc (A)	160.07	2	80.03	36.67
Own (B)	450.82	2	225.41	103.26
Source (C)	452.62	2	226.31	103.67
A × B	236.24	4	59.06	27.06
A × C	141.24	4	35.31	16.18
B × C	97.42	4	24.36	11.16
A × B × C	170.24	8	21.28	9.75
Error	530.45	243	2.18	
Total	2,239.12	269		

Note: All *F* values are significant at *p* <.01.

TABLE 2

Mean Belief Change Scores as a Function of Discrepancy, Source Confidence, and Own Confidence

| | Own confidence | | | | | | | | | |
| | High discrepancy | | | Moderate discrepancy | | | Low discrepancy | | | |
Source confidence	High	Moderate	Low	High	Moderate	Low	High	Moderate	Low	*M*
High	1.8	5.6	13.0	2.3	5.3	5.4	2.2	2.5	2.8	4.54
Moderate	1.7	1.6	6.1	.5	2.1	4.1	1.7	1.9	2.4	2.45
Low	.7	1.1	2.8	.9	1.5	1.8	.8	1.0	2.3	1.43
M	1.4	2.77	7.3	1.23	2.97	3.77	1.57	1.8	2.5	

In terms of goodness of fit, the present experiment indicated that the three summary variables were relatively good predictors of belief change as defined in this experiment. The percentage of variance accounted for by the between-groups variability relative to the total variability was .763 as indexed by eta-squared and .736 as indexed by the more conservative omega-squared. This represents reasonable predictive power, especially in comparison to previous studies.

DISCUSSION

The present experiment provides initial support for the approach suggested in this article. A threshold type model of belief change was observed such that whenever people are more confident in themselves than the source, relatively little belief change results. However, when the confidence in the source exceeds an individual's own confidence, belief change will be directly related to the discrepancy of the assertion. These variables, and the resulting function relating them to belief change, yielded relatively high levels of goodness of fit. Of critical importance, however, is the generality of the fit of the model and the function relating the key summary variables to belief change. This question can only be addressed through future research and requires the development of valid and reliable measures of the concepts of source confidence and own confidence. Such a set of measures are currently being developed.

The model developed in the present article is suggestive of psychological mechanisms underlying inconsistent data observed in some areas of persuasion research. For example, some studies have shown a direct linear relationship between source credibility and belief change, whereas others have shown no relationship between these variables. If two studies used a moderately to highly discrepant message, but one used a target belief that individuals had considerable confidence in while the other used a target belief that the individuals were not confident in, the threshold model would predict credibility effects in the latter but not the former study (see the pattern of means in Table 2 under these conditions).

The three summary variables suggested here may, admittedly, not capture the essence of all relevant distal variables. Future research could direct itself toward isolating other summary variables. The results of the present study, however, suggest that the three variables proposed may serve as important mediators of belief change. One possibility for future research focuses on the discrepancy variable. Although the present laboratory methodology rendered a distinction irrelevant, qualitative differences in discrepancy are probably critical to more socially relevant phenomena. This can be investigated by orthogonally manipulating the person's initial belief with the source's belief. It may be the case that a discrepancy of 3 units when the person is initially neutral on a belief is qualitatively different than a discrepancy of 3 units when the person's initial opinion is polarized.

If the present approach is substantiated in future research, then insights into studies that manipulate more distal variables may be possible. Given reliable and valid measures of source and own confidence, one should be able to predict a priori whether or not a manipulation will result in belief change, depending on the initial values of the three summary variables and the impact of the manipulation on them. In addition, "base rate" conditions (e.g., high own confidence with low source confidence, or vice versa) can be identified through pretesting and avoided to eliminate problems of "ceiling effects" (i.e., everyone will change) or floor effects (i.e., no one will change) in such studies.

Although the results of the present study are promising, it must be emphasized that the current research setting is rather restricted. The experiment was conducted in a laboratory context with an issue of little or no social relevance. The situation was one that minimized the influence of previous opinions, ego involvement, and the importance of the target belief for the individual. These conditions were necessary to orthogonally manipulate the three key summary variables and represent a reasonable first step in this research approach. Had the theory resulted in an unfavorable outcome at this stage, further research would not be called for. The results of the present study, however, indicate that the approach may be useful and further suggest an interesting threshold model of confidence that has not been previously considered. One experimental result in the present research that may not generalize to certain field settings are the findings in the high discrepancy conditions. Past research has shown that under very extreme discrepancy levels, the source will be derogated and source confidence will drop dramatically, yielding no belief change. The high discrepancy condition in the present experiment exhibited tendencies in this direction but did not yield the phenomenon unambiguously, probably because the high discrepancy level was not inordinately discrepant from the target belief. Such extreme discrepancies probably do not occur with great frequency in everyday life but nevertheless may produce a different pattern of results. Future research is needed on the extension of the approach to nonlaboratory settings.

Although relatively little attention has been given to the development of theories of variables that mediate source, message, audience characteristics, and belief change, there are two notable exceptions in the social psychological literature, McGuire's (1968) two-factor theory of persuasion and Anderson's (1971) information integration theory. McGuire's theory, which posits that opinion change is a multiplicative function of the probability of reception and the probability of yielding, has generated a number of interesting hypotheses in the persuasion area. However, several issues remain unresolved with the approach. One major problem concerns the measurement and conceptualization of the yielding parameter (Fishbein & Ajzen, 1975). McGuire (1968) has suggested that the reception mediator of his model can be measured directly but that the yielding mediator must be estimated on the basis of message reception and amount of belief change produced. Research in laboratory settings on source credibility has generally observed equivalent and high levels of reception across credibility conditions but inconsistent results on the effects of credibility on belief change. Given equivalent reception scores, differences in belief change as a function of source credibility must be due to differences in yielding. Since yielding is not directly assessed, and since McGuire has not extended the theory to incorporate the immediate psychological determinants of yielding, the theory does not offer sufficient explanation for these inconsistent effects of source credibility on belief change. If differential belief change occurs, we conclude that there were differences in yielding. If differential belief change does not occur, we conclude that there were no differences in yielding. A useful extension of McGuire's approach would be the specification of the psychological determinants of yielding, an issue that the present article addressed.

Anderson's (1971) information integration theory has been applied largely to persuasion situations involving multiple messages and multiple sources. In contrast, most of the research in the Hovland tradition has focused on a single source/message. Integration theory can be directly applied to this latter situation, as Anderson (1971) noted. According to integration theory, an individual's response on a scale after a persuasive message is a weighted additive function of the individual's premessage belief and the position of the source of the communication. Mathematically, this is expressed as

$$R = W_o S_o + W_l S_l,$$

where R = the person's belief after being exposed to the message, S_o = the "scale value" of the person's initial opinion, S_l = the scale value of the source's position, and W_o and W_l = weighting parameters reflecting the psychological importance of the individual's initial belief and the source's position. By making certain assumptions about the nature of the W_i and S_i in a given experimental situation and by then observing R, inferences are made about the integration (i.e., combinatorial) processes of the individuals. Estimates of the weights or scale values are then derived from these responses using functional measurement procedures (Anderson, 1962, 1971). From the present perspective, the key "summary" variables represent the Wi and S_i variables. The weight associated with the source's position should reflect such factors as expertise, trustworthiness, and any other relevant source perception. In addition, this weight could also reflect message variables. The weight associated with the individual's own belief should largely reflect audience characteristics as well as, possibly, message characteristics.

Integration theory has also generated a number of interesting hypotheses in the context of persuasion studies. However, several problems arise with the application of the approach to belief change. Some of the frequently cited problems include (a) the difficulty of obtaining estimates of *Wi* and *Si* simultaneously, outside of laboratory settings for a single source/message; (b) the exact conceptual and empirical meanings of the weighting variables and the problem of uniqueness (see Shönemann, Cafferty, & Rotton, 1973); and (c) the difficulty of testing the model without making a priori assumption about the values of the weights and/or scale values. In addition, empirical evidence reported by Anderson (1959) questions the applicability of an additive model to belief change for a single message.

The theoretical implications of the present research only pertain to the acceptance of simple assertions. The theory presented is consistent with, but more fully elaborated than, recent mediational models developed in conformity research (Endler, Wiesenthal, Coward, Edwards, & Geller, 1976; Wiesenthal, Endler, & Geller, 1973). As noted earlier, a theory of the acceptance of assertions seems to be a logical foundation for a more complex theory of the acceptance of elaborate persuasive messages. Perspectives developed in the context of cognitive responses to persuasion, balance theory, and subject-verb-object analysis may be useful in extending this research to complex messages.

NOTES

1. Although these measures were taken prior to the discrepancy manipulation, a discrepancy factor was included in the analyses to ensure that unanticipated sampling error due to random assignment would not bias the results.

2. The analysis of change in experiments such as the present one is controversial. One type of analysis, other than the present focus on change scores, is an analysis of covariance on the posttest scores with the pretest scores as the covariate. This form of analyses has been recommended by some statisticians but not others. The present analyses are reported in the context of raw change scores, since these illustrate nicely the trends in the data. A covariance analysis was also performed, and the results were comparable to the change score analysis.

REFERENCES

Anderson, N. H., Test of a model for opinion change. *Journal of Abnormal and Social Psychology,* 1959, *59,* 371-381.

Anderson, N. H. Application of an additive model to impression formation. *Science,* 1962, *138,* 817-818.

Anderson, N. H. Integration theory and attitude change. *Psychological Review,* 1971, *78,* 171-205.

Cliff, N. Adverbs as qualifiers. *Psychological Review,* 1959, *66,* 27-44.

Endler, N. S., Wiesenthal, D. L., Coward, T., Edwards, J., & Geller, S. Generalization of relative competence mediating conformity across differing tasks. *European Journal of Social Psychology,* 1976, *5,* 281-307.

Festinger, L. *A theory of cognitive dissonance.* Evanston, Ill.: Row, Peterson, 1957.

Festinger, L., & Carlsmith, J. M. Cognitive consequences of forced compliance. *Journal of Abnormal and Social Psychology,* 1959, *58,* 203-210.

Fishbein, M. & Ajzen, I. Attitudes and opinions. *Annual Review of Psychology,* 1972, *23,* 487-544.

Fishbein, M. & Ajzen, I. *Belief, attitude, intention and behavior.* Reading, Mass.: Addison-Wesley, 1975.

Himmelfarb, S., & Eagly, A. H. *Readings in attitude change.* New York: Wiley, 1973.

Jaccard, J., Knox, R., & Brinberg, D. Prediction of behavior from beliefs: An extension and test of a subjective probability model. *Journal of Personality and Social Psychology,* 1979, *37,* 1239-1248.

Johnson, D. M. *The psychology of thought and judgment.* New York: Harper & Row, 1955.

Lee, W. *Decisions theory.* New York: Wiley, 1972.

McGuire, W. J. Personality and susceptibility to social influence. In E. F. Borgatta & W. Lambert (Eds.), *Handbook of personality theory and research.* Chicago: Rand McNally, 1968.

McGuire, W. J. The nature of attitudes and attitude change. In G. Lindzey & E. Aronson (Eds.), *Handbook of social psychology.* Reading, Mass.: Addison-Wesley, 1969.

Schoñemann, P. H., Cafferty, T., & Rotton, J. A note on additive functional measurement. *Psychological Review,* 1973, *80,* 85-87.

Sherif, M., and Hovland, C. *Social judgment:* *Assimilation and contract effects in communication and attitude change.* New Haven, Conn.: Yale University Press, 1961.

Triandis, H. C. *Attitudes and attitude change.* New York: Wiley, 1971.

Triandis, H. C. *Interpersonal behavior.* Monterey, Calif.: Brooks/Cole, 1977.

Wiesenthal, D. I., Endler, N. S., & Geller, S. H. Effects of prior group agreement and correctness on relative competence mediating conformity. *European Journal of Social Psychology,* 1973, *3,* 193-203.

Wyer, R. S. *Cognitive organization and change.* Potomac, Md.: Erlbaum, 1974.

3   Stereotypes, Prejudice, and Discrimination

APPLYING SCIENTIFIC METHODS AND utilizing previously acquired knowledge to explain and change problematic behaviors in everyday life has been a noteworthy goal of many social psychologists. One area in which such applications are readily apparent is the study of stereotyping, prejudice, and discrimination. These three phenomena parallel the cognitive, affective, and behavioral components of attitudes. Stereotypes are beliefs about another elicited by salient characteristics of the person. Prejudices are affective or emotional reactions to an individual as a consequence of one's beliefs about that individual. Discrimination parallels the behavioral component of attitudes and refers to one's actions toward a person as a function of group membership.

Although the parallel between attitudes and these three new processes is clear, there are two additional characteristics that are typically associated with stereotyping, prejudice, and discrimination. While attitudes may be either positive or negative in valence and may be formed toward any object, stereotypes are generally elicited by an individual's membership in an identifiable group, and prejudices are typically negative feelings about those who belong to particular groups. As a consequence of the negative impressions that are formed via stereotyping and prejudice, the actions that follow these cognitive processes typically lead to negative discrimination as well.

In summary, stereotypes, prejudice, and discrimination are generalized beliefs, attitudes, and behaviors, respectively, toward an individual based on the person's perceived group membership. Unfortunately, these responses more often than not are unjustified, negativistic, and based on biased overgeneralizations of the true nature of the individual and the group to which the person belongs.

Because of the close correspondence between attitudes and stereotypes, prejudice, and discrimination, there has been considerable overlap in the research that has been pursued in these related areas. For example, it is not unusual for attitude researchers to select racial attitudes as the domain of interest in their investigation; this is true for researchers who are interested in studying attitude formation, attitude change, or attitude-behavior relationships. In addition, one of the foremost contributors to the attitude literature, Gordon Allport, also authored one of the most authoritative volumes concerning prejudice, *The Nature of Prejudice* (1954). It would be wise, therefore, to consider the study of stereotypes, prejudice, and discrimination as being something of a subset of the study of attitudes, with similar processes and mechanisms operating and affecting these two classes of phenomena.

The articles in this chapter provide a broad spectrum of issues that lie at the heart of stereotyping, prejudice, and discrimination, ranging from differential perception of in- versus out-group members, to sexism, and discrimination. The initial article, by E. E. Jones and his associates, describes a study in which subjects rated the personal characteristics of members of a group with which they were associated and the characteristics of

83

the members of several other groups with which they had had relatively little contact. Their findings suggest that people tend to perceive greater variability in the characteristics of their closest associates and less variability in the personal traits of those with whom they have had fewer interactions. These authors attempt to identify the reasons that lie behind this differential perception of in- and out-group members.

Berna Skrypnek and Mark Snyder report the results of an investigation of the processes that tend to perpetuate stereotypic beliefs about women and men in the second article in this chapter. Skrypnek and Snyder's findings suggest that differential expectations are elicited depending upon the gender of the coactor, that perceivers' expectations about others serve as guides for their interactions, and that the behaviors displayed produce a behavioral confirmation of the stereotypic beliefs that initially led to the interaction sequence. Because the initiator of the sequence sets the stage for the interaction, the stereotypes that the person holds may appear to be confirmed, even when the stereotype can objectively be shown to be erroneous.

Perceived Variability of Personal Characteristics in In-Groups and Out-Groups: The Role of Knowledge and Evaluation

Edward E. Jones, George C. Wood,
and George A. Quattrone

Members of four undergraduate clubs rated their own club as more heterogeneous on a series of personal characteristics than they rated the three other clubs. This tendency was unrelated to the number of in-group or out-group members known, or to the degree of preference for the in-group.

Quattrone and Jones (1980) have proposed that people generally perceive more variability within their own in-group than they attribute to out-groups. They suggest that this may be so for several reasons: (1) The individual knows a greater proportion of in-group members than out-group members. (2) The individual sees in-group members

"Perceived Variability of Personal Characteristics in In-groups and Out-groups: The Role of Knowledge and Evaluation" by E.E. Jones, G.C. Wood & G.A. Quattrone, 1981, *Personality and Social Psychology Bulletin, 7,* pp. 523-528. Reprinted by permission of the authors.

in a greater variety of contexts or roles than out-group members. (3) Knowledge of the out-group may be at an early stage where, as Campbell's (1956) data suggest, people look for similarities rather than differences. (4) The individual may be motivated to see out-group members as alike to facilitate predictability, whereas he may be motivated to discover heterogeneity within his own group so as to feel free of constraining expectations. It may also be true that (5) differences in perceived variability are a consequence of evaluative discrimination. That is, negative feelings toward the out-group stemming from whatever source may be justified or rationalized by attributing the same (negative) characteristics to most out-group members.

The results of relevant research to date offer encouraging support for the perceived variability proposition. Quattrone and Jones (1980) show in their main study that subjects who observe a target person making a decision tend to generalize to an expectation concerning the average member of that person's group. If the target person is from a rival college (out-group), the tendency to generalize is greater than if he is from the subject's own college (in-group), unless prior expectations have been well established. Quattrone and Jones reported additional evidence that premedical or nursing students consider their own groups as consisting of more distinct types of people than do the corresponding out-groups.

Although the existing data are thus consistent with the proposition concerning perceived variability in in-groups and out-groups, the direct evidence on differences in perceived variability is equivocal. In fact, in spite of Quattrone and Jones's generalization results, which strongly implied such differences in perceived variability, the subjects in the Quattrone and Jones experiment failed to rate the members of the in-group as any more variable than they rated the members of the out-group. Furthermore, compared to behavior predictions for an in-group member, there was no greater tendency to predict an out-group member's behavior from observing the response of another out-group member.

The present field study was conducted to pursue further the issue of direct perception of variability, when care is taken to clarify the variability estimation task for the subjects. In the Quattrone and Jones (1980) study, subjects were directly asked to rate the variability of their own group and the out-group, without reference to the particular dimension or dimensions involved. In the present study, not only was the task that of estimating variability within specific trait dimensions, but subjects were led to do this by concrete and clear instructions emphasizing inclusive range intervals for the target group. In addition, information concerning two mediating factors was sought. Subjects were asked to estimate the number of in-group and out-group members known. These data could be used to examine whether differences in perceived variability can be simply explained in terms of differential acquaintanceship. Finally, a discriminating index of evaluative preference for the in-group made it possible to study the relationship of attributed out-group homogeneity to negativity of evaluation.

METHOD

Subjects

The 13 Princeton "Eating Clubs" for undergraduate upperclassmen are relatively cohesive social units. Though nonresidential (except for the club officers), most members take all of their meals there and the clubs are important loci for parties and other recreational activities. The clubs have reputations or evoke stereotypes (e.g., "Southern Jocks," "Old New York Money"). This is especially true of those that select their own new members each year (rather than being open to all those who wish to join). Four of the five selective clubs were chosen to provide subjects for the present study, based on our judgment that the degree of acquaintanceship within and across the four clubs would be roughly comparable. Since one of these four clubs was coeducational, we focused only on male members providing data on other male members. The clubs ranged in male membership from approximately 60 to 120. Five sophomores, five juniors, and five seniors were randomly selected from each club, providing a total of 60 respondents.

Procedure

Each subject was contacted individually and invited to participate in a study concerning impressions of eating club members. All subjects contacted agreed to participate. Each was given a questionnaire which he was asked to return anonymously in an accompanying envelope addressed to the investigator.

The questionnaire incorporated eight trait dimensions thought to vary widely in their relevance to perceived differences in the average club members. The dimensions were identified by separating each of the following antonym pairs by a fourteen point scale: introverted—extroverted, refined—crude, athletic—nonathletic, arrogant—humble, deep—superficial, laid-back—uptight, optimistic—pessimistic, and low socioeconomic status—high socioeconomic status.

In making their ratings on the antonym scales, the subjects were asked to consider all Princeton males as their reference population. For each dimension, the subjects were instructed to mark the scale position of the average male member of the group being rated and then to mark the two scale values between which they believed 50% of the male members of the club fell (the interquartile range). They were then asked to underline the two numbers bracketing all members of the group (the total range). After instructions were carefully given and all questions answered, subjects rated the male members of their own club first and then proceeded to rate the males of the other

clubs in a standard order. Finally, the subjects were asked to indicate the approximate number of male students known personally in each of the clubs.

RESULTS

Perceptions of Variability Within In-Groups and Out-Groups

In order to test the proposed hypotheses concerning the perception of differential variability within in-groups versus out-groups, the assigned interquartile ranges were analyzed within a mixed design in which the "between" factor was class (sophomore, junior, senior), and the "within" factor was in-group versus out-group target. Table 1 shows that there was a main effect in the predicted direction for the in-group versus out-group perception of variability. $F(1, 57) = 6.22$. $p < .025$. None of the other factors produced significant results. Similar analyses of the total range scores also produced a significant effect for in-group versus out-group. $F(1, 57) = 5.44$. $p < .025$.

Acquaintanceship Volume and Perceived Variability

The average subject claimed to know personally 52% of the members in his own club and 16% of the members in the three out-group clubs. As one would expect, the average sophomore knew fewer of the members in his in-group (33%) than did the average junior and senior (roughly 60%). The acquaintance discrepancy (in-group percent known minus out-group percent known) was smaller for sophomores (20%) than for upperclassmen (43%). In spite of this large difference in acquaintanceship patterns, sophomores were no less likely to perceive greater in-group variability than upperclassmen. (In fact, on the range measure they were even more likely.) This suggests that the perceived heterogeneity of a group's members is not closely tied to the number of acquaintances one has in the group.

Since there were wide variations in acquaintanceship volume within each class, however, a more refined assessment seemed in order. To this end, two indices were devised for each subject. The first index was a measure of differential acquaintance. It will be recalled that each subject indicated the number of males personally known both in his own club and the three other clubs. The average number of members known in the three out-group clubs was subtracted from the number of members known in the subject's own club. A large positive value for this index indicates that the subject knew more members of his own club than in the average out-group about which he was questioned. The second index was a measure of differential variability perception. Each subject's average interquartile range estimate for the three out-group clubs was subtracted from his interquartile estimate for his own group. The differential acquaintance index and the differential perceived variability index were then correlated. Though the correlation for one club's members was barely significant ($r = .483$, $p < .05$), the other three coefficients were very close to zero (.090, .015, .017). The overall correlation was $r = .16$, a value that does not approach significance. Additional correlational analyses also showed no relationship between the number of members known and estimated variability among the three out-groups evaluated by each subject. Thus, variations in out-group variability estimates were unrelated to variations in the number of members known in each out-group.

Evaluative Preference and Perceived Variability

The typical subject was assumed to consider each of the following traits to be at the favorable end of its antonym pair continuum: extroverted, refined, athletic, humble, deep, laid-back, optimistic, and high socioeconomic status. The in-group means and the out-group means were totaled for each subject across the eight dimensions, so that a high score indicated a favorable rating. Not surprisingly, there was a strong evaluative preference for the in-group ($F = 105.11$, $p < .001$). Variations in an in-group preference index for each subject, however, were unrelated to variations in the perceived in-group/out-group variability index ($r = .021$). Thus it would appear that the tendency to perceive greater variability in the in-group is not closely related to the degree to which the in-group is favored. Certainly, there is no evidence in the present

TABLE 1

Analysis of Variance Summary: Interquartile Range Judgments

SV	df	MS	F
Between S	59	2.89	
A (class)	2	3.42	1.19
S/A	57	2.87	
Within S	60	.468	
B (in/out group)	1	2.80	6.22*
AB	2	0.35	
SB/A	57	0.45	

Note: *$p < .025$

study to suggest that perceived variability differences are a consequence of liking one's in-group and disfavoring comparable out-groups.

Rating Extremity and Perceived Variability

It is reasonable to expect that rating extremity would tend to be associated with lower perceived variability given the restrictions imposed by the scale endpoints. If the average member of target group X is judged to be rather extreme within a dimension, it is likely that the judged interquartile range for group X will be small relative to that of target group Y, whose average member is placed closer to the midpoint. Indeed, it does turn out to be the case that more extreme rated averages tend to go along with smaller variability ratings. The average correlation between extremity ratings on a given trait and perceived interquartile ranges on that same trait was $-.306$, a highly significant value since 16 correlations (4 in-group and 12 out-group), each involving 8 traits, were averaged. This cannot, however, explain the greater perceived variability of the in-groups relative to the out-groups, since the extremity scores of the two groups were almost identical. In fact, subjects were slightly more extreme in rating the average member of their own group ($M = 28.96$) than in rating the average member of the out-groups ($M = 28.33$).

DISCUSSION

The present results provide firm and direct support for the proposition that people tend to perceive the personal characteristics of those in their own membership groups to be more heterogeneous than the characteristics of out-group members. This at least appears to be the case when members select groups. The mediators of this differential variability perception are not obvious from the present data. One would presume that the in-group heterogeneity, out-group homogeneity effect is in some way a product of differential acquaintance with or knowledge about in-group and out-group members. After all, the respondents knew more in-group members than out-group members, and they also perceived more variability in the in-group. However, more refined analyses of the relationship between perceived variability and acquaintance volume suggest that the sheer number of people personally known is not a crucial mediating factor. It might be noted that logically, there is no reason why ignorance about most out-group members should not lead to larger, more safely inclusive variability estimates.

Nor is the perceived variability effect any simple function of evaluative preference for the in-group, since variation in such preferences are unrelated to differential variability estimates. The in-group is definitely preferred, and is seen as more heterogeneous, but variations in perceived out-group homogeneity are not associated with tendencies to deprecate a particular out-group. Furthermore, there is no overall tendency to use the extreme ends of the scale in rating the average out-group member and the middle of the scale in rating the average in-group member. Thus the tendency to see the out-group as more homogeneous cannot be explained as an artifact of rating extremity.

Future research should map out those features of group membership that promote assumptions concerning the homogeneity of out-groups. Voluntary selection, group rivalry, and the criteria for establishing group boundaries may turn out to be important determinants of the magnitude of the differential variability effect. Our own hunch is that the effect is a very general one stemming from the details of differential acquaintance and the greater variety of contexts in which in-group acquaintanceships are established. Given this contextual variety, the perceiver is in a better position to separate distinctive personal consistencies which generate the perception of individual differences from situationally induced similarities which lead to judgments of relative homogeneity.

REFERENCES

Campbell, D. T. Enhancement of contrast as a composite habit. *Journal of Abnormal and Social Psychology*, 1956, *53*, 350-355.

Quattrone, G., & Jones, E. E. The perception of variability within in-groups and out-groups: Implications for the law of small numbers. *Journal of Personality and Social Psychology*, 1980, *38*, 141-152.

On the Self-Perpetuating Nature of Stereotypes about Women and Men

Berna J. Skrypnek and Mark Snyder

An experiment was conducted to investigate an interpersonal process that contributes to the perpetuation of stereotyped beliefs about women and men. Male-female pairs of unacquainted individuals interacted to negotiate a division of labor on a series of work-like tasks (that differed in their sex-role connotations) in a situation that permitted control over the information that male perceivers received about the apparent sex of female targets. The perceivers' beliefs about the sex of their targets initiated a chain of events that resulted in targets providing behavioral confirmation for perceivers' beliefs about their sex. Targets believed by perceivers to be male chose tasks relatively masculine in nature, and targets believed by perceivers to be female chose tasks relatively feminine in nature. Although this behavioral confirmation effect was initially elicited as reactions to overtures made by perceivers, it persevered so that eventually targets came to initiate behaviors "appropriate" to the sex with which they had been labeled by perceivers. The specific roles of perceivers and targets in the behavioral confirmation process are examined. Implications of these findings for the perpetuation of stereotyped beliefs about the sexes are discussed.

Of men and women, it has been said that: "The courage of a man is shown in commanding, of a woman in obeying" (Aristotle), "We should regard loveliness as the attribute of woman, and dignity as the attribute of man" (Cicero), "Man is the will, and woman the sentiment" (Emerson), and "Woman is more impressionable than man" (Tolstoy). Literary and philosophical observers of the human condition are not alone in their beliefs about inherent differences between women and men. In fact, the existence of widespread stereotypes about sex differences has been well documented (e.g., Broverman, Vogel, Broverman, Clarkson, & Rosenkrantz, 1972; Fernberger, 1948; Lunneborg, 1970; Rosenkrantz, Vogel, Bee, Broverman, & Broverman, 1968; Sherriffs & McKee, 1957; Spence, Helmreich, & Stapp, 1975). According to this research, men are popularly believed to be relatively more dominant, independent, competitive, intellectual, athletic, unemotional, self-confident, ambitious, aggressive, decisive, logical, analytical, and objective. On the other hand, women are popularly regarded as relatively more submissive, dependent, emotional, excitable, irrational, conforming, affectionate, kind, sensitive, warm, sympathetic, understanding, gentle, and nurturant. These stereotypes have remained surprisingly consistent across the three decades spanned by the studies cited.

Although it is clear that there exist well-defined and pervasive stereotypes about the sexes, empirical research has not been able to demonstrate that women and men actually differ behaviorally in all the ways dictated by these stereotypes (for reviews, see Deaux, 1976; Maccoby & Jacklin, 1974; Tavris & Offir, 1977). Even when differences between the sexes have been found, these between-groups differences are often miniscule in comparison to within-

groups differences (cf. Maccoby & Jacklin, 1974, p. 9).

If little demonstrable validity of stereotypes about women and men exists, why do these essentially inaccurate, overgeneralized stereotypes persist? Part of the answer to this question is found in the well-documented tendency of stereotypes to influence perceptual/cognitive activities such that evidence that confirms stereotypes is more easily noticed, learned, and remembered than is nonconfirming evidence (e.g., Berman & Kenny, 1976; Chapman & Chapman, 1967; Rothbart, Fulero, Jensen, Howard, & Birrell, 1978; Snyder & Uranowitz, 1978; Zadny & Gerard, 1974). As a consequence of such perceptual/cognitive bolstering processes, people may overestimate the extent to which the behavior of women and men actually confirms their stereotypes.

Yet, we suspect that, over and above these perceptual/cognitive processes, there is a fundamentally *interpersonal* process that contributes to the persistence of inaccurate stereotyped beliefs about women and men. When individuals use their stereotyped beliefs about another person as guides for regulating interpersonal interactions with the other, they may constrain the other's behavioral options in ways that generate actual *behavioral confirmation* for their stereotypes (for demonstrations of behavioral confirmation in social interaction, see Snyder & Swann, 1978; Snyder, Tanke, & Berscheid, 1977; Swann & Snyder, 1980; Word, Zanna, & Cooper, 1974).

In fact, investigations of self-presentational processes by Zanna and his colleagues (von Baeyer, Sherk, & Zanna, 1981; Zanna & Pack, 1975) suggest that stereotypes about women and men may channel social interaction in ways that cause individuals to provide behavioral confir-

This research and the preparation of this manuscript were supported in part by a Canada Council Doctoral Fellowship and a Social Sciences and Humanities Research Council of Canada Doctoral Fellowship to Berna Skrypnek and in part by National Science Foundation Grant GNS 77-11346. "From Belief to Reality: Cognitive, Behavioral, and Interpersonal Consequences of Social Perception" to Mark Snyder. Portions of this manuscript were prepared while Mark Snyder was a Fellow of the Center for Advanced Study in the Behavioral Sciences. We thank Cheryl Wainio and Alma Woolf for their assistance in the conduct of this research.

mation for these stereotypes. Zanna and Pack (1975) had female undergraduates describe themselves (on a paper-and-pencil self-report measure) to a desirable male partner whose image of the ideal woman was either traditional or nontraditional. Women described themselves as quite conventional when his ideology was conventional, and as rather nontraditional when his ideology was nontraditional. Similarly, von Baeyer, et al. (1981) found that when female job applicants knew they would be interviewed by a male who held traditional views of women, they dressed more traditionally and provided more traditional answers during interviews than when they believed the interviewer held nontraditional views of women.

Clearly, in these experiments, expectations shaped self-presentations. But, these expectations were not transmitted from one person to another during the course of social interaction. Thus, it is unclear whether, in actual social interaction and in ongoing social relationships, one individual's stereotyped beliefs about the nature of the sexes can and will initiate a chain of events that actually cause another person to behave in accord with these stereotyped convictions, and whether this behavioral confirmation will persevere so that the latter person actually comes to initiate these stereotype-confirming actions.

To investigate these interpersonal consequences of stereotypes about women and men, we designed an experiment in which male-female pairs of unacquainted individuals (designated as "perceiver" and "target") were allowed to interact with each other in a situation that permitted us to control the information that each individual received about the apparent sex of the other. These individuals (who were located in separate rooms so that they could neither see nor hear each other) interacted with each other by means of a signaling system to negotiate a division of labor of a series of work-like tasks that differed in their sex-role connotations. In two of the experimental conditions, one member of the dyad (the male perceiver) was led to believe that the other member of the dyad (the female target) was either male or female. In the third experimental condition, the perceiver learned nothing about the sex of the other person. To measure the extent to which the actual behavior of the target in this interaction provided behavioral confirmation for general stereotypes about the sexes, we assessed the degree to which the target came to choose tasks "appropriate" to the "sex" to which the target had been assigned randomly by the experimental manipulation.

If behaviors associated with stereotypes may be generated in social interaction by behavioral confirmation processes, it is important to know whether some people are more "susceptible" targets than others, and to understand the processes that underlie and generate any such differences in targets' "susceptibility." Yet, the study of such "target factors" has been conspicuous in its absence from previous research on behavioral confirmation. Thus, in this investigation, we sought to specify theoretically and to identify empirically those targets most likely to provide behavioral confirmation for stereotypes about women and men. Some people may have greater flexibility and adaptiveness in the domain of sex role behaviors than others, and may be particularly able to adopt and enact the behaviors that provide confirmation for stereotypes about men and women. For example, one's self-image as a consistently feminine, a consistently masculine, or a non-sex-typed individual (cf. Bem, 1974) may influence one's willingness and ability to behave in relatively feminine or masculine fashion in response to the overtures of another person.

To examine the possible moderating influences of sex-role identity on the extent to which targets provide behavioral confirmation for another's beliefs about them, we classified targets as non-sex-typed (androgynous or undifferentiated) or as sex-typed (masculine or feminine) according to the Bem Sex Role Inventory (Bem, 1974, 1977). Programmatic research by Bem and her colleagues (Bem, 1975; Bem & Lenney, 1976; Bem, Martyna, & Watson, 1976) has found that non-sex-typed androgynous women demonstrate considerable behavioral flexibility, exhibiting appropriate masculine or feminine behavior depending upon situational requirements. Masculine women readily engage in masculine behavior, and although they generally do not avoid situations that call for feminine behavior, they sometimes show behavioral deficits in such situations. Feminine women appear to be the most rigid and limited in their behaviors; they express only certain stereotyped feminine behaviors. Moreover, feminine women try to avoid situations that call for masculine behavior; when thrust into such situations, they report psychological discomfort and loss of self-esteem.

Based upon this overall pattern of Bem's findings, we predicted that non-sex-typed targets would provide behavioral confirmation for perceivers' beliefs about them regardless of the sex to which they had been experimentally assigned. That is, they would come to display masculine behavior for perceivers who believed them to be male, and feminine behavior for perceivers who believed them to be female.[1] By contrast, we expected masculine and feminine targets to exclusively display behavior consistent with their sex-role identity across all conditions. Accordingly, these sex-typed individuals would provide behavioral confirmation only when interacting with perceivers whose stereotypes matched the targets' sex-role identity.

METHOD

Participants and Design

Students in introductory psychology (122 male and 122 female) at the University of Minnesota participated for course credit. Participants were scheduled in male-female pairs of previously unacquainted individuals. The male was always assigned to the role of *perceiver* and the female to the role of *targets*.[2] Each dyad was randomly assigned to one of three experimental conditions that manipulated the male perceiver's information about his partner's sex: Male Label, Female Label, or No Sex Label conditions. Targets were classified as feminine, masculine, or non-sex-typed according to previously gathered scores on the Bem Sex Role Inventory (Bem, 1974, 1977).

The Interaction between Perceiver and Target

To ensure that participants would not see each other before their interaction, they arrived at different waiting rooms on separate corridors. The experimenter escorted first the male, and then the female, to separate experimental rooms. She informed participants that she was studying the effects of different levels of communication on decision-making processes during division of labor in organizations, and that they are in a minimal interaction condition that involved communicating with another individual in the adjacent room by a system of lights.

The experimenter provided each participant with lists of 24 pairs of tasks, and informed them that their assignment involved negotiating a *successful* division of the 24 pairs. Success meant that, for each pair of tasks, one person agreed to do one task and the other person agreed to do the other task. She also explained that to make the negotiating process and the resulting division of labor personally meaningful, participants would actually perform five of the tasks they chose and would have their pictures taken while engaged in each. She displayed three Polaroid snapshots of an individual (who, supposedly, had already participated in the experiment) engaged in a masculine, a feminine, and neutral task.[3]

Activating the perceiver's stereotype. To perceivers assigned to the Male Label or Female Label conditions, the experimenter explained that since "usually we know something about the people we work with, here is the questionnaire your partner completed earlier this quarter. You'll probably remember filling out the same, or similar, questionnaire." The questionnaire was one of two prepared in advance to manipulate perceivers' beliefs about the sex of targets and to activate stereotyped conceptions of masculinity or femininity. Perceivers in the Male Label condition received a questionnaire purportedly completed by a 20-year-old male sophomore who described himself as almost always independent, athletic, assertive, masculine, competitive, ambitious, and almost never shy, feminine, soft-spoken, gullible, etc. Perceivers in the Female Label condition received a questionnaire purportedly completed by a 20-year-old female sophomore who described herself as almost always shy, feminine, soft-spoken, gullible, gentle, conventional, and almost never athletic, dominant, masculine, aggressive, etc. Perceivers in the No Sex Label control condition and targets in all conditions learned nothing about the sex of the other participant.

Negotiating the division of labor. Over an intercom from a control room, the experimenter instructed participants to begin negotiations. She explained that they could communicate their preference of tasks by the light system. This system was devised specifically to provide a means of communication between two parties without face-to-face interaction, oral communication, or written communication, thereby allowing the perceiver's beliefs about the sex of the target to be manipulated and the target's true sex to be kept anonymous. The signaling system provided each participant with a dial with discrete settings and a set of lights, connected to the identical set-up in the other's experimental room. The experimenter instructed participants to inform the other of their preference of tasks by using the dial located on the light system apparatus. She explained that their preference would light up the respective light on a panel in the adjacent room and advise the other person of their preferred choice of tasks. Similarly, they would know the other's choice by the light that lit up on their own panel.

Participants learned that, for each pair of tasks, they would have three possible communications (Interchange 1, 2, and 3) during which to negotiate a successful division of labor. Prior to each Interchange 1, the experimenter would instruct participants to consider a particular pair of tasks and advise their partner of their choice. Interchange 1 constituted a simultaneous exchange of preferences, where each informed the other of their preferred choice at the same time. This ensured that one participant would never know the other's choice before making an initial choice himself or herself. If participants did not successfully divide a given pair of tasks during Interchange 1, they would communicate again in Interchange 2, and if necessary, they would have one last attempt to negotiate in Interchange 3. During Interchanges 2 and 3, one participant would communicate his or her preference to the other, and then with that information, the other would respond by relaying his or her preference to the first participant. Thus, Interchanges 2 and 3 involved turn-taking to express preferences, providing one participant with the advantage of initiating the division of labor.

Each perceiver-target dyad then negotiated the division of a series of 24 work-like tasks. Negotiations involved two distinct and separate phases. Each phase consisted of the negotiation of the division of labor of 12 pairs of tasks. The 12 pairs of tasks for each phase were listed on separate pages.[4] In the first phase, the *perceiver* initiated the choices if the first communication resulted in conflict. In the second phase, the *target* initiated the choices if the first communication resulted in conflict.

Phase I: Behavioral Confirmation. To provide the perceiver with an opportunity to act on his stereotyped beliefs, we allowed the *perceiver* to *initiate* negotiation of tasks during Phase I whenever conflict arose. We could then assess the degree to which a target's actions during this phase provided *behavioral confirmation* for the perceiver's beliefs. Participants learned that Phase I involved the division of tasks on the first page. The experimenter explained that during this phase, if Interchange I (simultaneous communication) was unsuccessful, one member of the pair (the male perceiver was always delegated) gained the advantage

of designating a preference *first* during Interchanges 2 and 3. The female target responded, in turn, to each choice communicated by the perceiver.

Phase II: Perseveration. To free the target of constraints that may have governed her behavior during Phase I, we deliberately allowed the *target* to *initiate* the negotiation of tasks during the second phase, whenever conflict arose. This allowed us to examine the extent to which a target came to direct an interaction and actually initiate behaviors appropriate to the sex to which she was experimentally assigned. Participants learned that Phase II involved division of those tasks on the second page. During this phase, the experimenter requested that participants switch roles in initiating the relaying of preferences for tasks if conflict arose. Thus, whenever Interchange I was unsuccessful, the target relayed a preference of tasks to the perceiver first, and the perceiver responded, in turn, to each choice communicated by the target.

Postinteraction measures. After completing Phase II, participants rated themselves along two 10-point scales reporting how feminine and how masculine they felt during the experiment. Then, to assess suspicion and knowledge of experimental procedures, the experimenter separately questioned each. Participants were then introduced to each other and were thoroughly debriefed.

RESULTS

To assess the degree to which participants behaved in a stereotypically masculine or feminine manner, the following measure was constructed. First, from 59 independent raters, we obtained ratings of the degree to which each task was a stereotypically masculine or feminine activity.[5] The mean of these 59 ratings provided a single stereotyped value for each task: a higher value indicated greater stereotyped femininity. The sum of the stereotyped values of tasks chosen by each participant provided a measure of the relatively masculine or relatively feminine nature of that participant's actions.

Assessing Behavioral Confirmation (Phase I)

To assess the degree to which female targets behaved in a manner that would confirm their male partners' stereotyped beliefs about their sex, we subjected the sum of the stereotyped values of targets' final task choices from Phase I to a 3 × 3 analysis of variance (label × targets' sex-role identity). The analysis yielded a *single* significant main effect for label, $F(2, 102) = 18.39, p < .001$.[6] Planned comparisons revealed that those targets labeled Female chose tasks that were significantly more feminine in nature ($M = 56.60$) than did those who were not labeled ($M = 52.94$), $F(1, 102) = 16.34, p < .001$, and than did those who were labeled Male ($M = 51.17$), $F(1, 102) = 35.42, p < .001$. Tasks chosen by targets in the Male Label condition tended to be of a more masculine nature than did those in the No Sex Label condition, although this difference was not highly reliable, $F(1, 102) = 3.87, p < .10$. Indeed, we found evidence of behavioral confirmation: targets labeled Female behaved in a relatively feminine manner and those labeled Male behaved in a relatively masculine manner. Furthermore, no main effect for targets' sex role identity, $F(2, 102) = 1.49$, ns, and no interaction between label and targets' sex role identity, $F < 1$, in-

dicate that all targets, regardless of sex-role identity, provided the same degree of behavioral confirmation for perceivers in each experimental condition during Phase I (see Table 1).[7]

Assessing Perseveration of Behavioral Confirmation (Phase II)

To assess the extent to which the stereotype-confirming behaviors of targets persevered when targets were allowed to initiate the interaction, we subjected the sum of the stereotyped values of targets' final choices of tasks from Phase II to a 3 × 3 analysis of variance (label × targets' sex-role identity). The analysis revealed a significant main effect for label, $F(2, 102) = 11.34, p < .001$. Specifically, planned comparisons indicated that targets who were labeled Female chose tasks that were more feminine in nature ($M = 55.58$) than did those who were not labeled ($M = 52.77$), $F(1, 102) = 12.24, p < .001$, and than did those who were labeled Male ($M = 51.89$), $F(1, 102) = 20.80, p < .001$. There was no difference in the nature of the tasks chosen by the No Sex Label and Male Label conditions, $F(1, 102) = 1.21$, ns. As a consequence of the perceiver's *belief* about the targets' sex, targets actually came to initiate behaviors consistent with the sex to which they were assigned, and when they were not assigned to a particular sex they behaved as if they had been labeled Male.

The analysis also revealed a main effect for targets' sex-role identity, $F(2, 102) = 7.28, p < .001$. Newman-Keuls' multiple comparisons found no reliable mean differences in the sex-role connotations of tasks chosen by feminine ($M = 54.00$) and non-sex-typed targets ($M = 53.86$). However, comparisons revealed that masculine

TABLE 1

Stereotyped Value of Tasks Chosen by Targets

Targets	Phase I: behavioral confirmation			Phase II: perseveration		
	Condition			Condition		
	Female label	No sex label	Male label	Female label	No sex label	Male label
Feminine sex-typed						
Mean	56.93	52.88	51.71	$56.40_{a,c}$	52.90_b	$52.72_{b,d}$
SD	2.55	4.18	4.27	4.54	5.74	·2.43
n	16	15	17	16	15	17
Masculine sex-typed						
Mean	55.55	50.53	50.27	49.65_a	50.72_a	51.35_a
SD	7.31	4.94	5.18	2.33	4.16	3.72
n	6	6	6	6	6	6
Non-sex-typed						
Mean	56.68	53.85	50.90	57.19_e	53.39_f	51.11_f
SD	2.95	2.78	3.46	2.60	3.95	1.76
n	14	17	14	14	17	14

Notes: Higher means indicate greater stereotyped femininity of the target's behavioral choices. For planned comparisons in Phase II, means across the same row with different subscripts are significantly different at $p < .01$ (a,b) or $p < .005$ (c,d) or $p < .001$ (e,f)

targets chose tasks that were more masculine in nature $(M = 50.57)$ than did the other two groups, p's $< .01$.

These main effects are qualified by a label × targets' sex-role identity interaction, $F(4, 102) = 2.90$, $p < .05$. Targets of differing sex-role identities did not all behave in the same fashion in response to the perceiver's behavior in each of the three label conditions during the second phase. To specify the nature of this interaction, we conducted planned comparisons.

Did *non-sex-typed targets* provide behavioral confirmation for perceivers' beliefs in both experimental conditions? Indeed, as predicted, non-sex-typed targets behaved in a more feminine fashion in the Female Label than in the Male Label condition, $F(1, 102) = 11.46$, $p < .001$.

Did *sex-typed targets* fail to provide behavioral confirmation for perceivers' beliefs in both experimental conditions, and exclusively engage in behavior consistent with their sex-role identity? As predicted, masculine sex-typed targets behaved equally masculine in both experimental conditions, $F < 1$, providing behavioral confirmation for perceivers' beliefs in the Male Label condition, but disconfirmation in the Female Label condition, relative to other targets. Surprisingly, feminine sex-typed targets did not display the consistency or rigidity expected of them in the domain of sex-role behaviors. During Phase II, feminine targets continued to choose tasks of a significantly more masculine nature in the Male Label than in the Female Label condition, $F(1, 102) = 9.30, p < .005$.

Contrasts revealed no reliable differences for any classification of targets between No Sex and Male Label conditions, F's < 1. Targets whose sex was ambiguous behaved in as masculine a fashion as those labeled Male (see Table 1). Contrasts between Female and No Sex Label conditions, for targets of each sex-role identity, revealed the same pattern of data as that between Female and Male Label condition.[8]

Role of the Perceiver

When perceivers believed they were negotiating with another male student, their female targets behaved in a significantly more masculine fashion than when perceivers believed they were negotiating with a female student. How might have perceivers' stereotyped beliefs influenced targets' behaviors in ways that led targets to behaviorally confirm their beliefs?

Initial task choices. To examine how male perceivers behaved based upon their knowledge of the target's sex, we summed the stereotyped values of perceivers' *first* choices of tasks from Phase I and Phase II and entered these data into separate 3 × 3 analyses of variance (label × targets' sex-role identity). Indeed, perceivers behaved

quite differently depending upon what they believed to be the sex of the target, $F(2, 102) = 14.94, p < .001$ and $F(2, 102) = 17.31, p < .001$ for Phases I and II, respectively. Planned comparisons revealed that, during Phase I, perceivers were more likely to initially choose tasks of a more masculine nature when they thought the target was Female ($M = 41.10$) than when they had no information about the other's sex ($M = 44.29$), $F(1, 102) = 11.23, p < .005$, or than when they believed the target to be Male ($M = 46.31$), $F(1, 102) = 29.50, p < .001$. And, when they had no information about the target's sex, they chose tasks of a more masculine nature than when they believed the other to be Male, $F(1, 102) = 4.56, p < .05$. During Phase II, perceivers continued to behave in a more masculine fashion when they believed the target to be Female ($M = 41.08$) than when they had no information about the other's sex ($M = 44.32$), $F(1, 102) = 12.66, p < .001$, or than when they believed the target to be Male ($M = 46.44$), $F(1, 102) = 34.31, p < .001$. And, when they had no information about the target's sex, they continued to behave in a more masculine fashion than when they believed the other to be Male, $F(1, 102) = 5.48, p < .05$. As expected, these analyses revealed neither main effects for targets' sex-role identity nor label × targets' sex-role identity interactions, F's < 1.

Bargaining strategy. Furthermore, we found that not only did perceivers initially choose tasks that differed in their sex-role connotations depending upon their beliefs about targets' sex, but they also continued to treat targets quite differently during each step of the negotiations. For each phase, we calculated the frequency with which perceivers switched from their original choice of tasks to the alternative (when the perceiver and target initially chose the same task) and entered these data into separate 3 × 3 analyses of variance (label × targets' sex-role identity). Each analysis yielded a single significant main effect for label, $F(2, 102) = 3.68$, $p < .05$ and $F(2, 102) = 6.88$, $p < .005$ for Phases I and II, respectively. Newman-Keuls comparisons revealed the same bargaining strategy for both phases. During Phase I, when perceivers and targets initially chose the same task, perceivers were much less likely to agree to let the other person have the preferred task and switch to the alternative when they believed the other to be Female ($M = 1.97$) rather than Male ($M = 2.84$), $p < .05$, or than when they had no information about the other's sex ($M = 3.21$) $p < .01$. Similarly, during the second phase, those perceivers in the Female Label condition were much less likely to "give-in" and choose the alternative ($M = 2.03$) than were those in the Male Label ($M = 3.10$), $p < .01$, or No Sex Label conditions ($M = 3.42$), $p < .01$. During both phases, perceivers were equally likely in the Male Label and No Sex Label conditions to change their preference.[9]

DISCUSSION

Our research suggests that stereotypes about women and men can and do channel dyadic interaction in ways that produce actual behavioral confirmation for these stereotypes. In our investigation, pairs of unacquainted individuals interacted to negotiate a division of labor in a situation that allowed us to control the information that one member of the dyad (the male perceiver) received about the sex of the other person (the female target). As long as perceivers acted as initiators in this situation, all targets provided behavioral confirmation

for perceivers' beliefs. Targets believed by perceivers to be male displayed behavior relatively masculine in nature. Targets believed by perceivers to be female displayed behavior relatively feminine in nature. Furthermore, even when perceivers no longer had the same opportunity to guide the negotiations, many targets actually came to *initiate* behaviors "appropriate" to the sex to which they had been experimentally assigned. However, targets of differing sex-role identifications did not all demonstrate this *perseveration* of behavioral confirmation. To understand how, for which targets, and under what conditions behavioral confirmation for stereotyped beliefs may be generated in social interaction, we will first explore the role of the perceiver and then the role of the target.

Our results suggest that perceivers, based upon their knowledge of the apparent sex and sex-typed personalities of the target, developed expectations about the target. These beliefs and expectations then guided or directed the perceivers' behavior in the situation such that they adopted distinctly different strategies for interacting with targets believed to be male and those believed to be female. Perceivers initially chose tasks more masculine in nature and were less likely to "give-in" or change their choice of tasks when conflict arose when they believed the target to be female than when they believed her to be male. This differential treatment led targets to provide behavioral confirmation for perceivers' beliefs about their sex.

Interestingly, targets, whose sex was unknown to perceivers, behaved in a fashion indistinguishable from that of those believed to be male. This is not surprising since perceivers adopted very similar strategies for negotiating with targets labeled Male and those whose sex was unknown.

Perceivers likely developed similar impressions and expectations of targets whose sex was not defined and those labeled Male, and behaved accordingly (cf. Broverman, Broverman, Clarkson, Rosenkrantz, & Vogel, 1970).

Clearly, perceivers' beliefs about targets, based upon stereotypes about women and men, did indeed initiate a process that produced behavioral confirmation for those stereotyped beliefs. It is, however, more difficult to specify the role targets played in this process. We examined the thesis that individual differences in targets' sex-role identity affect the degree to which targets provide behavioral confirmation for perceivers' stereotyped beliefs about their sex. Contrary to our predictions, all targets provided behavioral confirmation for perceivers' beliefs when perceivers were the initiators of the interaction. However, not all targets continued to provide behavioral confirmation for perceivers' beliefs when targets became initiators during the latter phase of negotiations. As expected, non-sex-typed targets continued to demonstrate the same pattern of behavioral confirmation as they did when perceivers were initiating and guiding the course of labor negotiations. These non-sex-typed targets displayed feminine behavior when perceivers believed they were female, and displayed significantly more masculine behavior when perceivers believed they were male. Masculine sex-typed targets initiated the same degree of masculine behavior regardless of perceivers' beliefs about them. Thus, as predicted, masculine targets continued to provide behavioral confirmation for perceivers' beliefs only when those beliefs were congruent with their sex-role identity. But, contrary to prediction, feminine sex-typed targets persevered in their behavioral confirmation and initiated behaviors that provided confirmation for perceivers' beliefs about them, regardless of the nature of those beliefs.

Why might feminine targets have initiated behaviors that confirmed perceivers' erroneous beliefs that they were male? A successful division of tasks required cooperation between negotiators. Perhaps, since cooperativeness is a stereotypically feminine trait, feminine targets may have chosen to engage in cooperative behavior even if it resulted in agreeing to perform some traditionally masculine task. Or, feminine targets may simply be susceptible or responsive to others' influence in guiding or directing their behavior regardless of whether such behaviors are related to sex roles. In any event, it is clear that targets can and do play an active role in behavioral confirmation processes, and that relevant target factors help specify the "when" and "why" of behavioral confirmation and its perseveration.

Implications of our demonstration of the behavioral confirmation of sex-role stereotypes may be considerable. Behavioral confirmation processes may account, at least in part, for the reason why stereotypes about women and men, for which there is little empirical validity, have remained strong and stable over the years. Specifically, we have demonstrated how, at a dyadic level of interaction, one individual's beliefs about the sex of a target individual and the corresponding stereotypes can actually channel the interaction such that the target engages in behavior that confirms the former's stereotyped beliefs about the target. At the same time, this experience very likely confirms and strengthens the perceiver's stereotype about women and men in general. And, this individual may carry these beliefs into a new situation with another target and act on these beliefs in the same manner as before, once again eliciting behavior from the target that confirms these stereotyped beliefs, and the cycle repeats.

This is not to imply that stereotyped beliefs play a role in all interactions. Only some situations or interactions (e.g., husband-wife, boyfriend-girlfriend) will activate a perceiver's sex-role stereotypes. Only in these cases will behavioral confirmation or disconfirmation for stereotyped beliefs about the sexes occur, and only here will it be noticed. In many other situations or interactions (e.g., same-sex friendship, worker—co-worker, etc.), stereotyped beliefs about the sexes may not be activated in the mind of the perceiver. In such situations, the perceiver may simply not be in a position to notice whether the target has engaged in behavior that is or is not congruent with the target's sex, because such categories of behavior may not be relevant to the particular situation. Only in those situations where stereotypes about women and men are activated can the process of behavioral confirmation actually create concrete evidence that confirms these stereotypes. From this perspective, it becomes clearer why people's faith in stereotypes about women and men may remain strong whatever the actual empirical validity of these stereotypes.

NOTES

1. Although Bem's research provides reasons to predict that undifferentiated targets might provide weaker behavioral confirmation for perceivers' beliefs than androgynous targets, her research provides no reason to predict that undifferentiated targets would be more likely to behaviorally confirm one stereotype than the other. Thus, for our purpose we classified both these types of individuals as non-sex-typed.

2. Although desirable, it was not feasible to study perceivers of both sexes and targets of both

sexes in same-sex and opposite-sex dyads. Thus, we chose to study perceivers of one sex and targets of the other sex. Since much attention recently has been focused on the women's movement, the changing of women's roles in today's society, the working mother, the movement of women into traditionally masculine professions, etc., we decided to assign females to the role of target. Thus, our findings might more directly speak to these topics of controversy. However, for our purposes, the experiment would have addressed the same theoretical issues, and we would have expected the same results, had the roles of male and female participants been reversed.

3. Males saw a male stimulus person engaged in the following activities: drilling a hole into a board, photocopying, and ironing a shirt. Female participants saw a female stimulus person engaged in each of these tasks.

4. We developed a list of 48 tasks (some were adapted from those devised by Bem & Lenney, 1976) that included 16 "masculine" (e.g., fix a light switch, attach bait to a fishing hook, fix a window screen), 16 "feminine" (e.g., icing and decorating a birthday cake, grocery shopping, iron a shirt), and 16 "neutral" (e.g., coding test results, wash windows, paint a chair) tasks. With these we constructed two pages of 12 pairs of tasks. We randomly chose eight tasks of each kind for each page and then randomly paired the tasks in all possible combinations of masculine-masculine, masculine-feminine, masculine-neutral, feminine-feminine, etc. The order of the pairs on each page was also random, with exception that each page started with a neutral-neutral pair. (We did not want individuals to specifically focus on the masculine-feminine nature of the tasks.) We counterbalanced the order of the pages so that half the dyads received one page first and the other half received the other page first.

5. Thirty-one males and 28 females rated each of the 48 tasks on a 7-point scale ranging from "a completely masculine task" to "a completely feminine task" with a neutral midpoint. They rated the tasks according to current sex-role stereotypes about jobs and tasks. *No* student served both as a rater and a participant in the behavioral confirmation study. Mean stereotyped ratings of the tasks ranged from 1.5 for "clean a gun" to 6.2 for "polish silverware using cloth and polish paste." The variance was small for all tasks in-

dicating high consensus on the masculine-feminine nature of the tasks.

6. Of the original 122 dyads, data from seven pairs in the Male Label and four pairs in the Female Label condition were discarded from this analysis and all subsequent analyses because perceivers in these pairs expressed suspicion of the experimental manipulations during debriefing. Thus, all analyses are based upon 111 observations, 37, 36, and 38 in the Male Label, Female Label, and No Sex Label conditions, respectively.

7. Analysis of targets' *initial* choices during Phase I revealed a *single* significant main effect for targets' sex-role identity, $F(2, 102) = 4.57$, $p < .01$. Feminine targets chose tasks more feminine in nature ($M = 53.28$) than did androgynous targets ($M = 51.39$). And, masculine targets chose tasks the least feminine in nature ($M = 49.99$).

8. We also subjected targets' postexperimental self-perceptions of femininity and masculinity to 3×3 analyses of variance (label $\times$ targets' sex-role identity). Although targets behaved quite differently across conditions, the analyses revealed no effects for label on how feminine or how masculine targets reported that they felt during the experiment, F's < 1. No evidence for a label $\times$ targets' sex-role interaction emerged from the analysis on ratings of how feminine or how masculine targets felt during the course of negotiations, $F(4, 102) = 1.63$, ns, and $F(4, 102) = 1.05$, ns, respectively. However, a main effect for targets' sex-role identity on ratings of how feminine, $F(2, 102) = 3.40$, $p < .05$, and how masculine targets felt, $F(2, 102) = 6.67$, $p < .005$, emerged. These ratings were consistent with targets' classification by the Bem Sex Role Inventory. Specifically, masculine targets reported feeling least feminine ($M = 5.22$) and the most masculine ($M = 4.89$) of all classifications of targets. In contrast, feminine targets reported feeling the most feminine ($M = 6.72$) and the least masculine ($M = 3.27$) of all targets. Non-sextyped targets' self-perceptions of femininity ($M = 6.22$) and masculinity ($M = 3.93$) fell between the sex-typed targets on each dimension. Apparently, targets did not internalize the stereotype-confirming behaviors in which they had engaged during the division of labor interaction. Rather, they continued to report self-perceptions consistent with a stable sex-role identity.

9. Perceivers' postexperimental self-perceptions of femininity and masculinity were subjected to 3×3 analyses of variance (label $\times$ targets' sex-role identity). Analysis of perceptions of femininity revealed no effects. Analysis of perceptions of masculinity revealed a single main effect for label, $F(2, 102) = 4.15$, $p < .05$. When perceivers believed that they were interacting with a Female they reported feeling more masculine during the course of negotiations ($M = 8.06$) than when they had no information about the other's sex ($M = 6.79$) or than when they believed the other to be Male ($M = 7.03$).

REFERENCES

Bem, S. L. The measurement of psychological androgyny. *Journal of Consulting and Clinical Psychology*, 1974, *42*, 155-162.

Bem, S. L. Sex role adaptability: One consequence of psychological androgyny, *Journal of Personality and Social Psychology*, 1975, *31*, 634-643.

Bem, S. L. On the utility of alternative procedures for assessing psychological androgyny. *Journal of Consulting and Clinical Psychology*, 1977, *45*, 196-205.

Bem, S. L., & Lenney, E. Sex typing and the avoidance of cross-sex behaviors. *Journal of Personality and Social Psychology*, 1976, *33*, 48-54.

Bem, S. L., Martyna, W., & Watson, C. Sex typing and androgyny: Further explorations of the expressive domain. *Journal of Personality and Social Psychology*, 1976, *34*, 1016-1023.

Berman, J. S., & Kenny, D. A. Correlational bias in observer ratings. *Journal of Personality and Social Psychology*, 1976, *34*, 263-273.

Broverman, I. K., Broverman, D. M., Clarkson, F. E., Rosenkrantz, P. S., & Vogel, S. R. Sex-role stereotypes and clinical judgments of mental health. *Journal of Consulting Psychology*, 1970, *34*, 1-7.

Broverman, I. K., Vogel, S. R., Broverman, D. M., Clarkson, F. E., & Rosenkrantz, P. S. Sex-role stereotypes: A current appraisal. *Journal of Social Issues*, 1972, *28*, 59-78.

Chapman, L. J., & Chapman, J. P. The genesis of popular but erroneous psychodiagnostic observations. *Journal of Abnormal Psychology*, 1967, *72*, 193-204.

Deaux, K. *The behavior of women and men.* Monterey, Calif.: Brooks/Cole, 1976.

Fernberger, S. W. Persistence of stereotypes concerning sex differences. *Journal of Abnormal and Social Psychology,* 1948, *43,* 97-101.

Lunnenborg, P. W. Stereotypic aspects in masculinity-femininity measurement. *Journal of Consulting and Clinical Psychology,* 1970, *34,*113-118.

Maccoby, E. E., & Jacklin, C. N. *The psychology of sex differences.* Stanford, Calif.: Stanford Univ. Press, 1974.

Rosenkrantz, P. A., Vogel, S. R., Bee, H., Broverman, K. K., & Broverman, D. M. Sex-role stereotypes and self-concepts in college students. *Journal of Consulting and Clinical Psychology,* 1968, *32,* 287-295.

Rothbart, M., Fulero, S., Jensen, F., Howard, J., & Birrell, P. From individual to group impressions: Availability heuristics in stereotype formation. *Journal of Experimental Social Psychology,* 1978, *14,* 237-255.

Sherriffs, A. C., & McKee, J. P. Qualitative aspects of beliefs about men and women. *Journal of Personality,* 1957, *25,* 451-464.

Snyder, M., & Swann, W. B., Jr. Behavioral confirmation in social interaction: From social perception to social reality. *Journal of Experimental Social Psychology,* 1978, *14,* 148-162.

Snyder, M., Tanke, E. D., & Berscheid, E. Social perception and interpersonal behavior: On the self-fulfilling nature of social stereotypes. *Journal of Personality and Social Psychology,* 1977, *35,* 656-666.

Snyder, M., & Uranowitz, S. W. Reconstructing the past: Some cognitive consequences of per-son perception. *Journal of Personality and Social Psychology,* 1978, *36,* 941-950.

Spence, J. T., Helmreich, R., & Stapp, J. Ratings of self and peers on sex-role attributes and their relation to self-esteem and conception of masculinity and femininity. *Journal of Personality and Social Psychology,* 1975, *32,* 29-39.

Swann, W. B., Jr., & Snyder, M. On translating beliefs into action: Theories of ability and their application in an instructional setting. *Journal of Personality and Social Psychology,* 1980, *38,* 879-888.

Tavris, C., & Offir, C. *The longest war: Sex differences in perspective.* New York: Harcourt, Brace, Jovanovich, 1977.

von Baeyer, C. L., Sherk, D. L., & Zanna, M. P. Impression management in the job interview: When the female applicant meets the male "chauvinist" interviewer. *Personality and Social Psychology Bulletin,* 1981, *7,* 45-51.

Word, C. O., Zanna, M. P., & Cooper, J. The nonverbal mediation of self-fulfilling prophecies in interracial interaction. *Journal of Experimental Social Psychology,* 1974, *10,* 109-120.

Zadny, J., & Gerard, H. B. Attributed intentions and informational selectivity. *Journal of Experimental Social Psychology,* 1974, *10,* 34-52.

Zanna, M. P., & Pack, S. J. On the self-fulfilling nature of apparent sex differences in behavior. *Journal of Experimental Social Psychology,* 1975, *11,* 583-591.

4   Attribution Theory

IN 1958, FRITZ HEIDER published *The Psychology of Interpersonal Relations*, in which he attempted to explain how the layperson who has observed some event in the environment makes sense out of that observation. Heider posited that individuals act as naive scientists who observe some inexplicable event, sift through their observations of similar occurrences, and draw conclusions about the cause or causes of the event. The processes that yield such judgments of the causes for observed events constitute the subject matter of attribution theory.

Heider addressed a seemingly fundamental characteristic of human behavior—that we actively seek to understand our world in terms of stable properties of the environment and of the people involved, and we utilize this information to predict future events and behavior. Although relatively little research specifically designed to test Heider's insightful propositions and formulations immediately followed the publication of his book, in 1965, E. E. Jones and Keith Davis published their correspondent inference theory, which was an attempt to make Heider's formulations more amenable to empirical study. Shortly thereafter, in 1967, Harold Kelley published a more general theory of attribution processes that suggested causal inferences were made on the basis of discerning systematic covariation between possible causes and observed effects. Finally, in 1972, Daryl Bem extended attribution theorizing to describe the processes employed by individuals to determine the causes of their own behavior; Bem's self-perception theory suggested that we come to know our own attitudes and other internal states by observing our past behaviors and the contexts in which these behaviors were displayed. This list of attribution theories is not intended to be exhaustive, but these theories are primarily responsible for the large number of attribution studies carried out during the past fifteen years.

The rational approach to the attributional process (i.e., observation, analysis, attribution, and behavior) has been questioned in recent years. Ellen Langer (1978), for example, has suggested that we do not always utilize such complex attributional processes, especially under routine conditions in which the expected gain does not justify the cognitive effort that would be necessary for comprehensive analysis. Langer argues that on such occasions, most persons already possess basic action patterns that can be applied to those situations, and extensive information processing is not necessary. Instead, we rely upon sets of cues in the environment to evoke these previously learned behavior patterns, called scripts. However, under conditions in which no previously learned pattern of behavior exists, the more thorough information processing specified by the theories of Jones and Davis (1965) and of Kelley (1967) are assumed to occur.

Other researchers have also questioned the frequency with which the full attributional analysis actually takes place, and the first article of this chapter addresses this issue. Paul Wong and Bernard Weiner attempt to identify the situational factors that must be present to motivate individuals to engage in an attributional search. Additionally, Wong and Weiner tested the utility of a self-probe methodology for the study of attributional processes.

The second article, by Russell Fazio, Steven Sherman, and Paul Herr, deals with one aspect of self-perception theory. According to Bem, (1972), we determine our internal states and attitudes by observing our past behaviors and the circumstances surrounding them. Accordingly, if we were to attempt to explain our attitude toward some issue or object (e.g., nuclear disarmament), we would look at our past behavior toward this issue (e.g., voting for political candidates who support the issue, signing petitions, participating in rallies) to determine our true feelings about the topic. However, Fazio and his associates ask the pertinent question, "If such instances of past behavior can be used to infer internal states, can past failures to behave (e.g., not voting in an election) be equally informative?" The findings of these authors suggest that behavior is utilized for determination of internal states, but that failures to behave are not as influential in the self-perception process as overt actions by the individual.

The final article in this chapter focuses on more applied issues surrounding attribution theory. Richard Mizerski (1982) utilizes an attributional explanation to account for consumers' differential weighting of positive and negative information about products. In particular, Mizerski demonstrates that consumers utilize negative information to a greater extent than positive information in determining their attributions to product performance.

When People Ask "Why" Questions, and the Heuristics of Attributional Search

Paul T. P. Wong and Bernard Weiner

Five experiments making use of a self-probe methodology in both simulated and real conditions demonstrated that individuals do engage in spontaneous attributional search. This search is most likely when the outcome of an event is negative and unexpected. Content analysis of attributional questions also suggested that causal search is biased toward internality after failure but toward externality following success. This reverse of the oft-reported hedonic bias implicates the adaptive function of causal search. The data also revealed that the most commonly used heuristic in attributional search is to center on the locus and control dimensions of causality. The importance of heuristics in causal search and the advantages of the self-probe methodology employed in these investigations are discussed.

Central to attribution theory is the assumption that people spontaneously engage in attributional activities. But there is little or no published evidence to substantiate this claim (Bem, 1972; Wortman & Dintzer, 1978). In the literature of attribution research, subjects typically are asked to make attributions either by completing a fixed number of rating scales or by providing open-ended explanations for events. Both methods are highly reactive. In the absence of adequate methodology, the issue of whether lay people engage in *spontaneous* attributional activities remains unsolved. In this article, we re-examine this issue, identify the major preconditions for attributional search, propose a new self-probe methodology, and then present data yielded by this methodology.

A presumption guiding this article is that

it is more fruitful to ask *when*, rather than *if*, attribution occurs. No one has proposed that the attribution process goes on at all times. To the contrary, many investigators in the attribution area have contended that individuals carry with them sets of beliefs, schemas, or presuppositions as to how various causes and effects are related (see Kelley & Michela, 1980). If our experiences conform to our beliefs and expectations, then there is no need to search for explanations. For example, the conviction that "aptitude" is a relatively stable characteristic is generally accepted in our culture; students with proven aptitudes in, for example, math or artistic endeavors are expected to do well in those areas. Given this belief and expectation, success in these activities should not call for explanation or elicit attributional search.

A corollary of the above reasoning is that attributional search will take place when one's experiences cannot be readily assimilated into one's existing belief system. A frequently encountered difficulty in the assimilation of information results from disconfirmation of existing beliefs and related expectancies. Examples of this type of disconfirmation abound in real life: cheating by a person with a reputation for honesty and integrity; failure by a student known to be competent; or rejection of a manuscript submitted by an established author. In each of these cases, the disconfirmed expecta-

tions are based on the belief that perceived dispositions such as honesty, competence, and creativity are relatively stable. Disconfirmation of expectations based on consensus information, such as task difficulty, also is likely to trigger the attribution process. For example, failure at an "easy" task is inconsistent with the expectations generated by the concept of "easy."

The hypothesis that expectancy disconfirmation instigates attribution processes has been alluded to by a number of investigators (see Lau & Russell, 1980; Pyszczynski & Greenberg, 1981). For example, it has been suggested that atypical events are more likely to elicit multiple causality than typical events (Kelley, 1971). Furthermore, it has been demonstrated that novel or unexpected events promote exploration (Berlyne, 1960); attributional search can be considered one instance of the more general class of exploratory behaviors.

In addition to expectancy disconfirmation, frustration (failure) is hypothesized to be a second potent instigator of the attribution process. The law of effect dictates that organisms are motivated to terminate or prevent a negative state of affairs. But effective coping importantly depends on locating the cause(s) of failure. In this case, attribution serves an adaptive function. In support of this line of reasoning, there is evidence that rejection in an affiliative context is more likely to elicit attributional search and information seeking than is acceptance (Folkes, in press). Furthermore, it has been documented that failure in instrumental learning and at achievement-related tasks promotes exploration (Wong, 1979). Finally, there is evidence to suggest that people are motivated to preserve their self-esteem; attribution may also serve a defensive function when self-esteem is threatened (Zuckerman, 1979). In sum, it is hy-

This research was supported by a Leave Fellowship from the Social Sciences and Humanities Research Council of Canada to Paul T. P. Wong and a grant from the Spencer Foundation to Bernard Weiner.

The authors are grateful to Alan Worthington for statistical consultation.

"When People Ask 'Why' Questions, and the Heuristics of Attributional Search" by P.T.P. Wong & B. Weiner, 1981, *Journal of Personality and Social Psychology, 40,* pp. 650-663. Copyright 1981 by the American Psychological Assn. Reprinted by permission of the publisher and authors.

pothesized that expectancy disconfirmation (unexpected events) and frustration (nonattainment of a goal) will give rise to attributional search.

Unfortunately, the reactive methodologies currently in use do not permit an unambiguous test of these hypotheses. Diener and Dweck (1978) overcame the reactive issue and have reported a measure of spontaneous attributions. In one of their investigations, children were instructed to verbalize "what they were thinking about" while performing. But this procedure has a number of limitations. When one is still engaged in problem solving, it is only natural to be preoccupied with possible ways and means of solving the problem rather than explaining the anticipated outcome. The absence of attributional cognitions in their mastery-oriented subjects might be so explained.

The present self-probe methodology is a modification of Diener and Dweck's procedure. Instead of asking subjects to verbalize what they are thinking while performing, we asked subjects to report what questions, if any, they would ask themselves *following* a particular outcome. Since causal explanations are answers to "why" questions, self-questioning seems to be a direct and natural way to gauge the extent of attributional search, and it at least has the face validity of measuring the presence and depth of one's search for causal understanding. To broaden the sample of cognitions reported by the subjects, in our final experiment we instructed them to report whatever questions or thoughts came into their minds following an event.

EXPERIMENT 1

The main purpose of this experiment was to document that individuals do spontaneously ask "why" questions and that the extent of causal search is determined by the nature of the outcome (success vs. failure) and expectancy (expected vs. unexpected outcome). We predicted that both frustration (failure) and expectancy disconfirmation (unexpected outcome) would instigate more attributional search than success and an expected outcome.

Given the above contexts, most of the questions that people spontaneously ask were expected to be related to attributional search. However, individuals also may raise action-oriented questions (e.g., "What can I do about the situation?"). Studies of coping with stress (e.g., Folkman, Schaefer, & Lazarus, 1979; Lazarus, 1966) have documented the existence of "secondary appraisal," a process of evaluating one's coping resources and options. It was predicted that failure would also elicit more of such action-oriented questions than would success.

Finally, it was anticipated that unexpected outcomes would evoke more reevaluative questions than expected outcomes. Since in the present study expectancy was primarily based on the belief that one was a strong or weak student, expectancy disconfirmation should have resulted in a state of imbalance (Feather, 1971; Heider, 1958) or dissonance (Festinger, 1957) in regard to oneself. To maintain self-consistency, one may either "explain away" the unexpected outcome or modify one's beliefs to accommodate the outcome. The latter strategy may give rise to questions related to reassessment of one's competence (e.g., "Am I smarter than I think?")

Method

Seventy students (41 females and 29 males) participated in the study as part of their course requirement for introductory psychology at the University of California,

Los Angeles (UCLA). They were tested in two groups of approximately equal size.

The subjects were given a questionnaire containing four hypothetical situations (2 levels of outcome × 2 levels of expectancy). They were asked to imagine that they expectedly or unexpectedly succeeded or failed at a midterm test. For example, in the unexpected failure condition, they were to believe that they were "strong" in a subject, but they unexpectedly failed the midterm exam. The order of presentation of the four conditions was randomized, and the subjects were instructed that they could work on these conditions in any order. After the description of each condition, the subjects were asked, "What questions, if any, would you most likely ask yourself?" They were told not to write any questions if such inquiries would not characterize their thinking. No other instructions were given.

Results and Discussion

The responses were classified into four mutually exclusive categories: attribution, action, re-evaluation, and miscellaneous, with an interjudge agreement of 94%. Attribution questions are "why" questions concerned with the possible causes of the outcome (e.g., "Why did this happen?" "Did I study hard enough?"); action questions are concerned with possible courses of action and generally have a future orientation (e.g., "What can I do to pass?" "Shall I get a tutor?"); and re-evaluation questions are concerned with the reassessment of one's ability or aspiration (e.g., "Have I underestimated myself?"). Miscellaneous questions include any that cannot be classified into these three categories. (The distinctions and examples for each category were given to the judges prior to coding.)

Figure 1 shows the total number of questions asked (top panel) as well as the number of questions asked in the attribution (middle panel) and action and re-evaluation (bottom panels) categories. Only 5% of the questions fell in the miscellaneous category; they are not included in the figure. Concerning causal ascriptions, failure and unexpected outcomes generated more attributional questions than did success and expected outcomes, respectively, $F(1, 69) = 79.34, p < .001; F(1, 69) = 80.50, p < .001$. There also was a significant Outcome × Expectancy interaction, $F(1, 69) = 9.69, p < .001$, primarily due to the very low rate of responding in the expected success condition.

As hypothesized, failure generated more action-oriented questions than success, $F(1, 69) = 32.35, p < .001$. Expected failure gave rise to the greatest number of instrumental questions, resulting in a significant Outcome × Expectancy interaction, $F(1, 69) = 31.29, p < .001$. In fact, expected failure generated four times more instrumental questions than did unexpected failure. Perhaps expected failure (i.e., prolonged frustration) poses a greater threat and calls for more instrumental considerations. There is indeed some evidence that expected failure is more stressful, because 29% of the instrumental questions in the expected condition dealt with escape/avoidance (e.g., Should I drop the course?), whereas all of the instrumental questions in the unexpected condition were related to mastery-oriented coping actions (e.g., working harder, changing one's study habits, etc.).

Re-evaluation questions also conformed to prediction, occurring only following unexpected outcomes. There is some suggestion of a positivity bias in that people were more likely to re-evaluate themselves favorably following unexpected success than to consider downgrading themselves fol-

FIGURE 1.

Mean number of responses in the four categories, as a function of the experimental conditions.

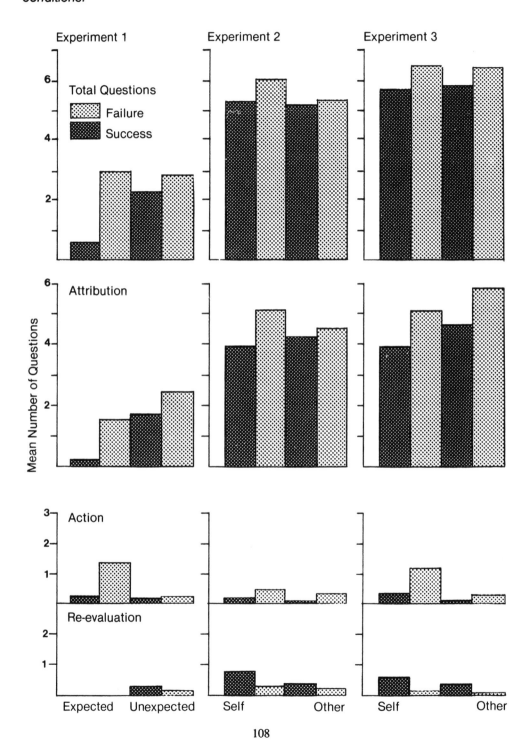

lowing unexpected failures, $F(1, 69) = 5.80, p < .05$.

In sum, it appears that individuals do engage in attributional search and are more likely to do so following failure and unexpected outcomes. There is also evidence of action-oriented questions, particularly after expected failure, and re-evaluation questions given unexpected events, particularly after unexpected success. Nearly all the questions that subjects asked can be classified into the three categories of attribution, action, and re-evaluation. But attributional questions comprised the largest proportion of the total questions asked.

EXPERIMENTS 2 AND 3

People do apparently engage in attributional activities, but it is not known how they search for causation. By causal or attributional search we simply mean the process of searching for causal understanding. Although it has long been recognized that how people search for causal ascription is vital to our understanding of the attribution process (Kelley, 1967, 1971), not much is known about causal search. We assume that this search probably takes the form of a series of implicit self-directed questions, for example, "Is it because of me?" Such questions are essentially hypotheses formulated by an individual concerning possible causes. (How these hypotheses are tested is another fundamental issue in attributional research that will not be dealt with in this article.) We also assume that individuals use heuristic rules that restrict causal search to selected areas of the total possible solutions (see Simon & Newell, 1971). That is, causal search is neither random nor exhaustive but is guided by a set of heuristics. We conceptualize these heuristics as various focuses of attention that guide individuals to formulate hypotheses

and seek relevant information in their search for causal understanding.

The psychological significance of perceived locus of causality (Lefcourt, 1976; Rotter, 1966) and perceived control (Bandura, 1977; Langer, 1975; Seligman, 1975) has been demonstrated in a variety of situations. It is hypothesized here that the process of causal search will first focus on the source or locus of causality (whether the cause resides within the person or in the external world) and then shift to the controllability of the cause (whether it is subject to personal influence). Finally, attention will turn toward causal stability (whether the cause is likely to change). These three focuses of attention correspond to the three primary dimensions or properties of causes specified by Weiner (1979). Intention and generality (globality) also have been suggested as possible dimensions of causality (Abramson, Seligman, & Teasdale, 1978; Rosenbaum, 1972). At present, there is no empirical evidence concerning which of the causal dimensions is of primary consideration in attributional search.

Each causal dimension is conceptualized as a continuum with opposite poles. For example, focusing on the locus dimension may be oriented toward the internal or the external pole, just as the focus on the control dimension may be toward the controllable or the uncontrollable pole. In the search for causality, if an individual implicitly asks "Is it because of me?" followed by "Could I have prevented it from happening?", then this sequence of self-directed questions reflects the heuristic of an initial search for internal causes, followed by a focus on controllable causes. Focus of attention in causal search may influence the kinds of causal explanations reached as well as the perceived dimensional properties of a given causal ascription.

Given the above assumptions concerning

causal search, the self-questioning methodology is suited for the investigation of searching heuristics. However, the problem remains as to how to identify the dimensional focus of each self-directed question. The traditional approach of dimensional categorization is to have raters code the responses. But one obvious shortcoming of this methodology is that the rater's coding may not correspond with that of the subject's. To circumvent this problem, subjects in Experiments 2 and 3 coded their own verbalizations into different dimensional focuses. Self-coding may be faulted as being just as artificial as coding by raters, but at least self-coding reflects the subject's own perceptions and phenomenological experience.

The self-probe methodology used here, consisting of both self-questioning and self-coding, provided evidence concerning the priority or temporal hierarchy of focuses of attention. In addition, it provided data concerning relative dimensional salience, which is here operationalized as the frequency of occurrence of dimensional focuses. Thus, the self-probe methodology revealed the relative priority and salience of various dimensional focuses in causal search.

Because causal search may differ for actors and observers (see Ross, 1977), perspective (self vs. other) was included as an antecedent condition in Experiments 2 and 3. Inasmuch as expected success yielded so few attributional questions in Experiment 1, an "expected' condition was not included in these experiments. Hence, Experiments 2 and 3 combined unexpected success and unexpected failure with a self- and other-perspective. In Experiment 2, a within-subjects design was used, whereas in Experiment 3 the four conditions were manipulated in a between-subjects design.

Method

The subjects in Experiment 2 were 56 introductory psychology students at UCLA (36 females and 20 males) who participated for course credit. The subjects in Experiment 3 were 86 females and 74 males from the same population, randomly assigned to one of the four treatment conditions. All subjects were tested in a group setting.

The subjects first received a questionnaire similar to that used in Experiment 1. In the other-failure condition, for example, subjects were told, "You know your friend is strong in a subject, yet he failed at the midterm exam." Following each description, the subjects wrote the questions they would most likely ask themselves. A minimum of five questions in each condition was required so that the temporal sequence of reported thoughts could be examined.

After completion of the questionnaire, the concept of causal dimensions was introduced. The subjects were told, "In seeking an explanation for success or failure, people often ask themselves certain questions regarding possible causes. Generally, these questions can be described in terms of five different dimensions, representing five different focuses of concern." The dimensions, presented in different predetermined random orders, were described as follows:

1. The *locus* dimension is concerned with the source of causality, this is, whether the cause resides in you, some other people, or in the situation.
2. The *control* dimension is concerned with the extent of one's control or mastery over various causal factors.
3. The *intention* dimension concerns responsibility and purpose.
4. The *stability* dimension is concerned

with prediction, that is, whether a causal factor will persist or change over time.

5. The *generality* dimension is concerned with the generalizability of a causal factor to other situations or to other people.

Each of the dimensions was illustrated with specific examples. In Experiment 2, the examples were drawn from achievement-related situations, whereas in Experiment 3, the examples were unrelated to achievement. For instance, the examples for the Intention dimension were "Did the teacher fail me on purpose?" (Experiment 2) and "Did he break my window on purpose?" (Experiment 3).

The subjects were instructed that a question could be classified into any number of dimensions, according to the focuses of concern that initially prompted the question. To facilitate the self-coding process, a grid was provided with the headings of the five dimensions randomly assigned to different columns, while the rows represented the order of the questions. Subjects coded the responses by placing a check mark in the appropriate dimensional column for each question (row). It was indicated that each question was to be coded independently of the preceding question.

Results and Discussion

The questions were again classified by two judges into the four categories used in Experiment 1, with an interjudge agreement of 97%. To further examine the contents of attributional questions, all attributional questions were then coded into different specific causes of ability, attitude, cheating, effort, emotion, error, general, help, knowledge, luck, motivation, physical conditions, situation, task, study method, and teacher. Several examples of each of the causal ascriptions were given to the judges. For instance, the "general" attributions were described as "nonspecific questions that are concerned with seeking explanations for an oucome," (e.g., "Why did that happen?" "How did I get an A?"). Interjudge agreement on this classification was 95%.

The mean number of questions in the three major categories for the four experimental conditions is shown in Figure 1. Analyses of the attributional questions revealed a main effect of outcome in both Experiments 2 and 3: $F(1, 55) = 14.60$, $p < .001$, and $F(1, 156) = 19.93$, $p < .001$, respectively. These results support the prediction that people ask more "why" questions after failure than after success. Only in Experiment 2 was there a significant Outcome × Perspective interaction, $F(1, 55) = 17.11$, $p < .001$, indicating that the outcome effect was more pronounced in the self than in the other condition. And, only in Experiment 3 was there a significant main effect of perspective, $F(1, 156) = 11.46$, $p < .001$, with more attributional questions raised in the other than in the self condition. In sum, the consistent finding across both studies, as was reported for Experiment 1, is that frustration (failure) is more likely to instigate attributional search than is goal attainment (success).

In the action category, the prediction that failure leads to more instrumental questions than does success was clearly confirmed in Experiment 3, $F(1, 156) = 9.89$, $p < .01$, and approached an acceptable level of significance in Experiment 2, $F(1, 55) = 3.67$, $p < .06$. Considering all three experiments, instrumental concern was consistently greater in the failure than in the success condition.

With respect to re-evaluation, the results again are consistent with Experiment 1.

Success led to more re-evaluation questions than did failure: $F(1, 55) = 4.89, p < .05$ (Experiment 2), and $F(1, 156) = 16.08, p < .001$ (Experiment 3). The positivity bias in reassessment is therefore reliably demonstrated. This bias may be more than self-serving, for it also is evident from the perspective of the observer. However, in Experiment 2 only, the tendency for greater reassessment given success rather than failure was higher in the self than in the other condition: Outcome × Perspective interaction, $F(1, 55) = 6.09, p < .05$. Thus, there is suggestive evidence that individuals may be especially concerned with improving their own self-concept or self-esteem (Zuckerman, 1979).

We turn next to the dimensional issues. The first topic to be examined was the temporal order of the search process. To determine this, the initial occurrence of a dimensional concern was ascertained. If, for example, the first question was judged as having a "control" focus, then control received a score of one, and so on. Given multiple classification of the same question (i.e., there was more than one focus of concern), all the dimensions involved received the same score. And if a dimensional focus was not used to code any question raised within a condition, then it received an arbitrary score of the total number of questions in that condition plus one.

The mean priority or sequence of each dimension is portrayed in Figure 2. The main effect of dimensions was significant in Experiment 2 and 3: $F(4, 220) = 85.87, p < .001$, and $F(4, 624 = 41.70, p < .001$, respectively. Linear contrasts confirmed the prediction that locus and control significantly ($p < .01$) differed from the other three dimensions. These results were exhibited across all the experimental conditions. In Experiment 2 only, locus was

temporally prior to control in the attributional search ($p < .01$). The inconsistency between the two experiments can be traced to the fact that in Experiment 2, subjects tended to use single-dimensional coding for each question ($M = 1.23$), whereas in Experiment 3 there was more double-dimensional coding ($M = 2.17$). Given this inconsistency, it is not clear whether a double-focus model is a more accurate description of the initiation of the attributional process than is a single-focus model. According to the former, the focus is on the locus and control dimensions simultaneously ("Am I personally responsible for what happened?"). According to the latter, there is a focus on one dimension at a time, with inquiry about locus ("Is it because of me?") preceding thoughts about controllability ("Did I have any control over what happened?"). However, the data clearly demonstrate that these two dimensions have the highest priority in attributional search.

In addition to the temporal hierarchy of dimensions, their relative salience was determined by the frequency of their occurrence. The more frequently a causal dimension is used to classify questions, the more salient this dimension is presumed to be. The frequency data yielded a pattern of results identical to the sequence findings, with locus and control significantly more salient ($p < .01$) than the other three dimensions. It appears that a dimensional focus occurring early in the attributional search also tends to be repeated.

Although in causal search the focus is primarily on locus and control regardless of treatment conditions, the *contents* of attribution questions are dependent on both the outcome and the perspective. Both experiments were very consistent in showing that several causal ascriptions are associated almost exclusively with only one or two treatment conditions. More specifically, in Experiment 2, questions regarding error (11.4%), emotion (7.9%), and physical condition (4.9%) were associated with failure, but not with success (where the frequency of these attributions was either 0 or less than 1%). Questions about luck (15%), on the other hand, were associated with success, but not with failure. Further, cheating (13.2%) and help (8.3%) were associated with others' success, but not with self-success. The same pattern of asymmetry was

FIGURE 2.

Mean temporal sequence of occurrence of the five causal dimensions (low values indicate high priority in the sequence). (For Experiment 4, the values are based on self-ratings.)

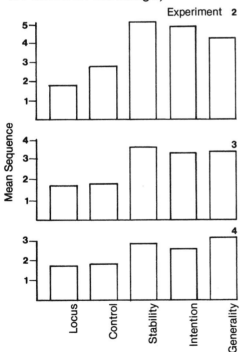

also obtained in Experiment 3, where error (11.6%), emotion (9.2%), and physical condition (8%) were exclusively connected with failure, luck (11.5%) was associated with success, and concerns about cheating (23.9%) and help (13%) were linked with others' success.

Effort, task, teacher, and general attributions were more evenly distributed across different treatment conditions. However, analyses of variance (ANOVA) revealed that in both Experiments 2 and 3, questions concerning effort were considered more frequently after failure (26.4% and 24%, respectively) than after success (17.2% and 6.8%): $F(1, 55) = 22.01, p < .001$, and $F(1, 156) = 25.00, p < .001$. Conversely, task attributions were considered more frequently following success (22.8% and 27%) than following failure (7.8% and 13.3%): $F(1, 55) = 9.17, p < .01$, and $F(1, 156) = 11.63, p < .001$. Other causal attributions, such as ability and attitude, occurred so infrequently (less than 5% in all conditions) that they will not be discussed here.

The priority of causal ascriptions was determined by their initial occurrence in the series of questions raised by the subjects. Once again priority data were identical to frequency data. For example, in the failure condition, effort had the highest frequency as well as the highest temporal priority (the mean initial occurrences being 2.6 and 2.4, respectively, for Experiments 2 and 3). ANOVAS showed that in both experiments, effort was considered earlier after failure than after success: $F(1, 55) = 24.60, p < .001$, and $F(1, 156) = 26.87, p < .001$, respectively. Task attribution on the other hand, was considered earlier after success than after failure: $F(1, 55) = 9.17, p < .01$, and $F(1, 156) = 23.48, p < .001$.

The above data suggest that both the salience (frequency) and the temporal priority (sequence) of specific causal ascriptions are dependent on particular conditions, whereas the dimensions (focuses) remain invariant across conditions. This is logically possible because given the same focus, the direction or orientation of the focus may be biased by the outcome. For example, given the locus dimension, it may be oriented to internal causes following failure but to external causes following success. To examine this possibility, all causal attributions were classified on the basis of logical analysis into either internal causes (e.g., effort, ability) or external causes (e.g., task, luck). ANOVA were performed on the total frequencies of all internal and external causes. In both experiments, failure gave rise to greater internal orientation than success, $F(1, 55) = 101.57, p < .001$, and $F(1, 156) = 47.72, p < .001$, whereas success resulted in greater external orientation than failure, $F(1,55) = 62.42, p < .001$, and $F(1, 156) = 14.18, p < .001$. (It should be noted that the internal cause considered most frequently—effort—is also controllable, whereas the most frequently cited external cause—task ease—is uncontrollable.) This result lends some credence to the notion that the orientation of a focus in causal search may be biased by the nature of the outcome.

The above attributional bias is in opposition to the well-known hedonic bias hypothesis, which posits that individuals internalize success but externalize failure (see Bradley, 1978; Wong, Watters, & Sproule, 1978; Zuckerman, 1979). In the introduction, it was suggested that attribution may serve either an adaptive or a defensive function. Perhaps defensive functioning predominates when one is publicly asked to give an explanation of a task already completed, whereas adaptive functioning pre-

vails when there is a search for a solution to problems that may recur. In our data, questions about internal and controllable causes (effort) for failure typically were followed by questions about possible coping actions. The adaptive advantage of this kind of bias in causal search is that one is motivated to plan constructive coping actions only when the cause is perceived as controllable by the actor.

EXPERIMENT 4

The prior experiments demonstrated that locus and control have the highest priority and salience among the five attributional dimensions. These results were based on self-coding of generated questions in an achievement setting. In Experiment 4, the generality of these findings was examined when the context in which the positive and negative outcomes occurred was not specified. In addition, in the prior investigations the importance of dimensional focus was determined after self-directed questions had been reported. In Experiment 4, subjects were asked to indicate the priority and salience of the different causal dimensions during the process of causal search.

Method

Sixty-one introductory psychology students at UCLA (35 females and 26 males) participated in the experiment for course credit. They were tested in a group setting.

The subjects received a questionnaire containing, in a fixed random order, the four experimental conditions (2 levels of outcome × 2 levels of perspective) used in Experiments 2 and 3. The self-success condition, for example, stated: "Suppose you just experienced an unexpected positive outcome. As you seek an explanation, what are your focuses of concern?" The subjects then were introduced to the five attributional dimensions discussed in the prior experiments; again the dimensions were characterized as focuses one might use in searching for an explanation. As in Experiment 3, the specific examples used to clarify the dimensions were unrelated to achievement events. In each of the four treatment conditions, the five dimensions were presented in a fixed random order, and the subjects rated the priority and the salience of each dimension in each condition. Priority was defined as "the order or sequence in which various focuses are considered by you." Salience was described as "the extent to which a dimension or focus of concern is persistent or prominent in your mind." For each dimension, rating scales ranging from 1 to 7 were provided.

Results and Discussion

The mean priority (sequence) ratings are shown in the bottom panel of Figure 2. An ANOVA revealed a significant main effect for dimensions, $F(4, 240) = 17.01, p < .001$. Again, the locus and control dimensions had a significant higher priority ($p < .05$) than the three remaining dimensions across all the conditions. The mean salience ratings were consistent with the priority ratings: Locus and control had a greater salience than the other three dimensions, as confirmed by a significant main effect for dimensions, $F(4, 240) = 16.97, p < .001$, and orthogonal comparisons contrasting the combination of locus and control with the average of the other three dimensions ($p < .05$ for all treatments). These data clearly replicated the findings in the prior investigations, even though in the present experiment the context of the outcomes was not

specified and the data were based on direct dimensional ratings. In the present study, we again failed to find any significant difference between locus and control; thus, there is additional support for a double-focus model of attributional search.

The correlations between the priority and the salience ratings, considered separately for each of the four conditions and for each of the five dimensions, yielded correlation coefficients ranging from .46 to .84, with all $ps < .001$. This finding is consistent with our prior results that dimensions considered earlier in time also persist longer in thought.

EXPERIMENT 5

Experiments 1-3 demonstrated that individuals do ask "why" questions, even when not specifically directed to do so. The finding that most of the questions generated were attributional indicates that causal search is prominent in people's minds. To increase the confidence in these findings, in Experiment 5 the effects of outcome and expectancy disconfirmation were examined in a more naturalistic setting, with subjects asked to report whatever questions or thoughts came into their minds regarding their exam results.

Students were recruited as subjects after they had completed a series of midterm exams and had received exam feedback on most, if not all, of their tests. Since there was considerable difficulty in finding students who actually expected to fail at their midterm tests, the words *success* and *failure* were defined as "doing well" and "not doing so well." In addition, because of the difficulty in obtaining students' expectancies prior to the midterm exams and maintaining their anonymity, we simply asked subjects at the time of experimental testing to indicate whether their overall midterm results were expected or unexpected.

To further document that individuals initially focus on the locus and control dimensions in causal search, in the present investigation self-coding was replaced by an objective, information-seeking behavior. Subjects were informed that prior research had produced information that might help them determine the causes of their performance on tests and that this information (contained in five separate envelopes) was organized into five categories, each reflecting a different dimension of causality. Subjects were asked to choose which envelopes they wished to examine first. The rationale for this new procedure was that in causal search, people use heuristics to formulate hypotheses (i.e., ask questions) as well as to seek out relevant information. Thus, the type of information they seek may reflect the heuristics they use. For example, if their heuristic is to focus on locus and control dimensions first, they will naturally first ask for the information pertinent to those two dimensions. This information-seeking behavior seems to be a more objective way of determining the heuristics of causal search than the self-coding method used in Experiments 2 and 3.

In sum, the present study was designed to replicate and extend the major findings of the preceding experiments in a more naturalistic achievement situation, with a broader self-probe methodology to sample attributional cognitions and a more behavioristic way of identifying the heuristics of causal search.

Method

One hundred volunteers from the introductory psychology class of Trent University were recruited as subjects. They were tested in small groups, with an average size of 15 subjects. The participants were first given a questionnaire to complete and were initially asked to indicate their own criteria for success and failure in the following manner: "For me personally, *doing well* means a grade of _____ or higher; *doing not so well* means a grade of _____ or lower." They were then instructed to "reflect on and assess your performance on all your midterm tests. According to your own criterion, do you think that you have done well or that you have not done so well? Was your overall midterm result expected or unexpected?" Subjects indicated their responses by circling a choice between doing well and not well and between expected and unexpected. Then they were told to write down in sequence what questions or thoughts, if any, came to their mind given the outcomes of their midterm exams.

In the second part of the experiment, the subjects were informed that they might ask for information yielded by past research to help them determine the cause(s) of their midterm exam performance. This information was contained in five different envelopes representing the five causal dimensions. The dimensions were introduced and defined in the usual manner on a sheet of paper. Several bundles of envelopes were observable to the subjects. The subjects were asked to indicate which envelope(s) they wished to examine first by circling the appropriate dimension(s). They were also told that they could examine the rest of the envelopes later. Following their choice, they approached the experimenter for the envelope(s). Each envelope actually contained information pertinent to that causal dimension. For example, the envelope on stability included the statement: "When people attribute success or failure to causes that are relatively stable, they tend to have strong expectancy of having the same outcome again in the future." Subjects looked at the information, returned it, and asked for their remaining selection(s).

Results and Discussion

Of the 100 subjects, 17 indicated that their failure was expected and 24 that it was unexpected; 43 reported expected success and 16 reported unexpected success. The subjective criterion for success revealed no significant differences between the outcome and expectancy groups ($F < 1$).

Responses were classified into the usual four categories, with an interjudge reliability of 95%. These data are shown in Figure 3. In view of unequal cells, planned orthogonal comparisons were executed. As predicted, failure produced a greater number of responses than success, $F(1, 96) = 23.00$, $p < .001$ (left panel). In addition, failure was associated with more attributional responses, $F(1, 96) = 17.87$, $p < .001$, and more action-oriented responses, $F(1, 96) = 18.94$, $p < .001$, than success. Concerning the expectancy variable, unexpected outcomes were related to a greater number of total responses, $F(1, 96) = 36.81$, $p < .001$, and more attributional responses, $F(1, 96) = 9.75$, $p < .001$, than expected outcomes. Also in accordance with the findings in Experiment 1, there was an Outcome × Expectancy interaction regarding action responses, $F(1, 96) = 5.01$, $p < .05$, with expected failure generating the most instrumental responses. There was, however, no significant difference in re-evaluation. Since expectancy was not explicitly derived from beliefs about one's competence, as in Experiments 1 to 3, it is not necessary to revise one's self-concept to accommodate the unexpected outcome; therefore, very rarely did subjects reassess their own competence. What seems to be unique to the present naturalistic study is that nearly all of the re-evaluation questions had to do with one's aspirations, values, or goals, as illustrated by these questions: "Is university what I really want?", "Is it worth my while to stay in university?", "What can I get out of a university education?". Apparently, subjects had some second thoughts (i.e., re-evaluation) about the value of a university education; this type of concern was not evident in our prior simulated studies.

The responses were then subdivided into questions and statements (thoughts). The patterns of data were quite similar, with the "thought" data somewhat less sensitive to the outcome and expectancy variables than were the "question" data. The contents of statements (thoughts) were very similar to those of questions except for the finding that emotional expressions occurred almost exclusively in the form of a statement (e.g., "I feel like getting violent with the marker," "I feel like crying," "Surprised how well I am doing").

The data pertaining to information seeking are depicted in Figure 4. The upper panel of Figure 4 portrays the data of all individuals ($n = 65$) seeking only one kind of information. The hypothesis that there is greatest choice of locus or control information is supported by a binomial test ($z = 3.79$, $p < .001$). The lower panel consists of the data of all individuals ($n = 28$) asking for two envelopes. Here again the prediction that most individuals would select the combination of locus and control evidence was confirmed by a binomial test ($z = 8.30$, $p < .001$). The seven individuals asking for more than two but fewer than five envelopes all included both locus and control in their request.

FIGURE 3.

Mean number of total responses (left panel), questions (middle panel), and statements or thoughts (right panel) in the four conditions.

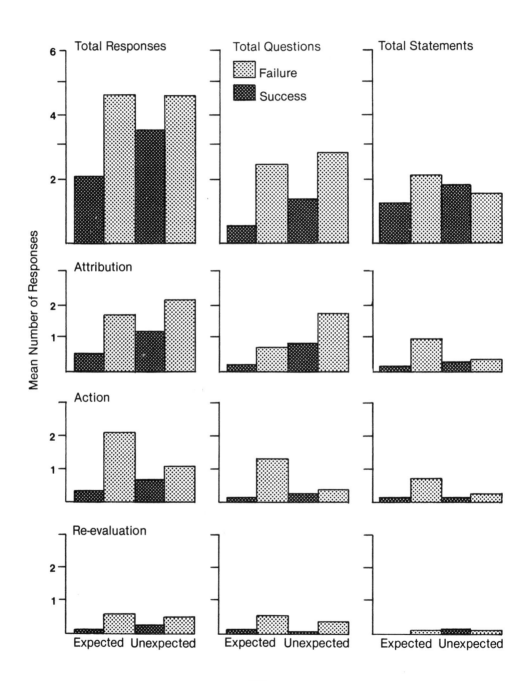

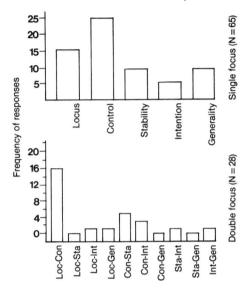

FIGURE 4.

Frequency of responses in seeking different types of information. (Data represent number of individuals.)

GENERAL CONCLUSIONS

The five experiments presented here provide evidence regarding several fundamental issues in attributional research. First, it can be concluded with reasonable confidence that people do ask "why" questions, even when they are not specifically directed to do so. The finding that most of their queries pertain to attributions indicates that causal questions are prominent in thought. In Experiment 1, subjects were instructed to report whatever questions, if any, they would most likely ask themselves in certain hypothetical situations. In Experiment 5, subjects were asked to report whatever questions or thoughts came to their minds. In these experiments, subjects were recruited to participate in experiments designed to study cognitive processes, and it was made clear to them in the instructions that they did not have to make any verbal responses. These procedures should not bias subjects toward asking *attributional* questions. The fact that subjects also asked other kinds of questions (i.e., instrumental and re-evaluation) indicates that they felt free to ask any kinds of questions. The only experimental constraint was that subjects were exposed to a specified set of outcomes. Such a constraint was necessary because we were primarily interested in whether this particular set of preconditions gives rise to attributional search.

Second, our results are very consistent in substantiating that frustration (failure) and expectancy disconfirmation (unexpected outcomes) promote attributional search. However, they are by no means the only preconditions for attributional search. One could readily identify a number of other preconditions. For example, stressful events (personal tragedy, interpersonal conflict, natural catastrophes, etc.) are likely to be potent instigators of attribution. Novel and unknown events may have a similar instigating effect. For example, young children are generally inquisitive, not only because they have not yet developed an adequate structure of causal beliefs and knowledge but also because many experiences are still new to them. Events of great personal importance may also be an effective antecedent for attribution.

Third, we have strong evidence that attributional search primarily is focused on the locus and control dimensions of causality. This finding is unlikely to derive from directive cues provided by our instructions or contexts, because it was obtained in three different experimental procedures: self-coding (Experiments 2 and 3), self-rating (Experiment 4), and information seeking

(Experiment 5). We also find that the focus was oriented toward internal and controllable causes (i.e., effort) after failure, but toward external and uncontrollable causes (i.e., task ease) following success, suggesting that the orientation of the search focus is dependent on the outcome. The significance of information on the locus and controllability of cause(s) is quite apparent, inasmuch as coping actions are very dependent on such information.

The present studies have also raised several new issues. First, the attributional bias in causal search is in direct contrast to traditional findings of success—failure bias that are based on overt explanations. This reverse hedonic issue may be resolved by testing the hypothesis that motivational forces at work in causal search may be different from those used to provide a public explanation. Research is needed to determine whether a control or competence motive operates primarily in causal search, whereas the self-enhancing or defensive motive predominates in public explanations.

A second unresolved issue is the extent to which the orientation of dimensional focus determines the causal explanation reached. It seems reasonable to assume that what we find depends to a great extent on where we look. If the heuristic used is one of searching for external and uncontrollable causes first before considering internal and controllable factors, it is likely that we will arrive at some acceptable external and uncontrollable causes if we search hard enough. A great void still exists regarding the heuristics that people use in attributional search and the effects of using different heuristics on causal ascriptions. The understanding of the attribution process will depend on further analysis of the heuristics of causal search.

We have demonstrated that the self-probe methodology is a sensitive and reliable way of monitoring the presence and the extent of spontaneous attributional search. It seems only logical that given any precondition or outcome, one must first establish the presence of spontaneous causal search before proceeding to investigate other aspects of the attribution process. The present simple and unobtrusive method has also provided evidence that action and re-evaluation related cognitions are sensitive to the major antecedents (i.e., outcome and expectancy) manipulated. Also, the self-probe methodology seems well suited to investigating the heuristics and the temporal course of attributional search. In sum, the present methodology has proven fruitful in unravelling the cognitive processes of causal search, and it has taken us at least one step closer to tapping the subject's phenomenological experiences than have the more reactive methodologies commonly employed in attribution research.

REFERENCES

Abramson, L. Y., Seligman, M. E. P., & Teasdale, J. D. Learned helplessness in humans: Critique and reformulation. *Journal of Abnormal Psychology*, 1978, *87*, 49-74.

Bandura, A. Self-efficacy: Toward a unifying theory of behavioral change. *Psychological Review*, 1977, *84*, 191-215.

Bem, D. J. Self-perception theory. In L. Berkowitz (Ed.), *Advances in experimental social psychology* (Vol. 6). New York: Academic Press, 1972.

Berlyne, D. E. *Conflict, arousal, and curiosity.* New York: McGraw-Hill, 1960.

Bradley, G. W. Self-serving biases in the attribution process: A reexamination of the fact or fiction question. *Journal of Personality and Social Psychology*, 1978, *36*, 56-71.

Diener, C. T., & Dweck, C. S. An analysis of learned helplessness: Continuous changes in performance, strategy, and achievement cognitions following failure. *Journal of Personality and Social Psychology,* 1978, *36,* 451-462.

Feather, N. T. Organization and discrepancy in cognitive structures. *Psychological Review,* 1971, *78,* 355-379.

Festinger, L. *A theory of cognitive dissonance.* Stanford, Calif.: Stanford University Press, 1957.

Folkes, V. S. An attributional analysis of affiliative behavior. *Journal of Experimental Social Psychology,* in press.

Folkman, S., Schaefer, C., & Lazarus, R. S. Cognitive processes as mediators of stress and coping. In V. Hamilton & D. M. Warburton (Eds.), *Human stress and cognition: An information-processing approach.* London: Wiley, 1979.

Heider, F. *The psychology of interpersonal relations.* New York: Wiley, 1958.

Kelley, H. H. Attribution theory in social psychology. In D. Levine (Ed.), *Nebraska Symposium on Motivation* (Vol. 15). Lincoln: University of Nebraska Press, 1967.

Kelley, H. H. *Attribution in social interaction.* Morristown, N.J.: General Learning Press, 1971.

Kelley, H. H., & Michela, J. L. Attribution theory and research. *Annual Review of Psychology,* 1980, *31,* 457-501.

Langer, E. J. The illusion of control. *Journal of Personality and Social Psychology,* 1975, *32,* 311-328.

Lau, R. R., & Russell, D. Attributions in the sports pages: A field test of some current hypotheses in attribution research. *Journal of Personality and Social Psychology,* 1980, *39,* 29-38.

Lazarus, R. S. *Psychological stress and the coping process.* New York: McGraw-Hill, 1966.

Lefcourt, H. M. *Locus of control, current trends in theory and research.* Hillsdale, N.J.: Erlbaum, 1976.

Pyszczynski, T. A., & Greenberg, J. Role of disconfirmed expectancies in the instigation of attributional processing. *Journal of Personality and Social Psychology,* 1981, *40,* 31-38.

Rosenbaum, R. M. *A dimensional analysis of the perceived causes of success and failure.* Unpublished doctoral dissertation, University of California, Los Angeles, 1972.

Ross, L. The intuitive psychologist and his shortcomings: Distortions in the attribution process. In L. Berkowitz (Ed.), *Advances in experimental social psychology* (Vol. 10). New York: Academic Press, 1977.

Rotter, J. B. Generalized expectancies for internal versus external control of reinforcement. *Psychological Monographs,* 1966, *80*(1, Whole No. 609).

Seligman, M. E. P. *Helplessness: On depression, development, and death.* San Francisco: Freeman, 1975.

Simon, H. A., & Newell, A. Human problem solving: The state of the theory in 1970. *American Psychologist,* 1971, *26,* 145-159.

Weiner, B. A theory of motivation for some classroom experiences. *Journal of Educational Psychology,* 1979, *71,* 3-25.

Wong, P. T. P. Frustration, exploration, and learning. *Canadian Psychological Review,* 1979, *20,* 133-144.

Wong, P. T. P., Watters, D. A., & Sproule, C. F. Initial validity and reliability of the Trent Attribution Profile (TAP) as a measure of attribution schema and locus of control. *Educational and Psychological Measurement,* 1978, *38,* 1129-1134.

Wortman, C. B., & Dintzer, L. Is an attributional analysis of learned helplessness phenomena viable? A critique of the Abramson-Seligman-Teasdale reformulation. *Journal of Abnormal Psychology,* 1978, *87,* 75-90.

Zuckerman, M. Attribution of success and failure revisited, or: The motivational bias is alive and well in attribution theory. *Journal of Personality,* 1979, *47,* 245-287.

The Feature-Positive Effect in the Self-Perception Process: Does Not Doing Matter as Much as Doing?

Russell H. Fazio, Steven J. Sherman,
and Paul M. Herr

Individuals are known to draw inferences about their attitudes from their decisions to perform a behavior. The present research examined whether individuals infer attitudes to as great an extent from logically equivalent failures to perform a given behavior. Recent research has documented the existence of a "feature-positive effect," a tendency of both animals and humans to exhibit greater difficulty in the processing of nonoccurrences than occurrences as positive cues for solving problems. On the basis of such research, it was predicted that individuals would infer less extreme attitudes from the nonoccurrence of a behavior than from the occurrence of a behavior. The results of an experiment confirmed this prediction. Relevant investigations from the self-perception literature are discussed in light of this feature-positive effect.

In 1965 Bem introduced his theory of self-perception. The basic postulate of this theory was that a major source of evidence for individuals' inferences about their attitudes and other internal states was the observation of their overt behavior and the circumstances under which that behavior occurred. Whenever internal cues are weak or ambiguous and whenever situational constraints on a behavior are minimal or unperceived, an individual will use that behavior as a basis for attitudinal inferences. According to Bem, an individual's answer to the question, "How do you feel about?' is achieved by reflecting on his or her behavior with respect to the object and arriving at the appropriate inference. Bem (1972) has presented much empirical support for his self-perception theory. In addition many social-psychological phenomena have been interpreted in terms of a process of self-perception (e.g., foot-in-the-door, Freedman & Fraser, 1966; overjustification, Lepper, Greene, & Nisbett, 1973).

The present research investigates the extent to which individuals use different kinds of behavioral information to arrive at attitudinal inferences. Although there is evidence that people use their own active behaviors to infer internal states, the question remains as to whether they will use in a similar way their failures to behave. That is, in the absence of situational constraints, is a person likely to use a freely chosen failure to act as strongly in the inference process as a freely chosen action? For example, loud and long clapping at a play or lecture should lead one to infer a positive

The authors thank Eliot Hearst and Mark Zanna for their helpful comments on an earlier draft of the manuscript.

attitude toward the event. Will the failure to clap at a similar event be used equally in the inference of one's attitude? Will the failure to vote in an election be taken as evidence of one's attitude toward the candidates as strongly as if one had actively voted for a candidate? According to the logic of Bem's theory, failures to behave (nonbehaviors) should be as useful and as informative about one's attitudes as overt behaviors. Provided there are neither strong internal cues nor strong situational pressures constraining one not to behave, a non-behavior should be a good indication of one's internal state.

Although nonbehaviors should logically be useful in the self-inference process, recent work suggests that both people and animals have a blind spot when it comes to nonbehaviors. There seems to be some difficulty in processing negative information and in using nonoccurrences as positive cues for making judgments or solving problems. Jenkins and Sainsbury (1969, 1970) used the term *feature-positive effect* to describe this phenomenon. First applied to animal behavior, the feature-positive effect described a strong asymmetry in a pigeon's ability to learn a discrimination based on the presence versus absence of a single distinguishing feature. Birds were involved in a discrimination task in which a response key was illuminated on each trial. On half the trials, a black dot was present on the key, and on the other half, it was absent. For some birds the presence of the dot constituted the food-reinforced trials (S +), and there was no reward on trials without the dot (S −). In other words, the feature (the black dot) appeared on positive trials. This is the feature-positive case. In the feature-negative condition, the black dot was present only on the nonreinforced S − trials, whereas the absence of the dot indicated an S + trial. Pigeons in the feature-positive case quickly acquired a discrimination between S + and S − trials, whereas pigeons in the feature-negative condition rarely showed much sign of learning. Only one of 50 pigeons ever mastered the feature-negative discrimination.

Newman, Wolff, and Hearst (1980) have recently shown the pervasiveness of the feature-positive effect in both human and animal behavior. In one of their experiments, human subjects were shown a series of cards, each with two trigrams on it. Subjects were told that one of the trigrams was "good," and they had to try to pick the right one on each trial. For the feature-positive subjects, the presence of a feature (e.g., the letter *T*) indicated the good trigram—the trigram with the *T* was good. For feature-negative subjects, the absence of the feature indicated the good trigram. The trigram without the *T* (regardless of what letters constituted it) was good. Feature-positive subjects required an average of 34.6 trials to arrive at the correct solution. *Not one* of the eight subjects in the feature-negative case ever found the solution on the 60 trials given. Five other experiments showed the feature-positive effect across a variety of stimulus materials, procedures, feedback, pacing and instructions.

Other work also suggests that people have difficulty in dealing with nonoccurrences. Research on judgments of contingency has shown repeatedly that human subjects will estimate the level of contingency between an event and an outcome (e.g. cloud seeding and rain) mainly by the number of positive-confirming instances. In other words cases where cloud seeding is followed by rain are used heavily in the judgment of contingency. Cases of cloud seeding without rain, rain without cloud seeding, and no seeding and no rain are used far less (Jenkins & Ward, 1965; Ward & Jenkins, 1965).

The literature on hypothesis testing further indicates that people generally do not seek out disconfirming information. They have a distinct bias to search for positive instances of a hypothesis, information that would serve as verification. They fail to search for negative instances that might disconfirm a hypothesis. Wason (1968) demonstrated in a simple yet dramatic way how people fail to seek out disconfirming evidence in hypothesis testing. Subjects were shown four cards on which one letter or number appeared (A, B, 2, or 3) and were asked to test the hypothesis that "all cards with a vowel on one side have an even number on the other." They were to test this hypothesis by turning over any or all of the four cards. The card wth a 3 on it (a useful choice providing possible disconfirmation) was almost never chosen. Snyder and Swann (1978) also have evidence of a hypothesis confirmation bias. Their subjects overlooked the importance of information indicating the nonoccurrence of a predicted outcome. When subjects were testing the hypothesis that a target was an extrovert, they asked few questions about the target engaging in introverted behavior.

Not only do subjects fail to look for disconfirming evidence, but they also fail to use it sufficiently when it is available. Einhorn and Hogarth (1978) showed that subjects making judgments discounted nonoccurrences of an action and instances of incorrect prediction. In an interesting application of this failure to process nonoccurrences sufficiently, Wells and Lindsay (1980) showed how nonidentifications in eyewitness testimony ("this is not the man") are considered uninformative and are not often used in court trials. Although such nonidentifications do have diagnostic value and should be used in judgments of innocence and guilt, they are treated as irrelevant.

Ross (1977) and Nisbett and Ross (1980) have suggested that nonoccurrences and nonbehaviors will not be sufficiently used either in the perception of other people or in self-perception. However, so far no empirical work has involved application of the feature-positive effect to the relative use of behaviors versus nonbehaviors in the self-perception of attitudes. Several studies have been concerned with the effects of *refusals* to act on subsequent attitudes and perceptions. For example, Zanna (1972) and Harvey and Mills (1971) looked at attitude change as a function of subjects' decisions *not* to alter a speech they were to deliver. Such refusals to behave do have effects on subsequent attitudes. However, a refusal to do something is an active behavior involving a readily observable set of responses. Thus, refusals to behave are quite different from simple nonoccurrences or nonbehaviors. It is a failure to do something rather than a refusal to do it that may potentially be underused in the inference process.

The present study proposes that subjects will use their own freely chosen behaviors more so than their freely chosen nonbehaviors in making attitudinal inferences. Subjects were shown a set of cartoons that they had previously rated as neutral and were asked to decide whether each was "very funny" or "very unfunny." Such a procedure has been proven effective in allowing attitudinal inferences (Bem, 1965). Some subjects (single-response/funny condition) indicated their choice of a cartoon as "very funny" by making an active behavioral response (e.g. pressing a button). Unfunniness was indicated only by the absence of this response. Other subjects (single-response/unfunny condition) indicated their choice of a cartoon as "very unfunny" by the active behavior and used the absence of behavior to indicate funniness. It was predicted that final scalar ratings of the cartoons would differ for these two groups of subjects despite the logical equivalence of their behaviors and nonbehaviors. Less extreme ratings were expected when judgments of the cartoon were associated with the absence of behavior than with the presence of behavior.

To gain further insight into the nature of this effect, two other groups were added. These groups were intended to provide data regarding the extremity of inferences when both funny and unfunny endorsements were associated with the occurrence of behavior. One possibility for establishing such a base rate was to provide subjects with two similar behavioral alternatives, for example, pressing one of two buttons, one of which indicated a funny endorsement, the other, an unfunny endorsement. We were concerned, however, that having the same type of behavioral response indicate both classes of cartoons might diminish the distinctiveness or salience of each response alternative and, hence, attenuate the extremity of inferences drawn from the behavior. F..rthermore, such a condition actually differs from the single-response conditions in two ways. Not only is each, as opposed to a single, class of endorsement associated with an active behavior, but also the two endorsements are indicated in identical rather than different manners, that is, pressing a given button as opposed to pressing or not pressing a single button. Given this reasoning, it was decided that a more appropriate base-rate condition would be one in which different behavioral responses—pressing a button versus blowing a whistle—were associated with funny or unfunny judgments. Nevertheless, to determine empirically whether the similarity of the two behavioral alternatives would generally diminish the extremity of inferences, a condition in which both judgments were indicated by a similar response, pressing one

button for funny and another for unfunny, was inciuded.

METHOD

Subjects

Fifty-two subjects participated in a two-session experiment concerning humor. Each subject was paid $3.50. Subjects were randomly assigned to a condition ($n = 13$). An additional nine subjects participated, but their data were excluded because they failed to meet an a priori criterion of behaviorally endorsing at least 25%, but no more than 75%, of the cartoons as funny. This criterion had been established because any response class including fewer than 25% of the cartoons would involve too small a number of observations to provide a good estimate of attitude change.

Procedure

During an initial session, subjects participated in groups of two to eight individuals. Each subject examined a set of 112 cartoons taken from *The New Yorker* and *Punch* magazines. The subject rated each cartoon by placing a slash along a 100 mm scale, divided into equal segments by the labels "Very Unfunny," "Unfunny," "Slightly Unfunny," "Slightly Funny," "Funny," and "Very Funny."

All subjects returned individually for a second session approximately 1 week later. During this session, each subject was exposed to the 20 cartoons he or she had earlier rated as most neutral, that is, closest to the midpoint of the scales. On arrival at the laboratory, the subject was seated in a cubicle and told to read a page of instructions. These instructions informed the subject that he or she would be asked to examine a series of cartoons and to make two judgments for each cartoon. The first judgment was to be a simple, two-choice response that endorsed the cartoon as either funny or unfunny. The instruction page presented a scale with the endpoints labeled "Very Unfunny" and "Very Funny" and the neutral point clearly demarcated. The subject was instructed to "Decide whether the cartoon in your opinion falls to the right or to the left of the neutral point. That is, decide whether the cartoon is closer to the VERY UNFUNNY end of the scale or closer to the VERY FUNNY end of the scale." After making this judgment and communicating it to the experimenter, the subject was to record his or her "exact opinion" of the cartoon on the same 100 mm scale employed for the preratings.

The form by which the two-choice response was to be communicated to the experimenter, who was seated in the adjacent cubicle, constituted the manipulation. Subjects in the two-similar-responses condition were equipped with two control buttons, one of which they were to press for a funny endorsement and the other for an unfunny endorsement. Each button controlled a light on a panel in the next room. This permitted the experimenter to record the response. Subjects in the two-different-responses condition were provided with one control button and a whistle. Half the subjects in this condition were told to press the button if they decided that the cartoon was funny and to blow the whistle if they believed it to be unfunny. The other half did the reverse. Thus, in both of these conditions, funny and unfunny endorsements involved the occurrence of behavior.

In the two single-response conditions, one endorsement was associated with the occurrence of behavior and the other with the nonoccurrence of behavior. In the single-response funny condition, only cartoons considered funny involved the presence of behavior. Half of the subjects were provided with a single button that they were to press if they believed that the cartoon was funny. The remaining subjects were to blow the whistle for a funny endorsement. Lack of a response indicated an unfunny endorsement. In the single-response/unfunny condition, either pressing the button or blowing the whistle served as the behavioral endorsement of a cartoon as unfunny. The nonoccurrence of a response was associated with cartoons perceived as funny.

These varying instructions appeared on the page that the subject was told to read and were reiterated verbally by the experimenter. Once it was clear to the experimenter that the subject understood the procedure, the cartoon evaluations began. Employing an intercom system that connected the two cubicles, the experimenter called out the identification number of the cartoon. (The set of 20 cartoons had been arranged randomly into a single stack and was located on the subject's table.) The subject then examined the cartoon and made the appropriate response, which the experimenter recorded. The experimenter allowed the subject time to complete the rating scale before calling out the next cartoon's identification number.

At the end of the session, subjects were fully debriefed and given their promised payment.

RESULTS

Preliminary analyses revealed that no differences occurred as a result of blowing the whistle versus pressing the button. Hence, all subsequent analyses collapsed the data across this dimension.

Behavioral Responses

It is first necessary to ensure that the availability of a single response versus two responses did not alter subjects' decision criteria as to what constituted a funny cartoon. Fortunately, this possibility can be examined easily. We simply compared the average proportion of cartoons labeled as funny in each of the four conditions. A one-way analysis of variance revealed no difference among the conditions ($F < 1$). On the average, subjects labeled 53.56% of the cartoons funny. This equivalence across the various conditions indicates that the number of cartoons judged as funny by the subjects was essentially identical despite differences in response modes.

Attitudinal Inferences

Having established the equivalence of behavioral responses, we can now examine the hypothesis concerning the extent to which the occurrence versus nonoccurrence of the behavior affected the extremity of the subsequent attitudinal inference. Since subjects' pre-experimental assessments of the cartoons were available, inferences were considered in terms of change from the prerating. For each subject the average change was calculated separately for those cartoons that the subject had judged by their behavior (or lack of behavior) as funny and those that the subject had judged as unfunny. Table 1 presents the mean change score for cartoons labeled funny and unfunny in each condition. In the case of funny cartoons, positive scores indicate deviation from the prerating in the direction of perceiving the cartoons as funnier than before the judgment. Likewise, positive scores for the unfunny cartoons represent change in the direction of perceiving the cartoon as less funny. In each and every cell of the design, the change scores were significantly greater than zero—smallest $t(12) = 6.44$, $p < .001$—thus replicating Bem (1965).

To examine the relative amount of rating extremity in the various conditions, a 4 (condition) × 2 (funny vs. unfunny behavioral response) analysis of variance, with the second variable as a within-subject factor, was performed on the rating change scores. No main effect of condition was apparent ($F < 1$). The analysis did reveal a main effect of behavioral response, $F(1, 48) = 9.60$, $p < .005$. Ratings of cartoons labeled unfunny were displaced more to the unfunny end of the scale (relative to initial ratings) than were ratings of cartoons labeled as funny displaced toward the funny end. This rating change effect reflects the fact that the initial ratings of those cartoons eventually labeled as funny were already more displaced from the neutral point in the funny direction than were the initial ratings of cartoons eventually labeled as unfunny displaced in the unfunny direction, $F(1, 48) = 32.60$, $p < .001$. Initial ratings of cartoons endorsed as funny averaged 52.90 (2.90 units in the funny direction). Initial ratings of cartoons endorsed as unfunny averaged 50.40 (.40 units in the *funny* direction). Indeed, final ratings of cartoons endorsed as unfunny were no more extreme with respect to the neutral point than were ratings of cartoons endorsed as funny, $F(1, 48) = 1.33$, $p < .25$.

More relevant to the present concerns is

TABLE 1

Mean Change Scores

Condition	Behavioral response	
	Funny	Unfunny
Single response/funny	16.99	17.86
Single response /unfunny	12.21	22.53
Two different responses	16.13	20.36
Two similar responses	16.13	17.69

Note: Higher scores indicate greater polarization in the direction of the behavioral response.

the nearly significant interaction that is observed on the rating change data, $F(3, 48) = 2.47$, $p < .08$. This finding indicates that the various conditions differed in the degree to which equivalent change regarding funny and unfunny cartoons was observed.[1]

As stated earlier, the critical hypothesis predicts a difference between subjects who made a single, overt behavioral response to funny cartoons and those who made a single response to unfunny cartoons despite their logical equivalence. This hypothesis calls for examination of the simple interaction between cartoons labeled as funny versus unfunny and the two single-response conditions. As predicted, this interaction was statistically significant, $t(48) = 2.44$, $p < .02$. Essentially, subjects inferred more extreme attitudes following the presence of a behavioral response (i.e., funny ratings in the single-response/funny condition and unfunny ratings in the single-response/unfunny condition) than following the logically equivalent absence of an overt response (i.e., unfunny ratings in the single-response/funny condition and funny ratings in the single-response/unfunny condition). Thus, a clear difference emerged between the two single-response conditions. Such a finding shows that differences in attitudes from the first session to the second session were not due to changes in attitudes or moods independent of the act of endorsement. If that had been the case, final attitudes toward the cartoon would not have differed with differences in the method of endorsement (response vs. no response). The fact that greater extremity was seen following active responding indicates that final attitudes were at least, in part, inferences derived from the observation of behavior.

The two-different-responses condition provides base-rate data regarding rating change when each response alternative is associated with a distinctive behavior. Within this condition, the difference in rating changes following the labeling of a cartoon as funny or unfunny (unfunny M − funny $M = 4.23$) was at an intermediate level relative to that in the single-response/funny condition (M difference $= 0.86$) and the single-response/unfunny condition (M difference $= 10.32$). Interactive contrasts revealed that the two-different-responses condition did not differ significantly from either of the single-response conditions.

The base-rate means from the two-different-responses condition also indicate that the effect observed in the two single-response conditions was due to an under-utilization of the information provided by the absence of an overt behavioral response. In fact the average of the means in the two cells involving the absence of behavior ($M = 15.03$) differed significantly from the average of the four cells involving the presence of a distinctive behavioral response ($M = 19.00$), $t(48) = 2.37$, $p < .025$.

Consideration of the data from the two-similar-responses condition reveals that our concern about an attenuation of rating change when the same type of behavior indicated funny and unfunny endorsements was unjustified. Although rating change tended to be generally less extreme in the two-similar-responses ($M = 16.91$) than in the two-different-responses condition ($M = 18.25$), the difference did not approach significance ($t < 1$).

DISCUSSION

The results basically support the existence of a feature-positive effect in the self-perception process. Subjects made more extreme attitudinal inferences from their judgmental behaviors than from their judgmental nonbehaviors. Logically, of course, there should be no difference in the information value of the behavior versus the nonbehavior in the present situation. Both were freely chosen and indicated the same kind of evaluation. Yet the absence of a response was treated as less informative. What subjects did not do did not matter as much as what they did do.

It is true that in many naturally occurring situations, nonoccurrences are actually less informative than occurrences. Not doing something leaves it unclear as to what *is* being done, and a great number of behavioral alternatives are possible. When someone eats, sleeps, or mows the lawn, we know what they are doing. However, the knowledge that one chooses not to eat, sleep, or mow the lawn does not tell us what that person has chosen to do. In the present study, actual differences in the information value of behaviors and nonbehaviors is not a problem, since we ensured that behavioral and nonbehavioral judgments were equally informative. However, it may be that because nonbehaviors are generally uninformative, people learn to ignore them—even when they might have great information value.

Interestingly, a careful examination of the relevant literature revealed three experiments in which the feature-positive effect was apparent (although not discussed) in the data. Consider the well-known test of Bem's self-perception theory by Bandler, Madaras, and Bem (1968). Subjects were given a series of 30 shocks of equal intensity. On 10 of these trials (when the red light went on), they were told that the experimenter preferred that they escape the shock by pressing a button (an active behavior). On another 10 trials, subjects were induced not to escape. When the green light

went on, they could escape by pressing the button but were told that the experimenter preferred that they experience the shock. Thus, in this case, subjects chose a nonbehavior (not pressing the button) to indicate their preference for receiving shock. In the yellow-light-control condition, subjects could not escape the shock but were asked to press the button as a measure of reaction time. In this condition, pressing the button terminated shock on 5 of the 10 trials. Interest was in ratings of the discomfort produced by the shock. According to Bem's theory, when subjects choose to escape the shock, they should infer greater discomfort and rate the shock as more severe than when they choose to endure the shock. Although this comparison yielded significant differences, a closer inspection of the data reveals that the difference was due only to inferences drawn in the escape-shock condition. When subjects actively escaped shocks, they rated these shocks as significantly more severe than terminated shocks in the reaction time trials. However, shocks that subjects chose to endure (which should have led to the inference that the shocks were mild) were not rated any less severe than the nonterminated shocks in the reaction time trials. Thus, although subjects were willing to make inferences from their active behavior, they were not willing to make such inferences from the failure to act. This asymmetry of drawing inferences in escape versus no-escape conditions is also apparent in subsequent studies by Corah and Boffa (1970) and Klemp and Leventhal (1972).

Nisbett and Valins (1972) explain this asymmetry by proposing that people feel less freedom of action when asked to perform a counterattitudinal behavior ("don't escape the shock") than when asked to do something they prefer to do anyway ("escape the shock"). This presumed absence of perceived freedom in the no-escape condition prompts subjects, according to Nisbett and Valins, to view the behavior as under external control and, hence, as attitudinally uninformative. Our interpretation is different. It is not the perception of freedom and control that matters so much as the presence versus absence of overt behavior. Our subjects were neither asked nor induced to perform or not to perform any particular behavior. Nor were there differential proattitudinal or counterattitudinal aspects to their behavior and nonbehavior. They simply judged cartoons by doing or not doing something. Yet as in Bandler et al., they failed to draw as extreme an inference from the nonoccurrence of behavior as from the occurrence of behavior.

Why should behaviors be more likely to serve as a source for attitudinal inferences than nonbehaviors? The relative salience of such responses appears relevant. Nonoccurrences and nonbehaviors may not be as cognitively available or as vivid as are overt actions. There is much research to indicate that salience and availability are important in the process of drawing attributions concerning others (Pryor & Kriss, 1977; Taylor & Fiske, 1978) and concerning self (Salancik & Conway, 1975). Both Kahneman and Tversky (1973) and Nisbett, Borgida, Crandall, and Reed (1976) noted that people rely heavily on direct, vivid, and concrete experiences in making their judgments. Reyes, Thompson, and Bower (1980) showed that more vivid information about a target person was disproportionately available in memory and had a correspondingly disproportionate input on evaluative judgments of that person. In the same way, the nonbehaviors of our subjects were not as salient and vivid as behaviors and were thus less likely to be used as a basis for judgments.

The present findings suggest that individuals generally fail to consider fully the implications of their nonbehavior. Attitudinal inferences from the occurrence of behavior tend to be more extreme than inferences from equivalently informative nonoccurrences of behavior. Consistent with Ross's (1977) basic thesis, the existence of a feature-positive effect with regard to self-perceptions provides yet another instance of individuals' shortcomings as intuitive psychologists.

NOTE

1. Since the extremity of inferences was equivalent in the two-different- and two-similar-responses conditions, a 3×2 analysis of variance in which these conditions were collapsed to form a single condition was also performed. This analysis revealed an interaction effect that attained a conventional level of statistical significance, $F(2, 49) = 3.51, p < .05$.

REFERENCES

Bandler, R. J., Madaras, G. R., & Bem, D. J. Self-observation as a source of pain. *Journal of Personality and Social Psychology,* 1968, *9,* 205-209.

Bem, D.J. An experimental analysis of self-persuasion. *Journal of Experimental Social Psychology,* 1965, *1,* 199-218.

Bem, D. J. Self-perception theory. In L. Berkowitz (Ed.), *Advances in experimental social psychology* (Vol. 6). New York: Academic Press, 1972.

Corah, N. L., & Boffa, J. Perceived control, self-observation, and response to aversive stimulation. *Journal of Personality and Social Psychology,* 1970, *16,* 1-4.

Einhorn, H. J., & Hogarth, R. M. Confidence in judgment: Persistence of the illusion of validity. *Psychological Review,* 1978, *85,* 395-416.

Freedman, J., & Fraser, S. Compliance without pressure: The foot-in-the-door technique. *Journal of Personality and Social Psychology,* 1966, *4,* 195-202.

Harvey, J., & Mills, J. Effect of an opportunity to revoke a counterattitudinal action upon attitude change. *Journal of Personality and Social Psychology*, 1971, *18*, 201-209.

Jenkins, H. M., & Sainsbury, R. S. The development of stimulus control, through differential reinforcement. In N. J. Mackintosh & W. K. Honig (Eds.), *Fundamental issues in associative learning*. Halifax, Nova Scotia, Canada: Dalhousie University Press, 1969.

Jenkins, H. M., & Sainsbury, R. S. Discrimination learning with the distinctive feature on positive or negative trials. In D. Mostofsky (Ed.), *Attention: Contemporary theory and analysis*. New York: Appleton-Century-Crofts, 1970.

Jenkins, H. M., & Ward, W. C. Judgment of contingency between responses and outcomes. *Psychological Monographs: General and Applied*, 1965, *79*(1, Whole No. 594).

Kahneman, D., & Tversky, A. On the psychology of prediction. *Psychological Review*, 1973, *80*, 237-251.

Klemp, G. O., & Leventhal, H. Self-persuasion and fear reduction from escape behavior. In H. London & R. E. Nisbett (Eds.), *Cognitive alteration of feeling states*. Chicago: Aldine, 1972.

Lepper, M. R., Greene, D., & Nisbett, R. E. Undermining children's intrinsic interest with extrinsic reward. *Journal of Personality and Social Psychology*, 1973, *28*, 129-137.

Newman, J., Wolff, W. T., & Hearst, E. The feature-positive effect in adult human subjects. *Journal of Experimental Psychology: Human Learning and Memory*, 1980, *6*, 630-650.

Nisbett, R. E., Borgida, E., Crandall, R., & Reed, H. Popular induction: Information is not always informative. In J. Carrol & J. Payne (Eds.), *Cognition and social behavior*. Hillsdale, N.J.: Erlbaum, 1976.

Nisbett, R. E., & Ross, L. *Human inference: Strategies and shortcomings of social judgment*. Englewood Cliffs, N.J.: Prentice-Hall, 1980.

Nisbett, R. E., & Valins, S. Perceiving the causes of one's own behavior. In E. E. Jones et al. (Eds.), *Attribution: Perceiving the causes of behavior*. New York: General Learning Press, 1972.

Pryor, J. B., & Kriss, M. The cognitive dynamics of salience in the attribution process. *Journal of Personality and Social Psychology*, 1977, *35*, 49-55.

Reyes, R. M., Thompson, W. C., & Bower, G. H. Judgmental biases resulting from differing availabilities of arguments. *Journal of Personality and Social Psychology*, 1980, *39*, 2-12.

Ross, L. The intuitive psychologist and his shortcomings: Distortions in the attribution process. In L. Berkowitz (Ed.), *Advances in experimental social psychology* (Vol. 10). New York: Academic Press, 1977.

Salancik, G. R., & Conway, M. Attitude inferences from salient and relevant cognitive content about behavior. *Journal of Personality and Social Psychology*, 1975, *32*, 820-840.

Snyder, M. & Swann, W. B. Hypothesis-testing processes in social interaction. *Journal of Personality and Social Psychology*, 1978, *36*, 1202-1212.

Taylor, S. E., & Fiske, S. T. Salience, attention, and attribution: Top of the head phenomena. In L. Berkowitz (Ed.), *Advances in experimental social psychology* (Vol. 11). New York: Academic Press, 1978.

Ward, W. C., & Jenkins, H. M. The display of information and the judgment of contingency. *Canadian Journal of Psychology*, 1965, *19*, 231-241.

Wason, P. C. Reasoning about a rule. *Quarterly Journal of Experimental Psychology*, 1968, *20*, 273-281.

Wells, G. L., & Lindsay, R. C. On estimating the diagnosticity of eyewitness nonidentifications. *Psychological Bulletin*, 1980, *88*, 776-784.

Zanna, M. P. Inference of belief from rejection of an alternative action. *Representative Research in Social Psychology*, 1972, *3*, 85-95.

An Attribution Explanation of the Disproportionate Influence of Unfavorable Information

Richard W. Mizerski

An attribution model of information processing is proposed and experimentally tested to explain the alleged disproportionate weighting of unfavorable product information. The findings of the experiment generally support hypotheses proposing that unfavorable ratings, as compared to favorable product ratings on the same attributes, prompt significantly stronger attributions to product performance, belief strength, and affect toward products.

One repeatedly finds discussions about how unfavorable product information appears to have a much stronger influence or prepotence than similar accounts of favorable information on consumer decision-making (see Weinberger, Allen, and Dillon 1981). However, there has been very little empirical testing of the reason(s) for this phenomenon. Given the increase of this information type—e.g., derogatory rumors about brands and manufacturers, counter-advertising, corrective advertising, and widely publicized tests of products by various media and government agencies—a better understanding of this alleged differential influence would be beneficial to a wide variety of principals in the marketplace. Toward that end, this investigation briefly explores the available literature for evidence of disproportionate weighting of unfavorable information; evaluates previ-

ously cited reasons for this phenomenon; proposes a more comprehensive attribution theory rationale; and tests that rationale experimentally in terms of several cognitive measures that appear to affect consumer decision-making.

RELEVANT LITERATURE

Evidence of Disproportionate Cognitive Weighting

Because unfavorable or "negative" product information is seldom disseminated by sponsoring companies, most early studies of its influence involved interpersonal or "word-of-mouth' communications. Initial research (e.g., Menzel and Katz 1955; Rogers 1962) simply noted that unfavorable information tended to retard new product adoption, although no quantifiable evidence was presented.

Arndt (1967) and Reynolds and Darden (1972) found evidence that consumers were significantly more responsive to unfavorable as compared to favorable information— i.e., they did not buy products as a result of it. However, the survey nature of both studies made it impossible to measure or

The author wishes to thank Michael B. Mazis and Jack Feldman for their helpful comments on developing the experiment and on an earlier draft of this paper; thanks also to a reviewer for comments on the present draft.

"An Attributional Explanation of the Disproportionate Influence of Unfavorable Information" by R.W. Mizerski, 1982, *Journal of Consumer Research*, 9, pp. 301-310. Reprinted by permission of The Journal of Consumer Research, Inc.

control for intensity of the message or accuracy of the response.

Wright (1974) investigated the use of information when the time allowed for decision-making was varied. The results suggested that individuals tend to place more weight on unfavorable product information as time is reduced, perhaps as a method of task simplification. In an experiment using Consumers Union as the source of detergent ratings, Lutz (1975) found that unfavorable information was more prepotent than favorable information on cognitive structure and attitude.

More recently, Weinberger and Dillon (1980) and Weinberger, Allen, and Dillon (1980) found that unfavorable information was more influential than favorable information on homemakers' evaluations of unbranded goods and services. However, this effect was moderated by the source of the information (e.g., trade source or other homemaker).

Perhaps the most rigorous clinical analysis of unfavorable or "negative" information has been conducted by social and cognitive psychologists who study how individuals combine information into the overall evaluation of others. Anderson (1965) had subjects evaluate a stimulus person based on manipulated sets of equally polarized positive and negative adjectives. His findings provided the first empirical evidence of the disproportionate influence of unfavorable information (negative adjectives) on forming impressions.

A similar result was reported by Rokeach (1968), who asked subjects to respond to assertions linking two concepts that they had rated separately. For example, "dishonest" and "dishonest athlete" were rated by each participant. In eight of the nine permutations rated, the overall evaluation was significantly more negative than would

be predicted by a simple averaging of the scale values for each of the two separate concepts. Feldman (1966) and Wyer (1973) have used other experimental approaches with similar results (see Fiske 1980 for measures of response).

Proposed Reasons for Differential Influence

Surprise and Frequency of Use. It has been proposed that differential influence may be due to unfavorable information having greater "surprisingness" (Feldman 1966) or less frequent use (Zajonc 1968). Derived from information theory, this rationale suggests that unfavorable information is somehow more shocking or surprising, and therefore has more influence on forming evaluations.

However, Kinder (1971) reanalyzed the data and noted that partialing out the effects of surprise and log frequency failed to account for the findings. A review of this topic led Kanouse and Hanson (1971) to concur with Kinder's conclusion.

Ambiguity and Uncertainty. Wyer (1974) proposes that unfavorable information may be viewed as relatively unambiguous, as compared to favorable information, which could prompt less uncertainty in the evaluation. However, the rationale for *why* less uncertainty is attached to the unfavorable information is untested.

Differences in Causal Attribution. A recent explanation is based on the concept that individuals differ in their processing of favorable and unfavorable information because of the perceived "cause" to which each information type is attributed. This perspective on information processing is referred to as attribution theory. It predicts that the more an individual attributes information about an entity that is obtained from another person to that entity's factual performance or actions (a stimulus cause), the more the individual will be influenced by that information. Therefore, an accurate report about an entity is perceived to be "caused" by that entity. In many cases, however, an individual may believe that the information was "caused" by another factor or factors, such as the extent of the communicator's knowledge or bias in reporting, which would then be considered "nonstimulus causes."[1]

One principle of attribution theory is that "the role of a given cause in producing a given effect is discounted if other plausible causes are also present" (Kelley 1973, p. 113). This concept, often referred to as the "discounting principle," has been demonstrated both in experiments of complaint behavior (Thibaut and Riecken 1955) and in the perceived sincerity of complimentary ratings (Jones, Gergen, and Jones 1963). The investigators in both studies suggested that their subjects perceived more nonstimulus causes (causes other than the entity on which information was being provided) for favorable behavior or information, and thus the possibility of the information having a stimulus cause (originating in the entity) was discounted. This discounting supposedly prompted a stronger inference of nonstimulus causation. Therefore, favorable information about an entity may work through the discounting principle to evoke its own unique attributions.

Attributions with unfavorable information are based on an extension of the "social desirability of effects" hypothesis initially proposed by Jones and Davis (1965). Viewed as a modification of the discounting principle, social desirability of effects has

two assumptions (Hastorf, Schneider, and Polefka 1970, p. 68).[2]

1. In general, people intend desirable effects from their actions.
2. Socially desirable effects provide relatively little information about causes for actions. When a person adheres to social norms, one is unsure whether the person's behavior was caused by stimulus (true intentions, beliefs) or nonstimulus (society, peer pressure) causes. Therefore, socially undesirable behavior tends to rule out stimulus causes, and leaves nonstimulus causes as the reason(s) for the effect.

Kanouse and Hanson (1971) have extended this rationale, suggesting that because of social norms concerning discussions about people or objects, most information is favorable in an individual's social environments. Therefore, unfavorable information about traits or behavior stands out, and has a tendency to be attributed to the person or object being evaluated (stimulus cause).

Differential Attributions and Information Influence

If these differences in attribution exist for processing favorable and unfavorable product information, the differential should affect the influence of each type of information. An individual should give more weight to information s/he feels reflects a product's characteristics than to information that is attributed to nonstimulus influences, such as social norms. This rationale assumes that the receiver's preinformation expectancies concerning the source's credibility, expertise, and manipulative intent (i.e., knowledge and reporting bias) are held constant across both information situations.

CONCEPTUAL FRAMEWORK

The Attribution Process in Attitude Formation

Linking Attribution and Belief Formation. It would seem to follow that if unfavorable information produces a stronger attribution to characteristics of the product, that would be the same as a *belief* that a relationship existed between the product and those characteristics (Ajzen and Fishbein 1975; Mizerski, Golden, and Kernan 1979). Such a belief should be much stronger than a belief formed from information that was attributed to causes other than a true evaluation of the product, the latter being the suggested attribution with favorable information. The stronger the stimulus attribution, the stronger the belief, assuming that the belief in question was originally neutral or initially perceived to bear a very weak relationship to the product.

In terms of expectancy—value attitude analysis (e.g., Fishbein 1963; Fishbein and Raven 1962), unfavorable information would prompt the consumer to attach a higher probability that the negatively rated characteristic (e.g., product attribute) was related to the object of belief (e.g., a goods or service). It is by this process that attribution is hypothesized to affect the formation of beliefs, which in turn affects other components in consumer decision-making.

The Effect on Inference. Unfavorable information's disproportionate impact on decision-making may extend *beyond* forming

beliefs about characteristics or attributes on which specific information is provided. For example, unless the information search is truly exhaustive in the purchase of a new automobile, information on such characteristics as reliability and operating expense must be inferred from inspection of and information on the more obvious aspects of the vehicle, such as a visual inspection of the engine, analysis of interior workmanship, or other clues on attributes the buyer cannot see or test.

Unfavorable information also appears to have a differential effect on this inference process. Goodman (1950) and Abelson and Kanouse (1966) found that information about negative traits tended to be more prepotent in forming impressions than information about positive traits. Thus, unfavorable information transmitted by a source on a central attribute[3] should lead the individual to put relatively more faith in the information s/he has received, and in turn, should prompt the consumer to make stronger inferences to other correlated attributes.

A Deductive Argument for the Disproportionate Weighting of Negative Information

As an example of the process, suppose that in the formation of an impression about an automobile, the attribute "good workmanship" is central on the correlated attributes "high reliability," "low maintenance cost," and "high durability." If a source provides favorable information about good workmanship, it will have a relatively greater tendency to be attributed to causes other than a true evaluation of that attribute. This tendency to attribute positive statements to causes other than the automobile leads the individual to assign a relatively low probability to the product possessing a positive value on this central attribute. This probability assignment produces a relatively weak belief about the central attribute of good workmanship. By the process of inference, low probabilities (beliefs) are also assigned to the correlated attributes of high reliability, low maintenance costs, and high durability.

Unfavorable information about workmanship is perceived as having relatively fewer possible causes than favorable information, with the most plausible being that of expressing one's own true feelings about the attribute. This prompts the individual to assign a relatively high probability that the automobile is negative (poor) on the central attribute of workmanship. In this case, the assignment of a high probability produces a belief that will have a greater weight in the final impression than a belief formed from favorable information on the same central attribute. This greater weight is augmented by the assignment of high probabilities (beliefs) to the correlated attributes of (low) reliability, (high) maintenance cost, and (low) durability.[4] By this process of differential causal attribution, belief formation, and inference, unfavorable information is suggested to have a disproportionate influence upon forming impressions, attitudes, and ultimate purchases:

H1: Individuals will tend to make relatively stronger stimulus attributions when provided with unfavorable, as compared to favorable, product information.

H2: The relatively stronger stimulus attributions evoked by unfavorable information will lead those individuals to form stronger central beliefs about the

product than individuals who received favorable product information.

H3: Unfavorable information on a product's central attribute will lead to more extreme beliefs on correlated attributes than will favorable information on the same central attribute.

H4: Individuals who receive unfavorable information about a product will tend to produce more extreme affect toward the product than subjects who receive favorable information.

METHOD

To determine whether there are social norms about product discussions, and thus some consensus about the type of information (favorable or unfavorable) expected, 97 pretest subjects were asked whether they would expect "favorable" or "unfavorable" information from (1) a student who had just tested a new automobile and (2) a student who had just previewed a new movie.

The responses to these questions revealed that a majority of individuals did expect favorable information about each product (78 percent for the automobile, 59 percent for the movie). Because similar tests in trait attribution have rarely been conducted, there are no previous measures from which to determine whether either product would have the minimum expectancy necessary to apply the proposed attribution principles. However, a simple majority does suggest a feasible application.

Subjects and Procedure

The main experiment was performed on nine classes (300 subjects)[5] of senior-level undergraduate and graduate business administration students. Each class was told the experiment was "part of a research project concerned with the way that individuals use other peoples' comments to form opinions about new products." The respondents then received a booklet that included the stimulus information and the dependent measures. The subjects were provided with both oral and written instructions for answering the questions. After the subjects completed the dependent measures, the booklets were collected. The subjects were debriefed about the true purpose of the experiment during the class meeting following completion of the data collection. None of the subjects said that they were aware of the specific hypotheses being tested.

Independent Variables

Three independent variables were manipulated in the experimental treatment: information type (favorable versus unfavorable), product (automobile versus movie), and the product attribute rated favorably or unfavorably (one of three presented). The treatments were described as follows:

Automobile treatment:

On the inside of this booklet, you will find a reprint of a page from an actual evaluation of an automobile that will be introduced in the near future. The opinions expressed are from *one* of 50 students who were randomly chosen to test the automobile for a period of one month. You will be asked to answer a number of questions based upon how you interpret the student's comments.

Movie treatment:

On the inside of this booklet, you will find a reprint of a page from an actual evaluation of a motion picture that will be showing in the near future. The opinions expressed are from *one* of 50 students who were randomly chosen to preview the movie. You will be asked to answer a number of questions based upon how you interpret the student's comments.

Pretests found that the subjects thought the one-month testing period for the automobile was necessary to provide valid ratings on the automobile attributes, while a single preview of the movie was deemed sufficient for its evaluation.

The reprinted evaluation was made to appear as realistic as possible. Toward that end, the (fictitious) rater's name was blacked out to avoid any bias from sex or surname and an unaltered social security number was provided. Instruction for the (fictitious) rater's answers were included so that the respondents could better understand the context of the product evaluations. These instructions asked, "How would you rate the (automobile or motion picture) you (tested or previewed) on the following?" Three product attributes for the relevant test product were listed, with a one-word, handwritten evaluation placed to the right of each attribute. Two of the three attributes were given an effective neutral rating with only one attribute (the treatment) rated favorable or unfavorable.[6] The modifiers used for rating were chosen after a pretest to determine equal polarity.

The three variables were incorporated into a complete 2 (information types) × 2 (products) × 3 (nested attributes) hierarchal design with control groups.[7] The subjects were randomly assigned to each of the 12 treatment and two control groups.

Central and Correlated Attribute Pretests. Wishner (1960, p. 108) has most precisely defined central and correlated traits as follows:

A trait is central for those traits correlated with it and peripheral for those traits uncorrelated with it.

A very large number of central/correlated attribute complexes could be formulated under this definition, yet it would be difficult to justify a better choice. If the concept is to be used in the context of impression formation, however, most researchers (e.g., Wilkie and Pessemier 1973) agree that only a few salient beliefs about product attributes are critical in forming an impression or attitude. Designating the most salient attributes as "central" provides a reasonable basis for a choice, and strengthens the implications if the experiment yields significant results. However, it should not be construed that salient attributes are always or must be highly correlated with other attributes. The emphasis here is on an operational—rather than on a purely conceptual—treatment in the experiment.

A number of methods have been used to elicit salient beliefs, but all have received mixed reactions from theorists. Since the Fishbein model has been used as a framework in this investigation, Fishbein's method of obtaining beliefs (Fishbein and Raven 1962) is a logical choice. It also has the advantage of not re.erring to the purchase decision when asking subjects for responses. This is important in that this study limits itself to impression formation and is not concerned with predicting a purchase decision.

Of the seven most mentioned attributes, four were chosen as possible central attributes, with three used in the final experiment. The attributes used were low maintenance cost, comfort, and low gas consumption for the automobile, and skilled acting, interesting plot, and expert photography for the movie. Final choice was contingent upon the number of times they were mentioned by respondents, whether the attribute could be realistically described in favorable and unfavorable

terms, and whether an individual would reasonably express an opinion about the attribute.

The four proposed central attributes were then used to elicit their correlated attributes. To accomplish this, a questionnaire asked subjects to respond to the following:

For the automobile:

If you heard an opinion expressed about the (e.g., *comfort*) of an automobile, what other characteristics or qualities of the vehicle would be suggested by that information?

For the movie:

If you heard an opinion expressed about the (e.g., *plot*) of a motion picture, what other aspects of the movie would be suggested by that information?

An attribute having a high degree of association (i.e., conditional probability) with one central attribute, and no or a low incidence of association with the other three central attributes, was considered to be the former's "correlated" attribute. An attempt was also made to choose central attributes having low association with other central attributes.

Modifier Choice Pretest. To control for the effect of the rating adjectives alone, and to test for perceived differences when the adjectives are paired to the attributes, the modifiers used for denoting favorable (positive) and unfavorable (negative) values must have equally polarized but affectively opposite psychological meaning to the respondents.

Myers and Warner (1968) conducted a study to determine the psychological meanings of 50 adjectives commonly used for evaluating products. This study was replicated with a sample of 54 subjects similar to those who were used in the final experiment. Of the 50 adjectives tested, the modifier that had the mean score closest to the midpoint on the 21-point response scale was "OK" ($\bar{x}_o = 10.9$). "Terrible" and "superior" had the most extreme means ($\bar{x}_r = 1.3$ and $\bar{x}_s = 19.8$), and were also almost equally distant from the neutral modifier. A pretest using these adjectives as they would appear in the treatments showed that the subjects perceived the modifiers as realistic comments about both products.

Product Selection. The choice of products in the experiments was subject to four criteria:

- Products should represent both an "important" and an "unimportant" purchase.
- Products should be items that the subjects (students) would plausibly purchase.
- They should be products on which individuals would reasonably express an opinion.
- Other individuals' opinions should have a strong impact on the evaluation of these products.

Because differences in importance may exert interesting effects, the experiment used two products with different levels of perceived (a priori) importance. Automobiles were chosen as an example of an "important" purchase because they fulfilled the other criteria and would be considered important using almost any measure. An example of an "unimportant" purchase is much more difficult to justify. The theory is ambiguous about the criteria upon which importance should be gauged, and suggests a relative rather than an absolute distinction. Motion pictures are unimportant relative to automobiles, and represent a product that readily lends itself to student

purchase, realistic expression of opinion, and incorporation of others' opinions into its evaluation (see Burzynski and Bayer 1977).

Dependent Variables

Following exposure to the experimental treatment, the subjects were asked to respond to attribution, belief (both central and peripheral), and overall affect questions. The attribution and central belief questions appeared first and were randomly ordered to control for any confounding that could result from their order of presentation. No significant order effects were detected.

The attribution measure asked the subjects "to what extent do you feel other reasons—reasons having *nothing to do with the automobile tested* (or *movie previewed)*—influenced the students' opinion about . . . (each of the products' three attributes)." The subjects responded on a seven-point scale ranging from "other reasons had no effect on the opinion" (1, an extreme stimulus attribution) to "other reasons were the only cause for the opinion" (7, a completely nonstimulus attribution). The smaller the scale value chosen, the stronger the stimulus attribution.

A series of questions that elicited beliefs about the relationship between the central attributes and the product appeared either before or after the attribution question. This procedure was used so that the subjects would not be forced to shift between making attributions and forming beliefs more than once. The initial format used to elicit the beliefs followed that developed by Fishbein and Raven (1962), and had a nine-point probability scale (-4 to $+4$) that has been used in a number of marketing studies.

Results from early questionnaire pretests revealed that affectively neutral modifiers, when used as ratings of product attributes, often did not prompt true neutral beliefs about the attributes. Two control groups received neutral information (a rating of "OK," which tested as neutral on the modifier pretest) on all three attributes. For all three of the movie central belief scales, and in two of the three automobile central belief scales, the control groups (one for each product) reported favorable beliefs ranging from 0.48 to 1.30. The remaining central belief mean was only slightly unfavorable (-0.04). Because this rather generalized positive bias was not caused by the experimental treatments, but resulted from the subjects' use of the scales, a "zero adjustment" procedure was used so that "adjusted" beliefs would serve as the dependent variable.

The actual adjustment procedure involved subtracting the appropriate mean belief score of the control group from each treated subject's belief score. This established the subject's adjusted belief in relation to the scale's actual affective neutral point.

Next, the respondents were asked to rate the attributes of the product (two correlated, four peripheral) on which no previous information had been given. Subjects were

TABLE 1

Mean Attribution to Product Performance

Product attributes	Information treatment		Across-information means
	Favorable	Unfavorable	
Automobile:			
(1) Low maintenance costs	4.38	4.59	
(2) Comfortable	2.58	3.31	
(3) Low gas consumption	3.22	2.64	
Automobile means	3.40	3.52	3.46
Movie:			
(1) Skilled acting	3.52	3.09	
(2) Interesting plot	3.47	2.95	
(3) Expert photography	3.69	2.65	
Movie means	3.56	2.90	3.23
Across-products means	3.48	3.21	3.53

Note: Scale end point ranged from "other reasons had no effect on the opinion" (1) to "other reasons were the only cause for the opinion" (7).

forced to make probability judgments about the extent to which the attributes were related to the stimulus object (i.e., belief strength). The question format and scale was similar to that used for scoring beliefs about the product's central attributes, and was also adjusted for deviations from affective neutral beliefs based on control group data.

Finally, the subjects were asked about their overall affect toward the stimulus product in terms of "how much would the (automobile tested/ movie previewed) appeal to you?" Scale values ran from "extremely low appeal (1)" to "extremely high appeal (7)."

RESULTS

The first hypothesis proposed that unfavorable information would have a greater tendency to be attributed to the actual performance of the product (stimulus cause) and requires lower mean scores under the unfavorable information treatments. All three of the movie attributes conformed to the hypothesis, but only one automobile attribute (low gas consumption) showed a significantly stronger product (stimulus) attribution with unfavorable information (Table 1). An unweighted means analysis of variance (ANOVA), with attributes nested within product, found a mean effect of attribute ($F = 7.46, p < 0.001$) and an interaction of product and information ($F = 4.33, p < 0.04$). However, the differences were independent of the information treatment and do not constitute a test of the first hypothesis. A Newman-Keuls Test was then performed to detect the source of the information by product interaction, and showed that only the movie attribution scores were significantly different ($p < 0.05$) in the two information conditions.

The second hypothesis stated that the differential attributions evoked by unfavorable, as compared to favorable, information on a product's central attributes would lead subjects to form relatively stronger, more extreme beliefs (i.e., extreme in the direction of the rating). Because differences in relative belief strength rather than direction were of interest, the sign of the beliefs formed in the unfavorable information condition (usually -4 to 0 on the -4 to $+4$ scale) were reflected for all analyses by multiplying the belief scores in the unfavorable treatment by -1. The mean adjusted central belief scores in Table 2 show that unfavorable information led to stronger beliefs about all the attributes. An unweighted means ANOVA on the adjusted central belief scores revealed that the across-products marginal means were significantly different ($F = 6.18, p \leq 0.025$), which supports the second hypothesis. An information-by-product interaction was marginally significant ($F = 2.70, p \leq 0.06$), and may be at least partially due to the relatively stronger attribution differential exhibited by the movie.

The third hypothesis (unfavorable information will lead to more extreme beliefs) requires higher mean correlated beliefs under the unfavorable information treatment. Belief scores for the two correlated attributes associated with each central attribute were averaged, to obtain a single more stable measurement of the correlated beliefs. Beliefs formed under the favorable information treatment were reflected so that the values could be contrasted on relative strength of belief. Mean correlated belief scores are presented in Table 3.

Relatively stronger correlated beliefs were formed for all of the movie attributes with unfavorable information, while only one of three pairs of automobile attributes conformed to the hypothesis. An un-weighted means ANOVA found that the effect of information ($F = 3.71, p \leq 0.06$) was marginally significant. In addition, there was a significant main effect of product ($F = 4.92, p \leq 0.03$), as well as an interaction of information by product ($F = 7.88, p \leq 0.005$). This interaction again points out the differential effect of unfavorable information on the two products, where only the movie conformed to all hypotheses concerning attributions, central beliefs, and correlated beliefs.

The fourth hypothesis proposed that un-favorable information would ultimately lead subjects to form relatively stronger or more extreme affect toward the stimulus product. As with the previous measures of the central and correlated beliefs, the original affect scores (based upon the original 1 to 7 scale) could not be used to test for differences in extremity. Each score was transformed to a -3 to $+3$ scale value, and affect ratings of those subjects who received unfavorable information were reflected.

The results, shown in Table 4, clearly indicate that more extreme or stronger af-

TABLE 2

Mean Central Belief Scores

Product attributes	Information treatment		Across-information means
	Favorable	Unfavorable	
Automobile:			
(1) Low Maintenance costs	2.23	2.37	
(2) Comfortable	1.99	3.71	
(3) Low gas consumption	2.29	3.42	
Automobile means	2.16	3.15	2.69
Movie:			
(1) Skilled acting	1.44	3.13	
(2) Interesting plot	1.95	2.83	
(3) Expert photography	1.33	3.48	
Movie means	1.56	3.15	2.32
Across-products means	1.95	3.15	2.47

Note: The adjusted scale ranged from 0 to $+4$, although some individual scores may have been negative due to the transformation procedure used. The original nine-point scale ranged from "unlikely" (-4) to "likely" ($+4$).

fect was formed with the unfavorable information for all attributes of both products. Application of an ANOVA to these results showed a very strong main effect of information treatment ($F = 12.99, p \leq 0.001$), as well as a main effect of attribute treated ($F = 3.05, p \leq 0.02$). Although the extremity of affect differed significantly in terms of the attribute the subjects received, all the differences were in the appropriate direction, and the final hypothesis was supported.

TABLE 3

Mean Averaged Correlated Belief Scores[a]

Product attributes	Information treatment		Across-information means
	Favorable	Unfavorable	
Automobile:			
(1)[b] { Has quality workmanship / Has a strong warranty	1.14	1.70	
(2) { Has plush upholstery / Has a spacious interior	3.03	2.15	
(3) { Has rapid acceleration / Has a large, high horsepower engine	2.72	0.78	
Automobile means	2.34	1.60	1.90
Movie:			
(1) { Had a large budget / Has well-known actors and actresses	1.15	1.42	
(2) { Had a talented producer / Had a creative scriptwriter	1.61	1.67	
(3) { Has imaginative use of color / Has an interesting location	1.73	1.82	
Movie means	1.50	1.64	1.57
Across-products means	1.90	1.62	1.77

[a] The original and adjusted scale ranges are the same as those used for eliciting central belief scores.
[b] Specifies the number of the central belief to which the correlated beliefs are related.

TABLE 4

Mean Relative Affect Scores

Product attributes	Information treatment		Across-information means
	Favorable	Unfavorable	
Automobile:			
(1) Low maintenance costs	.05	.64	
(2) Comfortable	.33	.36	
(3) Low gas consumption	.40	1.41	
Automobile means	.30	.75	.52
Movie:			
(1) Skilled acting	.36	1.18	
(2) Interesting plot	.78	.87	
(3) Expert photography	.15	.65	
Movie means	.42	.90	.65
Across-products means	.36	.83	.59

Note: The original scale and points ranged from "extremely low appeal" (1) to "extremely high appeal" (7). Transformation of the raw scores yielded a 0 (weak effect) to 3 (strong effect) scale range.

SUMMARY AND CONCLUSIONS

A larger proportion of pretest subjects said that they would expect favorable information about a new automobile (78 percent) more often than about a new movie (59 percent) from another individual. Although a simple plurality would suggest that "social desirability of effects" and "discounting" attribution activity would occur for both products, the greater expectancy associated with the automobile might lead one to expect it to experience stronger hypothesized effects than the movie.

The results did show differences across products on several of the hypotheses. Unfavorable information prompted the hypothesized stronger stimulus attributions for each of three movie attributes, while only one of the three automobile attributes conformed to that hypothesis. On the other hand, unfavorable information led to the predicted stronger beliefs from both products.

The hypothesized development of stronger correlated beliefs with unfavorable information was found for all three of the movie correlated attributes, yet only one of three automobile attributes showed this difference. Finally, both products exhibited stronger affect with unfavorable information.

There may be several reasons for these unexpected findings for the automobile. Perhaps the method for eliciting prestimulus expectancies should have addressed the specific attributes treated in the main experiment, rather than the more general, "would you expect favorable or unfavorable information about (a movie or an automobile)?"

There may be an attribution threshold operating. It is possible that, in situations where the expectancy of favorable information is particularly strong, unfavorable information would not be viewed as credible. This possibility is not addressed in the attribution literature and would seriously limit the applicability of the attribution principles studied. Future research may find it useful to investigate this possibility, and to compare both the expectancies and responses for each subject if the potential for demand characteristics (Orne 1962) can be controlled.

If the difference in information expectancy between the two products is valid, then several factors may explain the results. Post-test interviews revealed that some respondents tended to believe that automobiles were more homogeneous than movies. They viewed gas mileage, the product characteristic that conformed to the attribution hypothesis, as the treated automobile attribute with the greatest potential variation. If this feeling was generalized, individuals who received information about the automobile may have had a greater tendency to incorporate their previous experiences with the treated attributes than did those individuals who responded to information about the movie. This would result in a reduction of those subjects' potential use (and measurement) of the attribution process in developing beliefs based on the automobile information provided. This rationale would also explain the strong main effect of the attribute treated. Because the attribution process is thought to have its primary influence on belief formation, respondent use of exogenous information must be measured or eliminated, even when, as in the present situation, it is information involving a "new" product.

The degree to which an individual is seen as able to judge objectively the performance of the two products' attributes may also differ. If the movie has less objective criteria for evaluation (e.g., judgments about acting skill as compared to gas mileage), information about the movie would have a greater tendency to be viewed as reflecting the source's personal feelings and thus should prompt more potential nonstimulus causal attributions (reasons other than actual product performance). A larger potential causal array for the movie would then provide more latitude for differences in attributions with each information type. The stronger the attributional differences, the greater the impact on belief and effect formation. Mizerski and Weinberger (1977) tested and found support for this logic by comparing the attribution process of goods and services. Most of the criteria used to differentiate goods and services are readily applicable when comparing movies and automobiles.

The ability to generalize from the results is clearly limited by the sample composition, the products tested, and the attributes treated. One must also remember that a single measure of attribution was used. Although similar attribution differences were observed in a study that tested a measure of causal complexity (Mizerski 1978), future research would benefit from a multimethod approach.

Although some aspects of the model proved equivocal for the automobile, the proposed explanation appears to provide at least a partial rationale for consumers' disproportionate weighting of unfavorable information. The attribution belief process establishes a workable paradigm upon which other factors—such as source of message, product involvement, media, and various cognitive differences among subject populations—could be investigated. At the very least, the results strongly suggest that there are attributional differences in the way individuals process favorable and unfavorable information in the marketplace, and that the attribution process can have a significant effect on individual cognitions and feeling about products.

NOTES

1. This attribution may first involve, or be dependent on, the receiver's determination of the source's credibility. The terms "stimulus," "person," and "circumstance attribution" were used to alleviate conceptual problems when dealing with various attribution paradigms and any potential ambiguity when causal chains may be evident. For a more extensive discussion of the attribution process in consumer decision-making, see Mizerski, Golden, and Kernan (1979).

2. This view implicitly assumes that the actor has *knowledge* of the potential effects that will be produced from higher choice of action, as well as the *ability* to perform the action.

3. Asch (1952) and others have argued that traits could be considered either "central" or "peripheral" in terms of their influence upon further impressions, and that a "trait is central for those traits correlated with it and peripheral for those traits uncorrelated with it" (Wishner 1960, p. 108).

4. To avoid any confusion, note that the direction (favorable/unfavorable rating) and the strength (high/low probability assignment) of beliefs are separate concepts. It is in the *strength* of the belief that negative information exerts a disproportionate influence.

5. For the analyses, 30 subjects were deleted for missing data and for improper use of a scale. Although external validity of the results is limited with this sample, the study was primarily concerned with examining underlying psychological processes believed to be of a fairly universal nature. There were no significant differences in results between classes.

6. All three attributes were *not* rated identically in terms of favorability in the experimental groups because subjects might have viewed a consistency of such a strong response (e.g., identical favorable ratings of "superior" on all three) as reflecting a lack of care or some other inference that could confound the results.

7. The two control groups (one for the movie, one for the automobile) received "neutral" information on each of the three attributes. They were used to adjust the belief scores in order to test the second and third hypotheses. Further analyses were not attempted with these groups because their treatment, with *all* neutral ratings, would be confounded with more consistency over modality (the attributes rated) than the treatment groups (see Mizerski and Green 1978).

REFERENCES

Abelson, Robert P. & Kanouse, David E. (1966), "Subjective Acceptance of Verbal Generalizations, in *Cognitive Consistency: Motivational Antecedents and Behavioral Consequents,* ed. Sheldon Feldman, New York: Academic Press, 171-197.

Ajzen, Icek & Fishbein, Martin (1975), "A Bayesian Analysis of Attribution Processes, *Psychological Bulletin,* 82 (March), 261-277.

Anderson, Norman H. (1965), "Averaging Versus Adding as a Stimulus-Combination Rule in Impression Formation," *Journal of Personality and Social Psychology,* 2, (July), 1-9.

Arndt, Johan (1967), "Perceived Risk, Sociometric Integration, and Word-of-Mouth in the Adoption of a New Food Product," in *Risk Taking and Information Handling in Consumer Behavior,* ed. Donald Cox, Boston: Graduate School of Business Administration, Harvard University, 289-316.

Asch, Solomon E. (1952), *Social Psychology,* Englewood Cliffs, N.J.: Prentice-Hall.

Burzynski, Michael & Bayer, Dewey, (1977), "The Effect of Positive and Negative Prior Information on Motion Picture Appreciation,"

The Journal of Social Psychology, 101 (April), 215-218.

Feldman, Sheldon (1966), "Motivational Aspects of Attitudinal Elements and Their Place in Cognitive Interaction," in *Cognitive Consistency: Motivational Antecedents and Behavioral Consequents,* ed. Sheldon Feldman, New York: Academic Press, 75-87.

Fishbein, Martin (1963), "An Investigation of the Relationships Between Beliefs About an Object and the Attitude Toward the Object," *Human Relations,* 16 (September), 233-240.

_____ & Raven, Bertram H. (1962), "The AB Scales: An Operational Definition of Belief and Attitude," in *Readings in Attitude Theory and Measurement,* ed. Martin Fishbein, New York: John Wiley, 180-198.

Fiske, Susan T. (1980), "Attention and Weight in Person Perception: The Impact of Negative and Extreme Behavior," *Journal of Personality and Social Psychology,* 38 (June), 889-906.

Goodman, Stanley M. (1950), "Forming Impressions of Persons from Verbal Report," unpublished Ph.D. dissertation, Teachers' College, Columbia University, New York, N.Y.

Hastorf, Albert, Schneider, David, & Polefka, Judith (1970), *Person Perception,* Reading, MA: Addison-Wesley.

Jones, Edward E. & Davis, Keith E. (1965), "From Acts to Dispositions: The Attribution Process in Person Perception," in *Advances in Experimental Social Psychology,* Vol 2, ed. Leonard Berkowitz, New York: Academic Press, 218-266.

_____ , Gergen, Kenneth J., & Jones, Robert G. (1963), "Tactics of Ingratiation Among Leaders and Subordinates in a Status Hierarchy," *Psychological Monographs,* 77(3), 566-575.

Kanouse, David E. & Hanson, Reid L. (1971), "Negativity in Evaluations," in *Attribution: Perceiving the Causes of Behavior,* eds. Edward E. Jones et al., Morristown, NJ: General Learning Press, 47-62.

Kelley, Harold (1973), "Processes of Causal Attribution," *American Psychologist,* 28 (February), 107-128.

Kinder, Donald (1971), "Implicative Information of Positive and Negative Trait Adjectives," unpublished manuscript, Department of Psychology, University of California, Los Angeles.

Lutz, Richard J. (1975), "Changing Brand Attitudes Through Modification of Cognitive Structure," *Journal of Consumer Research,* 1 (March), 49-59.

Menzel, Herbert & Katz, Elihu (1955), "Social Relations and Innovation in the Medical Profession: The Epidemiology of a New Drug," *Public Opinion Quarterly,* 19 (Winter), 337-352.

Mizerski, Richard W. (1978), "Causal Complexity: A Measure of Consumer Causal Attribution," *Journal of Marketing Research,* 15 (May), 220-228.

_____ , Golden, Linda, & Kernan, Jerome B. (1979), "The Attribution Process in Consumer Decision-Making," *Journal of Consumer Research,* 6 (September), 123-140.

_____ & Green, Stephen (1978), "An Investigation into the Causal Links Between Attribution Schema and Decision-Making," in *Advances in Consumer Research,* Vol. 5, ed. H. Keith Hunt, Ann Arbor, MI: Association for Consumer Research, 126-130.

Myers, James H. & Gregory Warner, (1968), "Semantic Properties of Selected Evaluations Adjectives," *Journal of Marketing Research,* 5 (November), 409-412.

Orne, Milton T. (1962), "On the Social Psychology of the Psychological Experiment: With Particular Reference to Demand Characteristics and Their Implications," *American Psychologist,* 17 (November), 776-783.

Reynolds, Fred D. & Darden, William R. (1972), "Why the Midi Failed," *Journal of Advertising Research,* 12 (August), 39-46.

Rogers, Everett M. (1962), *Diffusions of Innovations,* New York: Free Press of Glencoe.

Rokeach, Milton (1968), *Beliefs, Attitudes, and Values,* San Francisco: Jossey-Bass.

Thibaut, John W. & Riecken, Henry W. (1955), "Some Determinants, and Consequences of the Perception of Social Causality," *Journal of Personality,* 24 (September), 113-133.

Weinberger, Marc C., Allen, Chris T., & Dillon, William R. (1980), "Assessing the Prepotency of Negative Information in the Marketplace," Working Paper 80-4, University of Massachusetts, Amherst.

_____ , Allen, Chris T., & Dillon, William R. (1981), "Negative Information: Perspectives and Research Directions," in *Advances in Consumer Research,* Vol. 8, ed. Kent B. Monroe, Ann Arbor, MI: Association for Consumer Research, 398-404.

————& Dillon, William R. (1980), "The Effects of Unfavorable Product Information," *Advances in Consumer Research*, Vol. 7, ed. Jerry C. Olson, Ann Arbor, MI: Association for Consumer Research, 528-532.

Wilkie, William L. & Pessemier, Edgar A. (1973), "Issues in Marketing's Use of Multi-Attribute Attitude Models," *Journal of Marketing Research*, 10 (November), 428-441.

Wishner, Julius (1960), "Reanalysis of Impressions of Personality," *Psychological Review*, 67 (January), 96-112.

Wright, Peter (1974), "The Harassed Decision-Maker: Time Pressures, Distractions, and the Use of Evidence," *Journal of Applied Psychology*, 59 (October), 555-561.

Wyer, R. S. (1973), "Category Ratings As 'Subjective Expected Values': Implications for Attitude Formation and Change," *Psychology Review*, 80 (November), 446-467.

————(1974), *Cognitive Organization and Changes: An Information Processing Approach*, Potomac, MD: Lawrence Erlbaum Associates.

Zajonc, Robert B. (1968), "Attitudinal Effects of Mere Exposure," *Journal of Personality and Social Psychology*, 9 (June), 1-29.

5 Interpersonal Attraction

THE RANGE OF EMOTIONS that we feel toward others with whom we interact on a daily basis is quite broad. Some persons arouse such negative feelings within us that we may negatively evaluate these people, their possessions, and their products. Other people arouse positive emotions within us and consequently are positively evaluated; these individuals constitute our network of friends. Of this group of friends, some subset may be extraordinarily close to us, and we refer to them as loved ones. The study of the social and psychological factors that promote such positive relationships with others constitutes the field of interpersonal attraction, a fertile field of investigation for social psychologists for well over thirty years.

Interest in the factors that attract persons to one another is certainly nothing new. Traditional folk wisdom (e.g., "Birds of a feather flock together", "Opposites attract") reveals many examples of attempts to find plausible explanations for the fact that we are attracted to some people but not to others. Although there seems to have been a continuing fascination among laypersons with the question of who likes whom and why, the utility of studying such processes scientifically has been questioned by some persons. For example, Senator William Proxmire has been an outspoken opponent of using federal funds for research on attraction and love; he has presented his Golden Fleece Award to Ellen Berscheid and Elaine Hatfield, two well-respected social psychologists who have contributed substantially to our understanding of interpersonal attraction, for their research investigating romantic attraction. It has been Senator Proxmire's contention that most Americans would rather leave some things, such as love, a mystery and do not want to know why men and women fall in love. Fortunately, as suggested by the sheer number of folk sayings that address the question of attraction and love, this view does not appear to be universally shared.

The articles selected for inclusion in this chapter represent two relatively recent shifts in social psychologists' investigations of interpersonal attraction and affiliative behavior. The first two articles are related in that they both refer to attributional processes (see Chapter 4) to understand the acquaintanceship process. In the first of these articles, Antonia Abbey suggests that men may regularly misinterpret the actions of women with whom they interact. Specifically, Abbey finds that men attribute friendly behavior by women as seductive attempts and expressions of desire for romantic involvement. Given that such messages are often not the intent of the women, interpersonal conflicts and misunderstandings may understandably result.

In the second article, William Bernstein and his associates studied male strategies for approaching attractive females. Arguing that the threat of rejection may inhibit males from approaching a woman, these authors suggest that if a man can make the reason for his approach ambiguous and rejection should occur, he can attribute the cause of the rejection to situational factors that have little or nothing to do with his own characteristics. By so doing, the rejected individual is able to maintain a reasonably positive self-image and avoid the negativity typically associated with rejection.

The final article by Susan Hendrick illustrates the new directions that much of the research on interpersonal attraction has begun to take during the past several years. Although the research conducted during the 1960s and 1970s tended to try to isolate initial determinants of liking (e.g., attitude similarity, physical attractiveness), more recent work has sought to understand the development of close relationships as they evolve across time. Hendrick's study demonstrates how attitude similarity and self-disclosure may be related to one's satisfaction with the individual with whom one expects to have the closest relationship, one's partner in marriage. Both of these factors are important for the process of attraction, and Hendrick shows how they play a role in maintaining harmonious marital relationships.

Sex Differences in Attributions for Friendly Behavior: Do Males Misperceive Females' Friendliness?

Antonia Abbey

This investigation tested the hypothesis that friendliness from a member of the opposite sex might be misperceived as a sign of sexual interest. Previous research in the area of acquaintance and date rape suggests that males frequently misunderstand females' intentions. A laboratory experiment was conducted in which a male and female participated in a 5-minute conversation while a hidden male and female observed this interaction. The results indicate that there were sex differences in subjects' rating of the actors. Male actors and observers rated the female actor as being more promiscuous and seductive than female actors and observers rated her. Males were also more sexually attracted to the opposite-sex actor than females were. Furthermore, males also rated the male actor in a more sexualized fashion than females did. These results were interpreted as indicating that men are more likely to perceive the world in sexual terms and to make sexual judgments than women are. Males do seem to perceive friendliness from females as seduction, but this appears to be merely one manifestation of a broader male sexual orientation.

The research described in this article grew out of the observation that females' friendly

Portions of this manuscript were based on the author's master's thesis. The author would like to thank Camille B. Wortman and Elizabeth Holland Hough for their thoughtful critiques of earlier drafts of this paper.

"Sex Differences in Attributions for Friendly Behavior: Do Males Misperceive Females' Friendliness?" by A. Abbey, 1982, *Journal of Personality and Social Psychology, 42*, pp. 830-838. Copyright 1982 by the American Psychological Association. Reprinted by permission of the publisher and author.

behavior is frequently misperceived by males as flirtation. Males tend to impute sexual interest to females when it is not intended. For example, one evening the author and a few of her female friends shared a table at a crowded campus bar with two male strangers. During one of the band's breaks, they struck up a friendly conversation with their male table companions. It was soon apparent that their friendliness had been misperceived by these men as a sexual invitation, and they finally had to excuse themselves from the table to avoid an awkward scene. What had been intended as platonic friendliness had been perceived as sexual interest.

After discussions with several other women verified that this experience was not unique, the author began to consider several related, researchable issues. Do women similarly misjudge men's intentions or is this bias limited to men only? How frequently do these opposite-sex misunderstandings occur? What causes them and what circumstances elicit them?

Research on other subcultural groups indicates that intergroup misperceptions may be common. For example, LaFrance and Mayo (1976, 1978a, 1978b) have examined racial differences in the interpretations of various nonverbal cues. They have found that black and white Americans frequently interpret the same nonverbal cues, such as a direct gaze, quite differently. For example, white listeners gaze at the speaker more than black listeners do. Consequently, interracial encounters may be cumbersome because the participants' signals for yielding the floor or ending the conversation may differ. Because neither individual realizes that their nonverbal vocabularies conflict, they are more likely to mistakenly attribute the awkwardness of the conversation to the other's dislike of them.

Although similar research has not been conducted concerning opposite-sex misunderstandings, a great deal has been written about date and acquaintance rape that may be applicable. Although a simple verbal misunderstanding is in no way comparable to rape in either magnitude or consequences, the underlying process that produces these two events may be related. Several authors have described how our cultural beliefs about the dating situation might lead

to sexual misunderstandings and, in the extreme case, rape (Bernard, 1969; Brodyaga, Gates, Singer, Tucker, & White, 1975; Medea & Thompson, 1974; Russell, 1975; Weis & Borges, 1973; Hendrick, Note 1; Goodchilds, Note 2). These authors argue that women are socialized to flirt and play "hard to get." Even when sexually attracted to a man, a woman is expected to say "no" to his sexual advances, at least at first. And, in a complementary fashion, men are taught to initiate all sexual encounters and to believe that women prefer lovers who are aggressive, forceful, and dominant.

According to this argument these social mores may cause men to unwittingly force sexual relations on their dates, mistaking their true lack of sexual interest for mere coyness. Date and acquaintance rape are prevalent. Researchers estimate that 48-58% of all reported rapes are committed by someone the victim knows (Amir, 1971; Kanin, 1957, 1967; Katz & Mazur, 1979; Kirkpatrick and Kanin, 1957). Kanin and Parcell (1977) found that 50.7% of the 292 female undergraduates they polled had experienced some level of sexual aggression on a date during the previous year. Of these, 23.8% involved forced intercourse (see also Kirkpatrick and Kanin, 1957, and Kanin, 1967). After interviewing college males who had engaged in sexual aggression toward their dates, Kanin (1969) argues that

The typical male enters into heterosexual interaction as an eager recipient of any subtle signs of sexual receptivity broadcasted by his female companion. In some instances, however, these signs are innocently emitted by a female naive in erotic communication. He perceives erotic encouragement, eagerly solicits further erotic concessions, encounters rebuff, and experiences bewilderment. (pp. 18-19)

Although many authors have speculated about the causes of date rape, little research has been conducted in this area. One notable exception is an experiment designed by Hendrick (Note 1) to examine sex differences in perceptions of the opposite sex. Male and female subjects viewed a videotape of a 12-minute interaction between a male and a female confederate. The tape ended with the male asking the female for a date and her acceptance. Subjects were also provided with a hypothetical scenario in which the couple went up to the woman's apartment and sexual intercourse occurred although she had said "no."

The results yielded several interesting findings. Male subjects rated the female actor as more physically attractive and sexually promiscuous than did female subjects. Surprisingly, males also rated the male actor as more physically attractive, sexually promiscuous, and provocative than females did. Males were less likely than females to believe that the female had really meant no. In fact, males were more likely than females to state that even if the female actor had meant no, the occurrence of sexual intercourse was her fault. The external validity of these findings is limited by the artificiality of the situation the observers rated and by the fact that they were passively watching rather than actively engaging in the interaction. Nonetheless, these results provide fairly strong preliminary support for the hypothesis that men and women perceive each others' sexual intentions differently.

In sum, the available literature on date and acquaintance rape suggests that males are unable to distinguish females' friendly behavior from their seductive behavior because of the differential meaning that the relevant cues have for the two sexes. Men may have been socialized to view any form of friendly behavior from a woman as an indication of sexual interest.

In order to test empirically the hypothesis that men misperceive women's intentions, an experiment was designed in which a male and a female would interact with each other while another male and female would observe this interaction. Hence, unlike Hendrick's (Note 1) experiment in which subjects reacted to the behavior of confederates on a videotape, in this case half of the subjects were participants in the interaction. This paradigm also permits examination of both actors' reactions to their partners. If the results do indicate that males misperceive females' intentions, such results would be difficult to interpret without knowing if females similarly misperceive males' intentions.

The observers were included in the design to provide greater insight into this phenomenon. Although it was hypothesized that males are unable to distinguish females' friendly behavior from their seductive behavior because of the differential meaning that the relevant cues have for the two sexes, other explanations of this effect are tenable. For instance, it could be argued that males mistakenly perceive sexual interest in females for ego-enhancing motives; it makes them feel good to think that a woman is sexually attracted to them. However, if male observers as well as male actors perceive the female as being sexually attracted to the male actor, then this lends support to the notion of a general male bias. By comparing the male actors' ratings of the female actor to the male observers' ratings of her, one can assess the extent to which these ratings are due to ego-enhancing motives as opposed to a more general masculine orientation toward female behavior.

The inclusion of female observers provides additional information about the boundaries of this effect. Again, because it was proposed that the hypothesized effect is due to differences in sex role socialization, one would expect the female observers' ratings to be similar to the female actors' ratings and unlike the males' ratings. However, alternatively, one could argue that this phenomenon is due to some kind of actor-observer difference. It may be that all outsiders, regardless of sex, misperceive the female actor's intentions. By comparing the female observers' ratings to the male observers' ratings, we can test these competing explanations.

Although it was predicted that male subjects would misperceive the female actor, it was less clear as to how female subjects would rate the male actor. The evidence in the nonverbal-cues literature, which indicates that women are better at interpreting nonverbal cues than men are (Buck, Miller, & Caul, 1974; Hall, 1978; Rosenthal, Hall, DiMatteo, Rogers, & Archer, 1979), suggests that women may be capable of correctly distinguishing men's friendly behavior from their seductive behavior. However, the pervasiveness of the cultural myth that men are primarily interested in women for sexual reasons may lead one to predict that women may also mistake a man's friendly behavior as a sign of sexual interest. Therefore, no predictions were made as to how the male actor would be judged by the female subjects.

METHOD

Subjects

Subjects were 144 white Northwestern University undergraduates who received credit toward a course requirement of research participation.[1] Subjects were scheduled in groups of four such that none of the students scheduled for the same session knew each other. In all, 36 complete sessions were run (72 males, 72 females).

Procedure

Subjects reported to a large anteroom with five connecting cubicles. Subjects were reminded by the experimenter that the study concerned the acquaintance process and were told that the purpose of the experiment was to determine the way in which the topic of conversation affects the smoothness of initial interactions. Pairs of subjects would each be assigned a different topic, which they would discuss for 5 minutes. Then they would fill out a questionnaire that would assess their opinion of the conversation. Finally, they would engage in a second conversation about a different topic either with the same or a different partner and fill out a second questionnaire. Subjects were told that the experimenter wanted a male and a female in each pair, and they drew pieces of paper to determine who would interact with whom. (Unbeknown to the subjects, this random draw was also used to determine their role assignment.) Although subjects were told by the experimenter that each pair would have a slightly different task, they were led to believe that both pairs would be engaging in conversations. This was done to keep the actors from correctly guessing that they were being observed.

After the draw the experimenter asked the subjects to fill out a brief questionnaire "before the actual study begins." Subjects were placed in individual cubicles to complete this questionnaire. They were given this questionnaire solely to provide the experimenter with the opportunity to give the observers their instructions. After waiting

3 minutes, the experimenter placed both observers in the same room and explained their task to them. Then they were asked to wait quietly and avoid talking while the actors were prepared.

The experimenter then escorted the actors into the "conversation" room in which the one-way mirror through which the observers were watching was hidden by sheer pastel curtains. The actors were seated in chairs facing each other about 4 ft. (1.2 m) apart. They were instructed to talk for 5 minutes about their experiences of that year at Northwestern.

The experimenter immediately joined the observers and turned on a microphone that allowed them to hear the conversation. The observers had a clear view of the actors' profiles. After 5 minutes the experimenter turned off the microphone, reminded the observers to remain silent, and returned to the actors' room to stop the conversation. The experimenter gave the actors questionnaires containing the dependent measures and asked them to fill them out in their individual cubicles. Then the experimenter gave the observers their questionnaires and asked them to return to their original rooms to complete them. When all four subjects were finished, they were brought together in the center room and thoroughly debriefed.

Dependent Measures

After the conversation, subjects completed a questionnaire that asked them to evaluate the quality of the conversation (this was included in order to make the cover story more convincing) and their reactions to the male and female actors. First, subjects were asked to describe one actor's personality in an open-ended question. Then

they rated that actor on a variety of trait terms using a 7-point Likert-type scale. Then they answered the same questions about the other actor.[2] The subjects were asked to base their ratings on how they thought the actor was "trying to behave" because according to the experimental hypothesis it is the target person's intentions that are misjudged. The key trait terms were the adjectives *flirtatious, seductive,* and *promiscuous;* these words were selected because they were thought to measure the construct "sexuality." Additional trait terms such as *considerate, interesting, likeable,* and *intelligent* were included to avoid alerting subjects to the true focus of the study. Other important dependent variables were subjects' responses to questions asking them if they would like to get to know the actors, if they were sexually attracted to the opposite-sex actor, if they would like to date him or her, and why or why not. The observers were also asked if they thought each of the actors was sexually attracted to and would like to date his or her partner and why or why not. Finally, the actors were asked to respond "yes" or "no" to a question asking them if they would like to interact with the same partner in the second half of the experiment.[3]

RESULTS[4]

Sex of Experimenter

Two male and two female experimenters conducted the study.[5] The results of a 2 × 2 × 2 (Sex of Subject × Role of Subject × Sex of Experimenter) analysis of variance indicated that the sex of experimenter did not have an effect on subjects' responses. Therefore, all further analyses were conducted by summing across this variable.

Sex Differences

As expected, there were no sex differences in subjects' ratings of the female actor's friendliness and these ratings were quite high (female M = 6.0; male M = 5.7). A multivariate analysis of variance combining subjects' ratings of the female actor on the three sexual adjectives—*flirtatious, seductive,* and *promiscuous*—into a Sexuality Index (interitem correlations ranged from .39 to .62, p < .001) indicated that there was a significant sex of subject effect for this variable, $F(3, 138)$ = 3.09, p < .03. An examination of the univariate findings indicated that, as predicted, male subjects rated the female actor as being significantly more promiscuous than female subjects did, $F(1, 140)$ = 7.67, p < .01 (see Table 1). Similarly, there was a marginal effect, $F(1, 140)$ = 2.98, p < .09. for males to rate the female actor as being more seductive than did females. However, there were no sex differences in subjects' ratings of the female actor's flirtatiousness.

A multivariate analysis of variance combining actors' responses to the questions "Would you like to get to know your partner better?"; "Would you be interested in becoming friends with your partner?"; "Are you sexually attracted to your partner?"; and "Would you be interested in dating your partner?" into a Future Interaction Index for actors (interitem correlations ranged from .56 to .88, p < .001) yielded a significant sex-of-subject effect, $F(4, 67)$ = 2.83, p < .03. Responses to the question asking the actors if they were sexually attracted to their partner indicated that the male actors were more sexually attracted to their partners than the female actors were, $F(1, 70)$ = 7.17, p < .01 (male M = 3.5, female M = 2.4). None of the other univariate results were significant.

Also, a multivariate analysis of variance combining observers' responses to questions asking them how sexually attracted they were to the opposite-sex actor and how interested they were in dating her or him into a Sexual Attraction Index for observers (r = .85, p < .001) showed a significant effect for sex of subject, $F(2, 69)$ = 4.83, p < .01, again indicating greater male interest than female interest. Univariate analyses indicated that the male observers were more sexually attracted to, $F(1, 70)$ = 9.10, p < .004, and eager to date, $F(1, 70)$ = 8.87, p < .004, the opposite-sex actor than were the female observers (sexually attracted: male M = 3.3, female M = 2.1; date: male M = 3.3, female M = 2.2). Similarly, the male observer thought that the female actor wanted to be friends with the male actor, $F(1, 70)$ = 3.25, p < .08, was sexually attracted to the male actor, $F(1, 70)$ = 6.58, p < .01, and wanted to date the male actor, $F(1, 70)$ = 6.80, p < .01, more than the female observer did (friends: male M = 4.1, female M = 3.5; sexually attracted: male M = 3.2, female

TABLE 1

Mean Scores for Ratings of the Female Actor on the Sexuality Items as a Function of Sex of Subject

Ratings of female actor	Sex of subject		
	Male	Female	p<
Promiscuous	2.2	1.7	.01
Seductive	2.3	1.9	.09
Flirtatious	2.9	2.8	*ns*

$M = 2.4$; date: male $M = 3.1$, female $M = 2.3$).

Analyses of subjects' ratings of the male actor exhibited some surprising sex-of-subject effects. A multivariate analysis of variance combining subjects' ratings of the male actor on the Sexuality Index (interitem correlations ranged from .40 to .72, $p < .001$)—flirtatious, seductive, and promiscuous—indicated that there was a significant sex-of-subject effect, $F(3, 138) = 2.99, p < .03$. The univariate analyses indicated that the male actors and observers rated the male actor as being significantly more flirtatious, $F(1, 140) = 4.21, p < .04$, and seductive, $F(1, 140) = 9.07, p < .003$, than the female subjects did. There was also a significant sex by role interaction for each of these variables, $F(1, 140) = 4.21, p < .04; F(1, 140) = 4.12, p < .04$, respectively. Tukey ($b$) tests indicated that the female actors' and the male actors' ratings were significantly different ($p < .05$) with the male actor rating himself as significantly more flirtatious and seductive than the female actor rated him (see Table 2).[6] There was a marginal trend for males to rate the male actor as being more promiscuous than females did, $F(1, 140) = 3.34, p < .07$. Male actors and observers also rated the male actor as being more attractive than females did, $F(1, 140) = 7.94, p < .01$ (male $M = 4.4$; female $M = 3.8$).

Gender of Stimulus

Because of the intriguing similarity of the males' ratings of both the male and female actor, the data were reanalyzed as a repeated measures analysis of variance. Gender of the stimulus was conceptualized as a repeated measure with respondents' ratings of the female actor representing one level of the variable and respondents' ratings of the male actor representing the second level of the variable. This analysis permits testing of the hypothesis that there is an overall sex-of-subject effect (same-sex subjects rate both actors similarly) or, alternatively, a gender-of-stimulus effect (both sexes rate actors of the same gender similarly).

For the dependent variable flirtatious, this analysis indicated a significant gender-of-stimulus effect, $F(1, 140) = 5.76, p < .05$. Examination of the means indicates that the female actor was rated as more flirtatious than the male actor by all respondents (female actor $M = 2.8$; male actor $M = 2.5$). However, this finding was not replicated with the other two dependent variables, seductive and promiscuous. For both of these variables there was a significant sex-of-subject effect indicating that male subjects rated both actors higher than female subjects did, $F(1, 140) = 6.98, p < .01; F(1, 140) = 6.52, p < .02$, respectively (seductive: male subjects $M = 2.2$, female subjects $M = 1.8$; promiscuous: male subjects $M = 2.2$, female subjects $M = 1.7$).

Role

There was a large and systematic role effect indicating that actors thought more highly of themselves and their partners than the observers did (see Table 3). The male actors and the female actors rated the female actor as being significantly more considerate, interesting, likeable, warm, intelligent, and sincere than did the male and female observers. Similarly, both actors rated the male actor as being significantly more cheerful, interesting, likeable, warm, intelligent, attractive, and sincere than the observers did. Actors also thought more highly of their conversation than the ob-

TABLE 2

Mean Scores for Ratings of the Male Actor on the Sexuality Items as a Function of Sex of Subject and Role of Subject

| | Rating of the male actor | | | | | | | | |
| | Flirtatious[a] | | | Seductive[b] | | | Promiscuous[c] | | |
Sex of subject	Actor	Observer	*M*	Actor	Observer	*M*	Actor	Observer	*M*
Female	2.1	2.4	2.3	1.5	1.9	1.7	1.8	1.8	1.8
Male	3.1	2.4	2.8	2.5	2.1	2.3	2.1	2.1	2.1

[a] Sex of Subject × Role interaction, $p<.04$. Sex-of-subject effect, $p<.04$.
[b] Sex of Subject × Role interaction, $p<.04$. Sex-of-subject effect, $p<.003$.
[c] Sex of Subject × Role interaction, *ns*. Sex-of-subject effect, $p<.07$.

servers did. Compared to observers, actors rated the conversation as more interesting and educational and their ideas as more creative and were more likely to say there was not enough time to talk, $F(1, 140) = 3.99$-36.57, $.001 < p < .05$ for all significant role effects.

DISCUSSION

Sex Differences

The results of the experiment were generally consistent with our predictions. Males rated the female actor as being more promiscuous and seductive than females did. Male actors were more sexually attracted to their partners than their partners were to them. Similarly, the male observers were more sexually attracted to and eager to date the opposite-sex actor than the female observers were. Finally, the male observers rated the female actors as being

more sexually attracted to and willing to date their partners than the female observers did.

It is noteworthy that most of the significant differences were found with the traits and behaviors most obviously sexual in nature. There were no sex differences in subjects' ratings of the female actor's flirtatiousness, the mildest trait term. In fact, the finding that both sexes rated the female actor as being more flirtatious than the male actor substantiates the interpretation that this term has a connotation that implies female gender. There were also no sex differences in actors' desire to get to know their partner better, to become friends, or to date their partner. This sex difference in perception of the opposite sex is only apparent when unmistakably sexual terms are used.

As mentioned earlier, if this effect was due to a self-serving bias on the male actors' part, then the male actors' ratings should

Mean Scores for Ratings of the Male Actor, the Female Actor, and the Conversation as a Function of Role of Subject

Rating	Actor	Observer
Female Actor		
Considerate	5.6	5.2
Interesting	5.4	5.0
Likeable	5.8	5.4
Warm	5.6	5.0
Intelligent	5.4	5.0
Sincere	5.9	5.2
Male actor		
Cheerful	5.4	5.0
Interesting	5.3	4.7
Likeable	5.8	5.4
Warm	5.2	4.8
Intelligent	5.4	5.0
Attractive	4.4	3.9
Sincere	5.8	5.4
Conversation		
Interesting	5.1	4.1
Educational	4.0	3.4
Presence of creative ideas	3.7	3.2
Not enough time to talk	4.5	3.2

have been significantly higher than the male observers' ratings. Similarly, if it was due to actor-observer differences, then the female actors' (the target persons') ratings should have been different from the other three participants' (her observers) ratings. Therefore, the absence of any significant sex by role interactions for these key dependent variables is consistent with the hypothesis that this effect is due to a general masculine style of viewing female behavior.[7]

In sum, the above results provide support for the hypothesis that men mistakenly interpret women's friendliness as an indication of sexual interest. According to the female actors' self-ratings, they intended to be friendly yet they were perceived as being seductive and promiscuous by the male subjects. Clearly, one has no way of judging if the women's behavior truly was seductive or not. What is important, however, is her own perception of her behavior. If she felt she was not being sexually provocative, then she would be offended if a man interpreted her behavior this way, regardless of how an unbiased observer would rate her behavior. In future research similar interactions can be videotaped and later rated by judges, thereby providing a clearer interpretation of these findings.

Although most of the predictions were substantiated by the results, an examination of the subjects' ratings of the male actor necessitated rethinking the initial hypothesis. Not only were males inclined to rate the female actor in sexual terms but they also rated the male actor in a similar manner. Male actors perceived themselves as being more flirtatious and seductive than the female actors rated them. Furthermore, male actors perceived themselves and male observers perceived the male actor as being more attractive and promiscuous than females did. The repeated measures analysis, which combined males' ratings of both actors and found a significant sex-of-subject effect for the variables seductive and promiscuous, corroborates this conclusion. These findings also replicate Hendrick's (Note 1) results; in his study, male subjects, who were observers, rated the male actor as being more physically attractive and sexually promiscuous than females did.

The results of this experiment indicate that men are more likely to perceive the world in sexual terms and to make sexual judgments than women are. The predicted effect that men misperceive friendliness from women as seduction, appears to be merely one manifestation of this broader male sexual orientation.

Alternatively, one could explain these findings by arguing that males and females in our experiment were equally likely to make sexual judgments but that males were simply more willing than females to admit them. Although this explanation is feasible, we consider it to be unlikely. Respondents' explanations as to why they were or were not interested in dating the opposite-sex actor were coded. Males and females were equally likely to mention sexual factors such as "I'm not physically attracted to her" or "The magnetism was not there" as influencing their decision (females = 22%, males = 25%; interrater reliability = .91). If females and males were equally willing to admit their sexual judgments in open-ended responses, then it is likely that they were both being equally honest about these feelings throughout the questionnaire. Also, an approximately equal number of males and females volunteered the information that they were currently dating (females = 19%; male = 17%.). Therefore, differential levels of sexual availability do not explain the findings.

Further verification of our revised hypothesis—that males perceive more sexuality in their own and in others' behavior than females do—comes from the recent work of Zellman, Johnson, Giarrusso, and Goodchilds (Note 3). Zellman et al. (Note 3) asked adolescents, ranging in age from 14 to 18 years, whether they view various cues in the dating situation as indicators that their partner is interested in engaging in sexual relations. They found "a consistent tendency for female respondents to view the behaviors of both male and female actors

as less expressive of an interest in sex than males did" (p. 11). Females were less likely than males to feel that the type of clothes either sex wore, the male's reputation, the setting in which the date occurred, or various dating behaviors (telling the date you love him or her, tickling, looking into the date's eyes, etc.) were signs of sexual interest. Not only do their findings provide independent support for the hypothesis that males view the world in a more sexualized manner than females do but they also extend it to a different age group.

A thorough explanation as to why males and females differ in their propensity to make sexual judgments is beyond the scope of this paper. An explanation based on differential socialization could probably be proposed. Certainly the stereotypes of our culture, as evidenced by the mass media's depiction of men and women, portray men as having a greater interest in sexual matters than do women. Once men develop this sexual orientation, it may act as a generalized expectancy, causing them to interpret ambiguous information, such as that presented in our study, as evidence in support of their beliefs. As Markus (1977) suggests, events that fit one's self-schemas have a greater impact than those that do not. Consequently, if the issue of sexuality is more central to men's concerns than those of women, then males may be more aware of the potential sexual meaning of others' behavior. Future research that delineates the extent of this phenomenon and the conditions under which it does and does not occur may help elucidate its origin.

Role Effects

The role effects, though unexpected, were both extensive and consistent. Actors had a higher opinion of themselves, their partner, and their conversation than observers did. This effect cannot be dismissed as a self-serving bias (Bradley, 1978; Miller & Ross, 1975; Snyder, Stephan, & Rosenfield, 1976), because it applies not only to the self and the conversation that one participated in but also to one's partner, a complete stranger, as well. Perhaps because the observers are not involved in the interaction they may remain more judgmental. Actors may be "caught up in" what is happening and, therefore, be unable to analyze it objectively. There may be a psychological reality to the situation for the actors that makes the experience more involving and pleasant, consequently inflating their ratings (Brickman, 1978). Observing, on the other hand, is a passive behavior that arouses only weak emotions and, therefore is likely to lead to lower ratings (Brickman, 1978).

Alternatively, one could argue that the role differentiation established a sense of "we versus them." This can cause the actors to inflate their 'in-group" ratings and the observers to deflate their "out-group" ratings (Tajfel, 1974, 1978).

SUMMARY AND CONCLUSIONS

Although the initial hypothesis appears to be only partially correct, its implications remain the same. Men do in some circumstances mistake friendliness for seduction. In fact, the whole issue of sexual availability appears to be more salient for men than for women, as evidenced by men's greater tendency to make sexual judgments.

In conclusion, the results of this laboratory investigation corroborate the author's personal experience: Men do tend to read sexual intent into friendly behavior. However, this appears to occur because of a general male bias rather than an attitude about females only. Evidently, women are not subject to this bias (at least not under these circumstances) and are, therefore, unlikely to misjudge male intentions in the way that men misjudge those of women. It is for future researchers to determine the underlying causal factors that contribute to this male bias and the specific circumstances that elicit it.

NOTES

1. It seemed unlikely that subjects would rate friendly behavior from opposite-sex individuals of a different race in the same manner as they would rate similar behavior from a member of the same race. Therefore, because it was desirable to have all four participants in a session be of the same race (and because the great majority of the students in the subject pool were white), the subject population was limited to white students.

2. The order in which the observers completed these questions was counterbalanced so that half of them rated the female actor first, whereas the other half rated the male actor first. The actors, however, always answered the questions about their partners before they answered the questions about themselves. This was done because during pilot testing actors asked to rate themselves first complained that this was too difficult to do, whereas actors who were asked to rate their partner first did not raise any objections.

3. Subjects were led to believe that two conversations would take place so that this behavioroid measure could be included. However, no significant differences were found; virtually all the actors preferred to interact with the same partner.

4. Because of a concern that the actors might not act particularly friendly during their interaction, two conditions were added to the design: one in which the female actor was instructed to act friendly and one in which the male was instructed to act friendly. There was also a control group in which neither actor received any instructions. A 2 × 2 × 3 (Sex of Subject × Role of Subject × Instruction Condition) analysis of the data indicated that subjects from all

three groups perceived the actors as being quite friendly. This manipulation did not affect subjects' responses to any of the key dependent variables, so subjects' scores were collapsed across this variable for all further analyses.

5. Special thanks to Lisa Schurer, Rich Mazanak, and Glenn Cohen for their assistance.

6. The Statistical Package for the Social Sciences (SPSS) Tukey (*b*) statistic averages the Tukey and Newman-Keuls range value at each step.

7. It is possible that the male observers thought they would have the opportunity to meet the female actor later. This could have caused them to rate her in a sexual manner for ego-enhancing motives also. Based on comments that respondents made during the debriefing, the author considers this to be unlikely. (Most observers reported that they thought it would be their turn to interact with each other next; they did not seem to think they would be asked to interact with either of the actors.)

REFERENCE NOTES

1. Hendrick, C. A. *Person perception and rape: An experimental approach.* Unpublished grant proposal, Kent State University, 1976.

2. Goodchilds, J. D. *Non-stranger rape: The role of sexual socialization.* Unpublished grant proposal, University of California, Los Angeles, 1977.

3. Zellman, G. L., Johnson, P. B., Giarrusso, R., & Goodchilds, J. D. *Adolescent expectations for dating relationships: Consensus and conflict between the sexes.* Paper presented at the meeting of the American Psychological Association, New York, 1979.

REFERENCES

Amir, M. *Patterns in forcible rape.* Chicago: University of Chicago Press, 1971.

Bernard, J. *The sex game.* London: L. Frewin, 1969.

Bradley, G. W. Self-serving biases in the attribution process: A reexamination of the fact or fiction question. *Journal of Personality and Social Psychology*, 1978, *36*, 56-71.

Brickman, P. Is it real? In J. H. Harvey, W. J. Ickes, & R. F. Kidd (Eds.), *New directions in attribution research* (Vol. 2). Hillsdale, N.J.: Erlbaum, 1978.

Brodyaga, L., Gates, M., Singer, S., Tucker, M., & White, R. *Rape and its victims: A report for citizens, health facilities, and criminal justice agencies* (National Institute of Law Enforcement and Criminal Justice, Law Enforcement Assistance Administration, U.S. Department of Justice). Washington, D.C.: U.S. Government Printing Office, 1975.

Buck, R., Miller, R. E., & Caul, W. F. Sex, personality, and physiological variables in the communication of affect via facial expression. *Journal of Personality and Social Psychology*, 1974, *30*, 587-596.

Hall, J. A. Gender effects in decoding nonverbal cues. *Psychological Bulletin*, 1978, *85*, 845-857.

Kanin, E. J. Male aggression in dating-courtship relations. *American Journal of Sociology*, 1957, *63*, 197-204.

Kanin, E. J. An examination of sexual aggression as a response to sexual frustration. *Journal of Marriage and the Family*, 1967, *29*, 428-433.

Kanin, E. J. Selected dyadic aspects of male sex aggression. *Journal of Sex Research*, 1969, *5*, 12-28.

Kanin, E. J., & Parcell, S. R. Sexual aggression: A second look at the offended female. *Archives of Sexual Behavior*, 1977, *6*, 67-76.

Katz, S., & Mazur, M. *Understanding the rape victim: A synthesis of research findings.* New York: Wiley, 1979.

Kirkpatrick, C., & Kanin, E. Male sex aggression on a university campus. *American Sociological Review*, 1957, *22*, 52-58.

La France, M., & Mayo, C. Racial differences in gaze behavior during conversations: Two systematic observational studies. *Journal of Personality and Social Psychology*, 1976, *33*, 547-552.

La France, M., & Mayo, C. Cultural aspects of nonverbal communication. *International Journal of Intercultural Relations*, 1978, *2*, 71-89. (a)

La France, & M., Mayo, C. Gaze direction in interracial dyadic communication. *Ethnicity*, 1978, *5*, 167-173. (b)

Markus, H. Self-schemata and processing information about the self. *Journal of Person-*

ality and Social Psychology, 1977, 35, 63-78.

Medea, A., & Thompson, K. Against rape. New York: Fa..ar, Straus & Giroux, 1974.

Miller, D. T., & Ross, M. Self-serving biases in the attribution of causality: Fact or fiction? Psychological Bulletin, 1975, 82, 213-225.

Rosenthal, R., Hall, J. A., DiMatteo, M. R., Rogers, P. L., & Archer D. Sensitivity to nonverbal communication: The PONS test. Baltimore: Johns Hopkins University Press, 1979.

Russell, D. E. H. The politics of rape. New York: Stein & Day, 1975.

Snyder, M. L., Stephan, W. G., & Rosenfield, D. Egotism and attribution. Journal of Personality and Social Psychology, 1976, 33, 435-441.

Tajfel, H. Social identity and intergroup behavior. Social Science Information, 1974, 13, 65-93.

Tajfel, H. The psychological structure of intergroup relations. In H. Tajfel (Ed.), Differentiation between social groups. New York: Academic Press, 1978.

Weis, K., & Borges, S. S. Victimology and rape: The case of the legitimate victim. Issues in Criminology, 1973, 8, 71-115.

Causal Ambiguity and Heterosexual Affiliation

William M. Bernstein, Blair O. Stephenson,
Melvin L. Snyder, and Robert A. Wicklund

A male's decision to approach a physically attractive female stranger may be fraught with ambivalence. He is drawn by her beauty but he may fear rejection. The conflict lessens, however, if approach can occur under the guise of a motive other than desire to be with the attractive woman. This is because keeping one's true approach motive ambiguous may make direct personal rejection less likely. The effect of ambiguity on males' tendencies to approach females was explored in two experiments. In the first study, presented to subjects as a movie rating exercise, an excuse to sit with an attractive female confederate (a movie preference) was available to some subjects but not to others. As predicted, males only sat with the confederate when a reason for their affiliative behavior, other than her attractiveness, was available. In the second study, male-female dyads were run through the film rating paradigm with the female subjects in the role played by the confederate in Study 1. The results of Study 1 were replicated for the dyads which included attractive females, as expected. The relationships between fear of failure and attributional ambiguity in social and achievement settings are examined. The tendency to discount a person's physical appearance as a cause of social behavior is discussed.

Physically attractive people are regarded more positively than unattractive people. Compared to unattractive individuals, attractive people are liked more (Byrne, Ervin, & Lamberth, 1970; Kleck & Rubenstein, 1975; Walster, Aronson, Abrahams, & Rottman, 1966), thought to be happier and more successful (Dion, Berscheid, & Walster, 1972), and even perceived as more intelligent (Clifford & Walster, 1973). That attractive individuals are assumed to possess many positive qualities may explain why we are desirous of affiliating with attractive others (e.g., Walster et al., 1966).

We tend to like people who can bring us rewards (e.g., Thibaut & Kelley, 1959), and those who are thought to be happy, intelligent, and successful (in addition to being pleasant to look at), should be seen as able to bring us much pleasure.

The desire to affiliate with the most attractive others is, of course, not the only motive operating to determine our choices of friends and lovers. For example, individuals seem to have a special affinity for those whose level of physical appeal is similar to their own (e.g., Berscheid, Dion, Walster, & Walster, 1971; Murstein, 1972). This tendency toward matching may be due, in part, to the risks involved in pursuing very attractive individuals. The positive attributes we project onto the physically attractive may give them the power to harm us. To be rejected by a wonderful person is perhaps more damaging than being rejected by a more average individual (cf. Jones, Bell, & Aronson, 1972; Sigall & Aronson, 1969). The fear of being rejected, then, may temper our drive to approach very attractive others (Kiesler & Baral, 1970).

The existence of tendencies to both approach attractive others in order to be rewarded, and to avoid attractive people so as not to risk rejection, may explain a common characteristic of the early acquaintanceship process. That is, individuals typically employ some excuse or pretense to affiliate with relative strangers. It is perhaps the rare Lothario, for example, who can calmly tell an attractive woman the real reason he is motivated to be with her (i.e., "I

This research was supported in part by National Science Foundation Grant BNS-7913828 to M. L. Snyder and R. A. Wicklund.

From "Causal Ambiguity and Heterosexual Affiliation" by W.M. Bernstein, M.L. Snyder, B.O. Stephenson, and R.A. Wicklund, 1983, *Journal of Experimental Social Psychology, 19,* pp. 78-92. (Copyright © 1983 by Academic Press, Inc.)

thought you were so beautiful that I wanted to meet you."). The more typical, less romantic, and slightly self-conscious individual may be unable to approach an attractive person without being somewhat indirect ("You're in my psychology class, aren't you? Look, I need to get the last reading assignment. Were you in class Monday?")

The indirect approach has clear advantages for the individual who may fear rejection. Both approaches result in contact with the desired target, but the indirect approach is unlikely to provoke a categorical rejection from the target person. With the indirect method, if the target is not desirous of future interaction, she can benignly play out the overt script about the class assignment and terminate the interaction. On the other hand, if she is interested in the indirect suitor, she may embellish the classmate script or improvise in order to keep the interaction going.

When the direct approach is used, however, the feedback received from the target person is more likely to contain information about her evaluation of the approaching individual himself. This may be because direct approaches are essentially self-disclosures. They are confessions of the approacher's attitude toward the other. The existence of a strong tendency to reciprocate self-disclosures (see Chaikin & Derlega, 1974) suggests that professing our attitude toward another will result in our hearing the other's attitude toward us. And, if we fear rejection, this type of feedback is precisely what we wish to avoid.

Snyder has argued for the existence of a general tendency for individuals to create and exploit ambiguity about the causes of their behavior (Snyder & Wicklund, 1981; Snyder, Kleck, Strenta, & Mentzer, 1979; Frankel & Snyder, 1978). For example, Frankel & Snyder (1978) showed that subjects who feared doing poorly on an intellectual task exerted minimal effort on the task in order to avoid having to attribute failure to a lack of intellectual ability. However, when informed that the threatening task was so difficult that almost all individuals fail, subjects exerted greater effort, presumably because a subsequent failure could be attributed to high task difficulty. Similar findings have been observed in analogous experimental contexts (e.g., Berglas & Jones, 1978; Snyder, Smoller, Strenta, & Frankel, 1981).

That the existence of convenient excuses for failure promote increases in efforts to succeed is consistent with our present hypothesis. The underlying assumption here is that individuals all desire to succeed with (or be liked by) the most attractive others. When efforts to achieve this goal will probably not engender ego-threatening feedback (i.e., when the motive to affiliate is kept covert), individuals will be more likely to act in accordance with their desire to be with attractive others.

The two studies reported here were designed to test the hypothesis that males are more likely to act on their motive to affiliate with attractive women when their motive for affiliating can be kept covert. Both studies involved modification of a paradigm first used to study the effect of situational ambiguity on avoidance of the handicapped (Snyder et al., 1979). These investigators assumed that their subjects were motivated to avoid sitting next to a woman wearing a leg brace because handicapped people tend to make others anxious (Kleck, 1966, 1968). But since individuals might feel ashamed or guilty about avoiding a disadvantaged person, they expected avoidance to be inhibited unless a plausible excuse for it existed in the situation. As predicted, subjects acted on their motive to avoid the woman only when their avoidance behavior

could be attributed to something other than her handicap.

In the first study reported here we merely replaced the handicapped confederate with an attractive woman. We expected our male subjects to affiliate with the attractive woman only when their approach could be made under the cover of a convenient excuse.

STUDY 1

Methods

Subjects. Thirty-three males enrolled in an introductory psychology class at the University of Texas at Austin participated as subjects as part of a course requirement. One subject in the different movie condition was dropped from the final analysis because he knew the confederate.

Confederate. An attractive female college student dressed in a halter top served as the confederate. The confederate was blind to the experimental hypothesis.

The setting. Two tables separated by a wooden partition were situated along the far wall of the room. On each table was a television monitor. Each table was just large enough to accommodate two chairs, that is, the adjacent sides of the chairs were only 3 in. apart. The confederate always sat in the chair farthest from the partition. The two chairs on the side of the partition without the confederate were empty. The subject entered the room at the opposite end from the monitors and the confederate, and he was seated in a chair positioned in line with the partition.

Procedure. When the subject had been seated the experimenter pointed and looked in the direction of the confederate who had been sitting facing the TV monitor. "As I have already mentioned to her," the experimenter began, "we are interested in peoples' reactions to silent comedy movies. You will be watching a film today and then we will ask you to evaluate the film." The confederate as previously instructed looked back briefly at the subject when she heard the cue "as I have already told her." After looking up briefly the confederate returned her gaze to the TV monitor in front of her and kept looking at the monitor until the subject had made his seating choice.

Same movie (low ambiguity) condition. In the same movie condition the experimenter told the subject that usually he gave people a choice between two movies but that one of the videotape machines was broken and therefore the same movie would be showing on both TV monitors. He then gave the subject a brief written description of the movie and instructed him to take a seat in front of whichever monitor he wished. At this point the experimenter left the room. He returned after 2 min. and told the subject, who had by now made his seating choice, that "unfortunately the other machine is broken and no film can be shown today." The subject was then told that another psychologist involved in the humor research was in the laboratory. Since the experiment had to be cancelled, this fellow said he would be glad to explain some more about the research to the subject. Subjects were then led to another room where the second experimenter probed for suspicion and administered the debriefing.

Different movie (high ambiguity) condition. The only change from the same movie condition was that subjects were told they had a choice of two movies and were given a

description of each. Signs taped to the side of the partition indicated which monitor was showing which film. Subjects were told to sit by the monitor showing the film they wanted to see. The two movies were described as follows:

Slapstick. This film covers the great era of visual comedy and the clowns who made it great. Included in the film are some of the top comics of the 1920s. Charlie Chase, Monty Banks, Fatty Arbuckle, Larry Semon, Andy Clyde, and others appear.

Sad Clowns. Charlie Chaplin, Buster Keaton, and Harry Langdon, Hollywood's comedy greats, all had widely differing styles and techniques, but a common ability to mix laughter and tears.

The side of the partition the confederate sat on and the movie she was associated with were counterbalanced.

Results and Discussion

As expected, most subjects in the same movie condition sat away from the confederate (Table 1). Their behavior was consistent with the social norm to not enter a stranger's intimate personal space (Hall, 1966). Of subjects in the same movie condition 75% chose to sit alone, on the vacant side of the room partition, rather than in the chair positioned just inches from the confederate, $\chi^2(1) = 4.00$, $p < .05$. This seating preference was entirely reversed in the different movie condition where subjects who wished to sit next to the attractive girl had an excuse to do so (i.e., a movie preference). In the different movie condition 75% of subjects decided to sit with the confederate, $\chi^2(1) = 4.00$, $p < .05$. The percentage sitting with the confederate was

TABLE 1

Number of Subjects in Study 1 Who Affiliated with and Avoided the Attractive Female Confederate as a Function of Ambiguity

	Affiliation	
Ambiguity	Yes	No
Low (same movie)	4	12
High (different movie)	12	4

significantly higher in the different movie condition, $\chi^2(1) = 8.00, p < .001$.

These results are consistent with the idea that males may be more likely to act on their desire to affiliate with an attractive woman if they can keep that desire covert. To interpret the results of Study 1 in this fashion, we must assume that the confederate's physical attractiveness per se caused the subjects to want to affiliate with her. But since only one confederate was employed, this assumption might reasonably be challenged. The use of only a single attractive confederate and the lack of an unattractive control raise the possibility that the results were due to some characteristic of the confederate other than her presumed physical attractiveness. In anticipation of these arguments, a second study was conducted.

STUDY 2

In this second study no female confederate was used. Instead, male and female subjects were paired and run through the "humorous films procedure" of Study 1. The female subject in each dyad, whose attractiveness was independently rated by two experimenters, took the role played by the confederate in Study 1. If our interpretation of the Study 1 findings is correct, we should be able to replicate those findings in dyads which include attractive females. In dyads with less attractive females, and, hence, less affilative motivation among males, we expect to find reduced affiliation regardless of ambiguity condition. Presumably the close positioning of the chairs in front of the TV monitors provides a reason for avoidance in both experimental conditions. It is only the combined effect of high motivation to affiliate (i.e., highly attractive female) and situational ambiguity (i.e., different movie condition) that should result in affiliation.

Besides eliminating the confound between a particular female and level of attractiveness, this more naturalistic design allows us to measure potential changes in females' reactions to males as a function of the ambiguity surrounding the males' seating choices. For example, are males more or less liked when the reason for their affiliation is ambiguous? Additionally, the extent to which both males and females attribute the males' seating choice to a movie preference, a measure not taken in Study 1, will be assessed in this study.

Methods

Subjects. Two hundred eight subjects (half males and half females) from introductory psychology classes at the University of Texas at Austin participated as subjects as part of a course requirement. One hundred four male-female dyads were recruited from different psychology classes. Members of each dyad were unacquainted prior to the experiment.

Procedure. The physical setting of the film viewing room was the same as in Study 1.

The female subject was always brought to the room first. A male experimenter, blind to the experimental hypotheses, told the female subject the humor research cover story and instructed her to choose a seat in front of one of the two TV monitors. The experimenter then left the room, informing the female subject that he was going to get another subject. He then returned with the male subject and seated him in a chair opposite the wall with the TV monitors and in line with the partition separating the two monitors. He then told the male the humor research cover story within earshot of the female subject who was by now seated in front of one of the two TVs.

Same movie condition. The cover story given to both the male and female subjects in the same movie condition was the same one given the male subjects in Study 1. The experimenter also made it clear to the male subject that he was being told the same thing about the experiment as the female subject had been told.

Different movie condition. The experimenter told female subjects in this condition that "although most subjects had a choice of either *Sad Clowns* or *Slapstick,* we need one more female to view *Sad Clowns* (or *Slapstick*) in order to have an even number of females who have seen each film." The male subject was told that the female had been assigned to a film and why they were assigned (to make the numbers in each cell equal). The experimenter told the male that he would have a choice of films, however. Assigning females to a film in this condition was done to assure that any differences in the females' impression of the males, assessed on a questionnaire given after the male had made his seating preference known, could not be attributed to assumed similarity (e.g., Byrne, 1971). That is, if

females had been permitted to choose a film of their liking, then their attitude toward the males might be a function of whether his film preference was the same as theirs.

After describing the humor study to the male subject, the experimenter left the room and instructed males in the same movie condition "to take a seat in front of whichever TV monitor you wish." In the different movie condition he instructed males "to sit in front of the monitor showing the film you wish to see." The experimenter was able to observe unobtrusively the males' seating choice, however, by leaving the door to the film viewing room slightly ajar as he left. As soon as the male subject had been observed pulling out the chair he intended to sit in, but before he actually sat down, the experimenter came back into the room. He then asked the male subject if he would come with him for a moment into an adjacent room. Once the experimenter had seated the male subject in a room adjacent to the film viewing room he told him that "this study is really concerned with first impressions." He then gave the male the postexperimental questionnaire. After getting the male started on his questionnaire, the experimenter returned to the female in the next room. He also informed her that the study was concerned with first impressions and started her on her questionnaire. All subjects were assured that no one besides the experimenter would see their questionnaire responses.

After both subjects had completed their questionnaires, they were taken to a third room and debriefed together by a female experimenter.

Experimenters' ratings of subjects' attractiveness. Both the male experimenter and the female debriefer were instructed to rate the "physical attractiveness" of the female and male in each dyad. The experimenter and the debriefer made their ratings covertly as soon as they saw the subjects. The ratings were made, therefore, before either rater had learned of the males' seating preference. Ratings were made on 8-point scales running from attractive (1) to unattractive (8).

Post-experimental questionnaire items. The questionnaires given to male and female dyad members contained three items. Both males and females were asked, "What was your first impression of the other subject?" Subjects responded on an 8-point scale running from "very positive" (1) to "very negative" (8).

Another item concerned the attractiveness of the female dyad member. Male subjects were asked to rate the physical attractiveness of the female in their dyad. Female subjects were asked to estimate the males' response to this last question ("In your opinion, how physically attractive does the other subject think you are?"). Responses to both items were made on 8-point scales running from "attractive" (1) to "unattractive" (8).

The last item concerned subjects' estimates of whether a movie preference influenced the male's seating preference. The item on the male's questionnaire read, "How much was your seating preference influenced by the movie?" The male's responses were made on a 13-point scale running from "My liking for the movie on the female's side greatly influenced my seating choice" through "The movie did not influence my seating choice" to "My liking for the movie on the empty side greatly influenced my seating choice." When the subject felt his seating choice, with or away from the female, could be attributed to a movie preference (e.g., he liked the movie on the female's side of the partition and he sat on that side), his movie attribution was scored positively. If he felt his movie preference

ran counter to his seating choice (e.g., he liked the movie on the female's side but he sat on the empty side), his movie attribution was scored negatively. The directionality of the scoring is derived from Kelley's (1971) analysis of facilitative and inhibitory causes. Facilitative causes are those that make the occurrence of an outcome more likely while inhibitory causes tend to prevent the occurrence of an outcome. The scoring system thus scores facilitative causes positively and inhibitory causes negatively.

The female members of each dyad were asked, "How much was the males' seating preference influenced by the movie?" The response format and scoring of their responses were handled in the same manner as the males' responses.

Results and Discussion

The one hundred four male-female dyads were grouped into three categories on the basis of the experimenters' ratings of the physical attractiveness of each dyad's female subject. The two experimenters' ratings ($r = .42$, $p < .001$) were combined to form a composite attractiveness score for each female. Dyads were trichotomized into those including high, moderate, and low attractive females on the basis of the composite attractiveness score. Male subjects' seating preferences were analyzed by means of a 2 (ambiguity) $\times$ 3 (female's attractiveness) ANOVA. The dependent variable was created by assigning affiliators values of 1 and avoiders values of 0. A regression model ANOVA was used due to the unequal cell frequencies.

The ANOVA yielded significant main effects for both ambiguity [$F(1, 103) = 10.38$, $p < .002$] and attractiveness [$F(2, 102) = 6.05$, $p < .003$]. The overall interaction was not significant. Inspection of the column percentages in Table 2 reveals that the attractiveness main effect was due to males' tendency to affiliate more with highly attractive females than with either low [$t(98) = -3.75, p < .002$] or moderately attractive females [$t(98) = -2.74, p < .01$]. More importantly, the effect of ambiguity on affiliation rates within the high attractiveness condition replicated the effect found in Study 1.

As expected, males were more likely to affiliate with attractive females when a plausible excuse to do so was present (72% affiliating) than when an excuse was absent (33% affiliating; $t(98) = -2.62, p < .01$). The 72% affiliation rate observed in the high ambiguity condition is also significantly greater than the 50% rate one might expect on the basis of random movie or seat preferences [$t(17) = 2.05$, two tailed, $p < .06$].

In the case of dyads with low attractive females, where approach rates and, presumably, approach motivation was low, males avoided females regardless of ambiguity. Only 13% of males in the same movie condition and 24% in the different movie condition affiliated with their unattractive female partners. Both the low and high ambiguity affiliation rates were below chance [$t(14) = -4.04$, two tailed, $p < .01$; $t(16) = -2.49$, two tailed, $p < .05$, respectively], suggesting that males' motivation to approach the unattractive females was less than their desire to conform with the social norm which discourages crowding.

The results from the moderately attractive dyads fell neatly between those from the other two attractiveness conditions. Males in the high ambiguity cell were more likely to affiliate than those in the low ambiguity cell (41% vs 9%; $t(98) = -2.34, p < .02$). But their behavior cannot be characterized as either pronounced approach (as in the high attractive, high ambiguity con-

TABLE 2

Percentages of Male Subjects in Study 2 Who Affiliated with Females as a Function of Ambiguity and Females' Attractiveness

| | Females' attractiveness | | | |
Ambiguity	Low	Moderate	High	Row percentage
Low (same movie)	13% (2/15)	9% (2/22)	33% (5/15)	17% (9/52)
High (different movie)	24% (4/17)	41% (7/17)	72% (13/18)	46% (24/52)
Column percentages	19% (6/32)	23% (9/39)	54% (18/33)	

Note: Actual affiliation ratios appear in parentheses.

dition) or pronounced avoidance (as in the low attractive, high ambiguity condition).

These results illustrate how ambiguity surrounding the cause of one's behavior may lead to disinhibition of desired action. We had assumed that men are more motivated to approach attractive women than to approach unattractive women. We further postulated that the costs associated with approach could be minimized by affiliating under a pretense. In the different movie condition, where a ready-made pretense to affiliate with females made approach less dangerous, the direct effect of females' attractiveness on males' affiliative desires was clearly manifest in behavior. We observed high affiliation with highly attractive women, low affiliation with unattractive women, and neither pronounced affiliation with, nor avoidance of, women of average attractiveness.

The behavior of males in the same movie condition appears constrained in contrast. Without the cover of ambiguity, subjects' affiliative motives were not manifest in their behavior. Instead, same movie condition subjects avoided affiliation, regardless of females' attractiveness. Their behavior may, however, be seen as consistent with a social norm, probably salient given the close placement of the chairs, not to encroach on another's personal space (Hall, 1966).

Experimenters' ratings of males' attractiveness. The two experimenters were asked to rate the attractiveness of male subjects as well as female subjects. Experimenters' ratings of the males' physical attractiveness ($r = .42$, coincidentally the same as the correlation between the experimenters' female attractiveness ratings) were combined to form a composite attractiveness score for each male. These scores were analyzed by

means of a 2 (ambiguity) × 2 (seating choice) × 3 (dyad female's attractiveness) ANOVA. A regression model ANOVA was used due to the unequal cell frequencies.

Since we hypothesized that avoidance of the attractive women in the same movie condition is due to fear of rejection, we had reason to expect that only highly attractive males might risk affiliating in that condition. Although no significant effects emerged from the overall ANOVA, there was some support for the prediction. Within the same movie condition, the 7 males who affiliated with high and moderately attractive females were rated as more attractive than the 30 males who avoided affiliating with high and moderately attractive females, $F(1, 92) = 4.40, p < .05$. On the other hand, no differences were observed in the attractiveness of different movie condition affiliators and avoiders within dyads containing high and moderately attractive females ($F < 1$). In dyads with unattractive women, the attractiveness of the few affiliators did not differ from that of the many avoiders in either ambiguity condition.

Questionnaire results. Responses to the three types of questionnaire items were analyzed separately by means of 3 between, 1 within ANOVAS. The between factors were always movie condition (same or different), females' attractiveness (high, moderate, or low), and males' seating choice (with or away from female). Whether the response was made by the male or the female was the within variable.

Female's attractiveness. Male subjects were asked to rate the physical attractiveness of their dyad's female subject. Females were asked to estimate how attractive the dyad's male found them to be.

The results confirmed that male subjects'

perceptions of female subjects' physical attractiveness were consistent with our experimenters' ratings (see Table 3). The female attractiveness by sex of subject interaction was significant, $F(2, 92) = 3.98, p < .02$. A significant linear trend, $F(2, 92) = 11.85, p < .001$ was found in the males' ratings of their dyad partners which paralleled the categorizations made by our experimenters. Individual cell comparisons using the overall male error term were also carried out. Males in dyads with females classed as highly attractive by our experimenters judged their partners to be more attractive than did males whose partners had been classed as moderately attractive by the experimenters, $F(1, 92) = 12.07, p < .001$. Males paired with moderately attractive females rated their partners as more attractive than did males paired with low attractive women, $F(1, 92) = 5.95, p < .05$.

In contrast to the males' ratings, females' estimates of their partners' assessment of their attractiveness only weakly tracked the experimenters' ratings. The main effect of attractiveness condition on attractiveness ratings was due primarily to variation in the males' ratings, $F(2, 92) = 12.10, p < .001$. In general, females tended to underestimate how attractive males found them to be. This is indicated by the significant sex main effect, $F(1, 92) = 36.64, p < .001$.

The only other significant effect on attractiveness ratings was the sex by attractiveness by seating choice interaction, $F(2, 92) = 3.22, p < .05$. The effect was due to a difference in the ratings of affiliating and avoiding males in the moderately attractive female dyads. Affiliators tended to perceive their partners as more attractive than nonaffiliators, $F(1, 92) = 10.63, p < .01$).

Movie attributions. Subjects in each dyad were asked to rate the extent to which the

TABLE 3

Male Subjects' Mean Perceptions of Females' Attractiveness and Female Subjects' Mean Estimates of How Attractive Males Perceived Them To Be

Sex	Female's attractiveness			Row means
	Low	Moderate	High	
Male	4.22 (32)	3.46 (39)	2.36 (33)	3.35 (104)
Female	4.94 (32)	4.74 (39)	4.12 (33)	4.60 (104)
Column means	4.58 (64)	4.10 (78)	3.24 (66)	

Note: Lower numbers indicate higher attractiveness. *Ns* appear in parentheses.

males' seating preference was influenced by his attraction or lack of attraction toward a particular movie (see Table 4). Results of the ANOVA confirmed the efficacy of the ambiguity manipulation. Different movie condition subjects (both males and females) attributed the males' seating choice to a movie preference more than did same movie condition subjects, $F(1, 92) = 33.59, p < .001$.

The ambiguity condition by female's attractiveness interaction was the only other significant finding for the movie attributions, $F(2, 92) = 4.71, p < .02$. The interaction indicated that high ambiguity condition subjects in dyads with high or low attractive females attributed males' seating choices more to a movie preference than did subjects in dyads with moderately attractive women.

First impressions. Both subjects in each dyad were asked for their first impression of their dyad partner. Because we had hypothesized, and indeed now have found, that males are more likely to affiliate with an attractive female under ambiguous conditions, we wondered if subjects' impressions of each other might be affected by the degree of ambiguity surrounding their first liaison. The results indicated, however, that first impressions were not affected by ambiguity. On the other hand, males' seating preferences, subjects' sex, and females' attractiveness did affect first impressions. Not surprisingly, when males affiliated with females, both dyad members had better impressions of one another than when the male avoided the female, $F(1, 92) = 4.75, p < .05$. Males in general tended to think better of females than females thought of males, $F(1, 92) = 4.40, p < .05$. And, lastly, subjects in dyads with highly attractive females tended to have better impressions of one another than did subjects in

dyads with moderate or low attractive females. The attractiveness main effect was of borderline significance $F(2, 92) = 3.05, p < .06$.

GENERAL DISCUSSION

The studies reported here demonstrate the usefulness of the attributional ambiguity concept (Snyder & Wicklund, 1981) for explaining affiliative behavior. We found in two separate experiments that movement toward an attractive other becomes more likely when one may advance under the cover of a convenient excuse. We assumed that affiliating for a plausible reason, ostensibly different than one's attraction for the other, makes a painful rejection less likely. If attention is focused on some nonpersonal cause of affiliation, the approaching individual has less chance of receiving a direct evaluation of himself from the other. By thus lessening the potential costs associated with approach, ambiguity about affiliation makes approach more likely.

Fear of Failure, Self-Handicapping, and Ambiguity

The results from Study 2 suggest that certain individuals may not need to camouflage their affiliative intentions as much as others. In the same movie condition, where no excuse for affiliating was available, attractive and, presumably, self-confident males were more likely to approach high and moderately attractive women than were less attractive males. That our male subjects' own attractiveness affected the boldness with which they approached attractive women may be seen as consistent with the findings of Kiesler & Baral (1970). They found that males who were induced to feel good about themselves were more likely to ask an attractive female for a date

TABLE 4

Mean Movie Attributions of Males and Females as a Function of Ambiguity Condition and Female's Attractiveness

| Ambiguity | Female's attractiveness | | | Row means |
	Low	Moderate	High	
Low (same movie)	0.03 (30)	0.89 (44)	0.80 (30)	0.62 (104)
High (different movie)	3.85 (34)	2.26 (34)	3.36 (36)	3.16 (104)
Column means	2.06 (64)	1.49 (78)	2.20 (66)	

Note: The higher the mean the more subjects attributed the male's seating choice to a movie preference. *Ns* in parentheses.

than were subjects whose self-esteem had been lowered.

When the risk or, at least, the fear of rejection is slight, then individuals seem to pursue attractive others nondefensively. Other results from less social achievement contexts support the complementary idea that when concern about failure is high, efforts to approach desired goals may be inhibited unless plausible, impersonal reasons for failure are available (Frankel & Snyder, 1978; Snyder et al., 1981). Not only may effort be inhibited if excuses are not available, but Berglas and Jones (1978) have shown that individuals may go out of their way to create them. In their study, subjects who were made uncertain about their ability to perform an anagram test were more desirous of taking a performance-inhibiting drug before attempting the task than were more self-confident subjects.

Jones and Berglas (1978) have dubbed such strategies self-handicapping since the cost of preserving self-esteem may be worsened performance. But we should note that there are ways of generating reasons for failure that do not promote it. For instance, choosing to work with others as a team rather than alone (Willerman, Lewit, & Tellegen, 1960). More generally, there are other strategies for increasing ambiguity besides generating multiple plausible causes. Snyder & Wicklund (1981) discuss two other strategies based on attributional principles: low consistency and high consensus.

Discounting Physical Appearance

When ambiguity was high our male subjects approached appealing women, avoided unappealing ones, and showed no marked tendency in regard to the moderately attractive. Since extreme levels of attractiveness engender more definitive behavioral tendencies, one might have expected subjects in the high and low attractive dyads to perceive of beauty and homeliness as sufficient causes of males' behavior. On the other hand, attributing males' behavior to a movie preference seems more plausible in the moderate dyads, where the females' appearance should have been less salient. These expectations are derived from a traditional attribution theory perspective, that is, one which views people as motivated to make sense of the world, to seek clarity.

The movie attribution results, however, were more in line with the attribute ambiguity viewpoint. Males and females in both the high and low attractive dyads saw the movie choice as a stronger cause of males' behavior than did subjects in dyads with females of unremarkable appearance (see Table 4). Regardless of whether these results are indicative of subjects' private beliefs or their attempts to manage the experimenter's impression of them, they seem to be evidence for ambiguity generation. Where the effects of physical appearance were greater, the movie attributions were higher and, presumably, the more strongly physical appearance was discounted (Kelley, 1971).

These results and those of Snyder et al. (1979) suggest that people may become upset if beauty, ugliness, or infirmity should appear to cause social behavior (cf. Becker, 1973). If generating ambiguity helps to relieve this discomfort, it may become habitual. That the attractive, for example, are generally thought to be intelligent, may be the result of habitually repeated rationalizations—socially evolved ambiguity.

REFERENCES

Becker, E. *The denial of death*. New York: Free Press, 1973.

Berglas, S., & Jones, E. E. Drug choice as an internalization strategy in response to non-contingent success. *Journal of Personality and Social Psychology*, 1978, *36*, 405-417.

Berscheid, E., Dion, K., Walster, E., & Walster, W. G. Physical attractiveness and dating choice: A test of the matching hypothesis. *Journal of Experimental Social Psychology*, 1971, *7*, 173-189.

Byrne, D., Ervin, C., & Lamberth, J. Continuity between the experimental study of attraction and real-life computer dating. *Journal of Personality and Social Psychology*, 1970, *16*, 157-165.

Byrne, D. *The attraction paradigm*. New York: Academic Press, 1971.

Chaikin, A. L., & Derlega, V. J. *Self-disclosure*. Morristown, N.J.: General Learning, 1974.

Clifford, M., & Walster. E. The effect of physical attractiveness on teacher expectation. *Sociology of Education*, 1973, *46*, 248.

Dion, K., Berscheid, E., & Walster, E. What is beautiful is good. *Journal of Personality and Social Psychology*, 1972, *24*, 285-290.

Frankel, A., & Snyder, M. L. Poor performance following unsolvable problems: Learned helplessness or egotism? *Journal of Personality and Social Psychology*, 1978, *36*, 1415-1423.

Hall, E. T. *The hidden dimension*. Garden City. N.Y.: Doubleday, 1966.

Jones, E. E., Bell, L., & Aronson, E. The reciprocation of attraction from similar and dissimilar others: A study in person perception and evaluation. In C. G. McClintock (Ed.), *Experimental social psychology*. New York: Holt, Rinehart & Winston, 1972.

Jones, E. E., & Berglas, S. Control of attributions about the self through self-handicapping strategies: The appeal of alcohol and the role of underachievement. *Personality and Social Psychology Bulletin*, 1978, *4*, 200-206.

Kelley, H. H. *Attribution in social interaction*. Morristown, N.J.: General Learning, 1971.

Kiesler, S. B., & Baral, R. L. The search for a romantic partner: The effects of self-esteem and physical attractiveness on romantic behavior. In K. J. Gergen & D. Marlowe (Eds), *Personality and social behavior*. Reading, Mass.: Addison-Wesley, 1970.

Kleck, R. E. Emotional arousal in interactions with stigmatized persons. *Psychological Reports*, 1966, *19*, 12-26.

Kleck, R. E. Physical stigma and nonverbal cues emitted in face-to-face interaction. *Human Relations*, 1968, *21*, 19-28.

Kleck, R. E., & Rubenstein, C. Physical attractiveness, perceived attitude similarity, and interpersonal attraction and opposite-sex encounter. *Journal of Personality and Social Psychology*, 1975, *31*, 107-114.

Murstein, B. I. Physical attractiveness and marital choice. *Journal of Personality and Social Psychology*. 1972, *22*, 8-12.

Sigall, H., & Aronson, E. Liking for an evaluator as a function of her physical attractiveness and the nature of the evaluations. *Journal of Experimental Social Psychology*, 1969, *5*, 93-100.

Snyder, M. L., Kleck, R. E., Strenta, A., & Mentzer, S. J. Avoidance of the handicapped: An attributional ambiguity analysis. *Journal of Personality and Social Psychology*, 1979, *37*, 2297-2306.

Snyder, M. L., Smoller, B., Strenta, A., & Frankel, A. A comparison of egotism, negativity, and learned helplessness as explanations for poor performance after unsolvable problems. *Journal of Personality and Social Psychology*, 1981, *40*, 24-30.

Snyder, M. L., & Wicklund, R. A. Attribute ambiguity. In J. H. Harvey, W. Ickes, & R. F.Kidd (Eds.), *New directions in attribution research* (Vol. 3). Hillsdale: N.J.: Erlbaum, 198?.

Thibaut, J. W., & Kelley, H. H. *The social psychology of groups*. New York: Wiley, 1959.

Walster, E., Aronson, V., Abrahams, D., & Rottman, L. Importance of physical attractiveness in dating behavior. *Journal of Personality and Social Psychology*, 1966, *4*, 508-516.

Willerman, B., Lewit, D., & Tellegen, A. Seeking and avoiding self-evaluation by working individually or in groups. In D. Willmer (Ed.), *Decisions, values and groups*. New York: Pergamon, 1960.

Self-Disclosure and Marital Satisfaction

Susan S. Hendrick

Self-disclosure is an influential factor in human relationships, and although various theories have been used to explain it, this complex behavior continues to require further research. The marriage relationship offers the most compelling situation in which to study self-disclosure; thus the present study examined the effect of self-disclosure on marital satisfaction in couples and also introduced attitude similarity as a possible predictor of marital satisfaction. Fifty-one couples completed five test instruments, including a self-disclosure scale, two marriage satisfaction scales, an attitude survey, and a demographic questionnaire. Results of the study revealed high reciprocity between spouses on most measures, found a consistent positive relationship between self-disclosure and marital satisfaction, substantiated self-disclosure as a significant predictor of marital satisfaction, and demonstrated that attitude similarity has a strong positive relationship to marital satisfaction. There were several subsidiary results of interest. The major findings of the study provide a firm basis for self-disclosure and attitude similarity as important predictors of marital satisfaction.

Relationships of one kind or another are part of our daily lives. Relationships exist in a romantic framework, in the structure of friendships, and in hundreds of casual daily encounters. The noncasual or "intimate" relationship has increasingly become the focus of psychological study in recent years (e.g., Burgess & Huston, 1979; Kelley, 1979; Levinger & Raush, 1977). Theorists and researchers strive to discover why and how such relationships are formed, maintained, and dissolved.

Communication is an important factor in relationship behavior, and a crucial modality of communication in relationships is self-disclosure (Morton, Alexander, & Altman, 1976). Although self-disclosure, or the verbal revelation of one's thoughts and feelings to another person, has been studied by various researchers (e.g., Jourard, 1971a), many questions about this important concept remain.

One crucial question concerns the best theoretical stance for self-disclosure. There is no unified theory of self-disclosure, and indeed, several social-psychological theories have been used to explain this behavior. From the general norm of reciprocity (Gouldner, 1960) has come the specific implication that "self-disclosure begets self-disclosure" (Jourard, 1971b). Several experiments have found reciprocal high disclosure between subjects (e.g., Ehrlich & Graeven, 1971; Worthy, Gary, & Kahn, 1969), although self-disclosure may be less reciprocal between friends than between strangers (Derlega, Wilson, & Chaikin, 1976).

Within an exchange theory framework (Hatfield, Utne, & Traupmann, 1979; Homans, 1961), self-disclosure can be seen as something that has both costs and benefits for discloser and listener. Cozby (1972) proposed a possible curvilinear relationship between reciprocity and self-disclosure, stating that the rewards of reciprocal self-disclosure increase to a certain point, but then increasingly intense intimacy causes self-disclosure to become so threatening and costly that reciprocity no longer operates.

This article is based on a dissertation submitted to Kent State University in partial fulfillment of the requirements for the degree of doctor of philosophy.

"Self-disclosure and Marital Satisfaction" by S.S. Hendrick, 1981, *Journal of Personality and Social Psychology, 40,* pp. 1150-1159. Copyright 1981 by the American Psychological Assn. Reprinted by permission of the publisher and author.

The focus on reciprocity of disclosure between strangers in a laboratory experiment is in some respects a rather narrow concern. A question that such studies tend to obscure is that of the causal status of self-disclosure. Many experiments treat it as a dependent variable. However, most relationships endure over time, and powerful variables that account for relationship formation and maintenance over time are not easily captured by "snapshot" independent and dependent variables. Self-disclosure is most likely to be bidirectional in its effects: It influences other variables and is influenced by them. Thus, a multivariate approach that allows for the possibility of bidirectional causality (McGuire, 1973) is most likely to lead to real-world correlations between self-disclosure and other important variables (e.g., marital satisfaction).

One approach that attempts to go beyond the confines of the issue of reciprocity of self-disclosure is Altman and Taylor's social penetration theory (e.g., Altman & Taylor, 1973; Taylor & Altman, 1975). This theory deals with the formation of social relationships, and self-disclosure is viewed as an important variable in relationship development. Altman and Taylor (1973) looked at both the depth and breadth of self-disclosure, seeing it as a conceptual wedge shape in a developing relationship, with the breadth of disclosure on many topics greater in the initial stages of a relationship and the depth or intimacy of topics increasing (while breadth may decrease) as the relationship continues into closeness. Taylor and Altman (1966) developed an instrument, the Social Penetration Scale, to assess an individual's amount of self-disclosure in a given situation.

The phenomenon of self-disclosure has often been studied as it occurs between two people in a dyadic relationship, but most of the research on the topic has been conducted in college settings with pairs of students who have no intimate relationship with each other. There is a notable lack of field research based on pairs of "significant others" (Altman, 1973). In no relationship is the other more significant, the commitment more profound, or the risk more intense than in marriage. It is of this relationship that Jourard (1971b) writes: "The optimum in a marriage relationship, as in any relationship between persons, is a relationship between I and Thou, where each partner discloses himself without reserve" (p. 46). Self-disclosure has been studied as one of several factors in the marriage relationshp (e.g., Miller, Corrales, & Wackman, 1975), and since self-disclosure is usually assumed to be a positive behavior, it has on a few occasions been studied in relation to marital satisfaction (e.g., Komarovsky, 1962; Levinger & Senn, 1967).

Komarovsky's (1962) classic study of 58 working-class couples was conducted in 1958-1959 and contains considerable useful information. She developed the term *self-disclosure* several years before it was more widely used by Jourard and found that self-disclosure seemed to be positively related to marital satisfaction in couples and that wives were more likely to disclose than were husbands. Although her study showed some reciprocity of self-disclosure, "in a number of marriages one partner was considerably more reserved than the other" (p. 353). Komarovsky's data are interesting and varied; however, they were gathered more than 20 years ago, and the sample was intentionally homogeneous and working class. The case study method was the only one used, and as Komarovsky noted, "one of the functions of case studies is to suggest explanatory clues for empirical

generalizations previously (and subsequently) derived by quantitative techniques" (p. 349).

In another important study, Levinger and Senn (1967) found reciprocity of self-disclosure among subject couples as well as limited support for the hypothesis that wives disclosed more than husbands did. The authors were interested in proportion of self-disclosure rather than amount or frequency, however, and they focused their attention on both positive and negative kinds of disclosure. Although it was an informative study, there were several problems with its design. First, the sample was composed of 15 couples seeking treatment for marriage problems and 17 couples not in treatment; thus, the group of nonclinical couples was a small one. Second, the self-disclosure questionnaire designed by the authors consisted of nine topics or "objects of communication." Each subject indicated his or her favorable feelings about each topic and also indicated the proportion of pleasant and unpleasant feelings disclosed to and received from the spouse. This instrument was considerably less comprehensive than the standardized instruments, such as the Social Penetration Scale (used in the present study), which have been extensively evaluated (Taylor & Altman, 1966). Third, Levinger and Senn (1967, p. 245) measured couples' self-disclosure 1 year after marital satisfaction was measured, and thus introduced the possibility of historical and maturational artifacts (Campbell & Stanley, 1963). The present study, in contrast, measured self-disclosure, marital satisfaction, and attitude similarity in one testing session.

In addition to the methodological problems and unanswered questions of previous studies of self-disclosure, there are other mixed findings that call for further clarification. For instance, Jourard (1971a) and Chelune (1977) found sex differences in self-disclosure, whereas Feigenbaum (1977) and Komarovsky (1974) did not. From another perspective, Altman and Taylor (1973) proposed that depth of self-disclosure increases as a relationship becomes more intimate, but Jourard (1971a) found that sheer *amount* of self-disclosure to a spouse increased right after marriage but then began to drop off after spouses reached age 40.

Although a few studies have examined the relationship between self-disclosure and marital satisfaction, virtually no research has related marital satisfaction to attitude similarity. A research paradigm relating attraction to attitude similarity (Byrne, 1971) has generated dozens of studies. Byrne (1971) found that "attraction between persons is a function of the extent to which reciprocal rewards are present in their interaction" (p. 266), and Byrne and Blaylock (1963) suggested that in a happy marriage, spouses exchange more positive reciprocal rewards than negative ones. Thus, attraction, and by implication attitude similarity, should have a positive relationship to marital satisfaction.

A major purpose of the present research was to study the joint effects of self-disclosure and attitude similarity in relation to marital satisfaction. Previous research and theorizing suggest that each variable should be related to marital satisfaction. However, no research has examined the relation between self-disclosure and attitude similarity. It could be argued that self-disclosure and attitude similarity are highly correlated. However, it is just as plausible that the two variables are independent of each other. If so, in a multivariate approach both variables should account for significant variance in predicting marital satisfaction when it is

taken as the dependent variable to be "explained."

The following general approach was used in the present study. Marital satisfaction was selected as the dependent variable of interest, and several possible predictive correlates were explored in multiple regression analyses. Self-disclosure and attitude similarity measures were the main predictors, but several demographic measures and a self-esteem measure were used as well. This approach allowed a systematic assessment of the variates relevant to marital satisfaction and at the same time extended the knowledge base for the phenomenon of self-disclosure.

METHOD

In order to examine the relationship among self-disclosure, marital satisfaction, and attitude similarity, a sample of 51 couples was recruited and given five research instruments including a self-disclosure questionnaire, two marital satisfaction instruments, a demographic questionnaire, and an attitude survey.

The Instruments

The Background Inventory, a demographic questionnaire designed by the author, collected data on age, sex, years of marriage, years of education, income level, and religious preference. The self-disclosure instrument is composed of three subscales of Taylor and Altman's (1966) Social Penetration Scale, a scale designed to include a wide variety of topics. Items on the scale are weighted for intimacy value. The three subscales included were (a) Own Marriage and Family, (b) Love, Dating, and Sex, and (c) Emotions and Feelings. Subjects were asked to rate their willingness to talk with their spouse about each item on a 5-point scale ranging from "always would talk about" to "never would talk about," with 5 assigned to "always" and 1 to "never." There were three subscale scores, and these were added for an overall summed score.

One marital satisfaction instrument used is the Marriage Adjustment Inventory (Manson & Lerner, 1962), which was developed primarily as a research and diagnostic tool for marriage counselors. This scale is a 157-item problem-oriented questionnaire on which a subject reads an item and indicates whether it applies to him or her within the marriage, applies to the spouse, or applies to the couple as a dyadic system. Each problem checked is scored as 1 point. This instrument thus offers three subscale scores (self score, spouse score, and couple score) and a total score based on the total number of problems indicated for the marriage.

The second marriage inventory is the Marital Assessment Questionnaire, an eight-item Likert-type scale with each item rated on a 5-point basis. The following questions were asked: (a) How well does your marriage partner meet your needs? (b) In general, how satisfied are you with your marriage? (c) How good is your marriage compared to most? (d) How often do you wish you hadn't gotten married? (e) To what extent has your marriage met your original expectations? (f) How much do you love your mate? (g) How many problems are there in your marriage? (h) Overall, how do you feel about yourself? Items d and g were reverse scored. The Marital Assessment questionnaire was constructd by the author and in final form correlated .48 with the more fully validated Marriage Adjustment Inventory.

The Survey of Attitudes was developed

by Byrne (1971) and has been widely used for several years. The survey contains 57 items, 45 of which were selected for this study. A subject indicated his or her attitude on each item by checking one of six answers ranging from "very much against" to "very much for." Subjects were also asked to complete the questionnaire a second time, placing an "s" next to the alternative for each item that best described their spouse's attitude.

The Sample

The sample consisted of 51 couples; for purposes of data analysis, the sample consisted of 51 men and 51 women, or 102 subjects. The average subject age was 30.6 years, and mean length of marriage was 8 years. Average educational level was 16.7 years, and mean annual income was $15,000. Approximately 48% of the subjects described themselves as Protestant, 21.6% as Catholic, 15.7% as Jewish, and 14.7% as other. Couples were recruited from several churches of different denominations in the local area as well as from married student housing at a nearby university. The church couples were approached personally by their ministers, who also made arrangements with the couples for the date and time of testing. The experimenter's first contact with the church couples was at the time of testing. The student couples were informed generally about the study by letter and given a card to return to the experimenter if they were interested in participating. When a card was received, the experimenter contacted the couple by phone and made arrangements for testing. Consistent telephone reminders proved effective in getting nearly all subjects to follow through in participating. A general script was used for both the phone calls and the introduction to the actual testing session. Subjects were told that they were participating in a dissertation study to examine patterns of marital communication and general marital satisfaction. A $10 honorarium was paid to each student couple, and a comparable contribution was made to each church from which couples were recruited.

Procedure

Couples were tested in groups ranging in size from 2 to 12 couples, and testing was usually done in the evening. People were asked to sit scattered throughout the room. After a brief introduction, the instruments were administered in the following order: the Background Inventory, the Social Penetration Scale, the Survey of Attitudes (first taken for own attitudes and then taken to predict spouse's attitudes), the Marriage Adjustment Inventory, and the Marital Assessment Questionnaire. The tests were given in this order because it was thought that the marriage inventories might be the most threatening of the instruments and should therefore be given last. In addition, the Survey of Attitudes was scheduled between the self-disclosure and marital satisfaction instruments to minimize any possible associations between these instruments. All data forms were coded for couples. Each couple was assigned a number and given two envelopes, one envelope marked with the couple's number and an "H" for the husband, the other envelope marked with the number and a "W" for the wife. Each subject marked all completed test instruments with his or her number and put them in the envelope. Testing usually lasted about 1½ hours, including a short debriefing.

RESULTS

Scoring

In the Background Inventory, the six demographic variables listed above were used for the analyses, and sex of subject was treated as a categorical variable. The Social Penetration Scale had three subscale scores and an overall summed score. Although the four scores were used separately in some analyses, they were highly intercorrelated, and only the overall score was used for the regression analyses. All items on the scale were weighted from 1 to 11 on intimacy value, and after analyses were conducted with both weighted and unweighted scores, all final analyses were done with the weighted scores, which gave slightly more significant values. The Marriage Adjustment Inventory had three subscale scores (self score, spouse score, and couple score) and a summed score consisting of the three subscales. Although all four scores were used for early data analyses, the total score was found to have the most consistent relationship with other variables, and it alone was used in the final regression analyses. Since that score describes the problems in a marriage, the lower the total score, the happier the marriage is assumed to be. Thus, a negative correlation between the Marriage Adjustment Inventory and another variable means a positive relationship between the two variables. The Marital Assessment Questionnaire was administered as an eight-item scale; however, when intercorrelations were conducted on these items, Items 1, 2, 3, 5, and 6 were highly intercorrelated, with correlations ranging from .41 to .76. Items 4 and 7 correlated poorly with the other items. A new Marital

Assessment Questionnaire was developed from the five items and was used in all further data analyses as a measure of marital satisfaction. The eighth item on the scale, a self-esteem item, correlated moderately well with the five-item questionnaire and was used in all analyses as a predictor of marital satisfaction. The Survey of Attitudes proved to be the most complicated instrument to score. Each subject received a score reflecting (a) the face discrepancy between the individual's own attitudes and his or her prediction of the spouse's attitudes and (b) a score based on the subject's ability to accurately predict the spouse's attitudes. In addition, each couple was assigned a score based on the *real* discrepancy between their attitudes.

Data Analyses

Correlational analyses. Reciprocity between spouses' scores was examined first. A simple Pearson correlation was computed between husbands' and wives' scores on all of the variables, and the results are shown in Table 1. Spouses exhibited a high degree of reciprocity on all variables except education, income, and self-esteem. There was a significant positive relationship between spouses' levels of self-disclosure on the Social Penetration Scale as well as on both measures of marital satisfaction. The same correlations were computed for 51 randomly paired couples as a control procedure, and results of these analyses are shown in Table 1. None of these correlations was significant. Analyses between variables were then conducted using the summed scores of a couple; the justification for this summing came from the high reciprocity between spouses' scores. The re-

sults of these analyses are found in Table 2. Real attitude similarity was significantly related to marital satisfaction as measured by the total score on the Marriage Adjustment Inventory. On the other hand, a couple's ability to accurately predict each other's attitudes, indicated by the attitude prediction score, did not relate to marital satisfaction. A major finding was the positive relationship between a couple's self-disclosure and their scores on both measures of marital satisfaction. These relationships were significant, with $r = -.37$ on the Marriage Adjustment Inventory and $r = .41$ on the Marital Assessment Questionnaire. (As noted above the Marriage Adjustment Inventory usually shows a negative correlation where a positive relationship exists. Thus, in this analysis, the higher the self-disclosure, the fewer the reported marital problems.) In addition, self-disclosure was found to have a significant negative relationship with the length of time a couple had been married and a highly positive relationship with a couple's education level. An interesting finding, shown in Table 2, is the positive relation between self-esteem and both measures of marital satisfaction.

Analyses of variance. Sex differences were found on several variables. Significant differences were found between men and women in education and income, with men having higher means on both variables ($p < .01$). The only other sex differences were reflected in the subscale scores and the total score of the Social Penetration Scale. Women scored higher than men on total score and on two of the three subscales ($p < .05$), thus indicating that women did have higher self-disclosure scores than men on this measure.

TABLE 1

TABLE 1

Correlations Between Husbands and Wives and Between Randomly Paired Couples

Variable	Husbands and wives	Random couples
Self-esteem	.20	−.15
Age of subject	.96*	−.15
Education	.09	.12
Income level	−.13	.20
Religion	.62*	−.22
Marriage Adjustment Inventory		
Self score	.33*	−.12
Spouse score	.37*	−.07
Couple score	.39*	−.09
Total score	.53*	−.08
Social Penetration Scale		
Subscale 1	.47*	−.22
Subscale 2	.48*	−.15
Subscale 3	.32*	−.03
Total summed score	.45*	−.13
Marital Assessment Questionnaire	.78*	−.09
Attitude prediction	.55*	.04

Note: Each correlation is based on a sample of 51 couples. *$p<.01$.

Prediction of marital satisfaction. Additional Pearson correlations were computed between the two measures of marital satisfaction and all other variables. These correlations, computed across 102 subjects, are shown in Table 3. Several demographic variables were positively related to marital satisfaction; however, the highest correlations with marital satisfaction were attained by self-esteem, self-disclosure, and face discrepancy on attitudes. (*Face discrepancy* represents the difference between a subject's own attitudes and the attitudes he or she predicts for the spouse; thus it represents the discrepancy a subject "perceives" between self and spouse attitudes.) A comparison of Table 2 with Table 3 indicates that the results were quite similar for individual data and summed couple scores.

In a second series of analyses, regression analysis was used to assess the prediction of marital satisfaction. Analyses were computed separately for persons and couples, using the Marriage Adjustment Inventory and the Marital Assessment Questionnaire as the dependent variables to be predicted and all of the other variables as independent predictors. A summary of the final regression analyses across all 102 subjects is shown in Table 4, and a similar summary across the 51 couples is shown in Table 5. The first obvious pattern in the regression scores for persons was the strong positive relationship of both self-disclosure and self-esteem to the measures of marital satisfaction. These two variables, along with years of marriage, were significant predictors of marital satisfaction on the Marriage Adjustment Inventory.

For couples, we again see the strong influences of self-disclosure on marital satisfaction. The self-esteem measure was also a significant predictor for couples' satisfaction on the Marital Assessment Questionnaire. *Real attitude similarity* was a powerful predictor of marital satisfaction for couples, as measured by the Marriage Adjustment Inventory.

DISCUSSION

The present study attempted to examine the relationship between self-disclosure and marital satisfaction with a new perspective and to provide a research base from which future studies can be developed. There were numerous secondary findings of interest in

TABLE 2

Correlations Between Variables for Spouses' Summed Scores

Variable	2	3	4	5	6	7	8	9	10	11
1. Age	.93**	−.09	.73**	−.48**	−.02	−.25*	−.21	−.27*	−.32**	−.13
2. Years of marriage		−.34**	.62**	−.44**	−.10	−.39**	−.10	−.17	−.22	−.18
3. Education			.14	.19	.20	.53**	−.31*	−.17	−.24*	.29*
4. Income				−.34**	−.20	−.02	−.27*	−.15	−.31**	−.08
5. Religion					−.03	.15	.25*	.14	.11	.14
6. Self-esteem						.30*	.003	−.08	−.32**	.45**
7. Social Penetration Scale							−.17	−.04	−.37**	.41**
8. Attitude prediction								.66**	.21	.06
9. Real attitude similarity									.38**	.13
10. Marriage Adjustment Inventory										−.48**
11. Marital Assessment Questionnaire										

Note: Each correlation is based on a sample of 51 couples.
*p<.05. **p<.01.

addition to the results for the primary variables.

Variable Matching

There was matching or high reciprocity of response between spouses on nearly all variables, and the strength of the reciprocity was confirmed by comparison of spouses' correlations against the correlations of randomly paired couples. In addition to the possible influence of a reciprocity norm (Gouldner, 1960), it may well be that people become more alike after they have been married awhile or that people who are similar tend to marry each other in the first place.

Sex Differences

Analysis of variance revealed some sex differences in self-disclosure, with wom-

TABLE 3

Correlations Between Predictor Variables and Marital Satisfaction Measures for Individuals

Variable	Marriage Adjustment Inventory	Marital Assessment Questionnaire
Self-esteem	−.30**	.42**
Age	−.27**	−.11
Years of marriage	−.19**	−.17*
Education	−.13	.20*
Income	−.21*	−.07
Attitude prediction	.20*	.02
Social Penetration Scale	−.31**	.36**
Face attitude discrepancy	.45**	−.28**

Note: Each correlation is based on a sample of 102 subjects.
*p<.05.** p<.01.

TABLE 4

Regression of Marital Satisfaction Measures Onto All Variables for Individuals

Variable	R	R^2	Beta	F
Marriage Adjustment Inventory				
Social Penetration Scale	.31	.10	−.33	12.07**
Years of marriage	.43	.19	−.38	5.84**
Self-esteem	.50	.25	−.29	9.99**
Income	.52	.27	−.18	3.52*
Marital Assessment Questionnaire				
Self-esteem	.42	.17	.35	15.70**
Social Penetration Scale	.50	.25	.29	10.39**

Note: Each regression is based on a sample of 102 subjects.
  *$p<.05$. **$p<.01$.

en's scores on two subscales of the Social Penetration Scale and on the total scale score significantly higher than men's scores. Although there were many young couples in the sample—couples whom one might expect to represent the new equality between men and women much talked about in present society—the sample still showed sex differences on variables that represent tangible success in society's terms—education and income—with men scoring higher on both. Interestingly, there was no significant difference in self-esteem between men and women, so both sexes appeared to feel equally good about their respective roles.

Correlates of Self-Disclosure

Self-disclosure by a couple was positively related to scores on the Marriage Ad-justment Inventory and the Marital Assessment Questionnaire. Since self-disclosure was a good predictor of marital satisfaction for persons as well as couples, it was examined in further analyses to see whether one spouse's self-disclosure was related to the other spouse's marital satisfaction. In fact, husbands' self-disclosure was significantly related to wives' marital satisfaction, and the reverse was also true.

Self-disclosure was also significantly related to years of marriage, with the scores for couples and for wives (not for husbands) showing a significant negative relationship between self-disclosure and length of marriage. This supported previous research by Jourard (1971a). Although there was a slight negative relationship between marital satisfaction and years of marriage, the relationship was not significant. Perhaps disclosing becomes less important to a couple when they have been married for a long

TABLE 5

Regression of Marital Satisfaction Measures Onto All Variables for Couples

Variable	R	R²	Beta	F
Marriage Adjustment Inventory				
Real attitude similarity	.38	.15	.37	9.02*
Social Penetration Scale	.52	.27	−.35	8.20*
Marital Assessment Questionnaire				
Self-esteem	.45	.20	.35	8.14*
Social Penetration Scale	.53	.28	.33	7.11*
Attitude prediction	.59	.35	−.26	4.81*

Note: Each regression is based on a sample of 51 couples.
  *$p<.01$.

time, know each other well, and are satisfied in their relationship; thus self-disclosure can decrease while marital satisfaction remains stable.

Attitude Similarity and Satisfaction

A major finding of the study involved the relationship of attitude similarity to marital satisfaction. Actual attitude similarity as well as perceived attitude similarity were both highly related to marital satisfaction, and actual or real attitude similarity served as a strong predictor of marital satisfaction on the Marriage Adjustment Inventory in the regression analyses. The latter finding was perhaps a logical extension of Byrne's (1971) research on similarity and attraction, on the assumption that marital satisfaction includes attraction as one important component. Since it was basically uncorrelated with either self-esteem or self-disclosure, attitude similarity proved to be a good independent predictor of marital satisfaction as indicated on one instrument. It was expected that spouses who could accurately predict each other's attitudes would have higher levels of marital satisfaction and/or self-disclosure; however, successful attitude prediction showed no relationship to either of these two major variables.

Wife Blame

One interesting finding involved individuals' assessments of problems that they and their respective mates felt contributed to the total problems experienced by the couples, as measured by the Marriage Adjustment Inventory. There was high agreement between husbands and wives on the problems wives contributed to marriages, $r = .68$, while there was low agreement between husbands and wives on the problems husbands contributed to marriages, $r = .17$. An inspection of the actual means of these four scores revealed that husbands' spouse score was .6 of a scale point higher than self score, while wives' spouse score was .6 of a scale point lower than self score. Thus both sexes blamed more marriage problems on wives. One possible explanation for this assignment of responsibility for marital problems may well reside in the traditional sex roles existing in marriages. Wives have customarily assumed responsibility for keeping marriages functioning smoothly and have often accepted a major share of the "blame" for marital problems, whereas men have less often been targets for criticism. Though this discrepancy will probably change as society moves toward equal rights for men and women, these scores indicate that women still are more likely than men to blame themselves and to be blamed for marital problems.

Scales

The five-item Marital Assessment Questionnaire showed a fairly high correlation with the Marriage Adjustment Inventory, $r = .48$, as well as a consistent relationship with other variables such as self-disclosure. It thus appeared to give a brief but adequate picture of marital satisfaction and could be useful in other testing and counseling situations. The self-esteem measure proved to be a major predictor of marital satisfaction for both individuals and couples. Though the validity of this single-item measure should not be overestimated, a subject's self-report of his or her own self-esteem did appear to relate significantly to other variables, particularly marital satisfaction.

Clinical Applications

Several of the study's findings also lend themselves to clinical application. Since self-disclosure is related to marital satisfaction, and since husbands generally disclose less than wives, training (e.g., role playing, communication exercises) in self-disclosure, especially for husbands, might become an integral component of marital counseling. Would healthy couples who were given self-disclosure training, perhaps as part of a personal growth experience, show greater marital satisfaction? Would such couples retain their self-disclosure levels over time rather than show the typical decline of self-disclosure with length of marriage? As suggested earlier, the Marital Assessment Questionnaire could be used with relative ease to assess present marital satisfaction of a couple beginning treatment.

The blaming of wives for marital problems has potential importance for marriage counseling, since blaming is often a fundamental problem for unhappy couples. Do couples who do more blaming (shown by the difference between self scores and spouse scores on the Marriage Adjustment Inventory) have more marriage problems and therefore lower marital satisfaction? Could couples in which the wife is blamed for marriage problems profit from early counseling intervention that "teaches" each spouse to accept half of the responsibility for both the positives and the negatives in a marriage? The opportunities for field research on self-disclosure and marital satisfaction are impressive.

CONCLUSIONS

This study established the importance of self-disclosure as a variable in marital satisfaction. Results of the analyses were consistent across individuals and couples. Generalizability of these results is enhanced because of the nature of the sample: average married couples without serious identified marital problems.

This study can provide the base for future studies in which the same instruments could be used with similar nonclinical samples and new variables introduced into the design. One question for future research is whether self-disclosure and marital satisfaction are causally related. Most likely, there is a two-way directionality between the two variables, with self-disclosure sometimes increasing marital satisfaction and marital satisfaction sometimes increasing self-disclosure. Self-disclosure is not always rewarding (Levinger & Senn, 1967) and can reduce satisfaction in marriage. Therefore, future studies of self-disclosure and relationships will need to take the discloser's intentions (and content) as well as the listener's receptivity into account when investigating self-disclosure in concrete situations.

REFERENCES

Altman, I. Reciprocity of interpersonal exchange. *Journal for the Theory of Social Behavior,* 1973, *3,* 249-261.

Altman, I., & Taylor, D. A. *Social penetration: The development of interpersonal relationships.* New York: Holt, Rinehart & Winston, 1973.

Burgess, R. L., & Huston, T. L. (Eds.)., *Social exchange in developing relationships.* New York: Academic Press, 1979.

Byrne, D. *The attraction paradigm.* New York: Academic Press, 1971.

Byrne, D., & Blaylock, B. Similarity and assumed similarity of attitudes between husbands and wives. *Journal of Abnormal and Social Psychology,* 1963, *67,* 636-640.

Campbell, D. T., & Stanley, J. C. Experimental and quasi-experimental designs for research on teaching. In N. L. Gage (Ed.), *Handbook of research on teaching.* Chicago: Rand McNally, 1963.

Chelune, G. J. Sex differences, repression-sensitization, and self-disclosure: A behavioral look. *Psychological Reports,* 1977, *40,* 667-670.

Cozby, P. C. Self-disclosure, reciprocity and liking. *Sociometry,* 1972, *35,* 151-160.

Derlega, V. J., Wilson, M., & Chaikin, A. L. Friendship and disclosure reciprocity. *Journal of Personality and Social Psychology,* 1976, *34,* 578-582.

Ehrlich, H. J., & Graeven, D. B. Reciprocal self-disclosure in a dyad. *Journal of Experimental Social Psychology,* 1971, *7,* 389-400.

Feigenbaum, W. M. Reciprocity in self-disclosure within the psychological interview. *Psychological Reports,* 1977, *40,* 15-26.

Gouldner, A. W. The norm of reciprocity: A preliminary statement. *American Sociological Review,* 1960, *25,* 161-179.

Hatfield, E., Utne, M. K., & Traupmann, J. Equity theory and intimate relationships. In R. L. Burgess & T. L. Huston (Eds.), *Social exchange in developing relationships.* New York: Academic Press, 1979.

Homans, G. C. *Social behavior: Its elementary forms.* New York: Harcourt, Brace & World, 1961.

Jourard, S. M. *Self-disclosure: An experimental analysis of the transparent self.* New York: Wiley, 1971. (a)

Jourard, S. M. *The transparent self.* Princeton, N.J.: Van Nostrand, 1971. (b)

Kelley, H. H. *Personal relationships: Their structures and processes.* Hillsdale, N.J.: Erlbaum, 1979.

Komarovsky, M. *Blue-collar marriage.* New York: Random House, 1962.

Komarovsky, M. Patterns of self-disclosure of male undergraduates. *Journal of Marriage and the Family,* 1974, *36,* 677-686.

Levinger, G., & Raush, H. L. (Eds.). *Close relationships: Perspectives on the meaning of intimacy.* Amherst: University of Massachusetts Press, 1977.

Levinger, G. & Senn, D. J. Disclosure of feelings in marriage. *Merrill-Palmer Quarterly,* 1967, *13,* 237-249.

Manson, M., & Lerner, A. *The marriage adjustment inventory.* Los Angeles: Western Psychological Services, 1962.

McGuire, W. J. The yin and yang of progress in social psychology: Seven koan. *Journal of Personality and Social Psychology,* 1973, *26,* 446-456.

Miller, S., Corrales, R., & Wackman, D. B. Recent progress in understanding and facilitating marital communication. *Family Coordinator,* 1975, *24,* 143-152.

Morton, T. L., Alexander, J. F., & Altman, I. Communication and relationship definition. In G. R. Miller (Ed.), *Annual review of communication research* (Vol. 5), Beverly Hills, Calif: Sage, 1976.

Taylor, D. A., & Altman, I. *Intimacy-scaled stimuli for use in studies of interpersonal relationships* (Research Report No. 9, MF022.01.03-1002). Bethesda, Md.: Naval Medical Research Institute, 1966.

Taylor, D. A., & Altman, I. Self-disclosure as a function of reward-cost outcomes. *Sociometry,* 1975, *38,* 18-31.

Worthy, M., Gary, A. L., & Kahn, G. M. Self-disclosure as an exchange process. *Journal of Personality and Social Psychology,* 1969, *13,* 59-63.

6 Altruism and Helping Behavior

SINCE LATANÉ AND DARLEY'S seminal series of studies investigating the reasons why by-standers often fail to render aid to those in distress, a growing number of social psychologists have begun to study altruism and helping behavior. The original Latané and Darley studies were stimulated by the unfortunate murder of Kitty Genovese who was killed early one morning in Queens, New York, while at least thirty-eight neighbors did nothing to help. Latané and Darley proposed a decision-tree model that attempted to specify the situational and personal considerations that potential benefactors evaluate when trying to determine if help should be given. Subsequent works, particularly by Piliavin, Dovidio, Gaertner, and Clark (1982), have expanded the number of factors taken into account by such models, but the basic notion—that the decision to provide aid is but the final step in an extended series of decisions—has been retained.

Although Latané and Darley and the Piliavins and their colleagues have focused upon the decision-making process per se in their works, other social psychologists have sought to determine the underlying motivations for helping others. Alternative views have been proposed by two of the major researchers in the field, and the first two selections of this chapter present their opposing views.

The first article in this chapter is the most recent of a series of studies that Robert Cialdini and his colleagues have been pursuing for the past ten years, investigating the possibility that acts of helping are made primarily for the egoistic benefit of the benefactor and only secondarily for the recipient of the aid. Early work by Cialdini, Darby, and Vincent (1973) suggested that people help in order to relieve their own negative affect that has been aroused either by transgressing against another or by simply observing the suffering of another person. Subsequent work by Cialdini and Kenrick (1976) demonstrated that this response to a negative mood state requires that the individual be sufficiently well socialized to understand that helping is a viable means of obtaining secondary reinforcements. In the present article, Baumann, Cialdini, and Kenrick attempt to show that helping is equivalent to other forms of self-gratification, to bolster their contention that the prime motive for aiding others is not the help that is provided but rather the relief of the helper's own negative feelings.

In the second article, Batson, Duncan, Ackerman, Buckley, and Birch argue that altruistic actions may be displayed primarily for the purpose of relieving the distress of another, without concern for any benefits that helpers might realize as a consequence of their acts. C. Daniel Batson and his collaborators suggest that it is not the act itself that is altruistic or egoistic, but rather the end-state goal of the action that determines the classification that should be attributed to an act. Although much of the current thinking about altruism assumes that purely selfless, altruistic acts are at best rare and possibly nonexistent, Batson has accumulated an impressive set of data that clearly imply that at least some aid is rendered to others due to a truly altruistic motivation.

The final selection in this chapter addresses a somewhat different aspect of situations in which help is given. For altruism to take place, there must be someone in need of assistance, and Arie Nadler, Jeff Fisher, and various associates have been investigating the impact that receiving aid from others has upon the recipient of an altruistic act. In a previous review paper, Fisher, Nadler, and Whitcher-Alagna (1982) discussed various reasons why the receipt of aid may have negative consequences for both the benefactor and the recipient: perceptions of participating in an inequitable relationship, the arousal of reactance, attributions of ulterior motives, and threats to the self-esteem of the recipient. The present research by Nadler, Fisher, and Ben-Itzhak examines the effects of single versus multiple acts of helping on ego-relevant or ego-irrelevant tasks by a close friend on the recipients' affective responses and self-evaluations. The idea that altruistic acts may be mixed blessings that yield both positive and negative consequences, even when the benefactor's intentions are purely altruistic, represents the latest research topic in the field of altruism and helping behavior.

Altruism as Hedonism: Helping and Self-Gratification as Equivalent Responses

Donald J. Baumann, Robert B. Cialdini, and Douglas T. Kenrick

An experiment was conducted to test the proposition that for adults, altruism and self-gratification are functional equivalents. It was predicted on the basis of this proposition that the effects of mood state on altruism would be parallel to the effects of mood on self-gratification. In support of this prediction, three separate findings from the mood-altruism literature were paralleled in the present study's investigation of the effects of mood on self-gratification. Specifically, it was found that (a) self-gratification increased under conditions of happy or sad mood; (b) for subjects in a sad mood, altruistic activity canceled the enhanced tendency for self-gratification; and (c) for subjects in a happy mood, altruistic activity did not cancel the enhanced tendency for self-gratification. Discussion focuses on the convergent evidence from the altruism literature and self-gratification literature that adult altruism functions as self-reward.

Cialdini and his associates (Cialdini, Darby, & Vincent, 1973; Cialdini & Kenrick, 1976; Cialdini, Kenrick, & Baumann, in press; Kenrick, Baumann, & Cialdini,

"Altruism as Hedonism: Helping and Self-gratification as Equivalent Responses" by D.J. Baumann, R.B. Cialdini & D.T. Kenrick, 1981, *Journal of Personality and Social Psychology, 40*, pp. 1039-1046. Copyright 1981 by the American Psychological Assn. Reprinted by permission of the publisher and authors.

1979) have taken the position that adult altruism is a form of hedonism. In this view, benevolent activity has been conditioned via the socialization process to be self-gratifying; therefore, individuals often behave charitably in order to provide themselves with reward. For these researchers, affect has played a prominent role in documenting the case for altruism as self-gratification. In an initial article, Cialdini et al.

(1973) argued for two propositions. First, on the basis of the results of prior studies, they maintained that a U-shaped relationship exists between temporary mood state and adult helping: Experiences likely to produce either happy or sad affective states in adults increase helping. Second, they proposed a negative state relief model to account for the direct relationship between sadness and benevolence: Helping increases under conditions of temporary sadness because altruism, as a self-gratifier, serves to alleviate the depressed mood state. Helping is seen as instrumental to the relief of negative mood.[1] Let us consider the existing evidence for each proposition.

THE U-SHAPED CURVE

The altruism literature provides solid ground for the belief that induced positive and negative moods lead to increased helping. Studies have unequivocally established that experiences likely to produce positive moods increase helping (see Cialdini et al., in press, and Rosenhan, Karylowski, Salovey, & Hargis, in press, for reviews). Studies have also demonstrated that for adults, a variety of negative-mood-inducing procedures (see Cialdini & Kenrick, 1976, and Krebs, 1970, for reviews) can lead to increased helping. Studies of helping by young children, however, typically have not demonstrated this relationship (Isen, Horn, & Rosenhan, 1973, Studies 1 and 3; Moore, Underwood, & Rosenhan, 1973; Rosenhan, Underwood, & Moore, 1974; Underwood, Froming, & Moore, 1977). This point will be addressed more fully below. Presently, we only wish to argue that, at least for adults, negative mood leads to increased helping and that for both adults and children positive mood leads to increased helping.

AN INSTRUMENTAL MODEL FOR NEGATIVE MOOD

The second proposition of the negative state relief model holds that because altruism is self-reinforcing in adults, helping while in a negative mood is instrumental to the removal of the mood state. Support for this instrumental view comes from several sources. Cialdini et al. (1973) argued that since altruism has been shown to have reinforcing properties (Weiss, Boyer, Lombardo, & Stitch, 1973; Weiss, Buchanan, Alstatt, & Lombardo, 1971), it is employed by individuals who wish to make themselves feel better. In a test of this notion, adult subjects were exposed to a negative-mood-inducing experience (performing or witnessing a transgression) and were then requested to perform a helping act. For half of these subjects, a gratifying event (the receipt of money or praise) occurred prior to the helping request. Results showed that the negative mood induction led to enhanced helping except in those subjects who also experienced the gratifying event. The authors argued that the rewarding event had canceled these later subjects' need to use the gratifying nature of altruism to relieve their negative mood.

Using the perceived reward value of the helping act as the critical factor in determining an individual's willingness to help, Weyant (1978) has provided further support for the instrumental view put forth here. Weyant suggested that the reward value of helping is a function of the perceived costs and benefits associated with the act. Weyant predicted and found that only when the costs of helping were low and the benefits high did individuals attempt to remove a negative mood state via prosocial action. Further, when both the costs and the benefits of helping were high, or low, helping while in a negative mood did not differ from a neutral mood control group. Finally, Weyant found that when the costs of helping were high and the benefits low, individuals in a negative mood helped less than controls. These results are completely in line with the instrumental view of the negative state relief model: Individuals help in a negative mood when the hedonic consequences of the act are sufficient to remove the mood. If increased costs or lowered benefits associated with the helping act prevent a response that is instrumental to the alleviation of negative mood, helping will not occur. In the case of Weyant's subjects, increased helping under negative mood was prevented by experimentally removing the ability of the act to serve as a self-gratifier.

Additional support for an instrumental interpretation of the effects of negative mood on helping comes from studies that have viewed altruism from a developmental perspective. Recall that although adults have been reliably shown to be helpful when in a negative mood, young children have not. Cialdini and Kenrick (1976) and Kenrick et al. (1979) sought to reconcile these conflicting results within the negative state relief model. These authors argued that young children have not completed the socialization process and as such have not been fully conditioned to find altruism rewarding in itself. Hence, they will not use it to relieve a negative mood. In support of this contention, it has been demonstrated that with increasing age, helping becomes a progressively greater response of sad subjects (Cialdini & Kenrick, 1976). Moreover, only when helping leads to external reinforcement (e.g., social approval) will saddened young children engage in helping activity to a greater degree than will neutral mood controls (Kenrick et al., 1979). Hence, it appears that benevolence may be

used by young children in the service of mood relief, provided that the act is made to be self-gratifying through its generation of external reward.

FUNCTIONAL EQUIVALENCE

Throughout the foregoing analysis, one of the basic tenets of the model provided by Cialdini et al. (1973) has been stressed: There is a functional equivalence between altruism and self-gratification. Therefore, an additional proposition can be derived from the negative state relief model: Because adult altruism acts as self-reward, the relationship between mood state and helping should be similar to the relationship between mood state and self-gratification. Although our own findings and those of other researchers have converged to support this view, the basic assumption of a parallel between self-gratification and altruism has yet to be directly tested. Three specific arguments in favor of the functional equivalence of adult altruism and self-gratification as interchangeable forms of reinforcement can be advanced. The present study provides a test of each of these arguments.

First, it can be reasoned that since adult altruism has been shown to increase as a function of direct positive and negative mood induction procedures, the same relationship should hold for self-gratification. It is therefore hypothesized that relative to a neutral mood control group, direct positive and negative inductions should result in increased self-gratification.

Second, it can be argued that since the effects of negative mood on helping appear to be instrumental, the same relationship should hold between negative mood and self-gratification. The logic of the negative state relief model provides the structure for a test of this view. Recall that in the Cialdini et al. (1973) experiment, for half of the subjects an event imbued with positive reinforcement characteristics (money or praise) was interposed between the manipulation of negative mood and the request for help. This nonaltruistic gratifier reduced benevolence to control levels. Receiving a gratifier removed the enhanced tendency for altruism among negative mood subjects. The present experiment proposes to test the converse of this finding: Acting altruistically should remove the enhanced tendency for self-gratification among negative mood subjects.

Our third argument concerns positive mood. Although we see altruism as functionally equivalent to self-gratification whether the subject is in a negative or a positive mood, the sequential interaction of altruism and self-gratification for individuals in a positive mood would not be expected to be the same. When an individual is in a negative mood, we hypothesize that self-gratification should serve to alleviate the unpleasant state. Once a neutral mood has been restored in a negative mood subject, subsequent instances of self-gratification (or altruism serving an equivalent function) should occur at about the same level they would for control subjects. Since altruism for an individual in a positive mood should generate additional positive affect, self-gratification should not serve a similar function here (i.e., to "restore" neutral mood). Thus, altruism and self-gratification should not have the same canceling effect for positive mood that we predict for negative mood. The results of the only study that we are aware of that allowed positive mood subjects to act charitably and self-gratify within the same context are in keeping with this suggestion. Rosenhan et al. (1974) found that the opportunity to self-gratify did not cancel the enhanced fre-

quency of helping behavior by their positive mood subjects (grade school children).[2] Therefore, based on the above analysis, we hypothesized that, unlike the circumstance of negative mood, an altruistic event interposed between positive mood and the opportunity to self-gratify should not reduce the heightened tendency to self-gratify.

METHOD

Subjects

Participants were 80 undergraduates (33 males, 47 females) who volunteered for this experiment as part of the requirements for an introductory psychology course. One subject was dropped from the analysis because of his suspicions regarding the nature of the experiment.

Procedure

Subjects were brought individually to an experimental room containing a desk, two chairs, a lamp, and a table. Subjects were told by a first experimenter that they would be participating in a two-part experiment designed to investigate the relationship between memory and perception. Subjects were informed that the experiment was specifically designed to investigate the effects of particular memory exercises on perception. They were further informed that the experimenter they were currently with would be working with them on the memory portion of the experiment and that a second experimenter would later be working with them on the perception segment. A partial blind procedure resulted from this tactic. In addition, each experimenter knew of the treatment he or she was to administer only when it was time to administer it.

Mood manipulation. Subjects were randomly assigned to a 5-min. positive, neutral, or negative mood induction procedure.[3] Approximately one third of all subjects were asked to reminisce about an experience that made them feel sad (negative mood), and approximately one third were asked to reminisce about an event that made them feel happy (positive mood). After 2 min., subjects were asked (dependent on condition) to recall and reminisce about a second happy or sad experience. Subjects were then asked to spend a final minute recalling the experience deemed by the experimenter to have had the most impact on mood. The neutral mood subjects were asked first to recall their route to school that day and second to imagine making a telephone call requesting the time of day. The experimenter then chose the more neutral topic for the subject to review during the final minute of the mood induction procedure.

Upon completion of the memory task, subjects were asked to fill out two scales. The first scale, a mood manipulation check, required subjects to rate on a 7-point scale their current mood state relative to their mood prior to the task. The scale category labels ranged from "a great deal happier" to "a great deal sadder." A second 7-point scale, included only to ensure believability of the memory task, required subjects to rate how well they felt their memory was functioning.

Interpolated task. At this point, and after the first experimenter left the room, the second experimenter entered and began the portion of the experiment ostensibly related to perception. Subjects were randomly exposed to one of two experimental conditions. The first condition (the altruistic task condition) involved participation in a stimulus discrimination task imbued with al-

truistic character and, therefore, presumably having a self-rewarding effect. Subjects in this condition were told: "This part of the study involves the development of a new technique which will help individuals who are gradually losing their eyesight learn to observe the world about them more efficiently so they can function better with their visual handicap."[4]

The other condition (the nonaltruistic task condition) also involved participation in a stimulus discrimination task and was designed to be unrelated to charitability. Subjects in this condition were told: "This part of the study involves the development of a technique that will enable us to better understand how individuals learn to observe the world about them."

Following these manipulations all subjects were required to decide, on four separate trials and for four separate pairs of figures, which figure in each pair was more complex (figures were drawn and judged by an artist to be of equal complexity).

Opportunity to self-gratify. The first trial was described as a practice trial. Following the second trial, subjects were provided with the opportunity for noncontingent self-reward. This was accomplished through informing subjects as follows: "Since we want to pay for your help, we are providing you with the opportunity to take some tokens for your responses. Tokens can be redeemed at the conclusion of the experiment for a prize. The more tokens you take the more valuable the prize. You can take up to seven tokens; you can take all, none, or some. How many would you like?" Subjects were then offered a box containing seven tokens. There was no mention of any connection between the correctness of their responses and the number of tokens they might take. The number of tokens subjects took from the box was unobtrusively recorded as the dependent measure. Following the recording of the dependent measure, subjects participated in the final two discrimination trials and were then debriefed. Debriefing consisted of allowing subjects to write open-ended statements about what they felt was the purpose of the experiment and their suspicions, if any. Subjects were then probed for suspicions, told the true nature of the experiment, and allowed to exchange their tokens for free fast-food coupons.

Independent variables. Subjects were randomly assigned to two conditions, mood (positive vs. neutral vs. negative) and type of task (altruistic vs. nonaltruistic). Sex of subjects was also varied.

Dependent variables. The major dependent measure was the number of tokens subjects took following the second trial. The manipulation checks consisted of subjects' responses to the mood scale and their statements regarding the purpose of the experiment.

RESULTS

Analysis of variance revealed that there were no significant effects for sex, except a marginal tendency on the part of females ($M = 4.95$) to self-gratify more than males ($M = 4.06$), $F(1, 73) = 3.45$, $p < .07$. Thus, all means are presented collapsed over the sex factor.

Manipulation Checks

The results of an initial analysis of variance revealed the predicted main effect for the mood induction procedure, $F(2, 73) = 22.97$, $p < .001$. However, subsequent planned comparisons suggested that although negative mood subjects ($M = 4.33$) differed significantly from neutral mood controls ($M = 2.72$), $F(1, 73) = 30.41$, $p < .001$, positive mood subjects ($M = 2.60$) did not, $F(1, 73) < 1$. We therefore inspected our mood data in order to determine whether there were occasions when a subject's self-reported mood was grossly at odds with the intended direction of our mood manipulation procedure. This process resulted in the removal of 5 subjects (3 in nonaltruistic task-negative mood, 1 in nonaltruistic task-neutral mood, and 1 in altruistic task-neutral mood) whose self-reported mood data differed by 3 scale points (on a 7-point scale) from the mood condition to which they were assigned. Planned comparisons of the remaining 74 subjects resulted in a significant effect between negative ($M = 4.96$) and neutral ($M = 2.86$) mood, $F(1, 68) = 47.87$, $p < .001$, and between positive ($M = 2.60$) and neutral mood, $F(1, 68) = 3.21$, $p < .04$ (one-tailed).

There was no explicit manipulation check performed on the type of test factor. However, because of subjects' open-ended written statements concerning their perceptions of the stated purpose of the experiment, we could see whether these statements described the altruistic nature of the task. Results of coding these responses showed that 33% of the subjects in the altruistic task condition spontaneously mentioned the helpful nature of the experiment whereas no subject in the nonaltruistic task condition mentioned this factor. A Fisher's exact test was performed on these data, which showed a significant effect, $p < .001$.

Self-Gratification

Since we made specific predictions concerning the amount of self-gratification that would be expected given our functional equivalence argument, we performed the following a priori contrasts (Hays, 1963): First, we tested our initial prediction that, relative to neutral mood, both positive and negative moods lead to increased self-gratification. This contrast compared, within the nonaltruistic task condition, the combined positive and negative mood groups with the neutral mood control group. The outcome of this comparison was marginally significant, $F(1, 68) = 3.61, p < .06$. Although this effect misses conventional levels of significance, it was predicted on the basis of considerable prior evidence; therefore, the reader may wish to apply a one-tailed test criterion here. Second, we performed a general contrast that simultaneously tested our second prediction that, relative to a neutral event, an interposed altruistic event would reduce to control levels the tendency for individuals in a negative mood to self-gratify and our third prediction that self-gratification in a positive mood would not be reduced by an altruistic interposing event. This contrast pitted the nonaltruistic task-negative mood, nonaltruistic task positive mood, and the altruistic task-positive mood groups against the altruistic task-negative mood group and the neutral mood control groups. Results showed that this contrast was significant, $F(1, 68) = 5.35, p < .02$. The means for these groups are presented in Table 1.

In addition, we also conducted specific tests of our second and third predictions. The test of our second prediction involved a contrast that pitted the nonaltruistic task-negative mood group against the combination of the altruistic task-negative mood group and the neutral mood control groups. The comparison resulted in a significant effect, $F(1, 68) = 5.35, p < .02$. In addition, the two negative mood groups were tested against each other. This test was also significant, $F(1, 68) = 4.47, p < .05$.

The specific test of our third prediction was embodied in a contrast in which the nonaltruistic task-positive mood group was compared with the combination of the altruistic task-positive mood group and the neutral mood control groups. As expected, this effect was not significant, $F(1, 68) < 1$. The comparison between the two positive mood groups was also not significant, $F(1, 68) < 1$.

TABLE 1

Mean Number of Tokens Taken by Type of Interposed Event and Mood Conditions

| | Mood | | | | | |
| | Positive | | Neutral | | Negative | |
Type of task	M	n	M	n	M	n
Nonaltruistic	5.00	16	3.69	13	6.10	10
Altruistic	5.07	14	4.30	10	3.63	11

Some readers may be concerned that the above effects occurred only when the five incongruent mood subjects were removed from the data. This was not the case. Our initial analyses performed on the data for all subjects revealed findings almost identical to those with the five incongruent subjects removed.[5] These tests confirmed our initial prediction that positive and negative moods lead to greater self-gratification than does neutral mood, $F(1, 73) = 5.18$, $p < .03$, our second, general prediction, $F(1, 73) = 5.86$, $p < .03$, as well as our specific predictions. Tests of these specific predictions revealed the following: (a) The nonaltruistic task-negative mood groups were significantly different from the combination of the neutral mood control groups and the altruistic task-negative mood group, $F(1, 73) = 5.61$, $p < .02$. (b) The two negative mood groups significantly differed from each other, $F(1, 73) = 4.33$, $p < .05$. (c) The nonaltruistic task-positive mood group was not significantly different from the combination of the neutral mood control groups and the altruistic task-positive mood group, and the two positive mood groups did not differ from each other (both $Fs < 1$). The reader should be apprised that because two sets of analyses were performed on the data, with 79 and 74 subjects, respectively, the possibility of alpha inflation exists to some degree.

DISCUSSION

Taken as a whole, the results of this investigation provide good support for our contention that adult altruism is the functional equivalent of self-gratification. Three separate effects involving mood and self-gratification in the present study were found to be similar in form to those effects characteristic of the mood altruism literature.

First, we observed a curvilinear relationship between mood and adult self-gratification (in the nonaltruistic task conditions) comparable to the U-shaped function defining the relationship between mood state and adult altruism (cf. Cialdini & Kenrick, 1976, for a review). Temporary states of happiness and sadness produced elevated levels of self-gratification as they had for altruism in the prior literature.

Second, previous work (Cialdini et al., 1973; Kidd & Berkowitz, 1976) had shown that the enhanced benevolence of adults exposed to negative mood procedures could be reduced to control levels by the interpolation of a self-gratifying event between the negative mood induction and the opportunity to help. Symmetrically, the present data indicate that the enhanced self-gratification of negative mood subjects can be eliminated by the interpolation of an altruistic event between the negative mood induction and the opportunity to self-gratify. This finding suggests the interchangeability of altruism and self-gratification for adults. It also implies an instrumental basis for increased self-gratification following sad mood inductions. The self-rewarding activity represents an attempt to dispel the negative mood. When some other gratifier, in this case the knowledge that one's actions have helped the blind, cancels the affective negativity, the increased need for further self-gratification is removed.

Finally, our analysis of the effects of positive mood on helping and self-gratification suggests that these behaviors would not have mutually canceling effects for positive affect subjects. While either self-gratification or altruism is seen to restore mood to control levels for those individuals in a negative mood, the converse was not expected to hold under positive mood. Accordingly, the introduction of an altruistic (and presumably rewarding) event did not nullify the tendency for high levels of self-reward within the happy condition, as it had for saddened subjects.

Some Parallels from the Developmental Literature

We began this paper by discussing some basic assumptions of the original model Cialdini et al. (1973) had developed to explain altruism in subjects exposed to negative-mood-inducing experiences. At this point it is fruitful to review several related assumptions that have served as underpinnings for our subsequent research in this area. As we have stated throughout the present article, altruism is seen to function as the equivalent of self-gratification in adults. For children, however, altruism has not yet acquired a self-gratifying function (Cialdini & Kenrick, 1976; Kenrick et al., 1979). We have assumed that the mood-altruism link found in adults is built on a basic relationship between mood and self-gratification—one that should be present in children as well as adults. Several findings from the developmental literature support this supposition.

Self-gratification. The present research demonstrates a U-shaped relationship between mood and self-reward in adults. Previous evidence on self-gratification in children is in line with the U-shaped model we have suggested to describe the relationship between mood and self-reward (or altruism) in adults. In a number of studies where affect was directly manipulated in children, Rosenhan and his colleagues (Rosenhan et al., 1974; Underwood, Moore, & Rosenhan, 1973) demonstrated that, compared with neutral controls, both positive and negative moods lead to increased self-gratification in children. The present study pro-

vides corroborative support for our assumption that the same relationship holds for adults.

Instrumental nature of self-gratification. The second hypothesis supported by the present research, and by the earlier research of Cialdini et al. (1973), is that self-gratification and altruism serve as (interchangeable) means of alleviating an unpleasant affective state in adults. Likewise, evidence from the self-gratification literature suggests that self-gratification by children in a negative mood is instrumental to the removal of that aversive state. A number of authors (Masters, 1972; Masters & Peskay, 1972; Rosenhan et al., 1974; Underwood et al., 1973) have argued from their data that increased self-gratification following negative mood induction is mediated by a "self-therapy" process that is an attempt at comforting oneself.

Positive mood and self-gratification. Our data provide an additional parallel between the adult literature and the findings that Rosenhan and his colleagues have obtained in their investigation of altruism and self-reward in children. The fact that altruism by our positive mood subjects did not eradicate the tendency for subsequent self-gratification is in line with the findings of Rosenhan et al. (1974). Further, it is clear from a number of other investigations that the relationship between positive mood and helping is not simply the mirror image of that between negative mood and helping. We will briefly note two of these asymmetries here.

First, negative mood leads to enhanced benevolence in adults but not in children, whereas positive moods lead to heightened altruism in both adults and children. Second, altruism by subjects in a negative mood appears to depend importantly on the potential instrumental costs and benefits of the altruistic behavior, whereas altruism by those in a positive mood does not (Weyant, 1978). Compared with neutral mood subjects, the positive mood subjects in Weyant's study were willing to act altruistically regardless of the potential costs and benefits of the helping act, whereas the negative mood subjects were willing to provide help only when it was low in cost and high in potential benefits.

An exciting task now facing researchers in this area is to determine the nature of the mediating processes underlying the positive mood helping relationship. While the present data cohere nicely with those of a number of earlier findings (Cialdini et al., 1973; Cialdini & Kenrick, 1976; Kenrick et al., 1979) to support the assumption that altruism by negative mood subjects is an attempt to remove the unpleasant affect, no clear mediational picture emerges in the positive mood literature.

As we stated in the introduction, we believe altruism and self-gratification are equivalent operations. Following a negative mood induction, either serves the same function (an instrumental one) in returning mood to a neutral point. In the case of positive mood, the function of altruism and/or self-gratification is not so clear; however, it appears that both operate similarly. Of course, we would not expect altruism and self-gratification to function equivalently when the net benefits associated with one are greater than those associated with the other. In general, though, it is our expectation that mood inductions that affect the incidence of self-gratification similarly affect the incidence of adult altruism.

NOTES

1. Cialdini and his co-workers have been careful to distinguish among types of negative affect in their relation to helping. Only such negative

moods as temporary sadness or depression are seen to lead to increased helping. Unpleasant moods such as frustration and anger, which are typically reduced through aggressionlike responses, are not predicted to enhance benevolence.

2. An instrumental model of altruism under conditions of positive mood, in which helping occurs to maintain positive affect, might suggest that such canceling would occur. However, the existing literature (e.g., Rosenhan et al., 1974; Weyant, 1978) seems to suggest that an instrumental model does not characterize helping under conditions of positive mood.

3. This technique was a modified version of one developed by Mischel, Ebbesen, and Zeiss (1972) for use with children. It has been shown to be effective in producing differences in adults' and children's altruistic responding (Cialdini & Kenrick, 1976; Moore et al., 1973; Rosenhan et al., 1974) and children's self-gratification (Rosenhan et al., 1974; Underwood et al., 1973).

4. This manipulation was based on an experimental procedure successfully used by Pisarowicz (Note 1).

5. The cell means for all 79 subjects were as follows: 5.00 (nonaltruistic task-positive mood), 3.42 (nonaltruistic task-neutral mood), 5.92 (nonaltruistic task-negative mood), 5.07 (altruistic task positive mood), 4.54 (altruistic task-neutral mood), and 3.63 (altruistic task-negative mood).

REFERENCE NOTE

1. Pisarowicz, J.A. *Self-reinforcement following altruistic behavior.* Paper presented at the meeting of the Rocky Mountain Psychological Association, Phoenix, Arizona, May 1976.

REFERENCES

Cialdini, R. B., Darby, B. L., & Vincent, J. E. Transgression and altruism: A case for hedonism. *Journal of Experimental Social Psychology,* 1973, *9,* 502-516.

Cialdini, R. B., & Kenrick, D. T. Altruism as hedonism: A social development perspective on the relationship of negative mood state and helping. *Journal of Personality and Social Psychology,* 1976, *34,* 907-914.

Cialdini, R. B., Kenrick, D. T., & Baumann, D. J. Effects of mood on prosocial behavior in children and adults. In Eisenberg-Berg, N. (Ed.), The development of prosocial behavior. New York: Academic Press, in press.

Hays, W. L., Statistics for psychologists. New York: Holt, Rinehart & Winston, 1963.

Isen, A.M., Horn, N., & Rosenhan, D. L. Effects of success and failure on children's generosity. Journal of Personality and Social Psychology, 1973, 27, 239-247.

Kenrick, D. T., Baumann, D. J., & Cialdini, R. B. A step in the socialization of altruism as hedonism: Effects of negative mood on children's generosity under public and private conditions. Journal of Personality and Social Psychology, 1979, 37, 747-755.

Kidd, R. F., & Berkowitz, L. Dissonance, self-concept, and helpfulness. Journal of Personality and Social Psychology, 1976, 33, 613-622.

Krebs, D. I. Altruism: An examination of the concept and a review of the literature. Psychological Bulletin, 1970, 73, 258-302.

Masters, J. C. Effects of success, failure, and reward outcome upon contingent and noncontingent self-reinforcement. Developmental Psychology, 1972, 7, 110-118.

Masters, J. C., & Peskay, J. Effects of race, socio-economic status, and success or failure upon contingent and noncontingent self-reinforcement in children. Developmental Psychology, 1972, 7 139-145.

Mischel, W., Ebbesen, E. B., & Zeiss, A. R. Cognitive and attentional mechanisms in delay of gratification. Journal of Personality and Social Psychology, 1972, 21, 204-218.

Moore, B., Underwood, B., & Rosenhan, D. L. Affect and altruism. Developmental Psychology, 1973, 8, 99-104.

Rosenhan, D. L., Karylowski, J., Salovey, P., & Hargis, K. Emotion and altruism. In J. P. Rushton & R. M. Sorrentino (Eds.), Altruism and helping behavior. Hillsdale, N.J.: Erlbaum, in press.

Rosenhan, D. L., Underwood, B., & Moore, B. Affect moderates self-gratification and altruism. Journal of Personality and Social Psychology, 1974, 30, 546-552.

Underwood, B., Froming, W. J., & Moore, B. S. Mood, attention, and altruism: A search for mediating variables. Developmental Psychology, 1977, 13, 541-542.

Underwood, B., Moore, B. S., & Rosenhan, D. I. Affect and self-gratification. Developmental Psychology, 1973, 8, 209-214.

Weiss, R. F., Boyer, J. L., Lombardo, J. P., & Stitch, M. H. Altruistic drive and altruistic reinforcement. Journal of Personality and Social Psychology, 1973, 25, 390-400.

Weiss, R. F., Buchanan, W., Alstatt, L., & Lombardo, J. P. Altruism is rewarding. Science, 1971, 171, 1262-1263.

Weyant, J. M. Effects of mood states, costs, and benefits on helping. Journal of Personality and Social Psychology, 1978, 36, 1167-1169.

Is Empathic Emotion a Source of Altruistic Motivation?

C. Daniel Batson, Bruce D. Duncan, Paul Ackerman,
Terese Buckley, and Kimberly Birch

It has been suggested that empathy leads to altruistic rather than egoistic motivation to help. This hypothesis was tested by having subjects watch another female undergraduate receive electric shocks and then giving them a chance to help her by taking the remaining shocks themselves. In each of two experiments, subjects' level of empathic emotion (low versus high) and their ease of escape from continuing to watch the victim suffer if they did not help (easy versus difficult) were manipulated in a 2 × 2 design. We reasoned that if empathy led to altruistic motivation, subjects feeling a high degree of empathy for the victim should be as ready to help when escape without helping was easy as when it was difficult. But if empathy led to egoistic motivation, subjects feeling empathy should be more ready to help when escape was difficult than when it was easy. Results of each experiment followed the former pattern when empathy was high and the latter pattern when empathy was low, supporting the hypothesis that empathy leads to altruistic rather than egoistic motivation to help.

Evidence indicates that feeling empathy for the person in need is an important motivator of helping (cf. Aderman & Berkowitz, 1970; Aronfreed & Paskal, cited in Aronfreed, 1970; Coke, Batson, & McDavis, 1978; Harris & Huang, 1973; Krebs, 1975; Mehrabian & Epstein, 1972). In the past few years, a number of researchers (Aronfreed, 1970; Batson, Darley, & Coke, 1978; Hoffman, 1975; Krebs, 1975) have hypothesized that this motivation might be truly altruistic, that is, directed toward the end-state goal of reducing the other's distress. If the empathy-altruism hypothesis is correct, it would have broad theoretical implications, for few if any major theories of motivation allow for the possibility of truly altruistic motivation (cf. Bolles, 1975, for a review). Current theories tend to be egoistic; they are built on the assumption that everything we do is ultimately directed toward the end-state goal of benefiting ourselves.

The egoistic orientation of modern psychology should not be dismissed lightly; it has prevailed for decades, and it can easily account for what might appear to be altruistic motivation arising from empathic emotion. To illustrate: You may answer the question of why you helped someone in other-directed, altruistic terms—you felt sorry for that person and wished to reduce his or her distress. But this apparently altruistic concern to reduce another's distress may not have been the end-state goal of your action but rather an intermediate means to the ultimate end of reducing *your own* distress. Your own distress could have arisen not only from the unpleasant emotions you experienced as a result of knowing that the other person was suffering (shock, disgust, fear, or grief) but from the increase in unpleasant emotion you anticipated if you did not help (guilt or shame). Interpreted in this way, your helping was not altruistic. It was an instrumental egoistic response. You acted to reduce the other person's distress because that reduced your own distress.

If we allow that apparently altruistic helping may be no more than an instrumental egoistic response, and we believe that we must, then there is no clear empirical evidence that empathic emotion leads to altruistic motivation to help. The difficulty in providing evidence is, of course, that egoism and altruism are motivational concepts, and we cannot directly observe motivation, only behavior. If we are to provide empirical evidence that empathic emotion leads to altruistic motivation, we need to identify some point at which the egoistic and altruistic interpretations differ at a be-

We would like to thank Edward Morrow, Elaine Alexander, Theresa Lahey, Paula Fremerman, and Martha Rosette for their assistance in making the videotapes used in these experiments. Jack Brehm, Jay Coke, Rick Gibbons, and Mary Vanderplas made helpful comments on an earlier draft of this mauscript.
"Is Empathic Emotion a Source of Altruistic Motivation?" by C.D. Batson, B.D. Duncan, P. Ackerman, T. Buckley & K. Birch, 1981, *Journal of Personality and Social Psychology, 40,* pp. 290-302. Copyright 1981 by the American Psychological Assn. Reprinted by permission of the publisher and authors.

havioral level. If no such point can be found, then we must conclude that the claim that empathy evokes altruistic motivation is of no real theoretical significance.

CONCEPTUAL DISTINCTION BETWEEN EGOISM AND ALTRUISM

In an attempt to find a point of behavioral difference, it is important, first, to be clear about the points of conceptual difference. Therefore, let us be explicit about what we mean by egoistic and altruistic motivation for helping. As we shall use the terms, a person's helping is egoistic to the degree that he or she helps from a desire for personal gain (e.g., material rewards, praise, or self-esteem) or a desire to avoid personal pain (e.g., punishment, social castigation, private guilt, or shame). That is, *egoistically motivated helping is directed toward the end-state goal of increasing the helper's own welfare.* In contrast, a person's helping is altruistic to the degree that he or she helps from a desire to reduce the distress or increase the benefit of the person in need. That is, *altruistically motivated helping is directed toward the end-state goal of increasing the other's welfare.*

This conceptual distinction between egoism and altruism leads to three observations: (a) Helping, as a behavior, can be either egoistically or altruistically motivated; it is the end-state goal, not the behavior, that distinguishes an act as altruistic. (b) Motivation for helping may be a mixture of altruism and egoism; it need not be solely or even primarily altruistic to have an altruistic component. (c) Increasing the other's welfare is both necessary and sufficient to attain an altruistic end-state goal. To the degree that helping is altruistically rather than egoistically motivated, increas-

ing the other's welfare is not an intermediate, instrumental response directed toward increasing one's own welfare; it is an end in itself. Although one's own welfare may be increased by altruistically motivated helping (for example, it may produce feelings of personal satisfaction or relief), personal gain must be an unintended by-product and not the goal of the behavior. This conception of altruism and of the distinction between it and egoism seem quite consistent not only with Auguste Comte's (1875) initial use of the term but also with modern dictionary definitions, for example, "unselfish concern for the welfare of others."

EMPIRICAL DISTINCTION BETWEEN EGOISM AND ALTRUISM

Equipped with this conceptual distinction, we may turn to the problem of making an empirical distinction between egoistic and altruistic motivation for helping. As we have said, all we can directly observe is the behavior, helping. The challenge is somehow to use the behavior as a basis for inferring whether the motivation underlying it is egoistic or altruistic.

Batson and Coke (in press) have recently proposed a technique for doing this. Building on the work of Piliavin and Piliavin (Note 1), they point out that the effect on helping of a cost variable—the cost of escaping from the need situation without helping—should be different, depending on whether the bystander's motivation is egoistic or altruistic. If the bystander's motivation is egoistic, his or her goal is to reduce personal distress caused by seeing the other suffer. This goal can be reached either by helping, and so removing the cause of one's distress, or by escaping (physically or psychologically) and so removing contact with the cause; either behavior can lead to the desired goal. The likelihood that the egoistically motivated bystander will choose to help should, therefore, be a direct function of the costs associated with choosing to escape. These costs include the physical effort involved in escaping from the need situation (often minimal) and, more importantly, the feelings of distress, guilt, and shame anticipated as a result of knowing that the person in need is continuing to suffer. Thus, if the bystander were egoistically motivated and all other variables were held constant, increasing the cost of escaping by, for example, preventing the bystander from leaving the scene of the accident and so making it hard to avoid thinking about the continuing distress of the unhelped victim should increase the rate of helping. Conversely, reducing the costs of escaping by, for example, making it easy for the bystander to leave the scene of the accident and thus avoid thinking about the victim's continuing distress should decrease the rate of helping.

If the bystander's motivation is altruistic, his or her goal is to reduce the other's distress. This goal can be reached by helping, but not by escaping. Therefore, the likelihood that the altruistically motivated bystander will help should be independent of the cost of escaping because escaping is a goal-irrelevant behavior. Increasing or decreasing the cost of escaping should have no effect on the rate of helping; the rate should remain as high when escape is easy as when it is difficult.

These predictions suggest a way of determining whether the motivation for helping is egoistic or altruistic. The motivation cannot be inferred from any single behavioral response, but it can be inferred from the *pattern* of helping responses presented

in Table 1. To the extent that the motivation for helping is egoistic, the helping rate should be affected by the difficulty of escaping. The easier it is to escape continued exposure to the need situation, the lower the cost of escaping and the less chance of a bystander's helping. But to the extent that the motivation for helping is altruistic, the helping rate should be unaffected by the difficulty of escaping; helping should be just as high when escape is easy as when it is difficult.[1]

APPLICATION TO THE PROBLEM OF THE MOTIVATION RESULTING FROM EMPATHIC EMOTION

Now let us apply this general technique for discriminating between egoistic and altruistic motivation to the specific question of whether empathic emotion leads to altruistic motivation to help. If the motivation associated with feeling empathy for the person in need is altruistic (the empathy-altruism hypothesis), individuals induced to feel a high degree of empathy should help regardless of whether escape is easy or difficult (column 2 of Table 1); individuals feeling little empathy should help only when escape is difficult (column 1). Thus, if empathy leads to altruistic motivation to help, one can relabel the columns in Table 1, as has been done in parentheses. If, however, the motivation to help resulting from empathic emotion is egoistic, as seems to be implied by those who speak of "empathic pain," helping in the high-empathy condition should be affected by the ease of escape. Then we would expect to observe two main effects: As in previous research, high empathy should lead to more helping than low empathy, presumably as a result of an increase in feelings of personal distress or in anticipated guilt or shame. And in each

TABLE 1

Rate of Helping When Difficulty of
Escape is Varied and Motivation is
Egoistic or Altruistic

Difficulty of escape	Type of motivation (level of empathic emotion)	
	Egoistic (low empathy)	Altruistic (high empathy)
Easy	Low	High
Difficult	High	High

empathy condition difficult escape should lead to more helping than easy escape.

Note that the entire one-versus-three interaction pattern depicted in Table 1 is important if one is to provide evidence for the empathy-altruism hypothesis. If, for example, one were to compare the easy and difficult escape cells only in the column marked altruistic motivation (high empathy), the altruistic prediction is for no difference in the rate of helping. Such a result could easily occur simply because the escape manipulation was too weak or the behavioral measure was insensitive. If, however, an escape manipulation has a significant effect on helping when a bystander feels little empathy but does not when a bystander feels much empathy, the evidence that empathic emotion evokes altruistic motivation is much stronger. Then the evidence cannot be dismissed as being the result of a weak escape manipulation or an insensitive measure.

It is also clear that one must be on guard for a possible ceiling effect. A ceiling effect in the high-empathy column could obscure the two-main-effect pattern that would be expected if the motivation were egoistic,

making it look like the one-versus-three interaction that would be expected if the motivation were altruistic.

PRESENT RESEARCH

We conducted two experiments to test the hypothesis that empathic emotion leads to altruistic motivation to help. As suggested by the preceding analysis, a 2 × 2 design was used in each. Subjects observed a young woman named Elaine receiving electric shocks; they were given an unanticipated chance to help her by volunteering to take the remaining shocks in her stead. Cost of escaping without helping was manipulated by making escape either easy or difficult. Subjects believed that if they did not take Elaine's place, either they would continue to observe her take the shocks (difficult escape condition) or they would not (easy escape condition). Level of empathic emotion (low versus high) was manipulated differently in the two experiments. Following the classic studies of Stotland (1969) and Krebs (1975), in Experiment 1 we used similarity information to manipulate empathy. In Experiment 2 we sought to manipulate empathy more directly through the use of an emotion-specific misattribution to a placebo. In both experiments, the empathy-altruism hypothesis predicted that helping responses would conform to the one-versus-three pattern depicted in Table 1.

EXPERIMENT 1

There is evidence (e.g., Hornstein, 1976; Krebs, 1975; Stotland, 1969) that people are more likely to identify with a person they perceive to be similar to themselves and, as a result, to feel more empathy for a similar than for a dissimilar other. In the clearest demonstration of this relationship,

Krebs (1975) manipulated male subjects' perceptions of their similarity to a young man (an experimental confederate) prior to having them watch him perform in a roulette game in which he received money if the ball landed on an even number and an electric shock if the ball landed on an odd number. Similarity was manipulated by telling subjects that their responses to a personality test completed several days earlier indicated that they and the performer were either similar or different. In addition, subjects received information suggesting that the performer's values and interests were either similar or different from their own. Compared with subjects in the dissimilar condition, subjects who perceived themselves to be similar to the performer showed greater physiological arousal in response to his pleasure and pain, reported identifying with him to a greater degree, and reported feeling worse while waiting for him to receive shock. These subjects also subsequently helped him more. But it was not clear whether the motivation to help was egoistic or altruistic. To clarify this issue, we used a procedure similar to Krebs's but varied perceived similarity and difficulty of escape in a 2 × 2 factorial design.

METHOD

Subjects

Subjects were 44 female introductory psychology students at the University of Kansas participating in partial fulfillment of a course requirement. They were randomly selected from those who had completed a personal value and interest questionnaire, which formed the basis for the similarity manipulation, at a screening session held a few weeks earlier. Subjects were assigned to the four conditions of the 2 (easy versus difficult escape) × 2 (similar

versus dissimilar victim) design through the use of a randomized block procedure, 11 subjects to each cell. Four additional participants, one from each cell, were excluded from the design because they suspected Elaine was not actually receiving shocks.

Procedure

All subjects were tested individually by a female experimenter. On arrival, subjects were told that they would have to wait a few minutes for the arrival of a second subject, Elaine (actually a confederate). They were given an introduction to read while waiting:

In this experiment we are studying task performance and impression projection under stressful condition. We are investigating, as well, whether any inefficiency that might result from working under aversive conditions increases proportionately with the amount of time spent working under such conditions.

Since this study requires the assistance of two participants, there will be a drawing to determine which role will be yours. One participant will perform a task (consisting of up to, but not more than, ten trials) under aversive conditions; the aversive conditions will be created by the presentation of electric shock at random intervals during the work period. The other participant will observe the individual working under aversive conditions. This role involves the formation and report of general attitudes towards the "worker" so that we may better assess what effect, if any, working under aversive conditions has upon how that individual is perceived.

After reading the introduction and signing a consent form, subjects drew lots for their role. The drawing was rigged so that they always drew the observer role.

Subjects were then escorted to the observation room and given more detailed instructions. They learned that they would not actually meet the worker but would instead observe her over closed-circuit television as she performed up to 10 2-min. digit-recall trials. At random intervals during each trial, the worker would receive moderately uncomfortable electric shocks. The instructions went on to explain that equipment limitations made it impossible to capture visually all of the worker's reactions and that this was a problem, since prior research suggested that nonverbal cues were important in assessing another person's emotional state. To compensate for this lost information, the worker would be connected to a galvanic skin response (GSR) monitor, which would be visible in the lower right-hand corner of the television screen. The level of arousal indicated on the monitor would enable the subjects to assess more accurately the worker's emotional response, and help them form an impression.

Difficulty of escape manipulation. To manipulate difficulty of escape without helping, the last line of the detailed instructions varied the number of trials that subjects expected to observe. In the easy-escape condition, subjects read: "Although the worker will be completing between two and ten trials, it will be necessary for you to observe only the first two." In the difficult-escape condition they read: "The worker will be completing between two and ten trials, all of which you will observe." All subjects were later to learn that Elaine agreed to complete all 10 trials, and they were given the chance to help her by trading places after the second trial. Therefore, in the easy-escape condition, subjects who did not help would not have to watch Elaine take any more shocks; in the difficult-escape condition they would.

Similarity manipulation. After the subject finished reading the detailed instructions, the experimenter handed her a copy of the personal values and interest questionnaire administered at the screening session, explaining that this copy had been filled out by Elaine and would provide information about her that might be of help in forming an impression. Elaine's questionnaire was prepared in advance so that it reflected values and interests that were either very similar or very dissimilar to those the subject had expressed on her questionnaire. In the similar-victim condition, Elaine's responses to six items that had only two possible answers (e.g., "If you had a choice, would you prefer living in a rural or an urban setting?") were identical to those the subject had given; her responses to the other eight items were similar but not identical (e.g., "What is your favorite magazine?" Answers: *Cosmopolitan* for the subject, *Seventeen* for Elaine; *Time* for the subject, *Newsweek* for Elaine).In the dissimilar-victim condition, Elaine's responses to the six two-answer items were the opposite of those the subject had given, and her responses to the other eight were clearly different (e.g., *Cosmopolitan* for the subject, *Newsweek* for Elaine).

The experimenter was blind to subjects' escape condition and to whether Elaine's questionnaire was similar or dissimilar. She remained blind to the similarity manipulation until after all measures were recorded, but she made herself aware of the escape manipulation just prior to presenting the opportunity to help Elaine. This was to allow her to remind the subjects how many more trials they would be observing if they did not help. Since the empathy-altruism hypothesis predicted that the two independent variables would interact, remaining blind to one independent variable was sufficient to rule out an experimenter-bias explanation (Rosenthal, 1966) for the predicted pattern of helping.

While the subject looked over Elaine's questionnaire, the experimenter left to see if Elaine had arrived. She returned to say that she had and that the subject could now begin observing her over the closed-circuit television. So saying, the experimenter turned on a video monitor, allowing the subject to see Elaine. Unknown to the subject, what she saw was actually a videotape.

Need situation. On the videotape, subjects first saw Elaine, a moderately attractive young woman, tell the research assistant (female) that she would complete all 10 of the digit-recall trials. As the assistant was going over the procedure, Elaine interrupted to ask about the nature of the electric shocks that were to be used. The assistant answered that the shocks would be of constant intensity and, although uncomfortable, would cause "no permanent damage." "You know if you scuff your feet walking across a carpet and touch something metal? Well, they'll be about two to three times more uncomfortable than that."

After GSR electrodes were attached to the first and third fingers on Elaine's non-dominant hand and a shock electrode was attached to her other arm, the digit-recall trials began. The experimenter left subjects alone at this point. As the first trial progressed, Elaine's facial expressions, body movement and the GSR monitor all indicated that she was finding the shocks extremely unpleasant. By midway through the second trial, her reactions were so strong that the assistant interrupted the procedure to ask if Elaine were all right. Elaine answered that she was but would appreciate having a glass of water. The assistant readily agreed to this request and went to get the water.

Manipulation check. During this 90-sec. break, the experimenter reentered the observation room and gave subjects a brief questionnaire, ostensibly assessing their impression of Elaine thus far. The questionnaire included six 7-point trait rating scales (attractive, intelligent, competent, friendly, mature, cooperative). Subjects were also asked how likable Elaine was and how enjoyable they thought it would be to work with her. To check on their perceptions of her distress, subjects were asked, "In your opinion, how uncomfortable were the aversive conditions (random shocks) for the person in the working conditions experiment?" Finally, to check on the effectiveness of the similarity manipulation, they were asked, "How similar to you is the person in the working conditions experiment?" Responses to each of these four questions were on 7-point scales (1 = not at all; 7 = extremely). When subjects finished the questionnaire, the experimenter collected it and left.

Returning with the glass of water, the assistant asked Elaine if she had ever had trouble with shocks before. Elaine confessed that she had—as a child she had been thrown from a horse onto an electric fence. The doctor had said at the time that she suffered a bad trauma and in the future might react strongly to even mild shocks. (This information was provided to ensure that subjects would view Elaine's extreme reaction to the shocks as atypical and would not expect to find the shocks as unpleasant if they chose to take her place.) Hearing this, the assistant said that she did not think Elaine should continue with the trials. Elaine replied that even though she found the shocks very unpleasant, she wanted to go on: "I started; I want to finish. I'll go on . . . I know your experiment is important, and I want to do it." At this point, the assistant hit upon an idea: Since the observer was also an introductory psychology student, maybe she would be willing to help Elaine out by trading places. Elaine readily consented to the assistant checking about this possibility. The assistant said that she would shut off the equipment and go talk with the experimenter about it. Shortly thereafter, the video screen went blank.

Dependent measure: Helping Elaine. About 30 sec. later, the experimenter entered the observation room and said:

> First of all, let me say that you're under no obligation to trade places. I mean, if you would like to continue in your role as observer that's fine; you did happen to draw the observer role. If you decide to continue as the observer, ([easy-escape condition] you've finished observing the two trials, so all you need to do is answer a few questions about your impression of Elaine and you'll be free to go) ([difficult-escape condition] I need you to observe Elaine's remaining trials. After you've done that and answered a few questions about your impression of Elaine, you'll be free to go.) If you decide to change places with Elaine, what will happen is that she'll come in here and observe you, and you'll do the aversive conditioning trials with the shocks. And then you'll be free to go.

> What would you like to do? [Experimenter gets response from subject.] OK, that's fine. [If subject says she wants to trade places with Elaine, the experimenter continues.] How many trials would you like to do? Elaine will go ahead and do any of the eight remaining trials that you don't want to do. [Experimenter gets response.] Fine.

The experimenter then left, ostensibly to go tell the assistant what had been decided. In fact, she recorded whether the subject wanted to trade places and, if so, how many

of the eight remaining trials she would do. This information provided the dependent measure of helping. Then the experimenter made herself aware of the subject's similarity condition.

Debriefing. The experimenter returned promptly and fully debriefed the subject. Subjects seemed readily to understand the necessity for the deception involved in the experiment, and none seemed upset by it. After debriefing, subjects were thanked for their participation and excused.

RESULTS AND DISCUSSION

Effectiveness of the Similarity Manipulation

To check the effectiveness of the similarity manipulation, subjects were asked how similar the worker (Elaine) was to them. On the 7-point response scale, subjects in the similar-victim condition perceived Elaine to be more similar to themselves ($M = 5.09$) than subjects in the dissimilar-victim condition ($M = 2.69$), $F(1, 40) = 39.56$, $p < .001$. No other effects approached significance ($Fs < 1.20$). Similar but weaker patterns were found for two related items: ratings of Elaine's attractiveness and likability. Subjects in the similar-victim condition perceived Elaine to be more attractive ($Ms = 5.86$ versus 5.14), $F(1, 40) = 4.38$, $p < .05$, and more likable ($M = 5.14$ versus 4.23), $F(1, 40) = 5.06$, $p < .03$. For each of these items, no other effects approached significance ($Fs < 1.30$). These results suggested that the similarity manipulation was successful, although as might be expected, manipulating similarity did not just affect perceived similarity; it had some effect on perceived attractiveness and liking as well.[2]

A formal check on the escape manipulation seemed impractical. It also seemed unnecessary, since subjects received the manipulation twice—once in their written instructions and again orally just prior to indicating whether they wished to help. Examination of debriefing notes indicated that, as expected, subjects were aware of their escape condition and its implications.

Perception of Elaine's Distress

As intended, subjects in all conditions perceived Elaine to be suffering. When asked on a 1-7 scale to indicate how uncomfortable the shocks were for her, subjects' modal response in each condition was 7 (extremely uncomfortable); the overall mean was 6.25. There were no reliable differences across conditions.

Relieving Elaine's Distress by Helping

The proportion of subjects in each experimental condition who offered to help Elaine by trading places is presented in Table 2. Following the procedure recommended by Langer and Abelson (1972) and Winer (1971, pp. 399-400), these dichotomous data were analyzed through analysis of variance by employing a normal approximation based on an arc sine transformation. The 2 × 2 analysis revealed a highly significant main effect for similarity, χ^2 (1) = 11.69, $p < .001$, qualified by a significant Escape × Similarity interaction, χ^2 (1) = 4.19, $p < .04$. The main effect for difficulty of escape did not approach significance, $\chi^2(1) = 1.34$, $p > .20$.

Inspection of the proportion of helping in each condition revealed that the interaction was of the form predicted by the empathy-altruism hypothesis; the proportion in the easy-escape—dissimilar-victim condition was much lower than in the other three conditions. To test the statistical significance of this predicted one-versus-three pattern, the rate of helping in this condition was contrasted with the rate in the other three conditions. This planned comparison

TABLE 2

Proportion of Subjects Agreeing to Trade Places with Elaine in Each Condition of Experiment 1

| | Similarity condition | | | |
| | Dissimilar victim | | Similar victim | |
Difficulty of escape condition	Proportion	*M* no.[a]	Proportion	*M* no.[a]
Easy	.18	1.09	.91	7.09
Difficult	.64	4.00	.82	5.00

Note: $n = 11$ in each condition.
[a] Mean number of shock trials (from 0 to 8) that subjects agreed to take for Elaine ($MS_e = 9.70$, $df = 40$).

revealed a highly significant difference, $\chi^2(1) = 14.62, p < .001$. Residual variance across the other three conditions did not approach significance, $\chi^2(2) = 2.60, p > .25$. Individual cell comparisons revealed that, as predicted, the proportion of helping in the easy-escape—dissimilar-victim condition was significantly lower than the proportion in each of the other three conditions (zs ranging from 2.27 to 3.87, all ps < .015, one-tailed). Comparisons among the other three conditions revealed no reliable differences (all zs < 1.60).

With one exception, an identical pattern of significant effects emerged from analysis of variance and planned comparisons on the number of shock trials subjects in each condition volunteered to take for Elaine. The one exception was that the number of trials was significantly lower in the two difficult-escape conditions (pooled) than in the easy-escape–similar-victim condition, $t(40) = 2.25, p < .03$, two-tailed.

These results were quite consistent with the empathy-altruism hypothesis; they were not consistent with the view that empathy simply increases egoistic motivation to help. In the dissimilar-victim condition, where empathic emotional response to Elaine's distress was expected to be relatively low and, according to the empathy-altruism hypothesis, the motivation to help was expected to be primarily egoistic, the difficulty of escape manipulation had a dramatic effect on helping. When escape was easy, subjects were not likely to help, presumably because a less costly way to reduce any personal distress caused by watching Elaine receive shock was to answer the experimenter's final questions and leave. When escape was difficult, subjects were likely to help, presumably because taking the remaining shocks themselves was less costly than sitting and watching Elaine take more.

In the similar-victim conditions, however, where empathic emotional response to Elaine's distress was expected to be relatively high and, according to the empathy-altruism hypothesis, the motivation to help should be at least in part altruistic, difficulty of escape had no effect on subjects' readiness to help. Presumably, because their concern was to reduce Elaine's distress and not just their own, they were very likely to help, even when escape was easy.

Nor could this pattern of results be dismissed as an artifact of a ceiling effect in the difficult-escape—similar-victim condition. Although the proportion of helping in both similar-victim conditions was high, there was a nonsignificant trend for the proportion to be higher under easy than under difficult escape ($z = -.63$). This was not what would be expected if a ceiling effect were operating. Moreover, a ceiling-effect explanation was even less plausible for the number of shock trials subjects volunteered to take, since the mean response on this measure in the difficult-escape–similar-victim condition was far from the upper endpoint of the scale. And on this measure too there was a nonsignificant trend for the number of trials to be larger under easy than under difficult escape, $t(44) = -1.58$.

Finally, internal analyses provide an opportunity to check on a possible alternative explanation for the low level of helping in the easy-escape–dissimilar-victim condition: derogation of Elaine. If derogation were inhibiting helping in this condition, we would expect positive correlations between the helping measures and the ratings of Elaine's attractiveness and likability. But these correlations appeared to be, if anything, negative (rs = -.08 to -.31). There was, then, no evidence that derogation was inhibiting helping in this condition. And covariance analyses indicated that derogation could not account for the pattern of helping across experimental conditions. Removing the effects of perceived attractiveness or of likability on either likelihood or amount of helping, the predicted one-versus-three pattern of helping responses remained highly significant (all Fs ≥ 13.63, all $ps < .001$).

Overall, the results of Experiment 1 seemed to conform closely to the one-versus-three pattern that, according to Table 1, would be expected if increased empathic emotion led to altruistic motivation; they did not conform to the two-main-effect pattern that would be expected if increased empathy led to egoistic motivation. Still, although Stotland (1969) and Krebs (1975) had provided rather strong evidence that a similarity manipulation like the one used in Experiment 1 manipulated empathic emotion, the manipulation was indirect. Therefore, a second experiment was conducted in which we sought to test the empathy-altruism hypothesis by manipulating empathic emotion more directly.

EXPERIMENT 2

Based on the results of four different studies, Batson and Coke (in press) have suggested that two qualitatively distinct emotional states are elicited by witnessing another person in distress: *empathic concern,* made up of emotions such as compassion, concern, warmth, and softheartedness, and *personal distress,* made up of emotions such as shock, alarm, disgust, shame, and fear. It seemed to us that in the absence of a similarity manipulation, watching Elaine take shocks should elicit a reasonably high degree of both of these emotional states. And, generalizing from the work on the misattribution of dissonance arousal (Zanna & Cooper, 1974; Zanna, Higgins, & Taves, 1976), we thought that if subjects could be induced to

misattribute one of these emotions to some other source, such as a placebo, they would perceive their response to Elaine's distress to be predominated by the other. That is, if they attributed their feelings of empathic concern to the placebo, they should perceive their responses to Elaine to be predominantly personal distress. If they attributed their feelings of personal distress to the placebo, they should perceive their response to Elaine to be predominantly empathic concern. So if empathic emotion leads to altruistic motivation to help, crossing such a misattribution manipulation with a difficulty-of-escape manipulation, like the one used in Experiment 1, should again produce the one-versus-three pattern of helping responses depicted in Table 1. Subjects induced to attribute their empathic concern to the placebo should attribute relatively little empathic concern to watching Elaine suffer, and as a result, their motivation to help should be predominantly egoistic. This egoistic motivation should be reflected in less helping under easy than difficult escape. In contrast, subjects induced to attribute their personal distress to the placebo should attribute a relatively large amount of empathic concern to watching Elaine suffer, and as a result, their motivation to help should be predominantly altruistic. This altruistic motivation should be reflected in a lack of effect for the escape manipulation; helping should be relatively high under both easy and difficult escape.

METHOD

Subjects

Subjects were 48 female introductory psychology students at the University of Kansas participating in partial fulfillment of a course requirement. They were assigned to the four conditions of the 2 (easy vs. difficult escape) × 2 (personal distress vs. empathic concern as response to watching Elaine) design through the use of a randomized block procedure. Twelve subjects were assigned to each cell. Five additional participants were excluded from the design because they did not believe that the placebo capsule contained a drug, and six more were excluded because they suspected Elaine was not actually receiving shocks. Although this relatively high suspicion rate (19%) was regrettable, it was not unexpected in an experiment using a placebo manipulation. Fortunately, there was no evidence of reliable differences across conditions in the number of participants excluded for suspicion, and data analyses, with all suspicious participants included, revealed the same, although somewhat weaker, pattern of significant effects reported below. Therefore, the relatively high suspicion rate did not appear to provide an alternative explanation for the results.

Procedure

The procedure was the same as in Experiment 1, except for three changes. First, instead of using a similarity manipulation, level of empathic response to Elaine's distress was manipulated by having subjects misattribute either empathic concern or personal distress to a placebo administered in the context of a separate study. Second, time constraints arising from employing two studies restricted the number of shock trials subjects watched and were given a chance to take for Elaine. This restriction led to a minor wording change in the escape manipulation and the use of only a dichotomous (yes–no) measure of helping. Third, since the change in the number of trials necessitated creation of a new video-

tape, two new actresses played the parts of Elaine and the research assistant. Except for minor changes required by the procedural differences, the script for the videotape was the same as in Experiment 1.

Introduction. The introduction subjects read on arrival informed them that we were running two studies concurrently because one involved a time delay and the other required the assistance of an observer. Through a drawing, subjects were assigned to the former study—the effect of Millentana on short-term memory—and Elaine was assigned to the second study—task performance under aversive conditions.

As a rationale for the first study, subjects read, "One of the enzymes in the drug Millentana is believed to increase the level of serotonin in the brain. This modification . . . results in greater ability for short-term memory recall." To test the possible effect of Millentana on short-term memory, subjects were to complete two brief memory tasks, one before and one after taking a capsule containing Millentana. Since it would take approximately 25 min. for the Millentana to be completely absorbed into their system, and absorption was necessary before the second memory task could be administered, subjects were to serve as the observer for the aversive conditions study in the interim.

Emotional response manipulation. After completing the first memory task, subjects were given a capsule containing Millentana (actually a corn starch placebo). Before taking the capsule, all subjects were informed on a typed statement that in addition to its brief effect on short-term memory, the oral form of Millentana we were using had a side effect. Subjects in the personal-distress condition read:

Prior to total absorption, Millentana produces a clear feeling of warmth and sensitivity, a feeling similar to that you might experience while reading a particularly touching novel. You should begin to notice this side effect sometime within the first five minutes after ingestion. The side effect will disappear within twenty-five minutes, when the drug is totally absorbed.

Subjects in the empathic-concern condition read the same statement, except that the side effect of Millentana was described as "a clear feeling of uneasiness and discomfort, a feeling similar to that you might experience while reading a particularly distressing novel." These manipulations were based on the assumption that subjects who were led to misattribute feelings of empathic concern to Millentana would perceive their emotional response to watching Elaine to be primarily personal distress, whereas those led to misattribute feelings of personal distress to Millentana would perceive their emotional response to Elaine to be primarily empathic concern. All subjects signed the statement to indicate that they had read and understood the information about the side effect of Millentana. The experimenter remained blind to the emotional response manipulation until debriefing.[3]

Escape manipulation. After ingesting the Millentana capsule, subjects were given instructions for their role as observer in the aversive conditions study. As in Experiment 1, the last sentence of these instructions contained the escape manipulation. In the easy-escape condition subjects read: "Although the worker will be completing two trials, you will be observing only the first." In the difficult-escape condition they read: "The worker will be completing two trials, both of which you will observe."

Need situation. As in Experiment 1, subjects watched over closed-circuit television as Elaine reacted very strongly to the moderately uncomfortable shocks. At the end of the first trial, the assistant interrupted the procedure and, at Elaine's request, went to get her a glass of water.

Manipulation check. During this break, subjects were given a list of 28 emotion adjectives and asked to circle any that they were experiencing as a result of taking the Millentana capsule. The list contained 10 adjectives that in previous research (cf. Batson & Coke, in press) had tended to load together on an empathic concern factor (sympathetic, kind, compassionate, warm, softhearted, tender, empathic, concerned, moved, and touched) and 10 that had tended to load together on an orthogonal, personal distress factor (alarmed, bothered, disturbed, upset, troubled, worried, anxious, uneasy, grieved, and distressed). Not only did completion of this form provide a partial check on the effectiveness of the emotional response manipulation, it also served to remind subjects of the possibility that any emotion they were experiencing could be due, in part, to the Millentana capsule.

Dependent measure: Helping Elaine. When the assistant returned, the conversation began about Elaine's reaction to the shocks. As in Experiment 1, it led up to the idea that the subject might be willing to help Elaine by trading places. Shortly thereafter, the experimenter entered the observation room and presented the subject with the opportunity to help. Paralleling the procedure in Experiment 1, in the easy-escape condition subjects were reminded that if they did not help they would not have to watch Elaine's second trial; in the difficult-escape condition subjects were reminded that they would. The dependent variable was whether or not subjects volunteered to trade places with Elaine for the second trial.

Response to Elaine and her need. After subjects indicated whether they wished to help, they were given a four-item questionnaire assessing their reactions to observing Elaine. The first two questions asked how much "uneasiness" and "warmth and sensitivity" observing the task performance study caused them to experience (1 = none, 9 = a great deal). The last two questions asked how likable the worker was and how uncomfortable the aversive conditions (random shock) were for her (for both questions, 1 = not at all; 9 = extremely).

Debriefing. On completion of this questionnaire, subjects were fully debriefed. As with Experiment 1, they seemed readily to understand the necessity for the deception involved, and none seemed upset by it. After debriefing, subjects were thanked for their participation and excused.

RESULTS AND DISCUSSION

Perception of Elaine's Distress

Ratings of how uncomfortable the shocks were for Elaine suggested that subjects in all conditions perceived her to be in considerable distress. On the 9-point response scale, the modal response in the difficult-escape–personal-distress condition was 8; in each of the other three conditions, it was 9. The overall mean was 8.07, with no reliable differences across conditions.

Effectiveness of the Emotional Response Manipulation

Perceived emotional response to Millentana. To check the effectiveness of the emo-tional response manipulation, subjects were first asked to circle adjectives describing the emotions that they were experiencing as side effects of Millentana. Because there were large individual differences in the number of adjectives circled, the most appropriate index of the type of emotion experienced seemed to be a simple classification: If a subject circled more empathic concern than personal distress adjectives, she received a score of 1; if she circled an equal number, she received a score of 0; and if she circled fewer, she received a score of −1. A 2 × 2 analysis of variance on this measure revealed only one reliable effect, a main effect for the emotional response manipulation, $F(1, 44) = 14.82$, $p < .001$. As intended, subjects in the personal-distress condition reported experiencing a relative predominance of empathic concern emotions as a result of taking the Millentana capsule ($M = .21$), whereas subjects in the empathic-concern condition reported experiencing a relative predominance of personal distress emotions ($M = −.46$). Thus, the emotional response manipulation appeared to produce the intended perceptions of side effects. But did it produce reciprocal perceptions of emotional response to Elaine's distress?

Perceived emotional response to Elaine's distress. Subjects' ratings of the amount of uneasiness and of warmth and sensitivity caused by observing the aversive conditions experiment provided indices of their emotional response to Elaine's distress. It was expected that subjects in the two emotional response conditions would not differ in the average amount of emotion attributed to watching Elaine, but they would differ in the nature of the emotion. To provide an index of the overall *amount* of emotion experienced, ratings of uneasiness and of warmth and sensitivity were averaged.

(Across the entire design, these ratings were positively correlated: r [46] $= .45$, $p < .01$, presumably reflecting individual differences in emotionality or in response set.) A 2 × 2 analysis of variance revealed no reliable differences on this index (overall $M = 4.59$).

To provide an index of the *nature* of the emotion experienced, a difference measure was created by subtracting the rating of uneasiness from the rating of warmth and sensitivity. Analysis of this index revealed only one reliable difference, a main effect for the emotional response manipulation, $F(1, 44) = 5.92$, $p < .02$. As intended, this main effect was a mirror image of the main effect on emotion experienced as a side effect of the placebo. Subjects in the distress condition reported a predominance of uneasiness in their response to observing Elaine ($M = -1.50$); subjects in the empathy condition reported more warmth and sensitivity ($M = .21$). Moreover, within-cell correlations between this index and the index of type of emotion experienced as a side effect of Millentana provided no evidence for differences independent of the experimental manipulations; none of the within-cell correlations differed reliably from zero. Looking separately at the ratings of uneasiness and of warmth and sensitivity, the main effect on the index of nature of emotional response was found to be primarily a result of a difference in reported warmth and sensitivity ($M = 3.46$ and 5.08 for the distress and empathy conditions, respectively), $F(1, 44) = 5.41$, $p < .03$; the difference in reported uneasiness was not reliable ($Ms = 4.96$ and 4.88, respectively). There were no other reliable differences on either emotional response item.

It appeared, then, that the emotional manipulation was effective. Although there was no difference across conditions in the total amount of emotion reported as a result of observing Elaine, there was a difference in the relative amount of empathic emotion reported. Significantly more empathy was reported in the empathic-concern than in the personal-distress condition. Moreover, unlike the similarity manipulation used in Experiment 1, the emotional response manipulation produced no reliable differences across conditions in how likable Elaine was perceived to be; she was seen as moderately likable in all conditions (overall $M = 6.04$ on the 9-point response scale).

As in Experiment 1, it was not considered practical or necessary to have a formal check on the escape manipulation. Debriefing notes again indicated that subjects were aware of their escape condition and its implications.

Relieving Elaine's Distress by Helping

Since the subjects reported less empathy as a result of witnessing Elaine's distress in the distress condition than in the empathy condition, it was possible to test the empathy-altruism hypothesis once again. The proportion of subjects offering to help Elaine in each experimental condition of Experiment 2 is presented in Table 3. As in Experiment 1, these dichotomous data were analyzed through analysis of variance and planned comparisons by employing a normal approximation based on an arc sine transformation. A 2 × 2 analysis revealed only one significant effect, an Escape × Emotional Response interaction, $\chi^2(1) = 6.10$, $p < .02$. As predicted by the empathy-altruism hypothesis, this effect was due to the proportion of helping being lower in the easy-escape distress condition than in the other three conditions. A planned comparison revealed that this predicted one-versus-three pattern was highly significant, $\chi^2(1) = 5.96$, $p < .02$; residual variance across the other three conditions did not approach significance, $\chi^2(2) = 1.94$, $p > .40$. Individual cell comparisons revealed that the proportion helping in the easy-escape–distress condition differed significantly from the proportion in the easy-escape–empathy condition ($z = 2.62$, $p < .01$, one-tailed), and the difficult-escape-distress condition ($z = 2.12$, $p < .02$, one-tailed), but not from the difficult-escape–empathy condition ($z = 1.24$). Comparisons among the other three conditions revealed no reliable differences (all zs ≤ 1.38).

These results were again quite consistent with the empathy-altruism hypothesis. In the distress conditions, where motivation was assumed to be egoistic, the rate of helping was significantly lower under easy than under difficult escape. In the empathy conditions, where motivation was assumed to be at least in part altruistic, the rate of helping remained high, even when escape was easy. In addition, the correlation between

helping and the index of nature of emotional response was significantly more positive in the easy-escape conditions, $r_{pb}(24) = .27$, than in the difficult-escape conditions, $r_{pb}(24) = -.32$, $z = 1.97$, $p < .05$, two-tailed. This indicated a more positive association between relative empathy and helping in the easy- than in the difficult-escape conditions, as would be predicted by the empathy-altruism hypothesis.

And again there was no evidence of a ceiling effect in the difficult-escape empathy condition. Instead, in the empathy conditions there was again a nonsignificant trend for the rate of helping to be higher under easy than under difficult escape ($z = -1.38$). Moreover, the rate of helping in the difficult-escape—empathy condition was near the midpoint of the response scale. Nor was there any evidence that derogation could account for the pattern of results. Paralleling results of Experiment 1, within-cell correlation and covariance analyses revealed no evidence of derogation in the easy-escape—distress condition.

GENERAL DISCUSSION

As we noted at the outset, the hypothesis that empathic emotion produces truly altruistic motivation contradicts the egoistic assumption of most, if not all, current theories of motivation. Because egoism is a widely held and basic assumption, it is only prudent to require that the evidence supporting altruism be strong before this hypothesis is accepted.

To the degree that the conceptual analysis and resulting predictions presented in Table 1 provide an adequate framework for an empirical test of truly altruistic motivation, the two experiments reported here seem to make an initial step toward providing such evidence. The results of the two experi-

TABLE 3

Proportion of Subjects Agreeing to Trade Places with Elaine in Each Condition of Experiment 2

Difficulty of escape condition	Subject's dominant emotional response to Elaine's distress	
	Personal distress	Empathic concern
Easy	.33	.83
Difficult	.75	.58

Note: $n = 12$ in each condition.

ments were highly consistent; in each, conditions assumed to produce relatively high empathic response to a person in distress led to helping regardless of whether escape without helping was easy or difficult. In contrast, conditions assumed to produce relatively low empathic response led to helping only when it was difficult to escape without helping. This was precisely the pattern of results predicted by the hypothesis that empathic emotion evokes altruistic motivation to see another's need reduced.

Still, two experiments are not many on which to base so radical a change in our view of human motivation, especially when they have at least two limitations. First, in each experiment the person in need was female, and because it seemed likely that subjects would be more likely to empathize with a same-sex individual, only female subjects were used. Although there is evidence that females report experiencing quantitatively more empathy than males (Hoffman, 1977), we know of no evidence nor any a priori reason why empathy, when experienced, would elicit qualitatively different kinds of motivation in males than in females. But future research should look more closely at the motivational consequences of empathy for males. Second, both experiments came out of the same laboratory—ours. Confidence in the hypothesis that empathic emotion elicits truly altruistic motivation would certainly be strengthened by converging evidence from other laboratories, especially ones with perspectives different from our own.

It may be, then, too early to conclude that empathic emotion can lead to altruistic motivation to help. But if future research produces the same pattern of results found in the experiments reported here, this conclusion, with all its theoretical and practical implications, would seem not only possible but necessary. For now, the research to date convinces us of the legitimacy of *suggesting* that empathic motivation for helping may be truly altruistic. In doing so, we are left far less confident than we were of reinterpretations of apparently altruistically motivated helping in terms of instrumental egoism.

NOTES

1. It is worth noting that another cost variable, the cost of helping, is frequently thought to be the key to altruism. If helping occurs when the cost of helping is high (at the extreme, when the helper's life is in danger), this is thought to be evidence of altruistic motivation. A little reflection shows that such an inference is unfounded, for even highly costly helping could easily be an instrumental egoistic response, motivated by a desire to avoid guilt or to attain praise and honor either in this life or an anticipated life to come.

2. There were no reliable differences across conditions in ratings of how enjoyable it would be to work with Elaine (overall $M = 4.57$) or in ratings of her intelligence (overall $M = 4.23$), friendliness (overall $M = 5.18$), maturity (overall 4.77) or cooperativeness (overall $M = 5.45$). On ratings of her competence, there was an unexpected, significant ($p < .03$) interaction; Elaine was perceived to be more competent in the easy-escape—similar-victim and the difficult-escape—dissimilar-victim conditions than in the other two conditions. Since there was no ready explanation for this interaction, it seemed best attributed to chance.

3. Unlike the typical placebo-misattribution manipulation, in which some people are told that the placebo will arouse them and some are told that it will not or some are led to expect side effects relevant to the arousal they are experiencing and others to expect irrelevant side effects, all subjects in Experiment 2 were told that the placebo would produce relevant arousal. What was manipulated was the *nature* of the arousal the placebo would produce—empathy or distress. Because the nature rather than the amount of arousal was being manipulated, a no-side-effect condition of the sort employed as a

control when amount of arousal is manipulated was not appropriate for our design.

REFERENCE NOTE

1. Piliavin, J. A., & Piliavin, I. M. *The Good Samaritan: Why does he help?* Unpublished manuscript, University of Wisconsin, 1973.

REFERENCES

Aderman, D., & Berkowitz, L. Observational set, empathy, and helping. *Journal of Personality and Social Psychology, 1970, 14,* 141-148.

Aronfreed, J. M. The socialization of altruistic and sympathetic behavior: some theoretical and experimental analyses. In J. Macaulay & L. Berkowitz (Eds.), *Altruism and helping behavior.* New York: Academic Press, 1970.

Batson, C. D., & Coke, J. S. Empathy: A source of altruistic motivation for helping. In J. P. Rushton & R. M. Sorrentino (Eds.), *Altruism and helping behavior.* Hillsdale, N.J.: Erlbaum, in press.

Batson, C. D., Darley, J. M., & Coke, J. S. Altruism and human kindness: Internal and external determinants of helping behavior. In L. Pervin & M. Lewis (Eds.), *Perspectives in interactional psychology.* New York: Plenum Press, 1978.

Bolles, R. D. *Theory of motivation* (2nd ed.). New York: Harper & Row, 1975.

Coke, J. S., Batson, C. D., & McDavis, K. Empathic mediation of helping : A two-stage model. *Journal of Personality and Social Psychology, 1978, 36,* 752-766.

Comte, I. A. *System of positive polity* (Vol. 1). London: Longmans, Green, 1875.

Harris, M. B., & Huang, L. C. Helping and the attribution process. *Journal of Social Psychology, 1973, 90,* 291-297.

Hoffman, M. L. Developmental synthesis of affect and cognition and its implications for altruistic motivation. *Developmental Psychology, 1975, 11,* 607-622.

Hoffman, M. L. Sex differences in empathy and related behaviors. *Psychological Bulletin, 1977, 84,* 712-722.

Hornstein, H. A. *Cruelty and kindness: A new look at aggression and altruism.* Englewood Cliffs, N.J.: Prentice-Hall, 1976.

Krebs, D. L. Empathy and altruism. *Journal of Personality and Social Psychology, 1975, 32,* 1134-1146.

Langer, E. J., & Abelson, R. The semantics of asking a favor: How to succeed in getting help without really dying. *Journal of Personality and Social Psychology, 1972, 24,* 26-32.

Mehrabian, A., & Epstein, N. A measure of emotional empathy. *Journal of Personality, 1972, 40,* 525-543.

Rosenthal, R. *Experimenter effects in behavioral research,* New York: Appleton-Century-Crofts, 1966.

Stotland, E. Exploratory investigations of empathy. In L. Berkowitz (Ed.), *Advances in experimental social psychology* (Vol. 3). New York: Academic Press, 1969.

Winer, B. J. *Statistical principles in experimental design* (2nd ed.). New York: McGraw-Hill, 1971.

Zanna, M. P., & Cooper, J. Dissonance and the pill: An attributional approach to studying the arousal properties of dissonance. *Journal of Personality and Social Psychology, 1974, 29,* 703-709.

Zanna, M. P., Higgins, E. T., & Taves, P. A. Is dissonance phenomenologically aversive? *Journal of Experimental Social Psychology, 1976, 12,* 530-538.

With a Little Help from My Friend: Effect of Single or Multiple Act Aid as a Function of Donor and Task Characteristics

Arie Nadler, Jeffrey D. Fisher,
and Shulamit Ben-Itzhak

The present study investigated reactions to receiving single or multiple act aid from a friend or a stranger, as a function of the ego relevance of the task on which help was given. Male subjects were asked to bring a good same-sex friend with them to the experiment. Half the subjects were told that their teammate, with whom they were to interact at a later stage of the experiment, was their friend. The other half were told that they had been teamed up with someone whom they did not know. Subjects were instructed to solve a detective story, the performance of which was presented to half as related to ego-relevant dimensions (e.g., intelligence, creativity) and to the other half as related to non-ego-relevant dimensions (e.g., luck, momentary mood). The assignment was insolvable, and subjects were helped by their supposed teammate to obtain the "correct" solution. Half received help on one detective story and the other half received help on two stories. Results show that subjects who had been helped twice on an ego-relevant task by a good friend had the least favorable affect and self-evaluations. Individuals who had been helped twice by a good friend on a non-ego-relevant dimension tended to have the most favorable affect and self-evaluations. Similar patterns were observed for measures of external perception (i.e., liking for helper, evaluations of helper and relations with him). The implications of these findings for research on recipient reactions to aid, social comparison processes, and close interpersonal relations are discussed.

Research on prosocial behavior has been concerned with the study of variables that predict and explain help giving (cf. Rushton & Sorrentino, 1981). Only recently has systematic attention been given to the other side of the helping paradigm, the recipient's reactions to being helped (cf. Fisher, Nadler, & Whitcher-Alagna, 1982). That body of research indicates that receiving help is a complex psychological phenomenon. At times it is a positive experience for the recipient and is associated with favorable responses. Under other conditions it is a negative, threatening experience associated with unfavorable responses. Further, past research has shown that conceptually relevant characteristics of the help (e.g., Fisher & Nadler, 1976; Gergen, Ellsworth, Maslach, & Seipel, 1975), the helper (e.g., DePaulo, 1978; Fisher & Nadler, 1974), and the recipient (e.g., DePaulo, Brown, Ishii, & Fisher, 1981; Nadler, Fisher, & Streufert, 1976; Nadler, Sheinberg, & Jaffe, 1981) affect the favorability of the

This research was funded by Grant 2290 from the U.S.-Israel Binational Science Foundation.
"With a Little Help from My Friend: Effect of Single or Multiple Act Aid as a Function of Donor and Task Characteristics" by A. Nadler, S. Ben-Itzhak & J.D. Fisher, 1983, *Journal of Personality and Social Psychology, 44*, pp. 310-321. Copyright 1983 by the American Psychological Assn. Reprinted by permission of the publisher and authors.

recipient's reactions to aid. The latter include self-perceptions (e.g., Nadler, Altman, & Fisher, 1979), evaluation of the helper and the help (e.g., Gergen & Gergen, 1971; Nadler, Fisher, & Streufert, 1974), and behavioral responses such as reciprocity (Clark & Mills, 1979) and self-help (Fisher & Nadler, 1976).

Within research on effects of *helper* characteristics, studies have investigated how donor-recipient similarity affects the responses of the beneficiary. Consistent with its theoretical underpinnings in the threat-to-self-esteem model of reactions to help (Fisher et al., 1982), the research focuses on how similarity moderates the intensity of the threatening and supportive self-relevant messages that may be inherent in help. Threatening self-information in aid includes cues of the recipient's relative dependency and inferiority, whereas supportive self-information includes cues of donor caring and concern. Social comparison theory (Festinger, 1954) and related empirical and conceptual developments (Brickman & Bulman, 977; Nadler, Jazwinski, Lau, & Miller, 1980) suggest that cues of relative inferiority and dependency in aid should be psychologically meaningful (and thus threatening) only when the helper is a similar other, because this promotes comparison stress between donor and recipient.

Past data have supported this expectation. Fisher and Nadler (1974) observed that when compared to individuals who did not receive help, those receiving help from an attitudinally similar helper had more negative affect and lower self-evaluations. However, receiving help from an attitudinally *dissimilar* other tended to have a positive effect on affect and self-evaluations. More recently, Fisher, Harrison, and Nadler (1978) found that the threat in aid from a

similar other generalized across different operationalizations of similarity (i.e., attitude similarity and similarity of task-relevant knowledge) and types of help (i.e., financial aid and verbal advice). Further research (Nadler et al., 1976) has replicated and extended these findings. Research has shown, in line with a consistency approach (cf. Bramel, 1968; Tessler & Schwartz, 1972), that high self-esteem individuals (for whom elements of dependency and inferiority are inconsistent with self-cognitions) are more sensitive than are those with low self-esteem to the comparison stress inherent in help from a similar other.

Thus, past findings corroborate the notion that help may contain varying degrees of positive, self-supporting and negative, self-threatening elements. Moreover, donor-recipient interpersonal similarity is one variable that determines the relative amount of self-threat and support in aid. Because of the greater psychological relevance of the fate of a similar other, such a donor highlights elements of relative inferiority and dependency for the recipient, which makes help an overall threatening experience.

This finding has implications for the understanding of helping relations between friends. A sizable body of data shows that interpersonal similarity is associated with interpersonal attraction (cf. Byrne, 1971), and relationships between friends potentiate more relevant social comparisons than relationships with strangers (cf. Tesser, 1980). Thus, the phenomenon of friendship may often include the pleasures of social proximity as well as the potential pains associated with comparison stress (cf. Brickman & Bulman, 1977). This suggests that the receipt of aid from a friend who has been able to succeed in a context where one has failed may be a mixed blessing. The present study is the first to assess reactions to help from friends in a controlled setting.

Although our previous data on donor-recipient similarity suggest that, due to a negative social comparison, help from a friend may be more aversive than help from a stranger, is this always the case? Both common sense and conceptual treatment of close relations suggest that under certain conditions the reverse may hold. An important characteristic of help that may moderate the effects of donor-recipient social proximity on recipient reactions is the ego-relevance of the helping task. Consistent with the logic of our earlier discussion, the comparison stress accompanying the receipt of aid from a socially close other should occur only when the receipt of help reflects inferiority on *ego-relevant* dimensions (e.g., intelligence). When the helping task reflects inferiority on a non-ego-relevant dimension (e.g., manual dexterity), aid from a similar other should not be aversive for the recipient, because the social comparison process is not likely to pose a threat to one's self-esteem. In this later case, the positive, supportive elements in receiving help (i.e., signs of another's concern) may become salient and meaningful, especially when the helper is a friend.

Our reasoning indicates that relative to help from a socially distant other, help from a friend may be *potentially* more painful or pleasant. The ego-relevance of the help determines which of these two consequences is likely to occur. When help reflects inferiority on an ego-relevant dimension, it should be an aversive, self-threatening experience. When it does not, its receipt should be a relatively positive, supportive experience. One should find a friend's help in changing a flat tire (a non-ego-relevant task) a relatively positive experience but be

threatened by help from a friend in solving a complex intellectual problem.

It was reasoned that the hypothesized effects should be mediated by the *duration* of the help. Because events that are consistent over time serve as more valid sources of information (cf. Kelley, 1967), the threatening effects of help from a friend on an ego-relevant task should be more evident when aid is given twice than once. Similarly, the self-support inherent in help from a friend that does not reflect inferiority on an ego-relevant dimension should be most evident when help is given twice.

Finally, in line with assertions made by the threat-to-self-esteem model of reactions to help (cf. Fisher et al., 1982), self threat and support in aid were expected to affect a wide range of affective and evaluative responses. Therefore, measures were taken of recipient affect, self-evaluation, evaluations of the donor and relations with him, and attributions of intent for the aid.

METHOD

Subjects and Overview

Ninety-six Israeli male students served as subjects in the experiment. Participants were randomly assigned to each of eight experimental groups in a 2 (friend vs. stranger) $\times$ 2 (ego relevant vs. non ego-relevant help) $\times$ 2 (help given once vs. twice) between-subjects design. Six of the experimental cells contained 12 subjects, whereas the seventh and eighth cells included 11 and 13 subjects, respectively.

Upon signing up for the experiment, each subject made a commitment to report with a good friend of the same-sex. The experiment was described as one involving problem solving. Half of the subjects were told that they were teamed up with the friend they brought with them, whereas the other half were informed that they were teamed up with a stranger. Also, subjects in the ego-relevant task condition were told that task performance was related to analytic and creative abilities, whereas the subjects in the other condition were told that task performance reflected the operation of chance factors (e.g., luck, momentary mood, etc.). Subjects could solve the problem only after the receipt of help from their partner. Half received help once and the other half received help twice. Following this, the dependent measures were taken. The experiment was run by a male experimenter.

Procedures

On arriving at the experiment, subjects were informed that they would participate in a study designed to investigate team and individual problem solving. Further, one of the experimental questions was said to center on differential performance by teams of friends and strangers. Half of the subjects were told that they were assigned to the "friend" condition (i.e., that their teammate was the friend they came with to the experiment). The other half were informed that they were randomly assigned to the "stranger" condition (i.e., that their teammate was someone whom they did not know). The experiment was described as having two parts. Subjects were told that in the first part, each of the team members would work alone, whereas in the second part, both team members would work together.[1] Further, subjects were told that following each phase of the experiment they would be asked to answer several questions about their feelings and thoughts. Next, subjects received the "Initial Report Forms," which included bogus questions and an item that asked each subject to in-

dicate the length of time (in months) he had known his teammate. This item was intended to provide a quantitative assessment of the friend-stranger variable. The mean acquaintance time of subjects in the friend-helper condition was 4.54 months.

Following this, the experimental task was introduced. Subjects were told that they would have to solve a mystery from a detective story by naming the murderer. Subjects in the ego-relevant condition were informed that based on past research with similar tasks, it was known that performance would be related to analytic abilities and creativity. Moreover, the importance of analytic abilities and creativity for general success in life was made explicit. Subjects in the non-ego-relevant condition were told that research indicated that performance on these problems had no relationship to abilities like creativity and analytic thinking. Rather, performance was said to be related to temporary factors like luck and mood.[2]

Subsequent to the instructions, each subject received the detective story. The subject's task was to identify the murderer. Five minutes later the experimenter returned and asked the subject to write down his solution. The subject was then told that his answer was wrong. Following this, the experimenter left the room, noting that he had to check the teammate's solution. On his return, the experimenter told the subject that his teammate had arrived at the correct solution and was willing to give the subject a clue to help him identify the murderer. Nearly all subjects agreed to receive the help. Six who declined the offer were excluded from the final analyses.[3] Following receipt of the clue (information about a character in the story not previously named by the subject as the suspected murderer) subjects were given 2–3 more minutes to reconsider their solution. Because of the nature of the clue, all subjects changed their answer. After the experimenter had reexamined the solution, he told the subjects that their new solution was correct.

Subjects in the one-act help condition were asked at this point to respond to the "2nd Report Forms," which included the dependent measures. For subjects in the continuous-help condition, the whole procedure was repeated with a different detective story. After the second helping event, subjects in that condition were asked to respond to the dependent measures.

Dependent Measures

Five major classes of dependent measures were employed. These included measures of (a) affect and self-evaluation, (b) liking for and evaluation of the helper, (c) subjects' perceptions of the helper's evaluation of them, (d) perceived quality of future relations with the helper, and (e) subjects' perceptions of the motivation underlying the helper's benevolence.

Affect and Self-Evaluation

Affect. Subjects were asked to rate how they "feel right now" on five, 7-point bipolar adjective scales. Three of the items (i.e., good-bad, pleasant-unpleasant, and tense-relaxed) were taken from a measure of affect used in past research (cf. Byrne, 1971; Nadler et al., 1976, 1979, 1980), and two were added because they tapped affective dimensions of special relevance in the present context (i.e., dependent-independent and able-unable to complete the task on my own). The intercorrelations between these items were high ($\alpha = .86$), and they were summed and averaged to obtain a single affect score.

Self-evaluations. In response to the statement "In comparison to other individuals my own age I evaluate myself as being," subjects were asked to rate themselves on three, 7-point bipolar adjective scales (intelligent-unintelligent, successful-unsuccessful, and above-below average). These items were highly intercorrelated ($\alpha = .81$) and summed and averaged to obtain a single self-evaluation score.

Subject's Liking for and Evaluation of the Helper

Subjects rated their teammate on seven 7-point bipolar adjective scales. A factor-analytic procedure using primary rotation yielded an "evaluative" factor and a "liking" factor. The evaluative factor included five items that loaded above a .40 preset criterion (i.e., intelligent-unintelligent, fair-unfair, good-bad, egoistic-not egoistic, and good-not good to be with). Alpha for this five-item scale was .85. Ratings on the five items were summed and averaged to obtain a single score for evaluation of the helper.

Liking toward the helper was assessed by the remaining two items (i.e., liking toward other, and willingness to work with other), which have been commonly used in past research to assess interpersonal attraction (i.e., the Interpersonal Judgment Scale; Byrne, 1971). Ratings on these two items were summed and averaged to obtain a single score for "liking for the helper."

Subject's Perceptions of the Helper's Evaluations of Them

To measure subjects' perceptions of the helper's evaluations of them, subjects were asked to indicate on three 7-point bipolar adjective scales their agreement with the following statements about their teammate: He appreciates my intellectual ability, he cares for me, he likes me. The interitem correlations between these items were sufficiently high ($\alpha = .75$) that they were summed and averaged to obtain a single score.

Expected Quality of Future Relations

To obtain an assessment of the quality of relations the subject expected with the helper when they were to work together in the second phase of the experiment, subjects were asked to rate their expectations on three 7-point bipolar adjective scales (pleasant-unpleasant, tense-not tense, and competitive-cooperative). The interitem correlations between these three items were high (alpha $= .84$) and they were summed and averaged to obtain a single measure of expected quality of future relations.

Perceived Reasons for Helper's Help

Following the completion of the above dependent measures, subjects were given an "Intermediate Report Form" on which to check any of four "occurrences" that had taken place during the experiment. This was said to be designed to provide the investigators with a detailed account of special occurrences during the session. The form included four events said to have occurred in past runs of the study: (a) equipment failure, (b) one of the participants was not performing because he felt ill, (c) one of the participants helped the other to arrive at the correct solution, and (d) some unexpected event interrupted the smooth running of the experiment. All subjects correctly reported that they were helped to arrive at the correct solution by their teammates and were subsequently given a short form asking them to answer some bogus questions (e.g., what kind of equipment

failure occurred, etc.) and to indicate their agreement, on 7-point scales, with three statements that described possible reasons for the helper's benevolence. The reasons were (a) "he gave because he really cares for me," (b) "because he wants me to help him in the future," and (c) "because he wanted to show me that he is more able than myself." Subjects' degree of agreement with each of these three statements served as a measure of perceived reasons for the helper's benevolence.

RESULTS

All of the measures were analyzed by a 2 (friend vs. stranger) $\times$ 2 (ego-relevant vs. non-ego-relevant help) $\times$ 2 (help given once vs. twice) between-subjects analysis of variance (ANOVA; Winer, 1971).

Affect and Self-Evaluation

Affect. The ANOVA for the measure of affect yielded a significant three-way interaction, $F(1, 88) = 4.12$, $p < .05$. None of the other main effects or interactions were significant.

To interpret the three-way interaction, separate 2 (identity of helper) $\times$ 2 (ego relevance) ANOVAs were conducted for subjects given help once and twice. When help was given only once, neither the identity of helper or ego-relevance main effects, nor the two-way interaction was statistically significant, $Fs < 1$ in all three cases. When help was given twice, the two-way interaction was significant, $F(1, 43) = 3.39$, $p < .05$. As can be seen in Table 1, this is because individuals who received ego-relevant help from a friend had significantly lower affect than did those who received non-ego-relevant help from a friend, $F(1, 43) = 6.57$, $p < .05$ (means were 3.98 and

TABLE 1

Mean Affect and Self-Evaluation Scores in All Eight Experimental Conditions

Ego relevance of help	Help given once		Help given twice	
	By friend	By stranger	By friend	By stranger
Affect				
Relevant	5.47	5.00	3.98	4.07
Not relevant	5.37	5.46	5.63	4.89
Self-evaluation				
Relevant	5.67	5.92	5.08	5.75
Not relevant	6.08	5.69	6.33	6.15

Note: N = 96.

5.63, respectively). For subjects who received help from a stranger, affect in ego-relevant conditions did not differ from that in non-ego-relevant conditions, $F < 1$ (means were 5.07 and 4.89, respectively).

Self-evaluations. The ANOVA revealed a main effect for ego relevance, $F(1, 88) = 5.97, p < .05$, indicating that subjects who received ego-relevant help had lower self-evaluations than did those who received non-ego-relevant help (means were 5.60 and 6.06, respectively). In addition, the two-way Identity of Helper × Ego-Relevance interaction was marginally significant, $F(1, 88) = 3.58, p < .06$. This indicates that, in line with expectations, ego-relevance of help did not affect one's self-evaluations when the helper was a stranger (means were 5.90 and 5.83 for the ego-relevant and non-ego-relevant conditions, respectively). Yet, individuals who re-

ceived ego-relevant help from a friend had significantly lower self-evaluations than did those who received non-ego-relevant help from him, $F(1, 88) = 4.47, p < .05$ (means were 5.38 and 6.21, respectively).

In addition, the two-way interaction between ego-relevance of help and the number of times help was given approached significance, $F(1, 88) = 3.46, p < .07$. This marginally significant interaction occurred because the discrepancy between self-evaluation scores in the ego-relevant and non-ego-relevant conditions was significant, $F(1, 88) = 4.47, p < .05$, when help was given twice (means were 5.42 and 6.24, respectively) and nonsignificant, $F < 1$, when it was given only once (cell means were 5.79 and 5.88, respectively).

In sum, these data indicate that help from a friend on an ego-relevant task is self-threatening, whereas such help on a non-ego-relevant task is self-supporting. Further, it seems that both the self-threat and self-support are more intense when help is given twice rather than only once.[4]

Liking for and Evaluation of Helper

Liking. The ANOVA on this measure yielded a significant two-way Identity of Helper × Ego-Relevance interaction, $F(1, 88) = 15.84$, $p < .001$. This indicates that those receiving ego-relevant help from a friend liked him less than those receiving non-ego-relevant help from him, $F(1, 88) = 6.53$, $p < .05$ (means were 4.58 and 5.81, respectively). An opposite tendency was observed for individuals in the stranger-helper condition (means were 5.17 and 4.46, respectively).

However, the above interpretation should be regarded in light of a marginally signif-

icant triple interaction, $F(1, 88) = 3.17$, $p < .08$. As can be seen from Table 2, this suggests that the two-way interaction described above was more pronounced when help was given twice than when it was given once—the F values for the two-way Identity of Helper × Ego-Relevance interactions were $F(1, 44) = 13.38$, $p < .001$, for help given twice, and $F(1, 44) = 3.27$, $p < .08$, for help given once, respectively.

Evaluations of helper. The ANOVA revealed a main effect for identity of the helper, $F(1, 88) = 7.09$, $p < .05$, indicating that a friend who helped was more positively evaluated than was a stranger. However, this should be viewed in light of a 2 (identity of helper) × 2 (ego relevance) interaction, $F(1, 88) = 3.98$, $p < .05$, suggesting that subjects receiving help from a friend on a non-ego-relevant task evaluated the helper

TABLE 2

Mean Liking For and Evaluation of Helper Scores in All Eight Experimental Conditions

	Help given once		Help given twice	
Ego relevance of help	By friend	By stranger	By friend	By stranger
Liking				
Relevant	5.33	5.08	3.83	5.25
Not relevant	5.75	4.42	5.88	4.50
Evaluation of helper				
Relevant	5.72	5.43	5.72	5.75
Not relevant	5.98	4.94	6.30	5.53

Note: N = 96.

more favorably than did those receiving such help from a stranger, $F(1, 88) = 5.62$, $p < .05$ (means were 6.14 and 5.21, respectively). There were no differences between the evaluations of the friend and the stranger who helped in the ego-relevant task conditions (means were 5.72 and 5.59, respectively). Thus, in line with the earlier findings, a friend who helped on a non-ego-relevant task was most favorably evaluated.

In all, these data show that, as with recipient affect and self-evaluations, expressed liking for and evaluation of the helper were determined by an interaction between the identity of the helper and the ego relevance of the help. Further, the data for the liking measure suggest that this interaction was more pronounced when help was received twice than once.

Subjects' Perception of Helper's Evaluations of Them

The ANOVA on the mean scores on this scale revealed a main effect for identity of the helper, $F(1, 88) = 15.53$, $p < .001$, indicating that subjects who received help from a friend expected the helper to view them more favorably than did those who received help from a stranger (means were 5.22 and 4.42, respectively). This main effect should be viewed in light of a 2 (identity of helper) $\times$ 2 (ego-relevance) interaction, $F(1, 88) = 6.06$, $p < .05$, suggesting that individuals receiving ego-relevant help from a friend thought the helper perceived them less favorably than did those receiving non-ego-relevant help from a friend (means were 4.99 and 5.44, respectively). With help from a stranger, an opposite pattern was observed: Subjects receiving help on an ego-relevant task thought the helper had more favorable perceptions of them than did those receiving help on a

non-ego-relevant task (means were 4.69 and 4.15, respectively).

Expected Quality of Future Relations with the Helper

The ANOVA on the mean scores of the expected quality of future relations scale revealed no significant main effects. Yet, the three 2-way interactions were all statistically significant. The Identity of Helper $\times$ Ego-Relevance interaction, $F(1, 88) = 6.17$, $p < .05$, indicates that those who received ego-relevant help from a friend expected more negative relations with him than did those who received non-ego-relevant help from a friend (means were 5.06 and 6.11, repectively). With a stranger as a helper, the ego-relevance of the help had negligible effects on expected quality of future relations (means were 5.29 and 5.00, respectively). The Ego-Relevance $\times$ Number of Times Help Was Given interaction, $F(1, 88) = 6.37$, $p < .05$, indicates that ego-relevant help given twice led to less-positive expected-future relations than did such help given only once (means were 4.75 and 5.6, respectively). An opposite pattern exists for non-ego-relevant help. Recipients of such help expected better future relations with the donor when help was given twice than when it was given only once (means were 5.81 and 5.33, respectively). Finally, the Identity of the Helper $\times$ Number of Times Help Was Given interaction, $F(1,88) = 5.1$, $p < .05$ indicates that in the friend conditions, subjects who received help once expected better relations with their helper than did those who had received help twice (means were 5.97 and 5.19, respectively). An opposite pattern occurred for the stranger-helper conditions (4.95 and 5.36, respectively).

However, these two-way interactions are

qualified by a marginally significant three-way interaction, $F(1, 88) = 2.27, p < .13$. Simple interaction-effects analyses suggest that the interaction between ego relevance of the task and the identity of the helper is more pronounced when help was given twice, $F(1, 43) = 7.2, p < .01$, than when it was given once, $F < 1$. In fact, as can be seen from Table 3, the least positive relations were expected with a friend who helped twice on ego-relevant dimensions ($M = 4.14$), and best relations were expected with a friend who helped twice on a non ego-relevant dimension ($M = 6.25$).

Perceived Reasons for Helper's Benevolence

Subjects rated their agreement with three statements describing possible reasons for the helper's benevolence. The first was "He gave because he really cared for me." An ANOVA on subjects' ratings of their agreement with this statement yielded a main effect for identity of the helper, $F(1, 88) = 8.17, p < .01$, indicating that those who had been helped by a friend endorsed it more than did those who had been helped by a stranger (means were 4.50 and 3.29 respectively). A marginally significant interaction of Ego Relevance × Number of Times Help Was Given, $F(1, 88) = 3.63$, $p < .06$, indicates that subjects who were helped twice on a non-ego-relevant task agreed more that the helper gave because he cared for them than did those who were helped once on a non-ego-relevant task (means were 4.65 and 3.32, respectively). No such difference was observed in the ego-relevant help conditions (means were 4.0 and 3.67, respectively).

An ANOVA on subjects' ratings of agreement with the statement that the helper gave because "he expected a future return" yielded no significant main or interaction effects.

Finally, ratings of agreement with the statement "the helper gave because he wanted to show he is more able than me" were subjected to a 2 × 2 × 2 ANOVA. This yielded a main effect for the number of times help was given, $F(1, 88) = 4.77$, $p < .05$, indicating that subjects who had been helped twice agreed more with this

TABLE 3

Mean Scores of "Expected Quality of Future Relations" Statement in All Experimental Cells

	Help given once		Help given twice	
Task	By friend	By stranger	By friend	By stranger
Ego relevant	5.97	5.22	4.14	5.36
Not ego relevant	5.97	4.69	6.25	5.36

Note: $N = 96$.

statement than did those who were helped once (means were 3.43 and 2.59, respectively). The interaction of Identity of the Helper × Ego Relevance of Help was statistically significant, $F(1, 88) = 7.98, p < .01$, and indicates that individuals who had been helped by a friend on an ego-relevant task agreed more with this statement than did those who had been helped by a friend on a non-ego-relevant task (means were 3.92 and 2.29, respectively). An opposite yet less pronounced pattern is evident in the stranger-helper conditions (means were 2.63 and 3.17, respectively). The interaction of ego-relevance and number of times help was given, $F(1, 88) = 8.92, p < .01$, indicates that individuals who had been helped twice on an ego-relevant task agreed more with this statement than did individuals who had been helped once on an ego-relevant task (means were 4.25 and 2.29 respectively). With non-ego-relevant help, the difference between help given once and twice was less pronounced (means were 2.57 and 2.88, respectively). The interaction of Identity of the Helper × Number of Times Help Was Given was also statis-

tically significant, $F(1, 88) = 5.38, p < .05$. This reflects the finding that subjects who had been helped twice by a friend agreed more with the statement that the helper provided the help because he wanted to show his relative superiority than did those who had been helped only once by a friend (means were 3.96 and 2.25, respectively). In stranger-helper conditions, there was no difference between the help given once condition and the help given twice condition (means were 2.87 and 2.92, respectively).

Although the three-way interaction for the above measure did not exceed the .05 level of significance, $F(1, 88) = 1.82, p < .18$, its conceptual importance to the issues under study called for its examination. This revealed that the interaction of Identity of the Helper × Ego Relevance of Help was significant only when help was given twice, $F(1, 44) = 8.81, p < .01$. When help was given once, this interaction was not significant, $F(1, 44) = 1.13, p < .30$. As can be seen from Table 4, subjects who had been helped twice by a friend on an ego-relevant task were most likely to agree

TABLE 4

Mean Agreement Scores on the Statement That Helper Helped Because He Wished to Show Superiority

Task	Help given once		Help given twice	
	By friend	By stranger	By friend	By stranger
Ego relevant	2.25	2.33	5.58	2.92
Not ego relevant	2.25	3.46	2.33	2.82

Note: N = 96.

that the helper's benevolence reflected his wish to show his superiority over the subject (mean agreement score in this cell was 5.58).

DISCUSSION

The results of the present study support the major assertion that the effect of donor-recipient social proximity on reaction to aid is determined by the ego relevance of the helping task. The findings show that when the help reflects the recipient's inferiority on ego-relevant dimensions (i.e., intelligence and creativity), its receipt from a friend is a negative experience. Such help leads to more negative affect and less favorable recipient self-evaluations than does aid from a friend that does not reflect inadequacy on an ego-relevant dimension. Subjects who receive ego-relevant help from a friend also indicate relative dislike and unfavorable evaluations of him, expect more negative future relations with him, and think that he evaluated them less favorably than did those who received non-ego-relevant help from a friend. This effect tends to be more pronounced when help is given twice than once. When the helper is a stranger, conditions associated with the receipt of help may not precipitate substantial changes in the recipient's reactions.

From a somewhat different perspective, an examination of the data indicates that help was most self-supportive and threatening when given by a friend. When a friend helped twice on an ego-relevant task, his help was most self-threatening (i.e., led to the lowest affect, self-evaluation, liking, and expected quality for future relations scores), and when help was given twice on a non-ego-relevant task it was most self-supportive (i.e., led to the highest affect,

self-evaluation, liking, and expected quality of future relations). This pattern of effects is consistent with the view of help from a socially close other as a "double-edged sword." Such help may contain intense elements of self-threat because of the inherent comparison stress in that a socially close individual (who serves as a social-comparison other) has succeeded to the point of providing help whereas the helpee has failed by needing it. On the other hand, such a receipt of help may contain a relatively high degree of self-support because it implies caring and concern from a psychologically significant other.

The data indicate that aid may be threatening only when its receipt reflects the recipient's inferiority on an ego-relevant dimension. Only then do the potential messages of relative inferiority and dependency become sufficiently stressful to induce a relatively high degree of self-threat. When help does not reflect inferiority on an ego-relevant dimension it holds no self-threat potential, and its favorable, self-supporting elements become psychologically salient and meaningful. Further, in line with the idea that events that are consistent over time are more likely to precipitate stable perceptions of interpersonal events (cf. Kelley, 1967), the self-threat or support was most apparent when help was given twice.

Further evidence that help from a friend that reflects inferiority on an ego-relevant dimension leads to increased comparison stress is available from the measure which assessed subjects' perceptions of the helper's motives. When asked why the helper gave aid, subjects who were given ego-relevant help twice by a friend agreed most strongly with the statement that the helper gave because he wanted to demonstrate his relative superiority.

Links with Past Theory and Research

What are the implications of these data for relevant research and theory? Conceptual and empirical aspects of the present research relate both to past research on recipient reactions to aid and to research on social-comparison processes. Regarding the former, the findings are in accord with earlier research that indicates that receiving help from a similar other arouses comparison stress and is therefore a self-threatening experience (Fisher & Nadler, 1974; Nadler et al., 1976). However, the present study importantly extends the range of this phenomenon in two respects.

First, it adds external validity by showing that this phenomenon is not unique to experimental manipulations of interpersonal similarity but is an integral part of helping relations between friends. This extension allows for a broader conceptual treatment of the issue at hand. It also suggests that the phenomena under study should be part of helping interactions between individuals in many types of close relations (e.g., relatives, romantic partners, etc.). Admittedly, what constitutes an ego-relevant task will change as a function of the specific relationship one focuses on (e.g., issues surrounding the "right way" to socialize children may be ego relevant for some, but not other, close relationships). However, once ego-relevant dimensions have been identified and defined, the same principles should hold.

Second, the present findings indicate some boundary conditions to earlier research by the present authors (e.g., Fisher & Nadler, 1974; Nadler et al., 1976) by suggesting that aid from a socially close other will not always be threatening. Rather, its effects depend on the *characteristics of the task* on which help is given (i.e., ego relevance of help) and *characteristics of the help itself* (i.e., whether it is given once or twice). This is especially noteworthy because past studies that demonstrated the threatening effects of help from a similar other all used ego-relevant tasks (e.g., various cognitive abilities). Even more important, by showing that help from a close other holds the potential for greater self-threat *and* self-support, the present findings reconcile the data that help from a similar other is an unpleasant experience (cf. Fisher & Nadler, 1974) with other data (e.g., Bar-Tal, Zohʾr, Greenberg, & Hermon, 1977; Clark & Mills, 1979; DePaulo, 1978) that help from a socially close other may be a relatively positive experience.[5]

Finally, the present findings are supportive of two major assertions of the threat to self-esteem model of recipient reactions to help (Fisher, Nadler, & Whitcher-Alagna, 1982). As hypothesized in the model, the data indicate that (a) receiving help contains a mixture of positive, self-supporting and negative, self-threatening elements for the recipient, and that (b) conceptually relevant variables moderate the relative amount of self-threat and self-support in aid. In addition, aid that is threatening is associated with a cluster of negative-defensive reactions (e.g., negative self and other perceptions and defensive behaviors) and supportive help is associated with a cluster of positive, nondefensive responses (i.e., positive self and other perceptions, and nondefensive behaviors).

The present findings are also relevant for recent developments in the study of social comparison processes. They support the notion that both greater pain and pleasure are potentially inherent in social comparison with others (cf. Brickman & Bulman, 1977;

Nadler, Jazwinski, Lau, & Miller, 1980). Further, our data and conceptualization are congruent with Tesser's recent development of the self-esteem—maintenance model, which asserts that a major variable that moderates the effects of the social comparison experience is the ego relevance of the task on which comparison occurs (cf. Tesser, 1980). The present findings may be viewed as complementing and extending Tesser's work. Tesser and Smith (1980) showed that the self-threat inherent in comparison processes moderates *help-giving*, whereas the present study shows conceptually similar patterns when the *recipient's reactions* to aid are concerned. Taken together, it seems that an important facet of interpersonal helping relations is the threat to self-esteem which accrues from social comparison processes.

Donor-Recipient Social Proximity and Recipient's Reactions: A Suggested Model

The preceding discussion can be viewed paradigmatically in terms of a model of the effects of donor—recipient social proximity on the recipient's reaction to aid. The utility of such a paradigmatic view (presented in Figure 1) is twofold. First, it provides an overview of the present findings and their conceptualization; second, it serves as a conceptual map to guide future research in this context. Figure 1 suggests the following:

1. Receiving help from a socially close other (i.e., a friend) is a more psychologically significant experience than help from a socially distant other (i.e., a stranger).

2. However, whether this greater psy-

FIGURE 1.

Effects of social proximity between donor and recipient on recipient's reactions.

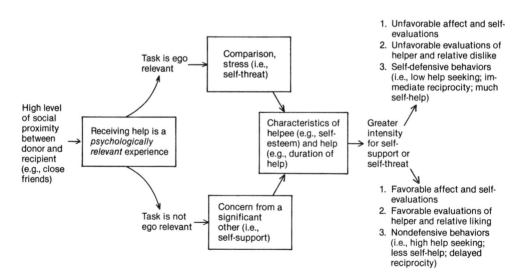

chological intensity translates to greater self-threat or support is dependent on the ego relevance of the task on which help was given. If the task is ego relevant, receiving help from a socially close other is self-threatening because of the greater intensity of the *comparison stress* involved. If, however, the task is not ego-relevant, help is more self-supportive due to the greater intensity of the positive elements involved (e.g., signs of concern from a friend, family member, etc.).

3. The intensity of the self-threat and self-support in aid is affected by other conceptually relevant situational and personality variables. Although the present study demonstrated that the consistency of helping (i.e., help given once or twice) moderates these elements, past research (Nadler et al., 1976; 1979; 1981) suggests that the recipient's self-concept should also moderate them.

4. In line with the threat-to-self-esteem model of reactions to aid (Fisher, Nadler, & Whitcher-Alagna, 1982), the self-threat and support in aid precipitate negative and positive clusters of reactions to help, respectively. Although the present study centered on affective and evaluative reactions, this model suggests that the recipient's behavioral responses should be affected in a similar manner. For example, people helped continuously by a friend on an ego-relevant task should engage in self-help efforts to terminate the uneasy dependency, choose not to seek help from their friend, and if possible, attempt immediate reciprocity.

NOTES

1. In actuality only the first part was run. The expectation for the second part of the experiment was incorporated because past research (i.e., Nadler, Shapira, & Ben-Itzhak, 1982) indicated

that such expectations increase the salience of self-related aspects inherent in receiving help.

2. Subjects were told that to increase motivation, monetary prizes would be awarded for correct solutions. It was indicated that if the two individuals solved the mystery correctly, they would both receive 2 Israeli Shekels (about twenty five cents at the time when the study was run); if only one reached the correct solution, he would receive 4 Israeli Shekels and his partner would receive nothing. Further, it was indicated to subjects that an individual's participation in the second part of the experiment—team problem solving—in which large sums of money could be won, was dependent on correct solution(s) in the first part. These instructions were introduced to insure a high motivation to solve the experimental task so that all subjects subsequently accepted their "partner's" offer of help. Also, the instructi ms established the fact that the helper was making a real and tangible sacrifice in helping the subject.

3. There were no differences between conditions in the attrition rate.

4. Although the three-way interaction was not significant for the measure of self-evaluation, both affect and self-evaluation scores were highest in the condition in which the friend helped twice on a non ego-relevant task (means were 5.63 and 6.33, respectively) and lowest in the condition in which the friend helped twice on an ego-relevant task (means were 3.98 and 5.08, respectively). Corroborating this statement is the fact that a multivariate ANOVA using the affect and self-evaluation scores as variates yielded a marginally significant three-way interaction, $F(2, 176) = 2.87, p < .06$.

5. For a detailed discussion of these two bodies of research and their integration, see Nadler and Fisher, in press.

REFERENCES

Bar-Tal, D., Zohar, Y. B., Greenberg, M. S., & Hermon, M. Reciprocity in the relationship between donor and recipient and between harm-doer and victim. *Sociometry*, 1977, *40*, 293-298.

Bramel, D. Dissonance, expectation and the self. In R. Abelson, E. Aronson, R. M. Newcomb, W. J. McQuire, M. J. Rosenberg, & P. H. Tannenbaum (Eds.), *Sourcebook of cognitive consistency*. New York: Rand-McNally, 1968.

Brickman, P., & Bulman, R. J. Pleasure and pain in social comparison. In J. M. Suls & R. L. Miller (Eds.), *Social comparison processes: Theoretical and empirical perspectives*. Washington, D. C.: Hemisphere, 1977.

Byrne, D. *The attraction paradigm*. New York: Academic Press, 1971.

Clark, M. S., & Mills, J. Interpersonal attraction in exchange and communal relationships. *Journal of Personality and Social Psychology*, 1979, *37*, 12-24.

DePaulo, B. M.. Help seeking from the recipient's point of view. JSAS *Catalog of Selected Documents in Psychology*, 1978, *8*, 62. (Ms. No. 1721)

DePaulo, B. M., Brown, P. L., Ishii, S. H., & Fisher, J. D. Recipient reactions to kindly and unkindly bestowed help. *Journal of Personality and Social Psychology*, 1982, *41*, 478-487.

Festinger, L. A theory of social comparison processes. *Human Relations*, 1954, *1*, 117-140.

Fisher, J. D., Harrison, C., & Nadler, A. Exploring the generalizability of donor-recipient similarity effects. *Personality and Social Psychology Bulletin*, 1978, *4*, 627-630.

Fisher, J. D., & Nadler, A. The effect of similarity between donor and recipient on reactions to aid. *Journal of Applied Social Psychology*, 1974, *4*, 230-243.

Fisher, J. D., & Nadler, A. Effect of donor resources on recipient self-esteem and self-help. *Journal of Experimental Social Psychology*, 1976, *12*, 139-150.

Fisher, J. D., Nadler, A., & Whitcher-Alagna, S. Recipient reactions to aid. *Psychological Bulletin*, 1982, *91*, 27-54.

Gergen, K. J., Ellsworth, P., Maslach, C., & Seipel, M. Obligation, donor resources, and reactions to aid in three nations. *Journal of Personality and Social Psychology*, 1975, *31*, 390-400.

Gergen, K. J., & Gergen, M. International assistance from a psychological perspective. *1971 Yearbook of world affairs* (Vol. 25). London: Institute of World Affairs, 1971.

Kelley, H. H. Attribution theory in social psychology. In D. Levine (Ed.), *Nebraska Symposium on Motivation* (Vol. 15). Lincoln: University of Nebraska Press, 1967.

Nadler, A., Altman, A., & Fisher, J. D. Helping is not enough: Recipient's reactions to aid as a function of positive and negative self-regard.

Journal of Personality, 1979, *47*, 615-628.

Nadler, A., & Fisher, J. D. Effects of donor-recipient relationships on recipient's reactions to being helped. In E. Staub, D. Bar-Tal, J. Reykowski, & J. Karylowski (Eds.), *Development and maintenance of pro-social behavior: International Perspectives*. New York: Plenum Press, in press.

Nadler, A., Fisher, J. D., & Streufert, S. The donor's dilemma: Recipient's reactions to aid from friend or foe. *Journal of Applied Social Psychology*, 1974, *4*, 272-285.

Nadler, A., Fisher, J. D., & Streufert, S. When helping hurts: The effects of donor-recipient similarity and recipient self-esteem on reactions to aid. *Journal of Personality*, 1976, *44*, 392-409.

Nadler, A., Jazwinski, C., Lau, S., & Miller, A. The cold glow of success: Responses to social rejection as affected by attitude similarity between chosen and rejected individuals. *European Journal of Social Psychology*, 1980, *10*, 279-289.

Nadler, A., Shapira, R., & Ben-Itzhak, S. Good looks may help: Effects of helper's physical attractiveness and sex of helper on males' and females' help-seeking behavior. *Journal of Personality and Social Psychology*, 1982, *42*, 90-99.

Nadler, A., Sheinberg, O., & Jaffe, Y. Coping with stress in male paraplegics through help seeking: The role of acceptance of physical disability in help seeking. In C. D. Spielberger, I. G. Sarason, & N. A. Milgram (Eds.), *Stress and anxiety* (Vol. 8). Washington, D. C.: Hemisphere, 1981.

Rushton, J. P., & Sorrentino, R. M. *Altruism and helping behavior: Social, personality and developmental perspectives*. Hillsdale, N.J.: Erlbaum, 1981.

Tesser, A. Self-esteem maintenance in family dynamics. *Journal of Personality and Social Psychology*, 1980, *39*, 77-91.

Tesser, A., & Smith, J. Some effects of task relevance and friendship on helping: You don't always help the one you like. *Journal of Experimental Social Psychology*, 1980, *16*, 582-590.

Tessler, R. C., & Schwartz, S. H. Help-seeking, self-esteem, and achievement motivation: An attributional analysis. *Journal of Personality and Social Psychology*, 1972, *21*, 318-326.

Winer, B. J. *Statistical principles in experimental design*. New York: McGraw-Hill, 1971.

7 Violence and Aggression

AS THE PAST TWO chapters have amply shown, social psychologists have a continuing interest in positive social relationships, as evidenced by their work in the areas of interpersonal attraction and altruism. Unfortunately, the dialectic nature of the human condition suggests that for every good there is a bad; such is the case in interpersonal affairs. Although our studies of prosocial behaviors reveal the good that people do, social psychologists' investigations of violence and aggression show the darker side of our social lives. Researchers from various disciplines have attempted to elucidate the causes of aggressive behavior, at both the infrahuman and human level of investigation. For example, ethologists, such as Konrad Lorenz, have focused on aggression as an adaptive, instinctual response in our behavioral repertoire that contributes to the survival of the species. Biologists and physiological psychologists have tended to implicate hormonal and genetic factors that may predispose some persons to exhibit high levels of aggressive behavior. Still others, such as Freud, suggest that aggression is the result of particular dispositional qualities and personality characteristics that can be modified and controlled via therapeutic intervention. Social psychologists, on the other hand, have focused on violence and aggression as responses to social and environmental stimuli.

One of the earliest attempts to explain aggression in the latter fashion was the frustration-aggression hypothesis of Dollard et al. (1939). In this formulation, aggression was perceived to be a consequence of external frustrations that blocked some goal-directed behavior. The notion that frustration and aggression were causally linked persisted with modification (e.g., Berkowitz, 1969) for many years. However, in the early 1960s, a new perspective began to take hold: the social-learning approach, as formulated by Albert Bandura (e.g., 1973; Bandura, Ross, and Ross, 1961, 1963).

Rather than consider aggression as a special type of behavior elicited from an individual by specific situational cues, Bandura (1973) viewed aggression as a behavior learned by one's observations of the actions of others and the consequences to which those actions led. The social learning approach also acknowledges the role of cognitive processes in the display of aggressive behavior to a much greater extent than previous theorists acknowledged. The success of Bandura's use of social learning theory to explain many of the complexities of aggressive behavior encouraged many others to use his work as a starting point for the development of programs designed to reduce the amount of violence in our society, and television, one of the primary sources from which aggressive behavior can be acquired, was one of the first targets.

The first article in this chapter directly addresses the question of the role that television may play in the acquisition and disinhibition of aggression. Leonard Eron reports on the progress of two longitudinal studies that indicate a link between the viewing of TV violence and the amount of aggressive behavior exhibited by children. Additionally, Eron cites parental factors that also appear to relate to children's aggressive tendencies. Finally, Eron confronts the topic of aggression reduction and suggests various methods that could conceivably be developed to promote the reduction of aggressive behavior in children.

The second article in this chapter, by Edward Donnerstein, also deals with the effects of viewing aggression, but in a more specific vein. Increasing violence toward women in recent years has led to a considerable amount of research on the antecedents of violent acts such as rape. Erotic reading materials and movies have been implicated as possible contributing causes of violent crimes against women. In the study presented, Donnerstein specifically attempts to assess the relationship between viewing aggressive erotica and the frequency of subsequent violence toward women.

The final article is an example of a field study that looks at another growing problem with respect to aggression—aggression at sporting events. Robert Arms, Gordon Russell, and Mark Sandilands demonstrate that viewing some sporting events may elicit more hostility on the part of the fans than others. Although observing aggressive sporting events (e.g., wrestling, ice hockey) increased the amount of hostility subsequently displayed, observing competitive but nonaggressive sports (e.g., swimming) did not lead to more aggressive behavior by observers. In addition to changes in the amount of aggression, observation of aggressive and competitive athletic events also appears to affect the quality of interpersonal relationships, decreasing the positivity of the observers' feelings toward others.

Parent-Child Interaction, Television Violence, and Aggression of Children

Leonard D. Eron

Abstract: The results of two large-scale longitudinal studies, one of which included an experimental manipulation, are summarized and integrated. The relation between television violence and aggression in children has been corroborated in two different geographical areas of the United States as well as in Finland, Poland, and Australia and has been found to hold for both boys and girls. Furthermore, the causal effect is seen as circular, with television violence affecting children's aggression and aggressive children watching more and more violent television. Contributing increments to a child's level of overt aggression are popularity, intellectual ability, and aggressive fantasy as well as extent of physical punishment and rejection by parents and the tendency of parents to endorse attitudes and behaviors often seen in sociopathic individuals. It has been demonstrated that it is possible to intervene in order to attenuate the relation between television violence and aggression with simple tuitional procedures that apparently supersede the influence of the parent variables studied. Important intervening variables in the television violence-aggression relation are the child's identification with aggressive characters and the extent to which the youngster believes television renders an accurate portrayal of life.

In the early 1960s I reported an incidental finding uncovered in a large-scale study in which we were attempting to determine the relation between child-rearing practices of parents and the aggressive behavior of their children in school (Eron, 1963). This finding, that there was a relation between the violence of the television programs children preferred and how aggressive they were in school, received a lot of attention, overshadowing other results of the study that I believe were equally important and theoretically just as interesting. As has been amply demonstrated by Bandura (1973), Berkowitz (1962), Buss (1961), Feshbach (1970), and my collaborators and me (Eron, Walder, & Lefkowitz, 1971; Lefkowitz, Eron, Walder, & Huesmann, 1977), aggression is to a great extent a learned behavior, and the findings in regard to television represent just one example of how aggression can be learned from the interaction of the individual with the environment. There are other ways in which aggression can be learned, however, than from viewing the behaviors of television characters. I will discuss these other processes and present some relevant recent data later in this article. However, now I would like to bring you up to date on the work that my colleagues and I have been doing, which is concerned with the television-aggression relation. Because the original finding was incidental and largely serendipitous does not mean that it is unimportant in adding to our understanding of how children learn to be aggressive and, also, how this behavior can be unlearned.

This article was presented as a Distinguished Professional Contribution to Knowledge Award address at the meeting of the American Psychological Association, Los Angeles, August 27, 1981, with the title "Mitigating the Modeling of Media Mayhem."

Thanks are due to Rowell Huesmann, with whom I have collaborated in most of these studies, and to Patrick Brice for help with the data analyses. Thanks are also due to the National Institute of Mental Health, which has supported this research with Grants M1726 and 34410 (L. D. Eron), Grants 28280 and 31866 (L. R. Huesmann), and Contract HSM 42-70-60 (M. M. Lefkowitz), and to the Office of Child Development for Grant CB364 (L. D. Eron).

"Parent-child Interaction, Television Violence, and Aggression of Children" by L.D. Eron, 1982, *American Psychologist, 37,* pp. 197-211. Copyright 1982 by the American Psychological Assn. Reprinted by permission of the publisher and author.

The original finding of a relation between television violence viewing and subsequent aggressive behavior in natural situations outside the laboratory has now been replicated by a number of investigators (Greenberg, 1975; Hartnagel, Teevan, & McIntyre, 1975; McCarthy, Langner, Gersten, Eisenberg, & Orzeck, 1975; Parke, Berkowitz, Leyens, West, & Sebastian, 1977). Further, my collaborators and I have demonstrated that the continued viewing of television violence is a very likely cause of aggressive behavior and that there is a long-lasting effect on children (Eron, Huesmann, Lefkowitz, & Walder, 1972; Huesmann, in press; Huesmann & Eron, in press). The causative direction of the relation has also been confirmed by other investigators (Belson, 1978; Singer & Singer, 1981).

The subjects of our original study, 875 eight-year-old children, included the entire third-grade population of a semi-rural county in upstate New York. This is referred to as the *Rip Van Winkle Study.* Ten years later we interviewed 475 of these subjects in a follow-up study. A surprising finding was that the correlation between television violence viewing and aggressive behavior was higher for boys over the 10-year period than it was contemporaneously. This led us to conclude that the effect of viewing violence was probably cumulative. Since there was no relation between the amount of violence viewed in the later period and aggression at that time, however, we further concluded that there must be a sensitive period, around age 8, when a youngster is especially susceptible to the effect of continued violence viewing. It was assumed this period began sometime before age 8 and was probably over by age 12.

Because our original sample included only eight-year-old children, it was impossible to determine when this sensitive period began and when it ended. Therefore, Rowell Huesmann and I undertook a new study, some 17 years later, in a different area of the country. In this new study we followed approximately 750 children for three years. By using two overlapping samples, we encompassed an age range of 6-10 years during this period. We were interested in determining the boundary conditions of the relation between television violence viewing and aggression that we and others had demonstrated. In addition, however, we were interested in learning more about the intervening variables. What were the essential child and parent factors that could mediate the relation between television violence viewing and aggressive behavior? And since the correlation between the two was far from perfect, were there certain kinds of parent and child variables that made some children more vulnerable than others to the effect of violence on television? Thus we interviewed as many of the parents of our child subjects as possible and obtained additional information from the children themselves. The variables we chose to investigate were primarily ones that had been suggested as likely precursors or mediators in our previous 10-year study. Another way in which we looked for important intervening variables was with a manipulative field experiment with sub-samples of the subjects from our longitudinal study. The manipulation was an intervention designed to attentuate the relation between exposure to TV violence and aggressive behavior among high violence viewers.

In this article, I will try to integrate the results of this manipulative field experiment with the findings in regard to precursor variables from the three-year longitudinal study. This longitudinal study, not including the manipulation, has been and is being replicated in Finland, Poland, Holland,

Australia, and Israel, and I will comment on the preliminary findings of this cross-national research that are now available. Finally, we are currently in the last stage of data collection in a 21-year follow-up of our original third-grade subjects . Of course since these data are not yet all collected, there are no analyses that I can report.

We turn now to the three-year longitudinal survey completed in the United States, which we will refer to as the *Chicago Circle Study*. Our original group included 672 children in the public schools of Oak Park, Illinois, an economically and socially heterogeneous suburb of Chicago, and 86 children from an inner city school in the Chicago Archdiocese. Half of these children were in the first grade and half in the third grade during the first year of the study, 1977. All of the children were tested in their classrooms in two hourly sessions a week apart in that year and then again in 1978 and 1979. In 1978 607 children remained in the sample, and in 1979 there were 505. In addition, 591 of their parents were also seen for individual interviews. Almost all of the subject attrition was attributable to children leaving the school system, and the attrition rate did not differ by grade or sex. Measures taken at the three points in time included peer-nominated aggression and popularity; self-ratings of aggression, fantasy, and preference for sex-typed behaviors; and various measures of television habits including frequency of viewing, violence of favorite programs, and identification with aggressive male and female television characters. The parent variables included rejection, nurturance, physical punishment for aggression, self-ratings of aggression, social mobility, and the violence of the television programs the parents themselves watched. A brief description of the measures follows.

Child Measures

Peer-Nominated Aggression and Popularity

Aggression and popularity of children were measured by a version of the Peer Rating Index of Aggression (Walder, Abelson, Eron, Banta, & Laulicht, 1961), in which every child in the classroom rates every other child on a series of 10 aggression and two popularity items embedded in a total list of 15 items. The reliability of this instrument as well as its concurrent predictive and construct validity have been amply demonstrated (Eron et al., 1971; Lefkowitz et al., 1977). In the current study coefficient alpha was .95 and test-retest reliability over one month was .91.

Self-Ratings of Aggression

This included four items in which the subject rates his or her similarity to fictional children described as engaging in specific aggressive behaviors; for example, "Steven often gets angry and punches other kids. Are you just like Steven, a little bit like Steven or not at all like Steven?" Test-retest reliability over one month was .54.

Sex-Typed Behavior

A measure of preference for sex-typed toys and games was used to determine appropriate sex role behavior. This measure of preference for sex-typed activities comprised a booklet of four pages, each of which contained six pictures of children's activities. Two pictures of each set had been previously rated as masculine, two as feminine, and two as neutral by 67 college students who had been asked to designate the activities as popular for boys or girls or both. The task for the children was to select the two activities they liked best on each page, and they received a score for the number of masculine, feminine, and neutral pictures they chose. The reason for including a neutral category is that even though less masculine boys may not like traditionally feminine activities, they might prefer neutral over traditionally masculine ones. Similarly, for girls we anticipated that those who did not prefer traditionally feminine activities might also eschew masculine activities but subscribe to neutral ones. Coefficient alpha is not an appropriate measure of reliability for this scale. However, one-month test—retest reliabilities ranged between .55 and .60. Only the masculine and neutral sex-typed preferences are included in the analyses, since preference for feminine activities did not relate to aggression either positively or negatively.

Fantasy

Two of the fantasy scales devised by Rosenfeld, Huesmann, Eron, and Torney-Purta (in press) were used to measure extent of aggressive fantasy and active heroic fantasy (each with six items; e.g., "Do you sometimes have daydreams about hitting or hurting somebody you don't like?" or "When you are daydreaming, do you think about being the winner in a game you like to play?"). Coefficient alphas for these scales were .64 and .61, respectively; one-month test—retest reliability, .44 and .62.

Frequency of Viewing

This measure was obtained from the subjects themselves, who rated the frequency with which they watched specifically named programs. These were the 80 television shows chosen from the Nielson data as the most popular for children of ages 6-11. The shows were divided into eight lists of 10 programs each. The lists were equivalent in terms of the violence and popularity of the shows in each list, the sex of the central character, and the time and day of the week in which the programs were shown in the Chicago area. The children were given booklets with each of the eight lists on a different colored sheet of paper and were asked to draw a line through the one program they watched the most on that list. They were then asked to indicate, by checking an appropriate box, whether they "watched every single time the program was on," or "watched a lot, but not every single time," or "just once in a while." A TV frequency score was then obtained by summing· the scores from all eight shows selected. Test-retest reliability over one month was .76.

Violence of Favorite Television Programs

Two psychology graduate students who had small children, but were not associated with this research project, rated all 80 programs for the amount of visually portrayed physical aggression in the show on a five-point scale from "not violent" to "very violent." Interrater reliability was .75. A child's TV violence score was the sum of the violence ratings of the eight shows that the child had indicated he or she watched, weighted by the frequency with which the child reported watching the program. Test-retest reliability over one month was also .75.

Realism of Television Programs

The children were asked to rate how realistic they judged television to be. They were given a list of 10 violent shows, in-cluding cartoons as well as police shows and "bionic" shows. They were then asked, "How true do you think these programs are in telling what life is really like: just like it is in real life, a little like it is in real life, or not at all like it is in real life?" The subject's total realism score was the sum of the ratings on all 10 items. One-month test-retest reliability was .74. Coefficient alpha was .72.

Identification with TV Characters

Ratings were made by the children to indicate how much they were like certain television characters. These characters included two aggressive males, two aggressive females, two unaggressive males, and two unaggressive females. From their responses a reliable identification with aggressive character score was derived. Coefficient alpha for this measure was .71, and test-retest reliability over one month was .60.

PARENT MEASURES

Rejection

This was a 10-item scale dealing with change-worthy behaviors, other than aggression, in the child. The greater the number of items on which the parent indicated disapproval of the child's current behavior, the higher the rejection score; for example, "Are you satisfied with Johnnie's manners?" "Does he read as well as could be expected for a child of his age?" "Is he too forgetful?" This measure has been demonstrated to be reliable and reasonably independent of rejectability of the child (Eron et al., 1971).

Nurturance

This scale included eight items having to do with the amount of attention the parent devotes to the child and the parent's awareness of the child's needs and activities. For example, "Do you usually have time so that Johnnie can talk to you about things that interest him?" "What does Johnnie dream about?" (scored + if parent can name at least one topic). The reliability and validity of this and the other parent measures have been reported by Eron et al. (1971) and Lefkowitz et al. (1977).

Punishment

This was a five-item scale tapping the parents' use of physical punishment; for example, "How many times in the past year have you spanked Johnnie until he cried?" Our previous research (Lefkowitz, Walder, & Eron, 1963) indicated that use of non-physical punishment by parents did not relate to aggression in children. It was only physical punishment by the parents that bore this relation to their child's aggression.

Self-Ratings of Aggression

There were two measures of the parents' own aggression. The first included the sum of Scales 4 and 9 (Psychopathic Deviate and Hypomania) of the Minnesota Multiphasic Personality Inventory (MMPI). These combined scales have been shown to be reliable and valid as a measure of antisocial behavior (Huesmann, Lefkowitz, & Eron, 1978). The other measure was a self-rating of how often the parents engaged in seven specific aggressive behaviors; for example, "Have you ever slapped or kicked another person?"

Social Mobility

This included five items designed to tap how strongly motivated the parent was toward occupational and social achievement; for example, "Would you give up your friends and move to a new location in order to get ahead?"

TV Violence

Sum of violence scores for parents' favorite program, weighted by the frequency with which the program was watched. This was identical to the child television measure (see above).

Aggressive Fantasy

This measure for parents included one of the six items used in the aggressive fantasy measure for child subjects (see above).

TELEVISION VIOLENCE AND AGGRESSION

The Chicago Circle Study and its replication in other countries were undertaken to determine the generality of the original findings obtained with eight-year-old children in a semi-rural area of New York state. As indicated in Table 1, the positive relation was found to hold up in a different geographical and more urban area of the United States and in three other countries with a range of political and economic systems as well as different organizations of control and distribution of television than in the United States. The correlations in all four countries are positive and, except for the first grades in Australia and Finland, are of roughly the same order and for the most part highly significant. Further, at least in the United States, the increasing size of the correlation with each succeeding year is consistent with our original assumption of a cumulative effect. Part of this trend may be the result of a methodological factor—the measures used are not as reliable with first graders as they are with older children. But probably even more important is a developmental factor. As demonstrated in an article by Eron, Huesmann, Brice, Fischer, and Mermelstein (in press), aggression, as measured by the peer rating index, increases significantly for both boys and girls from the first to the fifth grade, whereas the viewing of television violence increases up to the third grade and then starts to decline. Over the same period the child's perception of television violence as realistic is decreasing. Thus the third grade may be a period during which a number of factors converge and make the child unusually susceptible to the effects of television. It is interesting that the strongest relations between television violence and both simultaneous and later aggression have been reported for children of this age (Chaffee, 1972; Lefkowitz et al., 1977).

At any rate there is no denying that the relation between television viewing and aggressive behavior is ubiquitous. Indeed, although 20 years ago we found a significant relation only for boys, we now find the same effect for girls. In general, this is true in all four countries, Finland, Poland, Australia, and the United States (Lagerspetz, Note 1; Fraczek, Note 2; Sheehan, Note 3). The recent extension of the findings to include girls has been reported and commented on elsewhere (Eron, 1980; Huesmann, in press; Huesmann & Eron, in press). Though the existence of the positive relation between violence viewing and aggression is clear, the reasons for it are debatable. A number of processes have been hypothesized (Huesmann, in press).

suggesting various causes. The evidence seems compelling that excessive violence viewing is a cause of increased aggression in many children, but this does not necessarily eliminate other causal hypotheses as well. For example, on the basis of our most recent data, it appears that not only does continued exposure to violence on television influence a young person to be more aggressive, but aggressive youngsters continue to watch an increased amount of violence. It is quite possible that a number of processes in addition to observational learning account for the bidirectional nature of the relation between television violence and aggression. I will comment further on the likely circularity of the relation after discussing the evidence for the presence and effect of other intervening variables and processes.

TABLE 1

Correlations Between Television Violence and Aggression

Cohort	U.S.	Finland	Poland	Australia
1				
1st grade	.21**	.14	.23*	.02
2nd grade	.23**	.26**	.19*	
3rd grade	.25**	.20*		
2				
3rd grade	.22**	.16	.29**	.22**
4th grade	.23**	.23*	.23**	
5th grade	.26**	.22*		

Note: Ns = 758 in U.S.A.; 220 in Finland; 237 in Poland; 290 in Australia.
*p<.05 **p<.01.

INTELLIGENCE, AGGRESSION, AND TELEVISION VIOLENCE

In research in personality and child development, there is one variable that is invariably related to just about everything else, and that is intellectual ability. It is the prime example of a third variable that can often be invoked to explain away the correlation between two other variables. Thus it is usually necessary to control for intellectual ability, either in the experimental design by using randomized blocks or statistically by using partial correlation in the data analysis. Most observational and field studies have used the latter procedure. For example, Belson (1978) in England and Singer and Singer (1981) in New Haven partialed out the effect of intelligence and still detected a significant relation between television violence viewing and aggression. In our 10-year research in New York, we also found that low academic achievement was related both to television viewing and to aggression, but achievement could not account completely for the relation between the latter two. Again, in the Chicago Circle Study, as noted in Table 2, reading achievement is one of the highest correlates of aggression and, at least for boys, is also related to observation of violence. Further, for both boys and girls, the lower the intellectual ability, as indicated by scores on a reading achievement test, the more the youngster believes television violence is real. When achievement is partialed out, there is a substantial diminution in the relation between television viewing and aggression for boys, from .245 to .134, which, however, is still significant in this large group. Of course the partialed variable here is reading achievement, which may be influenced by television viewing as well as influencing both television viewing and

TABLE 2

Correlations Between Reading Achievement and Other Variables

Variable	Boys	Girls
Peer-nominated aggression	− .44***	− .24**
TV violence	− .30***	− .14
TV frequency	− .26**	− .05
TV realism	− .32***	− .30***
Identification with aggressive TV characters	− .20*	− .10
Parents' education	.35***	.21**
Fathers' occupation	− .19*	− .19*

*$p<.05$. **$p<.01$ ***$p<.001$.

aggression. As we see in Table 2, less-achieving children watch television more often, identify more strongly with aggressive television characters, and are more apt to believe aggressive television content is real. Thus they are more likely to be influenced by the behaviors they observe on the screen. In addition, they are likely to be frustrated more often. Thus intelligence, as reflected in reading achievement, accounts for some of the variance in the relation between television violence and aggressive behavior, but its role seems to be that of an exacerbating variable.

OTHER VARIABLES AND AGGRESSION

Although television violence by itself may be an important precursor of aggressive behavior, it would be foolish to maintain that it is the only one of importance. Ordinary common sense would tell us that other socializing agents, especially parents, should have at least equally as great an effect on children's behavior. Our previous research (the Rip Van Winkle Study) did indicate that parental punishment of aggression, the models of behavior parents provide, and the instigations to aggression implied in their rejecting and non-nurturant child-rearing practices all contribute to aggressive behavior in children. The Chicago Circle Study and the cross-national replications have furnished an opportunity to check further on the child-rearing antecedents of aggressive behavior as well as other child behaviors that might have some bearing on the relation between television vio-

lence and aggression, in addition to any independent influence they might have on aggressive behavior.

Table 3 presents those variables that, based on our previous findings in semi-rural New York, we posited would be most closely related to aggressive behavior of the children. The correlations of these variables with aggression are shown separately for boys and girls in Table 3. Most are significantly related to aggression, although not markedly so. Since most of the variables are not normally distributed, the correlation coefficient probably underestimates the true relation. A better understanding of the meaning of these relations can be obtained by dividing the male and female samples into high, medium, and low groups, according to each of the variables, and computing the mean peer-nominated aggression score for each level of the variable. It then becomes clearer how aggression increases with each of the hypothesized precursors or concomitant variables.

Let us look first at the measures obtained directly from the children. As noted in Fig-

TABLE 3

Correlations of Predictor Variables With Peer-Nominated Aggression Scores

Variable	Total	Girls	Boys
Child			
Self-rating of aggression	.322	.281	.300
Masculine sex role	.242	.163	.188
Neutral sex role	− .204	− .148	− .189
Aggressive fantasy	.164	.113	.195
Active heroic fantasy	.195	.171	.153
TV violence	.221	.171	.206
TV realism	.135	.115	.151
Identification with aggressive TV characters	.103	.122	.126
Popularity	− .372	− .355	− .409
Parent			
Mother's MMPI 4 + 9	.155	.062	.245
Father's MMPI 4 + 9	.191	.222	.187
Self-rating of aggression	.023	.001	.027
Rejection	.233	.132	.274
Nurturance	.053	− .023	.132
Mobility orientation	.034	− .01	.086
Punishment	.207	.175	.236
Television violence (parent)	− .060	− .058	− .063
Aggressive fantasy (parent)	.071	.053	.084
Father's occupation	.169	.085	.237

FIGURE 1.

Child aggression as a function of self-evaluation and peer popularity.

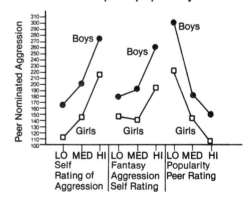

FIGURE 2.

Child aggression as a function of preferred sex-typed activities.

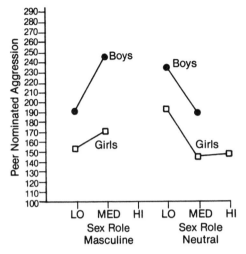

ure 1, self-ratings of aggression were significantly related to aggression. Children who were rated as more aggressive by their peers also said they had more aggressive daydreams. It seems that the more youngsters rehearse aggression in fantasy, the more aggressive they are in overt behavior. Generally the same results were found with both sexes and in the other two countries for which data have thus far been analyzed, Finland and Poland (Fraczek, Note 2; Lagerspetz, Note 1). Similarly, peer popularity, as also seen in Figure 1, was negatively related to aggression for both boys and girls. This was true in the other countries as well. The more aggressive youngsters are, the more unpopular they are. In Figure 2, it can be seen that preference for masculine activities is generally related to aggression for both boys and girls. This is true for all groups in all countries, and preference for neutral activities almost always

goes along with lessened aggression. Preference for feminine activities is not at all related to aggression, either positively or negatively, in any of the samples. These data have also been discussed elsewhere (Eron, 1980; Huesmann, in press; Huesmann & Eron, in press).

Television violence observed by children, as we mentioned previously (seen in Figure 3 for the United States only), is actually related to aggression in all four countries (as indicated previously in Table 1). As for the other television variables, the relation of aggression to TV realism or how realistic the youngster believes television to be does not reach significance in the United States. Nor does it in Finland, although it does in Poland. The results are the same for identification with TV characters.

Insofar as the parent-child interaction variables are concerned, in the United States, Finland, and Poland physical punishment by parents relates significantly to aggression of both boys and girls, as seen in Figure 4 for the United States. Rejection by parents is another important concomitant of aggression in school. The less satisfied

FIGURE 3.

Child aggression as a function of television habits and attitudes.

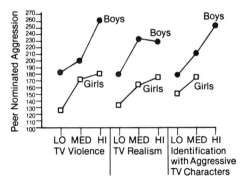

FIGURE 4.

Child aggression as a function of parent behaviors.

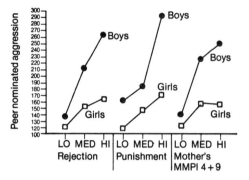

the parents are about their child's accomplishments, manners, and behaviors, the more aggressive is that child in school. In Poland and Finland results were essentially the same, but the relation seemed stronger for boys than girls, Nurturance by parents has no consistent relation to aggression in school. This was true in all three countries.

By and large, then, in terms of interaction between parent and child, those parents who punish their children physically and express dissatisfaction with their children's accomplishments and characteristics have the most aggressive children. This finding holds largely for both boys and girls and in Finland and Poland as well as the United States.

How about the characteristics of the parents themselves and how they relate to child aggression? One might guess from what we have said thus far that aggressive parents who watch violent television would have the most aggressive children. Well, not quite. We found no relation between either parent's television habits and the child's aggression in any of the three countries and no relation between parent and child aggres-

sion in Finland and Poland. In the United States, however, a mother's aggressiveness, as measured by Scales 4 + 9 of the MMPI (and as seen in Figure 4), was very highly related to her son's aggression. Father's aggression, as measured by these scales, also varied positively with son's aggression. There was no relation between either parent's aggression and daughter's aggressiveness in the United States.

Similarly, for sociological variables such as age, education, occupation, and mobility strivings of parents, there were no significant correlations with children's aggression in Poland and Finland. In the United States, however, fathers' age and education were related to boys' aggression. The younger and less educated the father, the higher the boy's aggression. For girls in the United States, fathers' occupation was related to aggression. The lower the occupation, according to census standards, the higher the aggression of girls. The relation was in the same direction for boys but did not reach statistical significance. The reason for the lack of relations in the other two countries may be their greater homogeneity on these characteristics. Social class distinctions are not widely prevalent, or at least so our foreign collaborators claim. One finding of considerable interest is that the children of working mothers obtain significantly higher aggression scores than children of nonworking mothers. This is probably not due to a confounding with social class in general, since 129 of the 352 working mothers were in Class 1 and 2 occupations (Huesmann & Eron, Note 4).

Except for these social variables, results in the three countries are remarkably similar and attest to the stability of the relations between aggression of children and their parents' personal characteristics and patterns of relation with their children. These findings essentially parallel the ones uncovered some 20 years earlier in New York state (Eron et al., 1971).

INDIVIDUAL CHILDREN AND CORRELATIONS BETWEEN GROUPS

As suggestive as these group results are in describing the variables that are important in influencing the aggressive behavior of children, they tell us nothing about individual children; for example, how many of these variables characterize a given aggressive child, and are they all or at least most of them absent in a given nonaggressive child? To accomplish this analysis we sampled the 10 most and 10 least aggressive boys in each cohort, as well as the 10 most and 10 least aggressive girls in each cohort—a total of 80 children in all, 40 high aggressive and 40 low aggressive, equally divided according to grade and sex. We compared these eight groups by inspection, first, in mean score on the nine child variables and eight parent interview variables previously described. Table 4 presents a sign analysis of the difference between the extreme subgroups on these variables. A plus indicates that the difference in means between the high and low aggression groups is greater than one *SE* of the means and in the direction hypothesized; a minus sign indicates the opposite direction from that hypothesized; a zero signifies there was less than one *SE* difference in mean score between the two groups. For third-grade boys 16 of the 17 comparisons are in the right direction; for first-grade boys 11 of the 17 are correct, three are in the wrong direction, and three show no difference between high and low aggression groups. For third-grade girls 15 of the 17 are in the correct direction, 1 is in the wrong direction, and on 1 variable there is no appreciable difference between high and low aggressive girls; for first-grade girls there are 14 in the predicted direction and 3 show no appreciable difference.

In general it can be said that these 17 variables do discriminate between the most and the least aggressive boys and girls in each cohort. Parental nurturance and parental preference for TV violence, however, are least likely to discriminate between the groups and, thus, will not be used here to characterize the background variables of extremely aggressive and nonaggressive children, leaving a total of 15 variables for this analysis.

Let us then look at these samples of the extremely aggressive and nonaggressive girls and boys and see how many in each group can be described as possessing many or most of the 15 discriminating group characteristics we have isolated. To do this we assigned each child a score of 0—4 on each of the 15 variables, corresponding to how far from the mean for his or her grade and gender group the specific score lay. A designation of 1 indicated that the subject's score was over .5 standard deviation from the mean; a designation of 2, that the score was greater than one standard deviation from the mean; 3, that it was more than two standard deviations removed; and 4, that it was three or more standard deviations removed from the mean. A plus sign was used to designate a deviation from the mean in line with the hypothesis; a minus sign, that it was in the opposite direction from the hypothesis.

Table 5 represents the deviation scores of each of the 10 most aggressive boys in the third grade on the 15 characteristics that we have indicated as important. The reason for less than 15 in some cases is that three of the mothers of these high aggressive chil-

TABLE 4

Agreement With Stated Hypothesis of Direction of Difference Between Most and Least Aggressive Boys and Girls

Variable	Third-grade boys	First-grade boys	Third-grade girls	First-grade girls
Child				
Aggression self-rating	+	+	+	+
Neutral sex role	+	0	+	+
Masculine sex role	+	−	+	0
Aggressive fantasy	+	+	+	+
Active fantasy	+	0	+	+
Popularity	+	+	+	+
TV violence	+	+	+	+
Identification with aggressive TV character	+	+	+	+
TV realism	+	+	+	+
Parent				
MMPI 4 + 9	+	+	+	+
Parent's self-rating of aggression	+	+	+	+
Rejection	+	+	+	+
Nurturance	−	−	+	0
Mobility orientation	+	+	0	+
Punishment	+	+	+	+
TV violence (parent)	+	−	−	+
Aggressive fantasy (parent)	+	0	+	0

Note: + indicates that the difference in means between the high and low aggression groups is greater than one standard error of the mean and in the direction hypothesized; − indicates the opposite direction from that hypothesized; 0 indicates that there was less than one standard error difference in mean score.

dren were unavailable for interview and one of the children was absent from school on one of the days we were collecting data. None of the children in this group has fewer than one half of the designated characteristics. Seven of the 10 have at least two thirds of them. The behaviors we have been discussing, then, are not merely group abstractions. Together they characterize spe-

cific children who have been designated by their peers as the most aggressive in the group.

We now look at Table 6, which contains similar data for the 10 least aggressive third-grade boys. All of the mothers of these children agreed to be interviewed, and none of the children was absent on the data collection day. None has as many as half

Table 5

Scores of the 10 Most Aggressive Third-Grade Boys in Terms of Their Distance From the Means for All Third-Grade Boys

Variable	Subject									
	1	2	3	4	5	6	7	8	9	10
Child										
Self-rating	+1	+4	−1	+4	−2	+1	+4	+3	+2	−2
Neutral sex role	+3	−1	+3	+1	+3	+1	+1	+1	+3	+3
Masculine sex role	+3	−1	+3	−1	+3	+2	+2	−1	+2	+3
Aggressive fantasy	+4	+3	+3	+3	−3	+3	+4	×	+3	−3
Active fantasy	+4	+3	+3	+3	−3	−1	+4	×	+3	−3
Popularity	+3	+3	−1	+2	+3	+3	+2	+3	+2	+3
TV violence	−1	+3	+3	−3	+3	+3	+3	×	+3	+3
Identification with aggressive										
TV character	+2	+3	−1	+1	−2	−2	+3	×	+3	+4
TV realism	+3	+2	−2	+4	+1	−1	−1	×	+3	+3
Parent										
MMPI 4 + 9	+3	−1	+3	×	×	+2	+1	−1	−1	×
Self-rating of aggression	−1	+1	+3	+2	−3	−2	−1	−1	+3	×
Rejection	−1	+2	+1	+3	−1	+3	−3	+1	+2	×
Punishment	+2	+3	+3	+4	+4	+3	+1	−1	+4	×
Mobility orientation	+1	+1	+2	−2	+1	−2	+3	−2	+3	×
Aggressive fantasy	+4	−1	+4	+4	−1	−1	−1	+4	+1	×

Note: A + indicates deviation in direction appropriate for hypothesis regarding high aggressive boys. A − indicates that it was in the opposite direction from the hypothesis. An × indicates data not available for that child or parent. 1 means subject's score was over .5 *SD* from the mean; 2, greater than one *SD*, 3, more than two *SDs*, 4, three or more *SDs*.

of these characteristics and half of the subjects have three or fewer. And so it is with the other groups, first-grade boys and first- and third-grade girls. Significantly more of the behaviors and attitudes we have been discussing are jointly present in the subjects and parents of the high aggressive than in those of the low aggressive group.

To illustrate the salience and concomit-ance of these characteristics in a specific individual, I would like to tell you about a subject in our 10-year longitudinal study, which is now a 21-year-old study. One of the bonuses of doing longitudinal research in a small community is that you get to know some of your subjects and the milieu in which they live quite well and from a number of perspectives. It is perhaps out of place in a scientific paper to give a case report, but I am after all a clinical psychologist and for a clinician the proof of a valid piece of research is whether it can be applied to a specific case in which the clinician has some interest.

CASE EXAMPLE OF A HIGHLY AGGRESSIVE CHILD

Ronald was first seen by me when he was eight years old and in the second grade. His teacher, who described him as "a likable and happy-go-lucky child," had referred him because of immature behavior and poor work habits. He had repeated first grade, but the teacher felt he was brighter than group tests indicated. Ronald was the youngest of three children. His brother, age 11, was out of the home at a special school for emotionally disturbed youngsters and his sister, age 12, was progressing normally in school. Ronald had been sickly from infancy, having suffered from severe attacks of asthma until the previous year. The parents reported that because the attacks were so frightening, they had overindulged him. However, the father, who had to hold two jobs to support the family, did not spend much time with the children. The mother's primary complaint about Ronald was that he was always hungry and "would eat from morning to night."

An intelligence test indicated that Ronald was of average ability. He was, however, one year retarded in reading due perhaps to a disturbance in spatial orientation that was apparent in the way he handled test materials. It was noted that he was impulsive and did not go about problem solving in any ordered, planned way, relying solely on trial and error. He was uncritical of his own performance.

Ronald was next seen by another psychologist when he was 12 years old and in the sixth grade. At this time he was failing in school, reading at a second-grade level, and a management problem in his class. He talked back to the teacher, provoked fights, and was constantly making noise. He was not allowed to go to the lavatory with his classmates because he would get into fights with them. Ronald was also having difficulty on the school bus and in the neighborhood, continually getting into fights with other boys by taunting them and egging them on. The parents did not seem to be concerned about the boy's behavior. The father never appeared for a parent interview and the mother said it was the school's problem, not hers. She usually took the boy's part and accused the school officials of picking on her son.

By coincidence Ronald was a subject in the longitudinal study of aggression. It was possible to retrieve the parent interviews conducted when Ronald was nine years old and his own interview, when he was 19. In the third grade Ronald was already seen by his peers as one of the most aggressive boys in class, doing things that bothered others, starting a fight over nothing, saying mean things, not obeying the teacher, and pushing other children. At the same time the father and mother indicated that Ronald was disobedient at home, that he annoyed and pestered them, had a bad temper, and used foul language. They did not approve of a number of things that he did, giving many indications of a rejecting attitude toward Ronald and little indication that they understood him or were concerned about him. They related having had many arguments between themselves that did not settle anything; they moved around a lot, so Ronald continually had to find new friends. These behaviors and occurrences must have created a very frustrating situation at home that probably instigated Ronald to be aggressive both there and at school. The father related using many physical punishments when Ronald was aggressive, including spanking him severely and washing out his mouth with soap, thus adding to the youngster's frustration and providing the model of an aggressive adult. Other aggressive models were furnished on Ronald's favorite TV programs, "Maverick," "Have Gun Will Travel," and "The Three Stooges." The parents indicated that Ronald showed few signs of internalized standards of behavior, such as feeling sorry after he disobeyed, worrying about telling a fib or a lie, or confessing when he had done something naughty. Thus according to information furnished by his parents at that time, Ronald

TABLE 6

Scores of the 10 Least Aggressive Third-Grade Boys in Terms of Their Distance From the Mean for All Third-Grade Boys

Variable	Subject									
	1	2	3	4	5	6	7	8	9	10
Child										
Self-rating of aggression	−2	−3	−2	−3	−3	−3	+2	−3	−2	−2
Neutral sex role	−1	+1	−3	+3	+1	−3	+1	+2	−3	−1
Masculine sex role	−1	−1	−4	+1	+1	−3	+1	+3	−3	−1
Aggressive fantasy	−2	+1	+1	−1	−3	−3	−2	−3	−3	−1
Active heroic fantasy	−1	+2	−2	+1	−4	−3	−1	−4	−2	−1
Popularity	−3	+1	−1	+1	+1	−4	−3	−4	−3	−4
TV violence	−2	0	−2	−1	−2	−3	−2	+3	−3	−2
Identification with aggressive TV character	−2	−2	−2	−2	−2	−2	+1	−2	−2	+2
TV realism	−3	−3	−3	−2	−3	−3	+1	−1	−2	−3
Parent										
MMPI 4 + 9	−3	−2	+2	+3	×	+2	−2	×	−2	−3
Self-rating of aggression	−1	−3	+1	−3	−2	+2	−3	−3	−3	−1
Rejection	+3	+3	+4	−3	−2	−3	−3	−2	−3	−3
Punishment	−1	−1	−2	−1	−2	−1	−2	−1	+2	−2
Mobility orientation	−1	+2	+2	+1	0	+1	+3	−1	−1	+2
Aggressive fantasy	+3	−1	+3	−1	−1	−1	+1	+1	−1	−1

Note: A + indicates deviation in direction appropriate for hypothesis regarding high aggressive boys. A − indicates that it was in the opposite direction from the hypothesis. An × indicates data not available for that parent. 1 means subject's score was over .5 *SD* from the mean; 2, greater than one *SD*, 3, more than two *SDs*, 4, three or more *SDs*.

at age nine was experiencing many insti-gations to aggression at home, had a phys-ically punitive father as well as other ag-gressive models, and showed little indication of having developed a con-science.

When Ronald was interviewed at the age of 19, he was on probation for three years for petty larceny. A few weeks after the interview, he was picked up by the police and charged with "criminal mischief in the third degree" and one week later with "criminal possession of drugs, fourth de-gree." During the interview it was revealed that he had dropped out of high school in the 10th grade, but he insisted that he ex-pected to go to graduate school so that he could eventually do research in "brain bi-ology." He admitted that he engaged in many aggressive behaviors. On the MMPI he had high scores on a pattern of scales characteristic of recalcitrant delinquents (Scales 4, 8, and 9—psychopathic deviate, schizophrenia, and mania, respectively). He continued to prefer violent television programs and thought that "Mod Squad," "Mannix," and "Dragnet" were very real-istic in showing what police work is really like.

Unfortunately Ronald is no longer a sub-ject in our 21-year longitudinal study. He was killed in a violent accident within a year of the second interview. In his brief life, however, we can discern the joint oc-currence of most of the factors, detailed in Table 4, that we have been discussing. And it is the joint occurrence of these factors, as demonstrated in Tables 5 and 6, that is important in determining the extent of ag-gressive and violent behavior in young peo-ple. Aggressive behavior, like most other behaviors, is overdetermined. But we have some knowledge about what many of those determinants are.

We know that observation of television violence is a cause of aggressive behavior in children, and we know that the effect is not confined to boys or to a certain geo-graphic or socioeconomic area in the United States. We know that because of a conver-gence of developmental trends occurring around age eight, children of that age may be unusually susceptible to the effect of vi-olent televison. Also, it seems likely that how closely a youngster identifies with ag-gressive TV characters and how realistic he or she believes aggressive television con-tent to be are related to both aggression and television viewing. We know further that academic achievement is negatively related to aggression and that aggressive young-sters tend not to be popular with their peers. We know that rejection and physical pun-ishment by parents are concomitants of aggression in children and that the attitudes and behaviors of parents, especially moth-ers, which are known predictors of anti-social behavior, are highly related to the aggressive behaviors of their sons. Is that sufficient knowledge to enable us to inter-vene sensibly with a program to counteract the influence of violent television and, in general, to reduce aggressive behavior in individual children?

THE CHICAGO CIRCLE STUDY

Huesmann and I (Huesmann, Eron, Klein, Brice, & Fischer, Note 5) were sim-ple-minded enough to think it might be. Therefore, we introduced an intervention into our Chicago Circle Study aimed at re-ducing the aggressive behavior of 169 high violence viewers. In the second year of the study, these high violence viewers were randomly assigned to one of two groups. The experimental group was exposed to three training sessions designed to help the children discriminate television fantasy from real life events. They were shown excerpts from violent programs and were informed about how the sound and visual effects were used to simulate reality. The control group spent a similar amount of time watching folk dancing programs and learning more about such activities. As I reported in 1980 (Eron, 1980) this effort did not appear to be successful, since on a posttest the experimental subjects did no better than the control subjects in discriminating between television fantasy and real life behavior. At that time we half-facetiously said that we were hoping for a "sleeper" effect that would show up later (Gruder et al., 1978). As a matter of fact, the next year a strong effect did show up that may be a confound of the effect of our new procedures with the sleeper from the old procedure, since at the beginning of the third year we instituted a new training procedure with the same subjects. This new procedure consisted of techniques traditionally associated with attitude change experiments and has been described in detail elsewhere (Huesmann et al., Note 5). I will mention them briefly here.

Each of the experimental subjects was asked to write a paragraph on "why TV violence is unrealistic and why viewing too much of it is bad." Over the course of two sessions, the children in the experimental group wrote the paragraph, received suggestions, and rewrote it; were taped reading the paragraph; and watched a TV tape of themselves and their classmates reading the paragraphs. The subjects were told that the tapes were going to be shown to the school children in Chicago. The placebo group also made a tape, but it was about "what you did last summer." Four months after this intervention, the final wave of data on all of the children in the study was col-

lected. Remarkably it was found that the mean peer-nominated aggression score for the experimental group was now significantly lower than the score for the placebo group, although a year previously the two groups were approximately equal in score. The difference was highly significant, as evaluated by analysis of covariance with sex, grade, and pretreatment aggression score as covariates (Huesmann et al., Note 5).

Even more striking was the lack of relation between television violence and aggression in the experimental group and the continued positive relation in the placebo group, almost the same degree of relation as in the general population. The best predictor in the experimental group, however, was identification with aggressive TV characters. Another good predictor was judgment of TV realism. Those subjects who had higher self-rated identification with TV characters had higher peer-nominated aggression scores. The more realistic the experimental subjects thought TV was,

FIGURE 5.

Change in attitude toward TV as a function of parent variables and experimental treatment.

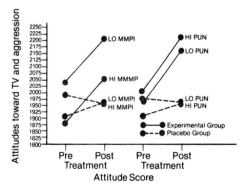

the more aggressive they were. In the placebo group there was no significant independent relation between realism or identification and aggression. For all boys in the Chicago Circle Study ($N = 375$), however, there was an interaction between identification and TV violence, so those who watched violent television and also identified with the aggressive characters were the most aggressive of all subjects.

Why were those subjects who identified with TV characters less susceptible to the treatment? The treatment attempted to change attitudes about television and about aggression as well. As a manipulation check six attitudinal questions were asked before and after treatment; for example, "How much of what kids see on television shows would make a kid meaner?" The subjects responded to these questions on a five-point scale. The score was the sum of the weighted responses. A change score was calculated for each child by subtracting the pretreatment score from the posttreatment score. The larger the score, the more the child changed toward the desired attitude. We found that the most important predictor of change was identification with TV characters. The more the subjects identified with TV characters, the less likely they were to change their attitudes toward television as a result of the intervention. It will be remembered that the more the youngsters identified with TV characters, the more aggressive they were. Extent of identification with TV characters is thus demonstrated to be an important mediating variable in the relation between television violence and aggression. The only other significant predictor was a self-report on the extent to which the subjects read fairy tales or had fairy tales read to them. The more extensive the reading of fairy tales, the more likely was the attitude toward television to

change. This latter finding is in keeping with the Singers' (Singer & Singer, 1981) contention that training in fantasy can affect the relation between television violence and behavior.

So with a very simple, brief technique, we were able to intervene in the real life relation between television violence viewing and aggressive behavior. It is almost too simple—almost unbelievable—that we who were strangers to the children could do this in three hours. What about the effect of parents—their personalities and behaviors? Is it possible that these brief procedures could overpower those effects? Figure 5 shows that indeed it is possible. The strongest parent predictors of aggressive behavior of their children were the sum of Scales 4 and 9 on the MMPI and the extent of parental punishment for aggression. This figure shows that whether a parent was a high or low punisher or was high or low in the behaviors and attitudes measured by Scales 4 and 9 had no effect on how much attitudes changed from the pretreatment to posttreatment sessions. This, of course, is just one study, which demands replication. But it certainly suggests that we are not helpless in the face of that insidious teacher in our living rooms. There are simple instructional procedures that can be used by parents and teachers to counteract the negative effects television is having on our children.

CONCLUSION

I have tried to summarize and integrate the findings to date of two ongoing, large-scale, longitudinal studies of the development of aggression. One, the Rip Van Winkle Study, located in semi-rural New York, is now in its 21st year, and we are in the midst of the third wave of data collection.

The second, the Chicago Circle Study, has drawn its subjects from suburban and inner-city Chicago, has completed three consecutive years of data collection, and is now being replicated in five other countries. The overriding conclusion, which should come as no surprise, is that aggression can be learned in many ways. Recourse to aggressive behavior as a way of solving problems is the result of a number of processes operating conjointly in the interactions of the youngster with his or her parents, peers, and other environmental figures. One persistent and ubiquitous finding deserves special consideration, and that is the relation between the continued observation of television violence and aggressive behavior. It is now apparent that the relation does not just go in one direction. Although we have demonstrated that television violence is one cause of aggressive behavior, it is also probable that aggressive children prefer to watch more and more violent television. The process is very likely circular. As we have seen, aggressive children are unpopular, and because their relations with their peers tend to be unsatisfying, they spend more time watching television than their more popular peers. The violence that they see on television reassures them that their own behavior is appropriate while teaching them new coercive techniques that they then attempt to use in their interaction with others, which in turn makes them more unpopular and drives them back to television, and the circle continues. Similarly, aggression is associated with low achievement—for reasons we may not yet know. But we do know that children who do not succeed in school spend more time watching television than scholastically successful children and therefore have more opportunity to observe aggressive models. They tend to identify with these models more than their achieving

peers and are therefore more influenced by the violent acts that they observe their favorite characters performing. Since their resources for problem solving are more limited than those of scholastically successful youngsters, the easy solutions they observe on television are more readily employed in their interactions with others. This type of behavior isolates them from their peers, leads them to more television, with less time for study, and so on and so on.

We have demonstrated, however, that it is possible to break into this cycle with simple interventions and short-circuit the connection between television violence and aggression. Unfortunately, with the procedures we have used, there is less chance for successful intervention when children identify strongly with TV characters and believe that the violence they observe on television is an accurate description of real life. The simple instructional procedures we have used may have to be modified for children already severely entrenched, by reason of constitution or environment, in these attitudes and beliefs.

REFERENCE NOTES

1. Lagerspetz, K. Personal communication, April 12, 1981.

2. Fraczek, A. *Cross cultural study of media violence and aggression among children: Comments on assumptions and methodology.* Paper read at the Twenty-Second International Congress of Psychology, Leipzig, Germany, July 6-12, 1980.

3. Sheehan, P. Personal communication, March 7, 1981.

4. Huesmann, L. R., & Eron, L. D. *The influence of mother's personality on child aggression* (Tech. Rep. No. 5). Chicago: University of Illinois at Chicago Circle, 1981.

5. Huesmann, L. R., Eron, L. D., Klein, R., Brice, P., & Fischer, P. *Mitigating the imitation of aggressive behaviors by changing children's*

attitudes about media violence (Tech. Rep. No. 3). Chicago: University of Illinois at Chicago Circle, 1981.

REFERENCES

Bandura, A. *Aggression: Social learning analysis.* Englewood Cliffs, N.J.: Prentice-Hall, 1973.

Belson, W. *Television violence and the adolescent boy.* Hampshire, England: Saxon House, 1978.

Berkowitz, L. *Aggression: A social psychological analysis.* New York: McGraw-Hill, 1962.

Buss, A. H. *The psychology of aggression.* New York: Wiley, 1961.

Chaffee, S. H. *Television and adolescent aggressiveness (overview).* In G. A. Comstock & E. A. Rubinstein (Eds.), *Television and social behavior.* Vol. 3: *Television and adolescent aggressiveness.* Washington, D.C.: U.S. Government Printing Office, 1972.

Eron, L. D. Relationship of TV viewing habits and aggressive behavior in children. *Journal of Abnormal and Social Psychology,* 1963, *67,* 193-196.

Eron, L. D. Prescription for reduction of aggression. *American Psychologist,* 1980, *35,* 244-252.

Eron, L. D., Huesmann, L. R., Brice, P., Fischer, P., & Mermelstein, R. Age trends in the development of aggression, sex typing, and related television habits. *Developmental Psychology,* in press.

Eron, L. D., Huesmann, L. R., Lefkowitz, M. M., & Walder, L. O. Does television violence cause aggression? *American Psychologist,* 1972, *27,* 253-263.

Eron, L. D., Walder, L. O., & Lefkowitz, M. M. *The learning of aggression in children.* Boston: Little, Brown, 1971.

Greenberg, B. S. British children and televised violence. *Public Opinion Quarterly,* 1975, *38,* 531-547.

Gruder, C. L., Cook. T. D., Hennigan, K. M., Flay, B. R., Allessis, C., & Halamaj, J. Empirical tests of the absolute sleeper effect predicted from the discounting in cue hypothesis.

Journal of Personality and Social Psychology, 1978, *36,* 1061-1074.

Hartnagel, T. F., Teevan, J. J., Jr., & McIntyre, J. J. Television violence and violent behavior. *Social Forces,* 1975, *54,* 341-351.

Huesmann, L. R. Television violence and aggressive behavior. In D. Pearl & L. Bouthilet (Eds.), *Television and behavior: Ten years of scientific progress and implications for the 80's.* Washington, D.C.: U.S. Government Printing Office, in press.

Huesmann, L. R., & Eron, L. D. Factors influencing the effect of television violence on children. In M. J. A. Howe (Ed.), *Learning from television: Psychological and educational research.* London: Academic Press, in press.

Huesmann, L. R., Lefkowitz, M. M., & Eron, L. D. Sum of MMPI Scales *F,* 4, and 9 as a measure of aggression. *Journal of Consulting and Clinical Psychology,* 1978, *46,* 1071-1078.

Lefkowitz, M. M., Eron, L. D., Walder, L. O., & Huesmann, L. R. *Growing up to be violent.* New York: Pergamon, 1977.

Lefkowitz, M. M., Walder, L. O., & Eron, L. D. Punishment, identification and aggression. *Merrill Palmer Quarterly of Behavior and Development,* 1963, *9,* 159-174.

McCarthy, E. D., Langner, T. S., Gersten, J. C., Eisenberg, J. G., & Orzeck, L. Violence and behavior disorders. *Journal of Communication,* 1975, *25,* 71-85.

Parke, R. D., Berkowitz, L., Leyens, P., West, S., & Sebastian, R. J. Some effects of violent and nonviolent movies on the behavior of juvenile delinquents. In L. Berkowitz (Ed.), *Advances in experimental social psychology* (Vol. 10). New York: Academic Press, 1977.

Rosenfeld, E., Huesmann, L. R., Eron, L. D., & Torney-Purta, J. V. Measuring patterns of fantasy behavior in children. *Journal of Personality and Social Psychology,* in press.

Singer, J. L., & Singer, D. G. *Television, imagination and aggression: A study of preschoolers' play.* Hillsdale, N.J.: Erlbaum, 1981.

Walder, L. O., Abelson, R., Eron, L. D., Banta, T. J., & Laulicht, J. H. Development of a peer rating measure of aggression. *Psychological Reports,* 1961, *9,* 497-556.

Aggressive Erotica and Violence Against Women

Edward Donnerstein

To examine the effects of aggressive-erotic stimuli on male aggression toward females, 120 male subjects were angered or treated in a neutral manner by a male or female confederate. Subjects were then shown either a neutral, erotic, or aggressive-erotic film and given an opportunity to aggress against the male or female via the delivery of electric shock. Results indicated that the aggressive-erotic film was effective in increasing aggression overall, and it produced the highest increase in aggression against the female. Even nonangered subjects showed an increase in aggression toward the female after viewing the aggressive-erotic film. Results are discussed in terms of the arousal and aggressive cue value of the films.

The National Institute of Mental Health recently concluded that an understanding of the conditions that lead to sexual attacks against women is a major goal for research. Although there are potentially many avenues of investigation, one topical area concerns the role of pornography in the elicitation of such aggressive attacks. The Presidential Commission on Obscenity and Pornography (1971) concluded that there was no evidence of a relationship between exposure to erotic presentations and subsequent aggression, particularly sexual crimes. Recent criticisms of these findings (e.g., Berkowitz, 1971; Cline, 1974;

Dienstbier, 1977; Wills, 1977), however, have led a number of investigators to reexamine this issue. Social-psychological research has indicated that under certain conditions, exposure to erotic forms of media presentations *can* facilitate aggressive behavior (e.g., Baron & Bell, 1977; Donnerstein, in press; Donnerstein & Barrett, 1978; Donnerstein, Donnerstein, & Evans, 1975; Donnerstein & Hallam, 1978; Jaffe, Malamuth, Feingold, & Feshbach, 1974; Malamuth, Feshbach, & Jaffe, 1977; Meyer, 1972; Zillmann, 1971, 1979). Although this research has been directed at the effects that erotica has on aggression in general, the more specific question of whether such media presentations are related to increased aggressive attacks against women has only recently been studied (i.e., Donnerstein, in press; Donnerstein & Barrett, 1978; Donnerstein & Hallam, 1978). The present study was designed to examine this latter issue by investigating the effects of specific types of erotica on aggression against women.

In past research two variables seem to have been most important in facilitating the aggression that follows exposure to erotic

This research was supported by Grant 1F32 MH07788-01 from the National Institute of Mental Health.

The advice of Len Berkowitz and Elaine Hatfield in the design and writing of this study is greatly appreciated. Thanks are also due Nancy De Franco, Fran Shefler, Hal Mallueg, Robert Berger, Ira Handler, and Tony Wen who served as research assistants. This research was conducted while the author was a visiting associate professor in the department of psychology at the University of Wisconsin.

forms of materials, anger arousal and increased arousal from erotic exposure. When male subjects have been insulted or attacked and later exposed to highly erotic materials, an increase in aggressive behavior has been observed (e.g., Baron, 1977; Donnerstein et al., 1975; Meyer, 1972; Zillmann, 1971). In contrast, when males have not been angered or have been exposed to mild erotica, aggressive behavior has been reduced (e.g., Baron, 1974; Baron & Bell, 1973; Frodi, 1977).

In the early research that examined the effects of erotica on aggression against women (e.g., Baron & Bell, 1973; Jaffe et al., 1974; Mosher, 1971a, 1971b), the general conclusion was that no differential sex effects occur. One major problem with these studies, however, is that anger arousal and high sexual arousal from film exposure were not systematically investigated. Recently, Donnerstein and his colleagues (Donnerstein, in press; Donnerstein & Barrett, 1978; Donnerstein & Hallam, 1978) examined the effects of both anger and highly arousing sexual films on aggression against females. The results of these studies indicate that when aggressive inhibitions are lowered in male subjects, there is a tendency for highly arousing sexual stimuli to increase aggression. Without lowered inhibitions, however, there is no evidence that sexual stimuli affect aggressive behaviors toward women. It would seem important, then, to examine additional factors that might be influential in lowering aggressive inhibitions, given the fact that this factor plays an important role in mediating the relationship of erotica and aggression against women.

Whereas initial research investigated factors external to film content as a means of influencing aggressive restraints (e.g., delayed aggression, aggressive models), there is evidence to suggest that aspects of the film itself could play a crucial role in affecting an individual's inhibitions to aggress. For example, there is ample documentation to suggest that the observation of aggressive films reduces restraints against subsequent aggressive behaviors (e.g., Geen, 1976). In previous research that has examined the link between erotica and aggression against women, erotic stimuli were chosen that excluded aggressive content. If aggressive content is a potentially important factor in the relationship between erotica and aggression toward women, there would be a number of reasons, beyond the aggressive restraint effect, to examine further the effects of aggressive erotica. First, there is recent evidence to suggest that aggression against women in erotica has increased in the past few years (e.g., Eysenck & Nias, 1978; Malamuth & Spinner, in press). Second, theoretical work suggests that aggressive erotica would have an effect on aggression against women. In particular, the work of Berkowitz (1974) has shown that one important determinant of whether an aggressive response is made is the presence of aggressive cues. Not only objects but individuals can take on aggressive cue value if they have been associated with observed violence. Thus viewing sexually aggressive films might facilitate subsequent aggression toward females because repeated association of females with the victim of observed violence increases the aggression-eliciting stimulus properties of a female.

The present study was designed, therefore, to examine the effects of aggressive cues juxtaposed with erotica on aggression against women. Male subjects were angered or treated in a neutral manner by a male or female confederate and were given the opportunity to view one of three types of films. Two of the films were selected to be highly sexually arousing, but differed in aggressive content. Since it was possible that any increase in aggression found for the aggressive-erotic film could be explained by increases in physiological arousal (e.g., Zillmann, 1971), the two erotic films were chosen to be equal in arousal level. The third film was neutral with respect to sexual and aggressive content.

It was predicted that angered subjects would display more aggression than non-angered individuals following exposure to either of the erotic films. This prediction was consistent with previous research which has shown that when individuals are predisposed to aggress, any source of high emotional arousal will tend to increase aggressive behavior. Second, based on a study by Tannenbaum (1971), it was predicted that aggression would be higher following exposure to the aggressive-erotic than to the nonaggressive-erotic film. It was expected that the differential impact of the two films would be higher for subjects angered by a female target of aggression due to the specific cue value of the aggressive-erotic film (e.g., Berkowitz, 1974). One question of interest in the present study is the effects of the aggressive-erotic film on nonangered subjects paired with a female target. It is possible that the interaction of arousal from the film and the aggressive cue value of the female target, through her association with observed aggression, could increase aggressive behavior. In addition to aggressive behavior, the present study also examined the physiological arousal (i.e., blood pressure) of subjects at various stages in the experiment.

METHOD

Subjects

The subjects were 120 male undergraduates enrolled in a course in introductory psychology. Subjects participated to receive extra credit toward their final grade in the course.

Apparatus and Selection of Films

Aggression, as measured by shock intensity ostensibly delivered to the aggressive target, was administered via a modified Buss (1961) aggression machine identical to that employed in previous investigations (e.g., Donnerstein, Donnerstein, & Barrett, 1976). A Narco Biosystem Electrosphygmomanometer was used to measure systolic and diastolic blood pressure. A Harvard Inductorium system was employed for the delivery of electric shock to the subject during the anger manipulation phase in the experiment.

Two neutral, two erotic, and two aggressive-erotic films were pretested and selected for presentation. Each film was 4 minutes long. The films were in black and white and presented over a SONY Video Recorder system. The neutral films were of a talk show interview and contained no aggressive or sexual content. The erotic films depicted a young couple in various stages of sexual intercourse. There were no scenes in which aggressive content was present. The aggressive-erotic films contained scenes in which an individual with a gun forces himself into the home of a woman and forces her into sexual intercourse. Pretesting indicated that the two types of erotic films were equal in their level of physiological arousal while differing significantly from the neutral films. In addition, the aggressive-erotic film was rated as more aggressive than the erotic film.

Design and Procedure

The basic design was a 2 × 2 × 3 factorial with anger (anger, no anger), sex of target (male, female), and films (neutral, erotic, aggressive-erotic) treated as factors. Four males were randomly assigned to the role of experimenter and confederate, with two females serving as confederates.

On arriving for the experiment, the subject was met by an experimental confederate (male or female) who posed as another subject. The experimenter then arrived and conducted the confederate and subject into the first experimental room.

Prerecorded taped instructions to the subject explained that the experiment was concerned with the effects of stress both on learning and on physiological responses. The subject and the confederate were informed that the experiment would involve both receiving and delivering mild electric shocks to the fingertips. The two were given the right to refuse to participate and still receive full experimental credit. Finally, an informed consent form was given to the subject. The subject was instructed to read and to sign the form, which acknowledged his agreement to participate in an experiment involving electric shock. The form also indicated that all information regarding the study would be given at the conclusion of the session. The taped instructions were started again and described the remainder of the procedure more fully.

The subjects were told that they would be asked to perform a task in a stressful situation. In addition to performance on the task, subjects were told that the experimenter was interested in their physiological responses to the task and the experimental situation. Consequently, readings of blood pressure would be taken from each subject at various specified times during the experiment.

At this point, the experimenter selected one subject (always the confederate) to go into a second room and begin studying for his/her task. The experimenter conducted the confederate into this room and after waiting about a minute, returned to the subject. He then showed the subject into a second room (adjacent to the one in which the confederate was placed). The subject was informed that his task was to assist the experimenter in administering the learning test for which the other subject (the confederate) was studying, but first, a base level measure of blood pressure would be needed. The experimenter then attached the arm cuff of the sphygmomanometer to the subject, returned to the adjoining room, and recorded the blood pressure reading (BP1-baseline).

Anger Manipulation

After taking the first blood pressure measure, the experimenter returned to the subject's room and presented the next segment of prerecorded instructions. Subjects were told that their task involved writing a short essay on the topic "We should completely legalize the use and distribution of marijuana." They were told to either state their agreement to, or disagreement with, the statement and to write a short essay (approximately 5 minutes) supporting their stand. Stress was induced in subjects by telling them that their essay would be evaluated by the subject in the other room who would write a short written evaluation and administer shocks. Since shock was involved, all subjects were asked to read and sign a medical health survey form. It was noted that the shock evaluation could range from no shocks for a good rating to 10 shocks for a poor rating, a procedure of anger manipulation similar to that employed in several other studies (e.g., Donnerstein & Wilson, 1976). The experimenter then left the room for 5 minutes while the subjects wrote their essays.

After time had elapsed, the experimenter

reentered the room and informed the subject that he would now give the essay to the other subject (the confederate) for evaluation. On returning to the subject (and while the confederate was "reading" the essay), the experimenter attached two electrodes to the fingers of the subject in preparation for the evaluation. The experimenter then went back into the confederate's room, picked up the written evaluation of the essay, and returned to the subject's room. He then contacted the confederate by intercom and instructed him/her to deliver the shock evaluation. For subjects in the anger condition, nine mild intensity shocks of .5-sec. duration were delivered; for the nonanger condition, only one shock was delivered. Following the evaluation the subject was presented with the written evaluation of his task performance. Four 5-point rating scales concerning the confederate's opinions about the subject's essay performance comprised the evaluation: overall quality, creativity, perceived intelligence of the subject, and knowledge of the subject matter. Consistent with the evaluation by shock, angered subjects were given poor ratings and nonangered subjects received good ratings on all of the scales. After the subject read his written evaluation, a second measure of blood pressure was recorded (BP2).

Film Exposure

The experimenter next returned to the subject and removed the electrodes. Subjects were then informed that the other subject (the confederate) would soon perform his or her task. It was explained that the subject would help in the administration of that task, but, as enough time had not elapsed for the confederate to finish studying for the task, there would be a few minutes delay in beginning that phase of the experiment.

At this point the rationale for viewing the different film segments was introduced. A subject assigned to the neutral condition was informed that while the "learner" was studying, the experimenter was interested in having the subject view a film that he (the experimenter) was hoping to use in future research. Since it was not part of the initial experiment, the experimenter asked the subject if he would be willing to view the film, rate it on a number of dimensions, and have his blood pressure taken immediately following the film. All subjects complied with the experimenter's request and subsequently viewed the film while the experimenter returned to the control room. On completion of the film (4 minutes later), the subject's blood pressure was taken and a short questionnaire regarding the film content was given to the subject. The subject was then informed that he could now proceed with the learning under stress experiment.

For the erotic and aggressive-erotic film conditions, in addition to the earlier described rationale and procedures, the subject was informed that the films to be viewed were highly erotic and depicted scenes of explicit sexual behavior. It was made clear that the subject was free to choose not to see the film and that credit for participation in the experiment would not in any way be affected by his decision. If the subject chose to continue and view the film (all did), he was given an appropriate informed-consent form to read and sign.[1] The subject then viewed one of the film segments, had the third blood pressure reading recorded (BP3), and completed the film rating scales.

Administration of Aggression

For the second task of the experiment, the subject was asked to present a prepared list of nonsense syllables to the confederate, ostensibly freeing the experimenter to monitor task performance and physiological responses of the confederates. The subject was supplied with the correct answer for each trial of the task and was informed that if the confederate responded correctly on a trial, he was to administer some number of points (1-8) with each point equal to 1¢. At the completion of the task, the confederate was to receive the amount of money he/she had earned for correct responses. If the confederate was incorrect, the subject was told to deliver some level of shock (1-8). The subject was also told that he could administer any number of points or level of shock he felt appropriate for any trial, since the particular number or level would have no effect on the confederate's performance. The task consisted of 24 trials with the confederate always making errors on the same 16 trials and giving correct responses on 8 trials. Following the last trial, a final measure of blood pressure (BP4) was taken.

Questionnaire and Debriefing

Following the last blood pressure measure, the subject completed a short questionnaire that asked him to rate, on a 5-point scale, how he felt his essay had been evaluated, how angry/not angry he felt after the rating, and how good/bad he felt. After completion of the rating scales, the subject was completely debriefed as to the nature of the experiment, and any questions were answered. The subject was then thanked for his participation and dismissed.

Calculation of Physiological Arousal

Three measures of blood pressure were calculated: systolic, diastolic, and mean

blood pressure. Mean blood pressure (cf. Zillmann, 1971) was computed as mean blood pressure = diastolic + ⅔ (systolic − diastolic). All change scores are in comparison to base level (BP1).

RESULTS

Effectiveness of Manipulations

Essay evaluation and anger. An analysis of the ratings that subjects indicated they received from the confederate for their essay revealed a main effect for anger, $F(1, 116) = 1,175.86$, $p < .001$; nonangered subjects reported a better rating ($M = 4.83$) than did angered subjects ($M = 1.30$). Significant effects for anger were also obtained on the measure of how good or bad subjects felt, $F(1, 116) = 229.96$, $p < .001$, and how angry they were, $F(1, 116) = 54.38$, $p < .001$. Angered subjects reported feeling worse ($M = 3.40$ vs. 1.39, respectively) and more angry ($M = 2.31$ vs. 1.11, respectively) than their nonangered counterparts.

Film ratings. A main effect for anger, $F(1, 108) = 6.16$, $p < .05$, and films, $F(2, 108) = 30.94$, $p < .001$, was obtained on the rating of the interest value of the film. Nonangered subjects found the films more interesting than did angered subjects. The two erotic films were rated as equal in interest to each other but were seen as more interesting than the neutral film ($p < .05$, Duncan's procedure). A main effect for films, $F(2, 108) = 96.65$, $p < .001$, was also obtained on the measure of how aggressive the film was. The means for the neutral, erotic, and aggressive-erotic films were all significantly different from each other ($ps < .05$, Duncan's procedure), with the aggressive-erotic film rated highest in aggression. An analysis on the measure of how erotic the films were revealed a main effect for films, $F(2, 108) = 135.80$, $p < .001$, as well as a significant Sex × Film interaction, $F(2, 108) = 6.20$, $p < .01$. The interaction indicated that the two erotic films were seen as more erotic than the neutral film. However, the aggressive-erotic film was rated higher than the erotic film when subjects were paired with a female, whereas the reverse was true when they were paired with a male. A final analysis on how arousing the films were revealed significant effects for films, $F(2, 108) = 64.64$, $p < .001$, and Anger × Film, $F(2, 108) = 3.28$, $p < .05$. The two erotic films were considered more arousing than the neutral film, and the aggressive-erotic film was seen as more arousing than the erotic film when subjects were angered.

Physiological Arousal

Mean blood pressure. A 2 × 2 analysis of variance (ANOVA) with anger and sex of target as factors was conducted on the BP2 (after anger manipulation) scores. This analysis yielded a significant effect for anger, $F(1, 116) = 43.76$, $p < .001$, with angered subjects revealing a larger increase in arousal ($M = 6.01$) than nonangered subjects ($M = .01$). Along with the self-report data reported earlier, this finding supports the effectiveness of the anger manipulation.

A 2 × 2 × 3 ANOVA with anger, sex of target, and films as factors was conducted on the BP3 scores (after film exposure). This analysis yielded a main effect for films, $F(2, 108) = 28.01$, $p < .001$, with the erotic ($M = 6.38$) and aggressive-erotic ($M = 5.45$) films not differing in arousal but differing significantly ($p < .01$, Duncan's procedure) from the neutral film (M

$= 2.86$). There were no other significant effects.

A final 2 × 2 × 3 ANOVA on BP4 (after aggression opportunity) revealed a significant effect for films, $F(2, 108) = 6.68$, $p < .01$, with the aggressive-erotic ($M = 4.69$) and erotic ($M = 3.58$) films not differing in arousal but higher ($p < .05$, Duncan's procedure) than the neutral film ($M = -.18$).

Systolic blood pressure. Similar analysis on systolic blood pressure revealed effects identical to that of mean blood pressure, except for a Sex × Film effect, $F(2, 108) = 3.67$, $p < .05$, on BP3 (after film exposure). This latter interaction indicated that although the two types of erotic films were higher in arousal level than the neutral film, subjects paired with a male target were more aroused when viewing the erotic film ($M = 8.05$) than the aggressive-erotic film ($M = 2.80$), whereas those paired with a female did not show a difference between the two films ($M = 6.45$ and $M = 9.80$, respectively). In addition, arousal was higher for the aggressive-erotic film when a female instead of a male target was employed ($p < .05$, all tests by Duncan's procedure).

Diastolic blood pressure. The analysis on diastolic blood pressure revealed results identical to those of mean blood pressure and consequently will not be elaborated on further.

Aggressive Behavior

A 2 × 2 × 3 ANOVA on the mean shock intensity administered to the confederate revealed significant effects for anger, $F(1, 108) = 49.50$, $p < .001$; films, $F(2, 108) = 18.84$, $p < .001$; Sex × Films, $F(2,$

108) = 5.02, $p < .01$; and Anger × Films, $F(2, 108) = 6.19$, $p < .01$. The two interactions are presented in Figure 1.

The Sex × Film interaction indicated that for subjects paired with a male target, both the erotic and aggressive-erotic films increased aggression beyond the neutral film, $F(1, 108) = 5.68$, $p < .05$, and $F(1, 108) = 7.25$, $p < .05$, respectively, while not differing from each other. For those subjects paired with a female, only the aggressive-erotic film increased aggression, $F(1, 108) = 33.51$, $p < .01$. In addition,

aggression was higher after viewing the aggressive-erotic film when subjects were paired with a female rather than a male target, $F(1, 108) = 10.23$, $p < .01$.

The Anger × Film interaction indicated that although there was no effect for films under nonangered conditions, the two types of erotic films did influence aggressive behavior for angered subjects. More specifically, the erotic film increased aggression beyond the level of the neutral film, $F(1, 108) = 4.63$, $p < .05$, whereas the aggressive-erotic film produced a higher level

FIGURE 1.

Mean shock intensity as a function of Sex × Film and Anger × Film interactions.

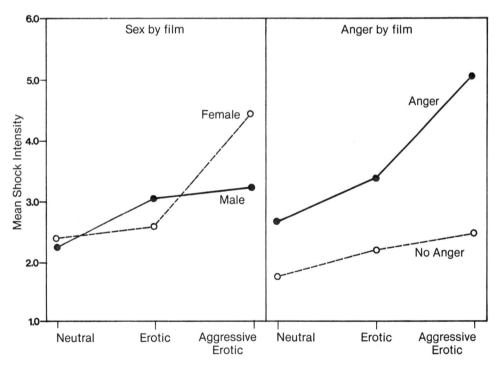

of aggression, $F(1, 108) = 19.50, p < .01$, than the erotic film.

One concern in the present study was the effect of the aggressive-erotic film on aggression against a female target when men were not angry. Although the Sex × Film interaction would indicate that, overall, the aggressive-erotic film facilitated aggression against a female, the Anger × Film interaction might suggest some qualification. Consequently, an examination of the means for the female target condition was undertaken. Results indicated that the highest level of aggression occurred for angered subjects exposed to the aggressive-erotic film ($p < .01$). Yet even when individuals were nonangered, the aggressive-erotic film did increase aggression against the female target in comparison to the neutral and erotic films ($p < .01$).

Rewarding Behavior

Reward was calculated as the mean number of points administered to the confederate on each of the eight correct trials. An ANOVA on these data revealed only a marginally significant effect for anger, $F(1, 108) = 3.36, p < .07$, with angered subjects tending to deliver fewer rewards ($M = 5.37$) than their nonangered counterparts ($M = 5.96$).

DISCUSSION

The purpose of the present study was to determine whether aggressive-erotic stimuli are, at least in part, responsible for aggressive responses against women. The results of the experiment suggest that such stimuli can lead to increased aggressive behaviors toward women. In addition, the results also extend the conclusions of previous investigators who have examined the effects of

highly arousing erotic, but nonaggressive, stimuli as a factor in aggression. Given the complexity of these issues, each of these implications will be addressed separately.

Effects of Nonaggressive Erotica on Aggression

The present results are supportive of past research which indicate that highly arousing erotic stimuli can increase aggressive behavior (e.g., Baron & Bell, 1977; Donnerstein et al., 1975; Zillmann, 1971). It was observed that aggression was increased on the part of angered males who were given an opportunity to aggress against another male. However, there was no effect seen for the nonaggressive-erotic film when subjects were paired with a female, even though arousal was increased after viewing the film. Since the effects of erotic films on aggression are often interpreted in terms of arousal produced by erotic exposure and the subsequent cognitive labeling of such arousal, it is interesting to speculate why no increase in aggression was observed toward females.

Consistent with recent theorizing in the area (e.g., Tannenbaum & Zillmann, 1975), nonangered subjects exposed to erotic films could have labeled their arousal from film exposure as sexual in nature. But what about the effects for angered subjects? Because the angered subjects exposed to the erotic film paired with a female also displayed high levels of arousal, one would have expected that these subjects would have labeled any residual arousal from film exposure as anger. Therefore, aggression would have been expected to increase. This, however, was not the case. One possibility is that subjects were inhibited from aggressing against a female target even though they were physiologically aroused by the erotic film. Taylor and Epstein (1967) have also found increased physiological arousal in angered male subjects who were less aggressive toward a female. Dengerink (1976) suggests one possible explanation for this type of finding: Since aggression toward females is generally disapproved of, fear of disapproval could act to inhibit its occurrence. The idea that inhibitions might be a contributing factor to the present findings is supported in a study by Donnerstein and Hallam (1978), which found that when male subjects were placed in a situation in which inhibitions were lowered, aggression toward a female was increased after exposure to a highly arousing erotic film.

In summary, the present results suggest that highly arousing nonaggressive-erotic stimuli can be a mediator of aggressive behavior by males toward other males under certain conditions. Likewise, under specific conditions (e.g., Donnerstein & Hallam, 1978) aggression could be increased against women, although this was not the pattern of results observed in the present study.

Effects of Aggressive Erotica on Aggression

The results showed that exposure to an aggressive-erotic film increased aggressive behavior to a level higher than was found for the erotic film. These findings were most noticeable in subjects who had previously been angered. This finding is similar to that obtained by Tannenbaum (1971), although the theoretical reasoning for these findings needs to be reconsidered. Independent findings by Tannenbaum and Zillmann (1975) indicated that the aggressive-erotic film in the Tannenbaum study produced higher arousal than the erotic film, suggesting that arousal may have been the prime mediating factor for the increase in

aggression. In the present study, however, arousal level was equal for the two types of erotic films. One explanation, then, for the present results is that suggested by Berkowitz (1970). This position would suggest that the aggressive responses elicited by the aggressive-erotic film were heightened by the arousal from previous anger and the arousal from the film itself. This position is of additional explanatory value when we examine the results of the aggressive-erotic film for differential aggression against males and females.

When angered subjects were paired with a male, the aggressive-erotic film produced no more aggression than exposure to the erotic film. Those subjects paired with a female, however, only displayed an increase in aggression after viewing the aggressive-erotic film. In fact, this increase occurred even if subjects were not angered, although the combination of anger and film exposure produced the highest level of aggressive behavior. Although there was some indication that arousal was higher for subjects who were paired with a female and had viewed the aggressive-erotic film, there was no difference in subject arousal level for the two types of erotic films. Why, then, would aggression be increased against the female after exposure to the aggressive-erotic film? One possible explanation is that the female's association with the victim in the film made her a stimulus that could elicit aggressive responses (e.g., Berkowitz, 1974). The combination of anger and arousal from the film heightened this response and led to the highest level of aggression against the female. But even in the nonanger condition, aggression was increased. This was not the case for subjects paired with a male. It would seem, then, that the female's association with the victim in the film was an important contributor to the aggression directed toward her. This

suggestion could be examined in future research by varying the sexual identity of the
film victim. Future research might also examine the victim's reactions to sexual
aggression (e.g., pleasure, pain) to determine if such reactions mediate the relationship of aggressive erotica and aggression
against women. These, and other studies
along the same lines, may be able to shed
more light on the controversial topic of erotica and human aggression.

NOTE

1. This additional procedure of the consent
form took approximately 1 minute. This time
was equated in the neutral condition by allowing
an additional minute before the film began.

REFERENCES

Baron, R. A. The aggression-inhibiting influence of heightened sexual arousal. *Journal of
Personality and Social Psychology*, 1974, *30*,
318-322.
Baron, R. A. *Human aggression*. New York:
Plenum Press, 1977.
Baron, R. A., & Bell, P. A. Effects of heightened sexual arousal on physical aggression.
*Proceedings of the 81st Annual Convention
of the American Psychological Association*,
1973, *8*, 171-172. (Summary)
Baron, R. A., & Bell, P. A. Sexual arousal and
aggression by males: Effects of type of erotic
stimuli and prior provocation. *Journal of Personality and Social Psychology*, 1977, *35*, 79-
87.
Berkowitz, L. The contagion of violence: An S-
R mediational analysis of some effects of observed aggression. In W. J. Arnold & M. M.
Page (Eds.), *Nebraska symposium on motivation* (Vol. 18). Lincoln: University of Nebraska Press, 1970.
Berkowitz, L. Sex and violence: We can't have
it both ways. *Psychology Today*, May 1971,
pp. 14-23.
Berkowitz, L. Some determinants of impulsive
aggression: The role of mediated associations
with reinforcements for aggression. *Psychological Review*, 1974, *81*, 165-176.

Buss, A. H. *The psychology of aggression*. New
York: Wiley, 1961.
Cline, V. B. Another view: Pornography effects,
the state of the art. In V. B. Cline (Ed.), *Where
do you draw the line?* Provo, Utah: Brigham
Young University Press, 1974.
Dengerink, H. A. Personality variables as mediators of attack-instigated aggression. In R.
Geen & E. O'Neal (Eds.), *Perspectives on
aggression*. New York: Academic Press,
1976.
Dienstbier, R. A. Sex and violence: Can research
have it both ways? *Journal of Communication*, 1977, *27*, 176-188.
Donnerstein, E. Pornography and violence
against women. *Annals of the New York Acad-
emy of Science*, in press.
Donnerstein, E., & Barrett, G. The effects of
erotic stimuli on male aggression toward females. *Journal of Personality and Social Psychology*, 1978, *36*, 180-188.
Donnerstein, E., Donnerstein, M., & Barrett,
G. Where is the facilitation of media violence:
The effects of nonexposure and placement of
anger arousal. *Journal of Research in Personality*, 1976, *10*, 386-398.
Donnerstein, E., Donnerstein, M., & Evans, R.
Erotic stimuli and aggression: Facilitation or
inhibition. *Journal of Personality and Social
Psychology*, 1975, *32*, 237-244.
Donnerstein, E., & Hallam, J. The facilitating
effects of erotica on aggression toward females. *Journal of Personality and Social Psychology*, 1978, *36*, 1270-1277.
Donnerstein, E., & Wilson, D. W. Effects of
noise and perceived control on ongoing and
subsequent aggressive behavior. *Journal of
Personality and Social Psychology*, 1976, *34*,
774-781.
Eysenck, H. J., & Nias, H. *Sex, violence, and
the media*. London: Spector, 1978.
Frodi, A. Sexual arousal, situational restrictive-
ness, and aggressive behavior. *Journal of Research in Personality*, 1977, *11*, 48-58.
Geen, R. G. Observing violence in the mass
media: Implications of basic research. In R.
Geen & E. O'Neal (Eds.), *Perspectives on
aggression*. New York: Academic Press,
1976.
Jaffe, Y., Malamuth, N., Feingold, J., & Feshbach, S. Sexual arousal and behavioral
aggression. *Journal of Personality and Social
Psychology*, 1974, *30*, 759-764.
Malamuth, N. M., Feshbach, S., & Jaffe, Y.

Sexual arousal and aggression: Recent experiments and theoretical issues. *Journal of Social Issues*, 1977, *33*(2), 110-133.

Malamuth, N. M., & Spinner, B. A. Longitudinal content analysis of sexual violence in the best-selling erotic magazines. *Journal of Sex Research*, in press.

Meyer, T. P. The effects of sexually arousing and violent films on aggressive behavior. *Journal of Sex Research*, 1972, *8*, 324-333.

Mosher, D. L. Pornographic films, male verbal aggression against women, and guilt. In *Technical Report of the Commission on Obscenity and Pornography* (Vol. 8). Washington, D.C.: Government Printing Office, 1971. (a)

Mosher, D. L. Psychological reactions to pornographic films. In *Technical Report of the Commission on Obscenity and Pornography* (Vol. 8). Washington, D.C.: Government Printing Office, 1971, (b)

Presidential Commission on Obscenity and Pornography. Washington, D.C.: U.S. Government Printing Office, 1971.

Tannenbaum, P. H. Emotional arousal as mediator of communication effects. In *Technical Report of the Commission on Obscenity and Pornography* (Vol. 8). Washington, D.C.: U.S. Government Printing Office, 1971.

Tannenbaum, P. H., & Zillmann, D. Emotional arousal in the facilitation of aggression through communication. In L. Berkowitz (Ed.), *Advances in experimental social psychology* (Vol. 8). New York: Academic Press, 1975.

Taylor, S. P., & Epstein, S. Aggression as a function of the interaction of the sex of the aggressor and the sex of the victim. *Journal of Personality*, 1967, *35*, 474-486.

Wills, G. Measuring the impact of erotica. *Psychology Today*, November 1977, 30-34.

Zillmann, D. Excitation transfer in communication-mediated aggressive behavior. *Journal of Experimental Social Psychology*, 1971, *7*, 419-434.

Zillmann, D. *Hostility and aggression*. Hillsdale, N.J.: Erlbaum, 1979.

Effects on the Hostility of Spectators of Viewing Aggressive Sports

Robert L. Arms, Gordon W. Russell, and Mark L. Sandilands

The effects on spectator hostility of viewing aggressive athletic contests were investigated using three diverse measures of hostility in a replication of the widely cited Goldstein and Arms (1971) Army-Navy football study. Male and female subjects were exposed to either stylized aggression (professional wrestling), realistic aggression (ice hockey), or a competitive but nonaggressive control event (swimming) in a before-after design. While the three measures of hostility yielded somewhat different results for the three events, general support was found for the earlier finding of increased spectator hostility as a result of observing aggression. Whereas hostility was shown to increase at wrestling and hockey, such increases did not occur at the swimming competition. Other aspects of mood change among spectators were also investigated. There was a blunting of the quality of interpersonal relations at the three events.

Hostile outbursts occurring at a number of spectator sports have contributed to a general international concern with escalating levels of violence. While that concern has primarily dealt with illegal aggression on the field of play, attention has also been focused on those relatively rare but newsworthy occasions in which violence has erupted among fans viewing sports contests. For example, soccer has been plagued by rampant hooliganism both in Britain and on the continent (e.g., Scottish Education Department, 1977). Elsewhere, soccer fans supporting their team in a losing cause in Guatemala recently attacked fans of the winning side with machetes, hacking five people to death (San Francisco Chronicle, 1977). Smith's (1978) archival study of collective violence among ice hockey fans found that approximately 74% of hostile outbursts were preceded by extraordinary displays of violence among the players.

At the level of public beliefs, the notion of a "safety valve" or catharsis enjoys widespread currency. This view, as it applies to spectators viewing aggression on the field of play, predicts that such displays serve to reduce hostility and physiological arousal in the viewer. This cathartic viewpoint is bolstered by the influential writing of Freud, Lorenz, Tinbergen, and their popularizers.[1] In general, the position has received little encouragement from the experimental literature (e.g., Geen and Quanty, 1977). Compelling as the notion of catharsis may be, vicarious participation in aggressive displays serves, with few exceptions (e.g., Doob and Wood, 1972) to enhance, rather than diminish, hostility in the onlooker.

Generalizations from the experimental laboratory to real-life settings inevitably

Portions of this paper were presented at the Canadian Symposium for Psycho-Motor Learning and Sports Psychology, Banff, Alberta, Canada, 1977. This project was supported by a University of Lethbridge research grant ULRF #86-1168. Authors are listed in alphabetical order. They wish to thank Stu and Helen Hart (Foothills Wrestling Association), Bill Burton and Dennis Kjeldgaard (Lethbridge Broncos), Andy Andrews, Keith Hart, the Morrow Brothers, Jon R. Amundson, Pat Dortsch, and Nicholas J. Previsich.

"Effects on the Hostility of Spectators of Viewing Aggressive Sports" by R.L. Arms, G.W. Russell & M.L. Sandilands, 1979, *Social Psychology Quarterly*, 42, pp. 275-279. Reprinted by permission of the American Sociological Assn. and the authors.

contain an element of risk. However, when the results of investigations conducted in the more complex naturalistic setting agree with lab findings, then confidence in their applicability is greatly enhanced. Unfortunately, complementary investigations of spectatorship reported in the literature have produced conflicting results. Kingsmore (1970) found professional wrestling fans showed less extrapunitive and intrapunitive aggression on the Thematic Apperception Test (TAT) and less self-reported aggression following the matches. Also, basketball fans showed less extrapunitive aggression after a game. Turner (1970) reported college males showed increases in TAT aggression at basketball and football, though not at amateur wrestling.

The annual Army-Navy football game provided the setting for a field study by Goldstein and Arms (1971) whose design pitted the cathartic against the enhancement position. A sample of males leaving the stadium after the game scored significantly higher on the Buss-Durkee hostility scale (Buss, 1961) than an equivalent sample entering the stadium before the game. Pre- and postevent measures for males at an equally competitive, but nonaggressive control event (gymnastics) did not differ. The major finding of an overall increase in hostility of *both* Army (winners) and Navy (losers) fans strongly supported a general disinhibition position (Bandura, 1973) which predicts that the observation of aggression leads to a lessening in the strength of inhibitions against expressing hostility.

Inevitably, a number of plausible rival interpretations remained to explain the heightened postevent hostility. The authors suggested a selection bias whereby football fans might be presumed to be more volatile than those attracted to a gymnastics competition. Other potential sources of bias include individual versus team competition and different norms governing expressive behavior at the events. Also cited (Goldstein and Arms, 1971) were differences in the density, numbers, and activity levels between the football and gymnastics fans. Goldstein (1976) has suggested that the student interviewers may have gained in confidence in the pregame stage, and unwittingly, approached and been successful in interviewing more aggressive-looking fans after the game. Furthermore, the differential consumption of alcohol at the two events cannot be discounted as a contributing factor, particularly if the football fans felt in any way "threatened" (Taylor *et al.*, 1976). Finally, Mann (1974) suggested the overall increase in hostility may have arisen from all fans experiencing a dull, lopsided game (Army 27, Navy 0).

The present investigation was designed as a systematic replication (Sidman, 1960) of the Goldstein and Arms (1971) study that would also test the merits of rival explanations advanced to account for their results. Departures from the original design were the inclusion of female spectators, the substitution of ice hockey for American football, and a provincial team swimming competition for gymnastics.

A special case for cathartic effects due to exposure to *stylized* aggression has been persuasively argued by Noble (1975). Cartoons, roller derby, or professional wrestling—displays in which interpersonal mayhem may be seen as fictional or a spoof—would qualify as stylized aggression. Thus, professional wrestling was chosen to represent stylized aggression, and hockey, realistic aggression.

PROCEDURE

Students (N = 127 females; N = 87 males) were recruited from an introductory psychology subject pool at the University of Lethbridge. Subjects received a 4% research participation bonus, free admission, and an offer of return transportation to their sporting event. The study was presented as an investigation of spectator's impressions of sports events.[2] Assignment to the events and to the pre- and postevent conditions was random within the female and male categories. Departures from the random assignment procedure to events proved necessary in 5% of the cases (exam conflicts).

Preevent subjects arrived 30 minutes before the event, were given their tickets, and were then escorted to a spare dressing room and were simply asked to complete a set of measures indicating their feelings at that time. Before taking their seats (dispersed) these subjects were asked not to discuss the measures with others. Postevent subjects arrived 15 minutes before game time, were given their tickets, and were asked to remain momentarily seated following the event. At the conclusion of the event, they were escorted to the same room to complete the hostility scales.

To ensure a more complete mapping of the multidimensional domain of hostility, the following measures of the dependent variable were administered: (1) the Buss-Durkee (Buss, 1961) subscales of *indirect hostility, resentment,* and *irritability* summed by Goldstein and Arms (1971) to provide an overall index; the aggression scale of the Nowlis (1965) Mood Adjective Check List (MACL); and a punitive measure (Goldstein *et al.*, 1975) based on the prison sentences subjects would assign to individuals convicted of serious crimes.

The complete MACL, including the *ad hoc* adjectives "sexy" and "aroused," were administered to provide the general pattern of mood changes at each event and as background against which any resulting change in hostility could be better understood. Earlier comment (Stone, 1973) and discussion with pilot subjects suggested that a sexual component may be inherent in contests involving either heavily padded athletes or contestants in swimsuits. An index of involvement was calculated for each subject by summing self-report ratings of frequency of TV viewing, actual attendance, and general interest in their assigned sport. Finally, subjects assigned to the wrestling match were asked: "What percentage of professional wrestling action do you think is 'faked' or just acting?"

RESULTS

Differences in pre- and postevent levels of spectator hostility were tested by t-tests

(two-tailed). As presented in Table 1, significant increases occurred at wrestling and hockey though no changes were observed at the control event. At wrestling, the MACL aggression measure proved sensitive to stylized aggression ($p < .01$), the combined pre- to postevent increase originating principally with females. The overall increase in hostility at the hockey game was significant ($p < .05$) using the punishment index, and marginally so ($p < .06$) with the Buss-Durkee scales. The distributions of involvement scores, and authenticity ratings by subjects assigned to wrestling, were too strongly skewed to permit meaningful analyses of these variables.

Changes in other dimensions of mood assessed by the MACL were tested by t-

TABLE 1

Mean Pre and Posttest Hostility Scores by Sex at Three Events

Event	MACL (Aggression)					Buss-Durkee			Punishment		
	N	Pre	N	Post	t[a]	Pre	Post	t	Pre	Post	t
Wrestling:											
Females	32	1.72	22	5.59	3.61***	13.39	14.55	.81	29.94	23.71	1.07
Males	16	3.06	20	3.80	.60	12.56	12.98	.24	18.72	34.85	1.72†
Combined	48	2.17	42	4.74	3.18**	13.11	13.80	.64	26.20	29.01	.55
Hockey:											
Females	24	2.08	23	3.52	1.02	12.23	14.50	1.60	18.52	22.74	.97
Males	17	2.29	16	2.50	.22	14.06	15.81	1.06	12.41	24.19	3.03**
Combined	41	2.17	39	3.10	1.02	12.99	15.04	1.90†	15.99	23.33	2.45*
Swimming (control):											
Females	12	3.08	14	1.36	1.24	13.00	14.86	1.05	25.17	33.82	1.05
Males	8	3.25	10	3.40	.13	11.38	13.40	.85	26.35	15.60	1.77†
Combined	20	3.15	24	2.21	.98	12.35	14.25	1.34	25.60	26.23	.11

[a] two-tailed tests
†p<.10
*p<.05
**p<.01
***p<.001.

tests. While anxiety and fatigue were un-affected by experiences at the events, *all* events produced a significant decline in feelings of Social Affection. Surgency de-clined significantly at hockey and swim-ming while feelings of sexiness dropped at the swim meet whereas arousal evidenced no change.

DISCUSSION

The coordination and movement of sub-jects at the venues was accomplished smoothly and without incident, mainly the result of improved procedures developed during the pilot stage. The local Western Canada Hockey League club (Tier 1, Junior A) badly outclassed the visiting Flin Flon Bombers, winning 11-1 in a lackluster con-test. In addition to being a rout, the game was devoid of major fights, with only the occasional flash of playmaking skill in evi-dence. The "good guys" also won the main tag-team event on the professional wres-tling card. Whereas students in the earlier pilot study remained aloof from the ring action, the present subjects entered whole-heartedly into the spirit of the evening, booing, cheering, and trading insults with the villains. The swim meet was fiercely competitive with the spectators easily as vo-ciferous as those at the other events.

Posttest hostility means were, almost without exception, greater than the mean pretest scores. Although aspects of the ca-thartic and enhancement viewpoints were conjoined in the present design, support was forthcoming for only the latter position. Subjects exposed to stylized aggression (wrestling) showed a significant increase on the MACL aggression scale, a combined effect arising principally from the female data. Furthermore, the choice of profes-sional wrestling to represent stylized

aggression was borne out insofar as subjects overwhelmingly saw it as a sham. Subjects at the hockey game showed increased hos-tility on the Buss-Durkee and punishment scales, the males in particular contributing to the latter increase. Spectators at the con-trol event showed no significant changes in hostility on any of the three measures. The present results are consistent with the earlier Goldstein and Arms (1971) findings and provide further support for a general dis-inhibition position (e.g., Bandura, 1973).

Although hostility increased through ex-posure to displays of both stylized and re-alistic aggression, such increases were not registered consistently on all three meas-ures. This makes it apparent that reliance on a single measure of aggression could be misleading. Nevertheless, each measure was shown to be sensitive on at least one occasion leading to a conclusion consistent with, but less decisive than that reached by Goldstein and Arms (1971). That is to say, the observation of aggression on the field of play leads to an increase in hostility on the part of spectators though displays of stylized aggression may increase one type of hostility in the viewer and realistic aggression, another.

The present results support Turner (1970) and, in extending the generality of the ear-lier Goldstein and Arms (1971) results, largely negate the rival explanations ad-vanced to date. Increases in spectator hos-tility have been demonstrated to occur in a different culture with two additional ag-gressive sports, one a stylized display. Fur-thermore, the increases in hostility found among avid Army and Navy fans seem also to be true of females and student spectators without strong sporting interests or team loyalties. The likelihood of a selection fac-tor operating to attract less volatile spec-tators to their control event (gymnastics) or the unwitting selection of less hostile pre-event males was negated by the random assignment of subject to events and to pre- and posttest conditions. With the number and density of spectators at wrestling and the control event equal in the present study and alcohol not present at the events, it seems unlikely that differences could have arisen from these factors. The hockey game was easily as lackluster as Army's runaway victory over Navy. However, the final wrestling bout was in doubt until the dying minutes of the match when the forces of good overcame the forces of evil. Mann's (1974) suggestion that increased hostility on the part of the Goldstein and Arms (1971) subjects arose from the dull, one-sided nature of the contest thereby seems less plausible. Lastly, while the football fans may have been thwarted in their efforts to beat the other 100,000 spectators onto a crowded freeway at the conclusion of the game, a similar challenge did not confront the Lethbridge (Pop. 50,000) subjects.

In addition to hostility, changes along other dimensions of mood were explored using the remaining MACL measures. There appeared to be a general deterioration in the quality of interpersonal relations. The most pronounced and consistent decrement occurred in Social Affection, a dimension characterized by the adjectives "affectionate," "forgiving," "kindly," and "warmhearted." It is particularly noteworthy that diminished social affection occurred at the nonaggressive control event as well as at wrestling and hockey. Thus, the reduction in social affection cannot be attributed to aggressive content but rather arises from other features of the spectator experience. Furthermore, postevent scores on the Surgency factor ("carefree," "playful," and "witty") were lower for males viewing the hockey game and for females attending the

swimming competition. Where changes in mood have occurred, such changes have consistently been toward a more negative emotional state. The present results call into question an assumption that sports events are necessarily rich social occasions where goodwill and warm interpersonal relations are fostered (Mehrabian, 1976:284).

NOTES

1. It should be noted that Lorenz (Evans, 1974) and Tinbergen (1968) have modified their views regarding the applicability of the cathartic viewpoint to mass spectator sports.

2. At the time of recruitment, subjects were told that they would be attending one of three sporting events: hockey, wrestling, or swimming. They were further informed that the experimenters were interested in assessing their impressions of the events. No mention was made of our specific interest in investigating the effects of viewing aggressive sports upon spectators' levels of aggression.

REFERENCES

Bandura, A. *Aggression: A Social Learning Analysis.* Englewood Cliffs, N.J.: Prentice-Hall, 1973.

Buss, A. H. *The Psychology of Aggression.* New York: Wiley, 1961.

Doob, A. N., & Wood, L. Catharsis and aggression: The effects of annoyance and retaliation on aggressive behavior. *Journal of Personality and Social Psychology,* 1972, *22,* 156-62.

Evans, R. I., A conversation with Konrad Lorenz about aggression, homosexuality, pornography, and the need for a new ethic. *Psychology Today,* November, 1974.

Geen, R. G., & Quanty, M. B. The catharsis of aggression: An evaluation of a hypothesis. Pp. 1-37 In L. Berkowitz (Ed.), *Advances in Experimental Social Psychology* (Vol. 10). New York: Academic Press, 1977.

Goldstein, J. H. Conducting field research on aggression: Notes on 'effects of observing athletic contests on hostility.' Pp. 248-57 In P. M. Golden (Ed.), *The Research Experience.* Itasca, Il.: F. E. Peacock, 1976.

Goldstein, J. H., & Arms, R. L. Effects of observing athletic contests on hostility. *Sociometry*, 1971, *34*, 83-90.

Goldstein, J. H., Rosnow, R. L., Raday, T., Silverman, I., & Gaskell, G. D. Punitiveness in response to films varying on content: A cross-national field study of aggression. *European Journal of Social Psychology*, 1975, *5*, 149-65.

Kingsmore, J. M. The effect of a professional wrestling and a professional basketball contest upon the aggressive tendencies of spectators. Pp. 311-15 in G. S. Kenyon (Ed.), *Contemporary Psychology of Sport*. Chicago: Athletic Institute, 1970.

Mann, L. On being a sore loser: How fans react to their team's failure. *Australian Journal of Psychology*, 1974, *26*, 37-47.

Mehrabian, A. *Public Places, and Private Spaces: Psychology of Work, Play and Living Environments*. New York: Fitzhenry & Whiteside, 1976.

Noble, G. *Chyildren in Front of the Small Screen*. Beverly Hills, CA: Sage Publications, 1975.

Nowlis, V. Research with the Mood Adjective Check List. In S. S. Tompkins and C. Izard (Eds.), *Affect, Cognition, and Personality*. New York: Springer, 1965.

San Francisco Chronicle. Five die in soccer melee. February 19, 1977.

Scottish Education Department, *Football Crowd Behaviour*. Edinburgh: Her Majesty's Stationery Office, 1977.

Sidman, M. *Tactics of Scientific Research*. New York: Basic Books, 1960.

Smith, M. D. Precipitants of crowd violence. *Sociological Inquiry* 1978, *48*, 121-131.

Stone, G. P. American sports: Play and display. Pp. 65-85 in J. T. Talamini and C. H. Page (Eds.), *Sport and Society*. Toronto: Little, Brown, 1973.

Taylor, S. P., Gammon, C. B., & Capasso, D. R. Aggression as a function of the interaction of alcohol and threat. *Journal of Personality and Social Psychology* 1976, *34*, 938-41.

Tinbergen, N. On war and peace in animals and man. *Science* 1968, *160*, 1411-18.

Turner, E. T. The effects of viewing college football, basketball and wrestling on the elicited aggressive responses of male spectators. *Medicine and Science in Sports* 1970, *2*, 100-05.

8 Interpersonal Influence

WHENEVER THE BEHAVIOR OF an individual is affected by the actions or presence of others, the resulting reaction is a product of interpersonal influence. The classic examples of interpersonal influence have focused primarily upon such phenomena as conformity (e.g., Asch, 1950), compliance (e.g., Freedman & Fraser, 1966; Kelman, 1958), and obedience (e.g., Milgram, 1963, 1975). One of the more enticing aspects of the study of interpersonal influence from the researcher's perspective is the fact that this broad area of study bridges the gap between primarily dyadic social phenomena, such as attraction and aggression, and the more group-oriented phenomena, such as leadership and intragroup relations. The virtually unlimited range of types of questions that the researcher can legitimately seek to answer while still remaining within the confines of the investigator's expertise represents an appealing characteristic of this field. The articles that have been chosen for this chapter represent the diversity of this area.

The first article approaches interpersonal influence at the level of individual-to-individual relations. Jerry Burger and Richard Petty report the results of three studies that attempt to identify the mediating mechanism responsible for the effectiveness of the low-ball compliance technique. Previous research by Cialdini, Cacioppo, Bassett and Miller (1978) demonstrated that individuals who first agreed to perform an act and subsequently had the costs of that action increased showed greater compliance than individuals who were simply asked to perform the more costly version. Cialdini et al. suggested that the commitment of the target person to the requested behavior in the low-ball situation led to the compliance advantage that was obtained. Burger and Petty argue that the original findings of Cialdini et al. may be due to a commitment to the requester rather than a commitment to the action. It is important to note that it is not sufficient for the social psychologist simply to identify successful means by which compliance to a request can be induced; for a significant contribution to be made to the field, the investigator must also elucidate the processes by which the technique is able to bring about the desired consequences.

Interpersonal influence, as suggested above, may bridge the gap between dyadic and group interactions, and the second article in the chapter reflects the group side of this area. Bibb Latané suggests that the effects of social forces on social behavior may be analogous to the effects of physical forces on physical actions. Beginning with three basic principles, Latané proceeds to show the generality of his theory of social impact by demonstrating its applicability to ten disparate domains, ranging from conformity and bystander intervention to tipping in restaurants and inquiring for Christ. Perhaps the most intriguing aspect of Latané's work is the demonstration that laws of social behavior are mathematically specifiable and therefore may lead to quantifiable and verifiable predictions that can be subjected to empirical validation.

Latané's social impact theory has recently begun to have an influence of its own, particularly in research investigating the social loafing effect. Latané and his coworkers Williams and Harkins (1979) have suggested that individuals in large groups may reduce the amount of effort they expend due to the fact that each member's personal contribution will not be identifiable to those monitoring the performance. In the third article in the chapter, Norbert Kerr and Steven Bruun report the results of three studies designed to clarify the roles of the type of task being completed, performance feedback, and group size on group performance. Although performance decrements were obtained, these authors argue that a social loafing explanation based simply on a lack of identifiability is not satisfactory to account for their findings. To account for their results, they introduce yet another possible explanation for reduced productivity in group situation: free-rider effects. As with the other phenomena discussed in this chapter, interpersonal influences are found to be important determinants of the actions displayed in either dyadic or group situations.

The Low-Ball Compliance Technique: Task or Person Commitment?

Jerry M. Burger and Richard E. Petty

Three experiments were conducted to examine the mediating process involved in the low-ball procedure for increasing compliance. In Experiment 1, subjects who agreed to but were not allowed to perform an initial request complied with a more costly version of the same request to a greater extent than did controls only when the second request came from the same person as did the first request and not when it came from a different person. In Experiment 2, subjects who agreed to but were not allowed to carry out an initial low-cost request complied with a larger request from the same person to the same extent, whether the first request was related or unrelated to the second. In Experiment 3, subjects were allowed or not allowed to perform an initial small request after agreeing to do so. Later, these subjects were approached by either the same or a different person with a larger second request. All groups showed increased compliance over a control cell. However, subjects not allowed to perform the initial request who were approached by the same person for the second request showed a higher rate of compliance than subjects in the other experimental conditions. The results from the three experiments suggest that an unfulfilled obligation to the requester, rather than a commitment to the initial target behavior, is responsible for the effectiveness of the low-ball technique.

Recent social psychological investigations have examined the effectiveness of techniques designed to increase compliance to requests in the absence of any obvious sources of pressure (cf. DeJong, 1979). The earliest compliance-without-pressure technique, the foot-in-the-door, was introduced by Freedman and Fraser (1966). Subjects who complied with an initial small request were found to be more likely to agree to a similar but larger request from a different person than were subjects contacted only with the second request. Freedman and Fraser suggested that as a result of performing the first request, the subject comes to see him- or herself as the type of person who favors such requests, resulting in an increased willingness to perform the second request.

The most recent procedure for increasing

compliance without pressure, the low-ball technique, was demonstrated by Cialdini, Cacioppo, Bassett, and Miller (1978). Subjects who agreed to but had not yet performed an initial small request (e.g., displaying a poster for a charity cause) were found to comply with that same request when it was subsequently made more costly (e.g., they had to pick up the poster at a distant location) at a higher rate than did subjects approached only with the costly version of the request. Additionally, Cialdini et al. demonstrated that the low-ball procedure was significantly more effective in increasing compliance than the foot-in-the-door technique. Although mere agreement to perform an initial small request may be sufficient to engender the same self-perception process that is operative with the foot-in-the-door technique (Bem, 1972), Cialdini et al. argued that the low-ball procedure requires an additional commitment to a particular behavior, which is absent in the foot-in-the-door procedure. This additional "cognitive commitment to the performance of the target behavior" (1978, p. 468) was advanced to account for the increased effectiveness of the low-ball procedure beyond that found with the foot-in-the-door technique.

Although Cialdini et al. successfully

Portions of this report were presented at the meeting of the Midwestern Psychological Association, Chicago, May 1979.

We would like to thank the many undergraduates who assisted in the data collection for these experiments, especially Steve Cole, Dan Kaline, Paul Marklin, Michael Oliveri, and Jim York. We are also indebted to the Columbia chapter of the Multiple Sclerosis Society for their cooperation and provision of materials for Experiment 3.

"The Low-ball Compliance Technique: Task or Person Commitment?" by J.M. Burger & R.E. Petty, 1981, *Journal of Personality and Social Psychology*, 40, pp. 492-500. Copyright 1981 by the American Psychological Assn. Reprinted by permission of the publisher and authors.

demonstrated the effectiveness of the low-ball procedure, a close examination of their experiments suggests an alternative interpretation of their findings. In all three of the Cialdini et al. (1978) studies, the same experimenter presented subjects with the first and second request. The possibility exists, therefore, that the subjects experienced an unfulfilled obligation to the specific requester in addition to or instead of a commitment to the target behavior. Individuals agreeing to the initial request may have felt as if they owed something to the requester, because they were unable to carry out the first request. Therefore, when asked by the same experimenter to engage in the behavior at an increased cost, subjects may have complied with the second request to fulfill their obligation to the requester.

Cialdini et al. (1978) provide the example of an automobile salesperson who secures an agreement to purchase a car and then increases the cost of the vehicle. The consumer is said to be committed to the action of purchasing the car and is more likely to purchase the car at an increased cost than if no initial commitment to the car had been made. However, it is reasonable to assume that an obligation to the salesperson has also developed in this situation and may be sufficient to account for the increased willingness to buy the car at the higher price. If the Cialdini et al. reasoning is correct—that as a result of the initial decision, persons become committed to the *car*—then even if a different salesperson were to return with the deal, increased compliance would result. However, if the low-ball procedure is effective because the initial agreement produces an unfulfilled obligation to the *salesperson*, then subjects would more easily reject the car at an increased price if the more costly deal were presented by a new salesperson.

EXPERIMENT 1

Our first experiment was designed to test the obligation-to-the-requester interpretation of the low-ball effect. Subjects who agreed to but did not perform an initial request were asked to perform the same behavior at a higher cost either by the same requester or by a different individual. Subjects in a control condition were presented only with the second request. It was reasoned that if a commitment to the target behavior is solely responsible for the low-ball effect, as suggested by Cialdini et al., then whether the second (more expensive) request is presented by the same or a different person should not affect the rate of compliance. Both conditions should show more compliance than the control condition. On the other hand, if an unfulfilled obligation to the initial requester is solely responsible for the low-ball effect, as suggested here, then persons receiving the first and second requests from the same individual should comply with the second request at a higher rate than persons who receive the requests from two different people. In fact, the latter condition should not differ from the control cell.

METHOD

Subjects

Sixty male and female undergraduate psychology students served individually as subjects. All subjects had just finished participating in an experiment on "advertising," for which they received class credit. Five undergraduate males served as experimenters for the study. Which experimenter made which request was determined randomly for each subject.

Procedure

Subjects were randomly assigned to one of three conditions. Upon completion of the "advertising" experiment, the experimenter gave the subject his or her credit point and then told the subject that he was also working on a class project and needed some students to serve as volunteers. The experimenter presented the subject with several sheets of long division problems and explained that he was conducting research on numeric skills. Each sheet contained 12 problems that required the subject to divide a multidigit number into another multidigit number. The first problem was completed to illustrate that several steps were required in answering each problem. The experimenter explained that the subject's task was to work on the problems until getting them all correct. He further explained that the task took about an hour to complete for the average college student.

All subjects except those in the control condition were then told that they could receive another hour of experimental credit by completing the division problems. The experimenter asked the subject if he or she would like to stay and participate. If the subject asked if he or she could complete only part of the problems, come back to participate, or finish participating in the experiment at a later time, the experimenter explained that he needed to have all of the problems completed at one sitting and the data collected that day.

If subjects declined to participate in the experiment on numeric skills, they were dismissed. If they agreed to participate (27 out of 40 agreed, see Table 1), the experimenter announced that he would have to go to his office to pick up the answer sheets. The experimenter asked the subject to wait in the room for a few minutes, and then he left with the problem sheets.

Same-requester condition. If subjects were assigned to the same-requester condition, the same experimenter returned approximately 2 minutes later with the experimental materials. The experimenter also held a memo, which he said he had just received from the chairman of the psychology department's Human Subjects Committee. He explained that due to a shortage of subjects, he would not be allowed to give any experimental credit for participating in class projects like the numeric skills study. The experimenter then briefly described the task again and asked the subject if he or she would still be willing to participate in the study for no credit. If the subject declined, he or she was debriefed and excused. If the subject agreed, he or she was handed the problem sheet and allowed to work on one problem before being stopped and debriefed.

Different-requester condition. If subjects were assigned to the different-requester condition, a second experimenter returned to the room approximately 2 minutes after the first experimenter had left. The second experimenter introduced himself as one of the persons working on the numeric skills project with the first experimenter. In addition to the experimental materials, he held the memo from the Human Subjects Committee. He explained that the first experimenter had to leave suddenly and would not be back. The experimenter said that he didn't know if the first experimenter had explained the project and briefly repeated the task requirements. He then announced that although they had initially planned to give subjects experimental credit for par-

ticipating in the numeric skills study, he had just received a memo from the chairman of the Human Subjects Committee that did not allow credit for participating in such projects. Subjects were then asked if they would be willing to participate in the study.

Control condition. Subjects in the control condition were not told about the possibility of earning experimental credit. Instead, when the experimenter presented the initial request he explained that although they had wanted to give 1 hour of credit, the Human Subjects Committee would not allow it. These subjects were thus presented with only the no-credit (more expensive) request.

RESULTS

The number of subjects complying with the first and second requests in each condition are presented in Table 1. As can be seen in the table, subjects in the two experimental conditions did not differ significantly in their rate of compliance with the initial request, $\chi^2(1) = 11$, *ns*. The investigation was concerned, however, with the rate of compliance with the second, more costly request. Two orthogonal contrasts were conducted. First, the compliance rate of subjects in the different-requester condition (including those declining the initial request) was compared with the compliance rate in the control condition. It was found that the conditions did not differ significantly in their rate of compliance, $\chi^2(1) = .17$, *ns*. Next, the rate of compliance in the same-requester condition was compared with that in the other two conditions. It was found that subjects receiving both requests from the same individual complied with the second request at a greater rate than did subjects in the other two conditions, $\chi^2(1) = 8.93, p < .005$.

When the subjects who declined the initial request are dropped from the analyses, similar results are obtained. Different-requester subjects did not comply significantly differently (21%) than control subjects, $\chi^2(1) = .01$, *ns*, and same-requester subjects complied at a rate significantly higher (85%) than that for subjects in the other two conditions, $\chi^2(1) = 10.78, p < .005$.

DISCUSSION

The results of Experiment 1 successfully replicated the increase in compliance over a control condition found with the low-ball technique, as operationalized by Cialdini et al. (1978). Subjects complied with a costly request more often when first presented with the same request at a lower cost than did subjects presented with only the most costly request. More importantly, however,

this effect was found *only* when the same requester presented the first and second requests. When a different experimenter presented the second request, subjects were no more likely to comply with this more costly request than were subjects not receiving the initial request.

The findings thus fail to support Cialdini et al.'s commitment-to-the-behavior explanation for the low-ball effect. Subjects should have been equally committed to performing the target behavior in both the same- and different-requester conditions. The finding that subjects increased their rate of compliance beyond that found in the control condition only when the same person presented both requests suggests that an obligation to the person instead of or in addition to a commitment to the behavior is responsible for the low-ball effect.

EXPERIMENT 2

One question that remains unanswered by the first experiment is whether a commitment to the target behavior is at all necessary for producing the low-ball effect. It may be that when a person agrees to but is unable to perform an initial task, the unfulfilled obligation to the requester makes the person more susceptible to a second, more costly request from the same person, even if the second task is unrelated to the first one. On the other hand, if a commitment to perform the target behavior is necessary for the low-ball effect, as suggested by Cialdini et al., then it would be expected that increased compliance would be found only when the second request is a more costly version of the initial request and not when it is unrelated. This question was examined in Experiment 2.

TABLE 1

Percentages of Subjects Complying With Initial and Second Requests

	Initial request		Second request	
Group	%	*n*	%	*n*
Same requester	65	13	55	11
Different requester	70	14	15	3
Control			20	4

Note: n = 20 for each cell.

METHOD

Subjects

Sixty university students were randomly selected from the university phone directory and assigned to one of three experimental conditions.

Procedure

Subjects were contacted by telephone in the evening. If a subject could not be contacted after three attempts, he or she was dropped from the sample and replaced by another randomly selected subject.

Related-request condition. Subjects in the related-request condition heard the following initial request:

> Hi. My name is _____ and I'm calling for the Committee for Student Awareness. We are a group of concerned students interested in demonstrating our opposition to further increases in student tuition and fee costs. What I would like to know from you now is, if we send a student by with a petition stating our position, would you be willing to sign it?

If subjects asked for further information about the petition, they were told, "The petition merely says that you, along with other signers, are in opposition to further tuition and fee increases." If subjects agreed to the initial request (only two refused and were replaced), the experimenter replied:

> Good. Oh, wait a minute, I'm sorry. I was looking at the wrong list. It looks like we have already filled several petitions. What I meant to call you about was not the petition, but a related task.

Subjects were then presented with the second, more costly request. They were told that in addition to the petitions,

> We would also like to get a large number of students to write letters or postcards during this next week to the Student Opinion Administrator here on campus to further demonstrate our opposition. If I give you the address right now, would you be willing to write a short postcard or letter just stating in a line or two that you, too, are opposed to any further increases in tuition and fees?

If subjects inquired about what to write in their letters, they were told, "Just write something like: I am writing to say that I am opposed to further increases in student tuition and fees at [the University of] Missouri." The experimenter waited until receiving a verbal reply to the request before ending the conversation. Thus, in this experimental condition, the cost (in terms of time, energy, and the expense of a stamp) of protesting an increase in tuition was increased. Subjects agreeing to the request were given a mailing address, which would allow the experimenter to record how many subjects in each condition showed behavioral as well as verbal compliance with the more costly request.

Unrelated-request condition. When the experimenter initially contacted subjects in the unrelated-request condition, he also identified himself as a member of the Committee for Student Awareness. Subjects in this condition were presented with the following initial request:

> We're calling students to get your opinion about the new campus shuttle bus system. Could you spare a few minutes now to answer about four or five short questions for us?

When subjects agreed to this request (none refused), the experimenter replied:

> Good. Oh, wait a minute. I'm sorry. I was looking at the wrong list. What I meant to call you about was not the survey, I've already reached my quota on that, but I wanted to ask you about helping us show our opposition to the suggested further increases in student tuition and fees here at [the University of] Missouri. We have already filled several petitions demonstrating our opposition to these increases.

This was followed by the same letter-writing request that was presented to the subjects in the same-request condition.

Control condition. Subjects in the no-initial-request control condition were also contacted by the experimenter, who identified himself as a member of the Committee for Student Awareness. These subjects were told:

> We're calling university students about helping us show our opposition to the suggested further increases in student tuition and fees here at [the University of] Missouri. We have already filled several petitions demonstrating our opposition to these increases.

This was followed by the letter-writing request as presented to subjects in the other two conditions.

Results

Subjects' responses were assigned the following values: 2 = verbal and behavioral compliance (agreed on phone and letter received), 1 = verbal compliance only, and 0 = no compliance. To test the specific hypotheses of interest, two orthogonal planned comparisons were performed.

First, as anticipated, a comparison between the related-request condition ($M = .70$) and the unrelated-request condition ($M = .65$) failed to find a significant difference between the compliance scores for these two groups ($F < 1$). However, as expected, when the combined compliance scores of subjects in the related-request condition and the unrelated-request condition ($M = .68$) were compared with the score of subjects in the no-initial-request control condition ($M = .35$), a significant effect emerged, $F(1, 57) = 4.70, p < .05$.[1]

Discussion

The results of Experiment 2 once again replicated the low-ball effect as operationalized by Cialdini et al. (1978). Subjects complied with a costly request at a higher rate when first presented with a similar low-cost request that they were not allowed to perform. More importantly though, the increase in compliance rate did not vary as a function of the specific behavior that the individual promised to perform in the initial request. When an unrelated behavior was requested by the same experimenter, subjects complied at a rate significantly higher than that of subjects presented with only one request but not significantly different from that of subjects presented with a similar first and second request.

The results thus suggest that a commitment to a specific task or issue (e.g., stopping tuition increases) may not be necessary for the increase in compliance found with the low-ball procedure. Instead, it appears that an unfulfilled obligation to the requester may be responsible for the low-ball effect. This unfulfilled obligation to the requester appears to increase compliance to a second request even when a very different issue is involved.

EXPERIMENT 3

Taken together, the results of Experiments 1 and 2 suggest that Cialdini et al.'s (1978) interpretation of the low-ball effect may not be correct. Instead of a commitment to the target activity, these two experiments suggest that an unfulfilled obligation to the requester may be responsible for the increase in compliance found with this technique. An important aspect of the Cialdini et al. studies and Experiments 1 and 2 is that subjects agreeing to the initial request were not allowed to perform that behavior at the original cost. If the unfulfilled-obligation-to-the-requester interpretation is correct, then it would be expected that if individuals are provided with an opportunity to fulfill the initial obligation, they will not feel a need to help the requester further and will therefore fail to show the increased rate of compliance found in the low-ball procedure.

Experiment 3 was designed to examine this possibility. Subjects were either allowed or not allowed to perform the initial low-cost request. The same or a different experimenter later presented the subject with a related but more costly request. It was anticipated that (a) when the subject was allowed to perform the initial request, compliance to the second request would not be affected by whether the same person made the request (since no unfulfilled obligation existed), and (b) when the subject was not allowed to perform the initial request, compliance to the second request would be greater when the same person made the requests than when the requests

came from different people (since it is hypothesized that the unfulfilled obligation is to a particular person).

METHOD

Subjects

Seventy-five college-age males and females served as subjects. Subjects were residents of on-campus dormitories or apartment complexes near the university campus.

Procedure

Subjects were randomly preassigned to one of the five conditions. That is, a random order of doors to be approached and a random order of conditions for subjects' answering their doors were predetermined.

Performance manipulation. In the first part of the experiment, the individual answering the door was presented with the following request by the experimenter:

> Hello. My name is _____ and I'm working for the National Multiple Sclerosis Society. We are interested in publicizing our current fund-raising drive and I was wondering if you would be interested in helping us by displaying a poster like this one on your door for the next two weeks.

All subjects agreed to this request. In the *perform conditions,* the experimenter thanked the person for helping and then taped an 8½ in. × 11 in. (21.5 cm × 27.9 cm) poster onto the front door. In the *no-perform conditions,* the experimenter reached into an envelope as if to pull out a poster but stopped and announced:

I'm sorry. It looks like I'm all out of posters. I guess I gave my last one away to the last person I talked to. I'm really sorry. But thanks anyway for offering to help.

Thus in the perform conditions, subjects were able to perform the initial small request, whereas in the no-perform conditions, subjects agreed to but were unable to perform the initial small request. In both conditions, the experimenter recorded the room number, first name, and experimental condition for each subject.

Requester manipulation. Approximately 10-15 minutes after the first request, either the same or a different experimenter returned to the door. In the *same-requester* condition, the experimenter explained "I forgot to mention last time I was here that . . . ." In the *different-requester* condition, the experimenter introduced himself with, "Hello. My name is ____ and I'm working for the National Multiple Sclerosis Society." In both conditions, the experimenter then said:

> The National Multiple Sclerosis Society is looking for people to serve as volunteers distributing envelopes for MS. There will be an MS representative at [a room in the lobby of the dorm or apartment] between [a 2-hour time interval] tonight handing out collection envelopes in which contributions can be made. Would you be interested in helping MS by going to ____ between ____ and ____ tonight and picking up a collection envelope and either collecting from others or taking the envelope for your own contribution?

Experimenters waited for an affirmative or negative reply before asking subjects for their first names, thanking them, and leaving. The experimenter then recorded the

room number, the subject's first name, and whether the subject had agreed to the second request.

Control condition. In the control condition, subjects were approached only once. The experimenter presented the subject with the different-experimenter request to pick up a volunteer packet.[2]

RESULTS

The names and room numbers of subjects who picked up packets were recorded. As in Experiment 2, subjects were assigned a score of 2 (verbal and behavioral compliance), 1 (verbal compliance only), or 0 (no compliance) for their responses to the second request. The mean scores for the five conditions are presented in Table 2. Four orthogonal contrasts in the context of a one-way analysis of variance were performed to test the specific hypotheses of interest. First, the four experimental conditions were compared with the control condition. This contrast revealed that experimental subjects complied more than controls, $F(1, 70) = 13.34$, $p < .05$. Next, no effect for the same-different requester variable within the perform conditions was found, $F(1, 70) = .37$, ns.

If the commitment-to-the-behavior interpretation of the low-ball effect is correct, subjects in the no-perform—different-requester condition should have complied with the second request more often than did subjects in the two perform conditions, because of their unfulfilled obligation to the task, helping MS. However, this effect failed to emerge, $F(1, 70) = 1.01$, ns. Finally, if an unfulfilled obligation to the person is responsible for the increased compliance with the low-ball procedure, then subjects in the no-perform—same-requester condition should have complied significantly more often than subjects in the other three conditions (because this is the only condition in which an unfulfilled obligation to a person exists). A significant contrast supported this viewpoint, $F(1, 70) = 4.51$, $p < .05$.[3]

Discussion

Experiment 3 once again demonstrated the effectiveness of the low-ball procedure for increasing the rate of compliance with a costly request by first securing agreement to perform but not allowing performance of a similar behavior at a lower cost. The results also replicated the foot-in-the-door effect, again demonstrating the effectiveness of this compliance technique. Subjects approached by a different individual with a larger request, after agreeing to perform or

TABLE 2

Effects of Same or Different Requester and Performance of Initial Request on Compliance Rates

Condition	VCF	BCF	CCI
No perform– same requester	13	4	1.13
No perform– different requester	8	1	.60
Perform– same requester	11	2	.87
Perform–different requester	10	1	.73
Control	5	0	.33

Note: VCF = verbal compliance frequency; BCF = behavioral compliance frequency; CCI = combined compliance index. $n = 15$ for each cell.

performing a smaller request, agreed to the second request at a higher rate than subjects approached only with the large request. The results also replicated the Cialdini et al. finding that the low-ball procedure (with the same requester) was more effective in inducing compliance than the foot-in-the-door procedure.

Of most importance in Experiment 3 was the finding that subjects not allowed to perform the initial request and approached by the same person for the second request had a rate of compliance significantly higher than that of subjects in the other three experimental conditions. This finding suggests that the higher rate of compliance for the no-perform—same-requester subjects is due to an unfulfilled obligation to the requester that developed from the inability to perform the initial request. Subjects approached by a different experimenter were not able to fulfill their obligation to the initial requester by complying with the second request. Subjects allowed to perform the initial request were able to fulfill their obligation to the requester and thus were not as likely to comply with the second request as were the no-perform same-requester subjects. The results thus provide additional support for the unfulfilled-obligation-to-the-requester interpretation of the low-ball effect.[4]

GENERAL DISCUSSION

Summary

The three experiments presented here suggest that the low-ball procedure, as operationalized by Cialdini et al. (1978), is a successful means of increasing compliance with a request. The effectiveness of the technique across three different types of requests indicates the robust nature of the effect. Consistent with the Cialdini et al. findings, the low-ball procedure also appears to be more effective in increasing compliance than the foot-in-the-door technique.

However, the effectiveness of the low-ball procedure does not appear to be due to the explanation proposed by Cialdini et al., namely, that a commitment to the target behavior develops. Instead, the results of all three experiments presented in the present research suggest that an unfulfilled obligation to the requester may be responsible for the effectiveness of the low-ball procedure. In Experiment 1, which provided the most direct test of the task versus person commitment hypotheses, the low-ball technique was effective only when the same person raised the cost of the initial request. When the higher cost version of the initial request was presented by a different person, no increased compliance over the control condition was found. Experiment 2 found that the second request did not have to be a higher cost version of the initial request. When subjects were unable to comply with the initial low-cost request, they showed enhanced compliance with a higher cost request from the same person, even when the second request was unrelated to the first. Finally, Experiment 3 demonstrated the importance of the nonperformance of the initial request. Individuals who were not allowed to perform the initial request were more likely to comply with the second request presented by the same person than were those allowed to perform the initial request. The results of all three studies provide support for the view that the effectiveness of the low-ball compliance technique is dependent on an unfulfilled obligation to a particular person rather than a commitment to a specific target behavior.

Low-Ball Versus Foot-in-the-Door

Given the above analysis, it seems necessary to clarify the relationship between the low-ball procedure and the foot-in-the-door technique as initially identified by Freedman and Fraser (1966). Cialdini et al. suggested that the difference between the two compliance techniques was that the low-ball procedure relied on inducing a commitment to the initial target behavior, whereas the foot-in-the-door procedure did not. However, Experiment 1 strongly indicated that the effectiveness of the low-ball procedure did not depend on inducing a commitment to the initial target behavior. If it did, enhanced compliance should have occurred even when the second request was presented by a different person, but it did not. Also, Experiment 2 demonstrated that the effectiveness of the low-ball procedure was not affected when the initial request was for a behavior very different from the second, more costly request. Thus, a commitment to the initial target behavior does not appear necessary for producing the low-ball effect and therefore cannot distinguish the low-ball from the foot-in-the-door technique.

Another apparent difference between the two procedures concerns the subject's performance of the initial request. Whereas Cialdini et al.'s low-ball subjects were not allowed to perform the request at the initial cost, foot-in-the-door subjects typically perform the initial request. Consistent with the self-perception interpretation of the foot-in-the-door phenomenon (Bem, 1972), the performance of this behavior can be seen as enhancing the subject's self-perception that he or she is the type of person who engages in such behaviors. However, some investigators (Snyder & Cunningham, 1975; Zuckerman, Lazzaro, & Waldgeir, 1979) have successfully produced a foot-in-the-door effect without the performance of the initial behavior (cf. DeJong, 1979). Consistent with this finding, subjects in Experiment 3 who agreed to but were not allowed to perform the initial request from one person complied significantly more often than the control subjects to a second, larger request presented by a different individual.[5] Thus, whether the subject is allowed to perform the initial request does not appear to be the crucial distinction between the foot-in-the-door and the low-ball procedures.

The foot-in-the-door effect appears to occur when an individual who agrees to perform (though does not necessarily perform) a small request comes to view him- or herself in a manner that makes him or her more susceptible to a second, more costly request from either the same or a different person. Thus, it is likely that there is a component of the foot-in-the-door effect in each of the four experimental conditions in Experiment 3.

However, one of the experimental conditions in Experiment 3 produced significantly more compliance than the others. Something unique appears to occur when (a) the person does not perform the initial agreed-upon smaller request, and (b) the second, larger request is presented by the same person. Joint occurrence of these two conditions produces an unfulfilled obligation to the initial requester, which is not present in the other three experimental cells (i.e., when the initial behavior is performed and/or the second request comes from a different person). This additional psychological process (an unfulfilled commitment to a person), called the low-ball effect, appears to be responsible for producing compliance above that which would be expected from the foot-in-the-door procedure alone.

NOTES

1. If the verbal and behavioral compliance frequencies are analyzed separately, then the same pattern emerges in each measure, though only the verbal measure produces a significant low-ball effect. Specifically, the rates of verbal compliance for the related (13/20) and unrelated (12/20) conditions did not differ significantly, but the combined rate was greater than the compliance rate in the control cell (7/20), $\chi^2(1) = 4.05, p < .05$. Only two letters in opposition to the tuition increase were received (behavioral compliance measure), one each from subjects in the two experimental cells. These letters were forwarded to the University chancellor.

2. Four male experimenters who were blind to the experimental hypotheses were rotated through the roles required in the various conditions. A fifth male acted as the MS representative in the dorm or apartment lobby.

3. These same four contrasts were computed separately on the frequencies of verbal and behavioral compliance (see frequencies in Table 2). Analyses on the verbal compliance measure produced one significant effect: There was greater verbal compliance in the experimental cells (42/60) than in the control cell (5/15), $\chi^2(1) = 6.89, p < .05$. Analyses on the behavioral compliance measure yielded one marginally significant result: Behavioral compliance was greater in the no-perform—same-requester condition (4/15) than in the other three experimental cells combined (4/45), $\chi^2(1) = 3.07, p < .10$.

4. In addition to the unfulfilled obligation to the requester, subjects in the same-requester conditions may have also been motivated by impression-management concerns. Tedeschi, Schlenker, and Bonoma (1971) have argued that people are motivated to present themselves in a consistent manner to others. However, a motive to appear consistent cannot by itself account for the increase in compliance found for the same-requester subjects not allowed to perform the behavior over that of the perform—same-re-

quester subjects. Because the experimenter saw them perform the initial behavior, perform—same-requester subjects should have been equally if not more motivated to present themselves in a consistent manner than the ho-perform subjects.

5. The foot-in-the-door effect did not emerge in Experiment 1 when a different requester presented the second request, because in that study, subjects had an external reason for agreeing to the initial request (i.e., getting an extra hour of credit), so there was no need to search for an internal explanation. Thus, the self-perception process would be unlikely to occur.

REFERENCES

Bem, D. J. Self-perception theory. In L. Berkowitz (Ed.), *Advances in experimental social psychology* (Vol. 6). New York: Academic Press, 1972.

Cialdini, R. B., Cacioppo, J. T., Bassett, R., & Miller, J. A. The low-ball procedure for producing compliance: Commitment then cost. *Journal of Personality and Social Psychology*, 1978, *36*, 463-476.

DeJong, W. An examination of the self-perception mediation of the foot-in-the-door effect. *Journal of Personality and Social Psychology*, 1979, *37*, 2221-2239.

Freedman, J. L., & Fraser, S. C. Compliance without pressure: The foot-in-the-door technique. *Journal of Personality and Social Psychology*, 1966, *4*, 195-202.

Snyder, M., & Cunningham, M. R. To comply or not comply: Testing the self-perception explanation of the "foot-in-the-door" phenomenon. *Journal of Personality and Social Psychology*, 1975, *31*, 64-67.

Tedeschi, J. T., Schlenker, B. R., & Bonoma, T. V. Cognitive dissonance: Private ratiocination or public spectacle? *American Psychologist*, 1971, *26*, 685-695.

Zuckerman, M., Lazzaro, M. M., Waldgeir, D. Undermining effects of the foot-in-the-door technique with extrinsic reward. *Journal of Applied Social Psychology*, 1979, *9*, 292-296.

The Psychology of Social Impact

Bibb Latané

Abstract: The author proposes a theory of social impact specifying the effect of other persons on an individual. According to the theory, when other people are the source of impact and the individual is the target, impact should be a multiplicative function of the strength, immediacy, and number of other people. Furthermore, impact should take the form of a power function, with the marginal effect of the Nth other person being less than that of the (N − 1)th. Finally, when other people stand with the individual as the target of forces from outside the group, impact should be divided such that the resultant is an inverse power function of the strength, immediacy, and number of persons standing together. The author reviews relevant evidence from research on conformity and imitation, stage fright and embarrassment, news interest, bystander intervention, tipping, inquiring for Christ, productivity in groups, and crowding in rats. He also discusses the unresolved issues and desirable characteristics of the theory.

People affect each other in many different ways. As social animals, we are drawn by the attractiveness of others and aroused by their mere presence, stimulated by their activity and embarrassed by their attention. We are influenced by the actions of others, entertained by their performances, and sometimes persuaded by their arguments. We are inhibited by the surveillance of others and made less guilty by their complicity.

We are threatened by the power of others and angered by their attack. Fortunately, we are also comforted by the support of others and sustained by their love.

I call all these effects, and others like them, "social impact." By social impact, I mean any of the great variety of changes in physiological states and subjective feelings, motives and emotions, cognitions and beliefs, values and behavior, that occur in an individual, human or animal, as a result of the real, implied, or imagined presence or actions of other individuals.

Clearly, this is a rather broad definition.

In the present article I offer a general theory of social impact. Depending on one's philosophy of science, one may wish rather to regard the theory as a quantitative description, an empirical generalization, a discovery, a set of fundamental laws, a model, an organizing theme, a framework, or a perspective. In any event, the theory is not itself very specific. It does not say when social impact will occur or detail the exact mechanisms whereby social impact is transmitted. It does not purport to "explain"

the operation of any of the number of particular social processes that are necessary to account for all the effects I have labeled "social impact" or to substitute for theories that do. It does, however, provide general overall rules that seem to govern each and all of these individual processes. The theory consists of three principles that represent an attempt to adapt, integrate, and formalize ideas initially developed by sociologist Stewart Dodd, astronomer J. Q. Stewart, anthropologist-geographer-linguist George Kingsley Zipf, and psychologists Kurt Lewin and S. S. Stevens, among others. Although the principles comprise a general theory, they lead to specific quantifiable and verifiable predictions. In the remainder of this article, I develop the theory and briefly review evidence from ten areas of application.

THREE PRINCIPLES OF SOCIAL IMPACT

To start I suggest that one can usefully think of social impact as being the result of social forces (like the physical forces of light, sound, gravity, and magnetism) operating in a social force field or social structure. As an example of what I mean by a social force field, Figure 1 depicts the plight of a hapless striped target beset by a variety of spotted sources, all having some impact.

PRINCIPLE 1: SOCIAL FORCES, $I = f(SIN)$

As a first principle, I suggest that when some number of social sources are acting on a target individual, the amount of impact experienced by the target should be a multiplicative function of the strength, S, the immediacy, I, and the number, N, of sources present. By strength, I mean the salience, power, importance, or intensity of

Previous versions of this article were presented at meetings of the Psychonomic Society, St. Louis, Missouri, 1973; the Conference on Mechanisms of Prosocial Behavior, Nieborow, Poland, 1974; the XXI International Congress of Psychology, Paris, 1976; the XVII InterAmerican Congress of Psychology, Lima, Peru, 1979; and as the presidential address of Division 8 at the meeting of the American Psychological Association, Toronto, 1978.

A large number of colleagues and students have shared in the development of these ideas and experiments. In particular, I want to mention Rodney Bassett, Richard Borden, Malcolm Brenner, James Dabbs, John Darley, Steven Freeman, David Hall, Stephen Harkins, Jack Keating, Lloyd Sloan, Marcus Walker, Carol Werner, and Kipling Williams.

This research was supported by National Science Foundation Grants GS 40194 and BNS 76-19629 and a Guggenheim fellowship.

"The Psychology of Social Impact" by B. Latané, 1981, *American Psychologist, 36*, pp. 343-356. Copyright 1981 by the American Psychological Assn. Reprinted by permission of the publisher and author.

FIGURE 1.

Multiplication of impact: I = f(SIN).

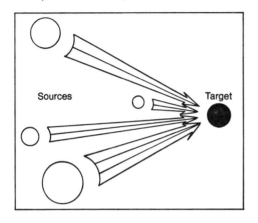

a given source to the target—usually this would be determined by such things as the source's status, age, socio-economic status, and prior relationship with, or future power over, the target. By immediacy, I mean closeness in space or time and absence of intervening barriers or filters. By number, I mean how many people there are.

This can be called a light bulb theory of social relations: As the amount of light falling on a surface is a multiplicative function of the wattage or intensity of the light bulbs shining on the surface, their closeness to the surface, and the number of bulbs, so the impact experienced by an individual is a multiplicative function of the strength, immediacy, and number of people affecting him or her. It seems reasonable to expect that an individual will experience more impact the higher the status, the more immediate the influence, and the greater the number of other people affecting him or her, and data typically bear this out. In general, I am suggesting that the laws governing the intensity of a social flux are comparable to

the laws governing the intensity of a luminous flux.

I concentrate on the number dimension here because this is the dimension for which there are the most data. The line of thought I shall pursue, however, is also translatable into the other dimensions, and I do not mean to imply that number is more important than strength or immediacy in moderating impact.

PRINCIPLE 2: THE PSYCHOSOCIAL LAW, $I = sN^t$, $t < I$

Any economist will tell you that the first dollar you have, devalued as it might be, is worth more than the hundredth. Likewise, I think, the first other person in a social force field should have greater impact than the hundredth. This is not to say that one wouldn't rather have $100 than $1 or that 100 people won't have more impact than a single person but that the difference between 99 and 100 is less than the difference between 0 and 1. Thus, I suggest there is a marginally decreasing effect of increased supplies of people as well as of money.

From Fechner's day, psychologists have studied similar relationships between objective and subjective reality, between external value and internal valuation, under the rubric of "psychophysics." In 1957, S. S. Stevens distilled all this activity into an elegant but simple law: $\psi = \kappa\phi^\beta$. For prothetic stimulus dimension (in which qualities vary in intensity), the subjective psychological intensity, ψ, equals some power, β, of the objective physical intensity of the stimulus, ϕ, times a scaling constant, κ.

I would like to suggest my own *psychosocial* law to parallel Stevens's psychophysical law: $I = sN^t$. When people are in a multiplicative force field, the amount of social impact, I, they experience will equal some power, t, of the number of sources, N, times a scaling constant, s. Further, the value of the exponent t should be less than one: Impact will increase in proportion to some root of the number of people present.

My task in this article is to convince you that SIN has a special role in psychology and that $I = sN^t$ is.

Application 1: Conformity and Imitation

Eighty years of experimental evidence strongly shows that individuals are influenced by the actions and expectations of others. These effects have long been studied under such rubrics as allelomimetic behavior, behavioral contagion, conformity, compliance, group pressure, imitation, normative influence, observational learning, social facilitation, suggestion, and vicarious conditioning. In general, the theory of social impact suggests that each of these kinds of influence can be understood as resulting from the operation of social forces in a multiplicative force field: Increases in the strength, immediacy, and number of people who are the source of influence should lead to increases in their effect on an individual. In this section, I discuss research on conformity, which presents only mixed support for the principles of social impact.

Asch and the magic number three. Ironically, some of the first and most famous research involving parametric variations in the number of people serving as the source of social impact appears to suggest a relationship quite different from that proposed here. In his classic studies on independence and conformity Asch (1951, 1952, 1956) asked Swarthmore College students to choose which of a set of three disparate lines matched a standard, either alone or after 1, 2, 3, 4, 8, or 16 confederates had first given a unanimously incorrect answer. Figure 2a shows the percentage of trials on which participants overruled their own senses and conformed to majority judgment. In discussing the implications of these data, Asch focused on the concept of group "concensus," concluding that increasing group size leads to increased conformity only to the point, 3, where there is a perception of consensus among group nembers.

Although the most striking feature of Asch's data is that conformity does not seem to increase with increases in group size beyond three members, the most troubling aspect for social impact theory is that people faced with but one or two incorrect conformers conformed so little—in the present theory, the first person added to a social setting is expected to have the most impact. However, for such counterfactual judgments, Swarthmore students may be sufficiently independent as to require a substantial amount of social pressure just to bring them up to a yielding threshold; the first one or two incorrect models may in fact reduce restraints, making it possible for the addition of further confederates to have a more visible effect.

In a replication by Gerard, Wilhelmy, and Conolley (1968) 154 high school students (who might not have had so much initial resistance to making counterfactual judgments) were exposed to one to seven confederates giving incorrect answers. Gerard et al. expected and found conformity to increase with group size. Furthermore, the first few confederates had the most impact. Figure 2b presents their data (circles) and the best fitting power function (dashed line) calculated from the formula $I = sN^t$, which does a good job in fitting these data, ac-

FIGURE 2.

Conformity and imitation as a function of a group size: a. Data from Asch (1951); b. Data from Gerard, Wilhelmy, and Conolley (1968); c. Data from Milgram, Bickman, and Berkowitz (1969).

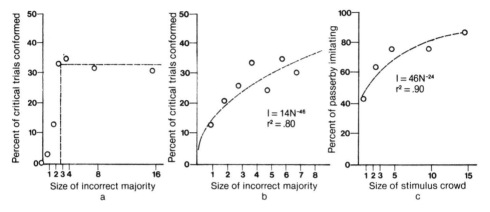

counting for 80% of the variance in means (better than the 61% best linear fit). In this case, the exponent is .46: Conformity seems to grow in proportion to the square root of majority size.

Craning and gawking. Milgram, Bickman, and Berkowitz (1969) conducted an interesting experiment at the Graduate Center of the City University of New York, where the laboratory facilities include 42nd Street. Confederates in groups ranging in size from 1 to 15 would stop, congregate, and crane their necks, gawking up at a window on the sixth floor, behind which, dimly visible, stood Stanley Milgram taking movies. These movies were later analyzed to see how many passersby were stimulated themselves to crane and gawk. Increasing the number of confederates craning and gawking led to an increase in the number of passersby craning and gawking, but the additional craning and gawking caused by each additional craner and gawker grew smaller with increasing numbers of confed-

erates. The fit between the data (circles in Figure 2c) and the best fitting power function (dotted line in Figure 2c) is again impressive, with the squared correlation coefficient indicating that the power law accounts for 90% of the variance in the percentage of passersby imitating. The exponent of .24 is less than one, as predicted, and craning and gawking is proportional to the fourth root of the number of craners and gawkers. On balance, research on conformity and imitation appears to support the general principles of social impact.

Application 2: The Social Psychophysics of Embarrassment

Although many of us have been exposed to the embarrassing or even debilitating experience of performing in front of an audience, the mechanism that mediates stage fright or performance apprehension is not at all well understood. In a study directly designed to provide exact tests of the relationships between audience size and strength and social impact, Latané and Harkins (1976) investigated anticipated stage fright using a technique borrowed from sensory psychophysics: cross-modality matching.

Sixteen college students tested individually in a soundproof booth were asked to imagine that they had memorized a poem and were to recite it in front of an audience. By pushing buttons, they could adjust the brightness of a translucent screen or the loudness of a tone to match their anticipated level of social tension about performing in front of audiences varying in size and status. They were asked to make the tone as loud or the screen as bright as they would be anxious, nervous, or tense. "Audiences" consisted of 1, 2, 4, 8, or 16 faces of persons, either all males or all females and either in their early teens or late thirties.

We predicted that (a) audience size and tension would be related by a power function with an exponent of less than one, (b) audiences composed of older, higher status people would engender more tension, and (c) since it was postulated that audience size and status would be multiplicatively related, there would be greater differences for larger audiences.

One of the elegant features of a power law is that simply by taking the logarithms of both sides of the equation $I = sN^t$, one obtains the equation $\log I = \log s + t(\log N)$, which has the form $\chi = a + by$, the formula for a straight line. This means that power functions are linear in logarithmic coordinates, allowing one to derive precise estimates of parameters and to make exact tests of predictions using standard regression and analysis of variance techniques after subjecting the data to logarithmic transformation.

As audience size increased, participants matched their subjective tension with increasing brightness and loudness of tone ($\omega^2 = 60\%$). The linear components accounted for 98% of the variance attributable to audience size, and deviations from linearity (i.e., deviations from a power function) were not significant. The slope of the linear trend for loudness, and therefore the exponent of the power function implied by it, was .99. Since in cross-modality matching this exponent should represent the ratio of the exponent for effect of audience size and the exponent for loudness, and since preliminary research showed the exponent for loudness in this setting to be .52, this result implies that the exponent for the effect of audience size on rated tension is also about .52, less than one, as expected. It appears that subjective tension in this situation grows in proportion to the square root of the number of people in the audience. Participants generated a similar exponent of .60 for their brightness matches.

In addition, audiences in their late thirties engendered more anxiety than audiences in their early teens ($\omega^2 = 14\%$), and male audiences elicited more tension than did female audiences ($\omega^2 = 3\%$). There were no interactions between age or sex and audience size. Since age and audience size did not interact, the main effects for these variables, expressed in logarithmic units, imply an additive relationship. However, adding logarithms is the same as multiplying the antilogarithms, and thus the data confirm the hypothesis that impact is a simple multiplicative function of status and number. This multiplicative relationship results in there being greater differences due to age and status for the larger audience sizes. Figure 3a displays this multiplicative relationship for the brightness matches; the comparable relationship for loudness is very similar.

FIGURE 3.

Social tension as a function of audience size: a. Data on matched brightness (footlamberts[54]) from Latané and Harkins (1976); b. Data on stuttering from Porter (1939).

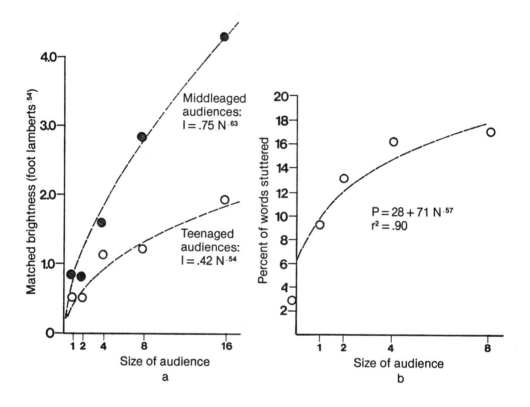

It is probably no surprise to psychologists familiar with cross-modality matching that people can do a good job on these tasks, but we were impressed by the remarkable ease and confidence with which our participants made these unusual comparisons. Not only were they able to equate such disparate commodities as nervousness, loudness, and brightness, but they did so in an impressively lawful manner. These results are based on subjective estimates about reactions to imagined situations, making them potentially responsive to such sources of bias as experimenter demand. Although cross-modality matching does not preclude expectations as to the existence or direction of effects, the complexity of the procedure would seem to make it unlikely that participants were merely responding to demand characteristics with respect to the shape of the functions. That we found the same functions and approximately the same exponent whether volunteers adjusted loudness or brightness increases our confidence that both results reflect the same underlying relationship.

Results of an experiment on stuttering reported by Porter (1939) provide evidence that the relationship we found between stage fright and audience size may also hold in situations involving natural behavior and real audiences. In Porter's experiment, 10 male and 3 female stutterers attending remedial speech courses at the University of Iowa were asked to read 500-word passages in front of audiences consisting of 0, 1, 2, 4, or 8 members. Since as audience size increased, stutterers were presumably faced with increasing social tension, we would expect stuttering to increase as a power function with an exponent of less than one. In fact, our reanalysis shows that Porter's data (open circles in Figure 3b) are well fit ($r^2 = .90$) by a power function of audience size with an exponent of less than one. Stuttering appears to grow in proportion to the cube root of audience size.

Application 3: Social Impact of News Events

Newspapers serve as a major source of information and as a topic for conversation: They help determine the content of our mental lives. However, not everything that happens gets printed in the newspaper, and not all that is printed is read or remembered. Obviously, a great many factors determine the interest value of news events—their rarity, their consequence, the extent to which they relate to our needs and aspirations. The theory of social impact suggests that among these determinants should be the strength, immediacy, and number of people involved.

In one of a series of studies, Bassett and Latané (Note 1) varied the status, the distance, and the number of others involved in catastrophes, asking 86 introductory psychology students to play the role of campus newspaper editors and recommend the amount of coverage (in newspaper column inches) to allocate to each story. At a single mass administration, each "editor" was given a booklet that contained 20 headlines about either a fire (e.g., "14 Professors Hospitalized After a Fire in Arizona State Lounge") or a bomb ("Bomb Disrupts Columbus Meeting of Business Leaders: Two Killed"), in which the status of those involved (secretaries or union members vs. professors or business leaders) and the distance of the event (Columbus or Arizona) were covaried with the number of people involved (0, 2, 5, 9, 14, 27, or 54). Before the editors made their decisions, they were shown samples of news stories of various lengths (2, 12, or 28 inches) to guide their decisions and were told to assume there was enough material for each story to be as long as they desired. Formally, this task can be considered an example of magnitude estimation or cross-modality matching, since participants were given the opportunity to adjust one dimension, column inches, to match another, news value. Such a procedure should provide ratio scaling of news interest.

Analyses of the data in logarithmic units indicated that the column inches assigned to news stories increased as a power function ($r^2 = .99$) of the number of persons involved with an exponent of about .5, which did not vary as a function of experimental condition. The interest value of news events seems to grow in proportion to the square root of the number of people involved. The severity of the event (bomb vs. fire) and the distance from Columbus also had strong main effects, but they did not interact in logarithmic units with the number of people involved. Again, this im-

FIGURE 4.

Interest value of news events as a function of number of people involved, based on data from Bassett and Latané (Note 1). Different circles reflect responses from different people exposed to different ranges of numbers of people involved.

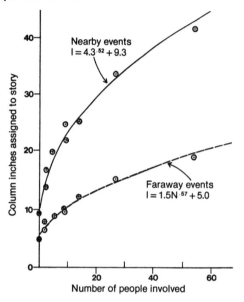

the test was sufficiently powerful to detect moderate effects, it is not clear whether this failure to find a difference represents a general exception to the theory or simply the operation of some factor related to catastrophes. For example, the idea that death is the great equalizer may be true in a new sense.

Evidence for the latter view comes from a second experiment in which participants rated the news interest value of two non-catastrophes: (a) "Fourteen (Fifty-Four) Minneapolis (Columbus) High School Students (Political Figures) Stage Unicycle Race for Charities" and (b) "Five (Twenty-Seven) University of Minnesota (Ohio State University) Nursing Students (Medical Students) Expelled in Cheating Scandal." This time, all three variables, status included, had very strong main effects. Again, there were no interactions in the logarithmic units, implying simple multiplicative relationships.

PRINCIPLE 3: MULTIPLICATION VERSUS DIVISION OF IMPACT

In addition to force fields in which a given individual is the target of social forces and experiences impact as a multiplicative function of the strength, immediacy, and number of sources, I now suggest that there exists a different type of force field or social structure in which other people stand with the individual as the target of forces coming from outside the group. In such situations, schematized in Figure 5, I suggest that increasing the strength, immediacy, or number of other targets should lead to a division or diminution of impact, with each person feeling less than he or she would if alone. For example, consider a person giving a speech. As the target of social forces emanating from each member of the audience

plies multiplicative relationships in normal units, as can be seen in Figure 4, which indicates that the difference in judged news value between the nearby (Columbus) and faraway (Phoenix) events grows larger the greater the number of people involved.

Status, in the present experiment, had no effect: Students considered it no more newsworthy for professors than secretaries to be hospitalized or for business leaders than union members to be bombed. Although separate manipulation checks did indicate that students do regard professors and business leaders as having higher status and

FIGURE 5.

Division of impact: I = f(1/SIN).

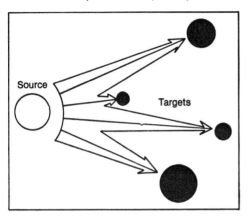

and the object of their attention, he or she is in a multiplicative force field and should feel greater tension the larger the audience. Members of the audience, on the other hand, stand, or rather sit, together as the target of forces coming from the speaker. Unfortunately, the impact of the speaker's arguments is probably divided, and the larger the audience, the less each member will be persuaded.

Consistent with my earlier arguments about marginal impact, I suggest that the psychosocial law still applies in divisive force fields and that the effect of a social force from outside the group is divided not by the actual number of people present, but by some root of that number, with $I = s/N^t$. This is mathematically equivalent to $I = sN^{-t}$, making the formula the same as in the case of multiplicative social structures but with the sign of the exponent changed. Thus, according to social impact theory, the exponent of t in divisive social structures should be negative with an absolute value of less than one.

Application 4: Social Inhibition of Emergency Response

The present theory grew out of a program of research with John Darley on bystander intervention in emergencies (Latané & Darley, 1970). One might recall that one of several processes we postulated to explain our finding that people are less likely to intervene if they believe other people are also available to respond was diffusion of responsibility—if others are present, the responsibility for intervention is psychologically diffused or divided among them, leaving each person less motivated to act. I suggest now that this process is more general and can lead to the diffusion or division of other social forces.

The discovery of the social inhibition of bystander intervention has been widely replicated: Latané and Nida (1981) cite 56 published and unpublished comparisons of helping by people who were alone with helping by those who were tested in the presence of confederates or believed other people to be present. In 48 of these 56 comparisons, involving a total of more than 2,000 people, there was less helping in the group condition. Overall, three quarters of individuals tested alone helped; only half of those tested with others did so. Further, in 31 of an additional 37 comparisons between persons tested alone and actual groups of 2-8 people, the effective individual probability of helping was less than the alone response rate, while in 4 others, the comparison was indeterminate. About half of the 2,028 individuals tested alone in these studies helped, whereas the effective individual response rate for the more than 1,600 people tested in groups was only 22%. Clearly, social inhibition occurs in both laboratory and field settings employing a wide variety of emergencies designed by a multitude of independent investigators.

According to the psychosocial law, the biggest increment in social inhibition should occur with the addition of the first other bystander; subsequent ones should have decreasing marginal impact. In fact, the results of the original Darley and Latané (1968) experiment bear out this expectation. In that experiment, speed of helping decreased in proportion to the cube root of the number of bystanders believed to be present.

Application 5: A Knock on the Door, a Power Failure, and a Request for Help

In order to test the effect of group size over several levels, Freeman (1974) asked 294 introductory psychology students at Ohio State to participate in an experiment "to help us pretest some materials for an experiment." Arriving in the laboratory alone, in pairs, in groups of four, or in groups of eight, participants sat in a room and watched slides.

Six minutes after the experimenter left the room, there was a series of knocks on the door. If there was no response within 10 seconds, the knocks were repeated. Participants had to decide whether to answer the door. Approximately five minutes later, all electricity was cut off from the experimental room and hallway, preventing all of them from continuing their task and leaving them in a pitch black room. Participants could then choose whether or not to leave the room. Finally, the experimenters started to move some boxes, and participants had to decide whether or not to help.

According to the results, if one needs help with some boxes or would like to have a power failure reported, one is no more likely to be obliged if eight people are available to respond than if only one or two are,

and when it comes to simply knocking on the door, one actually has only half the chance of getting a response. This comparison, however informative it may be as to one's chances of eliciting a response, does not provide a true picture of the effects of the presence of other people on an individual's response rate, since there were differing numbers of people available to respond. It is meaningless to compare directly individual with group responses, since with differing numbers of people available to respond there is a purely mechanical potential for getting more help with more people. However, one can use the obtained group response rate to calculate the effective individual probability of response under the null hypothesis that being in a group has no effects. The formula can easily be derived from a simple binomial, independent-trials model: $P_I = 1 - (1 - P_G)^n$, where P_I is the estimated effective individual probability of response, P_G is the obtained proportion of groups responding, and n is the size of the group. This formula makes it possible to compare effective individual rates across conditions involving groups of different sizes.

Figure 6a displays the results of Freeman's (1974) study. With the exception of a single inversion, the effective individual probability of response declines consistently, substantially, and significantly as group size increases. Analysis of speed scores based on the response latencies shows that the addition of the second person in these groups had an effect 8 times greater than that produced by the addition of the third or fourth person and 23 times greater than that produced by the addition of the fifth, sixth, seventh, or eighth person, supporting the prediction of decreasing marginal effect. Finally, there were no effects related to sex or to interactions of sex with group size. Social inhibition effects were

FIGURE 6.

Division of impact: a. Effective individual probability of response as a function of number in room, based on data from Freeman (1974); b. Picking up objects as a function of the sex and number of elevator passengers, based on data from Latané and Dabbs (1975); c. Size of tip as a function of number of people eating together, based on data from Freeman, Walker, Borden, and Latané (1975); d. Inquiring for Christ as a function of size of rally, based on data from Wilson (1970).

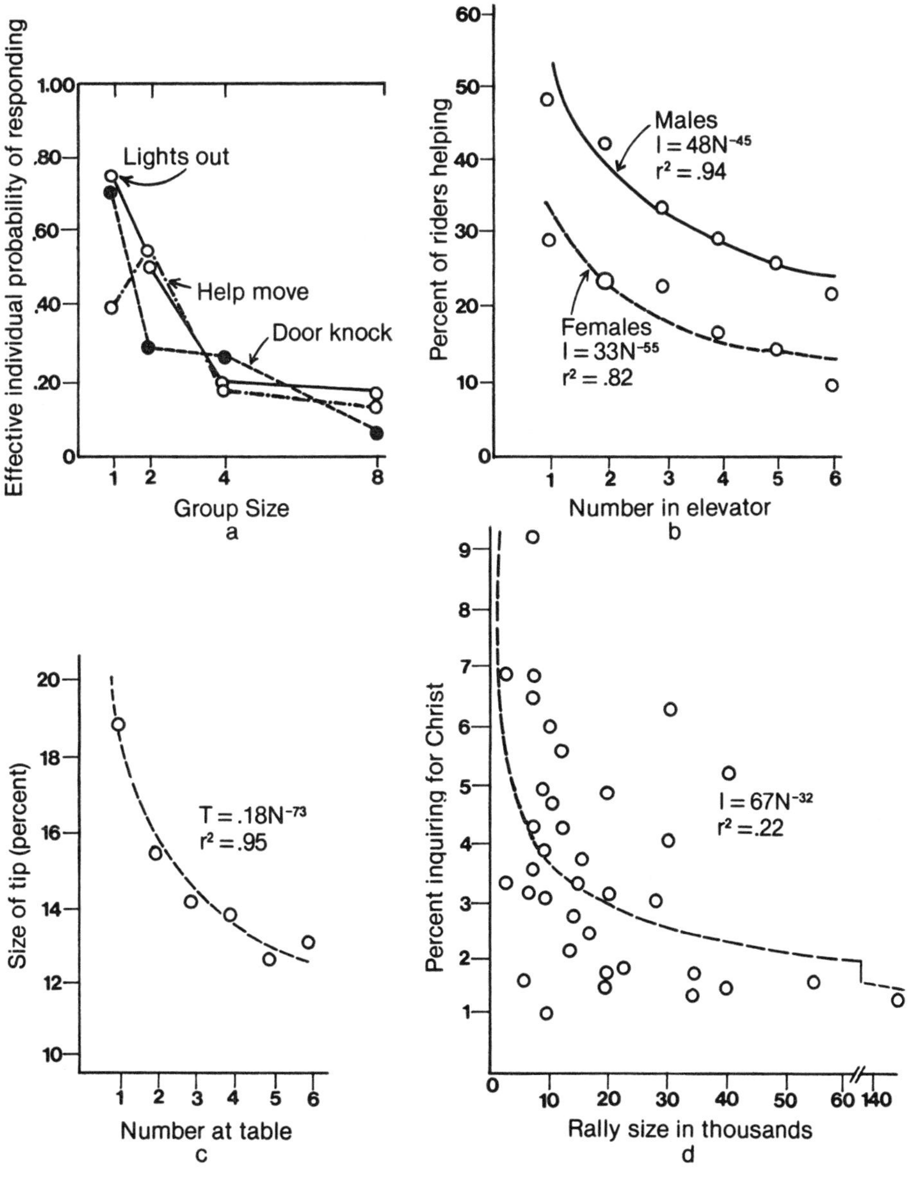

equally as pronounced for male as for female subjects.

Latané and Darley (1968, 1970, 1975) suggest several theoretical processes which, separately or in combination, may account for social inhibition effects. These include diffusion of responsibility from the knowledge that other people are also available to respond, embarrassment from knowing that other people may watch one make a fool of oneself, and social influence from seeing that other people are not responding. The present results can be interpreted in terms of diffusion of responsibility, with one to eight individuals standing as the target of needs for action caused by the door knock, power failure, or request for help. Although social inhibition may have also derived partially from processes related to social influence or embarrassment, in the power failure situation at least, the effect of these processes should have been reduced by the fact that individuals could not see or be seen by each other in the darkness.

Application 6: Chivalry in Elevators

In this and the next two sections I briefly describe three field studies which are consistent with the proposition that in social structures in which many people stand together as the target of forces from a single source, impact will be an inverse power function of the number of people with an exponent of less than one.

Figure 6b shows data reported by Latané and Dabbs (1975) and includes the responses of almost 5,000 elevator passengers in Atlanta, Columbus, and Seattle who were exposed to one of about 1,500 occasions on which a fellow passenger "accidentally" dropped a handful of pencils or

coins. In addition to our primary interest in regional differences in sex role differentiation, we found highly significant group size effects: As the number of people available to respond increased from one to six, the individual probability of response decreased from 40% to 15%. This systematic decrease can best be described as an inverse power function with an exponent of about .5. Although there were big differences between the sexes in the overall likelihood of helping, the effect of other people was similar for both sexes—helping to pick up objects decreased in proportion to the square root of the number of people available to pick up objects. The impact of the need for help shown by the clumsy coin dropper was seemingly divided among those who were the target of this need.

I might put in a parenthetical plug for the utility of elevators as portable psychological laboratories (see also Petty, Williams, Harkins, & Latané, 1977). Never cluttered up with surplus equipment or old data sheets, always available for scheduling, they generate a steady stream of subjects who come inside of their own volition and, once there, act with no more than their normal paranoia. Far more representative of the general population than the typical college sophomore, elevator passengers are far less suspicious or anxious to do the right thing for science. And unlike other public places, elevators are self-contained with clearly defined boundaries, so one knows exactly who is present and who is not.

Application 7: Tipping in Restaurants

The custom of tipping—leaving some money for the waiter after one has finished a meal—is interesting for several reasons. Unlike most other economic transactions, it is at least partly voluntary. Although most waiters have the reasonable expectation that one will leave a tip, whether one does and how much one leaves are personal choices. Unlike one's obligation to the restaurant owner for the price of the meal, one cannot go to jail or be forced to wash dishes if one chooses not to tip.

Reasoning that a primary motive for leaving a tip is a feeling of responsibility or obligation to the waiter, and that this feeling of obligation should be diffused or divided to the extent that several people eat together on the same bill, Freeman, Walker, Borden, and Latané (1975) enlisted the cooperation of 11 waiters, unfamiliar with the theory, who unobtrusively recorded size of party, amount of bill, and size of tip for 408 groups of 1,159 evening diners at the Steak and Ale Restaurant in Columbus, Ohio. Twelve parties had more than 6 members and were excluded from analysis, since they required special services; the remaining 396 parties consisted of an average of 2.67 people, who were billed an average of $6.95 per person and tipped an average of $1.00 per person.

Although the best linear prediction of tip from bill was 15.02% minus .09 cents, indicating rather close adherence to a 15% norm, group size also made a major contribution to tipping. As seen in Figure 6c, individuals dining alone tipped almost 19%, while groups of five to six people tipped less than 13%. This systematic decrease can best be described by an inverse power function with an exponent of about .2: Tipping seems to decrease in proportion to the fifth root of the number of people eating together. The impact of the responsibility for giving money to the waiter was seemingly divided among those who were the target of this responsibility.

This result has considerable practical significance. Americans spend about $30 billion a year in eating out and probably leave about $2 or $3 billion a year in tips, accounting for two thirds of the total income of the more than one million waiters in the United States. This result suggests, although it does not prove, that waiters might be far better off if they were a little more willing to write separate checks for large parties—this might short-circuit diffusion of responsibility and result in larger tips.

Application 8: Inquiring for Christ

Among the many evangelical crusades and rallies conducted by Billy Graham between 1947 and 1970 were 37 one-day events, varying in size from 2,000 to 143,000 persons, for which it is possible to determine how many people were present at one time and how many were moved to "inquire for Christ" (Wilson, 1970). These records are important to the Graham organization, for the inquiries lead to lists of names and addresses that form the basis for continued proselytizing at the local level. Figure 6d plots the percentage inquiring as a function of the size of the crowd and represents the behavior of 760,000 people.

Clearly, with increasing crowd size, the impact of Billy Graham grew less; fewer people were induced to inquire among those who shared Graham's persuasive powers with more than 12,000 others (2.6%) than among those who were in the presence of fewer others (4.5%, $p < .001$). This decrease can best be described as an inverse power function with an exponent of about .3: Persuasive impact seems to decrease in proportion to the cube root of audience size. It is interesting that the value of s in the power function plotted in Figure 6d is .67. This means that if we were to extrapolate to a situation in which Graham were to speak to an audience of one person, we should expect there to be about two chances in three of his eliciting an inquiry. Graham's impact was seemingly divided among those who were the target of the social forces he was able to generate.

Each of these three behaviors—chivalry in elevators, tipping in restaurants, and inquiring for Christ—is certainly affected by a host of other variables in addition to the number of people present, and there are certainly any number of more or less plausible alternative explanations as to each of the obtained inverse relationships between group size and impact. No one of the three studies, by itself, provides a very firm leg for a theory of social impact to stand on, and even when bound together, the tripod may still seem rather shaky. Nevertheless, in each of three widely different social settings involving significant real-world effects, social impact has operated in a fashion consistent with a simple theory, which has even succeeded in predicting the precise form of the relationships.

Application 9: Many Hands Make Light the Work

An unpublished experiment that has not perished is the classic study by Ringelman, reported only in summary form by Moede (1927) in German but cited and analyzed by many later scientists. In that experiment, the collective group performance of coworkers pulling on a rope was less than the sum of their individual performances, with dyads pulling at 93% of their individual capability, trios at 85%, and groups of eight at only 49%. As the old saw has it, "Many hands make light the work."

In a recently published replication (Latané, Williams, & Harkins, 1979), groups of six undergraduate males gathered in Ohio Stadium and were asked to make as much noise as possible by shouting or clapping hands alone, in pairs, or in groups of six. As in pulling ropes, it appears that when it comes to clapping or even shouting out loud, many hands do in fact make light the work: Even though total output increased with group size, the output of each member decreased, with six-person groups performing at only 36 % of capacity (see Figure 7, "actual groups"). Part of this deficit can be attributed to the fact that sound waves tend to cancel each other out, reflecting one form of faulty coordination of social effort (Steiner, 1972). Another part, however, may be due to the fact that participants did

FIGURE 7.

Sound pressure per person as a function of group or pseudogroup size, based on data from Latané, Williams, and Harkins (1979).

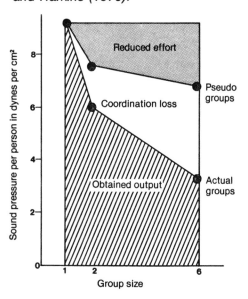

not shout as loud or clap as hard in groups as they did when alone (a process I call "social loafing").

Individuals in another set of conditions shouted in "pseudogroups" in which they believed that others were yelling with them, although they actually yelled alone. This change eliminates coordination loss as a factor, allowing social loafing to be measured directly. Consistent with the view that pressures to work hard in groups are diffused, individual effort decreased as pseudogroup size increased, and the addition of the second through fifth other pseudoshouters had much less negative effect than the addition of the first (see Figure 7, "pseudogroups"). The data are well fit by an inverse power function with an exponent of less than one: Effort seems to decrease in proportion to the sixth root of the number of people working together. Similar effects have been obtained in the case of cognitive effort (Petty, Harkins, Williams, & Latané, 1977).

Application 10: Crowding in Rats

Recently many commentators have focused on urbanization and its concomitant, crowding, as a root cause of social disorder. A number of studies, employing both human and animal participants, have investigated the physiological and psychological effects of population size or density. Amazingly few of these studies have tested the relationship parametrically over more than a very restricted range. Results of the few that have done so seem generally consistent with a power law.

A number of studies, for example, have housed rats or mice together in groups of varying size for varying periods of time to study the consequences (often discourag-

ing) of such crowding. In some of my own research on social attraction in rats, which basically deals with dynamic issues of social interaction rather than with the more static conception of social reaction treated here, we have varied the number of animals living together. Thus, Latané, Cappell, and Joy (1970) housed rats 1, 2, 3, 4, or 6 to a cage and then tested them in pairs for social attraction in an open field. As Figure 8a shows, isolated rats were the most gregarious, with each additional housing partner leading to decreased sociability. It should be no surprise, however, that the marginal impact of the first rat was much larger than that of the sixth. The effects of crowding seem to be in inverse proportion to the cube root of the number of rats living together. Hall and Latané (Note 2), sampling fewer data points but over a wider range, found similar results.

In addition to affecting sociability, the presence of other animals also affects physiological development. In a classic study, Christian (1955) compared the weights of reproductive organs of male mice housed in groups of various sizes (1, 4, 6, 8, 16, and 32) for one week before sacrifice. Significant overall differences were found on three dimensions: weight of preputial glands, weight of seminal vesicles, and, less strongly, overall body weight. Each of these relationships is more or less adequately described by a power function. Although it is unclear why the presence of other males should reduce the size of preputial glands or seminal vesicles, it is clear that the largest reduction came with the first few additional males, while the last 16 or 20 had relatively little impact.

Perhaps as a result of the effects cited above, group size also affects the rate of reproduction in closed rodent populations (Calhoun, 1967). As Figure 8b shows, the

FIGURE 8.

Social behavior in rats as a function of number housed together: a. Data on affiliation from Latané, Cappell, and Joy (1970) and Hall and Latané (Note 2); b. Data on reproduction from Calhoun (1967).

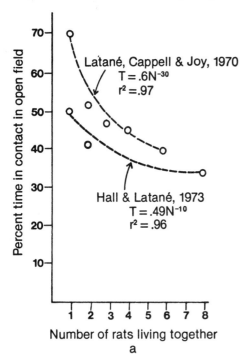
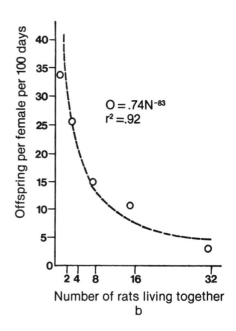

number of offspring per female per 100 days decreases as an inverse power function of the number of rats living together, with an exponent of less than one. Presumably, this would have the consequence of limiting the negative effects of overexposure to social impact for future generations.

The results of these studies, taken together, suggest that a power law has generality beyond human subjects and also beyond immediate impact effects. They also have implications for current discussions of crowding and its discontents. It seems that the effects of the presence of other organisms, whether beneficial or deleterious, are in the same direction whether there are few or many present (i.e., the relationships are monotonic). And the impact of additional organisms is largest not when there are already many present (as one might expect from some conceptions of crowding), but when the individual is isolated. As a matter of fact, after the first few others are present, additional crowding seems to have relatively little effect.

CONCLUSION

In the preceding sections of this article, I have discussed three principles of social impact and have presented data consistent with the principles from ten areas of empirical research. In conclusion, I briefly list six unresolved questions relating to the theory and two problems with it in its present form. Finally, I mention four characteristics of the theory that commend it, I believe, to our further attention.

Six Unresolved Questions

1. Can we achieve better measurement of social outcomes? This kind of theory, with its greater precision and specificity, requires ratio scaling. If it is to be useful in other domains of social psychology, we will have to improve our standards of measurement.

2. If indeed the psychosocial law involves a power function, what is the meaning of the exponent? Stevens (1975) believes there to be a characteristic psychophysical exponent for each sensory modality. Is there one for social impact?

3. How does one deal with individual differences in susceptibility to social impact? Perhaps individuals can be seen as differing in their mass, inertia, or resistance to change.

4. How do the acute effects of short-term exposure to impact transmute over time into chronic effects?

5. What happens when two or more groups act as simultaneous sources of impact, groups serve both as source and target of impact, social groups are heterogeneous with respect to the strength or immediacy of their members, and/or different psychological processes are triggered off at the same time? The general answer to these questions would seem to relate to how one combines and decomposes power functions.

6. Is the model descriptive or explanatory, a generalization or a theory?

Two Problems with the Theory

1. The model views people as passive recipients of social impact and not as active seekers. A more perfected theory would incorporate mechanisms for people to control and direct their exposure to social impact.

2. The model is static and at present does not have a needed dynamic aspect. A more perfected theory would specify the means whereby the consequences of social impact cumulate as the people in a social setting react to and interact with each other.

Four Characteristics of the Theory

1. It is a *general* theory, drawing on basic laws, predicting to many domains, and encompassing a variety of processes.

2. But it is also *specific* in the sense that it is quantifiable, deals with parametric variations, and makes precise predictions about observable aspects of the real world.

3. Thus, it is *falsifiable*—if relationships turn out to be nonmonotonic, or if exponents are greater than one or have the wrong sign, the theory will be disconfirmed.

4. The theory is *useful*. It not only can provide a baseline for assessing interesting exceptions to these general laws, but it can provide a foundation for the development of many areas of social engineering (Latané & Nida, 1980). Every day people need to decide on which people to appoint to a committee, on whether to make a telephone call or write a letter, on how many students should be in a classroom, or on any of a number of other choices concerning the strength, immediacy, and number of people to involve in a social setting. We live in a period of great societal growth—populations are getting larger and people are becoming more interdependent. It is becoming more and more important to understand

both the positive and the negative ways in which people have impact on each other and to design our physical and social environments so as to maximize the quality of life for all. I would like to think this theory will help.

REFERENCE NOTES

1. Bassett, R. L., & Latané, B. *Social influences and news stories.* Paper presented at the meeting of the American Psychological Association, Washington, D.C., September 1976.
2. Hall, D., & Latané, B. *Effects of social deprivation and satiation on social attraction and social attractiveness in rats.* Paper presented at the meeting of the Midwestern Psychological Association, Chicago, May 1973.

REFERENCES

Asch, S. E. Effects of group pressure upon the modification and distortion of judgments. In H. Guetzkow (Ed.), *Groups, leadership, and men.* Pittsburgh, Pa.: Carnegie Press, 1951.

Asch, S. E. *Social psychology.* Englewood Cliffs, N.J.: Prentice-Hall, 1952.

Asch, S. E. Studies of independence and conformity: I. A minority of one against a unanimous majority. *Psychological Monographs,* 1956, *70* (9, Whole No. 416).

Calhoun, J. B. Ecological factors in the development of behavioral anomalies. In E. Zubin (Ed.), *Comparative psychopathology.* New York: Grune & Stratton, 1967.

Christian, J. J. Effect of population size on the weights of the reproductive organs of white mice. *American Journal of Physiology,* 1955, *181,* 477-480.

Darley, J. M., & Latané, B. Bystander intervention in emergencies: Diffusion of responsibility. *Journal of Personality and Social Psychology,* 1968, *8,* 377-383.

Freeman, S. *Group inhibition of helping in nonemergency situations.* Unpublished master's thesis, Ohio State University, 1974.

Freeman, S., Walker, M. R., Borden, R., & Latané, B. Diffusion of responsibility and restaurant tipping: Cheaper by the bunch. *Personality and Social Psychology Bulletin,* 1975, *1,* 584-587.

Gerard, H. B., Wilhelmy, R. A., & Conolley, E. S. Conformity and group size. *Journal of Personality and Social Psychology,* 1968, *8,* 79-82.

Latané, B. Cappell, H., & Joy, V. Social deprivation, housing density, and gregariousness in rats. *Journal of Comparative and Physiological Psychology,* 1970, *70,* 221-227.

Latané, B., & Dabbs, J. Sex, group size and helping in three cities. *Sociometry,* 1975, *38,* 180-194.

Latané, B., & Darley, J. M. Group inhibition of bystander intervention in emergencies. *Journal of Personality and Social Psychology,* 1968, *10,* 215-221.

Latané, B., & Darley, J. M. *The unresponsive bystander: Why doesn't he help?* New York: Appleton-Century-Crofts, 1970.

Latané, B., & Darley, J. M. *Help in a crisis: Bystander response to an emergency.* Morristown, N.J.: General Learning Press, 1975.

Latané, B. & Harkins, S. Cross-modality matches suggest anticipated stage fright as a multiplicative power function of audience size and status. *Perception & Psychophysics,* 1976, *20,* 482-488.

Latané, B. & Nida, S. Social impact theory and group influence: A social engineering perspective. In P. B. Paulus (Ed.), *Psychology of group influence.* Hillsdale, N.J.: Erlbaum, 1980.

Latané, B. & Nida, S. Ten years of research on group size and helping. *Psychological Bulletin,* 1981, *89,* 307-324.

Latané, B., Williams, K., & Harkins, S. Many hands make light the work: The causes and consequences of social loafing. *Journal of Personality and Social Psychology,* 1979, *37,* 822-832.

Milgram, S., Bickman, L., & Berkowitz, L. Note on the drawing power of crowds of different size. *Journal of Personality and Social Psychology,* 1969, *13,* 79-82.

Moede, W. Die Richtlinien der Leistungs-Psychologie. *Industrielle Psychotechnik,* 1927, *4,* 193-207.

Petty, R. E., Harkins, S. G., Williams, K. D., & Latané, B. The effects of group size on cognitive effort and evaluation. *Personality and Social Psychology Bulletin*, 1977, *3*, 575-578.

Petty, R. E., Williams, K. D., Harkins, S. G., & Latané, B. Social inhibition of helping yourself: Bystander response to a cheeseburger. *Personality and Social Psychology Bulletin*, 1977, *3*, 579-582.

Porter, H. Studies in the psychology of stuttering: XIV. Stuttering phenomena in relation to size and personnel of audience. *Journal of Speech Disorders*, 1939, *4*, 323-333.

Steiner, I. D. *Group process and productivity.* New York: Academic Press, 1972.

Stevens, S. S. On the psychophysical law. *Psychological Review*, 1957, *64*, 153-181.

Stevens, S. S. *Psychophysics.* New York: Wiley, 1975.

Wilson, G. *Twenty years under God.* Minneapolis, Minn.: World Wide, 1970.

Dispensability of Member Effort and Group Motivation Losses: Free-Rider Effects

Norbert L. Kerr and Steven E. Bruun

Three experiments are reported that tested the hypothesis that group members exert less effort as the perceived dispensability of their efforts for group success increases. The resultant motivation losses were termed *free-rider effects*. In Experiment 1, subjects of high or low ability performed in two-, four-, or eight-person groups at tasks with additive, conjunctive, or disjunctive task demands. As predicted, member ability had opposite effects on effort under disjunctive and conjunctive task demands. The failure to obtain a relationship between group size and member effort in Experiment 1 was attributed to a procedural artifact eliminated in Experiment 2. As predicted, as groups performing conjunctive and disjunctive tasks increased in size, member motivation declined. This was not a social loafing effect; group members were fully identifiable at every group size. Experiment 3 explored the role performance feedback plays in informing group members of the dispensability of their efforts and encouraging free riding. Several issues for future research are discussed.

Reviews of small-group performance research (e.g., Davis, 1969; Steiner, 1972) indicate that task-performing groups rarely

The authors would like to thank Bill Persky, Phil Mercurio, and Megan Sullaway for their assistance. Support for this project was provided by National Science Foundation Grant BNS7927205 to the first author. Portions of this article were presented at the annual convention of the American Psychological Association, Montreal, Quebec, Canada, September 1980.

"Dispensability of Member Effort and Group Motivation Losses: Free-rider Effects" by N.L. Kerr & S.E. Brunn, 1983, *Journal of Personality and Social Psychology*, 44, pp. 78-94. Copyright 1983 by the American Psychological Assn. Reprinted by permission of the publisher and authors.

achieve their productive potential. Steiner (1972) termed the difference between a group's potential productivity and its actual productivity *process loss* and suggested two sources of such process loss. *Coordination losses* represent a group's failure to optimally coordinate or combine the contributions of a group's individual members. *Motivation losses* occur when members do not exert maximal effort in the group setting. The present article is concerned with the latter type of process loss. In particular, we empirically test the proposition that group members reduce their efforts at a group task as the dispensability of their efforts for group success increases.

Recently there has been a good deal of research on group motivation losses (e.g., Kerr & Bruun, 1981; Latané, Williams, & Harkins, 1979a; Williams, Harkins, & Latané, 1981). For example, several studies showed that member motivation drops with group size for certain tasks (Ingham, Levinger, Graves, & Peckham, 1974; Latané et al., 1979a), a phenomenon Latané et al. termed the *social loafing effect*. Recent work (Kerr & Bruun, 1981; Williams et al., 1981) showed that this effect is due to the fact that, for certain tasks, as the group gets larger it becomes more difficult to identify each member's contribution. Apparently, social loafing effects occur because group members' expectation of praise for working hard (and/or blame for hardly working) decreases with group size. Generalizing from this social loafing research, some researchers suggested (e.g., Latané et al., 1979a, 1979b) that suboptimal motivation may generally characterize large performance groups (except, perhaps, under certain limiting conditions such as when the group is highly cohesive). However, it seems unlikely that the motivational levels of group members are determined by a small set of factors or processes. Even a single variable may affect a group member's motivation in several ways. For example, variations in group size may not only affect member identifiability but may also affect a member's share of the payoff, proportional contribution to the group product, or uniqueness, all of which may have motivational significance. In sum, it seems likely that there are several distinct processes underlying group members' choices of how much effort should be expended on the group's task.

One such process is suggested by a common characteristic of collective performance settings. In many groups, the efforts of some member(s) may compensate for a lack of effort of some other member(s) or may even render their work superfluous. For example, consider a group working at an anagram task. All that is required for group success on this "eureka" task is for just one member to come up with the solution. The efforts of every nonsolving member will turn out to be superfluous. If group members anticipate or become aware of this, they may choose to just "let George do it." For many groups and tasks, the expectation that one can obtain the positively valued results of successful task performance may be nearly as high when one exerts little or no effort as when one exerts maximum effort because success can be achieved through others' efforts; the more dispensable one's efforts are for group success, the less well motivated one should be. Such effects will be referred to here as free-rider effects (see Olson, 1965). Olson advanced an economic analysis of the basis for apathy in seeking "public goods," outcomes shared by everyone in the group or organization (e.g., police and fire protection, air pollution abatement). In large groups (e.g., states, large organizations), Olson suggested that apathy may stem, in part, from the generally held assumption that someone else in the group can and will provide the needed public good.[1]

Olson (1965) suggested at least two distinct mechanisms that encourage inaction as group size increases: Members' behavior is usually less noticeable in larger groups, and members' perception of the perceived effectiveness of their efforts usually declines with group size.[2] The research on the social loafing effect (e.g., Ingham et al., 1974; Latané et al., 1979a) empirically demonstrated the former mechanism in small task-performing groups. The experiments reported here attempt to demonstrate the latter mechanism. It is important to note that the group size—free-rider effects hypothesized here are not merely replications of the already well-replicated social loafing effect. Social loafing has been obtained only for those tasks for which the individual members' contributions cannot be identified; when such a task is modified to permit such identification, the effect is eliminated (Kerr & Bruun, 1981; Williams et al., 1981). However, as described below, it is possible to create task situations in which group members are fully identifiable at every group size, yet the dispensability of their effort increases with group size.

The dispensability of members' efforts (and hence, the likelihood of free-rider motivation losses) depends strongly on task features. Steiner's (1972) task taxonomy lends itself particularly well to the analysis of such effects. Steiner focuses on *task demands,* which include the index of performance, the rules or "permitted processes" under which the task must be performed, and the task's "prescribed processes" that define the optimal way of combining member contributions. Steiner defines several task types with different permitted-prescribed processes. *Disjunctive* tasks permit the group to accept the contribution of only one member and prescribe that the group choose the most able member. Giving a group an anagram to solve is an example of a disjunctive task. *Conjunctive* tasks require that the group product be the contribution of the least able member (e.g., a group climbing a mountain linked together by ropes can go no faster than the slowest member). For *additive* tasks, the potential group product is the simple sum (or average) of the potential individual contributions. Most of the tasks used in the social loafing experiments

have been additive tasks, for example, a group tug of war.

In the present experiments, we explore the effects of group size and member ability on free-rider behavior. The effects of these variables on the dispensibility of member effort should depend strongly on task demands. All other things being equal, the larger the group, the more likely it is that there is someone more (and less) able than any particular member. Hence, for disjunctive and conjunctive tasks, member motivation should drop as group size increases. Note that these effects are predicted even if member contributions can be identified; again, the free-rider mechanism should be clearly distinguished from the mechanism shown to underlie the social loafing effect (e.g., Kerr & Bruun, 1981). It is less clear how group size should affect perceived member dispensability of effort for additive tasks. On the one hand, every member's performance affects the group product. For intergroup competitions, the effort ŏf every member might be indispensable (e.g., in a two-team tug of war, either team that loses a member would be at a serious disadvantage, regardless of the initial size of the two teams). On the other hand, the proportional impact of one's contribution declines with group size. Besides its effect on perceived dispensability, Shaw (1960) suggested that such a decline in the relative size of one's contribution should directly reduce one's willingness to work for the group.

The effect of member ability on perceived dispensability should have opposite effects for conjunctive and disjunctive tasks. On a disjunctive task, in which only the best member's performance matters, we predict that the less able members become free riders because their efforts are dispensable. However, on a conjunctive task, in which only the least able member's performance matters, we predict that high-ability members reduce their efforts, because any level of performance above that which the least able member is capable of is dispensable. Again, the effects of member ability for additive tasks are less clear. All member contributions have some impact on the group product, but the relative impact will vary with member ability.

Three experiments are reported that test the predictions derived from the free-rider analysis. Experiment 3 also examines the effects of performance feedback on strengthening group members' perceptions of the dispensability of their efforts.

EXPERIMENT 1

In this study, group size, member ability, and task demands were varied. The following predictions were made:

1. Member ability will have opposite effects on member task motivation for disjunctive and conjunctive tasks. Ability and effort will be positively related for disjunctive tasks but negatively related for conjunctive tasks.

2. Member effort will decline with group size for both conjunctive and disjunctive tasks.

3. Paralleling these effects on member effort will be effects on the perceived dispensability of effort for group success.

In light of ambiguity surrounding the effects of group size and member ability for additive tasks, no predictions were made for additive tasks.

METHOD

Design and Subjects

The experiment used a 3 (group size: two-, four-, and eight-person groups) × 2

(member ability: high, low) × 3 (task demands: additive, conjunctive, and disjunctive) × 2 (subject sex) factorial design. All factors were between subjects.

The analyses are based on data from 189 (87 male, 102 female) undergraduate students whose participation partially fulfilled a course requirement.[3]

Experimental Task

There were several requirements for the experimental task. First, the task had to allow direct assessment of each member's efforts by the experimenter. Generally, if one only assesses the group product, it may be impossible to attribute process losses to motivation losses rather than to coordination losses. Second, to take task performance as an index of task motivation, the task had to be one for which effort and performance were monotonically related. Third, to minimize variance due to noneffort factors, task performance should not be highly sensitive to such factors as insight or luck. And because one would not expect any group member to perform suboptimally unless there was a definite cost for optimal performance (e.g., fatigue), task performance had to be costly. Simple motor-production tasks best meet all of these requirements. In the present study (and in Experiment 3), we manipulated subjects' perceived task ability through false feedback. This meant that the motor task we chose also had to be fairly novel so that the performance feedback would not contradict subjects' firmly held prior beliefs about their task ability.

The task required subjects to blow as much air as they could through a mouthpiece during a 30-sec trial. The air blown was collected and measured in one of two Becker-Delft Godart Pulmotest spirometers. In the latex hose between the mouthpiece and spirometer was a cylindrical plastic plug with a small hole drilled through its axis. This plug created resistance to the subjects' blowing, making the task difficult. The primary costs of high effort were the same as the costs of blowing up balloons—fatigue and soreness in the jaws. Pretesting (on ourselves) and consultation with specialists in pulmonary medicine indicated that the task also entailed some risk of hyperventilation. Subjects were warned of this possibility and were told that the stated goal of doing their best at the task meant "the best you can do consistent with your own health and well-being." This instruction served not only to avoid undue risk to the subject; it also gave subjects leave to choose a reasonable level of effort.

Procedure

The procedures followed in all three studies were fairly similar. Common features are described in detail for Experiment 1 only.

Session one. At the conclusion of an unrelated experiment, subjects were individually pretested at the task for one trial. They were given no performance feedback. Subjects also completed a short questionnaire that allowed us to identify and screen out subjects who might have a preconception of their ability at such a blowing task (e.g., musicians who play a wind instrument) or subjects for whom the task might pose special risks (e.g., anyone with a respiratory ailment).

Session two. Eligible subjects were scheduled in same-sex groups of four. To keep subjects unaware of how many subjects were being run at any particular session, subjects reported individually to separate lab rooms.

Instructions were delivered over an intercom system. The study was allegedly concerned with the relative performance of groups whose members perform together or in isolation. All subjects were told that they were to be in the Isolated condition. The members of Isolated groups were to perform the task separately in different rooms. This isolation procedure avoided modeling, distraction, and mere presence effects on performance.

Subjects then performed a single trial. The alleged purpose of this trial was to verify the accuracy of all subjects' pretest trial scores, said to be important because the pretest trials had been used to compose groups such that all groups were equated for average ability. Prior to the trial, subjects were told that because task ability depended primarily on stable physical factors (e.g., lung capacity), scores tended to be stable, although scores could be affected by an individual's level of effort. The present trial was to be a safeguard against the possibility that any subjects had not tried as hard as they could during the pretest trial.

At the conclusion of the trial, subjects were directed to examine a sheet in a folder in their rooms while the experimenter scored the just-completed trial. This computer-generated sheet contained the purported pretest scores of all the members of the subject's group, including his or her own. The group-size and member-ability manipulations were achieved through these sheets. Subjects saw the names and scores of two, four, or eight people of the same sex. A unique set of feedback scores were defined for each subject using a normal distribution ($\mu = 651$ cl, $\sigma = 100$ cl). All groups had one member with high ability (feedback score randomly sampled between the 73rd and 77th percentile) and one member with low ability (score between the 23rd and 27th percentile). Each subject was randomly assigned one of these two scores as his or her own. In the four- and eight-person groups, there were also several members of moderate ability. In both groups, there was one member with fairly high ability (sampled in the 61st-72nd percentile range) and one member with fairly low ability (between the 28th and 39th percentiles). In addition, in the eight-person groups, there were two above-average (between the 50th and 61st percentiles) and two below-average (between the 39th and 50th percentiles) performers. The sheets also provided subjects with descriptive statistics that purportedly described the entire sample in the study. These were the overall mean (between the 49.4th and 50.6th percentiles), highest score (at the 89th percentile), and lowest score (at the 9th percentile) in the sample. The objective of this elaborate feedback procedure was to make the symmetry in the distribution of scores nonobvious. Two minutes after the subjects received their sheets, the experimenter informed them that the just-completed trial confirmed the reliability of the pretest scores. This step was designed to help establish confidence in the reliability of the feedback scores, particularly problematic for those in the low-ability condition (cf. Myers, 1980).

The task-demand manipulation was introduced at this point. To encourage good performance, a prize of $10 per member was offered to the group that performed best of all groups in the study. Depending on condition, the experimenter explained that on any given trial the group's score would be the highest score in the group (disjunctive task demands), the lowest score in the group (conjunctive task demands), or the sum of scores in the group (additive task demands).

Subjects then completed a series of six 30-sec performance trials with a 1-minute intertrial interval. Finally, they completed a brief questionnaire designed to check the ability and task-demand manipulations, to provide a direct assessment of the perceived dispensability of subject's efforts, and to check for subject suspicion or foreknowledge of the experiment. Subjects were then debriefed, thanked, and excused.

RESULTS

Manipulation Check

Subjects were asked to rate their own ability on a 7-point bipolar scale. As expected, subjects in the high-ability condition made significantly ($p < .001$) higher ability ratings than did subjects in the low-ability condition (highs = 5.79, lows = 3.48).

Performance Data

Performance scores were averaged across the six trials to yield an index of subjects' task motivation. Initial analyses consisted of a set of planned contrasts to test the predictions; when the predictions were directional, directional tests of significance were performed. To see if any unpredicted effects had occurred, the performance data were then analyzed in a 2 (sex) × 2 (ability) × 3 (task demand) × 3 (group size) least-squares analysis of variance (ANOVA).

As predicted, the ability of the group member had opposite effects on motivation for conjunctive and disjunctive tasks, $t(153) = 1.92$, $p < .03$, one-tailed. This effect is plotted in Figure 1. When only the best score counted (disjunctive task), the low-ability member was less motivated, but when the group score was defined by the worst score in the group (conjunctive task), the high-ability member worked less hard.

Contrary to expectations, none of the planned contrasts involving group size were significant. Combining the data for the conjunctive and disjunctive conditions, subjects did not work significantly harder in the dyads than in the tetrads, $t(153)$ = −1.60, *ns*, one-tailed; in fact, the trend was in the opposite direction (dyads = 95.9 cl, tetrads = 102.0 cl). Nor did subjects work less hard in the eight-person groups than in the tetrads, $t(153)$ = .73, *ns*, one-tailed (eight-person groups = 99.25). Finally, dyads did not work significantly harder than the eight-person groups, $t(153)$ = −.88, *ns*, one-tailed. The same set of contrasts was nonsignificant when applied to the disjunctive and conjunctive conditions separately. In summary, the predictions involving group size were not confirmed.

Two effects were significant in the overall ANOVA. The first was a main effect for sex, $F(1, 153) = 69.1, p < .001$. Males were more capable at the task than were females. The significant Ability × Task Demand interaction, $F(2, 153) = 3.15, p < .05$, reflected the predicted interaction effect on these variables. No specific predictions were advanced for the ability factor in the additive task-demands condition; subjects of greater ability might or might not perceive their inputs as less dispensable. The former possibility, as well as Shaw's (1960) conjecture, suggests a direct relationship between member ability and member effort at additive tasks. The simple main effect for ability was tested in the additive-task condition to test these conjectures. Member effort was not positively related to member ability in the additive condition, $F(1, 153) = .34$; the means were even in the opposite direction (highs = 102.1, lows = 105.0). Consistent with the test of planned contrasts, subjects' effort was not related to group size, neither generally— size main effect, $F(2, 153) = 1.18$—nor under specific task demands—Size × Task Demand, $F < 1$.

Perceived Dispensability of Effort

Subjects were also asked to rate "how much did the success of your group depend upon you, personally?" on a bipolar, 7-point scale. The same planned contrasts were performed on these data as on the performance data. First, ability and conjunctive/disjunctive task demands interacted as predicted, $t(152) = 7.57, p < .001$, one-tailed. This effect is plotted in Figure 2. The high-ability subjects felt more important than the low-ability subjects in the disjunctive condition; the opposite was true in the conjunctive condition. Paralleling this result, the Ability × Task Demand interaction ef-

FIGURE 1.

Task Demand × Ability interaction effect on performance: Experiment 1.

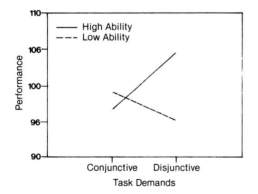

FIGURE 2.

Task Demand × Ability interaction effect on perceived dispensability: Experiment 1.

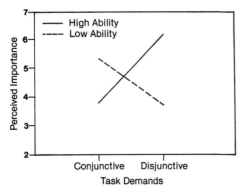

fect was significant in an overall analysis that included the additive condition, $F(2, 152) = 23.85$, $p < .001$. However, the simple ability main effect was not significant for the additive task. The group-size planned comparisons were all nonsignificant for the combined disjunctive and conjunctive conditions. The same comparisons were nonsignificant when performed on the disjunctive and conjunctive conditions separately with one exception—members of eight-person groups reported feeling less important than members of tetrads in the disjunctive condition, $t(152) = 1.98$, $p < .025$, one-tailed.

DISCUSSION

The free-rider predictions for the ability variable were confirmed. On disjunctive tasks, for which only the best score in the group counted, members with low ability felt that their efforts were more dispensable and they exerted less effort than did members with high ability. But when it was the

worst score in the group that counted, it was the high-ability member who felt more dispensable and who exerted less effort. Although these results nicely demonstrate the mediating role of the perceived dispensability of effort for reducing motivation, it might be argued that these effects on certain members' motivation would not result in any net process loss to the group; for example, what does it matter if the incapable members of the group don't exert themselves on a disjunctive task? However, this is only true if ability differences in the group are large, accurately perceived, stable, and the prime cause of performance differences. One can easily think of many exceptions to these conditions for which the free-rider effects found here might result in net group-motivation losses. For example, there seems to be a tendency to overestimate one's standing on most evaluative dimensions (Myers, 1980); our findings suggest that such exaggeration of personal ability could lead to group motivation losses for conjunctive tasks. Or, on many tasks, it is possible for capable members to occasionally perform badly (due to fatigue, inattention, misunderstanding of the task, etc.), just as it is possible for incapable members to perform well (due to luck or an extraordinary effort). Hence, sometimes the low- (high-) ability member's efforts will determine the group's performance level on a disjunctive (conjunctive) task, and any individual free riding could result in process loss to the group. Such motivation losses seem most likely for tasks that do not permit members to monitor one another's levels of productivity.

We also predicted that because the probability of a more (or less) productive member than oneself generally increases with group size, members ought to feel more dispensable and exert less effort as group size increased for both conjunctive and disjunctive tasks. These predictions were not confirmed. However, this could have been an unintended result of the ability manipulation. All the subjects were led to believe that they were far and away the most- or least-able member of their group. It was also stressed (to help establish the reliability of the pretest trial feedback) that "ability at the task depends upon physical factors which are fairly constant," although "performance does depend somewhat on how hard you try." If subjects assumed that their pretest ability rank would always be maintained during the performance trials—as these instructions imply—the size of the group would not affect the subjects' perceived dispensability. For example, it should not matter to a low-ability member how many others in the group are working at a conjunctive task if he or she is convinced that they will always perform better than he or she. If, however, group members are roughly equal in ability, or alternatively, are ignorant of one anothers' abilities, the group-size free-rider predictions should obtain. Experiment 2 was carried out to test this suggestion.

EXPERIMENT 2

In this study, subjects were given no performance feedback. With no explicit information available on one anothers' abilities, we assumed that subjects would assume a rough equivalence in ability. If members are essentially interchangeable, then the likelihood of being the best (or worst) member of the group should decline with group size. Thus, our first predictions were as follows:

1. For conjunctive and disjunctive tasks, the perceived dispensability of members' efforts should increase with group size.

2. For conjunctive and disjunctive tasks,

members' efforts should decrease with group size.

Again, for reasons given earlier, no specific group-size prediction was advanced for additive tasks.

A manipulation of task difficulty was also included. Task difficulty should directly affect members' perceived effectiveness although not necessarily their perceived dispensability of effort.[4] To consider the extremes, if a task were impossibly difficult, everyone in the group should have low-perceived effectiveness. Conversely, if the task were ridiculously easy, the group should probably succeed even if every member exerts little effort; this is clearly true for disjunctive tasks and likely for conjunctive tasks. This reasoning led to the following prediction:

3. Subjects will exert most effort when the task is moderately difficult.

METHOD

Design and Subjects

The overall design was a 2 (group size: dyads vs. tetrads) × 3 (task demand: additive, disjunctive, and conjunctive) × 2 (subject sex) × 3 (task difficulty) factorial with repeated measures on the last factor. The analyses are based on 73 subjects (37 males, 36 females) whose participation partially fulfilled a course requirement.[5]

Experimental Task and Apparatus

To avoid the risk of hyperventilation in the air-blowing task, the task was modified. Subjects were required to pump as much air as possible by squeezing a rubber sphygmograph bulb with the favored hand. Instead of using separate rooms, experimental sessions were conducted in a single large room, part of which had been partitioned into five curtained "isolation booths," each approximately 1.5 × 1.3 m. Each booth contained a desk with a pair of headphones attached to it through which the subject received instructions. Also on the desk was a single rubber bulb connected to a network of latex tubing routed to the data-collection apparatus. The plastic "resistor" plug was removed; the muscular fatigue resulting from squeezing the bulb made the task sufficiently costly. White noise was played over the headphones during each performance trial, effectively masking any sounds made by subjects performing in neighboring booths.

Procedure

The procedure was similar to that in Experiment 1. Subjects performed one trial early in the study, but its stated purpose was to familiarize subjects with the task, rather than to verify previous assessments of subjects' task ability. The same cover story was used—comparing performance of groups whose member were isolated versus being in view of one another. Again, there was to be a competition; each member of the most productive group would win a prize (their choice of $5 or 1 hour of experimental credit).

To manipulate task difficulty as a within-subjects factor, we had to change the purported task scoring. In Experiment 1, the group's average, best, or worst score on a trial was defined (by the task demands) as the group's score on that trial. In the present experiment, a performance criterion was established on each trial. If a member pumped more air than this criterion, he or she "succeeded" at that trial. In the disjunctive condition, the group succeeded on a trial if any member succeeded. In the conjunctive con-

dition, every member had to succeed for the group to succeed. In these conditions, the overall group score was the total number of trials at which the group succeeded. In the additive condition, the group score for a trial was the number of group members who succeeded, and the overall group score was the total number of successes across trials.[6] The criterion was varied from trial to trial. Subjects were told that previous research had established performance norms for the task. The moderate-difficulty performance criterion was the 50th percentile of this distribution; the high-difficulty criterion was the 80th percentile; the low-difficulty criterion was the 20th percentile.

Subjects performed nine 30-sec trials with 45-sec intertrial intervals. There were three 3-trial blocks. Within each block, a subject performed one trial at each difficulty level. The order of difficulty levels was constant across blocks within subjects. All six possible orders were used with approximately equal frequency across subjects. Subjects were given a sheet that specified their assigned difficulty level for each trial.

A brief questionnaire was administered at the end of the performance trials. The items of primary interest were subjects' understanding of the task demands, subjects' perceptions of the dispensability of their efforts, and checks on subjects' suspicion or foreknowledge of the experiment.

RESULTS

Performance Data

The amount of air pumped (in centiliters) was averaged across trial blocks within task-difficulty level. The initial analyses involved testing a set of planned comparisons derived from the theoretical predictions. These tests were followed by a 2 (sex) ×

2 (size) × 3 (task demands) × 3 (difficulty) least-squares repeated-measures ANOVA that explored for unpredicted effects.

The data of the conjunctive and disjunctive conditions were first combined to test the group-size predictions. As predicted, subjects in dyads worked significantly harder than subjects in the tetrads under these task demand conditions, $t(61)$ = 2.47, $p < .01$, one-tailed (dyad = 195.8 cl, tetrad = 182.3 cl).

It was predicted that subjects would work harder at the moderate-difficulty task than at the high- or low-difficulty tasks. Planned contrasts between the moderate-difficulty condition and the high- and low-difficulty conditions (in combination or separately) were not significant. The performance means varied little across difficulty conditions (high difficulty = 192.1 cl, moderate difficulty = 190.0 cl, low difficulty = 187.1 cl).

To determine whether there were any unpredicted effects and to examine member effort at the additive task, the overall ANOVA was performed. Two effects were significant. There was an unsurprising and uninteresting sex main effect, $F(1, 61)$ = 40.75, $p < .001$; males were generally able to pump more air than females. This analysis, which included the additive condition, also resulted in a significant overall group-size main effect, $F(1, 61) = 4.25, p < .05$. Like the subjects in the other task-demand conditions, subjects in the additive condition tended to work harder in dyads (193.2 cl) than in tetrads (187.3 cl), but this effect was much weaker; the simple group-size main effect in the additive condition was not significant, $F < 1$.

Perceived Dispensability

Subjects were asked to rate how important their contributions had been for the group's success on the high-, moderate-, and low-difficulty trials. In light of the irrelevance of the difficulty factor for effort, there was little point in testing a prediction that subjects felt least dispensable for moderately difficult tasks (they didn't, in any case). To test the group-size prediction, the three dispensability ratings were averaged. For the conjunctive and disjunctive conditions, the prediction that subjects would feel more dispensable in the tetrads than in the dyads was not confirmed, $t(47) = -1.70$, ns, one-tailed. One explanation for this may be that subjects were confused by the requirement of retrospectively assessing how dispensable they had felt for sets of trials with different assigned task difficulty.

DISCUSSION

This experiment empirically demonstrated free-rider effects due to group size. These effects were clearly not attributable to the identifiability mechanism underlying social loafing effects. In Experiment 2, all members' contributions could be identified (the scoring procedures inherent in the task demands required it), yet member motivation still declined with group size. Hence, it was not the identifiability or noticeability mechanism that mediated the present size effects but rather the dispensability or perceived effectiveness mechanism.

Both Experiments 1 and 2 reiterate the importance of task factors for group motivation losses. Significant motivation losses occurred when only one group member's score counted as the group's score (e.g., with conjunctive or disjunctive task demands). On a larger scale, it is interesting to note that the situations in large collectives that have been used to illustrate free riding (cf. Olson, 1965) are disjunctive-like in that a valued public good can be obtained through the efforts of a (sometimes small) subset of the collective. On the other hand, if every member's contribution had an effect on the group product, free riding should be reduced. And indeed, under additive task demands, the effects of group size on effort were similar to, but weaker than, those obtained under the other task-demand conditions. What little size effect there was can be attributed to the fact that the proportional impact of one's contribution declines with group size for an additive task.

Task difficulty had no effect on motivation. The reasons for this are not clear. It is possible that it was confusing for subjects to keep track of the difficulty level because it varied from trial to trial. Or, perhaps because most subjects tend to think of themselves as generally somewhat above average (Myers, 1980), the subjects may have felt capable of succeeding at every difficulty level.[7] More study of the task-difficulty variable seems warranted. We might note, though, that task difficulty may not be a particularly interesting variable in the study of group motivation losses. One would expect this variable to exert the same (although perhaps weaker) effects on individual performers as it does on members of cooperative task groups; hence, there is less that is uniquely social about the effects of this variable than, say, group size or ability ranking within the group.

EXPERIMENT 3

Several theorists (e.g., Abramson, Garber, & Seligman, 1980; Vroom, 1964) have stressed that it is the subjective, not the objective, dispensability of effort that mediates motivational deficits. For example, although the efforts of members of large groups performing a disjunctive task are objectively more dispensable than the efforts of members of small groups, group members may not always recognize this. This suggests that the more experience group members have with a task for which their efforts are dispensable, the more likely they are to become free riders. Experiment 3 was designed to test this hypothesis and to provide conceptual replications of the previous two experiments.

The basic plan of the study was to compare the incidence of free riding in groups before and after members received direct feedback of personal and group performance. In the first part of the study, subjects received no such feedback. They performed under disjunctive, conjunctive, or additive task demands. Perceived task ability was manipulated for some subjects (as in Experiment 1). For these subjects, the free-rider logic and the findings of Experiment 1 led to the following predictions:

1. Member ability should have opposite effects on member effort for conjunctive and disjunctive tasks. Low-ability members should exhibit motivation losses for disjunctive tasks, high ability members for conjunctive tasks. In Experiment 1, we argued that when ability rankings were fixed absolutely (i.e., no member could be expected to outperform [do worse than] the most [least] able member), the size of the group should not affect perceived dispensability. In the current experiment, the way in which member ability was manipulated assured clear, but not insurmountable, differences in ability. It was unclear, therefore, whether the most and least able members in Experiment 3 would or would not be sensitive to group size (on conjunctive and disjunctive tasks). For this reason, no group-size prediction was made for these conditions during the first part of the experiment. Like the subjects in Experiment 2, the rest of the subjects in Experiment 3 had no information about the distribution

of ability in the group during the first part of the study. For these "moderate-ability" subjects, the following prediction was made:

2. Member motivation should decrease with group size under conjunctive and disjunctive task demands.

During the second part of the experiment, all subjects received personal and group performance feedback. The following predictions were made:

3. Among moderate-ability subjects, the inverse relationship between group size and member effort in the disjunctive and conjunctive conditions will be stronger with feedback (Part 2) than without feedback (Part 1).

4. Among the highest and lowest ability subjects, the crossover interaction of member ability (high vs. low) and task demands (viz., conjunctive vs. disjunctive) will be stronger with feedback (Part 2) than without feedback (Part 1).

METHOD

Overall Design

Subjects were scheduled and run in groups of three. In each session, one subject was randomly assigned the role of high-ability member, another, the role of low-ability member; and the third, the role of moderate-ability member. The procedure for the moderate-ability subjects differed from that followed for the other two subjects. The high- and low-ability subjects were given information that indicated the relative task ability of every member of the group. Hence, like the subjects in Experiment 1, they knew the overall ability ranking of the group members. On the other hand, prior to the start of the performance series, the moderate-ability subjects only

received information indicating that they were about average in ability but received no information about the abilities of their co-workers. Like the subjects of Experiment 2, they were (initially) unaware of the ability ranking of the members of their groups.

Subjects performed a hand-pumping task for eighteen 30-sec trials. These trials were grouped into three 6-trial blocks. Block 1 replicated the no-performance feedback procedure followed in Experiments 1 and 2. In Blocks 2 and 3, subjects received performance feedback. This feedback was not precisely veridical. Rather, using the mean of each subject's performance during Block 1, a constant correction factor was calculated that would maintain the subject's purported ability levels when added or subtracted from their scores in Blocks 2 and 3. Generally, this meant that one constant was added to the true scores of the high-ability subject and a second constant was subtracted from the true scores of the low-ability subject. To make the performance feedback as salient as possible, subjects were not only informed after each trial of how well each group member had performed individually and of the group score for that trial (based on the assigned task demands), they also were informed of how much money each had earned on that trial. The payoff was determined from the purported group score and a fixed rate of pay (in cents per centiliter per member). Different rates were used for each task-demand condition to equate the expected payoffs to groups across conditions.

Group size was manipulated within subjects. Within each six-trial block, each subject performed two trials as an individual (solo trials), two as a member of a group of two (dyad trials), and two as a member of a group of three (triad trials). On her two dyad trials, the subject was paired once with each of the other two subjects.

The preceding distinctions define three subdesigns in Experiment 3. Analysis of the moderate-ability subjects' performance data during Block 1 (no feedback) used a 3 (task demands: additive, conjunctive, and disjunctive), × 3 (group size) design. This part of the experiment provided a conceptual replication of Experiment 2. The analysis of the high- and low-ability subjects' data during Block 1 (no feedback) used a 3 (task demands) × 2 (ability: high, low) × 3 (group size) design. This part of the experiment provided a conceptual replication of Experiment 1. It seemed probable that the longer subjects had received performance feedback, the stronger its effects would be. For this reason, we considered Block 2 to be a training period and analyzed only Block 3 data to determine the effects of such feedback. The overall design at Block 3 was a 3 (ability) × 3 (group size) × 3 (task demands) factorial.

Subjects

The subjects were 108 female undergraduate students. Of these, 54 were drawn from summer session classes and compensated with $1.50 plus their performance payoffs. The remaining 54 were drawn from introductory psychology classes and received, in addition to their performance payoffs, partial credit toward a course requirement for their participation.[8]

Experimental Task

The hand-pumping task used in Experiment 2 was used with only one modification. Instead of pumping a single bulb with the favored hand, subjects were provided with two bulbs. They were to take one bulb in each hand and pump as much air as possible by alternately squeezing the two bulbs. This change was introduced to circumvent a problem that had been detected by chance in an earlier study—at least one subject had violated instructions and switched hands from trial to trial to reduce muscular fatigue.

As in the previous experiment, there were five small booths along the rear wall of a large lab room. The curtains of the three central booths were open when the subjects entered the laboratory; each subject seated herself in one of these booths and occupied it throughout the experiment. The booths were labeled "green," "red," and "blue," and this color code was used throughout the study to refer to individual subjects. The spirometers sat on a table across the room from the booths and were clearly visible to all three subjects whenever their booths' curtains were open.

Three of the four available data-collection chambers were prominently marked with green, red, and blue tape, as were their latex hoses. Further, the graph pens charted performance in ink of the appropriate color to ensure that subjects would recognize their own (purported) scores. The fourth spirometer chamber had no color code and was used only by the experimenter to demonstrate the operation of the equipment.

One of the remaining two booths was never used during the experiment, but the other was occupied by a second experimenter (B) who controlled which of two audio input channels was fed into each subject's headset. In addition, all of the latex hoses passed through this booth. One of these (blue) was fitted with a variable pressure-relief valve. Another hose (green) could be disconnected completely and reconnected to a pair of large sphymograph bulbs that Experimenter B could use to simulate the green subject's performance. The purpose and use of this covert equipment is described more fully below.

Procedure

The first experimenter (A) seated the three subjects in the open booths. The initial instructions described the task as the experimenter demonstrated it. A horizontal yellow line marked on the spirometers' chart paper at 360 cl was said to represent average performance by women previously tested at the task. Maximal effort at the task was stressed, but the fatigue that might result from such exertion was also described.

At this time, subjects read and signed consent forms. The experimenter collected these along with the subjects' wristwatches. The rationale given for the latter step was "to minimize distraction caused by trying to time yourself." The curtain of the green booth was unobtrusively drawn shut at this point, but the curtains of the red and blue booths were left open so that their occupants could continue to monitor the spirometers.

A series of nine "ability test" trials was then run. Each subject participated once in each block of three trials. The order in which the color codes were called to perform was randomized across groups but was fixed within sessions. During these trials, the blue and red subjects could watch the spirometer chambers rise and the chart pens record as each subject (apparently) performed.[9] After each block of trials, Experimenter A reset the spirometers and announced each subject's score on that trial over the microphone. On each block of the three trials, one subject, red, consistently performed better than the "average'" of 360 cl and better than either of the other two subjects, achieving scores in the 400-440

cl range. Thus, the apparent performance of the high-ability subject was on average around 420 cl. The green subject appeared to perform near the purported population average and received scores of 340-380 cl. On average, the moderate-ability member's performance was about 360 cl. And the blue subject, the low-ability member, had scores consistently below average and well below the others. Blue's scores fell in the 280-320 cl range, with an expected value of 300 cl.

The intervention of Experimenter B made this manipulation possible. By opening the pressure relief valve described above, the experimenter could bleed off any fraction of the air actually pumped by the blue (low-ability) subject. With the curtain now open, Experimenter B had merely to watch the blue recording unit and moderate the valve aperture to insure that blue obtained the consistently low scores accorded this subject. Whenever the green (moderate-ability) subject was called to perform, Experimenter B wholly determined her scores by pumping the two large bulbs in his booth at a moderate pace. It was, in fact, the air he pumped that registered on the spirometer unit as the average-range scores accorded to green; this subject's input line remained unconnected to the equipment throughout this phase.

Despite the fact that subjects were told that the ability-test trials, like the performance trials, would each last 25 sec, the actual length of the test trials worked by blue and green was 30-35 sec. This was done in an effort to disguise the manipulation of the red (high-ability) subject's scores, which were affected simply by allowing her as much time as she needed to attain scores in the desired range, usually 35-40 sec. This was the actual reason for collecting subjects' wristwatches. No subject indicated any suspicion that the trial durations had varied.

Whenever one subject was performing a test trial, the other two subjects heard background music as masking noise. When individual subjects' scores were reported following each block of three trials, the red and blue subjects heard all three subjects' scores over their headsets. The green subject, however, heard only her own score; the music was fed to her headset during the report of red and blue's scores. Thus, the red and blue subjects had both visual (viz., the visible chart records) and verbal feedback confirming the manipulated ability levels, for all three subjects, whereas the green subject received only verbal feedback on her own, "average" performance.

Following the test trials, the prerecorded instructions were resumed and the curtains of the red and blue booths drawn shut. Subjects were then provided with the standard experimental cover story, reminders of the likelihood of fatigue and of their freedom to personally choose a reasonable level of effort, and the manipulation of task demands. On any given trial, the best (disjunctive), worst (conjunctive), or average (additive) score was counted as the group score. Every group score above a minimum criterion (250 cl, 50 cl below the apparent ability of the low-ability subject) would result in payoffs to the group. The rate of payoff varied with task demand. Additive groups were promised 9.5 cents per member per 100 cl above criterion, disjunctive groups received 7.5 cents per member per 100 cl above criterion; and conjunctive groups got 13 cents per member per 100 cl above criterion. These payoff rates were chosen so as to roughly equalize across task-demand conditions the net expected payoff to the three subjects at a session (near $5).[10]

The performance-trial series then began. Before each trial, the colors of those subjects to be working together were announced over the headphones. To help insure that subjects attended to the grouping structure, they were to record this information on a provided sheet. Each performance trial lasted 25 sec, and 78 dB of white noise masked the sounds of members' pumping. The intertrial intervals varied slightly in length (from 45-60 sec), depending on how long it took the experimenters to complete their scoring and transformations of the performance data.

During Block 1 (Trials 1-6), subjects received no performance feedback. Between Trials 6 and 7, subjects were told that after each of the remaining trials they would receive a report of all individual and group scores as well as each member's payoff. Subjects were to record all of this information on the provided sheet. The performance series was resumed. Following each trial, scores were read in an invariant order—blue, red, green, Group—as were subjects' payoffs on that trial. As noted above, the performance feedback a subject received was her true score plus a correction factor. The correction factors (K) were defined as follows: $K = A - X$, where $X =$ the subject's average performance on Trials 1-6 and $A = 405$ cl for high-ability subjects, 345 cl for moderate-ability subjects, and 285 cl for low-ability subjects, respectively. Hence, if a subject's average performance during Blocks 2 and 3 was identical to her performance during Block 1, her feedback during those blocks would indicate an average level of performance of A. The intent of this procedure was to simulate actual differences in ability while allowing scores to be responsive to variations in effort. (The A values represented somewhat lower average scores than subjects had received during ability test trials; this was intended to reflect the effect of fatigue during Block 1.)

At the conclusion of the performance trials, subjects completed a short questionnaire in their booths. Its purpose was to check the ability manipulation, subjects' understanding of task demands, and suspiciousness. Because group composition varied from trial to trial, it was not feasible to assess subjects' perceived dispensability to their group. All subjects were then thoroughly debriefed and paid. Because the task put the "low-ability" subjects at a disadvantage, all subjects were paid $2.50 regardless of their "earned" payoffs.

RESULTS

Manipulation Check

Subjects rated their personal ability on a bipolar 7-point scale and also estimated their own ability rank in the group. The only significant effect for either judgment was the ability main effect: $F(2, 99) = 73.6$, $p < .001$ for the rating; $F(2, 93) = 466.7$, $p < .001$ for the ranking. The means indicated that subjects perceived their relative abilities as intended. The rating means were high = 5.4, moderate = 4.3, and low = 2.7; the mean ranks were high = 1.1, moderate = 2.0, and low = 2.9.

Performance Data

Subjects' actual performance scores were averaged across trials within group size and block. The predictions were tested with a set of planned comparisons. When the predictions were directional, directional statistical tests were performed. These were followed by overall ANOVAs that probed for unpredicted effects.

Performance with no-feedback—no-ability manipulation (Block 1, moderates). The basic design was a 3 (task demand) × 3 (group size) factorial. The design essentially paralleled that of Experiment 2 (minus the task-difficulty factor), the major difference being the current use of a within-subjects group size manipulation.

The pattern of means for the conjunctive and disjunctive conditions was as predicted; effort tended to decline as group size increased (solo = 343.3, dyad = 342.1, and triad = 340.5). However, unlike Experiment 2, none of the planned contrasts designed to test this prediction achieved statistical significance, $t < 1$ for all. Nor were any of these group-size contrasts significant when tested on the conjunctive and disjunctive conditions separately. A 3 (task demands) × 3 (group size) least-squares ANOVA on the moderates' data also resulted in no significant effects. In summary, Hypothesis 2 was not supported.

Performance with no-feedback—ability manipulation (Block 1, highs and lows). The design was a 2 (ability) × 3 (task demands) × 3 (group size) factorial. Except for the repeated measures on the group-size factor, this portion of the study was a conceptual replication of Experiment 1. It was predicted, as in Experiment 1, that ability and conjunctive/disjunctive task demands would interact. This prediction was confirmed, $t(63) = 2.04$, $p < .025$, one-tailed. This effect is plotted in Figure 3. As in Experiment 1, varying task demands had opposite impact on high- and low-ability members; for high-ability members, motivation was higher in the disjunctive condition, whereas for low-ability members, motivation was higher in the conjunctive condition. Hypothesis 1 was confirmed.

Another effect evident in Figure 3 and

FIGURE 3.

Task Demand × Ability interaction effect on performance: Experiment 3, Block 1.

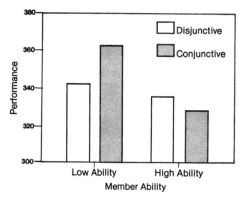

which emerged from the overall ANOVA was a main effect for ability, $F(1, 63) = 8.17$, $p < .01$; lows worked significantly harder than highs (lows = 351.5 cl, highs = 325.4 cl). To probe whether this effect represented heightened efforts by lows, lowered efforts by highs, or both, we compared them to the moderates' Block 1 performance. The overall average for the moderates was 336.3 cl. Newman-Keuls analysis with a pooled error term indicated both that lows worked significantly harder and highs significantly less hard than moderates ($p < .05$). This effect probably reflects the relative ease with which the highs apparently outperformed the other subjects during the ability test trials, and the apparent difficulty the lows had in reaching even an "average" level of performance. It appears that the highs relaxed somewhat and the lows redoubled their efforts to "catch up."

Group size significantly affected effort in the conjunctive and disjunctive conditions, $F(2, 126) = 3.48, p < .05$ (solo =

347.1 cl, dyad = 341.2 cl, triad = 336.0 cl). The overall ANOVA (which included the additive condition) also produced a significant group-size main effect, $F(1, 126) = 3.75, p < .05$; again, effort declined monotonically with size (solo = 342.1 cl, dyad = 339.2 cl, triad = 332.5 cl). As reasoned in Experiment 1, this effect suggests that the high and low subjects felt that they might sometimes (respectively) be outperformed by or outperform other group members.

Performance with feedback (Block 3). The initial analyses were the planned contrasts derived from the predictions. By Block 3, after considerable feedback had been given to subjects, the moderates (in the conjunctive and disjunctive conditions) began to be responsive to the group-size variable. Effort declined monotonically with size (solo = 360.9, dyad = 358.6, triad = 347.8); both the planned comparisons of solo versus triad, $t(66) = 1.80, p < .05$, one-tailed, and of dyad versus triad $t(66) = 2.19, p < .025$, one-tailed, were significant. Thus, the prediction that performance feedback would strengthen the group-size—free-rider effect, that is, Hypothesis 3, was confirmed.

The Ability × Conjunctive/Disjunctive Task Demand contrast was tested for highs and lows again at Block 3. The predicted interaction effect was again significant, $t(66) = 1.70, p < .05$, one-tailed, mirroring the pattern observed at Block 1 (cf. Figure 3). There was no indication, however, that this effect was stronger after having received feedback (Block 3) than without such feedback (Block 1); that is, Hypothesis 4 was not confirmed. There was also no evidence that the group-size effect that had been observed among highs and lows at Block 1 was stronger by Block 3,

By Block 3, highs, lows, and moderates had received considerable performance feedback. Therefore, all three ability conditions were included in an overall 3 (ability) × 3 (task demands) × 3 (group size) analysis. Two effects were significant. Ability and effort were inversely related, $F(2, 99) = 12.41$, $p < .001$ (highs = 321.8 cl, moderates = 346.7 cl, lows = 365.8 cl). And group size and member effort were inversely related, $F(2, 198) = 8.05$, $p < .001$ (solo = 349.8 cl, dyad = 344.7 cl, triad = 340.3 cl).

DISCUSSION

The results of Experiment 3 were generally consistent with those of the two previous experiments. First, member ability clearly interacted with conjunctive/disjunctive task demands, just as in Experiment 1. High-ability members worked harder under disjunctive task demands; low-ability members worked harder under conjunctive task demands. Second, we argued previously that under disjunctive and conjunctive task demands, member motivation should decline with group size, but only if a person's dispensability increased with group size. In Experiment 1, subjects were led to believe that their ability was extreme (viz., above or below everyone else in the group and very near the population extremes) and very stable (viz., dependent on stable physical factors). For these subjects, dispensability should not and did not increase with group size. In Experiment 2, in which subjects were given no explicit information about member ability, members of larger groups should have felt more dispensable and have expended less effort than members of smaller groups. The latter prediction was confirmed. The situation in Experiment 3 appears to be intermediate to the first two

experiments. High- and low-ability subjects clearly perceived themselves, respectively, to be the most and least able members of their groups. The manipulation checks and the Ability × Conjunctive/Disjunctive Task Demand interaction effects confirm this. But subjects could also reasonably imagine exceptions (at least on occasional trials) to the usual performance rankings. Subjects were not told that their abilities were extreme or stable, and furthermore, the ability test trials clearly demonstrated within-subject variability in performance. Under these conditions, the larger the group, the better the chance that some other member could both outperform and underperform one, the more dispensable one should be (for disjunctive or conjunctive tasks), and the less hard one should work. The high- and low-ability subjects exhibited just such a group-size effect.

The only finding that was inconsistent with the previous experiments was for the moderates in Block 1; the relationship between group size and effort (for conjunctive and disjunctive tasks) was not statistically significant, although it was in the predicted direction. The basic design used in Experiment 3 was very similar to the one used in Experiment 2, in which a significant group-size effect was obtained. For several reasons,[11] this failure to replicate may be attributed to a weaker test in the present experiment.

The primary objective of Experiment 3 was to examine the effects of performance feedback on free-riding behavior. There was some evidence that such feedback could make the dispensability of members' efforts more apparent. The predicted group-size effect was nonsignificant for moderates when they received no performance feedback but was significant after they received such feedback. Unexpectedly, the observed

Ability × Task Demand free-rider effects were not strengthened through performance feedback. Our general expectation had been that the more experience one had with working in a group under specific task demands, the better one would recognize opportunities to free ride. However, it may be that the opportunity for a high-ability (low-ability) member to free ride on a conjunctive (disjunctive) task is fairly self-evident. Even if this was not the case, the feedback highs and lows received during the ability test trials could have revealed the opportunities to free ride. These subjects learned during these trials which members were most and least able. When they later received instructions defining the task demands, they could have retrospectively applied those task demands to the results of the ability test trials, which would have provided a kind of "feedback." The point is that the performance feedback the highs and lows received during Blocks 2 and 3 may have added little to their recognition of free-rider opportunities. Intuitively, the free-riding opportunities created by increasing group size are not as self-evident. And, because moderates received only their "own" scores during the ability test trials, they had no opportunity either to apply the task demands or to determine just how variable each member's performance was. The feedback in Blocks 2 and 3 should have been much more informative for these subjects, and indeed, it was only for these subjects that feedback enhanced free riding.

GENERAL DISCUSSION

The studies reported here demonstrate that the task motivation of group members is sensitive to the perceived dispensability of their efforts for group success and they identify some of the group (e.g., size),

member (e.g., ability), and task (e.g., task demands) factors that may promote free-rider behavior. We would like to conclude with a brief discussion of some of the interesting research questions suggested by this work.

First, how do group members decide that their efforts are dispensable? What, besides objective dispensability, are the most salient cues? For example, is dispensability sensitive to the overall probability of group success?[12] Is dispensability sensitive to irrelevant factors like attraction to the group or liking for the task? One could easily imagine group members subjectively exaggerating the dispensability of their efforts as a way of rationalizing reduced effort for unpleasant tasks.

A second issue is the impact of individual differences on the propensity to free ride. A number of personality constructs have been linked to generalized expectancies of personal ineffectiveness (e.g., helplessness, depression, locus of control). These seem likely to facilitate judgments of dispensability in social contexts.

These conjectures raise the larger question of how to deter or reduce free riding short of making every group member indispensable. An expectancy-value analysis suggests several ways of doing this (cf. Orbell & Dawes, 1981) for example, adding or increasing incentives for high effort, introducing disincentives for low effort, or selectively altering expectancies of certain outcomes. A class of socially mediated outcomes that seem particularly relevant in the small-group setting are those associated with "normative systems" (cf. Orbell & Dawes, 1981), for example, the reactions of other group members to one's level of performance. The motivational effects of variables that are central to social norms' formation (e.g., communication), internalization (e.g., commitment), strength (e.g., group cohesiveness), and enforcement (e.g., anonymity) deserve systematic study.

Because most external social sanctions or rewards require the group to monitor the behavior of individual members, the anonymity or noticeability of member effort should exert a particularly powerful influence on motivation. Stroebe and Frey (in press) suggest that the high noticeability of input in most small, face-to-face groups may effectively discourage free riding. Our results demonstrate that free riding can occur even when every member's contribution is made public (e.g., in Experiment 3), but it seems probable that increasing member anonymity would remove powerful restraints against free riding. The results of a recent study by Harkins and Petty (in press, Experiment 3) nicely corroborate this. Group members performing a recognition task monitored either separate stimulus displays or the same display; the dispensability of member effort was presumably greater in the latter condition. Crossed with this manipulation was an anonymity factor. Harkins and Petty found reduced performance in the "same stimulus" condition only when subjects were anonymous. Essentially the same result has been reported by Sweeney (1973). These findings suggest that member anonymity may not only directly induce reductions in motivation through the identifiability mechanism, but may also serve to amplify the dispensability mechanism.

A final set of questions is suggested by research on learned helplessness. The intriguing thing about the original findings (e.g., Seligman & Maier, 1967) was not that restrained dogs would eventually stop trying to escape inescapable shock, but that the dogs tended to remain helpless after the restraints were removed. Like the dog's harness, a group task for which the members' efforts are dispensable reduces the contingency between effort and outcome, and indeed, we found that group members "struggled" less under these circumstances. But it is unknown whether eliminating the group's "restraints" leaves the group member with a lasting motivational deficit. Stated another way, will the effects of free riding generalize from situations in which the subject is dispensable to situations in which he or she is not? For instance, consider an assembly line worker whose errors can routinely be corrected by another worker further up the line. If the assembly line were redesigned to eliminate such corrections, would the formerly dispensable worker work as hard as, say, a new worker? Abramson, Seligman, and Teasdale (1978) proposed an attributional model that holds that helplessness will generalize when it is attributed to stable, global causes. Although this attributional approach is promising, the group situation introduces additional complexities. For example, a low-ability member's efforts are dispensable when the task demands are disjunctive. However, if the task demands suddenly became conjunctive, would the motivational deficit generalize because low-ability is a stable cause or not generalize because task demands are unstable? Clearly, both theoretical and empirical work is required on the generalization issue.

NOTES

1. When group members' efforts are sufficiently dispensable, such free-rider situations may become social dilemmas (Dawes, 1980; Orbell & Dawes, 1981) in which each individual will receive a higher payoff for a socially defecting choice (e.g., exerting no effort) than for a socially cooperative choice (e.g., exerting high effort) regardless of what others do, but all individuals are better off if all cooperate than if

all defect. Stroebe and Frey (in press) extended and elaborated on Olson's reasoning in the small-group case. The basic free-rider logic has been applied widely in psychology. For example, Barker and Wicker's (e.g., Barker & Gump, 1964; Wicker, 1968, 1969) concept of manning involves a similar reasoning. They present evidence that when the number of members of a group exceeds the number of task roles (i.e., the group is overmanned), members' motivation is lower than when there are fewer members than task roles (i.e., the group is undermanned).

Another application of the free-rider logic appears in Darley and Latané's work on bystander intervention in emergencies (Latané & Darley, 1970). They reason that the probability of an individual bystander intervening in an emergency may decline as the number of bystanders increases due to, in part, diffusion of responsibility (i.e., one's help is more dispensable in a large group of bystanders). A final illustration is Seligman's work (e.g., Seligman, 1975) on learned helplessness. When there is little or no contingency beween one's task efforts and effective performance, the likelihood drops that a person will initiate and sustain task-relevant behavior.

2. Olson includes two processes in his notion of perceived effectiveness. The first is the perception of how much difference an individual's contribution is likely to make in the provision of the public good. This is similar, but not identical, to the notion of dispensability considered here. The perceived difficulty of a task may increase with group size without perceived dispensability being affected (e.g., a citizen of a metropolis may perceive it to be a much more difficult task to mount an effective "community clean-up" campaign than would a citizen of a small village, but both may consider their own efforts to be equally dispensable to a successful campaign). Perceived dispensability depends not only on one's own perceived effectiveness, but on one's perception of the other group members' effectiveness. Olson's second process is the perceived difference one's contribution is likely to make in one's personal payoff. Of course, for a true public good, there is little if any additional payoff for having helped supply the public good but there is considerable cost. In the small-group case, if the group's payoff is a fixed quantity, increasing the group size will usually decrease the size of each member's share. We controlled this motivational mechanism in the present research by offering a fixed cash prize for each member of the winning groups (e.g., $5 per member, regardless of group size).

3. An additional 47 subjects (30 males, 17 females) were also run but not included in the analyses. They had all failed a stringent test of their understanding of the task demands in a postexperimental questionnaire. Subjects were given member scores for several hypothetical groups and required to identify (in a multiple-choice format) the correct group scores. Confusion was most likely to occur when different rules were used for combining scores within and across trials. In all conditions, the overall score of a group was the sum of its trial scores. Hence, the most common errors were inferring additive task demands for conjunctive or disjunctive tasks.

4. See Footnote 2, supra.

5. Two other subjects were run but dropped from the analyses. One had been a subject in a related previous study and the second received the wrong instructions.

6. A secondary benefit of this method of defining task demands was that they were somewhat clearer than in Experiment 1. Unlike Experiment 1, the conjunctive groups' success required that every member succeed. It might appear at first glance that every member of these groups is indispensable. However, it is the dispensability of one's effort that is significant. In both experiments, the conjunctive group's performance is defined by the worst member performance, and any effort by another member in excess of that level is entirely dispensable. In short, the conjunctive task demands in Experiments 1 and 2 should be functionally equivalent for producing free-rider effects.

7. The suggestion that subjects may have considered themselves to be "somewhat above average" does not preclude subjects "assuming rough equivalence" in abilities. For a novel and non-ego-involving task like the present one, the self-serving bias is likely to be fairly weak and uncertain. In any case, an egocentric self-assurance need not necessarily imply low ability for one's partners.

8. Data from an additional seven sessions (involving 9 summer-session and 12 regular-term students) had to be discarded. For five of these

sessions there were equipment malfunctions; for one session, one of the subjects clearly misunderstood the instructions; and in another session, one member was observed to blatantly cheat at the task.

9. The reason for allowing the high- and low-ability subjects to see the spirometers was that, unlike the air-blowing task, subjects might have some preconception of their own ability at the hand-pumping task and might disbelieve false verbal feedback. This procedure provided subjects with direct evidence that they were well above or below average in ability.

10. It can be proven that it is not possible to control the expected payoffs exactly. However, the payoff rates used here did accomplish a rough equivalence. In any case, because our interest was primarily in the differential effects of group size or member ability within task demands, small differences in payoff among task-demand conditions were not of concern.

11. The sample size was smaller in Experiment 3 (36 moderate-ability subjects vs. 64 in Experiment 2); there were fewer performance trials in Experiment 3 (2 per size level in Block 1 vs. 9 per size level in Experiment 2); the range of actual group sizes was narrower in Experiment 3 (dyads vs. tetrads in Experiment 2; dyads vs. triads in Experiment 3); and subjects in Experiment 3 had to monitor the size of their work group from trial to trial (whereas group size was constant across trials in Experiment 2). These between-experiment differences tended to reduce the impact of the manipulation, the precision of measurement of the dependent variable, and the power of statistical tests in Experiment 3.

12. Framed in this way, the question is closely akin to a controversial issue in the learned-helplessness literature. Do noncontingent positive outcomes reduce motivational deficits like noncontingent negative outcomes? Free-rider behavior supports this conjecture and provides a useful research paradigm within which to further explore the issue.

REFERENCES

Abramson, L. Y., Garber, J., & Seligman, M. E. P. Learned helplessness in humans: An attributional analysis. In J. Garber & M. E. P. Seligman (Eds.), *Human helplessness: Theory and applications.* New York: Academic Press, 1980.

Abramson, L. Y., Seligman, M. E. P., & Teasdale, J. Learned helplessness in humans: Critique and reformulation. *Journal of Abnormal Psychology,* 1978, *87,* 49-74.

Barker, R., & Gump, P. *Big school, small school: High school size and student behavior.* Stanford, Calif.: Stanford University Press, 1964.

Davis, J. H. *Group performance.* Reading, Mass.: Addison-Wesley, 1969.

Dawes, R. M. Social dilemmas. *Annual Review of Psychology,* 1980, *31,* 169-193.

Harkins, S., & Petty R. E. The role of intrinsic motivation in eliminating social loafing. *Journal of Personality and Social Psychology,* in press.

Ingham, A. G., Levinger, G., Graves, J., & Peckham, V. The Ringelmann effect: Studies of group size and group performance. *Journal of Experimental Social Psychology,* 1974, *10,* 371-384.

Kerr, N. L., & Bruun, S. E. Ringelmann revisited: Alternative explanations for the social loafing effect. *Personality and Social Psychology Bulletin,* 1981, *7,* 224-231.

Latané, B., & Darley, J. *The unresponsive bystander: Why doesn't he help?* New York: Appleton-Century-Crofts, 1970.

Latané, B., Williams, K., & Harkins, S. Many hands make light the work: The causes and consequences of social loafing. *Journal of Personality and Social Psychology,* 1979, *37,* 822-832. (a)

Latané, B., Williams, K., & Harkins, S. Social loafing. *Psychology Today,* April 1979, pp. 104-110. (b)

Myers, D. G. *The inflated self.* New York: Seabury Press, 1980.

Olson, M. *The logic of collective action: Public goods and the theory of groups.* Cambridge, Mass.: Harvard University Press, 1965.

Orbell, J., & Dawes, R. Social dilemmas. In G. Stephenson & J. H. Davis (Eds.), *Progress in applied social psychology* (Vol. 1). New York: Wiley, 1981.

Seligman, M. *Helplessness.* San Francisco: Freeman, 1975.

Seligman, M. E. P., & Maier, S. Failure to escape traumatic shock. *Journal of Experimental Psychology,* 1967, *74,* 1-9.

Shaw, D. Size of the share in task and motivation in work groups. *Sociometry,* 1960, *23,* 203-208.

Steiner, I. *Group process and productivity.* New York: Academic Press, 1972.

Stroebe, W., & Frey, B. S. Self-interest and collective action: The economics and psychology of public goods. *British Journal of Social Psychology,* in press.

Sweeney, J. W. An experimental investigation of the free-rider problem. *Social Science Research,* 1973, *2,* 277-292.

Vroom, V. *Work and motivation.* New York: Wiley, 1964.

Wicker, A. W. Undermanning, performances, and students' subjective experiences in behavior settings of large and small high schools. *Journal of Personality and Social Psychology,* 1968, *10,* 255-261.

Wicker, A. W. Size of church membership and members' support of church behavior settings. *Journal of Personality and Social Psychology,* 1969, *13,* 278-288.

Williams, K., Harkins, S., & Latané, B. Identifiability as a deterrent to social loafing: Two cheering experiments. *Journal of Personality and Social Psychology,* 1981, *40,* 303-311.

9   Group Dynamics

A GROUP IS GENERALLY considered to be two or more persons who interact with and influence one another in pursuit of some common goal. The fact that each person spends approximately half of his or her waking hours in the company of at least two other people demonstrates the potential impact that group activities may have on our lives, and the importance of understanding these situations to ensure that group interactions are efficient and productive. The import of group dynamics is also demonstrated by the wide variety of disciplines that devote significant attention to group processes: social psychology, clinical psychology, anthropology, sociology, political science, and management.

Although each of these disciplines is interested in group processes, the focus of investigations in group dynamics varies somewhat as one shifts from one field to the next. For example, most sociologists studying groups are primarily interested in understanding intergroup relationships, often at societal or cultural levels of analysis. Clinical psychologists, on the other hand, are more concerned about utilizing their understanding of group phenomena to help their clients cope with or solve their psychological problems. From the social psychology perspective, the primary focus of studies of group processes has traditionally been the impact of the group on the behavior of the individual group member. The articles that have been selected for this chapter exemplify the traditional social psychological approach.

The presence of other people may affect the degree to which an individual monitors his or her own actions as compared to the actions of the group as a whole. Although it was originally felt that being in a group may cause individuals to lose their identities and to "deindividuate," Ed Diener and his associates contend that deindividuation causes the individual to refocus attention to external factors that may affect behavior. The principal consequence of deindividuation is an increase in the frequency of counternormative activities, as immediate situation cues replace internalized normative standards as the primary determinants of one's behavior. In a series of three studies reported in this article, Diener and his colleagues examine the effects of group size, group density, and gender similarity on deindividuation, predicting that being a member of a larger group would lead to greater deindividuation and less self-consciousness than being a member of a smaller group.

Finally, in the article in this chapter, Milton Rosenbaum and his associates examine various factors that may affect group productivity. Group activities arise frequently in our everyday lives, so it is advantageous to understand the means by which we can maximize the productivity of groups of which we are members, whether they are such important groups as business associates without whom we would have no livelihood, or relatively trivial groups such as recreational teams. In particular, Rosenbaum and his coauthors manipulated the reward structures that were operating as small groups of subjects completed a block-stacking task. It was predicted that reward structures that emphasize cooperative behavior among group members would result in greater group productivity than reward structures that encouraged competition. Even when the dominant aspect of the reward structure was cooperation among peers, the mere presence of a competitive component substantially reduced efficiency and productivity.

Deindividuation: Effects of Group Size, Density, Number of Observers, and Group Member Similarity on Self-Consciousness and Disinhibited Behavior

Ed Diener, Rob Lusk,
Darlene DeFour, and Robert Flax

Predictions about the social causes of self-consciousness in groups were derived from the theory of deindividuation and tested in three experiments. In Experiment 1 it was found that increasing group size was related to a decrease in self-consciousness. Group density did not influence self-consciousness. In Experiment 2 it was found that increases in the number of observers increased self-consciousness. In Experiments 1 and 2, self-reports of self-consciousness were independent of one's group, whereas the degree of behavioral disinhibition was highly correlated within groups. In Experiment 3 it was found that gender similarity within a group was related to lower self-consciousness. These findings offer support for a perceptual/attentional model of self-consciousness within groups. Contrary to deindividuation theory predictions, however, behavior intensity did not vary across conditions in Experiments 1 and 2, even though self-consciousness did differ. This finding suggests that deindividuation theory is incomplete in its present form, and several potential inadequacies are discussed.

The concept of deindividuation was derived from the Gestalt idea of perception of whole figures (Festinger, Pepitone, & Newcomb, 1952). Festinger and his colleagues maintained that just as visual attention can be directed by the characteristics of visual figures, so one's attention to persons and oneself when one is in a group may be directed by the characteristics of the group. The theory of deindividuation suggests that the characteristics of certain groups may serve to draw the group members' attention away from themselves and toward the group as a whole. In other words, persons in groups

"Deindividuation: Effects of Group Size, Density, Number of Observers, and Group Member Similiarity on Self-Consciousness and Disinhibited Behavior" by E. Deiner, R. Lusk, D. DeFour & F. Flax, 1980, *Journal of Personality and Social Psychology, 39,* pp. 449-459. Copyright 1980 by the American Psychological Assn. Reprinted by permission of the publisher and authors.

with certain characteristics may be less self-conscious or self-aware because their attention is directed to the groups in which they are immersed. Diener (1979, 1980) further developed the theory of deindividuation by hypothesizing that when one's attention is drawn outward toward the group, one will rely less on one's own standards and be more influenced by external cues. Diener (1980) maintained that the deindividuated person's behavior is less inhibited by long-term norms and long-term consequences because of a lack of self-monitoring and other self-regulatory processes. Therefore, the person whose attention is focused on the group is more reactive to immediate emotions, motives, and situational cues. Since deindividuated persons are less likely to self-regulate their behavior in accord with long-term norms, they are more likely to perform disinhibited behaviors.

The purpose of the present experiments was to test deindividuation predictions that were derived from perceptual/attentional principles. More specifically, group characteristics such as size and homogeneity were varied and self-consciousness and disinhibited behavior were measured. Based on the theories of deindividuation, we predicted that a number of social factors could decrease self-consciousness—large groups, dense groups, similar groups, and few observers—and thus lead to more disinhibited behavior. Thus, the present studies allowed both a test of deindividuation predictions and an exploration of some of the natural causes of self-consciousness.

In addition to the reasoning of a gestalt-oriented theory of deindividuation, the importance of group size and number of observers to the self-focusing of attention was suggested by Latané and Nida's (1979) social impact theory, which hypothesizes that the impact of onlookers is lessened by increases in the number of people in a group. In Experiment 1, subjects performed potentially embarrassing tasks in groups composed of 1, 2, 4, 8, or 16 participants. We predicted a decreasing marginal impact on self-consciousness as the group grew. The idea of marginal effect, borrowed by analogy from economics, is that as more individuals are added, each additional person has less impact than the individuals added earlier. Group density was manipulated simultaneously with group size, since it was reasoned that persons in more dense groups may be less self-conscious. In Experiment 1, the number of observers was held constant. In Experiment 2 the same tasks were performed, but the size of the group was held constant, and the number of observers was manipulated (1, 2, 4, 8, or 16). Latané's social impact theory predicts that more observers should result in the multiplication of impact and thus in increases in self-consciousness. Again, a marginal effect was predicted—that is, each additional observer should add less impact than the previous observer added.

Taylor and Fiske (1978) reviewed evidence which indicates that when a person is made distinct in a group, that person becomes more salient, and causal attributions to that person become more likely. Distinctiveness has been manipulated in past research by external characteristics such as sex and race. By extension, it seems likely that being dissimilar to others within a group on an external variable such as sex can result in an individual's focusing attention on the self, thus becoming self-conscious. In Experiment 3, each group of four persons contained one female subject and three confederates who acted in a standard manner. Three types of groups were compared—one female and three males, two females and two males, and three females and one male. Based on gestalt principles and the findings reviewed by Taylor and Fiske, we predicted that in Experiment 3 participants who were more outwardly similar to the group would be less self-conscious than those who were dissimilar.

Current thinking indicates that variations in self-awareness and self-consciousness are essential in the theory of deindividuation. This suggests that the theory of self-awareness as developed by Duval and Wicklund (1972) and Wicklund (1975) is related to deindividuation, and indeed, research has shown that loss of individuality and self-awareness covary (Ickes, Layden, & Barnes, 1978). A basic premise of the theory of self-awareness is that there are two directions to conscious attention—inward on the self or outward on the environment. The theory of self-awareness has generated research on diverse phenomena such as aggression (e.g., Rule, Nesdale, & Dyck, 1975), cheating (Diener & Wallbom,

1976), and stealing (Beaman, Klentz, Diener, & Svanum, 1979). However, research in this tradition has relied on artificial devices such as mirrors and television cameras to produce self-awareness and self-consciousness. It is unlikely that these apparatuses are the usual causes of self-awareness or self-consciousness in naturalistic settings. Thus, the present experiments should aid research in the self-awareness tradition by uncovering natural social-situational variables that influence self-consciousness. Although Buss and his colleagues hypothesized that there are several types of self-awareness (Buss, 1980; Fenigstein, Scheier, & Buss, 1975), in this initial examination, we have focused on one—public self-consciousness—that may be the more important type of self-awareness in social situations.

In conclusion, in the present experiments the effect on self-consciousness of four variables was explored: group size, group density, number of observers, and similarity to the group. In addition, disinhibited behavior was measured to test the prediction that behavior would become more reactive to external cues, or more disinhibited, as attention to the self decreased.

EXPERIMENT 1

Method

In Experiment 1 the size and density of the participant groups were varied, and self-consciousness was measured. The number of subjects in the experimental groups was 1, 2, 4, 8, and 16. Groups of more than one were composed of equal numbers of males and females. Both high-density and low-density conditions were run with groups greater than one. Subjects participated in four potentially embarrassing activities while being rated by observers.

After each activity the participants indicated their level of self-consciousness during the previous task. On completion of the activities, the participants completed a questionnaire and a personality scale.

Participants and Procedures

The 408 participants were undergraduate students at the University of Illinois fulfilling a requirement for an introductory psychology course. Two subjects withdrew from the experiment after hearing the initial instructions. Since no-shows are a frequent occurrence, additional participants were scheduled for the group sessions to insure adequate numbers in each group. Despite this precaution, several groups fell below the intended number. When this occurred in a smaller group, participants were dismissed to obtain the next smaller group size. However, in a number of cases, groups of Sizes 8 and 16 were run with fewer participants because of the large amount of subject time involved. The number of subjects per condition was as follows (with the number of groups shown in parentheses): Size 1—19; Size 2—28 (14) Size 4—60 (15); Size 8—108 (14); and Size 16—191 (13).

A male experimenter informed participants that the study would concern aspects of task orientation, situational factors, and self-consciousness. He also informed participants that they would be watched by observers. The instructions were memorized so that the experimental protocol was standardized word for word at every session. Participants were told that the first task would be "making something out of paper," that this would get them "warmed up and motivated," and that they would be competing against other groups in the experiment for a prize of $10 for each participant. The purpose of the cohesiveness task was to allow subjects to get to know each other and to produce a sense of unity in the group. The experimenter told participants that they next would be performing "silly and probably embarrassing tasks." He made it clear that they could refuse to perform particular tasks or withdraw from the experiment at any time.

The experimenter next brought the participants to a large experimental room and positioned them on the floor facing the observers. There were eight observers, four male and four female, who were undergraduate research assistants. They were trained to remain expressionless and nonreactive during the self-consciousness tasks. The observers were seated behind a table at one end of the room. Participants in the low-density condition were seated about 3 ft. (.9 m) apart in rows about 4 ft. (1.2 m) apart. Those in the high-density condition were seated as close together as possible in a roughly square array.

The observers rated the behavior of each subject on each task on a 0 to 10 scale for intensity, with 0 being "did not do" and 10 being "highly intense." For smaller group sizes, there were two or more raters per subject. The embarrassing tasks were acting like a chimp, making "gross" sounds, "finger-painting" with one's nose, and sucking on a baby bottle. The following estimates of interrater reliability were obtained: chimp activity—.86; nose painting—.67; baby bottle—.66; and gross sounds—.81. These intensity ratings were used as an estimate of level of disinhibited activity. When two observers rated the same subject, their intensity ratings were averaged in determining the intensity scores for that participant.

Each task lasted for 30 sec. After each task, participants filled out forms, which read as follows: "During the last activity, how self-conscious or embarrassed were you? Make a check at the appropriate place on the line." Below was a 100-mm line anchored by "Not at all self-conscious" and "Extremely highly self-conscious." The order of the four tasks was randomly determined prior to each session.

After the disinhibition session, participants completed two forms in an adjacent room. The first asked various questions dealing with their reactions to the session. Items were also included to assess subjects' memory of the experimental room. There were seven posters on the wall in the activity room, and participants were asked questions about these posters. The accuracy of participants' responses was used to indicate how free they felt to look around the room, especially in the direction of the observers (since most of the posters were on the wall above the seated observers' heads). There was a question on how worried participants were about what the observers would think of them. The questionnaire also contained questions to assess foreknowledge of the experiment and the extent to which subjects could guess the specific purpose of the study. The second questionnaire was the Self-Consciousness Scale (Fenigstein et al., 1975). This instrument contains three subscales—Private Self-Awareness, Public Self-Consciousness, and Social Anxiety. Finally, there was a thorough debriefing in which participant reactions were elicited and discussed. The scientific purpose of the study was carefully described. Subjects signed a form promising not to discuss the study with others in introductory psychology. They were also given a form with the experimenter's office address and phone number in case they had questions, were upset by participation, or wanted to learn the results of the study. In general, the ethical precautions suggested by Diener and Crandall (1978) were followed, with particular emphasis on the informed consent and debriefing procedures.

RESULTS

Five variables were analyzed: memory, summed self-consciousness, concern about what the onlookers would think of the subject, and behavior intensity. The memory score was the sum of correct responses to six questions on the post-questionnaire asking about the content of six posters in the experiment room. The summed self-consciousness score was the sum of the four 0-100 scales that participants completed after each task, whereas the overall self-consciousness score was a self-report item on the final questionnaire. This item asked participants how self-conscious on the average they were during the four tasks and was answered on a 7-point scale anchored by "Not at all self-conscious" and "Extremely highly self-conscious." Two self-consciousness measures were used to capture both participants' immediate reaction and a more global longer-term response. The final questionnaire also contained a question about participants' concern for what the onlookers thought of them, and this question was answered on a 7-point scale anchored by "Never entered my mind" and "Extremely concerned." Finally, the behavior intensity was the sum of the four intensity scores (ranging from 0 to 10) for each subject.

Group Influence and Data Independence

In most conditions participants were run in groups with other participants. Thus, a question arises regarding the statistical independency of participants run together. In addition, a theoretically interesting question was whether participants in certain conditions behaved more similarly. The theory of deindividuation predicts that non-self-conscious persons should behave more similarly because they are more influenced by external situational cues that are similar for everyone.and because they are less influenced by idiosyncratic personal factors. Correlations within each condition were computed on the data for all possible pairings of participants from the same groups. Computing the correlations based on subjects within conditions was desirable so that overall differences between conditions would not spuriously raise the values. The average Pearson product-moment correlation (McNemar, 1969) over the four group size conditions for the sum of self-consciousness between pairs of subjects run together was .15 (*ns*). The average correlation across conditions for overall self-consciousness was .09 (*ns*); for memory it was .03 (*ns*); and for what onlookers would think of you, it was .05 (*ns*). The correlations did not reach significance in any of the conditions, suggesting that these internal events were not substantially influenced by others. The lack of correlation also indicates that these data can be treated on an individual basis for purposes of statistical analysis.

Only behavioral intensity showed non-independence for subjects run together, $r(44) = .51$, $p < .01$. Thus, when this variable was analyzed, the analyses were based on group means as observations. Interestingly, the behavior intensity of subjects run together appeared to be more highly correlated in the smaller groups (Group Size 2, $r = .77$; Group Size 4, $r = .59$; Group Size 8, $r = .45$; and Group

Size 16, $r = .14$). The only difference between these correlations that reached significance was between Group Size 2 and Group Size 16, $t(22) = 2.1, p < .05$. The group size correlations suggest that conformity or situational influence effects were greater in small groups, perhaps because in larger groups any particular pair are less likely to be close physically and are less likely to be able to see each other.

Effects of Group Size and Density

Experiment 1 was an unbalanced design because there was no density condition for the Size 1 condition. Therefore, the data were analyzed in two stages for differences between conditions. A $2 \times 2 \times 4$ (Sex $\times$ Levels of Density $\times$ Group Sizes) was first conducted, with subjects tested alone omitted from the analysis. Density did not produce a significant main effect for any dependent variables, nor did it significantly interact with sex or group size. The mean overall self-consciousness score and the mean behavioral intensity score were 4.2 and 19.2 for the high-density group and 4.3 and 19.7 for the low-density group. Sex produced a significant effect for summed self-consciousness, $F(1, 371) = 6.49, p < .01$, with males reporting less self-consciousness (males 179.5 vs. females, 207.8). However, sex did not interact significantly with group size or density for any variable.

Next, trend analyses of the dependent variables for linear and higher order trends across group size were calculated after collapsing data across sex and density. Once the data were collapsed, the alone condition participants could be included in the analyses. Means for the five dependent variables and five group size conditions are

shown in Table 1. As can be seen, four of the five dependent variables showed highly significant linear trends. Higher order trends did not approach significance for any of the variables. Thus, the effects of group size were linear when the increase in group size was logarithmic.

Correlational Analyses

Personality effects. The personality subscales of the Self-Consciousness Scale were each correlated with the dependent variables to determine whether individual differences in trait self-awareness and self-consciousness correlated with state self-consciousness in this situation. Since there were a large number of correlations across the three studies, an alpha level of .01 was adopted. Private self-awareness and public self-consciousness did not correlate significantly with any of the variables. However, the Social Anxiety subscale correlated with a number of variables: concern about what the onlookers would think ($r = .42$), overall self-consciousness ($r = .40$), and summed self-consciousness, ($r = .40$, all $ps < .001$).

Self-consciousness and behavior intensity correlation. There was a relatively strong negative correlation ($-.47, p < .001$) between summed self-consciousness and behavioral intensity, indicating that less self-conscious persons exhibited more intense behavior. To determine whether this relationship was due to condition, a multiple regression was computed in which behavioral intensity was predicted by condition (entered as 1 to 5) and self-consciousness. A large standardized beta weight emerged for self-consciousness ($-.50, p < .001$), although the beta weight for condition was also significant ($-.11, p < .05$). Thus, independently of condition, behavioral intensity and self-consciousness were negatively correlated.

Analysis for artifacts. Sixty-three participants (16%) claimed to have heard of the study beforehand. When this foreknowledge (coded as a 0 or 1) was correlated with the dependent variables, the resultant values were all close to 0. Participants' guesses about the study's purpose were coded 0 (no idea whatsoever), 1 (some vague idea), and 2 (an idea closely related to the specific purpose). The mean value was .44, and the correlation between a subject's score and the other values never exceeded .1.

Experiment 2

Method

In the second experiment, the number of observers was varied. Four subjects, two male and two female, participated in each condition. Observer group sizes of 1, 2, 4, and 16 were used. The data from the first experiment (for high-density groups of 4 subjects) were used for the 8-observer condition. In other respects this experiment was identical to the first one. A majority of this experiment was conducted concurrently with the first experiment, with the same experimenter, room, and obervers used in both experiments.

A total of 158 subjects participated— eight groups of four persons in each of the five conditions. Two additional participants withdrew from the experiment after hearing the initial instructions. Two groups were short one person and were thus comprised of only three subjects each. All groups were seated close together as in the high-density condition in Experiment 1. Once again

TABLE 1

Experiment 1 Means and Trend Analyses

Dependent variable	Number of persons in groups					Linear trend F^a
	1	2	4	8	16	
Overall SC	5.2	4.9	4.4	4.1	3.7	23.9*
Summed SC	243.3	221.4	206.4	185.1	161.7	30.6*
Memory	.2	.4	.6	.8	1.1	23.1*
Concern for onlookers	4.7	4.5	4.1	3.8	3.5	16.0*
Behavior intensity	19.3	20.4	18.0	19.9	19.4	0^b

Note: For overall self-consciousness (SC) and concern for onlookers, subjects responded on 7-point scales. Summed SC was the sum of four behaviors on 0-100 scales, and thus this score could vary from 0 to 400. Behavior intensity was the sum of the four behaviors each scored on a 10-point scale and therefore varied from 0 to 40. The memory score could vary from 0 to 6.

  [a] $df = 1,401$.
  [b] The df for this variable are only 1 and 70 based on groups as the number of observations in the group conditions
  * $p < .001$.

there were conditions in which two raters observed each subject, and thus the following interrater reliabilities were calculated: chimp activity—.81; baby bottle—.56; nose painting—.58; gross sounds—.85.

RESULTS

The data of participants run together were checked for independence by correlating for each condition the scores of all pairs of participants run together in the same groups. The mean correlation for the summed self-consciousness score was .20 (*ns*). The correlations for overall self-consciousness (mean $r = .05$) memory (mean $r = -.10$), and what onlookers think of you ($r = .10$) were also low and not significant. However, the correlation for behavior intensity was significant, $r (25) = .60, p < .01$. Thus, the data analysis for this variable was again based on group means.

The means for Experiment 2 are shown in Table 2. An initial analysis of variance was computed to analyze for sex. Males were again significantly less self-conscious, $F(1, 148) = 6.0, p < .05$. However, sex did not interact with condition for any variable. The data were thus collapsed across sex, and a trend analysis was conducted. As can be seen, summed self-consciousness and memory for cues in the room showed significant linear trends. There were no significant higher order trends.

Private self-awareness and public self-consciousness did not correlate above .2 with any of the dependent variables. Once again, social anxiety did so (concern about what onlookers would think, $r = .40$; overall self-consciousness, $r = .40$; and summed self-consciousness, $r = .37$, all $ps < .001$). There was again a negative correlation between summed self-consciousness and behavioral intensity, $r = .42, p < .001$. A regression analysis on

TABLE 2

Experiment 2 Means and Trend Analyses

Dependent variable	Number of persons observing groups					Linear trend F^a
	1	2	4	8	16	
Overall SC	4.2	4.1	4.5	4.3	4.4	.5
Summed SC	180.1	182.6	191.8	197.7	218.0	4.5**
Memory	1.0	.9	.5	.6	.2	11.6***
Concern for onlookers	3.6	3.5	3.9	3.9	4.1	2.8*
Behavior intensity	16.0	18.7	19.4	17.2	19.3	.9^b

Note: SC = self consciousness.
[a] $df = 1,153$.
[b] The *df* for this variable are only 1 and 35 based on groups as the number of observations.
* $p<.10$.   ** $p<.05$.   *** $p<.001$.

behavioral intensity showed that there was a self-consciousness effect (B = 4.5, $p <$ .001) independent of condition (B = .16, $p <$ .05). Thirty subjects (19%) claimed foreknowledge of the experiment, and subjects averaged a score of .43 in guessing the purpose of the experiment. Neither factor showed a significant correlation with any of the dependent variables.

EXPERIMENT 3

Method

In this study, the real subject was always female, and the effect of a participant's gender similarity or dissimilarity to others in her group was manipulated. Groups of four persons were used. However, only one was an actual subject—the other three were confederates. Subjects participated in the four self-consciousness tasks as in the earlier studies. Twenty-eight of the participants were undergraduate students at the University of Illinois who were fulfilling a requirement for an introductory psychology course. The remaining 25 participants were recruited by advertisements posted around the campus and in the campus newspaper and were paid $3.50 for being in the experiment. The data for one of them were not used because she suspected the confederates during the session, and the experiment was terminated. One subject was randomly discarded to achieve equal cell sizes.

The confederates reported to the waiting room along with the subject and were treated like real subjects throughout the experiment. They were instructed on what to say and how to act so that their behavior would be constant from session to session and from individual to individual. The confederates acted friendly but reserved in the waiting room. They responded if the participants talked but otherwise did not initiate conversation. During the activities the confederates performed in a rehearsed, moderate way. The cohesiveness task was eliminated from this study because it did not seem to be essential to the purpose of the study and because it would introduce additional interaction between subjects and confederates.

The subject and confederates were seated in a manner similar to the high-density condition in the first experiment. The seat positions of the confederates were varied randomly, but the subject was always seated in the right rear corner of the group. Eight observers were used throughout the experiment. In this experiment it was possible to always have two observers rating each subject, and thus the following interrater reliabilities were based on all participants: chimp activity—.93, baby bottle—.77, nose painting—.92, and gross sounds— .90.

The sex of the confederates was varied to make the group similar or dissimilar to the subject. In the dissimilar condition, there was one female (the subject) and three males. In the similar condition, there were three females (including the subject) and one male. In the intermediate condition, there were two males and two females. At least one male was included in every condition to help counter the possibility that an apparent similarity effect could be due to subjects' being more at ease when no male colleagues were present. In addition, the experimenter and half of the observers were also males.

RESULTS

There was no problem of independence of subjects in the present study, since true participants were not run together. The data and the results of a trend analysis are shown in Table 3. The trend here is based on proportion of females in the group, not on number of persons as in the earlier trend analyses. In this case overall self-consciousness showed a significant linear trend, whereas the summed self-consciousness means fell in the appropriate pattern but were not significantly different. Behavior intensity also showed a significant effect due to group similarity.

Once again, private self-awareness did not correlate highly with the dependent variables, but in this study public self-awareness did so (concern about what onlookers would think, $r = .36$; overall self-consciousness, $r = .44$; and memory, $r = -.41$, all $ps < .01$). Once again, social anxiety correlated strongly with several variables (concern for onlookers, $r = .40$; overall self-consciousness, $r = .60$; and summed self-consciousness, $r = .51$, all $ps < .01$). The correlation between summed self-consciousness and intensity was significant ($r = -.52, p < .001$), and a regression analysis indicated that this ef-

fect ($B = -.48, p < .001$) occurred even when the effect of condition ($B = .21, ns$) was taken into account.

Foreknowledge about the study was indicated by 20 subjects (39%). Subjects averaged .27 on the measure of their ability to guess the hypothesis. An additional question queried participants about whether they were suspicious of the confederates, and 5 subjects (10%) responded affirmatively. Subjects' ability to guess the hypothesis correlated with their memory ability ($r = .43, p < .01$), as did foreknowledge ($r = .25, p < .05$). Foreknowledge also correlated negatively with concern for observers ($r = -.27, p < .05$). Although artifacts presented more of a potential problem in this experiment, it does not appear that they had an influence on the behavioral intensity or the direct self-consciousness measures.

DISCUSSION

Three of four group characteristics appeared to influence self-consciousness. The

TABLE 3

Experiment 3 Means and Trend Analyses

Dependent variable	Sex composition of groups			Linear trend F^a
	3 M, 1 F	2 M, 2 F	1 M, 3 F	
Overall SC	5.6	5.1	4.0	5.6**
Summed SC	225.4	193.3	179.9	2.2
Memory	.7	.2	.3	1.2
Concern for onlookers	4.8	4.2	3.5	3.1*
Behavior intensity	21.1	20.4	26.1	5.5**

Note: M means male; F means female. SC = self-consciousness.
  $^a df = 1,48$.
  $^* p<.10$. $^{**} p<.05$.

impact of group size was most clear—the larger the group, the less self-conscious were group members. In Experiment 1, for all measures that reflected self-consciousness, there was a linear decrease when plotted against the log increase in group size. There did not appear to be any effect of group density on self-consciousness. In Experiment 2, self-consciousness seemed to increase as the number of observers increased. Although the effect of number of observers on self-consciousness was not as consistent as the group size effect, there did appear to be an influence that was reflected in at least two of the measures. In both studies, although each added person had an effect, his or her impact was less than that of the previously added person. In the third study, the effect of group similarity on self-consciousness was assessed. Although three of the indicants of self-consciousness seemed to be linearly related to degree of group similarity, the linear trend was significant for only one of these measures. (Since this study had a smaller sample size, the significance levels do not necessarily suggest weaker effects for the similarity variable.) In conclusion, when one examines all of the self-consciousness means, it appears that group size, number of observers, and group homogeneity have an influence on self-consciousness, whereas group density does not.

An influence of group size and number of observers on embarrassment and stage fright analogous to the results that we found have been uncovered by Latané and Harkins (1976) and Jackson and Latané (Note 1). In role-playing studies on embarrassment, Latané and his colleagues administered measurement scales with known ratio properties and employed a repeated measures design. They found that embarrassment and stage fright increased as a multiplicative

power function of number of observers but decreased as a power function of the number of performers.[1] The embarrassment and stage fright examined by Latané and his colleagues in role-playing paradigms appear to be similar to the self-consciousness studied in the present experiments. However, in the present experiments, measures of self-consciousness were taken after subjects had actually performed the embarrassing tasks, and observer size and group size were varied in reality (not in imagination or in pictures). In addition, the between subjects design of our experiments makes our findings less susceptible than a within-subjects design to a demand characteristic interpretation. Since the methodology of Latané and his colleagues was complementary to ours, increased confidence can be placed in the similar patterns of findings. In one last study, Jackson and Latané found a power function effect based on group size for stage fright in a field situation. In all, then, there is good support for a log-linear relation between group size, as well as audience size, and self-consciousness.

The correlational data for pairs of subjects run together for the behavioral intensity measure yielded an unexpected but interesting finding. In both Experiments 1 and 2, the correlations for the internal self-consciousness measures were uniformly low, whereas the correlations for pairs of participants from the same groups for behavioral intensity were much higher. This difference suggests that social influence can impact on a person's behavior but have little influence on conscious cognitions. It appears that a person might conform behaviorally to the group, whereas his or her level of self-consciousness may remain unaffected by the self-consciousness of other group members. The plasticity of behavior compared to cognition may be partly responsible for the fact that an individual's behavior is often situationally specific, whereas cognitions, as reflected in personality inventories and so forth, are often much more stable (Mischel, 1968). Another interesting finding emerging from the correlations in Experiment 1 was that the behaviors of subjects in the same group were more highly correlated in small groups. Behavioral conformity of different individuals in smaller groups may be due to the greater physical proximity of all persons, the ability to see all other group members, or a greater feeling of group unity. In small groups in which there is physical proximity and visual access to all members, both modeling influences and social conformity pressures are probably enhanced. As the group size grows, the behavior of group members becomes more heterogeneous, which is congruent with observational data on large crowds.

The personality results based on the Fenigstein et al. (1975) Self-Consciousness Scale were also interesting. The personal self-awareness scale, measuring something akin to introspectiveness, usually did not correlate with the dependent variables. Undoubtedly, the type of self-consciousness produced or measured in this study was not similar to an introspective form of self-awareness. Public self-consciousness also did not correlate highly with the dependent variables in Experiments 1 and 2, suggesting that the chronic trait form of self-consciousness measured by the personality scale does not predict the intensity of self-consciousness felt in a highly evaluative situation. However, this conclusion must be tempered by the fact that public self-consciousness did correlate with several of the measures in Experiment 3. Social anxiety was a significant predictor of self-con-

sciousness in all three studies, suggesting that it measures people's propensity to become self-conscious in evaluative or embarrassing situations. The public self-consciousness scale may tap the extent of a person's self-consciousness, whereas the social anxiety scale may measure its intensity, especially in evaluative situations. The findings of the present study indicate that the relationships between trait and state self-awareness and self-consciousness should be explored, as they are affected by various situational factors.

The lack of predictable behavioral differences between conditions in Experiments 1 and 2 raises questions about the theory of deindividuation. Since self-consciousness did vary between conditions, the theory would predict that disinhibited behavior should also vary, which did not occur. Even in Experiment 3, in which behavior varied significantly between the three conditions, the pattern did not seem to have a direct relationship to the variations between conditions in self-consciousness. Although there was a strong relationship between self-consciousness and the behavior of individuals, this effect appeared to be due to individual difference factors and was not clearly related to situationally produced variations in self-consciousness. The lack of behavioral differences between conditions represents a challenge to deindividuation theory that predicts that lowered self-awareness will be accompanied by disinhibited behavior. The behavioral findings also stand in contrast to the findings of Diener (1979) and Prentice-Dunn and Rogers (in press), who found that a deindividuated internal state did lead to disinhibited behavior.

Several arguments may be marshaled to defend deindividuation theory. First, it is unclear which behavior was most disinhibited in the experimental situation. It might be, for example, that intense behavior was normative because it followed the experimenter's directions and that refusal was most disinhibited. Thus, the lack of behavioral differences in the present experiments could be due to the fact that disinhibition could be expressed in unanticipated, diverse ways. However, our inability in the present experiments to tell whether intense behavior, refusal to act, or both were disinhibited suggests that clearer definitions of disinhibition are required of the theory, along with ways to identify and measure the construct. The difficulty in defining disinhibited behavior and the difficulty in telling beforehand which responses were disinhibited limit the importance of the theory in understanding the behavior that it is often invoked to explain. Furthermore, the failure to clearly specify which behaviors are disinhibited makes it difficult to rigorously test or reject the theory. Finally, the within-group correlations in Experiment 1 suggested that subjects in large groups were least influenced by the group, and yet it was subjects in the larger groups who were least self-conscious. This finding is not consistent with Diener's (1980) contention that deindividuated persons are more susceptible to the influence of environmental cues. This discussion suggests that a revised theory of deindividuation must deal with both the definition and measurement of disinhibition, as well as the types of behavioral cues that are likely to emerge in various types of deindividuated groups.

A second possible defense of the deindividuation theory in light of the behavioral findings of our experiments is related to the self-awareness versus self-consciousness distinction. Self-consciousness was measured in the present experiments, not the self-monitoring type of self-awareness on

which the theory of deindividuation seems to be based. However, the work of Buss (1980) and Fenigstein et al. (1975) suggests that private self-awareness and public self-consciousness are distinct in their effects. Nevertheless, although the self-consciousness versus self-awareness distinction can be used to explain the problematical absence of behavioral findings in two of the present experiments, this distinction also points to a limitation of the theory. Even Diener's (1979, 1980) more recent version of deindividuation treated self-awareness as a unitary phenomenon, whereas this does not appear to be the case. A comprehensive theory of deindividuation must come to grips with various types of self-awareness and how they relate to disinhibition. In conclusion, the behavioral intensity findings of the present study do not disprove the theory, since a number of arguments can be made as to why the findings do not contradict the theory. (See Kuhn, 1970, for why such disproof is unlikely.) However, the anomalous behavioral data do point to shortcomings in the theory and suggest the need for revisions.

CONCLUSION

In summary, Diener's (1979) model of deindividuation and the earlier gestalt formulations of deindividuation (Festinger et al., 1952), suggested several group factors that should affect self-consciousness. The self-consciousness findings were largely supportive of the predictions derived from deindividuation theory, with the most supportive data emerging for group size. As group size increased, participants were less self-conscious. An additional finding was that it required more individuals to create the same effect as group size increased. Weaker effects in the predicted direction were also found for number of observers and group dissimilarity, which both led to increased self-consciousness. Group density did not appear to influence self-consciousness. Behavioral intensity did not clearly follow the pattern predicted from deindividuation theory. Two areas of revision or further explication of the theory are therefore suggested: a clearer definition of disinhibition and operational measures of this construct and a description of how awareness to different aspects of the environment, the group, and the self relate to deindividuation. In other studies (Diener, 1979; Prentice-Dunn & Rogers, in press) a relationship between internal deindividuation and disinhibited behavior has been uncovered. The present experiments failed to replicate these earlier behavioral findings. An understanding of these discrepant empirical findings would appear to depend on further theoretical statements that explain under what circumstances disinhibited behavior will follow from internal deindividuation.

NOTE

1. Latané and Nida's (1979) theory of social impact contains a mathematical formulation of social impact that was not given a strong test in the present experiments because the exact scaling properties of our scales are not known with certainty. However, since the effects of group size were often log linear, it seems probable that subjects responded to our scales as though they were ratio in nature.

REFERENCE NOTE

1. Jackson, J. M., & Latané, B. *All alone in front of all those people: Stage fright as a function of number and type of coperformers and audience.* Unpublished manuscript, Ohio State University, 1979.

REFERENCES

Beaman, A. L., Klentz, B., Diener, E., & Svanum, S. Objective self-awareness and transgression in children: A field study. *Journal of Personality and Social Psychology,* 1979, *37,* 1835-1846.

Buss, A. H. *Self-consciousness and social anxiety.* San Francisco: Freeman, 1980.

Diener, E. Deindividuation, self-awareness, and disinhibition. *Journal of Personality and Social Psychology,* 1979, *37,* 1160-1171.

Diener, E. Deindividuation: The absence of self-awareness and self-regulation in group members. In P. Paulus (Ed.), *The psychology of group influence.* Hillsdale, N.J.: Erlbaum, 1980.

Diener, E., & Crandall, R. *Ethics in social and behavioral research.* Chicago: University of Chicago Press, 1978.

Diener, E., & Wallbom, M. Effects of self-awareness on antinormative behavior. *Journal of Research in Personality,* 1976, *10,* 107-111.

Duval, S., & Wicklund, R. A. *A theory of objective self-awareness.* New York: Academic Press, 1972.

Fenigstein, A., Scheier, M. F., & Buss, A. H. Public and private self-consciousness: Assessment and theory. *Journal of Consulting and Clinical Psychology,* 1975, *43,* 522-527.

Festinger, L., Pepitone, A., & Newcomb, T. Some consequences of deindividuation in a group. *Journal of Abnormal and Social Psychology,* 1952, *47,* 382-389.

Ickes, W., Layden, M. A., & Barnes, R. D. Objective self-awareness and individuation: An empirical link. *Journal of Personality,* 1978, *46,* 146-161.

Kuhn, T. S. *The structure of scientific revolutions.* Chicago: University of Chicago Press, 1970.

Latané, B., & Harkins, S. Cross-modality matches suggest anticipated stage fright as a multiplicative power function of audience size and status. *Perception & Psychophysics,* 1976, *20,* 482-488.

Latané, B., & Nida, S. Social impact theory and group influence: A social engineering perspective. In P. Paulus (Ed.), *The psychology of group influence.* Hillsdale, N. J.: Erlbaum, 1979.

McNemar, Q. *Psychological statistics*, New York: Wiley, 1969.

Mischel, W. *Personality and assessment*. New York: Wiley, 1968.

Prentice-Dunn, S., & Rogers, R. W. Effects of deindividuating situational cues and aggressive models on subjective deindividuation and aggression. *Journal of Personality and Social Psychology*, in press.

Rule, B. G., Nesdale, A. R., & Dyck, R. Objective self-awareness and differing standards

of aggression. *Representative Research in Social Psychology*, 1975, *6*, 82-88.

Taylor, S. E., & Fiske, S. T. Salience, attention, and attribution: Top of the head phenomena. In L. Berkowitz (Ed.), *Advances in experimental social psychology*. New York: Academic Press, 1978

Wicklund, R. A. Objective self-awareness. In L. Berkowitz (Ed.), *Advances in experimental social psychology* (Vol. 8). New York: Academic Press, 1975.

Group Productivity and Process: Pure and Mixed Reward Structures and Task Interdependence

Milton E. Rosenbaum, Danny L. Moore, John L. Cotton,
Michael S. Cook, Rex A. Hieser, M. Nicki Shovar,
and Morris J. Gray

Two experiments were conducted in which triads participated in multitrial block-stacking tasks that allowed for objective measures of productivity and process. In Experiment 1, the task was executed either interdependently in the form of a single tower or individualistically in the construction of three separate towers. Reward points were distributed equally (cooperative), in relation to contribution (independent), or only to the most productive group member (competitive). Results indicated that cooperative and independent systems were associated with greater productivity than competitive systems only under conditions of high task interdependence, but there was no relation between reward system and productivity for the individualistic task. Competitive systems also impaired facilitative process events (e.g., turn taking) and led to less efficient, poorer quality products than cooperative systems. In Experiment 2, independent and competitive allocations were each combined in varied proportions with cooperative allocations to examine the effects of mixed reward systems on productivity and process. The results of this second study showed that even a modicum of competitive reward led to lowered efficiency and productivity.

Three decades ago, Deutsch (1949a) outlined a theory of cooperation and competition that emphasized the group processes emerging from cooperative and competitive reward structures. The main prediction of

From *Journal of Personality and Social Psychology*, 1980, *39*, pp. 626-642. Copyright 1980 by the American Psychological Assn., Inc.

Deutsch's theory is that cooperative reward structures yield greater group productivity than competitive structures. Although this prediction is not unique to Deutsch's theory, the implication of process variables in the effects of reward structure on group productivity was a milestone in the cooperation and competition literature. Despite a surge of research (see Rosenbaum, 1980; Steiner,

1972) aimed at elucidating the effects of reward structures on group productivity, there has been little progress in providing adequate tests of Deutsch's contentions concerning group process events.

In his original article, Deutsch noted that studies of cooperative and competitive reward structures prior to 1949 ignored the interactions between individuals. These early studies were largely concerned with the effects of cooperation and competition on an individual's motivation to achieve. Deutsch proceeded to fill the void created by this early research with a number of hypotheses concerning the effects of cooperation and competition on small (face-to-face) group functioning. Cooperative reward structures allow for substitutability of action, mutual reward, and positive cathexis of others and their actions. That is, an action by one individual not only facilitates the attainment of reward by the actor, but promotes reward attainment for other group members as well. As a consequence, Deutsch hypothesized that cooperative structures should facilitate role differentiation, coordination, and helpfulness, which in turn should result in greater, more efficient productivity than possible with competitive structures. Competition, in contrast, pits individuals against one another in attempting to gain a scarce reward. Thus competitive structures do not involve mutual reward because goal attainment by one individual precludes goal attainment by others. In such situations, actions are not substitutable, role differentiation is unlikely, individuals may obstruct one another's efforts, and consequently, group productivity can be expected to suffer.

Although Deutsch outlined process events related to "purely" cooperative and competitive structures, he acknowledged that most real-life situations have mixed motives. For example, members of a basketball team may be cooperatively interdependent with respect to winning a game, but simultaneously competitively interdependent with respect to being a star on the team. In the present article, we present two studies that examine group process events emerging from cooperative and competitive reward structures as well as the effects of mixed reward structures on group process and productivity.

Much subsequent research was engendered by Deutsch's (1949a) formulation that gave primary attention to the effect of cooperative and competitive reward structures on productivity. This research produced conflicting findings with respect to Deutsch's contention that cooperative reward structures result in greater productivity than competitive structures; several studies reported greater productivity with competitive reward structures (Scott & Cherrington, 1974; Weinstein & Holzback, 1972), whereas others found greater productivity with cooperative reward structures.

A number of contributors (Raven & Eachus, 1963; Thomas, 1957) noted that these conflicting findings may have arisen because Deutsch considered goal interdependence but not task interdependence in his formulation. Thus reward structures may have different effects on tasks that require concerted efforts among group members to attain a group product compared with tasks that simply require the summation of independent, individual efforts for attainment of a group product.

Miller and Hamblin (1963) conducted an experiment in which they included a high and a low task interdependence condition as well as three variations in reward structure. In a cooperative condition, members of triads shared equally in group rewards on each of 10 trials. In an extreme competitive condition, on each trial the most successful member received two thirds of the group reward, the next most successful member received one third, and the least successful member received nothing. In an intermediate competitive condition, the most successful member received half of the reward, the next most successful member received one third, and the least successful member received one sixth. Miller and Hamblin found an inverse relation between group productivity and differential rewarding under high task interdependence: Cooperative reward structures resulted in highest productivity, and productivity was lowest in the extreme competitive condition. No relation between productivity and differential rewarding appeared for low interdependence conditions, although Miller and Hamblin predicted a positive relation between productivity and rewarding in the low interdependence conditions. However, subsequent studies (Scott & Cherrington, 1974; Weinstein & Holzbach, 1972) have shown greater productivity under competition than cooperation when task interdependence was low.

Following the precedent set by Deutsch (1949a), Miller and Hamblin (1963) emphasized the group process events likely to result from various combinations of reward structures and task structures. Low interdependent tasks present group participants with few strategic choices for reward attainment. The only available choice for competitors is to work hard and exceed the output of others. Thus competitive reward structures can be expected to facilitate productivity on low interdependent tasks by increasing the individual participants' motivation. Cooperators may exhibit elevated motivation to maintain equity or to compete with another group (an issue fully discussed by Steiner, 1972, but not to be developed

in the present context), but motivational factors play a secondary role in the analysis of cooperative reward structures. Despite the strategic relevance of motivation for competitors in low interdependent tasks, Miller and Hamblin concluded on the basis of their own results and a careful review of the literature that the influence of higher motivation by competitors was a weak effect at best.

Unfortunately, few data have been obtained concerning group processes in the study of cooperation and competition. Many studies contain postexperimental self-report data, some of which are retrospective ratings of process events, obtained from the subjects. Only occasionally have studies included data obtained by observers concerning group process, but in the few instances in which interjudge reliabilities have been reported (Deutsch, 1949b; Hammond & Goldman, 1961) correlation coefficients have been uncomfortably low (average $r = .50$). Miller and Hamblin (1963) provided graphic representations of productivity by groups over trials, and from productivity fluctuations they inferred more hindering of members' efforts by competitive groups under high task interdependence than by cooperative groups.

French, Brownell, Graziano, and Hartup (1977) reported a study of the effect of reward structures on group productivity. They utilized a task that permits objective measures of group process. Until this time, reports of objective quantitative measures of ongoing group process that test the various theoretical contentions of Deutsch and Miller and Hamblin had been absent from the literature. In their basic procedure triads of children erected a single tower of small wooden blocks over six 15-sec trials. Three reward conditions were employed. In the cooperative condition, the number of blocks in a tower standing at the end of a trial were counted, and each child received tokens equal to one third of the total. The tokens were redeemable at a later point for toys. In an independent condition, each child received tokens following each trial based on the number of blocks the child had contributed to a tower standing at the end of a trial. In a competitive condition, the child that had contributed the greatest number of blocks received tokens equal to that contribution and others received nothing. In the event of a tie, no reward was distributed. Color coding of blocks allowed an accurate count of each child's contribution.

If the independent condition may be regarded as an intermediate reward condition, the productivity results obtained by French et al. (1977) supported Miller and Hamblin's (1963) finding that productivity is inversely related to differential rewarding in the highly interdependent block-stacking task. In addition, falls of the towers over trials were more frequent in the competitive and individualistic conditions than in the cooperative condition. Falls may be indicative of heightened arousal or possibly direct interference effects. The authors noted some tendency for role differentiation in cooperative triads when one member on occasion stopped adding blocks to the tower and either held the shaky tower or straightened it while the other two members continued to add blocks. A discrepancy measure, the difference between contributions of largest and smallest producer during a trial, was employed to reflect this type of role differentiation, but significant differences were not found in this portion of the research. In another aspect of the work of French et al. (1977), the discrepancy measure proved fruitful.

It can be seen that the block-stacking task shows promise of illumination of process events as well as being an objective test of group productivity hypotheses. The task has a variety of meritorious qualities. The units of work (block handling) are identical for all group members and are well within the competence of all participants. Relative contributions are immediately quantifiable and readily apparent to both subjects and the experimenter during and at the end of a trial. The requirement of contribution to a single tower imposes the necessity for direct interaction. Positive as well as negative contributions to the task can be made. On the positive side, these may include role differentiation (as when members hold or straighten the tower) or coordination (as when blocks are added by members in a systematic rotational manner). Negative events are primarily those producing tower falls that may result from careless placements, highly aroused movements, or deliberate sabotage. Finally, the task is readily adaptable for low interdependence treatment by having each member build his or her own individual tower.

In Experiment 1, cooperative, independent, and competitive reward structures were manipulated along with task interdependence. The block-stacking task was presented to adult triads under instructions to build either a single tower (high task interdependence) or individual towers (low task interdependence). Productivity, measured by the number of blocks in the towers, was expected to be greatest in cooperative groups and lowest in competitive groups under high task interdependence. Following Miller and Hamblin's (1963) original contentions and subsequent findings by others (Scott & Cherrington, 1974; Weinstein & Holzbach, 1972), we expected competitive groups to be most productive under low task interdependence, and cooperative groups to be least productive in this condition. Productivity for independent groups was expected to be between the cooperative and competitive groups in both high and low task interdependence.

Several process events were also monitored. These included the number of tower falls, turn taking, efficiency of work, and differential input by individual group members. In general, the cooperative reward structure was expected to produce a variety of facilitative process events such as turn taking, efficient work, role differentiation (i.e., reflected in the discrepancy between the most productive and least productive individuals' contributions), and low number of falls. Competitive and independent reward structures, in contrast, were expected to exhibit few of these facilitative process events and perhaps, in the case of the competitive structure, to show evidence of direct interference. A final set of measures was obtained from a questionnaire, previously used by Scott and Cherrington (1974), designed to assess self-report of task attractiveness, arousal, interpersonal attraction, and the affective tone of the group interaction.

EXPERIMENT 1

METHOD

Subjects

The subjects were introductory psychology students who participated as part of a course requirement. Four subjects of the same sex were recruited for each session; if all appeared, one of them was randomly assigned to be an observer. Although it was planned to have six groups participate in each cell of the $2 \times 3 \times 2$ design comprised of two levels of interdependence (high and low), three levels of reward structure (cooperative, independent, and competitive), and the two sexes, only five triads were obtained in two of the cells. These instances were the male, cooperative, single-tower condition and the male, independent, individual-tower condition. Therefore data were collected from 102 male and 108 female subjects. Six graduate students served as experimenters, and except for the failure of one experimenter to obtain two triads as noted above, all experimenters completed one full replication of the entire design.

Task

The tower-building task originated by Goldberg and Maccoby (1965) for use with children and recently adapted by French et al. (1977) was used. The subjects either worked together to build a single tower of blocks (single tower conditions), or each subject constructed his or her own tower (individual tower conditions). Each subject was given twenty 8.9-cm wooden blocks, which were painted with a different striped pattern for each subject. The blocks for each subject were arranged on the floor within squares (63.5 cm on a side) of red, yellow, or blue tape. The three squares projected from the sides of an equilateral triangle (63.5 cm on a side) of white tape that had a small white square (12.7 cm on a side) located in the center. There were also small solid red, yellow, and blue squares located adjacent to the three colored block squares. The central small square was the site of the tower in the single tower conditions, and the small colored squares were the sites of the three towers in the individual tower conditions. The task was conducted in a large room (8.3 m × 7.4 m), with videotape equipment placed approximately 4.3 m from the site of tower building.

Procedure

The subjects were told that their basic task was to obtain points for themselves. They were told to use one hand when adding blocks to a tower. The points were awarded on the basis of the number of blocks in the tower (in the single tower conditions) or the three towers (in the individual tower conditions), with each block in the tower(s) being worth 1 point. The points were distributed in one of three different ways:

Cooperative conditions. The experimenter told subjects in these conditions that each of them would receive points equal to one third of the total number of blocks in the tower(s). For example, if subjects in the single tower condition constructed a 15-block tower, each subject would receive 5 points regardless of how many blocks each subject had contributed to the tower. If subjects in the individual tower conditions constructed three towers totaling 21 blocks, each subject would receive 7 points, regardless of how many blocks were in each subject's own tower. Points were awarded by giving the subjects play money and poker chips, with each point worth $1 and the poker chips denoting fractions of a dollar.

Independent conditions. The experimenter told these subjects that each of them would receive 1 point for each block they contributed to the tower (single tower conditions) or for each block in their own tower (individual tower conditions). Therefore, in the single tower condition, if a 15-block tower was constructed with 7 blocks from one subject, 5 blocks from another, and 3 blocks from the third, the first subject would receive 7 points, the second subject would receive 5 points, and the third subject 3 points. In the individual tower conditions, if the three towers were constructed of 14, 12, and 11 blocks, the subjects would receive 14, 12, and 11 points, respectively.

Competitive conditions. The experimenter told the subjects in these conditions that the member of the triad who contributed the most blocks to the tower (single tower conditions) or constructed the tallest tower (individual tower conditions) would receive points equal in number to that subject's contribution. The other two subjects would receive nothing. If there was a tie for the most blocks contributed, or for the tallest individual tower, no points would be awarded. Therefore in the single tower condition, if a 15-block tower was constructed with 7 blocks from one subject, 5 blocks from another, and 3 blocks from the third, the first subject would receive 7 points and the other two subjects would receive nothing. In the individual tower condition, if three towers were constructed of 14, 12, and 11 blocks, the subject who built the 14-block tower would receive 14 points and the other subjects would receive nothing.[1]

In all conditions, the task consisted of 10 trials. For each trial, the subjects had 15 sec for tower building. At the end of the 15 sec, the experimenter counted the blocks in the tower(s) or portions of towers that remained standing and distributed points according to one of the three procedures described above. If a tower fell during the 15-sec building period, subjects were allowed to rebuild until time was called. After time was called, subjects were not allowed to add blocks to the tower, and if part of a tower fell before the experimenter finished counting the blocks, only blocks remaining standing were counted. After each trial, payment was distributed and collected in bowls provided to each member. After the 10th trial, the subjects counted their points and filled out the self-report measures.

During the task, the experimenter recorded the number of times the tower(s) fell and at the completion of each trial recorded the contribution of each member to the final tower(s). Payment was distributed based on these records. Reliability of recording was without question. Subjects participated actively and challenged, usually without foundation, incorrect recording.

Dependent Measures

Five measures of group performance were obtained. In each case, the triad was the unit of analysis, not the individual.

Blocks. For each triad, the number of blocks in each tower standing at the end of each trial was summed across trials.

Falls. For each triad, the number of times towers collapsed was summed across trials.

Discrepancy. For each triad, at the end of each trial, the contribution of the member with the least number of blocks was subtracted from the contribution of the member with most blocks and summed across trials.

Turn taking. Each tower in the single tower condition standing at the end of a trial was divided into groups of three blocks counting from the bottom. The percentage of occasions in which the blocks of each member of the triad appeared in each group of blocks was counted across trials.

Total blocks handled. Using the videotapes, each block contributed by a member was counted, including those in a tower that fell,

and summed across trials. The ratio of blocks to total blocks handled was treated as a measure of efficiency.

Four self-report measures were obtained from each subject on the basis of responses to a semantic differential instrument that was adapted from the questionnaire employed by Scott and Cherrington (1974) and described by them in detail. Sets of bipolar adjectives comprising scales were presented for three concepts, "How I felt while doing the task," "How I felt about the task," and "How I felt about my fellow workers." Responses were scored 1-7 for each scale, with 7 representing the extreme of each self-report measure, and then summed across the number of scales associated with the measure. The measures were (a) general affective tone (4 scales), (b) general arousal (3 scales), and (c) task attractiveness and interpersonal attractiveness (5 scales each).

RESULTS

The results for the performance measures were analyzed by considering the single tower and individual tower conditions separately. As Table 1 shows, these two conditions produced very different patterns of performance. In the analyses of the self-report measures (Table 2), however, the scales of measurement were similar, and hence the single tower and individual tower conditions were evaluated together.

For each dependent measure, 3 (Reward Structure) × 2 (Sex) unweighted-means analyses of variance (Winer, 1971) were conducted. In those cases in which significant results are reported, Newman-Keuls tests were used to examine simple effects. Effects associated with sex will be presented only in the few instances in which significant results were obtained.

Blocks

In the single tower condition, a significant main effect was found for reward structure, $F(2, 29) = 5.37$, $p < .05$. Tests for simple effects showed that both the cooperative ($p < .01$) and the independent ($p < .05$) conditions produced towers in which the mean number of blocks was greater than in the competitive condition, but the cooperative and independent conditions did not differ from each other. No significant effects were found in the individual tower condition.

Falls

A significant main effect, $F(2, 29) = 3.75$, $p < .05$, for reward structure in the single tower condition was based on significantly more mean falls of towers in the competitive condition than in the cooperative condition ($p < .05$) and somewhat more mean falls in the competitive than in

TABLE 1

Means for Group Performance Measures in Experiment 1 by Reward Structure in the Single and Individual Tower Conditions

Reward structure	Dependent variable					
	Blocks	Falls	Discrepancy	Turn Taking	Total blocks handled	Efficiency
	Single tower					
Cooperative (n = 11)	87.00$_a$	5.00$_a$	10.27$_a$	.730$_a$	158.27$_a$	.55$_a$
Independent (n = 12)	79.33$_a$	6.92$_a$	9.58$_a$	.745$_a$	171.67$_a$	.46$_a$
Competitive (n = 12)	60.00$_b$	13.75$_b$	11.17$_a$	.703$_a$	188.42$_a$	.32$_b$
F(2, 29)	5.37, p<.02	3.75, p<.05	<1.00	<1.00	2.70, p<.08	5.13, p<.02
	Individual towers					
Promotive (n = 12)	299.25$_a$	2.25$_a$	30.33$_a$	—	319.92$_a$	.94$_a$
Independent (n = 11)	303.82$_a$	1.64$_a$	25.36$_a$	—	319.92$_a$	.95$_a$
Competitive (n = 12)	281.08$_a$	3.92$_b$	46.42$_b$	—	323.17$_a$	.87$_a$
F(2, 29)	<1.00	5.04, p<.02	6.50, p<.01	—	<1.00	<1.00

Note: Means in each group of three means that share a common subscript are not significantly different by Newman-Keuls, $p<.05$.

the independent condition ($p < .10$). The independent and cooperative conditions did not differ significantly. In the individual tower condition, there was also a main effect for reward structure, $F(2, 29) = 5.04$, $p < .05$, again based on significantly more falls in the competitive condition than in the cooperative ($p < .05$) and the independent ($p < .02$) conditions. The cooperative and independent conditions did not differ from each other in mean number of falls.

Discrepancy

In the single tower condition, no significant differences in mean discrepancy (difference between largest and smallest contributor's number of blocks) were found. In the individual tower condition, a significant main effect for reward structure appeared, $F(2, 29) = 6.50, p < .01$. Subsequent analysis indicated that mean discrepancy was significantly greater in the competitive condition than in the cooperative ($p < .05$) and the independent ($p < .05$) conditions, which did not differ from each other.

Turn Taking

This measure was appropriate only for the single tower condition, and analysis of the data revealed no significant effects.

Total Blocks Handled

In the single tower condition, the pattern of means of total blocks handled was the reverse of those for total blocks remaining in towers at the end of each trial. That is, competitive groups handled more blocks than the independent groups, which in turn handled more than the cooperative groups. However, the analysis indicated that the dif-

ferences fell short of a significant level, $F(2, 29) = 2.70, p < .08$. No differences approached significance for the individual tower condition.

Efficiency

Efficiency of task performance was determined by dividing the number of blocks in a tower by the total number of blocks handled. For the single tower conditions a significant effect for reward structure appeared in the analysis, $F(2, 29) = 5.13, p < .02$. Follow-up analyses on the reward structure effect indicated that efficiency was significantly greater in the cooperative and independent conditions compared to the competitive condition ($p < .05$). Analysis of the efficiency measure in the individual tower conditions revealed no significant effects.

Self-Report Measures

The means for each self-report measure are presented in Table 2 in terms of reward structure condition, sex, and tower condition. The analysis of general affective tone showed a significant main effect for reward structure, $F(2, 198) = 6.18, p < .01$. Comparisons between reward structure conditions indicated that the cooperative and independent groups reported higher (more positive) affect than competitive groups did ($p < .01$); the cooperative and independent groups did not differ significantly in self-report of general affect.

The analysis of the general arousal measure indicated a significant main effect for interdependence, $F(1, 198) = 4.79, p < .03$, and a Reward Structure × Sex interaction, $F(2, 198) = 3.95, p < .03$. Inspection of Table 2 indicates that subjects in the individual tower conditions reported

TABLE 2

Means for Self-Report Measures in Experiment 1 by Reward Structure and Sex in the Single and Individual Tower Conditions

	Dependent variable											
	General affective tone			General arousal			Task attractiveness			Interpersonal attractiveness		
Reward structure	M	F	Combined	M	F	Combined	M	F	Combined	M	F	Combined
Single tower												
Cooperative (*n* = 33)[a]	20.00	19.50	19.72	12.67	11.72	12.15	22.67	22.00	22.12	27.80	28.44	28.15
Independent (*n* = 36)	17.33	20.28	18.81	12.33	13.39	12.86	21.28	23.11	22.19	20.94	26.00	23.64
Competitive (*n* = 36)	15.78	17.39	16.58	12.39	12.00	12.19	21.67	20.78	21.22	21.94	24.89	23.42
Individual towers												
Cooperative (*n* = 36)	18.94	19.78	19.36	13.33	11.22	12.78	22.67	22.33	22.50	23.83	26.00	24.92
Independent (*n* = 33)[b]	19.00	19.39	19.21	13.27	14.94	14.18	22.53	22.06	22.27	24.33	24.39	24.36
Competitive (*n* = 36)	19.39	18.00	18.69	14.61	13.00	13.80	22.33	22.11	22.22	21.33	25.22	23.28

Note: M = male; F = female.
[a] There were 15 males and 18 females in the cooperative condition for the single tower task.
[b] Fifteen males and 18 females participated in the independent condition for the individual tower task.

higher levels of arousal than those in the single tower conditions ($M = 13.40$ vs. $M = 12.42$). The Reward Structure × Sex interaction reflected a tendency for females to report lower arousal than males in cooperative and competitive conditions, but females in the independent condition reported higher arousal than males.

There were no significant effects uncovered in the analysis of the task attractiveness measure.

The analysis of the interpersonal attraction measure revealed significant main effects for reward structure, $F(2, 198) = 9.90$, $p < .001$, and sex, $F(1, 198) = 15.69$, $p < .001$. In general, females reported greater interpersonal attraction ($M = 25.81$) than males did ($M = 23.29$). The reward structure effect resulted from greater interpersonal attraction in the cooperative conditions than in either the independent or competitive conditions ($p < .01$). However, this effect was qualified by a Reward Structure × Interdependence interaction, $F(2, 198) = 3.92, p < .02$. Simple main effects tests for this interaction indicated a significant reward structure effect in the single tower conditions ($p < .001$), whereas reward structure had little effect on interpersonal attraction in the individual tower conditions. As can be seen in Table 2, cooperative reward structures were associated with greater interpersonal attraction than independent and competitive reward structures in the single tower conditions, but not in the individual tower conditions.

EXPERIMENT 2a

A portion of Experiment 2 was a replication, with only minor changes, of the single tower conditions of Experiment 1. The entire design was considerably more elaborate and will be described in detail in Experiment 2. In the interest of clarity of presentation, the results of the replication will be considered along with those of Experiment 1. Only departures in method will be described. All other features of the procedure were the same as those for the single tower conditions in Experiment 1.

METHOD

Subjects

In the 3 (Reward Structure) × 2 (Sex) design, 12 triads of each sex participated in the cooperative condition, and 6 triads of each sex participated in the independent and competitive conditions—producing a total of 72 male and 72 female subjects drawn from an introductory psychology course.

Task

The blocks were painted yellow, blue, and red. Fifteen blocks of each color were placed within corresponding colored tape squares (55.9 cm on a side). The experiment was conducted in two small rooms (3.8 m × 3.6 m) and was not videotaped (this prevented obtaining data on total blocks handled). The self-report measures (presented after the block-stacking task) consisted of the three concepts, "me at this task," "my task," and "my fellow workers."

RESULTS

Blocks

A main effect was found for reward structure, $F(2, 42) = 12.44$, $p < .01$, as well as a Reward Structure × Sex interaction, $F(2, 42) = 3.85$, $p < .05$. Tests for simple effects showed that all reward conditions differed from each other ($p <$ .05) with the greatest productivity associated with the cooperative condition and the least with the competitive condition (see Table 3). The Reward Contingency × Sex interaction was based on a significant difference for males between the competitive condition and both the cooperative and independent conditions, whereas for females the competitive and independent conditions were not different from each other, but both differed from the cooperative condition.

Falls

A significant main effect for reward structure, $F(2, 42) = 11.07, p < .001$, was based on a greater mean number of falls in the competitive condition than in both the cooperative and independent conditions ($p < .05$), which did not differ from each other.

Turn Taking

A significant main effect for reward structure was found, $F(2, 42) = 8.60, p < .001$. Analysis of simple effects indicated that the cooperative condition resulted in a significantly greater amount of turn taking than did the independent or competitive conditions ($p < .05$), which did not differ from each other.

Discrepancy

The analysis of discrepancy scores revealed no significant effects.

Self-Report Measures

Only the main effect for reward structure for the interpersonal attraction measure was significant, $F(2, 138) = 9.77, p < .01$. This was based on significantly greater attraction in the cooperative condition ($M =$

TABLE 3

Means for Group Performance Measures in Experiment 2a

Reward structure	Blocks	Falls	Discrepancy	Turn taking
Cooperative				
Males	103.75	4.25	7.33	.81
Females	117.33	3.75	11.50	.83
Overall	110.54	4.00	9.42	.82
Independent				
Males	103.33	6.50	10.83	.45
Females	77.17	7.33	9.33	.59
Overall	90.25	6.92	10.08	.52
Competitive				
Males	57.17	13.50	11.17	.40
Females	80.88	10.33	11.00	.69
Overall	69.00	11.92	11.08	.55

27.17) than in the independent (M = 24.19) or in the competitive conditions (M = 23.22), which did not differ from each other.

DISCUSSION

The results of Experiments 1 and 2a generally support Miller and Hamblin's (1963) findings and analysis of the relationship between reward structure and task interdependence. Under high task interdependence an inverse relation between differential rewarding and productivity was obtained, whereas no relation between these variables appeared under low task interdependence. Findings that illuminate some of the group process events responsible for the results are perhaps the most significant.

First, let us turn to the evidence concerning interference with group productivity demonstrated in the competitive conditions. In executing the single tower task in Experiment 1, competitors were clearly more inefficient. Only one third of the effort expended was translated into acceptable standing towers at the end of trials, although triads in this condition handled more blocks. In contrast, close to one half of the work of cooperative and independent triads resulted in rewarded towers. The major contributor to the difference in inefficiency would seem to be the significantly greater number of falls that occurred under the competitive reward structure that appeared in both Experiments 1 and 2a.

Why did falls occur? High arousal may produce activity that is not constructive in a task that requires at least some degree of care and precision. An example of this activity would be rapidly adding a block to an already unstable tower, possibly resulting in a fall. Although poor placement is a likely product of haste, it may also be a strategic choice. In the competitive condi-

tion it is better to add one block that produces a fall than not to add at all, particularly if the contributor is behind. There is also the choice of deliberate sabotage. This tactic was difficult to document, even with careful review of videotapes. Observer agreement on what was a judgment of intent was not possible. An anecdote that documents the possibility of deliberate sabotage can be drawn from the low interdependence condition.

During one of the first occasions on which the competitive-individual towers condition was conducted, a male subject, at the conclusion of the instructions, asked how much time was allowed per trial. The experimenter responded that the time allowed was 15 sec. The triad proceeded to build their individual towers, and the inquiring subject repeatedly consulted his wristwatch as he added blocks. At approximately 14 sec into the first trial, he rapidly flicked his hand at the base of each of the towers of his co-workers, producing a collapse of their towers and a reward for himself. He continued the same behavior over the 10 trials. Although there was much defensive maneuvering by the others, only an occasional assault was made on the tower of the instigating subject. The data provided by this triad were discarded because it was the only occasion on which the time limit of a trial was specified to subjects. The anecdote does produce an explicit example of the type of sabotaging strategy that may have been implicit in many of the falls in the competitive condition.

Facilitation of group process was shown in Experiment 2a by the cooperative triads in the considerably greater tendency to take rotating turns in placing blocks. This technique of coordinated responding was highly efficient in that triad members were at any moment executing different components of the necessary motions for tower construction. The failure for coordination to occur in a similar manner in competitive groups is quite understandable. It is potentially beneficial for a competitor to move as rapidly as possible and to ignore the contributions of others. It is not clear why turn-taking differences were manifested in Experiment 2a and not in Experiment 1, in which turn taking was plentiful in all high interdependence conditions.

Although it was expected that the discrepancy measure would be related to other aspects of facilitation in cooperative triads, no differences among conditions were obtained. French et al. (1977) had noted that in cooperative groups a child would sometimes cease adding blocks to stabilize or straighten a tower while others continued to contribute blocks. No instances of these activities were noted in the present experiments, which may have been due to misinterpretation of a portion of the instructions. The subjects were told to use only one hand in adding blocks to the tower. This instruction was inserted because in pretest it was found that some adults would assemble a horizontal train of blocks and then, grasping the ends with both hands, turn the train into a vertical tower. Most subjects responded to the instruction by obviously removing one hand from action.

Miller and Hamblin's (1963) original analysis suggested that under low interdependence, differential rewarding and productivity would be positively related. It should be noted, however, that Miller and Hamblin failed to confirm this contention in their own research and subsequently viewed the hypothesis as tentative at best. The present research also failed to show a positive relation between productivity and differential rewarding under low task interdependence. In contrast, several reports of such a positive relation appear in the literature (Scott & Cherrington, 1974; Shaw,

1958; Weinstein & Holzbach, 1972). Thus it is unclear whether differential rewarding facilitates productivity under low interdependence or has no effect on productivity.

Perhaps the major difference between studies that show a positive relation between differential rewarding and productivity under low interdependence and studies that show no relation lies in the nature of the task. If we assume, as Shaw (1958) and others do, that competition increases arousal and leads to the adoption of a speeded response set, then the effects of competition on productivity will depend on the nature of the task. For example, certain tasks may show both facilitated productivity and more errors under competitive reward structures. However, if productivity measures are not independent of errors, then the final measure of productivity may show no differences between reward structures. In the block-stacking task, task errors and productivity are intimately related; poor construction results in falls and consequent low productivity. Thus subjects who hastily built towers increased their efforts but produced no more than those who constructed towers in a slow and deliberate manner. In short, this analysis suggests that productivity under low interdependence depends on the trade-off between speed and accuracy. Competitive structures may indeed lead to greater productivity under low interdependence than cooperative structures do, but certainly such facilitation must be corrected for by the decreased quality of the product. The present data do show significantly more falls in the competitive condition than in other conditions.

EXPERIMENT 2

Research on the effect of reward structures on group productivity and process has concentrated attention on pure allocation systems. As Deutsch (1949a) noted, most real-life situations involve complex conditions that mix motivational goals and subgoals. For theoretical development, Deutsch felt that it was preferable to confine attention to pure cases, but that "in many circumstances not much theoretical extrapolation is necessary to handle the more complex situations" (p. 133). In laboratory research thus far there has been no effort to make the extrapolation. Experiment 2 was designed to address the issue of mixed reward structures.

Mixed reward structures are employed quite deliberately in work situations. Controllers of pay create varied incentive plans to motivate job performance either as a direct function of reward-related arousal or by means of improved morale. Many of the plans can be seen as mixing cooperative disbursement with independent or competitive features. For example Lawler (1971), in a major contribution to the analysis of pay in work settings, describes what he calls a "widely applicable model for an incentive plan" as follows:

Each person's pay would be divided into three components. One part would be for the job the employee is doing, and everyone who holds a similar job would get the same amount. A second part of the pay package would be determined by seniority and cost-of-living factors; everyone in the company would get this and the amount would be automatically adjusted each year. The third part of the package, however, would not be automatic; it would be individualized so that the amount paid would be based upon each person's performance during the immediately preceding period. The poor performer in the organization should find that this part of his or her pay package is minimal, while the good performer should find that this part of his or her pay is at least as great as the other two parts combined. (p. 167)

The first and second components may be viewed as approximating a cooperative pay structure, whereas the third component adds an independent pay feature. Competitive features may also be added to what is essentially a cooperative structure by giving prizes to the highest producers (e.g., a trip to Hawaii for two, a very special bonus). Some complex incentive plans, such as the Scanlon plan and the Lincoln Electric plan, have achieved considerable fame following claims of remarkable effectiveness. However, the presence of many confounding variables associated with company organization makes it difficult to evaluate these claims (Lawler, 1971).

As Duetsch (1949a) suggested, theoretical extrapolation to mixed conditions from information derived from research on pure conditions would seem possible. Experiments 1 and 2a showed that when the task demands high interdependence, cooperative reward structures lead to facilitation of productivity, whereas competition is detrimental. When reward structures are combined, one can anticipate that, depending on the weighting of cooperative and competitive orientation, at some point the deleterious effects of competition will interfere with the promotive aspects of cooperation. If such factors as arousal and sabotage are stimulated by competition, then facilitative activities like turn taking and role differentiation are less likely to occur. Although a prediction may be made that some combination of cooperative and competitive allocations will be deleterious to productivity, no guidance from previous research is available to indicate the degree of effect of various proportionate combinations. Accordingly, it would seem valuable to employ several different combinations of proportions of cooperative and competitive reward in an experiment in which combined reward structures are manipulated.

TABLE 4

Means for Group Performance Measures and Interpersonal Attraction for Various Proportions of Cooperative and Competitive Rewards in Experiment 2

Dependent variable	Cooperative-competitive reward proportion				
	$1.00 - 0$	$.80 - .20$	$.50 - .50$	$.20 - .80$	$0 - 1.00$
Blocks	110.54$_a$	84.50$_b$	88.04$_b$	75.58$_b$	69.00$_b$
Falls	4.00$_a$	9.83$_b$	6.33$_{a,b}$	11.58$_b$	11.92$_b$
Turn taking	.82$_a$	.71$_{a,b}$	.72$_{a,b}$	.68$_{a,b}$	.54$_b$
Interpersonal attraction	27.17$_a$	26.08$_a$	22.36$_b$	24.47$_b$	23.22$_b$

Note: Means for each dependent variable that do not share common subscripts are significantly different at $p < .05$.

In a similar vein, combinations of cooperative and independent reward structures may be considered, but the results of Experiments 1 and 2a provide an unclear basis for extrapolation. In Experiment 2a, evidence was obtained indicating less productivity in the high interdependence condition under independent reward than under cooperative reward, but this finding was not supported by a difference in frequency of falls. In Experiment 1, differences between cooperative and independent reward did not appear. It is possible that combinations of independent and cooperative allocations are deleterious to productivity. However, Lawler's (1971) evaluation of incentive plans suggests that the cooperative-independent combination may have a salutary effect on productivity.

To examine the effects of mixed reward structures on triads that constructed single towers, two concurrently executed designs were composed. In one design cooperative and competitive rewards were combined in differing proportions, and in the other design combinations of cooperative and independent reward were employed. In the cooperative-competitive design, a fully cooperative condition and a fully competitive condition described in Experiment 2a were included as well as conditions involving the following varying proportions of combined allocations: .80 cooperative-.20 competitive, .50 cooperative-.50 competitive, and .20 cooperative-.80 competitive. As an example of a mixed allocation, if in the .50-.50 condition A contributed 12 blocks and B and C 6 blocks each to the resultant 24-block tower, each member would receive 4 points as his or her portion of the cooperative allocation. A would receive an additional 6 points, derived from .50 of the competitive payment. The five conditions of cooperative-independent design were similarly constructed, and referring to the above example for the .50-.50 condition, each member received 4 points, A received an additional 6 points, and B and C each received an additional 3 points.

METHOD

The basic features of Experiment 2 were described earlier under Experiment 2a.

Other than the physical changes already described, the only further changes from the single tower procedures of Experiment 1 were those involving reward allocation in the mixed incentive conditions.

Design and Subjects

In two separate but simultaneously executed experiments involving cooperative-independent reward structures and cooperative-competitive reward structures, 5 × 2 factorial designs composed of five conditions of reward allocation and two conditions of sex were employed. Six triads of each sex participated in each of the cells of the design, producing a total of 90 males and 90 females in each of the experiments. For the data analysis, the 12 male and 12 female triads that experienced the 1.00 cooperative conditions were combined.[2]

Procedure

Only the details for reward allocation in the mixed incentive conditions will be described. At the end of each trial, the number of blocks remaining in the tower were counted and a portion of the points, .80, .50, or .20, was distributed cooperatively to members of the triad; the remaining points were distributed either competitively or independently. For example, if a 15-block tower was constructed in the .80 conditions, 12 points were distributed equally, providing 4 points for each triad member. The remaining 3 points were distributed according to either an independent or competitive rule.

The mixed incentive systems often necessitated somewhat complex calculations to arrive at each member's reward. To facilitate these calculations, the experimenters were provided with a schedule of reward allocation for each of the mixed

TABLE 5

Means for Group Performance Measures and Interpersonal Attraction for Various Proportions of Cooperative and Independent Rewards in Experiment 2

	Cooperative-independent reward proportions				
Dependent variable	$1.00-0$	$.80-.20$	$.50-.50$	$.20-.80$	$0-1.00$
Blocks	110.54_a	$85.17_{a,b}$	73.58_b	$94.25_{a,b}$	$90.25_{a,b}$
Falls	4.00_a	8.67_a	8.17_a	9.33_a	6.92_a
Turn taking	$.82_a$	$.70_{a,b}$	$.82_a$	$.71_{a,b}$	$.51_b$
Interpersonal attraction	26.83_a	25.94_a	25.92_a	24.25_a	24.19_a

Note: Means for each dependent variable that do not share common subscripts are significantly different at $p < .05$.

incentive systems. Subjects were given a detailed example of the reward allocation procedures prior to the first trial. Throughout the course of the experiment, the experimenter first distributed the cooperative portion of the reward and then distributed the competitive or independent portion. As a check on subjects' understanding of the procedures, each subject was given a description of one possible outcome and asked to write down the distribution of rewards. Examination of subjects' responses indicated that the vast majority were quite facile in determining the proper allocation of rewards.

RESULTS

Two separate 5×2 analyses of variance were conducted for each dependent variable. As indicated earlier, all 24 triads in the 1.00 cooperative condition were employed for both the cooperative-independent and cooperative-competitive analyses. In Tables 4 and 5, the mean performance measures associated with the independent variables are presented for the cooperative-competitive conditions and the cooperative-independent conditions, respectively.

Blocks

The analysis of the cooperative-competitive conditions resulted in a significant main effect for reward structure, $F(4, 62) = 7.14, p < .001$, and a significant Reward Structure $\times$ Sex interaction, $F(4, 62) = 3.18, p < .02$. The mean number of blocks in towers produced in the 1.00 cooperative condition was significantly greater than in all other conditions ($p < .05$), which did not differ from one another. The Reward Structure $\times$ Sex interaction was produced by a crossover for males and females in the

.20 cooperative-.80 competitive and 1.00 competitive conditions; males built taller towers than females in the .20 cooperative-.80 competitive condition (97.00 for males vs. 54.17 for females), whereas females produced taller towers than males in the 1.00 competitive conditions (57.17 for males vs. 80.83 for females). In the remaining conditions, males and females showed parallel patterns of responses.

Analysis of the cooperative-independent conditions revealed only a main effect for reward structure, $F(4, 62) = 4.83, p < .01$. Follow-up tests indicated that the number of blocks in towers produced in the 1.00 cooperative condition was significantly greater than in the .50 cooperative-.50 independent condition ($p < .05$) and marginally greater ($p < .10$) than in the remaining conditions. There were no significant differences among conditions that included a portion of independent reward.

Falls

The number of tower falls summed across trials in the cooperative-competitive conditions showed a main effect for reward structure, $F(4, 62) = 5.35, p < .002$, and a Reward Structure $\times$ Sex interaction, $F(4, 62) = 2.61, p < .05$. As in the analysis of blocks, the Reward Structure $\times$ Sex interaction reflected a crossover for males and females in the .20 cooperative-.80 competitive and 1.00 competitive conditions. Males had fewer falls than females (6.50 vs. 16.67) in the .20 cooperative-.80 competitive condition, whereas females had fewer falls than males (10.33 vs. 13.50) in the 1.00 competitive condition. Follow-up tests for the reward structure main effect showed that there were significantly fewer falls in the 1.00 cooperative condition than in all other conditions except the .50 cooperative-.50 independent conditions, ($p <$ .05). There were no significant differences among conditions containing a portion of competitive reward.

The analysis of falls for the cooperative-independent conditions resulted in a significant main effect for reward structure, $F(4, 62) = 2.52, p < .05$. The number of falls in the 1.00 cooperative condition was only marginally lower ($p < .10$) than in the .20 cooperative-.80 independent, .50 cooperative-.50 independent, or .80 cooperative-.20 independent conditions. However, the number of falls in the 1.00 independent condition was not significantly greater than in the 1.00 cooperative condition.

Discrepancy

Neither the cooperative-competitive nor the cooperative-independent analyses revealed significant effects for the discrepancy score measure.

Turn Taking

Turn taking in the cooperative-competitive conditions showed a main effect for reward structure, $F(4, 62) = 3.65, p < .01$, and a main effect for sex, $F(1, 62) = 4.22, p < .05$. The sex effect resulted from more turn taking on the part of females ($M = .78$) than males ($M = .67$). Comparisons among the reward structure means indicated that groups in the 1.00 competitive condition engaged in significantly less turn taking than those in the 1.00 cooperative conditions ($p < .05$). In addition, the 1.00 competitive groups engaged in somewhat less turn taking than groups in the remaining conditions ($ps < .10$).

The analysis of the cooperative-independent conditions also resulted in a main effect for reward structure, $F(4, 62) =$

3.99, $p < .01$, and a main effect for sex, $F(4, 62) = 4.00, p < .05$. Females in the cooperative-independent conditions engaged in more turn taking ($M = .79$) than males ($M = .68$), which parallels the findings for cooperative-competitive conditions. Groups in the 1.00 independent condition engaged in significantly less turn taking than those in the 1.00 cooperative condition or the .50 cooperative-.50 independent condition. Turn taking was also marginally more frequent ($p < .10$) in the .80 cooperative-.20 independent and .20 cooperative $-$ .80 independent conditions than in the 1.00 independent conditions.

Self-Report Measures

The analysis of interpersonal attraction ratings resulted in a significant main effect for reward structure in both the cooperative-competitive conditions, $F(4, 206) = 7.40, p < .0001$, and the cooperative-independent conditions, $F(4, 206) = 2.96, p < .02$. The mean interpersonal attraction ratings for each reward structure condition are included in Tables 4 and 5. Comparisons among the means for the cooperative-competitive conditions indicated that both the 1.00 cooperative and .80 cooperative-.20 competitive conditions were associated with higher attraction ratings than the remaining conditions ($p < .05$). However, follow-up analyses for the cooperative-independent conditions indicated only a marginally significant ($p < .10$) higher attraction rating for subjects in the 1.00 cooperative condition compared to the .20 cooperative-.80 independent and 1.00 independent conditions. Apparently, interpersonal attraction does not suffer as severely from the inclusion of independent rewards as it does from the inclusion of competitive rewards. None of the remaining analyses of self-report measures resulted in significant effects.

DISCUSSION

The results of Experiment 2 indicate that a modicum of competitive reward is sufficient to disrupt the facilitated productivity associated wtih cooperation. A mere 20% competitive allocation resulted in impaired productivity and an increased number of falls even though 80% of the reward was distributed cooperatively. This is a sobering finding for advocates of mixed cooperative-competitive incentive plans and suggests that the competitive portion of such plans will exert the greatest behavioral control. The suggested hypothesis will require test in contexts involving more enduring group association and more realistic incentive conditions.

What accounts for the powerful impact of competitive reward structures in a mixed reward system? On the one hand, our results appear to confirm Deutsch's (1949a) assertion that little theoretical extrapolation is necessary to account for mixed reward structures. The degree of impairment in productivity in the mixed reward systems was approximately equivalent to that evidenced under a purely competitive reward system. Likewise, the number of falls for the mixed reward systems was approximately equal to the number of falls in the purely competitive system. Thus one might posit that the addition of any amount of a competitive allocation to a cooperative reward structure creates a psychological environment in which individuals view goal attainment by any one group member to be negatively correlated with goal attainment by others: Actions are no longer considered to be substitutable, role differentiation does not appear, and overt or covert sabotage

lowers the productivity of the group. In short, the competitive portion of a mixed cooperative-competitive reward structure may stimulate the identical process events associated with a purely competitive reward structure.

Two findings in Experiment 2, however, suggest that additional factors may need to be considered in accounting for the effects of mixed cooperative and competitive reward structures on group process and productivity. First, the turn-taking measure indicated that groups under mixed reward systems engaged in somewhat more turn taking than the groups in the purely competitive reward system ($p < .10$). Secondly, individuals in the .20 competitive-.80 cooperative conditions reported more interpersonal attraction than individuals in the remaining competitive conditions. Thus despite the equivalence of the mixed reward systems and the purely competitive system in terms of productivity, there is some indication that the process events were not equivalent.

The effect of mixtures of competitive and cooperative rewards on group process can be addressed from several perspectives. Competitive allocations in mixed reward systems may increase arousal or increase attempts to sabotage the group product. The failure to witness direct sabotage events coupled with somewhat higher turn taking in the mixed reward systems suggests that the competitive portion of a cooperative-competitive reward structure is unlikely to lead to overt attempts to obstruct attainment of the group product. This points to arousal as one possible explanation for the poor productivity in cooperative-competitive groups. As indicated earlier, high arousal may reduce the care and precision taken in creating the group product and therefore lower productivity. In the present experiments self-reports of arousal failed to provide support of this explanation, but in previous work (Scott & Cherrington, 1974) arousal was reported to be greater under conditions of competition than under cooperation. Future documentation of sabotage and use of tasks that separate total productivity from errors will allow for more direct tests of the arousal hypothesis.

A final explanation for the effect of competitive rewards in a mixed cooperative-competitive reward structure should be discussed. The addition of competitive rewards to a cooperative system creates a situation qualifying as a social dilemma (Dawes, 1980). Consider the case in which a tall unstable tower has been constructed and each member has contributed equally to the tower. Each individual is now faced with the decision to add one more block to the tower, which would result in acquiring the competitive allocation, or to refrain from adding to the tower and be content with the cooperative allocation. Either of these decisions incurs some potential cost: Adding to the tower can result in a fall and all reward is lost, and failing to place the last block on the tower results in a loss of the competitive reward. A large body of research indicates that the competitive alternative is most frequently chosen in such situations, and thus one would expect lowered productivity in a mixed cooperative-competitive reward system (Dawes, 1980; Pruitt & Kimmel, 1977). With respect to the group processes engendered by social dilemmas, one may need to consider the attributions that are made for behavior in the mixed reward system. When the proportion of competitive rewards is small, choosing to add a block to a wobbly, unstable tower may be seen as an attempt to increase everyone's payoff, and the behavior may be interpreted as a cooperative,

trustworthy (although perhaps foolhardy) gesture rather than as a selfish attempt to increase personal gain at the expense of others. Such attributions can indirectly influence group processes by defining the group enterprise as a competitive or cooperative venture. Brickman, Becker, and Castle (1979) have recently shown that in continuing interactions the decision to trust others is a dilemma and depends on the particular choices made by others, which supports the current analogy. However, the adequacy of comparing mixed cooperative-competitive reward systems to a social dilemma requires a clear demonstration that such variables as the magnitude of the incentives, communication, and requiring simultaneous or alternating actions affect productivity (cf. Brickman et al., 1979; Dawes, 1980).

Turning now to the results for the cooperative-independent mixed reward systems, one finds a pattern of results that are somewhat more complicated. Productivity was marginally higher in the 1.00 cooperative condition compared to the remaining conditions. Falls, however, were marginally greater in the mixed reward conditions than in the 1.00 cooperative conditions, whereas the 1.00 independent condition did not differ from the 1.00 cooperative condition. Turn taking was greatest in the 1.00 cooperative condition and marginally greater in the mixed reward conditions than in the 1.00 independent condition. Finally, the interpersonal attraction measure revealed only weak differences between conditions for pairwise comparisons. If one overlooks several minor deviations in this pattern, it appears as if the results for the cooperative-independent reward systems provide a weak, albeit imperfect, reflection of the cooperative-competitive reward systems. The implication is that independent reward structures may contain some component common to competitive structures.

Conceptually, one can view the choice presented to group members in an independent reward structure as containing both cooperative elements and competitive dilemmas. Certainly, combining efforts promotes the acquisition of rewards by all members of the group as in cooperative reward structures. However, any one individual's efforts result in payoff only to that individual. It is thus difficult for an individual to consider the group product as a truly joint effort because rewards are distributed on the basis of individual efforts: The group is merely a medium for self-reward. Alternatively, independent reward structures only provide secondary reinforcement for working together with others because rewards for any given individual are not perfectly correlated with the total group product. These considerations lead to the conclusion that responses to independent reward structures will be highly variable and that the specific process events that occur will reflect the particular mix of people one assembles in the group, the interpretations placed on the actions of each individual, and the scarcity of rewards. In a highly competitive society, competition may be fostered by independent reward structures through various social comparison processes, whereas more cooperatively oriented societies may foster cooperative process events with independent reward structures.

Although the present study cannot resolve the complexities involved in the use of independent reward structures, our results do suggest that mixtures of independent and cooperative reward structures are less costly than competitive-cooperative combinations. However, independent reward allocations did not facilitate productivity as Lawler (1971) suggested. Instead, mixtures of independent rewards and cooperative rewards produced a modest decrease in productivity and were associated with disruptive group process events. It would thus appear unwise to introduce a mixed reward structure with the expectation that individuals inevitably will be motivated to produce more, especially when the task confronting the group requires interdependent actions for successful completion.

NOTES

1. The allocation of the competitive reward is similar to the procedure employed by French et al. (1977), and it is recognized that the total allocation is different than in other conditions. The principal alternative procedure would involve giving the largest contributor an amount equal to the total number of blocks in the tower(s). This method would then lead to allocations to single participants that are clearly larger than in any other condition.

2. To achieve the comparison presented in Experiment 2a, it seemed advisable to combine the data from the two 1.00 cooperative conditions that were conducted as part of the present two experiments. No clear basis for choice of one or the other two conditions was apparent, nor did random discard of half of the data seem desirable. The use of the combined conditions was maintained for the present analyses. It is recognized that the larger number of subjects in the cooperative condition may provide somewhat more reliable estimates of the means and variances than those obtained in the various conditions involving competitive or independent reward.

REFERENCES

Brickman, P., Becker, L. J., & Castle, S. Making trust easier and harder through two forms of sequential interaction. *Journal of Personality and Social Psychology*, 1979, *37*, 515-521.

Dawes, R. M. Social dilemmas. *Annual Review of Psychology*, 1980, *31*, 169-193.

Deutsch, M. A theory of cooperation and competition. *Human Relations*, 1949, *2*, 129-152. (a)

Deutsch, M. An experimental study of the effects of cooperation and competition upon group process. *Human Relations*, 1949, *2*, 199-231. (b)

French, D. C., Brownell, C. A., Graziano, W. G., & Hartup, W. W. Effects of cooperative, competitive, and individualistic sets on performance in children's groups. *Journal of Experimental Child Psychology*, 1977, *24*, 1-10.

Goldberg, M. H., & Maccoby, E. E. Children's acquisition of skill in performing a group task under two conditions of group formation. *Journal of Personality and Social Psychology*, 1965, *2*, 898-902.

Hammond, L., & Goldman, M. Competition and noncompetition and its relationship to individual and group productivity. *Sociometry*, 1961, *24*, 46-60.

Lawler, E. E., III *Pay and organizational effectiveness: A psychological view.* New York: McGraw-Hill, 1971.

Miller, L. K., & Hamblin, R. L. Interdependence, differential rewarding and productivity. *American Sociological Review*, 1963, *28*, 768-778.

Pruitt, D. G., & Kimmel, M. J. Twenty years of experimental gaming: Critique, synthesis, and suggestions for the future. *Annual Review of Psychology*, 1977, *28*, 363-392.

Raven, B. G., & Eachus, H. T. Cooperation and competition in means—interdependent triads. *Journal of Abnormal and Social Psychology*, 1963, *67*, 307-316.

Rosenbaum, M. E. Cooperation and competition. In P. B. Paulus (Ed.), *Psychology of group influence.* Hillsdale, N.J.: Erlbaum, 1980.

Scott, W. E., Jr., & Cherrington, D. J. Effects of competitive, cooperative and individualistic reinforcement contingencies. *Journal of Personality and Social Psychology*, 1974, *30*, 748-758.

Shaw, M. E. Some motivational factors in cooperation and competition. *Journal of Personality*, 1958, *26*, 155-169.

Steiner, I. D. *Group process and productivity.* New York: Academic Press, 1972.

Thomas, E. J. Effects of facilitative role interdependence on group functioning. *Human Relations*, 1957, *10*, 347-366.

Weinstein, A. G., & Holzbach, R. L. Effects of financial inducement on performance under two task structures. *Proceedings of the 80th Annual Convention of the American Psychological Association*, 1972, *7*, 217-218. (Summary)

Winer, B. J. *Statistical principles in experimental design* (2nd ed.). New York: McGraw-Hill, 1971.

10   The Environmental Context
of Behavior

SINCE KURT LEWIN (1951) originally proposed the notion that behavior is a joint function of an individual's personality and the environmental influences operating on the individual at a particular time, social psychologists have tried to identify the factors within the social environment that affect a person's social behavior. Other professionals, many of whom were originally trained as social psychologists and were also influenced by Lewin's insightful comments, have similarly tried to determine the effects of environmental factors on behavior. But these researchers have been as concerned about the effects of the physical environment as they have been about the effects of the social environment. They now represent the field of environmental psychology—a field that was virtually nonexistent in the 1950s but now is represented by chapters in many social psychology texts and by a growing number of environmental texts as well (e.g., Fisher, Bell, and Baum, 1984; Holohan, 1982).

There are a variety of areas within the field of environmental psychology that may be of interest to the social psychologist. The three articles that are presented in this chapter are concerned with a rather diverse set of environmentally related phenomena. In the first article, Yakov Epstein briefly reviews the literature concerning crowding stress in several different situations and attempts to provide a critical assessment of our current understanding of the phenomenon. In addition, he discusses several lines of research in the general area of crowding that he perceives as deserving of additional research attention.

In the second article, Gary Evans, David Marrero, and Patricia Butler discuss the ways in which one's perceptions of the environment appear to be represented cognitively and, particularly, how these perceptions may change as more information about the environment is acquired. Evans and his colleagues initially address the question of whether the identification of particular landmarks or of specific paths through an area is the first step toward understanding a particular environmental setting. The second question addressed is whether there are distinct, qualitatively different stages of environmental cognition or whether differences that are observed are simply a matter of quantity and degree. While reading this article, consider carefully the methodology these authors have employed as compared to the methods used in the majority of the preceding articles. These methodological differences are characteristic of the differences between mainstream environmental psychology research and mainstream social psychological research.

While the first two articles deal with cognitive and emotional effects that result from environmental factors, the final article, by Anne Vinsel, Barbara Brown, Irwin Altman, and Carolyn Foss, describes how individuals may use the environment to affect their social interactions and to regulate their contacts with others. They also show how persons who drop out of college differ from their peers in their use of such environmental adornments, particularly in the diversity of the decorations used and in the degree of association between

369

the decorations and their school. This article clearly demonstrates the reciprocal nature of environmental influences: not only may the environment limit and constrain the range of behaviors that may be displayed by an individual, but the individual may also modify the environment so that the range of behaviors that others may display may also be restricted.

Crowding Stress and Human Behavior

Yakov M. Epstein

A model of crowding highlighting the importance of perceived control and group orientation is discussed. The literature on crowding in residential and laboratory settings is reviewed. Control and group orientation are shown to mediate reactions to high density environments, both in residential and laboratory settings. Needed future directions in research on crowding are discussed. These include intensive case studies focusing on the processes used to cope with crowding, paying greater attention to the role of group phenomena, and studying the effects of crowding in classroom settings.

During the 1970s, well over 200 studies examined some aspect of crowding. A number of monographs dealing with various aspects of crowding have also recently appeared (cf. Aiello & Baum, 1979; Altman, 1975; Baum & Epstein, 1978; Baum & Valins, 1977; Esser & Greenbie, 1978; Freedman, 1975). This paper emphasizes the need to think of crowding as a *group* phenomenon. In this vein, it highlights the role of group orientation in explaining the results of studies of crowding. In addition to group level issues, individual attempts to cope with the problems of crowding also need to be considered in accounting for the effects of crowding. This paper utilizes the concept of perceived control as a salient person level concept. The literature on crowding is organized into two settings—residential and laboratory. Residential studies are further grouped into studies of fam-

"Crowding Stress and Human Behavior" by Y.M. Epstein, 1981, *Journal of Social Issues, 37*, pp. 126-144. Reprinted by permission of The Society for the Psychological Study of Social Issues and the author.

ily, dormitory, and prison settings. The role of group orientation, and of perceived control, are considered as processes accounting for the results of studies in each of these settings. The paper ends with a discussion of some shortcomings in current theorizing about crowding related phenomena, and describes some directions for future research.

A MODEL OF CROWDING

In any setting, crowded or uncrowded, occupants must manage the environment in order to achieve their goals. For example, most people clear their desks before attempting serious writing. In so doing, they provide a work space needed to accomplish their goal. When other persons become a part of the individual's environment, he or she must coordinate his or her need for resources, activities, level of interpersonal interaction, and spatial location with theirs. As the number of people populating an individual's environment increases, the task of managing and coordinating that environment increasingly drains attention ordinarily available for goal attainment. Further, each individual has a unique set of goals that he or she wishes to attain in a given setting. Assuming that at any one time the goal of any particular individual may be incompatible with the goal of another person, increasing the number of occupants increases the number of potentially conflicting goals. At the very least, this presents a problem in coordination. In addition, it may make some individual goals impossible to attain.

When an environment becomes crowded: resources may become scarce; activities of one person may interfere with the activities of another person; unavoidable interpersonal interaction may distract the individual or may create group maintenance behaviors which prevent the individual from attaining his or her personal goals; while violations of spatial norms may increase arousal and discomfort.

When individual goal attainment is thwarted in one or more of these manners, the individual may feel threatened. Under conditions of perceived threat, the individual attempts to cope by using behaviors he or she has learned that are compatible with the norms of the culture in which he or she lives.

Several factors are involved in the attempt to cope. The first is the individual's appraisal of the severity of the threat to goal attainment posed by the high density environment. The second is the goal structure of the group occupying the high density environment. The group occupying a high density environment may have a cooperative or a competitive goal structure. The third factor is the set of internal resources that the individual has available for coping with the problems caused by the high density environment.

If the potentially thwarted goals are im-

portant to the individual, if the threat is appraised as severe, if the individual cannot induce other occupants to engage in behaviors that will facilitate his or her goal attainment, and if an alternate path to the goal that does not require coordinated activities with others is unavailable, then the individual may perceive that he or she lacks control over his or her environment. If she or he cannot escape from this environment and find an alternate environment in which her or his goals can be attained, she or he will experience stress as a concomitant of the perceived lack of control.

This model suggests that high density *alone* does not lead to stress reactions—a conclusion amply demonstrated by the program of research of Freedman and his colleagues (Freedman, 1975). Yet the lay person holds a naive model which posits that high density may be the cause of his or her inability to attain desired goals in the setting. Thus, when the occupant labels a setting as crowded, she or he is attributing the problems experienced to the presence of others. The likelihood that the person will attribute outcomes to the presence of others depends upon cues in the environment, situational norms, and his or her social learning history. Additionally, the act of attributing problems to the "crowdedness" of the environment has important consequences. For example, it may reduce the likelihood that the individual will attribute malevolent intentions to the behaviors of others that block her or his goal attainment. If a stranger presses against you in a crowded bus, you are less likely to consider him or her a pervert than if the same act occurred on a bus with only two other occupants.

For the scientist, on the other hand, the question is not whether high density has major negative consequences but rather under what conditions such negative consequences are likely to occur. The model suggested above provides a basic outline for specifying the conditions under which we may expect high density to have such negative effects. Let us examine the literature to see how well the model explains the data.

Before turning to such an examination, it is important to note that the nature of the setting specifies to some degree which goals are important to the person and the relationship between group members. Therefore, the literature will be organized as a function of the major types of settings that have been investigated.

Research on crowding has focused mainly on two settings: residential settings and laboratory settings. Some additional research has investigated the effects of crowding in public settings while a very small number of studies have investigated crowding in classrooms. We will review studies of residential and laboratory settings since the bulk of the research has been conducted in these settings. We begin with studies of residential crowding.

RESIDENTIAL CROWDING

Three types of residential settings have been studied: family dwellings, dormitories (either in college or non-college environments) and prisons. Given the model proposed above, high density can be expected to produce different types of results in these settings. Family dwellings house families—that is, groups of people who are normatively expected to be cooperatively interdependent. Further, alternate paths outside the home can be used to obtain many of the important goals in the home. For example, if the home is too congested to permit TV viewing, the neighborhood bar or a friend's home can provide an alternative. Further, given their cooperative orientation and the

obligations owed and sanctions available to family members, the possibility of inducing other family members to engage in behaviors which will facilitate the individual's goal attainment are relatively high. We can speculate that this is even more the case for adult family members than for children, since adults are, for the most part, better able to induce children to enact desired behaviors than vice versa. This observation suggests that youngsters should be more adversely affected by crowding than adults, a conclusion reached by Evans in his review of developmental aspects of crowding (Evans, 1978). The cooperative interdependence and high level of inducibility in families should prevent a feeling of loss of control, thereby minimizing the negative effects of crowding.

Two types of strategies have been used to investigate the effects of crowding in family dwellings. Prior to 1970, the method of ecological correlation was the typical mode of investigation. This method is described in detail elsewhere, and its serious shortcomings are described in Epstein and Baum (1978). Despite the drawbacks of this approach, however, one can, to some degree, generalize about the findings drawn from this literature. In general, it fails to provide clear evidence that crowding causes major ill effects. Measures such as juvenile delinquency, crime, mortality and the like, fail to show clear and consistent relationships with crowding (see Freedman, 1975, for a summary of this literature). In addition, one study of this genre which adequately controlled for the major statistical artifacts generally found in these studies found essentially no evidence of pathology associated with high density (Freedman, Heshka & Levy, 1975). It is interesting to note that the single exception in this study was the relationship between density and psychiatric hospitalizations: higher density was associated with increased rates of psychiatric hospitalization. We can speculate that the mentally ill, being constrained by their individual needs, are less likely to cooperate with other family members (cf. Johnson & Matross, 1977). One strategy for dealing with this problem is to hospitalize these individuals.

The second type of study utilized interviews with residents. Two large scale interview studies of residents living under conditions of high density have been reported in the literature. The first, and perhaps most dramatic, study was conducted in Hong Kong by Mitchell (1971). The average occupant shared a 400 square foot dwelling with 10 or more persons. This averages out to 40 or less square feet per person, which is less than half of the 85 square feet per person considered a minimum in households in which all of the occupants are normally healthy (see Committee on the Hygiene of Housing, American Public Health Association, 1950). In many cases, the dwelling was shared by two unrelated families. Despite these conditions, Mitchell found no evidence of deficits in emotional health related to density. Of greater interest, in light of the coping formulation suggested previously, are Mitchell's data on the presence of an unrelated family within the household and the floor level on which the household was located. Mitchell finds that these two factors combine in an interactive way to produce greater levels of emotional illness. Persons living on the sixth floor and above in households containing two or more unrelated families showed the greatest degree of emotional illness and the highest levels of hostility. Additionally, the presence of an unrelated family increases the likelihood of stressful interactions when persons are trying to coordinate activities under conditions of resource scarcity. Although Mitchell does not say so, we can speculate that the ability to adopt cooperative strategies to cope with these demands is reduced by the presence of two groups rather than a single related one. Floor level affects the occupants ability to monitor the activities of their children and to escape from the problems of the household. Those living on a lower floor of a walkup can retreat to the sidewalks to find a respite from the heat, congestion, and arguments in the household. Those living on higher floors are less likely to take advantage of this alternative. In terms of behavioral control, they have less of a choice in their exposure to the noxious aspects of overcrowding.

Booth (1976) assessed both objective measures of density and subjective measures of perceived crowding in Toronto. He found no important differences related to varying levels of density. One finding that is of interest, however, is that men who grew up in crowded households were less likely to experience stress related diseases under conditions of high density than men who grew up in less crowded households. This study suggests that individual difference variables related to prior experience are important contributors to experiencing problems posed by residential crowding. However, this study did not attempt to shed light on what coping mechanisms are involved.

Finally, in a study of smaller scope, Rohe (Note 1) examined reactions to a stratified sample of residents of State College, Pennsylvania, to dwellings differing in density. Density had little direct effect on behavior. However, Rohe reports that in competitively structured dwellings, reports of interpersonal stress were highly correlated with persons per room. The effect was sig-

nificantly weaker in cooperatively structured homes.

Three field experiments have been performed assessing the effects of crowding on
children. Rodin (1976) and McConohay
and Rodin (Note 2) studied the social behavior of lower class children. Crowded
lower class children showed higher levels
of learned helplessness and competed even
when competitive behavior minimized their
own rewards. Shapiro (1974) studied the
effects of crowding and socio-economic
status on motor task behavior of Israeli children. Crowding predicted poor task performance among lower class boys, but it
had no effect on lower class girls or on
middle class children of either sex. These
three studies present a contrast of sorts to
the pattern of results previously discussed.
In accordance with the model presented earlier, we can speculate about several variables that may be contributing to these differences. We noted that the ability to induce
others to act in ways that facilitate one's
own goal attainment is important. We can
conjecture that children have less ability to
induce family members to facilitate their
goal attainment than adults have. This
would be consistent with the findings of
more negative effects observed amongst
children than amongst adults. Second,
lower class households have greater scarcity than middle class households. Increasing scarcity heightens the probability of
competitive behavior (cf. Deutsch, 1973).
Thus, lower class children may be at greater
risk than middle class children regarding
negative effects of crowding. Finally,
crowding seemed to have little effect on
children in Hong Kong, whereas it has some
effects on children in American and Israeli
cultures. We can speculate that differing
cultural norms may mediate the effects of
high density for children.

We now turn to an examination of the
effects of dormitory crowding. Unlike the
situation faced by families, who are normatively expected to maintain a high degree
of cooperation, we may consider the basic
orientation of dormitory residents as individualistic. As Deutsch (1973) has demonstrated, however, individualistic orientations are unstable and are likely to become
either cooperative or competitive depending upon important features of the social
situation. One such feature is resource
scarcity. Ordinarily, scarce resources increase the likelihood of competitive behavior. However, it is possible to create a social
structure that will minimize competition in
the face of scarce resources and, under unusual circumstances, may even promote cooperation. Thus, the effects of crowding on
the social behavior of dormitory residents
should be quite variable—at times reflecting the adverse effects of competitive orientations while at other times responding
to the positive effects of a cooperative orientation.

In terms of control, dormitories also provide a more variable environment than do
family dwellings on the one hand, or prisons on the other. Young people live in dormitories because they have chosen to be a
part of a particular social world. Thus, they
exercise some voluntary control over the
choice of a place to live. But for many
students, roommates are assigned, resources are limited, and their ability to exert
decisional control over the allocation of
those resources that are available is lower
than the control available to adults in family
residences. Some youths may treat such circumstances as a desirable challenge,
thereby avoiding feelings of loss of control
over the environment. Others may find their
goals thwarted, thereby experiencing low
levels of environmental control.

In an early study, MacDonald and Oden (1973) demonstrated that youths living in crowded dormitory style accommodations, but having a high degree of perceived control and a strongly cooperative orientation, showed positive effects. Five married couples, all Peace Corps volunteers, volunteered to share an unpartitioned 30 by 30 foot room for 12 weeks of training. They made this choice so as to experience some of the hardships that they expected during their Peace Corps assignment. They were compared to Peace Corps volunteer couples who lived in hotel accommodations. The crowded couples not only failed to show adverse effects but showed enhanced marital relationships, were chosen as socioemotional leaders by other volunteers, and regretted leaving their living accommodations more than those living in hotel accommodations. The authors' description makes it clear that these couples developed a high degree of cooperation with each other and with their spouses while dealing with adversity. Further, they had volunteered to enter the setting, saw it as a challenge and as part of their training. Thus, they experienced a high degree of decisional control over their environment. Under such circumstances, it would seem that crowding can lead to positive rather than negative effects.

In an interesting program of research, Baum, Valins and their colleagues investigated the effects of dormitory architecture on social behavior. In some of their studies, they compared groups of students living in traditional double loaded long corridor dormitories with students living in suite style accommodations. In other studies, long corridor dormitory residents were compared with residents of short corridor dormitories. All residents had equivalent square footage of living space available to them. However, long corridor residents were more likely to encounter unwanted social interaction than were short corridor or suite residents. The investigators suggest that excessive unwanted social interaction decreases feelings of control over the environment. Additionally, we can speculate that the desire to avoid interaction with others minimizes the possibility of cooperation, a condition requiring coordinated efforts with others. Indeed, these investigators found that long corridor residents felt more helpless and acted more competitively than did students living in accommodations of a different architectural variety (Baum, Aiello, & Calesnick, 1978; Baum & Valins, 1977; Baum & Gatchell, Note 3). In addition, such students perceived a high degree of crowding and experienced greater overall stress than did their counterparts (Baum & Valins, 1977). Two other sets of investigators have found similar effects (Zuckerman, Schmitz, & Yosha, 1977; Stokols & Resnick, Note 4).

In a program of research conducted at Rutgers University, students living two to a room were compared with students who were tripled in traditional double loaded corridor dormitory rooms intended for two person occupancy. Tripled students were more disappointed and stressed than doubled students. These results were especially severe for tripled women who, in an attempt to make a home-like environment, spent significantly more time and invested more in their rooms than did men. Crowded men escaped to alternate locations (Karlin, Epstein & Aiello, 1978). Both tripled men and tripled women, however, showed equivalent reductions in grade point averages when crowded. This effect disappeared in subsequent years, however, when they no longer lived in high density environments (Karlin, Rosen & Epstein, 1979). Clearly, these tripled students all experienced goal blockage as a result of resource scarcity. Among other things, dormitory rooms were unavailable for adequate studying. Hence, grades suffered. Faced with this situation, men pursued their goals in alternate settings. Women, on the other hand, wanted to create a home-like environment in their rooms. To do so, they needed to coordinate activities with their roommates. Lacking specialized training, they were unable to accomplish this difficult task given the problems created by resource scarcity. Attempts by these women to form cooperative groups failed. Instead, coalitions emerged; and by the end of the semester, all of the tripled women disbanded their threesomes in favor of alternate living arrangements. Men, on the other hand, did not form coalitions and continued to live as threesomes (Karlin et al., 1978).

Baron, Mandel, Adams, and Griffen (1976) also investigated the effects of tripled living conditions amongst college dormitory residents. Consistent with the formulation advanced above, these investigators found evidence indicating that tripled students perceived less control over their environment.

In addition to studies in college dormitories, studies of dormitory living have been conducted with Naval personnel. Dean, Pugh and Gunderson (1975) found that crowding had few effects. Smith and Haythorn (1972), using a simulated undersea laboratory, also found few main effects attributable to crowding. However, crowding interacted with other factors to produce important effects on social behavior. For example, when crowded groups consisted of men whose personalities were incompatible with one another, men withdrew from social interaction to a greater extent than less crowded men whose personalities were in-

compatible. However, crowded men with compatible personalities spent more time together in recreational activities than noncrowded compatible individuals.

Thus, in general, crowded dormitory living, as predicted, has widely variable effects which may be understood in light of the perceived control and interpersonal orientation of residents.

In family residences, adults have a high degree of control and usually cooperate with one another. Dormitory residents, who are usually young adults, generally experience less control over their environment and tend to be less cooperatively oriented. We now turn to a discussion of the results of studies conducted in prisons, where inmates have very little control and are likely to be competitively oriented towards one another. Under these conditions, we would expect crowding to lead to more negative effects than it would in family residences or in college dormitories.

McCain, Cox and Paulus (1976) found that prisoners sharing a dormitory cell with others had higher numbers of illness complaints than those housed in single cells. Persons living in single cells have more control over their environment than persons sharing a cell with others. Apparently, this modicum of added control in a rather uncontrollable environment influences the amount of stress experienced. D'Atri (1975) compared blood pressure of inmates living in dormitory type cells with those housed in single cells. Consistent with the McCain et al. (1976) findings and the control formulation suggested above, he found that both systolic and diastolic blood pressure was higher for inmates sharing a cell. Paulus, McCain and Cox (1978) used archival data to examine the relationship between crowding in prison and various measures of pathology. They found that the more crowded the prisons were, the higher were: the death rates, the number of psychiatric commitments, and inmates' blood pressure. Cox, Paulus, McCain and Schkade (1979) found a positive correlation between level of density and palmar sweat for prisoners in a Texas County jail. In sum, as expected under a formulation highlighting the central role of control and cooperation in adverse reactions to crowding, studies conducted in prison environments where prisoners have very little control show consistent evidence of adverse effects.

Thus, if one organizes the literature on residential crowding in terms of the degree of cooperation and control available to residents, the findings present a fairly clear picture. The lower the degree of cooperation and control, the more adverse the effects.

CROWDING IN LABORATORY SETTINGS

Studies of the effects of crowding in residential environments have clear implications for policy decisions. A large number of studies, however, have been conducted in laboratory settings in which crowding is usually engendered by placing a relatively large number of people in a relatively small room for short periods of time. Unlike residential environments, crowding is not usually engendered in laboratories by creating a scarcity of resources or a reduction in desired levels of privacy. Rather, normative expectations about appropriate interaction distances between strangers are violated. Thus, at first glance there is little resemblance between crowded homes and crowded laboratory rooms. Some investigators have argued that findings from laboratories are therefore of little use for understanding crowding in the "real world"

(Baldassare & Fisher, 1976). However, in our view the basic psychological processes responsible for the effects of crowding in residences—that is, degree of control over an environmental stressor and group orientation for dealing with this stressor—should also be the critical variables determining the effects of crowding in the laboratory. Below, we will briefly review studies of crowding which have been conducted in laboratory settings.

Studies of laboratory crowding vary in the degree to which they subject participants to violations of expectations about appropriate social behavior amongst strangers. At one extreme, subjects are so closely spaced that they are forced to touch one another and are unable to avoid eye contact with one another. Under these circumstances, subjects almost universally show stress reactions. Stress reactions have been demonstrated physiologically by increases in skin conductance level (Aiello, DeRisi, Epstein & Karlin, 1977; Aiello, Epstein, & Karlin, 1975; Nicosia, Hyman, Karlin, Epstein, & Aiello, 1979; Epstein, Teitelbaum, Karlin, Katz, & Aiello, Note 5) and in cardiac function (Karlin, Katz, Epstein & Woolfolk, 1979; Epstein, Lehrer & Woolfolk, Note 6). In the latter study, the stressful effects of crowding persisted after three weekly exposures to crowding. Similar effects have been found on task measures (Aiello et. al., 1977; Epstein & Karlin, 1975). In addition, crowded subjects show lower tolerance for frustration (Nicosia et al., 1979) and report more negative mood, greater discomfort, and more symptoms of physiological arousal than their noncrowded counterparts (Aiello et al., 1977; Epstein & Karlin, 1975; Nicosia et al., 1979; Epstein et al., Note 5; Epstein et al., Note 6). If this level of social inappropriateness is reduced by eliminating bodily contact or eye contact at close range, the stressful effects of crowding tend to be lessened (Freedman, 1975; Freedman, Kelvansky & Ehrlich, 1971; Kutner, 1973; Nicosia et al., 1979; Paulus, Annis, Seta, Schkade, & Matthews, 1976; Epstein et al., Note 6). Epstein et al. (Note 6) report that crowded subjects report less control over the environment than do noncrowded subjects. This is consistent with observations of increased defensive posturing (Epstein & Karlin, 1975; Evans, 1979; Epstein et al., Note 6) during crowding and even prior to crowding but following the anticipation of future crowding (Baum & Greenberg, 1975). When subjects are given a means to control this otherwise uncontrollable situation, stress reactions are ameliorated. Sherrod (1974) provided crowded subjects with a button which, if pressed, would signal the experimenter to remove them from the crowded environment. Although subjects did not, in fact, press the button, the sense of control which it offered reduced adverse reactions to crowding.

In addition, a number of studies have shown that the social orientation of the group mediates reactions to crowding. For example, in situations which require the formation of an achievement oriented team, males more easily form cooperative groups than do females. Under such circumstances, crowded males become even more cooperative and crowded females less cooperative than their noncrowded counterparts (Marshall & Heslin, 1975). Alternately, in situations requiring a high degree of socioemotional group maintenance, women are more likely to band together cooperatively than are men. Under these circumstances, it has been found that crowded females become more cooperative and crowded males more competitive than their noncrowded counterparts (Epstein & Karlin, 1975). Fol-

lowing an extensive program of research, Freedman (1975) has concluded that high density intensifies the prevailing social orientation amongst group members. The results cited above are consistent with his formulation.

Thus, the effects of laboratory crowding, like those of residential crowding, are ameliorated when subjects perceive a high degree of control. In addition, the social effects of crowding, such as mood and liking for others, are largely determined by the interpersonal orientation of the group.

This review has focused on crowding in residential settings and in the experimental laboratory. Research conducted in public settings such as supermarkets (Langer & Saegert, 1977), department stores (Saegert, McIntosh & West, 1975) or city streets (Heshka & Pylypuk, Note 7) also suggests that crowding may be stressful, and that strategies which afford control to the crowded individual help to alleviate this stress. We turn now to a consideration of the unique features of crowding stress and some of the ways in which it differs from other stressors discussed in this volume.

CROWDING AND OTHER STRESSORS

This volume has focused on the effects of several environmental stressors. I would like to briefly highlight an important difference between crowding stress and some of the other environmental stressors discussed in this issue. My argument follows from the analysis presented in this paper and hinges on the fact that crowding, in contrast to stressors such as heat, noise, and air pollution, is of necessity a *group* phenomenon.

It is certainly true that spatial restriction is an important component of crowding.

Yet, if an individual were to be placed alone in an extremely small and confined environment, he or she would be cramped, but not crowded. To be crowded, one must share an environment with others. The problems created by crowding are problems arising from difficulties in interaction and the coordination of activities with others.

Let me amplify this point by considering one set of findings discussed in this review. I have reported the findings of Baum and Valins (1977), which demonstrate the stressful consequences of being subjected to unwanted interactions with others. The problem is one of inadequate coordination of activities with others. Individuals are expected to talk with others when they don't wish to do so. The problem is amenable to solution if members of the group could discuss their difficulties, examine the prevailing norms, and determine whether they wish to substitute a different set of norms more appropriate to the situation. Baum and Valins show that suite architecture promotes a different form of group organization, which minimizes these problems of coordination. One concomitant of this differing architecture is that it creates meaningful small groups for those living in suites while organizing residents of corridor dormitories into dyads, cliques, and collectivities of hallmates. The differential effects of corridor and suite architecture can then be traced to the differing properties of meaningful intact groups compared with loosely organized collectivities. Suitemates have obligations to one another comparable to the obligations that family members have to one another. They learn to coordinate their activities with each other and have a basis for inducing others in their suite to cooperate so as to facilitate their goal attainment.

Because crowding is a social phenomenon and the salient causes of the problem are other individuals, we can speculate that many of the important consequences of crowding will be social. If others in the home prevent the individual from achieving privacy, for example, they may be seen as the source of the individual's frustration; and it is quite likely that they may become the objects of his or her response to frustration. We can speculate that this should not be the case for noise, heat, or air pollution. The problems created by noise, heat, or air pollution may sometimes be attributable to the behavior of other persons, but oftentimes they can be attributed to more impersonal agents. Moreover, of those times when noise, heat, and air pollution are blamed on the behavior of others, it is probably the case that in a large proportion of the instances, the others responsible are not linked to the individual in a close relationship.

From the above discussion, it follows that the problems created by crowding are more likely to be ameliorated by concerted group action than are the problems arising from noise, heat, or air pollution. In residences, persons living together must learn to communicate in ways that will allow them to indicate how the behavior of the other person may be interfering with their own goal attainment. Methods of interpersonal negotiation and persuasion can then be used to change behaviors that are causing problems. For example, in families living in quarters with insufficient space for studying and watching TV or listening to music simultaneously, rules for cooperatively scheduling these activities can help to ameliorate these problems. I am assuming that some of the internal stress and tension that the crowded individual experiences may arise from failures to communicate with other group members about the problems that their behaviors are creating for that person. Airing these grievances and successfully inducing others to take corrective action is one way to reduce stress. It is also likely to induce the belief that one has some control over the environment.

This analysis has concentrated on the problems created by crowding in residences. I believe that chances of reducing the stressful effects of crowding in mass transportation or in public settings are smaller, because the problems are attributable to others who are not cooperatively linked to the individual. Hence, the task of inducing these individuals to coordinate their activities to facilitate joint goal attainment is more difficult, and is more comparable to the difficulties encountered in attempting to induce strangers making noise or polluting the environment to desist from these activities.

FUTURE DIRECTIONS

Research on crowding has done little to examine the processes that persons use to cope with the problems created by crowding. It would be extremely enlightening, for example, to conduct case studies of families living under conditions of high density who, nevertheless, manage to adapt successfully. This presupposes that we have adequate measures of good vs. poor adaptation. Assuming that we can identify persons who adapt successfully, can we discover what it is that they do? Studying the process of adaptation requires a longitudinal approach. We also need to learn how experience with crowded conditions over a long period of time influences the appraisal of the problem, and how it changes behavior. Several studies have begun to use this approach (cf. Baron et al., 1976; Karlin et al., 1978; Karlin et al., 1979; Baum &

Gatchel, Note 3). More such longitudinal research is needed.

In accordance with the theme presented in this paper, another fruitful direction for crowding research would be to explore how group phenomena affect the crowding experience (Stokols, 1972). How do variables such as status within a group, the organization of the group, the group's norms of cooperativeness or competitiveness, or social roles, influence reactions to crowding? A beginning has been made by Baum, Harpin and Valins (1975). More is needed.

There is a paucity of research on crowding in work settings and classrooms. With respect to the latter, there have been numerous studies relating class size to pupil achievement and these have reported contradictory findings. In a thorough review of that literature, Blake (Note 8) summarized the results of several hundred studies by noting a slight majority showing better achievement in smaller classes. But none of these studies examined the processes that occur in crowded, as opposed to uncrowded, classrooms. It would be useful to know, for example, how teachers allocate their attention, what differences there are in planned activities, and whether there is a greater disparity in the attention teachers pay to poor vs. good students, as crowding increases.

Relatively little crowding research has focused on individual and cross cultural differences. For example, there is some research (see Evans, 1978, for a summary) indicating that young children are more adversely affected by crowding than older persons. But this doesn't hold across cultures. While crowding may have negative effects on youngsters in Western cultures, children in the Kung society don't suffer ill effects (Draper, 1974). While studies of crowded residential living in Chicago show that the higher the density the greater the pathology (cf. Galle, Gove & MacPherson, 1972), a study in the Netherlands (Levy & Herzog, 1974) shows the reverse relationship, while a study of residential crowding in Hong Kong—perhaps as crowded a residential setting as can be found anywhere—revealed no overall adverse effects of high density living (Mitchell, 1971). Studies conducted in laboratory settings indicate that variables such as personal space preferences (cf. Aiello et al., 1977) or locus of control (cf. Schopler, McCallum & Rusbult, Note 9) may mediate reactions to crowding. We would hope that one important direction in which future research on the effects of crowding can move is toward an Actor by Setting by Process model of the sort advocated by Altman (1976) in his discussion of the fruitful integration of environmental and social psychology. Perhaps the ideas offered in this article, and this issue of *JSI*, will encourage such directions.

REFERENCE NOTES

1. Rohe, W. *Effects of mediating variables on response to density in residential settings.* Paper presented at the American Psychological Association Meeting, Toronto, 1978.
2. McConahay, J. & Rodin, J. *Interactions of long and short term density on task performance.* Unpublished manuscript, Yale University, 1976.
3. Baum, A. & Gatchel, R. *Cognitive determinants of reaction to uncontrollable events: Development of reactance and learned helplessness.* Unpublished manuscript, Uniformed Services University of the Health Sciences, 1980.
4. Stokols, D., & Resnick, S. *The generalization of residential crowding experiences to nonresidential settings.* Paper presented at the annual Meeting of the Environmental Design Research Association, Lawrence, Kansas, 1975.
5. Epstein, Y., Teitelbaum, R., Karlin, R., Katz, S., & Aiello, J. *An assessment of the effectiveness of two tactics to reduce arousal in mass transit settings.* Unpublished manuscript, Rutgers University, 1979.
6. Epstein, Y. M., Lehrer, P., & Woolfolk, R. L. *Physiological, cognitive and behavioral effects of repeated exposure to crowding.* Unpublished manuscript, Rutgers University, 1978.
7. Heshka, S. & Pylypuk, A. *Human crowding and adrenocortical activity.* Paper presented at meeting of the Canadian Psychological Association, Quebec, Canada, June 1975.
8. Blake H. *Class size: A summary of selected studies in elementary and secondary schools.* Unpublished doctoral thesis, Teachers College, Columbia University, 1954.
9. Schopler, J., McCallum, R., & Rusbult, C. *Behavioral interference and internality-externality as determinants of subject crowding.* Unpublished paper, University of North Carolina, 1977.

REFERENCES

Aiello, J., & Baum, A. (Eds.). *Residential Crowding and Design.* New York: Plenum, 1979.

Aiello, J. R., DeRisi, D. T., Epstein, Y. M., & Karlin, R. A. Crowding and the role of interpersonal distance preference. *Sociometry,* 1977, *40*, 271-282.

Aiello, J. R., Epstein, Y. M., & Karlin, R. A. Effects of crowding on electrodermal activity. *Sociological Symposium,* 1975, *14*, 43-57.

Altman, I. *The environment and social behavior: Privacy, Territoriality, Crowding and Personal Space.* Monterey, CA: Brooks/Cole, 1975.

Altman, I. Environmental psychology and social psychology. *Personality and Social Psychology Bulletin,* 1976, *2*, 96-113.

Baldassare, M., & Fisher, C. The relevance of crowding experiments to urban studies. In D. Stokols (Ed.), *Psychological Perspectives on Environment and Behavior.* New York: Plenum, 1976.

Baron, R. M., Mandel, D. G., Adams, C. A., & Griffen, L. M. Effects of social density in university residential environments. *Journal of Personality and Social Psychology,* 1976, *34*, 434-446.

Baum, A., Aiello, J., & Calesnick, L. Crowding and personal control: Social density and the development of learned helplessness. *Journal of Personality and Social Psychology*, 1978, *36*, 1000-1011.

Baum, A., & Epstein, Y. (Eds.). *Human Response to Crowding*. Hillsdale, NJ: Erlbaum, 1978.

Baum, A., & Greenberg, C. Waiting for a crowd: The behavioral and perceptual effects of anticipated crowding. *Journal of Personality and Social Psychology*, 1975, *32*, 671-679.

Baum, A., Harpin, R., & Valins, S. The role of group phenomena in the experience of crowding. *Environment and Behavior*, 1975, *7*, 185-198.

Baum, A., & Valins, S. *Architecture and social behavior: Psychological studies of social density*. Hillsdale, NJ: Erlbaum, 1977.

Booth, A. *Urban crowding and its consequences*. New York: Praeger Publishers, 1976.

Committee on the Hygiene of Housing, American Public Health Association, *Planning the home for occupancy: Standards for healthful housing series*. Chicago, IL: Public Administration Service, 1950.

Cox, V. C., Paulus, P. B., McCain, G., & Schkade, J. K. Field research on the effects of crowding in prisons and on off-shore drilling platforms. In J. R. Aiello & A. Baum (Eds.), *Residential crowding and design*. New York: Plenum, 1979.

D'Atri, D. A. Psychophysiological responses to crowding. *Environment and Behavior*, 1975, *7*, 237-250.

Dean, L. M., Pugh W. M., & Gunderson, E. K. Spatial and perceptual components of crowding: Effects on health and satisfaction. *Environment and Behavior*, 1975, *7*, 225-236.

Deutsch, M. *The resolution of conflict*. New Haven, CT: Yale University Press, 1973.

Draper, D. Crowding among hunter-gatherers: The Kung Bushmen. *Science*, 1974, *182*, 301-303.

Epstein, Y. M., & Baum, A. Crowding: Methods of study. In A. Baum & Y. M. Epstein (Eds.), *Human response to crowding*. Hillsdale, NJ: Erlbaum, 1978.

Epstein, Y. M.. & Karlin, R. A. Effects of acute experimental crowding. *Journal of Applied Psychology*, 1975, *5*, 34-53.

Esser, A., & Greenbie, B. (Eds.). *Design for communality and privacy*. New York: Plenum, 1978.

Evans, G. W. Crowding and the developmental process. In A. Baum & Y. Epstein (Eds.), *Human response to crowding*. Hillsdale, NJ: Erlbaum, 1978.

Evans, G. W. Behavioral and physiological consequences of crowding in humans. *Journal of Applied Social Psychology*, 1979, *9*, 27-46.

Freedman, J. *Crowding and behavior*. San Francisco, CA: Freeman, 1975.

Freedman, J. L., Heshka, S.. & Levy, A. Population density and pathology: Is there a relationship?. *Journal of Experimental Social Psychology*, 1975, *11*, 539-552.

Freedman, J., Klevansky, S., & Ehrlich, P. The effect of crowding on human task performance. *Journal of Applied Social Psychology*, 1971, 1, 7-25.

Galle, O., Gove, W., & McPherson, J. Population density and pathology: What are the relations for man? *Science*, 1972, *176*, 23-30.

Johnson, D. & Matross, R. Interpersonal influence in psychotherapy: A social psychological view. In A. Gurman & A. Razin (Eds.), *Effective psychotherapy: A handbook of research*. New York: Pergamon, 1977, 395-432.

Karlin, R. A., Epstein, Y. M., & Aiello, J. R. Strategies for the investigation of crowding. In A. Esser & B. Greenbie (Eds.), *Design for community and privacy*. New York: Plenum, 1978.

Karlin, R. A., Katz, S., Epstein, Y. M., & Woolfolk, R. L. The use of therapeutic interventions to reduce crowding related arousal: A preliminary investigation. *Environmental Psychology and Nonverbal Behavior*, 1979, *3*, 219-227.

Karlin, R. A., Rosen, L., & Epstein, Y. M. Three into two doesn't go: A follow-up on the effects of overcrowded dormitory rooms. *Personality and Social Psychology Bulletin*, 1979, *5*, 391-395.

Kutner, D. H., Jr. Overcrowding: Human responses to density and visual exposure. *Human Relations*, 1973, *26*, 31-50.

Langer, E. J., & Saegert, S. Crowding and cognitive control. *Journal of Personality and Social Psychology*, 1977, *35*, 175-182.

Levy, L., & Herzog, A. Effects of population density and crowding on health and social adaptation in the Netherlands. *Journal of Health and Social Behavior*, 1974, *15*, 228-240.

MacDonald, W. S., & Oden, C. W., Jr. Effects of extreme crowding on the performance of five married couples during twelve weeks of intensive training. *Proceedings of 81st Annual Convention of the American Psychological Association*, 1973, *8*, 209-210.

McCain, G., Cox, V. C., & Paulus, P. B. The relationship between illness, complaints and degree to crowding in a prison environment. *Environment and Behavior*, 1976, *8*, 283-290.

Marshall, J. & Heslin, R. Boys and girls together: Sexual composition and the effect of density and group size on cohesiveness. *Journal of Personality and Social Psychology*, 1975, *31*, 952-961.

Mitchell, R. E. Some implications of high density housing. *American Sociological Review*, 1971, *36*, 18-29.

Nicosia, G., Hyman, D., Karlin, R. A., Epstein, Y. M., & Aiello, J. R. Effects of bodily contact on reactions to crowding. *Journal of Applied Social Psychology*, 1979, *9*, 508-523.

Paulus, P., Annis, A. B., Seta, J. J., Schkade, J. K., & Matthews, R. W. Density does affect task performance. *Journal of Personality and Social Psychology*, 1976, *34*, 248-253.

Paulus, P., McCain, G., & Cox, V. Death rates, psychiatric commitments, blood pressure and perceived crowding as a function of institu-

tional crowding. *Environmental Psychology and Nonverbal Behavior*, 1978, *3*, 998-999.

Rodin, J. Density, perceived choice and responses to controllable and uncontrollable outcomes. *Journal of Experimental Social Psychology*, 1976, *12*, 546-578.

Saegert, S., Mackintosh, E., & West, S. Two studies of crowding in urban public spaces. *Environment and Behavior*, 1975, *7*, 159-184.

Shapiro, A. H. Effects of family density and mothers' education on preschoolers' motor skills. *Perceptual and Motor Skills*, 1974, *38*, 79-86.

Sherrod, D. R. Crowding, perceived control and behavioral after-effects. *Journal of Applied Social Psychology*, 1974, *4*, 171-186.

Smith, S., & Haythorn, W. Effects of compatability, crowding, group size, and leadership seniority on stress, anxiety, hostility and annoyance in isolated groups. *Journal of Personality and Social Psychology*, 1972, *22*, 67-79.

Stokols, D. On the distinction between density and crowding: Some implications for future research. *Psychological Review*, 1972, *79*, 275-277.

Zuckerman, M., Schmitz, M., & Yosha, A. Effects of crowding in a student environment. *Journal of Applied Social Psychology*, 1977, *7*, 67-72.

Environmental Learning and Cognitive Mapping

Gary W. Evans, David G. Marrero, and Patricia A. Butler

THE PRESENT STUDY examined changes in adults' cognitive maps of novel environments as a function of increased environmental experience. Two independent samples recalled information about their residential settings during their first week in each respective setting and one year later. Two samples were chosen that differed both in personal characteristics and physical setting to provide conservative estimates of the external validity of the data. Furthermore, several important advances in the analysis of cognitive mapping data were demonstrated.

In his seminal work on environmental cognition, Lynch (1960) hypothesized that people more familiar with a city relied primarily on specific landmarks for navigating and less on paths and regions that served as early learning frameworks. Similar arguments were made by Appleyard (1970, 1976). Conversely, both Hart and Moore

(1973) and Siegel and White (1975) theorized that adult learning sequences parallel ontogenetic spatial development. The child's first structuring of the environment is in terms of egocentric location with respect to actual body position in space. This is followed in development by a stable, landmark-based cognitive representation. Path structures are elaborated subsequently, using the original landmark points as anchors. Thus, for one scheme, landmark learning precedes path elaboration, whereas in the other the opposite sequence occurs. Currently, there is little data in the literature that decisively differentiate these two hypotheses. The first aim of the present study is to empirically evaluate these two competing hypotheses.

Appleyard (1970, 1976) compared the sketch maps of adults who had lived in an urban area for less than six months, six months to one year, one to five years, and longer than five years. People who had lived in the city for one year or less produced more sequentially dominant maps, characterized by greater path usage. More long-term residents drew spatially dominant maps that emphasized schematic boundaries and landmarks. Additionally, Devlin (1976) found that newcomers to an area (two weeks) used nearly the same pathways six weeks later in sketch maps, but showed greater variability in landmarks. Initial paths seemed to establish initial structures that were then elaborated on with continued setting experience. Thus, both of

The authors thank John Baird, Iseli Krauss, Gary Moore, Robert Newcomb, Kathy Pezdek, and Daniel Stokols for their comments on earlier drafts of this research. We are especially grateful to James Lovins for his production of our graphics.

"Environmental Learning and Cognitive Mapping" by G.W. Evans, D.G. Marrero & P.A. Butler, 1981, *Environment and Behavior, 13*, pp. 83-104. Reprinted by permission of the authors.

these studies are consistent with Lynch's and Appleyard's hypothesis that path structures are most critical as early learning cues in the macrophysical environment. Appleyard's map-classification scheme includes other criteria as well, and thus may not directly isolate the two important features. Devlin's data clearly support the primacy of path structures in early learning but may not generalize well, since her setting was a small town with few distinct, easily visible landmarks. Therefore, it remains important to critically test these competing hypotheses on the relative salience of landmarks and path structures in early environmental learning.

A second objective of this research was to examine changes in the accuracy of cognitive maps with learning. Both Hart and Moore (1973) and Siegel and White (1975) have theorized that adult learning in the macroenvironment resembles a Piagetian, ontogenetic sequence of spatial cognition (Piaget and Inhelder, 1967). These models propose three stages of accuracy. First, topological comprehension is manifested by an egocentric orientation in which the relative positions of items in space with respect to the body is understood. Thus, the relative location of objects close in space can be correctly processed, provided no perspective shifts are demanded. Projective accuracy follows and is reflected by a fixed frame of reference in which items throughout a given setting are comprehended in terms of their relative positions with respect to various fixed points in space. Thus, rather than orienting in space by noting where something is in relationship to the body, the individual orients in terms of where things are in relationship to each other. Finally, Euclidean comprehension emerges wherein space is encoded as a unit in which items are located with respect to their position in two- or three-dimensional space.

There are a few findings in the environmental cognition literature generally consistent with the Piagetian trend. Appleyard (1970, 1976) found that newcomers to the city (less than six months) were more apt to reverse the location of different city zones than long-term residents, but placed roads and landmarks within zones equally accurately. Moore (1973) had independent judges sort young adults' sketch maps of familiar and unfamiliar city areas into three classifications. Area familiarity was determined by subject's ratings. Level I maps contained unorganized elements or elements organized topologically only vis-à-vis egocentric perspective. Level II maps were partially differentiated and coordinated into fixed subgroups with good intracluster accuracy. Intercluster elaboration and accuracy were poor. Level III maps were abstractly coordinated and hierarchically organized, reflecting a schematic reference system wherein Euclidean accuracy of elements and element cluster location were high throughout the map. Significantly more subjects drew Level II maps of unfamiliar areas and Level III maps for familiar areas. Beck and Wood (1976) have also examined microgenetic changes in adults' cognitive mapping. They found that long-term residents of cities drew more accurate maps of their city than recent arrivals did (less than three years); recent arrivals in turn drew more accurate maps than tourists who had recently seen the city for the first time. Unfortunately, no data or measurement information were presented in this article, precluding evaluation of their conclusions.

Siegel and Schadler (1977) asked five- and six-year-olds to construct models of their classroom in a sandbox physically separated from the classroom. They found that, independent of age, increased experience in the classroom (eight months) significantly enhanced Euclidean accuracy, but had no impact on topological or projective accuracy. Topological relationships were operationalized as the relative location of objects within clusters, projective accuracy as intercluster relative location, and Euclidean accuracy as exact object placement (i.e., Euclidean distance from object placement to its correct, scaled location in the sandbox).

On the other hand, Acredolo et al. (1975) found that while foreknowledge and environmental differentiation (unique landmarks) facilitated location task performance, environmental familiarity did not. Children accurately recalled where a particular event had occurred equally well in familiar and unfamiliar hallways. Accuracy was measured as the distance between where an object had previously been dropped and the child's location of that event.

The operational distinctions among the Piagetian stages may reflect scalar differences instead of distinct stages of spatial cognition. One could argue that as the number of paths between a given set of points in space increases, there is increased restriction on the possible locations of items in space. Given a large enough set of points, if the relative position of items is accurate, then each item can only exist in one particular locus in space. Thus, a second major aim of this research is to examine how mapping accuracy changes with experience.

A major problem in cognitive mapping research has been the development of suitable, objective quantitative techniques for the measurement of accuracy in maps (Golledge, 1977). Most previous environmental cognition research has relied on interjudge reliability data to measure and validate accuracy in maps (cf. Downs and Stea, 1973; Moore and Golledge, 1976). It is important to improve our measures of accuracy, complexity, and so forth by operationalizing such constructs more specifically, and by developing more quantitatively powerful dependent measures. The present study demonstrates the utility of multidimensional scaling techniques for measuring accuracy in sketch-map data, and how other multivariate techniques can be applied to measure structural variations in environmental cognition.

METHOD

Subjects

Twenty freshmen from the University of California, Irvine served as volunteer subjects in the Irvine sample. All of the students lived on campus and were attending Irvine for the first time. Fourteen junior and senior volunteers from the University of California Education Abroad Program, living in Bordeaux, France, made up the Bordeaux sample. All of the students lived within the city limits of Bordeaux and were newcomers to the area. While the Irvine sample was a random sample of Irvine freshmen volunteers, the Bordeaux group was a highly selective group of especially intelligent, mature, and independent upperclassmen drawn from the University of California system at large.

Settings

The Irvine campus is in its eleventh year, and has a generally modern architectural style. Figure 1 illustrates typical views of the campus. The campus is organized in a concentric circular pattern. Bordeaux is a very old city which dates from the medieval period. The predominant architectural style of the downtown area is eighteenth-century French. The city is organized on a grid pattern, although numerous winding, nonperpendicular paths violate the basic grid pattern. Figure 2 depicts typical scenes of the city.

Procedure

Within the first two weeks of their arrival in each novel setting, subjects were asked to draw as detailed a diagram as possible of the Irvine campus or the city of Bordeaux. Subjects were given as much time as they desired to work on their drawings. Subjects did not know that they would be asked to repeat the procedure ten months later.

DEPENDENT VARIABLES

(1) Element composition: The number of paths, landmarks, and nodes (path intersections) was determined for each map. A path was defined as any continuous line drawn between two or more points without a break or section labelled to indicate a path change. If the latter occurred, then two paths or more would be indicated. Nodes were defined as the intersection of two or more paths. If three paths came together at the same point, it was scored as one intersection. Most landmarks were buildings, although, in Bordeaux, other examples included parks, squares, and statues. Semantic labels and/or figurative drawings of landmarks were counted as landmarks, provided they indicated distinct landmarks; i.e., a label and drawing of the same landmark were counted as one landmark.

The number of alternative paths between two major points in Bordeaux was calculated for each time frame. This analysis was impossible for the Irvine maps because of the circular structure of the Irvine path system. The number of alternative paths was defined as the total number of routes drawn between two specific landmarks present on all the Bordeaux maps that were located at extreme eastern and western points of the city. Each continuous path that exhibited either forward or parallel progress from one point to the other was counted. Direction reversals or backtracking were disallowed. Finally, the number of linkages between major landmarks and other points was determined (Milgram and Jodelet, 1976). Two points were linked if they were connected by a continuous path without any intervening points. Thus, if A was linked to B, which in turn was linked to C by the same path, A and B and B and C would each be considered linked, but A and C would not. A line connecting A and C without passing through B, however, would produce a linkage judgment for A and C.

(2) Accuracy: Ordinal accuracy was defined similarly to Siegel and Schadler's (1977) analysis. The relative location of landmarks within clusters was scored as intracluster accuracy. Each correct horizontal relationship between two items was scored one point. Similarly, each correct vertical relationship was scored as one point for each pair of items. Total points were adjusted for the total number of possible points, given the number of landmarks depicted in the cluster. Clusters were defined by independent, resident judges (nonsubjects) who were asked to indicate which landmarks clustered or grouped together. Greater than 90% agreement among observers was achieved for the cluster judgments. Intercluster accuracy was scored similarly for intercluster, relative vertical. and horizontal relationships.

Euclidean accuracy was measured by nonmetric multi-dimensional scaling techniques. For each individual map, the distances between the most frequent landmarks (Irvine, n = 12; Bordeaux, n = 9) were rank ordered. The mean rank orders for Time 1 and Time 2 for each sample were scaled to yield an aggregate solution (Young and Torgerson, 1967). Each aggregate was then compared to the nonmetric scaling solution of the real distances for each setting. Euclidean accuracy was defined as the canonical correlation between each comparison (see Oliver's CONGRU program, 1970). It is important to note that these scaling techniques provide quantitative estimates of the Euclidean metrics of the interitem distance matrices from the hand-drawn maps without assuming interval or ratio level of measurement (Golledge, 1977). When an individual draws AB = 3 units and CD = 6 units, it is questionable to assume that therefore CD = 2AB in the cognitive representation of that space. It is more reasonable to assume only that CB > AB in the cognitive representation, as we have done here.

Map accuracy was also assessed by Moore's map-classification scheme as outlined in the introduction. Two blind, independent judges highly trained on Moore's classification criteria scored each map within the two samples as Level I, II, or III (moore, 1973).

RESULTS

Element Composition

The mean numbers of elements depicted on maps for Time 1 and Time 2 for each sample are shown in Table 1. Alternative routes between two major landmarks in Bordeaux are also shown in Table 1. For

FIGURE 1.

Irvine Setting.

FIGURE 2.

Bordeaux Setting.

389

TABLE 1

Element Frequencies

	Irvine[1]		Bordeaux[2]	
	Time 1	Time 2	Time 1	Time 2
Landmarks	19.90	23.55	12.92	13.92
Paths	3.85	4.05[a]	21.28	30.50[b]
Nodes	2.65	3.85[a]	25.78	40.21[b]
Alternative Routes			8.40	12.10[a]

1. Irvine element composition: 89 landmarks, 110 paths, 144 nodes.
2. Bordeaux element composition: 120 landmarks, 310 paths, 500 nodes.

Univariate t test (one tailed)
 a: $p < .025$
 b: $p < .005$

the Irvine data, Hotelling's T^2 analysis was significant, $F(4, 14) = 3.8, p < .05$. Number of landmarks did not change as a function of time, $t_{17} = 1.18$, *ns*. Paths and nodes significantly increased over time, however, $t_{17} = 2.10, p = .025$, one tailed, and $t_{17} = 2.20, p < .025$, one tailed respectively. For Bordeaux maps, Hotelling's T^2 was marginally significant, $F(5, 9) = 3.14, p < .10$. Number of landmarks did not shift as a function of familiarity, $t_{13} < 1.0$, whereas paths, $t_{13} = 2.29, p < .005$, one tailed and nodes, $t_{13} = 3.39, p < .005$, one tailed, both significantly increased with environmental experience. Alternative routes between two landmarks in Bordeaux also significantly increased with experience, $t_{13} = 2.29, p < .025$, one tailed. To examine the relative stability of landmark usage over time, the rank order correlation was calculated between the frequency of

landmarks used in Time 1 and Time 2 for each sample. For Irvine, the correlation was significant, $.64, p < .002$, and, similarly, for Bordeaux the samples were highly correlated, $.92, p < .001$.

The data in Table 1 and the significant correlation data indicate that for both samples the number and relative familiarity of landmarks remained stable over time, whereas the number of paths and nodes increased substantially. The increased elaboration of element linkages over time within the identical landmark configuration is further illustrated in Figures 3 and 4, which depict the linkage data.

Accuracy

Ordinal data are shown in Table 2. As predicted, no significant shifts in either type of accuracy occurred as a function of increased familiarity. All *t* values were nonsignificant.

In order to determine the validity of the nonmetric multi-dimensional scaling technique to adequately mirror Euclidean accuracy, the actual interlandmark distances were rank ordered for each setting and entered into the TORSCA program. Goodness of fit values (stress) were very low for both solutions, $.008, p < .05$ for Irvine, and $.033, p < .05$ for Bordeaux (Klahr, 1969). Furthermore, the resultant two-dimensional configurations closely resembled the actual settings with minimal directional or distance distortion. Golledge has also found close correspondence between actual maps and nonmetric, multidimensional scaling solutions of the interitem distance matrix (Golledge et al., 1976).

The scaling solutions of the mean rank orders across subjects for interlandmark distances at Times 1 and 2 for each sample were also scaled and compared to the actual interlandmark rank ordered distance scaling solutions (CONGRU algorithm, Oliver, 1970). Visual inspection of Figures 5 and 6 reveals that Euclidean accuracy increased for each sample with greater environmental experience. The Time 2 solutions for each sample more closely resemble the real solutions than the Time 1 solutions do. This conclusion is supported by the finding that the correlations between the Time 2 solutions and the real solutions exceed the correlations between the Time 1 solutions and the real solutions in each sample. The canonical correlations between the real-world space solutions and Times 1 and 2, respectively, are .81 and .92 for Irvine, and .67 and .84 for Bordeaux.

A nonparametric procedure, the Sign Test, was utilized to analyze the frequency of Time 1 and Time 2 maps classified as Level II or Level III maps according to the Moore classification scheme described in the introduction (Moore, 1973). No significant relationship was found for the Irvine sample, $n = 5$, $\chi = 2$, *n.s.* The Bordeaux data, however, indicated a significant relationship in the predicted direction, $n = 4$, $\chi = 0$, $p < .05$. Thus, for the Bordeaux sample, Time 2 maps were classified more often as Level III maps, whereas Time 1 maps were classified more often as Level

TABLE 2

Ordinal Accuracy

	Irvine		Bordeaux	
	Time 1	Time 2	Time 1	Time 2
Intracluster	1.93	2.32	1.49	1.41
Intercluster	.84	.86	.90	.92

II maps. This trend did not hold for the Irvine data.

DISCUSSION

This research addressed two basic issues. The first question was the relative saliency of items in the physical setting as initial cues in environmental learning. The data generally support the position that landmarks are used as initial anchor points in the environment and path structures are elaborated within the initial landmark network. The second set of issues centered on changes in accuracy as a function of experience. The data suggest that basic ordinal accuracy of landmarks does not shift with experience, but that exact location in space improves.

Element Composition

These data support Hart and Moore's (1973) and Siegel and White's (1975) hypothesis of cognitive microgenesis in complex environments. Subjects from both samples recalled significantly more paths and nodes after nearly a year's experience in an initially novel setting (see Table 1). At the same time, people in both samples did not recall more landmarks as a function of experience (see Table 1). As evidenced by the correlational data, they recalled essentially the same landmarks one year later that they had during initial test probes. The elaboration of the path system in a networklike fashion within the context of initial anchor landmarks is illustrated by the substantial increase over time in alternative routes between two points in Bordeaux (see Table 1) and by Figures 3 and 4, which depict the element linkage data. These data are consistent with the hypothesis that people rely heavily on initially encoded land-

FIGURE 3.

Irvine Linkage Data.

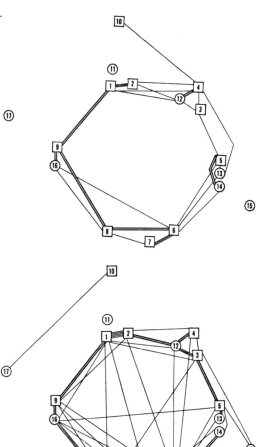

Time 1

Time 2

LEGEND		PRIMARY LANDMARK	SECONDARY LANDMARK

LEGEND

——— 10%-29%

━━━ 30%-49%

≡≡≡ 50%-69%

≡≡ ≥70%

PRIMARY LANDMARK

1 = Humanities Hall
2 = Humanities Office Building
3 = Library
4 = Administration Building
5 = Social Science Tower
6 = Engineering Building
7 = Computer Sciences Building
8 = Physical Sciences Building
9 = Steinhaus Biology Building
10 = Mesa Court Dorms

SECONDARY LANDMARK

11 = Fine Arts Center
12 = Gateway Commons
13 = Social Science Lab
14 = Social Science Hall
15 = Middle Earth Dorms
16 = Science Lecture Hall
17 = Crawford Hall Gym

marks as anchors for subsequent environmental knowledge acquisition. Route learning appears to occur within the context of one's initial landmark configuration pattern.

Accuracy

The ordinal accuracy results shown in Table 2 are consistent with the prediction that little or no improvement would occur for non-Euclidean measures of accuracy as a function of environmental experience. The Euclidean accuracy data, however, reflect improvement with experience. Inspection of Figures 5 and 6 suggests that for both samples, individuals' cognitive maps of the environment made after nearly a year's experience resemble the real-world configuration more closely than their initial maps. This conclusion is bolstered by the increase in canonical correlation found for each sample when comparing Time 2 maps and Time 1 maps to their respective real-world maps.

In addition to the above analyses of accuracy, the data were also classified according to Moore's (1973) tripartite classification scheme. The Bordeaux data are in accord with previous work in that the Time 2 maps were more often rated as Level III, whereas Time 1 maps were more often scored as Level II. This finding was not replicated in the Irvine sample. A possible reason for this discrepancy may be physical differences between the respective settings. Irvine can be viewed from a variety of points on the campus in its entirety. Moreover, all of the major buildings on campus are connected by one major path which forms the boundary of the circle on which they stand. Bordeaux, on the other hand, is developed on a grid pattern which provides no vantage point from which the ma-

jor sections of the city can be viewed in their entirety. The view from any vantage point is restricted by the presence of closely placed buildings.

Overall, the accuracy data indicate that as people learn about a setting, information changes as a function of scalar differences. Individuals initially comprehend the relative positions of items in space, but fine tune the exact location of items in space with increasing experience. One model of how this process may occur is that as more routes between various landmarks are filled in, there are fewer degrees of freedom to locate each landmark in space. This model presupposes that a relatively finite set of points in space is maintained over time with increasing environmental experience. The linkage data and high correlations found between the Time 1 and Time 2 landmark samples are congruent with this presupposition.

Methodology

In addition to the conceptual issues discussed above, this study makes several important methodological contributions to the environmental cognition literature. First, the use of a replicated sample in vastly different settings suggests considerable robustness in the cognitive processing trends postulated during adult microgenesis. Randomly selected college freshmen living on a modernistic Southern California campus, and a very select group of upperclassmen from the entire University of California system residing in a medieval European city yielded remarkably similar data patterns with regard to cognitive representation of their respective surroundings as a function of experience. Only the map classification data did not replicate.

The second major methodological con-

FIGURE 4.

Bordeaux Linkage Data.

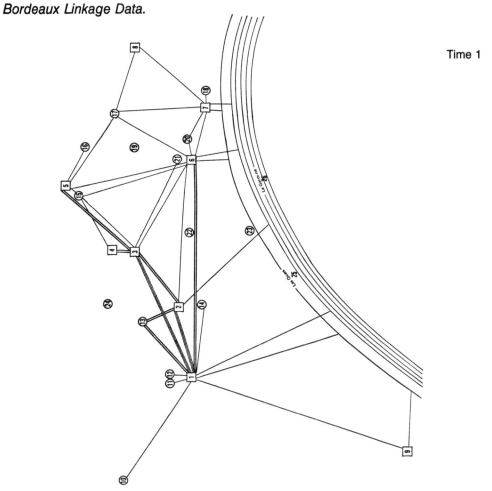

Time 1

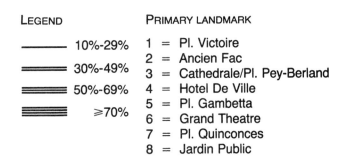

LEGEND		PRIMARY LANDMARK
———	10%-29%	1 = Pl. Victoire
		2 = Ancien Fac
═══	30%-49%	3 = Cathedrale/Pl. Pey-Berland
≡≡≡	50%-69%	4 = Hotel De Ville
		5 = Pl. Gambetta
≣≣≣	≥70%	6 = Grand Theatre
		7 = Pl. Quinconces
		8 = Jardin Public
		9 = Gard St. Jean

394

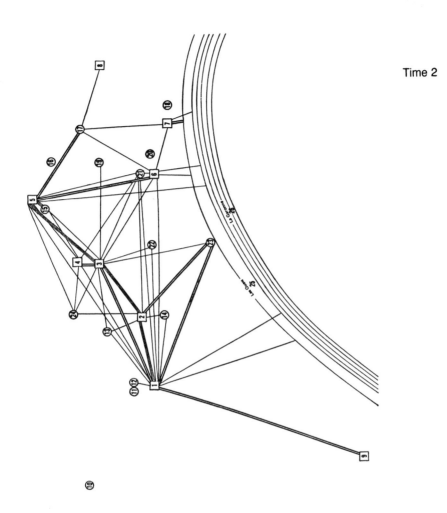

Time 2

SECONDARY LANDMARK

10	= Campus	19	= Marche Des Grands Hommes
11	= CROUS (Student Union)	20	= Syndicat D'Initiative
12	= Central Student Restaurant	21	= Pl. De La Comedie
13	= BEC (Student Restaurant)	22	= Pl. St. Projet
14	= Grosse Cloche	23	= Porte Cailhau
15	= Porte Dijeaux	24	= Pl. De La Republique
16	= Movie Theatres	25	= Les Quais
17	= Pl. Tourny	26	= La Garonne
18	= Program Director's Home		

FIGURE 5.

Bordeaux Euclidean Accuracy.

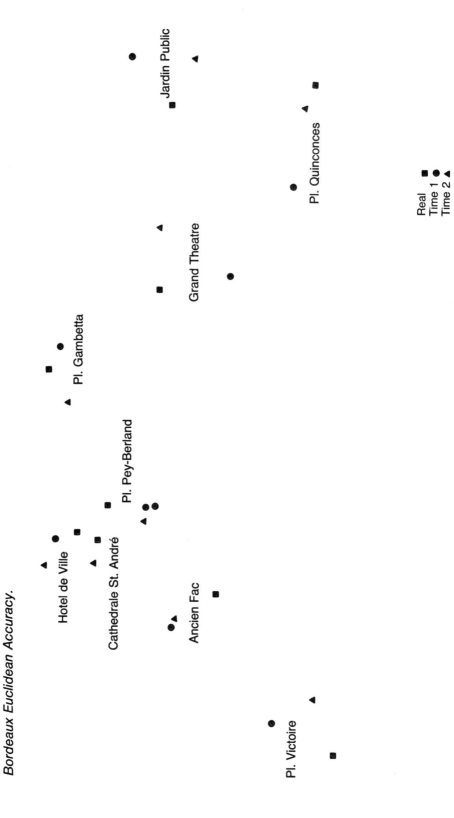

tribution of this work is its operationalization of mapping complexity and accuracy constructs. While previous work has relied primarily on highly subjective, qualitative analyses of sketch maps (cf. Downs and Stea, 1973; Moore and Golledge, 1976), the present analyses employed multivariate, quantitative assessments of relative landmark, path and node stability, and/or elaboration. Furthermore, the multidimensional scaling data provide an objective way to illustrate aggregate map data and analyze accuracy without assuming more than ordinal measurement level. Golledge's pioneering work in behavioral geography has also demonstrated the utility of multidimensional scaling approaches to environmental cognition research using paired comparison judgments of interitem distances (Golledge, 1976, 1977; Golledge et al., 1976).

In summary, this study makes three contributions to the environmental cognition literature. First, several methodological techniques are demonstrated that provide sophisticated, quantitative analysis of cognitive map data without straining assumptions about the measurement level of the data. Second, structural assessments of the learning data support the hypothesis that landmarks function as initial anchor points in environmental learning. Third, an environmental learning model is proposed which suggests that human beings initially learn the relative position of landmarks in space. Exact landmark location emerges as a function of increasing path interconnection among the initial anchor points. As more routes are filled in between these points, the exact locus of each point is fine tuned, since fewer alternative loci are possible given the dual constraints of interlandmark position and spatial relationships with the emerging path network .

Several issues for future consideration

are raised by the present study. First, an important theoretical question to ponder is the nature of the microgenetic sequence. Do changes in environmental comprehension reflect an invariant, qualitative progression of learning stages that resembles a Piagetian developmental sequence, or are changes in accuracy more simply quantitative, scalar differences in precision? Second, how exactly do landmarks facilitate learning a new setting? Hart and Moore's important early work stressed the functional nature of landmarks as sequential place markers that facilitated one's knowledge of relative position in space over them. Lynch and Appleyard emphasize instead the architectural and sociocultural features of landmarks that enhance distinctiveness. Finally, to what extent does microgenesis imply a transactional process between learner and setting? The role of landmarks in shaping structure and influencing accuracy over time, as suggested herein, is consistent with a transactional view of environmental development and learning developed by Piaget and elaborated on by Hart and Moore. Many theoretical issues in the environmental cognition literature beg further empirical examination. Recent methodological advances in various multivariate data techniques have provided us with improved tools to tackle some of these issues.

REFERENCES

Acredolo, L. P., Pick, H. L., & Olsen, M. (1975) "Environmental differentiation and familiarity as determinants of children's memory for spatial location." *Developmental Psychology*, 11: 495-501.

Appleyard, D. (1976) Planning a Pluralistic City. Cambridge, MA: MIT Press.

———(1970) "Styles and methods of structuring a city." *Environment and Behavior* 2:100-116.

FIGURE 6.
Irvine Euclidean Accuracy.

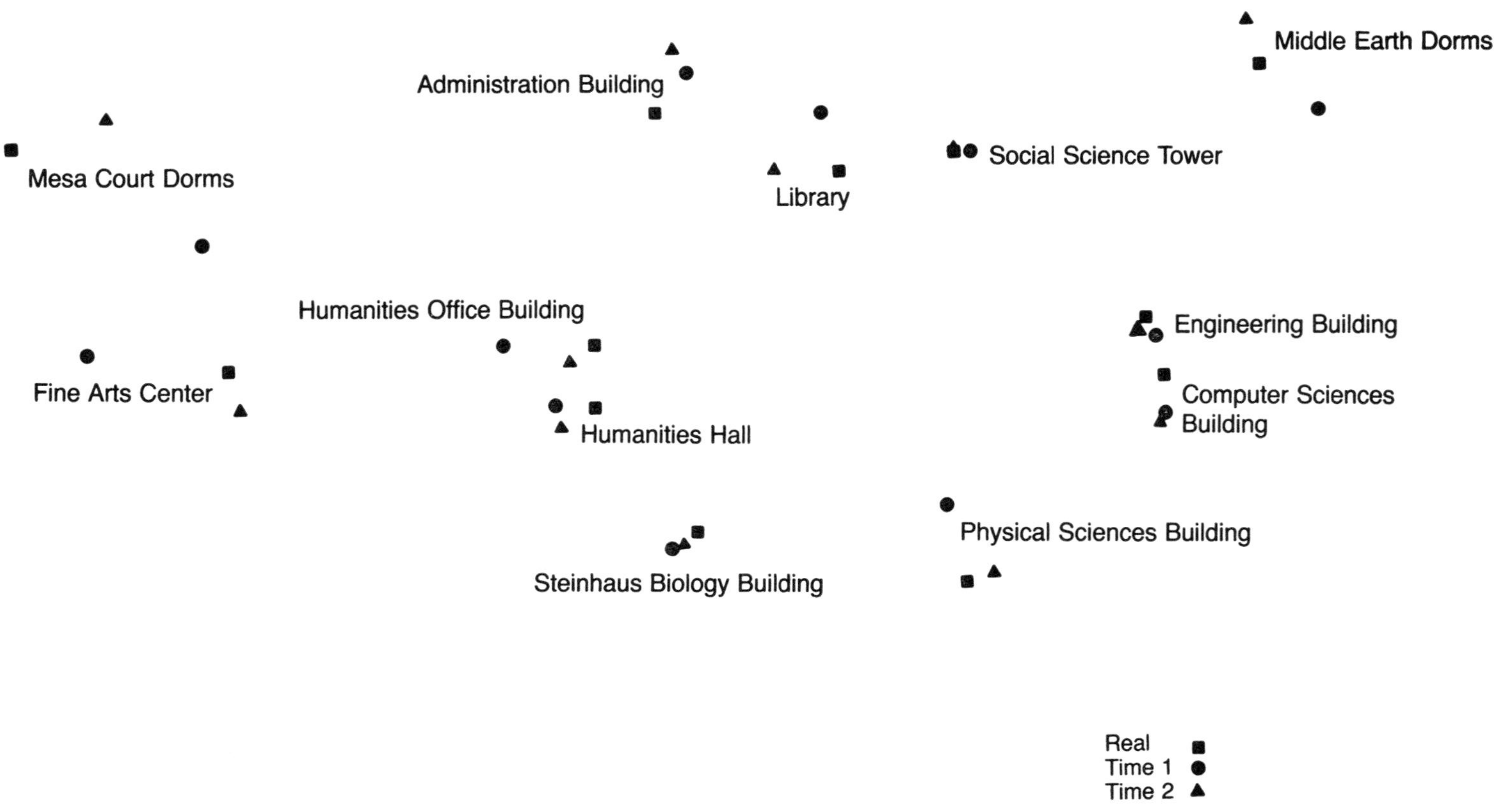

Middle Earth Dorms

Engineering Building

Computer Sciences
Building

Social Science Tower

Physical Sciences Building

Library

Administration Building

Steinhaus Biology Building

Humanities Office Building

Humanities Hall

Mesa Court Dorms

Fine Arts Center

Real
Time 1
Time 2

Beck, R. & Wood, D. (1976) "Cognitive transformation of information from urban geographic fields to mental maps." *Environment and Behavior* 8:199-238.

Devlin, A. S. (1976) "The small town cognitive map: adjusting to a new environment," in G. T. Moore and R. G. Golledge (Eds.) *Environmental Knowing.* Stroudsburg, PA: Dowden, Hutchinson & Ross.

Downs, R. & Stea, D. (1973) Image and Environment. Chicago: AVC.

Golledge, R. G. (1977) "Multidimensional analysis in the study of environmental behavior and environmental design," in I. Altman and J. Wohwill (Eds.) *Human Behavior and Environment.* New York: Plenum.

_____(1976) "Methods and methodological issues in environmental cognition research," in G. T. Moore and R. G. Golledge (Eds.) *Environmental Knowing.* Stroudsburg, PA: Dowden, Hutchinson & Ross.

_____, Rivizzigno, V. L., & Spector, A. (1976) "Learning about a city: analysis by multidimensional scaling," in R. G. Golledge and G. Rushton (Eds.), *Spatial Choice and Spatial Behavior.* Columbus, OH: Ohio State Press.

Hart, R. A. & Moore, G. T. (1973) "The development of spatial cognition: a review," in R. Downs and D. Stea (Eds.) *Image and Environment.* Chicago AVC.

Klahr, D. (1969) "A Monte Carlo investigation of the statistical significance of Kruskal's nonmetric scaling procedure." *Psychometrika* 34:319-330.

Lynch, K. (1960) The Image of the City. Cambridge, MA: MIT Press.

Milgram, S. & Jodelet, D. (1976) "Psychological maps of Paris," in H. Proshansky et al. (Eds.) *Environmental Psychology.* New York: Holt, Rinehart & Winston.

Moore, G. T. (1973) "Developmental differences in environmental cognition," in W. Preisser (Ed.) *Environmental Design Research.* Stroudsburg, PA: Dowden, Hutchinson & Ross.

_____& Golledge, R. G. (Eds.) (1976) *Environmental Knowing.* Stroudsburg: PA: Dowden, Hutchinson & Ross.

Oliver, D. (1970) "Metrics for comparison of multidimensional scalings." Harvard University. (unpublished)

Piaget, J. & Inhelder, B. (1967) The Child's Conception of Space. New York: Norton.

Siegel, A. W. & Schadler, M. (1977) "Young children's cognitive maps of their classroom." *Child Development* 48:388-394.

Siegel, A. W. & White, S. H. (1975) "The development of spatial representations of large-scale environments," in H. W. Reese (Ed.) *Advances in Child Development and Behavior.* New York: Academic.

Young, F. W., & Torgerson, W. S. (1967) "TORSCA, a FORTRAN IV program for Shepard-Kruskal multidimensional scaling analysis." *Behavioral Sci.* 12:498.

Privacy Regulation, Territorial Displays, and Effectiveness of Individual Functioning

Anne Vinsel, Barbara B. Brown, Irwin Altman, and Carolyn Foss

This study examines privacy regulation in terms of mechanisms used by college students to make themselves more or less accessible to one another, dormitory room decorations, and the relationships between privacy regulation, personal displays, and short- and long-term adjustment to a university setting.

Newly entering 1st-year students completed a questionnaire that assessed privacy mechanisms, satisfaction with the university, and other topics. Content analyses of photos of room decorations were also completed. Those who eventually dropped out of the university over a year later had fewer and less effective privacy mechanisms, were less satisfied with university life, and were less active in various campus events. Although dropouts tended to decorate their rooms more than "stayins," their decorations showed less diversity and less commitment to the university setting.

This study examines privacy regulation in a college dormitory setting in terms of the mechanisms used by students to make themselves more or less accessible to one another, the personal displays or decorations exhibited by students, and the relationships between privacy regulation, personal displays, and short- and long-term adjustment to a university setting.

The study was designed in accordance with a model of privacy regulation proposed by Altman (1975, 1976, 1977a). This framework defines privacy as "the selective control of access to the self" and as a dialectic process that includes both the opening and closing of the self to others. At certain times people seek contact with others, and at other times they desire to avoid social contact. Althoughᵣseeking and avoiding social interaction are opposites, a dialectic perspective treats them as part of a unified social system. A related aspect of Altman's approach is that privacy regulation is hypothesized to involve a variety of behavioral mechanisms such as verbal and paraverbal behavior, nonverbal behavior, environmentally oriented behaviors of personal space and territoriality, and culture-specific norms and rules that help regulate social interaction. Through different combinations of such behaviors, a person can convey a desire for more or less openness to others. One aim of the present study is to describe the range of mechanisms used

by 1st-year university students to regulate their openness and "closedness" to others in the new and strange setting of dormitories. How do they reach out to others for social contact? How do they avoid and shut off contacts with other people?

One of the mechanisms to regulate privacy that is of interest in the present study is territorial behavior. According to Altman (1975), Altman and Chemers (1980), Edney and Buda (1976) and others, human territorial behavior has at least two functions: (a) communication of personal identity, whereby people display their personalities, values, and beliefs on the physical environment and (b) regulation of social interaction, which is achieved by control of spatial areas and objects. The latter function has received considerable attention in the psychological literature in studies of territorial marking, the relationship between dominance and territoriality, and the effective functioning of social systems. The present study focuses on the personal identity function of territoriality through examining decorations used in dormitory rooms.

In addition to descriptions of how students seek out and avoid others and how they display personal identity, a major focus of the present study is on effectiveness of functioning in relation to privacy regulation. According to Altman (1975), privacy regulation plays a crucial role in the well-being of individuals and groups. Hypothetically, people who successfully regulate openness-closedness to others, in accord with personal desires and demands of situations, function better than those unable to regulate self-other accessibility. One goal of the present study is to examine the relationship between privacy regulation

"Privacy Regulation, Territorial Displays, and Effectiveness of Individual Functioning" by A. Vinsel, B.B. Brown, I. Altman & C. Foss, 1980, *Journal of Personality and Social Psychology, 39,* pp. 1104-1115. Copyright 1980 by the American Psychological Assn. Reprinted by permission of the publisher and authors.

mechanisms and several possible indicators of well-being and adjustment of new freshmen at a university. Such indicators include personal feelings of satisfaction with the university, use of facilities and participation in activities, and dropping out of or staying in the university over a year beyond the first freshman quarter. In accordance with one aspect of Altman's approach, our expectation was that students who were proficient in the use of privacy mechanisms would function more effectively than those who had difficulty with privacy regulation.

A second aspect of privacy regulation in relation to viability concerns territorial displays. We expected that students who functioned well or poorly in a university would exhibit different territorial displays in the form of room decorations. There is considerable research on the relationship between territorial behavior and individual and group functioning. For example, Altman and Haythorn (1967) and Altman, Taylor, and Wheeler (1971) reported that members of effective groups in long-term social isolation quickly established territories for chairs, beds, and areas of living space. Similarly, Sundstrom and Altman (1974) found that the breakdown of territoriality in a boys' rehabilitation setting was associated with poor group functioning. And Edney and Buda (1976) reported that establishment of individual territories led to greater feelings of personal control. Comparable ideas were proposed by Brower (1980), who theorized that urban residents established individual and group territories by means of surveillance and personal displays in response to threats of crime and intrusion by outsiders. These and related studies focused on that aspect of territorial behavior which involved control and regulation of space in the form of marking and/or occupancy. The present study examined the relationship between personal identity displays and individual functioning. Our expectation was that 1st-year students who functioned more effectively would exhibit forms of personal display that were different from those who adapted less well to the new environment.

In summary, the present study was largely a descriptive analysis of the privacy regulation practices of 1st-year university students. Specifically, we described the behavioral mechanisms used by students to either gain social contacts or avoid social interaction with others. In addition, the study described the personal identity displays, in the form of wall decorations, used by students during their first quarter at the university. A final purpose of the study was to examine the possibility that variations in use of privacy regulation mechanisms and personal identity displays would be related to adjustment to the university, as reflected in short-term satisfaction, participation in activities, and long-term staying in or dropping out of the university. Although the study was influenced by Altman's (1975, 1976, 1977a) model of privacy regulation, we did not intend to test directly the dialectic aspect of that model. Instead our primary goal was to provide descriptive baseline information about privacy mechanisms and territorial displays used by students and to explore in a preliminary way the relationship between these behaviors and indicators of adjustment to the university.

METHOD

Procedure and Participants

During the first 8 weeks of the 1975 autumn quarter, 102 male and female freshmen at the University of Utah were randomly selected to participate in the study. A letter describing the research was sent to dormitory residents, and a follow-up visit was made 7-10 days later. No students who were contacted refused to participate. With their permission, we photographed the walls over students' beds. Because the camera malfunctioned during initial data collection, some photography was repeated during the last weeks of the autumn quarter and, in some instances, during the first 2 weeks of the winter quarter.

Photographs of wall decorations above beds were obtained from 51 males and 32 females. Nineteen of the initial 102 students were eliminated from the study because either they were not available, or they had arranged their beds in double tier bunks, thereby eliminating decorating space, or there were photography problems.

Students also completed a questionnaire that assessed the types and effectiveness of their privacy regulation mechanisms, their satisfaction with the university and dormitory, and their participation in university activities. The questionnaire also included health and biographical information. Questionnaire data were available for 73 students, including 28 males and 45 females. The reduced sample was due to unavailability of students or to questionnaires that were not completed properly.

Over a year later, at the end of the 1977 winter quarter, we examined university records to determine which students were still enrolled in the university. Those no longer at the university were classified as dropouts, and those still enrolled were categorized as "stayins." Students on academic probation were eliminated from the sample to ensure that the dropout category excluded students who left the university for academic reasons.

Dependent Measures

Participants completed a questionnaire that contained the following types of items:[1]

1. *Privacy regulation.* This 18-item scale assessed the technique used by students to seek out or avoid contact with others. It consisted of a checklist of nine contact-seeking and nine contact-avoiding mechanisms that the students might have used during their time at the university. In addition, the students indicated the effectiveness of these mechanisms on a 4-point rating scale.

2. *Satisfaction with dormitory and university life.* A 22-item scale assessed facets of student satisfaction with both social and academic aspects of dormitory and university life.

3. *Participation in university activities.* Five items measured student involvement as spectators at athletic and other events; four items assessed their active participation in various social and sports activities; and one item measured their involvement in religious groups.

4. *Health.* 18 questions addressed aspects of students' physical and mental health during and immediately preceding their first quarter at the university.

5. *Knowledge of university services.* A group of 16 items assessed students' familiarity with a variety of university services.

A second group of measures involved content analyses of room decorations. An Olympus OM-1 35-mm single lens reflex camera with a Vivitar strobe flash attachment was used to take color slide photographs of the wall above each student's bed. Photographs were taken from a standard distance and angle, approximately 10 feet (3 m) from the wall.

Photographs were analyzed by means of a matrix of 840 1-inch (2.6 cm) squares projected on a wall screen. Each photograph was content analyzed by using the categories described in Table 1.

This category system is a modification

of one developed by Hansen and Altman (1976). Decorations were scored in terms of *area,* or the number of squares covered by an item in a particular content category, and *number* of separate items in a particular category.

In addition, we also measured *diversity,* or variation in decorations, and *commitment,* or involvement with the university and the local Salt Lake City region. A diversity score was calculated by dividing the number of decorating categories used (according to an expanded system containing 45 content categories) by the total number of separate items appearing on a wall. Two commitment measures were calculated: (a) the number of decorating items that reflected involvement with the university, dormitory, or Salt Lake City region, such

as schedules of events, scenes depicting local activities, and the like, and (b) the number of items that referred to home and high school events, pictures of parents and friends, high school mementos, and so forth.

The main content analysis procedure used three coders: One coder rated all slides for area and number of decorations, and the other two coders rated separate sets of 25% of the slides; thus, reliability data were available for 50% of the decorating material. Coder reliability, based on intraclass correlations for individual categories, ranged from .64 to .98 and averaged .94 and .91 for the number and area scores, respectively. For the diversity and commitment measures, half the slides were coded by two raters: The average intraclass correlation of coder agreement was .95.

TABLE 1

Content Analysis Categories for Wall Decorations

Category	Decorations
Entertainment/equipment	Bicycles, skis, radios, stereos or components, climbing gear, tennis racquets
Personal relationships	Pictures of friends and family, prom flowers, snapshots of vacations, letters, drawings by siblings
Values	Religious or political posters, bumper stickers, ecology signs, flags, sorority signs
Abstract	Prints or posters of flowers, kittens, landscapes, art reproductions, etc.
Reference items	Schedules, syllabi, calendars, maps
Music/theater	Posters of ballet, rock or musical groups, theater posters
Sports	Ski posters, pictures of athletes, motorcycle races, magazine covers, mountain climbing-hiking posters
Idiosyncratic	Handmade items (macrame, wall hangings, paintings), plants, unique items (stolen road signs, bearskins, etc.)

RESULTS

Analysis Strategy

Because of the limited number of cases, it was not always possible to do comprehensive statistical analyses on all facets of the data. Instead, we will present descriptive data about privacy regulation and decorating behavior and conduct multiple regression analyses on privacy regulation and decorating behavior in relation to dropping out or staying in the university. These analyses are supplemented by univariate analyses of variance (ANOVA) to test for sex differences and to examine specific items as selected subscales of the questionnaire.[2]

Privacy Regulation

Table 2 summarizes reports of use and effectiveness of nine contact-seeking and nine contact-avoidance mechanisms. Overall, students employed an average of 7.9 of a possible 18 mechanisms, with slightly greater use of contact-seeking techniques. The most popular contact mechanisms were direct approaches to specific people, such as calling them on the telephone, looking for them in their rooms, or inviting them to one's own room. Less specifically targeted techniques (not directed at particular other people) included going to the dormitory lounge and opening the door to one's room. Infrequently used techniques, also not directed at particular other people, included studying at a time or place where people were apt to be around, going to popular places, turning on music, or using the bathroom at a busy time.

Students also employed a number of direct behavioral means to avoid others, such as shutting the doors to their rooms, going for a walk alone, or finding a quiet place. They also reported using cognitive techniques such as "tuning out" noise when sleeping or studying. Less frequently used avoidance mechanisms included playing loud music, getting ready for bed away from the presence of others, using the bathroom at quiet times, or arranging their rooms to achieve privacy.[3]

Table 2 also describes the initial use of privacy regulation mechanisms by students who remained in the university 1½ years later compared with those who had dropped out. In general, stayins used 8.5 of 18 possible mechanisms, whereas dropouts used only 6.7 mechanisms. Furthermore, those who stayed in the university reported using a greater number of both contact-seeking (8/9) and contact-avoiding mechanisms (8/9). Students also rated the effectiveness of their privacy mechanisms. Based on a comparison of means, stayins were consistently more satisfied than dropouts with how well their privacy mechanisms worked on 16/18 items.[4]

Certain techniques used more frequently by dropouts were interesting. They reported using loud music to avoid hearing others, whereas stayins used music to attract others. Furthermore, dropouts sought social contacts in the dormitory lounges to a greater extent than did stayins; yet, the folklore of these dormitories is that the lounge is not the best place to meet people.

In summary, these descriptive data suggest that students who remained in the university over a year later reported using a greater variety of techniques for seeking out and avoiding others during their first quarter and that these techniques worked relatively well. On the contrary, students who later dropped out of the university reported using fewer and less successful privacy regulation mechanisms. Multiple regression analyses employing subscales developed from these individual mechanisms are presented later.

Participation in and Satisfaction with University Activities

The questionnaire also measured several aspects of reaction to university life, as summarized in Table 3. Multiple regression analysis yielded an R^2 of .21; $F(3, 69) = 6.01$, $p < .01$; adjusted $F(3, 69) = 4.80$, $p < .01$. These data indicate that students who remained in the university were more satisfied with the university and dormitory

TABLE 2

Use and Effectiveness of Privacy Mechanisms

Mechanism	Proportion using mechanism			Greater mechanism effectiveness
	All students	Dropouts ($n = 19$)	Stayins ($n = 54$)	
Contact seeking				
Open door to room	.64	.47	.70	Stayins
Go to student union	.22	.11	.26	Stayins
Phone someone	.74	.68	.76	Stayins
Visit others' rooms	.71	.63	.74	Stayins
Attract others with music	.21	.16	.22	Stayins
Use bathroom at busy time	.10	.05	.11	Stayins
Invite people to own room	.64	.58	.67	Stayins
Study in busy place	.30	.21	.53	Stayins
Go to dorm lounge	.70	.78	.67	Dropouts
Average number mechanisms used	4.3	3.7	4.5	
Contact avoidance				
Shut door to room	.92	.84	.94	Stayins
Find quiet place	.62	.42	.69	Stayins
Arrange room for privacy	.16	.11	.19	Stayins
Tune out noise to study	.52	.47	.54	Stayins
Go for walk alone	.49	.37	.54	Stayins
Use bathroom at quiet time	.12	.00	.17	Stayins
Prepare for bed in quiet place	.16	.00	.22	Stayins
Tune out noise to sleep	.59	.53	.61	Stayins
Use loud music to cover noise	.19	.26	.17	Dropouts
Average number mechanisms used	3.8	3.0	4.1	
Total privacy mechanisms used	7.9	6.7	8.5	

life, had more positive expectations about the university in relation to their academic and career goals, were more active in university affairs, and were less involved than dropouts in religious activities. Although the differences were not significant, stayins also had more knowledge of university services and facilities and engaged less in spectator activities. A discriminant function analysis of these data yielded a correct classification of 72.2% for stayins and 73.7% for dropouts. Students who dropped out also reported more health problems during the first quarter, although these data did not contribute to the multiple regression. There were no indications that any of these differences were systematically linked to gender.[5]

In summary, students who dropped out of the university over a year later reported a lower number and lesser effectiveness of both contact-seeking and contact-avoiding privacy mechanisms than did the stayins, suggesting that they did not use appropriate techniques for establishing relationships with others during their first weeks at the university. Although more active in religious activities, dropouts were also less active in participatory university affairs and were less satisfied with university and dormitory life. Mean differences indicate that subsequent dropouts had more symptoms of poor health and were more likely to participate in spectator activities.

Combined Privacy Regulation and Participation/Satisfaction Analyses

To ascertain the joint contributions of privacy regulation and satisfaction/participation in university life to long-term viability,

TABLE 3

Multiple Regression of Satisfaction and Participation for Stayins and Dropouts

Student reaction	Mean		r	Beta	R^2	Adjusted R^2
	Dropout	Stayin				
Satisfaction with the university and with future plans (22 items)[a]	49.58	44.24	$-.32^{***}$	$-.28$	$.10^{***}$	.09
Active participation in extra-curricular activities (5 items)	1.37	1.98	$.28^{**}$	.29	$.15^{***}$	.13
Active participation in religious activities (1 item)	.32	.15	$-.19$	$-.23$	$.21^{***}$	.17
Participation in spectator activities (4 items)	3.47	3.20	$-.11$	$-.17$	.22	.18
Knowledge of university facilities (16 items)	11.84	12.15	.05	.14	.24	.18

Note: In this and subsequent tables, variables with $F \geqslant 1.0$ were included in the table. Significance of the semipartial correlations was tested, following Kerlinger and Pedhazur (1973, p. 286).

[a] Low scores on the satisfaction scale indicate greater satisfaction.

$^*p < .10.$ $^{**}p < .05$ $^{***}p < .01.$

we conducted additional multiple regression analyses. The first analysis included satisfaction/participation questionnaire subscales, with scales based on the use and effectiveness of the total number of privacy contact and avoidance mechanisms. Table 4 summarizes the results of this analysis.

The R^2 of .21, overall $F(3, 69) = 6.01$, $p < .01$; adjusted $F(3, 69) = 4.80$, $p < .01$; and/or Pearson rs of each subscale with the drop-stay criterion support earlier analyses and descriptive data. That is, stayin students were more satisfied with university life, were more active participants in university activities, and participated less in religious activities. There was also a trend ($r = .21$, $p < .10$) for stayin students to use a greater number of privacy mechanisms. Mean differences also suggest that dropout students engaged in more spectator activities such as concerts, sporting events, and so forth. A discriminant function analysis using all variables in Table 4 indicates a correct classification of dropouts of

78.9% and a correct classification of stayins of 74.1%.

Given these results, we next conducted a multiple regression analysis using the same satisfaction/participation subscales. However, the privacy use and effectiveness scales were divided into subscales involving contact mechanisms and avoidance mechanisms.

The results of this analysis (Table 5) yielded essentially similar findings, with respect to satisfaction and participation by stayins and dropouts. However, this analysis suggests that stayin students used a greater number of privacy mechanisms directed at avoiding others compared with dropouts, overall $F(4, 70) = 5.79$, $p < .01$; adjusted $F(4, 70) = 4.52$, $p < .01$. Thus, although the descriptive data presented earlier suggest that stayins used a greater number of both contact and avoidance mechanisms and that they felt that their mechanisms were more effective, the analysis in Table 5 indicates that it is pri-

TABLE 4

Multiple Regression of Privacy Regulation and Participation/Satisfaction Indices for Dropouts and Stayins

| | Mean | | | | | Adjusted |
Activity	Dropout	Stayin	r	Beta	R^2	R^2
Satisfaction[a]	49.58	44.24	−.32***	−.26	.10***	.09
Active participation	1.37	1.98	.28**	.26	.15**	.13
Religious activities	.32	.15	−.19	−.23	.21**	.17
Number of privacy mechanisms used	6.68	8.52	.21*	.22	.23	.19
Spectator activities	3.47	3.20	−.11	−.15	.25	.19
Effectiveness of privacy mechanisms	2.99	3.05	.05	.16	.27	.20

[a] Low scores on the satisfaction scale indicate greater satisfaction.
* $p < .10$. ** $p < .05$. *** $p < .01$.

TABLE 5

Multiple Regression of Contact and Avoidance Privacy Subscales and Partici-
pation/Satisfaction Indices for Dropouts and Stayins

| | Mean | | | | | Adjusted |
Activity	Dropouts	Stayins	r	Beta	R^2	R^2
Satisfaction[a]	49.58	44.24	−.32***	−.28	.10***	.09
Active participation	1.37	1.98	.28**	.27	.15**	.13
Religious activities	.32	.15	−.19	−.22	.21**	.17
Number of avoidance mechanisms	3.00	4.06	.23**	.22	.25**	.21

[a] Low scores on the satisfaction scale indicate greater satisfaction.
* $p < .10$. ** $p < .05$. *** $p < .01$.

marily use of avoidance mechanisms that
differentiates the two types of students. Discriminant function analysis of these data
indicated a correct classification of dropouts of 78.9% and of stayins of 74.1%.

Wall Decorations and Personalization

The study also analyzed decorations displayed on students' walls during their first
quarter. Photographs of wall decorations
were content analyzed according to area of
wall space covered and number of items in
the eight categories of the coding system
described earlier. Table 6 summarizes descriptive data for the combined sample and
for both males and females. Although students used many personal relationship
items, they decorated with a smaller but
relatively equal number of items in the other
categories. With respect to area, walls were
dominated by abstract, sports, and idiosyncratic items. Abstract and sports decorations usually were commercially produced
posters. These tended to be relatively large-

sized items, with an average of one to two
such decorations on walls. Idiosyncratic
items, or one-of-a-kind decorations, included handmade planters, rugs, stolen
signs, and the like. These also were large,
and they covered substantial areas of the
wall.

Other types of items included reference
items (calendars and schedules), equipment
(radios, skis), and posters containing music, theatre, and personal values themes.
Thus, students used a wide range of decorations, a finding reported earlier by Hansen and Altman (1976).

There also were differences in the decorating done by men and women. Females
decorated their walls with a greater number
and larger area of personal relationship
items, such as photographs of family and
friends and other personal mementos.
Males, on the other hand, decorated their
walls with a greater number and larger area
of sports posters and reference items, such
as schedules, calendars, and announcements. In addition, males used larger idiosyncratic items, such as rugs and wall hang-

TABLE 6

Wall Decorations of Male and Female Students

	Area			Number of items		
Category	Males	Females	Combined	Males	Females	Combined
Personal relationships	8.5	20.1	12.6	2.0	8.6	4.3
Abstract	66.1	80.7	71.1	1.5	2.1	1.7
Music/theater	24.4	20.3	23.0	.8	.4	.7
Sports	77.4	21.1	57.7	2.0	1.2	1.7
Values	9.4	16.8	12.0	.9	1.2	1.0
Reference items	18.7	5.8	14.2	1.4	.8	1.2
Idiosyncratic	46.4	17.8	36.4	1.1	1.5	1.2
Entertainment equipment	15.4	10.0	13.5	.9	1.0	.9

ings. The impact of sex differences on the drop-stay criterion is discussed later.

Decorating by Stayins and Dropouts

Descriptive statistics and multiple regression analyses for area and number of wall decorations in relation to staying in or dropping out of the university are presented in Tables 7 and 8.

Although the Rs were relatively small, students who eventually left the university tended to be more extensive decorators than stayins. Dropouts tended to cover their walls with a greater number of items in the personal relationship and music/theater categories. Although the difference is not significant, dropouts also seemed to use a greater area of decorations for reference items and idiosyncratic categories. On the other hand, stayins decorated more with entertainment/equipment items. Multiple regressions on area yielded $F(1, 71) = 2.10, ns;$ adjusted $F(1, 71) = 1.08, ns;$ and on number of items, $F(2, 70) = 3.36, p$

$< .05;$ adjusted $F(2, 70) = 2.29, ns.$ These data were associated with correct classifications on discriminant function analyses as follows: area—dropouts, 62.5%, stayins, 78.0%; number—dropouts, 33.3%, stayins, 79.7%.

These data do not replicate earlier pilot data of Hansen and Altman (1976), who conducted a study in the same university a few years earlier. In that study, stayins generally exhibited a greater area and number of decorations. However, those data were based on only six male dropouts and on a much shorter time frame.

The limited number of cases ruled out the possibility of multivariate analyses to assess the interaction of dropping out and sex. Univariate 2 × 2 ANOVAs (Male-Female × Drop-Stay) on each content analysis category yielded only one significant interaction in 16 analyses. Female dropouts displayed a greater number of personal relationship items, suggesting that the tendency for dropouts to display more personal facets of their lives may be attributable primarily to female students.

TABLE 7

Decorating by Stayin and Dropout Students

	Area decorated		Number of decorations	
Category	Dropouts	Stayins	Dropouts	Stayins
Personal relations	18.5	10.2	7.0	3.2
Abstract	68.8	72.1	1.7	1.8
Music/theater	34.7	18.2	1.2	.4
Sports	59.8	56.8	1.2	1.9
Values	12.2	11.9	1.0	1.0
Reference items	21.1	11.4	1.2	1.2
Idiosyncratic	50.9	30.5	1.1	1.2
Entertainment/equipment	8.0	15.8	.7	1.0

Diversity of Decorations

Content analyses based on the original category system did not wholly capture certain features of student decorating. In particular, students seemed to vary widely in the diversity of their decorating practices. That is, some students decorated in only a single category, such as sports posters, whereas others used a wide variety of decorations. To measure diversity, we expanded the 8-category content analysis system to a 45-category one that used a more fine-grained breakdown within each of the original categories. For example, *personal relationships* was further subdivided into cards and letters, postcards, high school nostalgia items, and family items; *values* was expanded to include religious, political, and related items; *reference items* was divided into maps, schedules, phone numbers, announcements, calendars, and so on for the other categories.

A diversity score for each student was computed as follows:

$$D = \frac{\text{Number of different categories used}}{\text{Number of total items used}}$$

A score approaching 1 indicated a great variety of items; a score approaching 0 suggested homogeneity of decorating practices.[6]

A 2 × 2 univariate ANOVA (Drop-Stay × Sex) yielded neither a main effect for sex nor an interaction of sex and drop-stay. However, dropouts had a significantly lower diversity score than stayins, $F(1, 65) = 9.8, p < .003$, indicating that dropouts decorated their walls in a less varied fashion than stayins. Examples included one dropout student whose wall was completely covered with posters depicting ballet scenes and another student who had only ski posters on the wall. So, although the walls of dropout students tended to have a greater area and number of decorations, as indicated by

TABLE 8

Multiple Regression Analyses of Wall Decorations for Dropouts and Stayins

Category	Mean		*r*	Beta	R^2	Adjusted R^2
	Dropout	Stayin				
		Area decorated				
Reference items	21.1	11.4	−.17	−.17	.03	.02
Music/theater	34.7	18.2	−.14	−.19	.05	.03
Entertainment/equipment	8.0	15.8	.17	.16	.08	.04
Personal relations	18.5	10.2	−.15	−.16	.10	.06
Idiosyncratic	50.9	30.5	−.10	−.13	.12	.06
		Number of decorations				
Music/theater	1.2	.4	−.22*	−.24	.05*	.04
Personal relations	7.0	3.2	−.18	−.24	.09*	.06
Entertainment/equipment	.7	1.0	.09	.15	.11	.08

* $p < .10$.

descriptive data, their personal displays were less diverse than those of stayins.

Commitment in Decorations

Another analysis involved the use of an index that assessed the extent to which wall decorations reflected students' commitment to the new environment of the university and region rather than to their earlier home and setting. (See Footnote 6.) Items counted in the university/region commitment category included maps of campus and schedules of campus events, maps of Salt Lake City and the surrounding region, skiing and mountain posters, and so forth. A 2 × 2 ANOVA (Sex × Drop-Stay) yielded no significant sex or Sex × Drop-Stay differences. However, stayins had higher university/region commitment than dropouts, $F(1, 65) = 5.33, p < .02$.

In addition, a measure of home and hometown commitment was based on a count of photos of high school friends and parents, drawings by younger siblings, and other mementos such as prom flowers. Because of the small number of cases, it was not possible to do more than simple mean comparisons. The results indicated that dropouts displayed an average of 17.8 home commitment items, compared with 7.8 for stayins, $t(22) = 1.97, p < .05$. In summary, stayin students decorated more with items symbolic of their commitment to their present university environment, whereas dropouts used more items reflecting commitment to their home environments.

DISCUSSION

One descriptive goal of the present research was to illustrate techniques used by students to regulate their privacy. The results indicated that students used an array of mechanisms to make themselves more or less available to others, with an approximately equal distribution of techniques for contacting and avoiding others. In seeking contact, students were quite direct. They called particular people on the phone, visited others' rooms, or invited specific individuals to their rooms. They generally did not seek out others in an indirect fashion; for example, they less often went to places to meet someone by chance. Similarly, when students wanted to avoid others they were quite direct—they closed their doors, they left the dormitory and went for a walk alone, or they sought out a quiet place on campus. Sometimes they used more indirect techniques, such as "tuning out" others, although these were employed less often.

We also described personal identity aspects of territorial behavior. Most current research on territoriality examines how people mark territories to protect space, the relationship between social structure and space use, and the relationship of territoriality to group functioning. (See Altman, 1975, and Altman & Chemers, 1980, for a review of this literature.) Another facet of territorial behavior, of particular interest to the present study, concerns how students use territories to display aspects of their personalities, interests, and values. A salient feature of students' decorations was that most of them had put up at least one item on their walls. Their personal displays were a blend of easily available, low-cost, commercial material, such as posters, and more idiosyncratic items, such as homemade wall hangings. However, personal displays were somewhat different for men than for women. Females more frequently used personal relationship items, such as mementos and photographs. Males more

often decorated with idiosyncratic items, such as sports posters and reference items.

The present study also explored the relationships between privacy regulation, decorating displays, satisfaction, and long-term viability of students. These relationships have been well documented for marking and occupancy of territories by Altman and Haythorn (1967), Altman, Taylor, and Wheeler (1971), Sundstrom and Altman (1974), and others. Our goal was to extend these findings in relation to privacy regulation mechanisms and territorial displays.

The data yielded a coherent profile of stayins and dropouts that confirmed our expectations. The student who remained at the university over a year later used a wide variety of privacy regulation mechanisms during the first quarter. He or she apparently had a larger number of techniques to contact or to avoid others, and these privacy techniques were direct and targeted at specific people.

In particular, stayins had more avoidance techniques than did dropouts. Given that the dormitory environment inherently provides many opportunities for social contact, it may be more important to develop effective avoidance techniques in such a setting. Stayins were also positive about dormitory living and about the university as a whole, and they were active participants in sports and other activities. They were also confident about remaining in the university, and they were satisfied with the career path and major they were considering. In short, they quickly adjusted to the demands of university life and seemed to handle their day-to-day social relationships quite well.

Stayin students decorated somewhat less than their dropout counterparts except in the entertainment/equipment category. However, they decorated with considerable diversity and richness of material, thereby revealing several facets of themselves. In addition, stayins' decorations indicated commitment to the university and region. They displayed such items as scenes of the Salt Lake City region or the nearby mountains. Furthermore, they used fewer items reflecting attachments to their hometowns, such as high school mementos and photographs of high school scenes.

Dropouts revealed the opposite pattern of behavior. In their first quarter they were less satisfied with the university and dormitory, they were less certain about their major and career plans, and they participated in fewer activities (except religious groups). Furthermore, eventual dropouts had a smaller range of privacy regulation mechanisms, especially avoidance techniques. And the data suggest that the privacy mechanisms they emphasized were somewhat inappropriate. For example, they sought out people in the dormitory lounge, a reputedly poor place to meet others. They also used loud music to drown out noise, whereas stayin students reported using music to attract others.

Dropouts were more extensive decorators, and their pattern of decorations differed from those of stayins. They tended to be less diverse in their decorations, perhaps because they had fewer interests or because they chose to reveal only a few facets of themselves to others. Furthermore, their decorations symbolized a lack of commitment to the university and community. Instead, their displays suggested a greater commitment to their past life and to their parents and friends. Thus dropouts seemed to show low social competence, manifested by ineffective privacy regulation techniques, more dissatisfaction with the university and dormitory, and limited participation in university activities. Furthermore, their pattern of territorial displays reflected

less imagination or diversity of interests and an absence of commitment to the new university environment.

These profiles of dropouts and stayins need to be qualified. The data do not permit identification of causal relationships between components of the dropout and stayin profiles. Thus, one cannot attribute lack of satisfaction with the dormitory and university to poor privacy regulation or vice versa. Nor can one establish causal linkages between decorating practices and privacy regulation. Instead, we have presented a social unit analysis (Altman, 1977b) in which a variety of behaviors from several levels of functioning fit together in a coherent profile. All one can say at this juncture is that privacy regulation, territorial displays, and various measures of satisfaction and participation seem to fit with one another and with indicators of viability. Further research is necessary to tease out specific cause-effect relationships among these variables and the relationship of these factors to other variables, such as personality and family history. For our purposes, however, these profiles are important because they show an interrelation among privacy regulation and territorial displays and a variety of other behaviors, especially indicators of short- and long-term adjustment, and they demonstrate the value of a social unit analysis that involves the quantitative description of "types" of intact social units—people and groups—as an interesting and useful approach to the study of social psychological processes.

This study also suggests some theoretical and applied directions for future research. At a theoretical level, the data suggest the need to weave in more facets of student behavior to better understand the profiles described above. How do well and poorly adjusted students regulate privacy in their ongoing relationships? How are they viewed by others in terms of social competence? To what extent are they "smooth" in their development, management, and closing off of social interactions? What social histories do dropouts and stayins have with friends, family, and others? Or, in the realm of personal identity displays, do students reveal different conscious motives and plans regarding decorations? Are differences in personal identity displays associated with personality qualities? How do personal identity displays affect the initial development of relationships? Do different combinations of privacy mechanisms work better or worse in different settings?

At an applied level, the present research suggests some intervention programs. For example, one could use the data of the present study to identify potential dropouts during their first weeks at a university. Intervention programs could be developed to train resident counselors to deal with student dissatisfaction, to provide career counseling, to train students in privacy regulation, to communicate the possible meanings of decorating, and so forth. Assessment of the effectiveness of such intervention programs could be charted for intervention and appropriate control groups. In addition, such programs could vary their content and emphasis on various facets of the data and theory discussed here in order to assess the relative contribution of different factors to viability.

NOTES

1. The complete questionnaire is available from the authors.

2. Allen Cole and Charles Turner were especially helpful in providing advice about multivariate analyses of the data.

3. There were no main effects for sex in relation to use and effectiveness of individual contact-seeking or contact-avoidance mechanisms, based on univariate ANOVAS.

4. To examine sex differences in relation to privacy regulation, we conducted 2 × 2 univariate ANOVAS (Male-Female × Stay-Drop) on use and effectiveness of contact-seeking and contact-avoidance mechanisms. Although 7/36 interaction items were significant, they followed no consistent pattern.

5. There was some suggestion that females tended to be more active in extracurricular activities, were more satisfied with and knew more about university facilities, and engaged in more religious activities than did males.

6. The complete diversity and commitment category systems are available from the authors. As a percentage score, the diversity index is susceptible to wide variation in the case of a small amount of decorating. For this reason, scores were computed only for students who had more than three items on their walls.

REFERENCES

Altman, I. *The environment and social behavior: Privacy, personal space, territory and crowding.* Monterey, Calif.: Brooks/Cole, 1975.

Altman, I. Privacy: A conceptual analysis. *Environment and behavior,* 1976, *8,* 7-29.

Altman, I. Privacy regulation: Culturally universal or culturally specific? *Journal of Social Issues,* 1977, *33,* 66-84. (a)

Altman, I. Research on environment and behavior: A personal statement of strategy. In D. Stokols (Ed.), *Perspectives on environment and behavior.* New York: Plenum Press, 1977. (b)

Altman, I., & Chemers, M. M. *Culture and environment.* Monterey, Calif.: Brooks/Cole, 1980.

Altman, I., & Haythorn, W. W. The ecology of isolated groups. *Behavioral Science,* 1967, *12,* 169-182.

Altman, I., Taylor, D. A., & Wheeler, L. Ecological aspects of group behavior in social isolation. *Journal of Applied Social Psychology,* 1971, *1,* 76-100.

Brower, S. Territory in urban settings. In I. Altman, A. Rapoport, & J. F. Wohlwill (Eds.),

The environment and culture: Vol. 4. Human behavior & environment. New York: Plenum Press, 1980.

Edney, J. J., & Buda, M. A. Distinguishing territoriality and privacy: Two studies. *Human Ecology,* 1976, *4,* 283-296.

Hansen, W. B., & Altman, I. Decorating personal places: A descriptive analysis. *Environ-ment and Behavior,* 1976, *8,* 491-504.

Kerlinger, F., & Pedhazur, E. *Multiple regression in behavioral research.* New York: Holt, Rinehart & Winston, 1973.

Sundstrom, E., & Altman, I. Field study of dominance and territorial behavior. *Journal of Personality and Social Psychology,* 1974, *30,* 115-125.